CHINA AND THE SEARCH FOR HAPPINESS

CHINA
AND THE SEARCH FOR HAPPINESS

Recurring Themes in Four Thousand Years of Chinese Cultural History

---

WOLFGANG BAUER

Translated from the German by Michael Shaw

A Continuum Book

THE SEABURY PRESS · NEW YORK

1976

The Seabury Press, Inc.
815 Second Avenue
New York, New York 10017

Printed in the United States of America

Library of Congress Cataloging in Publication Data

Bauer, Wolfgang, 1930–
China and the search for happiness.
(A Continuum book)
Translation of China und die Hoffnung auf Glück.
Bibliography: p. 461 Includes index.
1. China—Civilization—History. 2. Philosophy, Chinese—History.
3. National characteristics, Chinese. I. Title.
DS721.B3413 951 76-10679 ISBN 0-8164-9276-X

CONTENTS

PREFACE

Every form of happiness, the happiness of the individual as well as that of a community, is ultimately indescribable. It is invisible like the air we breathe and yet recognize only at a distance where it takes on color. If happiness is to be described faithfully, it always appears either so close as to blind the eye or, more frequently, so distant as to allow only faint, shadowy contours to be perceived. Thus there can be found in all cultures many descriptions of the places of desolation of these and of the infernos of other worlds, terrifyingly present and menacing in their palpable cruelty, almost familiar in all their torment. But when it comes to paradises, it is only the portals barring entry that have been written about with the same clarity. All paradises are lost paradises, lying in a distant past or a distant future, in a different country, on a different star, in a different sky.

Surely this is the reason that all images men have created of the countries of happiness seem so unreal and ghostlike, "sicklied o'er by the pale cast of thought." Somehow they violate a law difficult to express and according to which genuine happiness causes time and space to collapse and can only be seized in its movement, not in contemplation. All directly intuited ideal worlds are thus characterized by a hint of embarrassed boredom, of naiveté, indeed of untruthfulness, because they can be experienced only indirectly: in the growing joy at their emergence, in the sadness that settles as they vanish.

All the more astonishing is the constant, enormous power of the visions, the degree to which they influence decisions of men and nations. It is not their realism, but precisely their unreality which exerts an invincible magic. For in a world which is seen as unhappiness and injustice, happiness can only consist in a precise reversal of reality. This background lends even a faded paradise, a colorless ideal, a quality of exuberant vividness. Even when there is nothing, that nothing is nonetheless the open gate, the way out, the delivery from evil, an evil whose immediate reality thus spontaneously and with great force suffuses its opposite with its glow.

Seen from this point of view, the apparent general sameness of these visions of happiness and their stereotyped formulations dissolve into a number of highly differentiated and sometimes even opposing concepts. The identical image, the identical word acquire an unexpected sharpness through juxtaposition. It is defined through its opposite. Only when peace, love and life, for example, are coupled with dissension, hatred and death—concepts which unfortunately seem much more rigorously elaborated—does it become apparent that not infrequently they are used on different levels and thus pass through the most remarkable metamorphoses, their meanings occasionally coming to contradict each other.

In the search for happiness, it is important to ask whether it is primarily the happiness of the individual or that of society which is sought. This dividing line cuts across another, equally important one: is happiness to be hoped for in a beyond, or here on earth? Both questions are so closely connected that while they appear in the most various aspects and proportions, they must always be answered at the same time. In the individual's striving for happiness, a certain pessimistic quality is never absent. It may include the undiluted contempt for society where man is viewed as the means to implement its egoistic purposes. This cold hunger for power may be attenuated occasionally by the feeling that the vanquished many, obliged to identify spiritually with the splendor and magnificence of the conqueror, thereby also participate in the happiness of the man at the top. Much more frequently than in this self-fulfillment of the "strong," however, the pessimism shows itself in the resigned philosophy of the "weak" who turn their back on society and look for happiness in other spheres. The forms such escapist tendencies assume vary considerably. Ultimately, they depend as much on the structure of the society they turn against as on the intensity with which that society dominates the inhabited world. The archetypal image is that of the hermit who, abandoning the noise of the cities, escapes into the wilderness of mountains and deserts. There he loses his identity by returning to the childhood of the race. Becoming once again a part of nature, he no longer experiences himself as something alien in the world. But if the radius of civilization lengthens, if its periphery comes to coincide with the world at large and no islands of wilderness remain, the hermits are driven to seek refuge within themselves. They become subject to a strange split: while compelled to continue living within society, they descend in meditation—and not infrequently in a state of ecstasy—into deeper layers of the personality which seem closer to the core and thus resemble in a certain sense the wild paradise of childhood which their more fortunate brethren of earlier times could still experience bodily in nature. The emigration from the Here and Now often coincides with the vision of a voyage which creates the impression that a spreading civilization has not overgrown the paradises and made them disappear, but that they have merely moved further away as civilization itself has advanced. They still exist, as they always have, awaiting in quiet sunshine those worthy of them—be it on inaccessible mountain peaks where the gods reside, on remote islands, the habitation of genii, or in heaven, the last, unconquerable domain of the blessed.

Quite unnoticeably and with many intermediate steps, the gradual detachment from the unconscious which lies in the development of civilization but is also repeated in every individual life allows the "beyond" to develop from untamed nature. This domain may exist in the outside world, in geographically almost identifiable areas, but also in the depth of the individual's soul. Yet it is curious that it should always be tied to a condition predating the coming of consciousness and the knowledge of the self in all its nakedness. The further the road back seems to stretch, the greater the longing to return; the greater also the bliss, should that desire be realized. The sensation of a joyful surrender of the self, its concurrent absorption in a larger self, the feeling of a liberation from the self when the walls of the individual soul seem to dissolve has been described by many mystics. But one can also discern its traces in the faces of the disciples of important, religiously tinged mass movements. The happiness of the individual and that of the mass may thus well coincide.

But the paradises outside society, beyond the world, always retain their character as places of refuge, as oases of bliss. Outside or below, the evil world continues to lie in wait. Perhaps it was only created when Adam and Eve were driven from Eden. But it does not vanish when one retreats into paradise. This is the reason escape is usually of short duration. As though subject to an invincible law of gravity, the self, humiliated, usually returns to the dust of this world after a brief flight. Born without wings, man does not seem to have been created for heaven. For this reason, other searchers for happiness did not believe that bliss could be attained by raising man to the heavens since only a few, and these only for a short while, seemed to succeed. They chose the opposite path: to bring heaven down to earth. Those who conceived this thought were always of a temperament different from that of the refugees from this world. Their image of civilization and society is optimistic. They believe, or hope at least, that what is bad can be improved, that all suffering can be alleviated. This is so even when they agree with the others that a steady, ever-deepening deterioration of the world is the cause of all evil. Of course, even among the optimists there are essential differences in attitude, some being active, others rather more passive. Some believe that the time will come when heaven with all its bliss will mercifully descend to earth; they "wait." Others are confident that they can seize the helm by their own effort and give a different direction to the course of development. They do not walk on clouds but have their feet solidly planted on the ground, prepared to wrest happiness from heaven. Yet both are turned toward society and understand that happiness on earth can only be the happiness of society as a whole, that enclaves cannot be tolerated. Such men also focus on history, either merely observing its course in wonder and seeking to discern in its movement the hoped-for coming of salvation, or else proposing to make it themselves.

This bold speculation that seeks to join heaven and earth, this reaching for the stars, pulls down those walls that stand between the vale of misery that is this world and the land of eternal happiness, walls that can never be high enough for those that seek to flee this world. Somehow, the light of paradise thus falls on earth, but paradise thereby also loses its value as a place of refuge. Suddenly, the stakes become total: if salvation is attained in this world, heaven and earth are joined. No place remains where new danger could breed. All are redeemed, and no one is left whose foolishness or suffering could make one's own happiness problematic. But if salvation cannot be realized, only a dull hopelessness is left which even a hint of better things to come in some distant future can barely alleviate. Because the individual can occasionally, if only momentarily, experience happiness in all its plenitude in this world, his certain expectation of it in a beyond can accept infinite delay much more readily than the belief of the many that happiness in society will materialize. For it promises everything to those yet unborn, yet nothing to the living.

China is a great land with a great people. One might almost say that it was born old, like certain legendary figures, and precisely because of this it always renews itself. It sometimes sleeps, but it never dies. In its long history of three or four thousand years, it has experienced all these forms of the hope for happiness in its very veins. And yet it is not true that all those curious contrasts to be found here cancel each other out and simply leave the picture of a grey, pervasive sameness. Hard as bone in its unshakable, this-worldly confidence in the blessings of antiquity, Confucianism contrasts starkly with the overflowing abundance of divine figures imagined by Taoism and its always repeated, always vain promise of a "long life" for man. Notwithstanding all these contradictions, a certain continuity is present in all the doctrines concerning the salvation of the individual and of society. In this pulsating of clashing opinions, certain elements constantly recur, while others surface astonishingly rarely or are altogether lacking. A certain profile thus unmistakably emerges.

The importance accorded the past in almost all the world views that originated in China is generally known. But the ultimate implications of this phenomenon have perhaps not yet been fully understood. It is obvious that its role differs substantially from that in western thought where, as most strikingly illustrated in the image of the hourglass, it forms a kind of correlate of the future and is always connected with it in the compressed, point-like "Now." In China, the past was something like a widening of the present; it was indeed the present itself in the sense that it almost always constituted the ground on which intellectual conflicts were fought which had the Here and Now as their stake. Besides, it furnished most of the concepts used in debate. By comparison, the future ordinarily had much less importance. It was simply the nonexistent, though not in the sense of non-being from which something startlingly new might spring, but rather in the sense of an as yet unaccomplished reproduction of an atemporal, archetypal image whose ideal form had been known from the beginning. Not only the much discussed Confucians, but most Chinese thinkers considered it their primary task to see to it that the "new" resemble this archetypal image as closely as possible. What in a more dynamic form of thought constitutes the appeal of every dispute and every decision—the fundamental separation of past and present—was thus gratifyingly eliminated. Both past and present collapse in a single present widening from a point to a spacious plain. Even if happiness is situated in the remotest past, it is not thereby removed from the sphere of human endeavor. It does not happen to be here, but it is attainable.

Perhaps this is the reason for the diligence and assiduity, the frequently praised industriousness of the Chinese, which still manifests itself in the highly conscious and even strained not-doing of the Taoist sages. Yet pure waiting for the return of happiness has been much less frequent in China, and the waiting for salvation through the sudden transformation of the world into a new paradise, through a comet never seen before and appearing in a blinding light, has been even rarer. This is probably one of the decisive differences between China and Russia which, in many respects, is both a geographic and a spiritual neighbor today and whose philosophies throughout history were suffused with messianic ideas. This is demonstrable not only in the many instances where religious communities enthusiastically expected the coming of the Savior, but even in Goncharov's *Oblomov.* The shock created in China by its clash with Western world views which, in spite of their many differences, were almost wholly oriented toward the future, was all the greater. The explosive force, the dynamic power that quite obviously inhered in these views and revealed itself massively in the technological and military superiority of the West, left China no choice. It had to adapt itself to the new insight that the future belongs to those who made it the goal of all their endeavor. The question remains, however, whether China thereby really adopted the western concept of time and historical movement, or whether past and future did not merely change places without modifying the system of thought in any way. For both past and future and consequently the concepts of "movement" and "history" have an entirely different meaning here than in western systems.

These reflections indicate that it is actually impossible to arrive at even an approximate view of the idea of happiness of a people without also grasping the background of time and space onto which they are necessarily and always projected. This is particularly true of China which sensed these reciprocal relations with an unbelievable alertness and sobriety from its very beginning. Of course, the complex of questions then widens to such a degree as to almost reduce itself to absurdity. Because of the early invention of printing more than a thousand years ago, the incredibly rich Chinese literature is remarkably well preserved. Literally thousands of texts, relevant to some aspect of this question, could be mentioned. For although it is true that a great many, indeed the majority of these writings are nothing but the result of untiring, reciprocal quotation, it would be a serious mistake to believe that old wine always remains old when poured into new bottles. On the contrary. Whenever a certain ideology attains a total dominance, as has been true of Confucianism during the last eight hundred years, the most important thoughts emerge in Hermeneutics. They are difficult to spot behind this mimicry, for at first glance they appear merely to repeat what had always been stated before. This is particularly true for outsiders who did not grow up in a milieu where thought pursues a single line of inquiry, and who therefore lack the sensitivity to the delicate change frequently wrought by a single word not found in the canon.

Not a scarcity, but an abundance of material, and the difficulty of its interpretation would seem to make it an almost hopeless task to derive a total picture of Chinese concepts of the ideal, unless the greatest restraint is used in limiting the field of investigation. In this connection, it is important that the portrayal be confined to China, however frequent and obvious the parallels to thought processes in other countries and other nations that may emerge and demand comparison. This necessary and conscious limitation of the field also has its advantages, however. For the perspective from which China has viewed its own ideals down to the present is brought out much more sharply. After all, it was not until the beginning of this century that China could survey the worldwide and thus necessarily confusing panorama of the most widely differing and often opposing conceptions of happiness.

It is a consequence of some importance that a descriptive rather than a constantly evaluative and argumentative mode of presentation must be employed, although occasionally judgments may indirectly result from the course of political history, for sometimes utopias were realized, at least in part, if not at the time originally foreseen. The attempt to systematize Chinese ideals of man and society, to assign them a place within an encompassing framework of values, can be meaningfully undertaken only when it has been successful within the smaller compass of Chinese intellectual history. It may be assumed with certainty that these ideals will not only appear in a new light, but also add new dimensions to similar conceptions of other nations, once it becomes possible to compare them. But for this reason it is also a precarious undertaking to try to do justice here to foreign ideas which entered China from the outside in the course of history, and were diffused there. Without Buddhism in the Chinese "Middle Ages" for example, and without the complex of western world views in modern times, the entire development of Chinese ideas of happiness would be altogether inconceivable. If one were also to trace these foreign ideas to their roots, the subject matter would become infinite. For the time being, therefore, only the reactions of the Chinese mind to these stimuli can be noted in their essential characteristics. We cannot also consider the changes such teachings underwent in a new and strange environment. For their importance for China lay not in their original form but precisely in the shape they took in that country. Quite often, indeed, it was merely the indirect influence they had on the further development of indigenous systems of thought. Depending upon the point of view, such adaptation may either be called "falsification" or "further development."

Once it has been decided that the presentation should be concentrated and limited in scope, choices regarding the selection and evaluation of material can be facilitated by consulting those modern Chinese scholars who have themselves investigated the conceptions of the ideal found in their own cultural past and present. In their writings, one ordinarily finds a much more precise knowledge of the sources and, more importantly, a finely honed perception of the influence these writings had on the development of Chinese thought, an ear for the nuances which, particularly in these texts, are frequently decisive for their understanding. On the other hand, a new and unexpected difficulty is encountered at this point. What becomes visible is not only the interplay of philosophy and its history, of modern and traditional thought, but also the complex opposition between foreign, i.e. western and indigenous thought. Most of these Chinese scholars, those belonging to the last century and working with traditional methods but an astounding knowledge of the texts, but also the more modern ones, usually viewed matters from a definite, subjective point of view. This was all the more pronounced when the problems serving as points of departure for their inquiries into the question of happiness were topical and urgent. Not infrequently, they produced what may be termed autobiographies of the ideals of their great and ancient culture. As such, they have all the advantages and disadvantages common to autobiographic documents as compared to biographies composed by outsiders. A very intimate knowledge is coupled with an invincible bias. Totally unprejudiced works by Chinese scholars dealing with the role played by utopias, paradises and conceptions of the ideal in Chinese intellectual history are consequently rare. The hyperacuity of an insight resulting from their knowledge of western systems of thought often leads the more modern among them to read more into a text than is contained in it. Without their being aware of it, a vision shaped by the West may sometimes significantly modify their findings. Yet even if their interpretation of the sources occasionally reflects the influence of modern western thought, their choice of these sources is of enormous help. For it shows which texts were relevant to given conceptions of the ideal; what associations they evoked and with what historical personalities they were connected.

The opposite phenomenon, however, is more important. As already suggested, the metamorphosis of western ideals under Chinese influence, rather than the reverse, is also much more directly tied to the question of Chinese conceptions of happiness as a whole. For in the one case, we are dealing merely with shifts in the perspective of scholars; in the other, with changes in the ideals themselves which usually set in shortly after their penetration into China. Indigenous Chinese culture began to exert its unavoidable influence on foreign thought as soon as it came into contact with the Chinese language. However new a concept or value might be, it had to be articulated in some fashion, and this meant that it had to be translated if the constant intrusiveness of its foreign origin was to be avoided. For Chinese, and particularly for a fundamentally ideographic form of writing, it is much more difficult to create and integrate foreign terms than it is for our languages and systems of writing. But this act of translation always necessarily created a connection with the past, with the many-layered world of images made up of written signs, proverbs, anecdotes and historical figures which had sustained thought for thousands of years in a language poorly suited for pure abstractions because formative elements were inadequately developed. Today, we witness a deliberate, logical and vigorous drive to make Chinese "grammatical," to enable it to formulate abstract concepts, to deemphasize the ideographic character of the writing and, most importantly, to create a new network of images, categories and historical precedents in the innumerable political movements and the daily inthronization of new heroic figures. Perhaps, and in the course of time, this will bring about a fundamental change not just in a language fixed on the past, but also in modes of thought. This is, of course, the intended result. But at present, the old patterns still unmistakably suffuse innumerable concepts and phrases, and many of the conceptions of the ideal. How extensively this will affect the actions and thoughts of the Chinese of our time may be difficult to gauge, but that it exerts an influence cannot be denied.

These are complex presuppositions. If we keep them in mind and muster the courage to view the often conflicting, yet also complementary forms which shifting conceptions of happiness assumed in Chinese thought; if we remain aware that we shall not discover all but perhaps those most essential shapes which continue to influence and fascinate contemporary Chinese scholars and politicians, we shall always have to remember two different yet related goals: first, to appreciate the hope of traditional China for a new and better world, a hope that has survived all disappointments. Secondly, there should be a consideration of the hopes of contemporary China from an unusual perspective, from what, metaphorically speaking, may be called a vantage point behind the stage. For the confidence we encounter in the faith of contemporary China does not spring merely from those ideals which were once brought from West to East, but also from others that originated in China long ago. A knowledge of them and their reciprocal relations may be rewarding at a time when certain western conceptions, curiously transformed by the distant East, appear to be returning home.

CHINA AND THE SEARCH FOR HAPPINESS

I

DEFINING THE DIMENSIONS (ca. 1500 – 200 B.C.)

1 / *THE UNITY OF THIS WORLD AND THE BEYOND*

THE INTEGRAL WORLD

A judgment about the great land in the East, which is disputed almost nowhere and enjoys almost universal acceptance, informs us that China, a country without a childhood, has marched through the centuries down to our day with its head turned backward and all its ideals in the past, looking for almost none in the future. This view often implies a reproach that is sometimes explicitly stated and is indeed easily justified at first glance by a variety of arguments. Yet, like all generalizations, it requires considerable modification. For it is untrue that China was always and everywhere animated by a longing for the past. This is naturally most evidently the case in the beginning of its unimaginably long history when it did not yet really have one, but was only making halting efforts to become conscious of itself. Nor is it true that this earliest period coincides with the "Golden Age," as the Confucians believe, who, as is well known, revered antiquity more than all others. For the Western Chou dynasty (1050–770 B.C.), which the Confucians later felt obliged to hold up as a model to a disintegrating world, was certainly not the beginning of China, but a new beginning at best. Certainly the half century of the Shang dynasty (ca. 1500–1050) which predated the Chou period, and the even remoter Hsia dynasty, allegedly founded in 2205 B.C. and constituting the beginning of traditional Chinese historiography, were history for Confucius.[1] It is true, of course, that his conception of the thought and sentiment of these earliest epochs was necessarily false and hazy in many respects. The long shadows of dawn falling over the beginnings of Chinese civilization may have suggested to him that these early dynasties were less well suited as an image of the ideal. In any event, the first millennium of Chinese history, the period of the country's youth, hardly ever became the object of nostalgic reminiscence, nor did they produce conceptions which viewed antiquity as an ideal. However strongly Confucius and his disciples may have felt that this period was genuinely historical, they knew even less than we do about this reciprocal relation and the degree to which it may have been due to the particular intellectual factors shaping this early stage. For it is a curious though not unique fact of scholarship that we are much better informed about this remote period than those men of two and one-half millennia ago, much closer to it though they were, and still dominated by its influence in certain respects. Our knowledge is even more precise than that of the more critical seventeenth-century Chinese literati. Up to the turn of the century, for example, the Shang dynasty was considered "half legendary" by modern western and eastern scholars, and to some extent this is still true of the Hsia dynasty today. It was only the accidental discovery of inscribed and dated parts of animal bones and tortoise shells during the construction of a railroad line and a subsequent, uninterrupted chain of similar finds with thousands upon thousands of individual pieces that caused this period to burst into the bright light of history and thus opened a perspective on a curious, very early mentality for which reality and imagination were still one.

The "bone inscriptions" from the Shang dynasty were not ordinary documents of secular correspondence (just as the bones, so difficult to use, were not ordinary writing surfaces). Scratched into a durable material which had become nearly petrified in the course of time, they lent remarkable support, as regards names and dates, to traditional, oral historiography and had served a single purpose: the fathoming of the future. We know from the literature that these bones were pierced with glowing iron tools to make one or more holes, after a question addressed to the spirits had been written down on them. The cracks, resulting from the sudden heat and corresponding in a way to scratchings made by a human hand, represented the answer from the spirit realm. An immense number of questions addressed to destiny has thus come down to us. The bones seldom gave the answers, but due to a curious form of pedantry, the date, i.e. the day of the oracle, was added.[2] They show quite clearly on what depended the weal and woe of mankind or, perhaps more accurately, of the aristocracy of the time. Most questions concerned natural events of all kinds such as rain and sunshine, floods, the failure of harvests, and the right time for hunting and fishing. No less important was the advice sought in all human affairs such as the sending of envoys, the founding of cities, sacrifices to the spirits of nature and the dead, military expeditions, illnesses and dreams, to mention only the most important.[3] The questions are phrased very tersely in a kind of telegraphic style, and read as follows: " 'On the day Ting-ssu oracle. [Oracle priest] K'o asks: Rain? Asks: No rain?' 'On the day Kuei-mao oracle. [Oracle priest] Pin asks: Expedition to area X[4] lucky and promising?' 'On the day Kuei-yu oracle. [Oracle priest] Cheng asks: King has stomach ache. Unfavorable course?' 'On the day Ken-tzu oracle. [Oracle priest] Pin asks: King dreamt of white oxen. Omen?' "[5]

This laconic diction, abandoned only in rare cases, is of course dictated primarily by the writing material. It was difficult to work with and simply did not leave much room for an inscription. But another kind of limitation relates to the contents, for almost all questions follow the "yes-no" schema. When the matter concerns the outcome of an event under way (dream, illness) or a human enterprise (campaigns, sacrifices), it follows the form: "auspicious-disastrous." In spite of the required terseness of the formulation, the entire question was often repeated in the negative form (as still frequently happens today in ordinary speech). The reason for this is probably that when a question was so "clearly" phrased, it was much easier to decipher the answer shown in the cracks on the surface of the bone because only two possibilities existed. It should be remembered, however, that reality thus became a matter of black and white, presenting itself as made up of fortunate and unfortunate events.[6] In this form of thought, nothing could occur spontaneously, let alone as the result of human will. Everything that happened was "sent," in some way. In a manner hardly imaginable today, yet typical of the early phases of all high cultures, all major decisions including political ones may be said to have first been projected into a vacuum. Decisions were first made in the realm of the supernatural. Only afterwards were they given their definitive implementation on earth.

This attitude, childlike in the best sense if one wishes to call it that, enlarged what was then the geographically still relatively limited Chinese civilization by a vertical dimension, the dimension of spirits. During the Shang period, the nuclei of this civilization, surrounded by dark-skinned original inhabitants, lay along the middle course of the Huang-ho in north central China. They radiated in a northeasterly, a southeasterly and a southwesterly direction into what are today the Liaoning and Ssuch'uan provinces. The lines separating the beyond and this world were experienced as no less shifting than the borders of civilization itself, and as it was being extended in constant struggles, its perimeters were blurred time and again. Because this world was almost disturbingly open in all directions, the oracular sayings were an indispensable means of orientation. They reduced the abundance of possibilities to a measure bearable for man. Because they could be grasped, they gave him the feeling of a certain security, for even calamity and danger, when viewed calmly and assigned to categories, become significantly less threatening. The oracle priests thus became indispensable guides in a world divided into both wilderness and civilization, this world and the beyond. Yet the partitions were so thin that an uninterrupted exchange took place between all of its parts, and even the means for attaining joy and wellbeing were the same on both sides. An army of spirits spun its possibly invisible yet quite palpable threads behind those changes in nature which brought man food and clothing, but also death and catastrophes, in the cycle of the seasons. Their world was no stranger than that of the barbarians living in the surrounding primeval forests. They also were sometimes friendly, and if more frequently they acted as enemies, it was simply that their life seemed to follow a different rhythm. Death itself was thus no absolute barrier. The dead merely changed his life rhythm in some way, yet not to such an extent that his desires were not directed toward the same things and could not be satisfied in the same way as in the Here and Now. The innumerable burial gifts[7] found in the graves of the Shang kings and their high functionaries show this quite clearly: from rings and cowry to entire carriages, horses, dogs and groups of servants and women, they all accompanied the dead to continue giving him pleasure in the beyond. The constant sacrifices to the dead were merely a continuation of this concern. All scrupulously observed distinctions notwithstanding, they underlined the similarities between the dead and other natural spirits who demanded the same attention (the bone inscriptions employed a complex vocabulary in the terminology of sacrifice, part of which is no longer decipherable today). The bronze vessels also found in the graves, used exclusively for sacral purposes and justifiably admired for their great artisanal skill and artistic quality, often suggest by their symbolic ornamentation that perhaps the way back from the beyond to this world, the return of the dead, also played a role and became connected with the symbolism of light and darkness as expressed in the eternal succession of day and night.[8] It is probable that intercourse with the realm of the dead was also maintained by shamans and mediums, although we have no reports about them from this early period but merely know that they existed.

The coalescence of such wholly different worlds had its parallel in the merging of two realms that are contraries for us: the past and the future. Although the oracle priests ostensibly confined their interests to prognostication, they were actually primarily concerned with the present. They intended to provide guides for action in the Here and Now.[9] Nothing fundamentally new or different was expected from the future. Had that been the case, their questions would have had to be phrased quite differently. What was expected was the repetition of what had long been known, and whose particular form depended on a decision made by the spirits in the beyond. The oracle priests were anything but prophets. Indeed, prophecy and oracles do not complement each other; they rather tend to be mutually exclusive. They were sober experts who attempted to uncover the mechanism of world events as it affected human life, just as they tried to discover the mechanism of the weather and of celestial phenomena. In their thought, the future played the same role as it does in meteorology: it was both the reason for, and the object of, all their endeavors. But as a concept, it was altogether meaningless. This almost scientific joy of discovery probably also led to the creation of the archives of inscribed bones on which all our knowledge is based. For it seems extremely likely that even at this early time an exploration of the future went hand in hand with an exploration or, at least, a preservation of the past which was to facilitate prognostication. This in turn would show that with the passage of time, the answers given by the oracles came to be understood not just as the independent decisions of more powerful spirits, but also as the pronouncements of more perceptive powers closer to the principle governing the course of the world. This early conception of time, which was still ignorant of the *Origin and Goal of History* (Jaspers) and surfaced time and again in later Chinese thought, had another important characteristic: stories about the creation of the world were unknown. This wholly undynamic conception of time which lacked any and all orientation, even toward the past, excluded the concept of a beginning as naturally as it did one of the end of the world.[10]

The extent to which this still undeveloped idea of time may have been influenced by the language is an extremely interesting though not easily settled question. For at that period, it was probably in the most pronounced phase of its "isolation" (perhaps still retaining vestiges of inflexional endings) and thus lacked nearly all means of assigning a statement to the past, the present or the future (as we do all the time without being aware of it). There can hardly be any doubt that this phenomenon, the result of a process continuing through millennia of prehistory, influenced thought in some fashion. The development of certain though only sporadically used auxiliary terms such as "already" (from "to stop") for the past, "soon" (from "to bring") for the future, or the negation "*wei*," "not yet" interesting as a concept and related to other negations in a series of vowel gradations, were hardly of a kind to make up for the fact that the temporal aspect could not be changed. For these auxiliaries came to occupy the same position as the auxiliaries used to designate space, so that the difference between "I do" and "I shall do" was the same, and no more important than, the difference between "I do here" and "I do there." One has to become aware of this curious spell exerted by atemporality if one wishes to understand what "hope" could have meant in traditional China. It required a second shift—still under way at the present time though proceeding more rapidly—until the language could gradually free itself by forming temporal suffixes, a development which surely further modified modes of thought.

It has been shown that the "isolating" character of the language was also decisive for the special quality of written Chinese. It is peculiar not because it was originally ideographic (all systems of writing began in this way), but because it always remained such, some unmistakable rudiments of a phonetic system notwithstanding. But this unwieldy and yet so seductively decorative script, itself the result of a lack of temporal differentiation, in turn acted as a brake on the development of Chinese language and culture, since it swallowed all phonetic changes that might have occurred in the course of time, and which undoubtedly also frequently indicated shifts in the meanings of concepts. It remained a silent communications system in the sense that, like the language of numbers in mathematics, something new could only be conveyed by a different grouping of the many individual elements, but not through the change in value of any single one whose meaning was fixed and axiomatic. Since the characters, once created, could obviously assimilate any phonetic or semantic shift a concept might undergo, it is understandable that for some the written language became a symbol of unchangeable, almost sacred ideas, while others saw it as the very image of a petrified doctrine choking a living culture with an icy hand. A step-by-step reform of the written language has been under way since 1956. While it is true that the principle of ideographic writing could not be abandoned lest the spatial unity of the country be endangered, it is probably no accident that the written language changed so fundamentally that even the layman cannot fail to notice it. As a result of the many abbreviated characters largely derived from variants of cursive, the stroke of the pen becomes surprisingly rapid, fleeting, almost hasty as compared to the solemn fixity of the old, complete characters. In its daring equilibrium, it is reminiscent of the Japanese brush stroke which, although derived from the Chinese, already at a very early date gave visual expression to the more dynamic national character of the Japanese, so different from the more tranquil Chinese, at rest within itself.[11]

FUNDAMENTAL CONCEPTIONS OF HAPPINESS

The ideographic character of the written language, which had nonetheless absorbed phonetic elements as well, permits a kind of etymology on two planes: the phonetic and the graphic, when one examines the basic meaning of a word-sign complex. This is true for the period extending to the third century B.C., when a systematization gave the characters a definitive form which remained unchanged for more than two thousand years. Yet the greatest caution is necessary for two reasons: an enormous quantity of unrelated homonyms induces the false belief that these words were originally pronounced the same way. Also, many graphic symbols look so much alike in their old form that they are easily confused with one another. In order to determine what was considered "happiness" during the Shang period, it is therefore certainly safer to examine the previously mentioned burial gifts since they are like those cherished objects taken along on a journey because without them life seems to lack savor. It is tempting, nonetheless, to glance briefly at the words and signs connected with the term "happiness" during earliest times since the bone inscriptions, which inquired how best to adapt to what lay in store, contain an abundance of expressions of this kind. In contrast to the burial gifts, they tell us not merely what constituted material happiness, but provide a psychological insight into the conceptions of happiness in earliest China, although it is true that they reflect somewhat onesidedly the associations formed in the minds of priests or the ruling upper class.

Viewed purely in terms of language, three large areas seem to emerge. Each of them demarcates one of the three principal aspects of happiness: the religious, the social and the material. "Word families" can be constituted for each of them. Both phonetically and semantically, their individual components developed along divergent paths in the course of the centuries. But precisely for this reason, we can discover the original seeds that ultimately produced the tree and its ramification.

In the religious sphere, we note the following integrated field:

(1) **t̯i̯ĕng*> *chen*[1] "beneficial."

---

1. 禎

(2) **tsâng> tsang*[2] "bringing happiness."
(3) **dzi̯ang> hsiang*[3] "promising happiness," "happiness."
(4) **dz' âg> tso*[4] "blessing," "happiness," "honor."

In the sphere of social life, i.e. wherever men bring each other joy and happiness albeit never wholly independently of nature and the supernatural, we have the following configuration:

(5) **k'ăng> k'ang*[5] "an abundant year," "prosperity," "peace."
(6) **k'i̯ăng> ch'ing*[6] "blessing," "happiness."
(7) **g'ĕng> hsing*[7] "happiness," "bringing blessings."
(8) **g'i̯ag> ch'i*[8] "happiness," "blessing."
(9) **χi̯ag> hsi*[9] "joy," "to be pleased," "joyful exclamation," "to have a good time."
(10) **χôg> hao*[10] "to take pleasure in," "to love."
(11) **nglŏg> yao*[11] or **lo* "joy."[13]

A second series which might be added here, although it could have developed independently because of the final dental, comprises the following terms:

(12) **g'ăn> hsien*[12] "happy and content."
(13) **χwân> huan*[13] "to be pleased."
(14) **χi̯an> hsin*[14] "joy," "happiness."
(15) **ki̯ĕt> chi*[15] "happiness," "promising happiness."[14]

The sphere of material well-being contains considerably fewer terms and is clearly distinct from the other two:

(16) **pi̯ŭk> fu*[16] "happiness," "prosperity," "many children."
(17) **pi̯ŭg> fu*[17] "wealth."[15]

This tripartition may be somewhat blurred in certain places, particularly in the second area where the dividing line between the "blessing" sent from the sphere of the supernatural on the one hand, and the "pleasure" found in human society on the other, understandably blend into each other, for every festive occasion was primarily a religious event, at least for the priest. Nonetheless, the demarcation was certainly experienced as a reality. For it recurs in identical fashion when we look at the Chinese signs signifying the various forms of happiness not as phonetic but as graphic entities. It is true that the number of relevant signs is relatively small if we confine ourselves to those going back in their entirety to an old pictograph. But the somewhat more frequent signs where only the one half has a semantic element (while the other half refers to pronunciation) can be used for purposes of interpretation. For since in the case of the semantic elements we are dealing with

2. 臧
3. 祥
4. 祚
5. 康
6. 慶
7. 幸
8. 祺
9. 喜
10. 好 
11. 樂 
12. 憪
13. 歡
14. 欣
15. 吉 
16. 福 
17. 富 

what are clearly signs for categories, so-called radicals, the larger part of which was added at a relatively late date, though some of which were already in use during the Shang period, we can be certain that the concepts used by them reflect categories already in existence in the most remote times.

In a number of the words listed, the element of the supernatural is represented by the categorical sign "God" or "spirit," which is joined to a phonetic element not essential to the meaning here. This applies to (1), (3), (4), (8), (16). (4), belonging to the group of concepts of religious happiness, is introduced through phonetic derivation without secondary additions, and therefore asserts nothing. But perhaps (15) should be included in the religious sphere. It recurs constantly in the bone inscriptions. But precisely because of this fact, it was represented in so many different and rapidly developing pictographs that its true original meaning is difficult to determine. In the oldest forms,[16] however, there is fairly good reason to believe that the lower element meant "mouth." In the case of the upper element, it is unclear whether it originally designated a house (place of worship with talking spirits) or an altogether different object.

If the element "mouth" alone is considered, it could of course just as easily be assigned to the second group to which it belongs phonetically, for song and music did constitute the most essential characteristics of the Chinese conception of happiness in society. We encounter them in the form of several pictographs, the most important being the two signs (9) and (11). As can be incontestably shown by a comparison with other material, the old form of the first represents "kettle drum" and "mouth." This combination is sometimes supplemented by an additional radical, "mouth" or "woman," which shows rather prettily the idea the old Chinese had of merry celebrations. The other sign is the drawing of a complicated musical instrument, probably of a set of bells of varying size, which were common during the Shang period if we can judge by burial finds. The sign (10) is also very impressive, representing "woman" and "child" happily united. The signs (5), (6), and (7) again seem to belong to the type of simple phonetic derivation and are therefore useless for an interpretation of pictographs. At best, the radical "rain" in sign (5) might perhaps be considered significant. The three remaining signs of the group, however, are clearly formed with radicals: (12) with the conceptually somewhat indistinct radical "heart," which is present in an enormous number of characters denoting emotions, while (13) and (14) are formed with the much rarer radical "yawning," which is truly memorable in this context. In (16) and (17), the last of the signs listed, we find a common basic element for the concept of material happiness. While it does not appear in isolation in the written language, it is wholly unambiguous nonetheless. It denotes a jug of wine. In the first sign, (16), which stands for material happiness in the most comprehensive sense, only the previously mentioned radical "spirit" is added, and in the second, (17), the radical "roof." Either partly or in their entirety, all of these signs derive from pictographs. Among them, (11), the set of bells, is undoubtedly the most interesting. Both graphically and phonetically, the exceptionally important connection between "happiness-joy" and "music" is demonstrable here. Even today, this very sign, though with a different pronunciation, is used to denote music in general. But this different reading *yüeh* goes back to an old **nglŏk* which in turn is closely related to the two old forms for the two further readings, **nglŏg* and **glak,* which the sign has in the meaning "joy." The written language thus preserved a genuine relationship between two words which gradually disappeared in the spoken language due to progressive phonetic differentiation. While Chinese philosophers also frequently adduced rather questionable verbal parallels not unlike our popular etymologies, this connection between joy and music led many of them to speculate about the nature of language at an early date. Particularly the distinction made by the Confucian Hsün-tzu (ca. 298–238 B.C.)[17] had a profound effect. Because it was most probably based on earlier reflections, it must be briefly mentioned here. He considered music as that element of culture that united men beyond all their differences, while its no less important opposite pole, "ritual" *(li),* supposedly had the function of separating them according to their different classes. But some especially important, perhaps indeed the most important, provisions of "ritual" referred to the instructions concerning the various forms of mourning for the dead. Particularly with respect to the kinds of garment and the length of time they were to be worn, these rules made such subtle distinctions that the severely hierarchical social structure found an exceptionally clear expression here. It would therefore appear that from the very beginning, "ritual" evoked associations of "misfortune," "mourning," and class-conscious dress in Chinese thought, and also the "distinction" created by social categories. Conversely, "music" evoked such concepts as "happiness," "joy," "nakedness," and the union of men irrespective of class and sex. Hsün-tzu wished to assure "ritual" the most important place in the Confucian system. Although his strict views did not find unanimous acceptance, it seems almost an omen that of the "Five Classics" most deeply respected in Confucianism, one, originally the sixth according to tradition, should have been lost. It was the "classic of music." Conversely, the "classic of ritual" became so voluminous that it had to be reedited in three separate works.[18]

THE PROBLEM OF CHANGE

In the second millennium B.C. of course, the period of Confucianism still lay far in the future. Many profound changes were necessary to create the conditions from which the specifically Confucian world view could arise. The first, probably most decisive event in this context was the decline of the Shang dynasty. It was brought about by the Chou who invaded China from the west. Still viewed as semi-barbarians in central China, theirs was a strictly patriarchal organization and they consequently only worshipped heaven and the stars. They thus differed from the Shang, where matriarchal elements still survived. The ruler, who now took the title of king, enjoyed a much stronger position than the Shang king ever had, particularly because he evidently performed the most important of all rites, the rite of heaven, in his own person. While the Shang kings thus lost their position of leadership and sank to the level of ordinary feudal princes, the oracle priests who had formed a kind of second government up to that time because their predictions had also influenced politics, suffered an even worse fate. They literally lost their entire existence—at least the existence which they had always considered ideal, i.e. their position as councillors of the king and as men whose word was all-powerful. The new rulers had sufficient confidence in themselves to eliminate them rigorously from this position. At the same time, they were intelligent enough to continue occupying them in the administration as slave officials of a sort. For their knowledge of the written language and of astronomy was simply irreplaceable. This is also the reason that the old Chinese word for "slave" underwent a curious change in meaning, becoming the term for "minister." The classical *Book of Songs (Shih-ching)* contains some songs which express the lament of these educated men who were being wasted as simple scribes and administrators.[19]

Under these conditions, it cannot have been easy for the Chou to make the people and, more importantly, the not entirely replaceable upper stratum (the nobility was taken over from the Shang without change) believe that this change in leadership was just. Quite a number of documents that have come down to us clearly show that the Chou engaged in very intensive political propaganda which suddenly introduced an entirely new category never mentioned previously: morality. It is true that all these texts later passed through the hands of the Confucians. According to tradition, it was even Confucius himself who compiled them. Nonetheless, the parts that concern us here are undoubtedly genuine. In some of the speeches allegedly made by the first two Chou kings, the theory is developed that they had not acted on their own authority in driving the Shang from their throne, but that this had been accomplished with the will of "heaven." In view of the infamous excesses the last kings had supposedly indulged in, heaven had withdrawn its "mandate" *(ming)* from them. (It is possible that the reference here is to certain matriarchal orgiastic cults whose origin the Chou did not understand.) To give a solid foundation to this idea, it was extended backward in time. It was suddenly discovered that a precedent existed, for the Shang themselves had usurped the place of the still earlier Hsia dynasty in an analogous manner. Speeches by king T'ang, the first Shang ruler, were invented and studded with the same reproaches against the last Hsia kings as seemed apposite at this later time.[20] There was no escaping the force of this cleverly constructed argument which gave the Shang their due and even beat them with their own arms. The Chou probably owed the success of the first centuries of their reign to its persuasiveness.

The downfall of the oracle priests necessarily resulted in a change or, perhaps more accurately, a shift in emphasis in the practice of oracles. The oracle using pieces of bone and tortoise shells was completely abolished. Its place was taken by the oracle with dried milfoil stalks counted according to fixed rules. It is very probable that this form of oracle, known simply as the "oracle of the Chou," already existed during the Shang period. Given the nature of the material, it is obvious that no trace of it has been found. What is essential is that this kind of oracle came to be used to the exclusion of all others. Actually, the two forms of oracle were not so different as may appear. For like the bone oracle, the milfoil stalk oracle only answered questions framed according to the yes-no or favorable-unfavorable schema. The opposites were symbolized by a straight or a bent stalk which remained after all the stalks had been counted out.[21] But an important difference emerges here. In a certain sense, the answer was calculated; it was already given in the way the stalks were thrown or chosen and not wholly subject to the accidents of nature or the varying temperature on the surface of the bones, as in the earlier oracle. Even more important is the fact that the milfoil stalk oracle was subject to a measure of verification. The bone oracle, on the other hand, could be manipulated at will, as has been proven in certain instances where the answer was also noted.

On the one hand, this simplification of the oracle eliminated the possibility of discovering any number of nuances in a positive or negative, a favorable or unfavorable response in the network of cracks. But there also arose the temptation to increase the number of possible answers, to enlarge the scope of the entire system after that of the individual imagination had first been restricted to a minimum. A similar development can be observed in almost all forms of divination. Spontaneous prediction is followed by systematization, which assures even the person without prophetic gifts access to this art and thus abruptly turns seers into scientists. In the case of the milfoil stalk oracle, a decision was obviously made to maintain a degree of tension between positive and negative prior to their resolution. This was accomplished by leaving not just one, but three, and ultimately six stalks. If their position was also taken into account, this meant eight and sixty-four answers respectively. Obviously, these answers were no longer a simple "yes" or "no" but defined a specific situation. The origins of the *I-ching*, the *Book of Changes,* can be traced back to this method. In its sixty-four "hexagrams," broken—(being "divided in two," they always counted as even numbers) and unbroken lines were combined in groups of six (as, for example, ䷅) and described in terse aphorisms as cosmic or human situations. But these situations were not conceived as rigidly isolated but in constant movement, as indeed taking on meaning only when in movement, since one or several lines in such a hexagram were always about to turn into their opposite and thus to become part of any other hexagram. In a numerologically, carefully constructed network with enormous possibilities of variation (more precisely 64 x 64, or 4,096 different situations), "all" forms of reality in their reciprocal causal and temporal effects were included at a single stroke. Under these circumstances, it is only natural that the single lines which originally merely symbolized "yes" or "no" as alternative answers suddenly appeared in a wholly changed light. They became symbols of the oppositions which pervade all of nature, which constitute the tension, the movement in all life processes. However various their forms might be—light and darkness, male and female, origin and decline—they had an identical essence consisting of complementary opposites. The pervasively dualistic Chinese world view thus developed from the interpretation of these two fundamental forces, Yang and Yin, and their varying effects. They could be gleaned from the *Book of Changes* and commentaries and appendices of which more and more were added, beginning in the fifth century B.C. Like annual rings, they began to surround the slender stem in greater and greater quantities.[22]

In this conception, past and future play a role not dissimilar to the one we noted in our discussion of language. They collapse in the present since every actualized situation contains all others in a state of latency. Such a view, where time is conceived of as two dimensional[23] may, but need not, include cycles. But even without them, the passage of time can be easily surveyed. Speaking figuratively, thought about time moves on a disc rather than along a circle. The present is never limited to the narrow area of a line, let alone that of a point. The system has its critical limitation elsewhere, for the number of possible situations is necessarily finite. It follows that all movement occurs within a closed system, proceeds at an even speed. It takes its cue from a nature that "makes no jumps." The very premise that everything is change endows change with a curiously static quality, something suspiciously homogeneous which precludes development properly so-called. The ideograph for the concept "*i*"[1] "change," which gave the *I-ching* its name, also seems to point in this direction. On the oldest bone inscriptions, it has a form which probably represents a juxtaposition of "darkness" (hatches) and "moon." In spite of the slight deviation in the stylization of the sign for "moon"[2] this interpretation is supported by the fact that on the bones "hatches" appear with some regularity as an independent sign only in front of "sun" or "moon."[24] The change from full moon to new moon was thus the original concept of "change." By its very nature, such change is not just cyclical but merely apparent since it owes its existence to the varying illumination of something which is itself unchangeable.

Whether this shift in the nature of oracles, and the profanization implicit in it was accomplished by the oracle priests of the Shang period is difficult to determine. Some facts support such a hypothesis. There are, for example, certain parallels in the formulations found in the bone inscriptions and the *I-ching.* It is also true that clearly historical events in back of some of the sayings of the *I-ching* were intentionally stripped of their historical characteristics. Having thus been turned into abstractions, they were used to illustrate recurring developmental tendencies. This would fit in well with the systematic work of the oracle priests and their "archives."[25] For that this unchanging intellectual class had at least an indirect influence on all activities connected with the mastery of writing may be

1. 易    2. 月 

taken for granted. But it is possible that their influence extended even further. It is true that the *I-ching* has a static quality. Yet it is possible that from the very beginning they infused something like a hope for a future in Chinese thought, although that future was a cyclically recurring one. During the first third of our century when an entire generation of Chinese intellectuals undertook a remembrance of things past in their own culture because they were profoundly disturbed by the vehemence and force of western civilization that seemed to result from its belief in development and progress, the ingenious scholar Hu Shih (1891–1962) developed the exciting theory that not only the Jews but also the Shang people had been animated by messianic ideas. He further suggested that the Shang had also transferred these messianic hopes to the religious sphere after they had been disappointed in the political arena. Hu Shih's starting point was the self-designation of the "Confucians" which is indeed much older than Confucius. The term in question, **ńi̯u>ju*[1] originally meant "weak," (later also "dwarf") and is obviously related to the terms **ńi̯u>ju*[2] "child" and **sni̯u>hsü*[3] "to wait," where it is of course in "child" that the bifurcation of concepts begins (in the written language also, these words use the same element combined with "rain"). For it is characteristic of the child that its weakness is a function of time, that it need only wait to lose it. But Hu Shih not merely stresses the meaning "weak," which is uncontested in this connection and simply distinguished the scribes from armed knights, but also the meaning "to wait." He tried to prove that the *Ju*-"Confucians" still wore the garments of the Shang, that they observed their ritual, particularly the ceremony of mourning, and that they played the leading role in the state of Sung and the regions east of it, the states of Ch'i and Lu (the state where Confucius was born), the domain of the Shang. According to Hu Shih, they did not simply resign themselves to the decline of the Shang but hoped for a restoration of their rule and thus of their own position of dominance.[26] Hu Shih seems to have believed that many prophecies to this effect were hidden in the classical writings, such as the old chronicle *Tso-chuan,* but also in the *Book of Changes,* specifically in hexagram 5, which is entitled *Hsü* ("waiting") and attempts to portray this situation. In the interpretations of the six lines, the phases of waiting are described as follows:

1. Waiting along the borders. If one helps oneself by being constant, there will be no misfortune.
2. Waiting in the sand. Little talk, but ultimately salvation.
3. Waiting in the mud. One attracts misfortune.
4. Waiting in blood. One leaves the cave.
5. Waiting while eating and drinking wine. Happiness and salvation.
6. One returns to the cave. Three unknown guests have arrived without having been urged. If one pays them respect, salvation will come in the end.[27]

---

1. 儒 2. 孺 3. 需

In these sentences, Hu Shih sees an allusion to the fate of the oracle priests who had to wait "in blood," lost their domicile, but believed that they would some day return in splendor under new rulers. The following poem from the section "Songs of the Chang" from the classical *Book of Songs* where the greatness of this dynasty is celebrated, suggests a similar allusion to him:

> Heaven bade the black bird/descend and give life to the Shang./ Living in the land of Yin, they multiplied./Thus the god emperor commanded the warlike T'ang ages ago,/to order the frontiers in the four directions of heaven.//
>
> He then ordered his princes to proceed to the four directions of heaven,/and thus possessed the nine domains in splendor./In this way, the first princes of the Shang received their orders without danger,/and this is also true of the descendant of king Wu-ting.//
>
> There is no one who is not defeated by the descendant of king Wu-ting,/the "Warrior King"/with only ten chariots decorated with dragon banners he removed the great misery./It is in the royal land of a thousand miles/that the people finds rest,/where the borders begin, which extend as far as the four oceans.//
>
> They come hurrying from the four oceans to participate./They hurry to participate in great numbers./The splendor radiates roundabout as far as the Yellow River./It is proper in every respect that Yin [i.e. Shang] receives the order of heaven,/hundredfold is the happiness that thrives.//[28]

The important thing in this poem is that actually all traditional commentators have been puzzled about the identity of the "Warrior King" mentioned in the central section. Because Chinese does not differentiate between the various tenses, it cannot even be determined whether the descriptions in the last two stanzas, given in the present tense in this translation, refer to the past, the present or the future. Hu Shih boldly assigns them to the future. Because he cannot identify a historical successor of Wu-ting to whom the exploits so fervently celebrated can be ascribed or who may have had this title of honor, he sees in the "Warrior King," the "descendant of Wu-ting," a Messiah who would free the Shang people of their great "misery" (this word appears in the text only because a philologically correct but nonetheless risky substitution has been made by replacing the similarly written sign "millet" which occurs in the *textus receptus*).[29] A scholar of equal, worldwide renown, the much more sober Feng Yu-lan (born in 1895), has rejected Hu Shih's theories as too improbable, particularly the messianic prophecies.[30] But they have not been decisively disproved and are too fascinating not to be mentioned. For even if they were to have no significance in an evaluation of the intellectual situation of China during the early Chou period, their import is all the greater for the China of early modern times, which attempted to become conscious of itself. In any event, Hu Shih's researches into the intellectual origins of Confucianism—and they are not confined to what has been set forth here—have directed attention to the dynamic components in its development. They are not subject to any doubt, and have been neglected for too long.

2 / *TURNING AWAY FROM THE PRESENT*

HEAVEN

The power of the Chou kings collapsed about 770 B.C., not quite three centuries after their victory over the Shang. This did not lead to a restoration of the Shang empire, however, but to an interregnum of nearly half a century's duration. The Chou kings, driven from their crown lands in the West by foreign tribes, at first remained the nominal rulers, but their functions were restricted to matters of cult and religion. Thus they retained their influence the longest in a sphere from which they had once driven the oracle priests. Yet it was generally felt that this division of powers between the king as a kind of high priest conducting the sacrifices to heaven, and the "protectors of the realm," powerful princes of individual, now independent but formerly feudal states who were the real rulers, turned the right order upside down. This view was confirmed by the gradual disintegration of all order, the unending wars between the states, and the increasing misery of the population. In addition, there was a certain dishonesty in intellectual matters. When the Chou had assumed power, many, but especially religious concepts coined by the Shang either had to be equated or combined with those used by the Chou, although originally they had had nothing to do with each other. Their ambiguity increased as a result, and while they became superficially more interesting perhaps, they actually suffered a loss of substance because the various meanings cancelled each other out.

A quite characteristic and important example of this trend is the word *t'ien*[1] "heaven," which at first clearly represented the ancestor of the Shang rulers. The old pictograph distinctly shows a human figure with a large head and powerfully developed limbs. It was only natural that the Chou should not have been interested in obeisance to the Shang ancestors, yet they did not simply want to drop this weighty concept. Because heaven was worshipped in their religion, they

1. 天

identified this earliest ancestor with Shang-ti, the "God-emperor on high,"[31] who was revered by the Chou. But in the process, he lost much of his distinctness. Gradually, he also came to be used to merely designate the place where the earliest ancestors of the Chou sat on their thrones "to the left and the right of the God-emperor on high." Thus he lost not only his character as a person but also the personal closeness that had been his up to this moment. The consequence was that those passages in the documents where "heaven" itself "speaks" and not merely acts spontaneously (which is a wholly different matter) became increasingly rare. Conversely, we encounter more and more passages where, in direct opposition to the original meaning of the word, it is the difference between heaven and man that is stressed. In the previously mentioned chronicle *Tso-chuan,* for example, we find the following observation entered under the year 524 B.C.: "The way of heaven is far away from us, only the way of man is close. Since we do not reach heaven, how could we succeed in understanding it?"[32]

Hesitantly but unmistakably, a split between this world and the beyond, between these two realms which had still been so closely integrated during the Shang period, becomes noticeable. Given the immeasurable expanse of heaven, this gap had already been implicit in the equation of *t'ien* and "heaven." The sacrifice to heaven and the use of the *I-ching,* viewed increasingly as a symbol of the world principle, meant that a direct intervention of the beyond in this world was no longer expected. What is reflected here is a more sceptical attitude, a spirit that had returned to itself. Besides, the dualism of the *Book of Changes,* reinforcing already accepted polarizations of being, suggested the opposition of heaven (Yang) and earth (Yin). This new conception worked in two directions. Psychologically, the recognition of heaven meant that a new world was created which might well serve as a place of refuge, of distant vistas and of happiness. But it also established clear boundaries; it made the earth more of a place for men, living men, than ever before and suggested that these boundaries against the spirits be made as impenetrable as possible (and this included those spirits whose home was not "heaven" but other spheres in the beyond).

It is probably the Shamans who discovered heaven as a quasi-spatial dimension of bliss. Many of them were women and had, together with the oracle priests, already played a role during the Shang period, especially in rain magic. Even later, they continued their activity in a tradition that was principally connected with southern China. It lies in the nature of the case that they should have left no literary documents, least of all from this early period. But in a collection of song-like poems, the *Elegies of Ch'u (Ch'u-tz'u)* which goes back to the second century B.C. and whose earliest parts date back to the fourth century, we find a number of pieces which convey a very clear if stylized concept of the mystical and religious experiences of these Shamans. In an incredibly spirited language scanned by the word *hsi* and which resembles a moan, the Shaman's ecstatic flights to heaven are described. They culminate in an almost erotically experienced encounter with the god residing there, and usually end with an anguished return to earth. The collection contains a total of nine of these elegies with the title, "Nine Songs" *(Chiu-ko).* One of them reads as follows:

> Open wide the gate of Heaven!/I ride in splendor on a black cloud,/commanding the whirlwind to drive ahead of me,/commanding the rain to scatter the mist in front of me!//
>
> You descend in wide circles, o Master,/let me follow you over the K'un-sang mountain!/Do you see down below the milling crowds on the nine continents?/What does the span of a single life mean to me?//
>
> Vaulting upward, he floats on serene heights,/riding on pure vapor, guiding Yin and Yang./Quickly, o Master, I wish to move with you to guide the god above on his way to the Chiu-kang mountain.//
>
> In undulating folds, my garment of clouds falls down,/my belt of jade gives off a deep sound./A Yin, a Yang, a Yin, a Yang, no mortal knows what we are doing.//
>
> I have plucked the iridescent flower of the sacred hemp,/to give it to one living far away./Age has overtaken me,/I have lost him and have rapidly become a stranger to him.//
>
> He drives a dragon chariot with thundering wheels/up high on his way heavenward,/but I stand here, turning the cinnamon branch in my hands/while I pine away.//
>
> My heart aches, what am I to do?/I wish moments could last an eternity./But fate governs the life of man,/meeting and parting are not his decision.//[33]

There is also another, probably later poem to be found in the *Elegies of Ch'u.* It is entitled, "The Calling Back of the Soul" *(Chao-hun),* and is closely connected with certain ceremonies for the dead which developed toward the end of the Chou period. In a rich vocabulary and a language celebrating triumphs, all the beauties of the world are described in the most glowing colors for the soul of the dead as it flies heavenward (of course, beauties in such abundance were available only to princes). At the same time, unpleasant things are mentioned about all the worlds in the beyond so that at the last moment the fleeing spirit might perhaps be induced to return to his body. Even heaven itself is not excluded from this warning, as can be seen in the following verse: "O return, soul, do not ascend to heaven!/For tigers and leopards guard its gates./Their jaws ever open to attack mortals. . . ./All the corners of the world are filled with evil and terror."/[34]

In a certain sense, they thus show the opposite attitude: if happiness can be found at all, it is on earth, not in heaven. The this-worldly orientation of this thought, a this-worldliness which can be persuaded only with difficulty that things are better "beyond" than on this earth, is really much more typical of Chinese thought generally than the belief in a beyond. The mere fact that we encounter it in texts as evidently religious as these is convincing proof. But this element is even more pronounced in texts which confine themselves to descriptions of the world here and now, and view everything outside it exclusively from this perspective. These are primarily the writings which have been classified as "Confucian."

CONFUCIUS AND CHINESE HUMANISM

Confucius (551–479 B.C.) was indeed the first Chinese philosopher to formulate these earthbound thoughts which had been developing gradually and for centuries before his birth. He brought them together in a kind of system, although he himself does not seem to have left any writings but exerted his influence entirely through his disciples. His great discovery was man and the virtue of "humanity" (there is no distinction between the two words in ancient Chinese). However nebulous it might be in every respect, this concept brought a shift in thought of epochal proportions.[35] For seen from its perspective, the charisma of kings, a kind of axiom which could at best be derived from the supernatural, the existence of spirits, of the dead, and of a variety of beings in nature, all of them values that had governed life up to this point, shrank to the status of mere ornaments. They retained a value, of course, but it was one that had its source wholly in man, and was moral and esthetic in nature. As "heaven" became an ordering power which did not intervene arbitrarily in the course of history but was bound to human, moral norms and could even less be a place detached from the world, the wall separating this world and a possible beyond was strengthened further. The *Book of Conversations (Lun-yü),* the only authoritative source of the teachings of Confucius, states that "the master never discussed magic powers and demons."[36] This is no mere agnosticism but a clear rejection of all commerce with this sphere. It was meant to counter the danger that laws, which were irrational and not of this world should find acceptance among men and thus abolish the pervasive law of "humanity." Two passages in the *Lun-yü* leave no doubt about this:

> Fan Ch'ih asked what wisdom is. The master answered: "To dedicate oneself seriously to the duties toward men, to honor spirits and gods but to stay away from them. That can be called wisdom."
>
> Chi-lu asked how spirits should be served. The master answered: "If it is impossible to do justice to men, how can one do justice to the spirits?" And when Chi-lu asked further if he might find out something about the nature of death, Confucius answered: "How can one understand death as long as one does not yet understand life?"[37]

All energy and all hope were thus to be concentrated on the here and now. For the split between a beyond and a world here below created an urgent task which Confucius saw facing his time: the rebirth of a world with a new kind of hierarchy and under the leadership of a ruler who derived his legitimacy from the abundance of his human virtues. While Confucius expressed himself at length about such a "prince's son" (Chün-tzu), he said much less about the kind of government he would institute and the nature of the ordered world he would create. He was to govern through "virtue" (**tak>te*).[1] But "virtue" itself was apparently one of the values to be included in a transvaluation of all values. In its old form, the sign was graphically and phonetically related to "straight" (**d'i̯ək>chih*),[2] where "eye" and "straight line" represent the essential elements in both of the old written forms. Its basic meaning, particularly in matters relating to magic, seems to have been "to fix with one's eyes," "to look at fixedly," "to bind by a spell," from which both the meaning "(magical) power" and "orientation toward" could be derived.[38] Seen from this perspective, many of Confucius's sayings concerning the right form of government acquire a very concrete meaning, and almost come to resemble plays on words, such as the following: "The master said: 'To govern through "virtue" is, figuratively speaking, to act like the north star: it does not move from its place, and all stars gather around it.' "[39]

Powerful calm which by its own concentrated lack of movement assigns to all that happens its unalterable course, is thus the key to peace and order in the world. It is supplemented by "ritual"[40] which represents a unified, yet internally finely gradated system: "The master said: 'If the people are governed by a bureaucracy and by equal punishments, they will slip away and no longer feel shame. If the people are governed by "virtue" and made equal by "ritual," they will be modest and also have social categories.' "[41]

This term "to make equal" *(ch'i)* is an expression which was originally used to distinguish the woman who had attained "equality" through betrothal and by being declared of age, from the mere girl. The word shows strikingly the Confucian concept of "equality": equality rests on the consistency of the system of government in its totality and as it affects everyone. It does not function by extending the sanctions of its every component to every single person. On the contrary: "virtue" and "ritual" bring the people to accept social categories as a matter of personal concern. This is much more effective than a bureaucracy which allows the people to break away from the sphere of influence of the ruler or a penal code which permits it to "shamelessly" pull down the barriers between the various classes: "Superior men find themselves in harmony *(ho)* with each other, but they are not equal *(t'ung)*. The lower classes are equal, but are not in harmony with each other."[42]

The following quotation must be understood in the same way. Here, the concept "equal," although again conveyed by a different word having the basic meaning "level" *(chün)*, signifies the same thing: "The master said: . . . 'I have heard that the person who calls a state or a family his own should not be troubled if [the people] are few, but that he should be troubled if they are not "equal";

1. 德 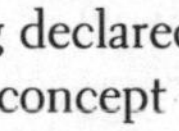 2. 直 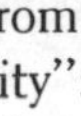

that he should not be troubled if they are poor, but should be troubled if they have no peace. For if they are "equal," they will not be poor; if there is harmony, they will not [remain] few in numbers; [if they live] peacefully, there will be no overthrow.' "[43]

The fundamental equation of an ideal world order, calm and equality can thus already be found in Confucius, although its form rather reminds us of a uniform stabilization of inequality. The period where this kind of government seems to have been fully realized in Confucius's opinion was the western (or "earlier") Chou dynasty (about 1050–770 B.C.). Later, this period tended to become increasingly the "golden age" for the Confucians, as mentioned before. But it is important to realize that from the perspective of the sixth century B.C., this meant that it was not situated in remotest antiquity but still stood in the brightest light of history, having ended little more than two hundred years earlier.

Originally, Confucius's teaching thus had none of the orientation toward the past which appeared to characterize it at a later date. Compared with its competitors, it even seemed relatively modern. Emotionally, Confucius felt close to the duke of Chou. This was the brother of the founder of the dynasty, Wu-wang ("warrior king") who for years acted as regent for Ch'eng-wang (governed 1115–1078 B.C. according to tradition), Wu-wang's son and successor. This tie to a person who had lived half a millennium earlier and which appears time and again in the *Lun-yü* certainly did not rest on an exaggerated archaism but on a certain self-appraisal. For Confucius, and not only for him, the "duke of Chou" was the spiritual founder of the Chou dynasty, just as king Wu-wang had been the political one. Everything indicates that Confucius longed for a similar role. It is possible that this marked esteem for the position of regent and imperial councillor, in some respects even more important than that of the emperor himself, was not unrelated to memories of the indirect power of the oracle priests, although the functions of a councillor and regent of Confucian stamp were clearly of an ethical, not a religious character. Many remarks that have come down to us prove that Confucius was firmly convinced of his world-shaking, "heaven-sent" mission. He may already have known of a tradition whose existence during the century following his death is verifiable beyond a doubt and according to which the realm would be saved and restored every five hundred years by a truly spiritual ruler. Along with his previously discussed theories concerning the messianism of the oracle priests, Hu Shih has done impressive work in bringing out and documenting the existence of such a tradition for the period *following* Confucius.[44] Yet it seems odd that even at a later time we never hear about this matter from the lips of prophets but only from those who, basing themselves on a rather dubious arithmetic, thought that they were the anxiously awaited restorers. This shows not merely a crude egotism but underlines again, if from a different perspective, that passive waiting was not a developed idea in Chinese thought. Similar to the belief in a heavenly "mandate" to rule the world being passed from one dynasty to the next, the conviction that a great restorer would appear every five hundred years thus more probably arose from the precedent created by Confucius's repeated emphasis on the close tie between himself and the duke of Chou. Among those who always saw themselves as the longed-for redeemers when one of these periods approached (and our own time is one of them), there were men of influence close to potentates, emperors and pretenders to the crown. Whether the melioration of the world was to proceed in two simultaneous or successive phases (a political and a cultural reform), or in a single movement through the emergence of a "philosopher king" was a question that was never unambiguously answered.[45]

MENCIUS AND THE FIRST SOCIAL UTOPIAS

If credence can be given to Confucian writings—and presumably they are never more genuine than when they discuss defeat—the last years of Confucius's life were filled with profound disappointment over his lack of political impact. At the time of the early death of his favorite disciple Yen Hui whom he perhaps even hoped at times to train as the future king, he complained that "heaven had abandoned him,"[46] a melancholy phrase whose tone is echoed in many other formulations of his last years. Indeed, the direct political influence of his teaching was minimal. Yet a single human life would not have sufficed to measure the full extent of an indirect effect that was to transform the future. It was probably not without justification that Mencius, Confucius's famous successor, looked upon himself as having brought his work to fruition, for it was only with him that Confucianism took on a clearly political stamp. Mencius was much more sober than his venerated model. He adopted—or perhaps established—the tradition of the periodic return of a world savior. Making no secret of his view, he immediately claimed that role for himself, and sought to dismiss the temporal discrepancy in a subordinate clause according to which the time was more than ripe. He strengthened the tradition with the doctrine of a rhythmically recurring self-purification of the world. "It is long ago that the empire (*t'ien-hsia* "that below heaven") came into being," he said. "There have always been periods of order, and periods of confusion."[47] The tone of this statement is composed and rests on his firm belief in the "goodness" of a nature which would always reassert itself, and this was true both of nature in general and human nature in particular. This also accounts for his regard for the "people." Elaborating on the lapidary phrase that "heaven does not speak," he represents it as a true "vox dei," more valuable than the king, more valuable even than the gods of nature. For, according to him, the people are the only court of appeal and decide whether or not a dynasty has the "mandate." A new ruler must be "introduced" to both heaven and the people before he can be certain of his office.[48] It is therefore a basic premise of every ideal government that the prince own everything in an "equal manner" with the people. At every opportunity, Mencius describes this form of government and quotes supporting instances from antiquity:

King Hsüan of Ch'i asked: "Is it true that the park of King Wen-wang [of Chou] comprised 70 square miles?" "Thus it is written," Mencius replied. "What, that large?" the king exclaimed. "The people still considered it too small," Mencius answered. "My park covers only 40 square miles, and yet the people consider it too large. What is the reason?" "The park of Wen-wang," Mencius replied, "comprised 70 square miles, it is true, but whoever wanted to cut grass or firewood, whoever wanted to hunt pheasants or rabbits, could enter it. [King Wen] thus owned it in the same manner *(t'ung)* as the people. Is that not a reason that the people still considered it too small?"[49]

Under such a government, it is naturally also impossible for the people to be exploited, and this results in a well-being that benefits all:

"If one does not arbitrarily ignore the work in the field that each season demands," [by the imposition of irrelevant forced labor] Mencius taught King Hui of Liang, "more grain will be harvested than can be eaten. If nets that are too narrow are not allowed in ponds and lakes, there will be more fish and tortoises than can be eaten. If the axe and the hatchet can only be taken into the mountain forests at the proper time, there will be more timber than can be used. If all this happens, the people are given an opportunity to feed the living and to mourn the dead without grief. And this in turn is the first step toward a truly royal government *(wang-tao).* Let mulberry trees be planted around the estates of more than five *mou,* and those fifty years and older will be dressed in silk. Do not let the right time for the breeding of cattle pass by, and those seventy years and older will always have meat to eat. Don't steal from the people the time required to till their land of 100 *mou,* and even families with several mouths to feed will not have to suffer hunger. Turn your attention to the education in the schools, let the people be taught the sentiments of piety and brotherly love, and you will no longer see the grey-haired carrying heavy burdens in the streets. It has never yet happened that royal dignity was not conferred on the ruler of a state where all this is done."[50]

This rather detailed description of a state functioning ideally in the Confucian sense is of a sobriety that could hardly be expected of Confucius. Its characteristics recur in the account of the "well field system," designed by Mencius as a key to the just distribution of goods between the people and its ruler. This system owes its name to the form of the Chinese character *ching*[1] (well). Its central idea is the division of the empire into a network of units of land. Each of these consists of nine fields, eight of which serve a family group for its needs while the ninth, which lies in the center, is tilled for the ruler and the state. Mencius said about this system:

Under a government with "humanity" [according to the well field system], one begins with demarcation [of the land]. For if the boundaries are not drawn correctly,

---

1. 井 丼 丼

> the land within the well units is not of equal quality and the amount of grain grown and used for pay not the same everywhere . . . I therefore propose to divide the new land [along the periphery of the state] into units of nine fields, and to let one of them be tilled according to the rules governing compulsory service. In the center of the state, on the other hand, a tenth is to be raised as tax and paid by those subject to it. [The high officials] from the minister on down must have a "scepter field" of fifty *mou,* the other dignitaries one of 25 *mou.* When someone dies or moves away, the village community does not lose any land, for it always retains the same *(t'ung)* share in the well field units [comprising its area]. [All members of the community] become friends through constant intercourse, they help each other maintain and guard their land, and care for each other when ill and in distress. Thus the "hundred families" become affectionate and content. One well field unit measures one square mile, a total of 900 *mou.* The "public field" lies in the center. Eight families till their private piece of land of 100 *mou* each and the "public field" jointly. Only after they have finished work on the "public field" do they dare work on their private field.[51]

It is not entirely clear from these comments whether this system, whose administrative schematism is a typically Chinese phenomenon, was developed by Mencius as a sort of governmental program, or whether he was referring to actual models of either the past or his own time. Although not realizable in practice in this form, the idea as such had considerable influence on the development of all conceptions of the ideal state in China although, or perhaps precisely because, the tone was so sober. As late as the twenties and thirties, and even thereafter, when modern socio-political ideas became influential, east-Asian and some western scholars engaged in vigorous disputes concerning the historicity of these well fields. Their discussion created a special branch of scholarly literature in the field of Chinese social history. The problem was not resolved, of course, but the dispute did reveal the various subjective views of the authors concerning the ideal state in general.[52]

MO TI AND THE FUNDAMENTS OF CHINESE SOCIALISM

The passion with which Mencius stressed the importance of the people and his appeal to the ruler to share everything with it in an "equal manner"; and even his use of the expression *t'ung* for "equal," a term Confucius had still called the "connecting element" among the lower classes and therefore rejected as inapplicable to "superior men" certainly do not mean that this "equality" implied a blurring of status distinctions in the ideal state. Quite the contrary. Since Mencius's thought was considerably more sober than that of Confucius, distinctions of status find an even clearer expression in his writings. The community intended to link all classes lies on a completely different, purely human plane which does not eliminate the structure of society but merely imbues it with a higher meaning. This attitude surfaces most unmistakably in a dialogue Mencius is said to have had with a disciple of the school which traced its origin to the legendary Shen-nung, the "divine farmer," the "inventor" of farming. No documents have been preserved of this "School of Agriculture" *(Nung-chia),* yet it was important enough to be mentioned in works of the second century B.C. alongside the writings of Confucians and Taoists.[53] In contemporary China, there has been a tendency to regard its members as precursors of communism (in part because of the coarse work clothes they wore).[54] But whether this is accurate can neither be proved nor disproved since our knowledge is largely based on this comment in the book Mencius:

> At that time there appeared in the state of T'eng a man by the name of Hsü Hsing from the state of Ch'u, who claimed to represent the teachings of the "divine farmer." He went directly to the gate of the prince's residence and said to prince Wen: "As a man from distant regions, I have heard of your princely conduct and your humane rule. I wish to live in your country and to belong to your people." Prince Wen granted him domicile. The disciples [of Hsü Hsing], a few dozen, all wore simple hair shirts, sandals made of hemp, and wove mats for a living. At about this time there also came Ch'en Hsiang and his younger brother Ch'en Hsin, a disciple of a certain Ch'en Liang. Carrying ploughshares and agricultural implements on their backs, they traveled from the state of Sung to T'eng, and said: "We have heard that you, [Prince], rule like a saint and therefore are a saint. We wish to belong to the people of Your Holiness." When Ch'en Hsiang met Hsü Hsing, he was very pleased, gave up his own teachings, and became his disciple. It was he who [later] visited Mencius and told him about the teachings of Hsü Hsing: "The prince of T'eng," he said, "is truly a worthy prince, although he has no knowledge as yet of the true form [of government]. A worthy ruler should eat only after having tilled the soil together with his people, nor should he govern unless he also prepares his breakfast and his supper with his own hand. The prince of T'eng, however, owns granaries and treasuries which he uses to suppress his people to nourish himself. How can he be a [real] worthy ruler?" "Master Hsü surely only eats the grain he has sown himself?" Mencius asked. "Indeed," was the answer. "And he only wears the clothing he has woven himself?" "No, he wears a hempen garment." "And does he wear a cap?" "Yes." "What kind of cap?" "A very simple one." "Did he weave it himself?" "No, he traded it against grain." "Well, why did he not weave it himself?" "That would interfere with his work in the fields." "Does master Hsü use pots and jugs for cooking, and iron ploughshares?" Mencius continued asking. "Yes." "And does he make all these things himself?" "No, those things he also exchanges for grain." Mencius replied: "In that case, his obtaining all these things for grain is no suppression of the potter and the smith, nor do potter and smith suppress the farmer when they trade their implements for grain. Why does master Hsü not work as potter and smith to provide himself with all those things he needs at home? Why does he barter so much with all craftsmen? Would it not be better if he saved himself all that trouble?" "It is simply unavoidable. One cannot do all the work required of a farmer, and something else besides," Ch'en Hsiang replied. "In that case," Mencius exclaimed, "is the governing of the realm the only activity one can engage in along with agriculture? [No], there are the affairs of the important

people, and there are the affairs of the small people. If every single person were to use all the things made by craftsmen only if he made them himself, all the people in the empire would have to be constantly travelling. Therefore it is said: some work with their heart, others with the strength of their bodies. Those who work with their heart rule the rest. Those who work with their body are governed by the others . . . [And in this way Mencius explained to Ch'en Hsiang how society had only gradually and through the efforts of the sages developed from an oppressive and dangerous natural condition and become a civilization where social differentiation preserved by piety made possible the happiness of the entire people, a notion which Hsü Hsiang, coming from the southern barbarian state of Ch'u, naturally could not grasp.] By way of a final objection, Ch'en Hsiang replied: "But if master Hsü's teaching were followed, there would no longer be two different prices in the market place, and no more lying in politics. One could send a boy five feet tall to market, and no one would cheat him. Linen and silk goods of equal length would be traded at the same *(t'ung)* price, just like hemp and silk yarns of equal weight. And similarly, the same price would obtain for the five kinds of grain, and for shoes, whether large or small. "Ah," Mencius replied, "but it is in the nature of things to be unequal *(ch'i)*. Some are twice, five, ten, a hundred, a thousand or ten thousand times as valuable as others. If you want to make them all equal, you would throw the whole realm into confusion. If large and small shoes were to cost the same, who could be found to make shoes? If people followed the teachings of master Hsü, they would merely delude each other. How could a state be governed in this way?"[55]

The eloquence and polemics apparent in this dialogue are very characteristic of all the writing in the book Mencius. Confucius could still "preach," Mencius had to engage in disputes. Yet the "agriculturists" were the weakest adversaries. The really dangerous opponents came from a school which may be traceable to a secondary branch of the Confucian school and actually drilled its rigorously organized disciples in the techniques of debate: the school of Mo Ti (?479–381 B.C.). Nearly forgotten for more than two millennia, this philosopher was almost something like a rediscovery for the Chinese and Westerners of the last two centuries, if in two quite different ways. On the one hand, he astonished western scholars, including missionaries, by his advocacy of general, mutual love among men, for it went back to the fourth century B.C. On the other, the Chinese (justifiably) recognized in this love of men a clear, early form of a western type of socialism. At the same time, they were surprised to find in the Mohist writings the rudiments of those very sciences which had led the West to power and success: logic and technology. In a sense, it might therefore seem that the victory of Confucianism over the school of Mo Ti had caused China to abandon a path which might have taken it into the modern world much earlier than the West. Besides, our century lent Mo Ti the romantic aura of the man engaged in the class struggle. For scholars of repute (Chiang Ch'üan and Ch'ien Mu [born 1895]) developed the very plausible theory that Mo, not Ti, was the actual family name of the philosopher, stating that Mo ("india ink") had to function here as a by-name meaning "branded (slave)."[56] They maintained that this interpretation would readily fit in with the teaching of a left splinter group of Confucianism where suddenly such an indelicate concept as "profit" began to play the principal role. This profit would not be shared according to the principles of the traditional class and family hierarchy, but in a truly equal manner.

Various components make up Mo Ti's ideal state. An undifferentiated love which was not confined to the family, as in Confucianism; a marked religiousness viewed as a guarantee for an improved morality; strict parsimony; an iron will to work on everyone's part (a concept previously unknown in this form); and, finally, peace among nations. He was optimistic enough to believe that this could be achieved by perfecting defensive rather than offensive weapons. The pervasive element connecting all these ideas is again the concept of "equality," which has once again changed its form here. For Mo Ti, it means something like "porousness," a constantly renewed bond between all parts of society. This is already apparent in the chapters of the book *Mo-tzu,* ("[sayings] of the philosopher Mo [Ti]") dealing with "universal love." As is true of all parts of the work, their rhetoric is worked out to the last detail:

> What constitutes the way of "universal love" *(chien-ai)* and of mutual aid? Master Mo explained it as follows: "It means that one makes no distinction between the state of others and one's own; none between the houses of others and one's own; none between the other person and oneself. If princes love each other, there will be no more wars. If heads of families love each other, there will be no more taking of advantage; and if individual men love each other, there will be no more injustice. If ruler and ruled love each other, they will be magnanimous and loyal; if father and son love each other, they will be devoted and respectful toward each other; if older and younger brothers love each other, they will live together in harmony. If all the people in the world love each other, the strong will not overpower the weak, the many will not suppress the few, the rich will not mock the poor, the highly placed will not despise the lowly, nor the clever take advantage of the simple[57] . . . If one tries in this way to benefit the world through 'universal love,' attentive ears and keen eyes will assist each other, bodies will be strengthened through exercise, and those who know the True Way *(tao)* will indefatigably instruct the rest. The aged, having neither wife nor child, will be supported and spend their last days peacefully. The young, the weak and the orphans will be cared for and taught so that they may grow up and thrive. Such are the benefits that spring from 'universal love.' "[58]

Three synoptic chapters also discuss the problem of learning this "universal love" through constant practice. Their title is *Shang-t'ung,* a concept coined by the Mohists. Literally translated, it means "to assimilate to what is above." There is a certain ambiguity or, perhaps better, bipolarity here. For what is meant is both the assimilation of those below to those above, and also the reverse, although the latter is emphasized much less strongly and recognized only as receptiveness to advice. This reciprocal communication is necessary precisely because of the differences between men. In the following words, Mo Ti describes how it is to take place:

> When human life first arose in antiquity and now law of government yet existed, there was the rule: men have different opinions. Therefore one person had one opinion, two persons had two, and ten had ten. The greater the number of people, the greater the number of opinions expressed. And therefore everyone also [naturally] considered his opinion correct and that of others false. Thus all people began to criticize each other. Within the family, father and son, the older and the younger brother, became hostile toward each other, and estranged. They ran from each other, unable to come to an agreement. Everyone in the empire tried to harm everyone else, using water, fire, and poison. Surplus energy was not used for mutual help, surplus goods were allowed to rot rather than shared, and the best methods of work were kept secret from one's neighbor instead of being passed on by instruction. The confusion of the empire was [as severe as] that reigning among wild animals. When attempts were made to discover its cause, [it was noted] that there were no leaders. Therefore the most capable person in the realm was sought out and made the Son of Heaven. Because his abilities were limited, the Son of Heaven sought out the most capable in turn, and made them his three ministers. Having been appointed, the ministers in turn divided the country among the feudal lords because it was so large. In view of their limited abilities, the latter now chose the most capable in their states and made leaders of them. After the leaders had been appointed in this manner, the emperor issued a decree to the people which said: "If a person hears something good or something bad, he is to report it to his superior. What the superior [in question] considers proper, all those [below him] are also to consider proper. What he considers incorrect, they also are to consider incorrect. If a superior commits an error, he is to be admonished, and if an inferior shows virtue, a general recommendation [for his promotion] is to be made. To adapt *(t'ung)* in this fashion to those above, and not to descend to the level of those below (*pi*, "comparable"), deserves encouragement from above and praise from below . . . [while the opposite] deserves punishment.[59] An old proverb says: 'One eye does not see as much as two, one ear does not hear as well as two, one hand does not grasp as firmly as two.' . . . Therefore the holy kings of antiquity had a government that enabled them to reward a righteous person living one thousand miles away before all the people living in his own country knew him, just as they could punish a wicked person under the same conditions. . . . They could see without changing place, and hear without drawing close . . . because they understood how to make assimilation to those above a principle of government. . . . But whoever commands his people to become like him, the leader, must love it without violence. A people only become unmanageable when one tries to lead them with a violent love. But if one approaches them with trust, and takes them by the hand, if one lures them forward with riches and drives them from behind with just punishment and governs in this fashion, there will not be a single one [among the subjects] who will not adapt himself to the ruler even if he should be asked not to do so."[60]

Through the system of adaptation (or assimilation) to what is above, the thinking of the entire people is to be developed in many individual cells and by degrees. It is to be focused on the leader and to become strong and unified in him. The knowledge and the will of the ruler are thus greatly strengthened, and it is in them that the thinking of the people will find its fulfillment. This "adaptation" of the people is not simple subjection. Through the reports about good and evil deeds that are to flow in a steady stream from below to above, and the "advice" the subjects not only can but must give to the leadership when glaring mistakes are made, a kind of feedback system is created. While this may not directly compel those above to change their objectives, it enables them to learn from the experience of the masses. Abuse is not possible, for this mysterious influence works only when it is supported by, and directed toward, love.

The gulf separating the Mohists from the Confucians was a wholly different concept of love. Having been made more comprehensive, it lost its intimate warmth.[61] The "love of men," as the expression *jen* "Humanity," may also be translated, consisted for the Confucians in directing the love between parents and children to all of humanity. For the Mohists, this love among relatives was only one case among many. It was a sublime form of egoism. If given preeminence, it would become the root of all the evil in the world. In contrast to the Confucians, the Mohists acted consistently in their advocacy of an elective monarchy. For them, it was the period predating the Hsia dynasty that was exemplary. For the sage rulers Yao and Shun were careful not to make their own sons their successors because they wished to raise the worthiest person to the throne. It is interesting to observe how the rivals of the Confucians imitated them in presenting the past as a model. They simply situated their own golden ages in periods still more remote, thereby opening up the past to an ever greater depth. Negating the progressive differentiation of society, they felt not without some justification that social "equality" increased as one went back in time. In his reflections about these matters, Mo Ti had not really traced this conception to its logical limit. For the "primordial condition" he discusses in his description of the development of the *Shang t'ung* idea was no more a paradise for him than for Mencius, where we find a more concise formulation of the same thoughts. Rather, it was a wilderness where nature still remorselessly overwhelmed man. Only with the order created by sage rulers did the world become a world of men which deserved the honorific title "under Heaven."

Yet the dogma of the Agriculturists already suggests that there must have been still other teachings which promoted a kind of primitivism, and represented a radically different conception. Already in the *Analects,* there is a curious passage pointing in this direction. Once, when Confucius was traveling with his disciple Tzu-lu, and the latter asked two farmers tilling the soil along the edge of the road about a ford across the river ahead of them, and mentioned the name of his teacher, these people only showed contempt, and said: "The whole world is in uproar, who can do anything about it? Instead of rushing from one lord to the next with this fellow, it would be better for you to attach yourself to someone who has completely turned his back on the world."[62]

It is possible that these men also were disciples of the "School of Agriculturists." The somewhat pessimistic note in the characterization of the "world in uproar" however, suggests another school which probably arose at the same time as the Confucian but only took on a character of its own through its opposition to Confucianism, and that is Taoism. For in Taoism we can find doctrines which managed to reconcile even such extreme opposites as the Shamans' imaginative flights to heaven and the social programs of the "School of Agriculturists," and to provide a common basis for them.

3 / ESCAPE FROM SOCIETY

NATURE AND LIFE ACCORDING TO THE TAOISTS

However great the contrast between the thought of Confucians and Mohists may have been, it shared one assumption of extreme importance to our inquiry: in all their reflections, both stayed within the framework of social existence. They never considered the individual as other than part of mankind as a whole, and believed that his happiness was inseparably connected with that of the mass. And while intensively searching the past for models, they never went beyond the bounds of historicity which coincides with the rise of human society. The time of the sage kings constituted an absolute limit for them. It was they who had taught men to distinguish themselves from "four-legged creatures and birds." For them, the "world" was actually identical with the "realm" *(t'ien-hsia),* and the creation of this world by the culture-bearing sages—an event of infinitely greater significance than the creation of the universe to which they gave no thought—was the first and also the most decisive historical event. The idea of turning one's back on this world, either temporally by an attempt to return to the period predating the inception of civilization, or spatially by an escape into the wilderness, not only seemed barbaric to them but was simply unimaginable. Yet it was precisely at this point that the reflections of the Taoists set in. They viewed all the theories of the Confucians and Mohists concerning the right culture and government, and thus the right relations between men as a hopeless attempt to cure the symptoms of an illness whose real causes had to be looked for in the development of culture and government and the well-meant but harmful activity of the sage kings. Because Taoism was both hostile to civilization and ahistorical, our knowledge of its beginnings is much more limited than in the case of Confucianism. In many respects, it seems, it was originally a reservoir of various traditions. As these subsequently diverged, various polarizations were created. Sometimes, curious shifts in accent also occurred and gave the impression that wholesale reorientations of the teaching had taken place. An important component apparently was the tradition of certain practices—breathing exercises, dietetics, sexual teachings

—whose aim it was to prolong human life. They also seem to have been coupled with meditation exercises which may in turn suggest a link to the ecstasies of the Shamans, although it is true that these states were attained in a wholly different manner.[63] What all these efforts had in common was that they had little to do with society and the state. Indeed, they were based on a certain withdrawal of the individual, on isolation and quiet, which guaranteed that he was protected from the distracting and wearing effects of the outside world. The life of solitude, a part of Taoism from the very beginning, thus presumably had much deeper roots which did not necessarily have any connection with a philosophy of whatever kind.

This is equally true of the anonymity so eagerly sought by the earliest Taoist personalities. The enormous expansion of the self during meditation, its submergence in the rushing stream of eternal nature in macrobiotic exercises, also meant the total effacement of its contours and its complete extinction. Ordinarily it is therefore extremely difficult to ascribe early Taoist writings to identifiable personalities, all the more so since usually only a meaningless name has come down to us. Furthermore, the important texts are collections and consist of quite various parts. The two most important Taoist collections of texts, the *Tao-te-ching*[64] ascribed to Lao-tzu (the "Old Master") and the book *Chuang-tzu* ("Master Chuang"),[65] allegedly written by the philosopher Chuang Chou, are no exception in this regard. The temporal relationship between them appears to be such that the older parts of the book *Chuang-tzu* are earlier (end of the fifth or beginning of the fourth century B.C.) than the *Tao-te-ching* (middle to end of the fourth century B.C.). The latter, which is a more unified whole, in turn dates back to an earlier period than the later sections of the *Chuang-tzu*, parts of which did not come to be written before the second century B.C. Yet the continuity between the two collections is nowhere broken, not even where the development of the thought and its gradual change can still be clearly recognized. But there are many passages where the same idea is merely viewed from two perspectives. One may say that the *Tao-te-ching*, written in a concise, simple style, gives the contours of the image, while the *Chuang-tzu* gives it fire and color through its ecstatic abundance of words and allegories. The *Tao-te-ching* develops political programs, while the *Chuang-tzu* rises to a magic height of imagination.

The Taoist descriptions of the ideal life among men take us into a wholly different, new world. Its most immediately striking characteristic is its small scale which makes possible its simplicity and closeness to nature. These accounts take us into a bygone world of tiny villages which were content with their state until startled out of their paradisiacal condition by the sages coming like invaders upon them.

"The people," we read in *Chuang-tzu*,

> have a natural instinct implanted in it from the very beginning, for the weaving of fabrics, thus to clothe itself, and for the tilling of the fields, thus to nourish itself.

This is what is called a "uniform virtue" *(t'ung te).* Since it is common to all and knows no difference between groups, it is also called "granted by the heavens" *(t'ien fang).* This is the reason man was clumsy in his movements and steady in his gaze during the age of the "highest virtue" *(chih-te).* In that age, there were no paths over the mountains, no boats and bridges to cross rivers. The ten thousand creatures grew abundantly, each in its sphere. Birds and animals formed herds, plants and trees shot up as they pleased. Therefore birds and animals could be led by hand (and they did not try to run away), and one could climb to the nests of ravens and look into them (without disturbing them). Indeed, in the age of highest virtue, man had the same habitation as birds and animals and constituted a single race with the ten thousand creatures. Nothing was known of a "superior" and a "common man." People were equal *(t'ung)* in their not-desiring. That is what was called plain and simple. In plainness and simplicity the people had discovered its nature. But when the holy men appeared and constricted the people through love, and fettered it with duties toward its neighbor, doubt was born in the world. And with their talk about music and their prattle about ritual, the realm collapsed in dissension.[66]

"Equality," this keyword for access to paradise which had already been of so much concern to Confucians and Mohists, is also of decisive importance for the Taoists. But this equality is much more rigorously carried through in their ideal society. It comprises not only all people, but even includes animals with which one shares a place to live and constitutes a single race. With great boldness, the Taoists thus discarded the notion of "humanity," that most sacred of Confucian discoveries. The magnificently primitive condition of "simplicity and plainness" was obviously situated in a time predating the creation of civilization, which is what the Confucians meant by the world. Yet at least initially, the Taoists hoped to be able to discover the way back. In the *Tao-te-ching,* all the characteristics of Taoist ideal society are offered as recipes for a just government, not without pointed allusions to Confucians and Mohists, who preached the very opposite:

Banish wisdom, throw away knowledge,/and the people will benefit a hundred-fold!/Banish "humanity," throw away righteousness, and the people will become conscientious and full of love!/Banish skill, throw away profit/and thieves and robbers will disappear!/Yet even if one should let these three principles redound to one's honor, that will not suffice./One should therefore let the people have something it can hold on to./It should be given simplicity to look at, and the unhewn to grasp./It should be given selfless desires!/[67]

As in *Chuang-tzu,* we also find a passage in the *Tao-te-ching* where an ideal Taoist community is described. But characteristically it contains no concrete historical allusions, and thus fails to provide a temporal determinateness. In view of the temporal neutrality of Chinese, it can thus be transposed at will into the past, the present or the future, "as the reader may desire" (this touch of irony is Arthur Waley's, the famous English sinologist, to whom we are indebted for one of the best among the excessive number of translations of this book[68]). If situated in the past, it will read like a romantically-resigned reminiscence, if in the present, as an open possibility, if in the future as a revolutionary, almost dangerously anarchical program for a high civilization, considering its invocation of neglected, rotting ships and chariots:

> Assume a small country with few inhabitants: one could see to it that, even if there existed inventions which would save ten or even one hundred times the labor power otherwise expended, the people would not use them. One could bring it about that the people would rather die twice, than emigrate. Perhaps there would be boats and chariots, but no one would travel by them. Perhaps there would be weapons, but no one would train himself in their use. One could bring it about that the people knew no writing other than knotted ropes, was content with its food, pleased about its clothing, happy with its dwelling, and took pleasure in [simple] ways of doing things. The next place might be so close that one could hear the crowing of cocks and the barking of dogs, but the people would become old and die without ever having visited there.[69]

The members of such a community seemed to the Taoists to be on their way to becoming "true human beings" *(chen-jen),* relieved of all human concerns precisely because of their "pre-human" existence. In a manner of speaking, they would be like beings who had not yet eaten from the tree of knowledge. As can be seen in *Chuang-tzu,* it is precisely this lack of awareness which gave them seemingly supernatural capabilities. But these were just the powers of an unfalsified nature of which they partook fully because they did not shut themselves off from it:

> The "true men" of antiquity did not object to limitations, they were not proud of success, they never planned how to become people of rank. If they achieved nothing, there was no reason for remorse, and if they accomplished something, no reason for satisfaction. Thus they could climb the greatest heights without fear, go into the water without getting wet, and pass through fire without being burnt. This is how close their knowledge had taken them to the "Way." The "true men of antiquity" slept without dreaming and had no worries when they woke up. They ate without searching for delicacies and breathed with their lungs wide open; for the "true men" draw their breath down to their heels, ordinary men only down to their throat. . . . The "true men" of antiquity took no delight in life, and felt no distaste for death. They rejoiced neither because they were born, nor did they try to prevent their dissolution: they came and passed quickly—that was all. They did not forget where they came from, nor did they strive mightily to arrive where they would end. They were pleased with what they had received, and they returned to what they had forgotten. This is what is called "not to divert one's attention from the 'Way,' " and not to try to help heaven with something human. This is the form of action of the "true man." Such men are strong willed, have dignity in their demeanor, serenity in their expression. They are cool like autumn, warm like spring. Their passions arise like the four seasons, in harmony with the ten thousand creatures, and no one knows their limits.[70]

The happiness these "true men" experience is thus anything but a rush of feeling. It expresses itself rather in a calm balance. Even heat and frost are attenuated and become the temperatures of the temperate, yet much more lively seasons. Another passage in *Chuang-tzu* even states unambiguously that "when the holy emperor Yao governed, he caused excessive joy in the hearts of men and thereby aroused their discontent. [He was thus no better than] the tyrant Chieh, who created excessive grief in the hearts of men and thus made them resentful."[71] Most surprising perhaps is the indifference with which these true men are said to have faced death, particularly when one considers that macrobiotic exercises are among the oldest roots of Taoism. And yet this contradiction can be fairly easily resolved. As so often, absolute opposites are closer here than appears at first glance; they collapse into unity when carried to a higher plane.

The difference in premises between Taoists on the one hand, and Confucians and Mohists on the other, unquestionably derives from the divergent interpretation of a central concept, the concept of "life."[72] Interestingly enough, it never became an important issue because the Chinese language had already clearly distinguished its two aspects. In all western languages, this concept comprises two ideas which are really surprisingly different: life as a force that holds together all of "living" nature, everything, that is, which is subject not only to movement but to metamorphosis. Secondly, life is also an individually "experienced" span of time shaped either by fate or individual will. As such, it is man's unique possession in the sense that he does not merely live in the moment but can use his memory to unify isolated events and endow them with meaning. Just as often, of course, he may question that they have one. It could be asked whether this conceptual linkage of human and non-human life may not have been one of the major decisions made by language before philosophic thought had arisen, and that this accounts for the personal tone of western thought. In any event, there can be no doubt that this concept of life combined what were disparate elements from the Chinese point of view. It thus aroused particular interest (and this is true of all western cultural phenomena for which no parallel can be found in China). A book by the scholar Fu Ssu-nien (1896–1950), which appeared in 1938 and created a considerable stir, is a typical example. For the first time, the two Chinese conceptions of life were juxtaposed in a study which traced their etymologies and investigated the different meanings they had had in the works of philosophers.[73] It clarified not only the concepts themselves but also their relationship to other, obviously connected terms.

The old form of one of the two words for "life," **mi̯ăng>ming*[1] shows a kneeling man next to a mouth under some kind of roof, probably of a cultic nature (interpreted as "roof" and also as "bell" [Karlgren]).[74] The concept is rather complex. First of all, it means "command." Derived from this, it also means

---

1. 命

"mandate" (as, for example, the heavenly mandate on which every dynasty based its claim to power, as mentioned previously).[75] Then, it signified "to give a name" on the one hand, and "fate," "life," on the other. There is a clear graphic and phonetic connection with the word **mi̯ĕng > ming*[1] "personal name," "to give a name," in whose old written form only the roof is missing. The graphic and signific relationship to the expression **li̯ĕng > ling*[2] "to command," is just as certain. In its written form, the roof is retained, but the mouth has disappeared. In old inscriptions, it is used interchangeably with *ming,* "command," and is probably related to it phonetically. Certain phonetic connections with the word **mi̯ĕng > ming*[3] "to shout," may also exist, but this term is represented by an entirely different sign ("mouth" and "bird").[76] *Ming,* "life," is thus originally life as decreed by fate. Together with his name, it is imposed on man by the gods, as it were. This form of life, which initially did not have a moral but rather a charismatic nuance, was the domain of the Confucians. For them, this *ming* was nothing other than the *Tao,* the "way," a mission heaven assigns to man as it gives him life, and to which he had to adapt as closely as possible by conscientiously fulfilling his part in human society. Like every command, this conception of life had a clear goal, and also a strict temporal aspect: during the span allotted him, man must carry out his mission. Time and again, he must compare what has been attained with what remains to be done, he must incessantly "accumulate knowledge" (these are the terms that constantly recur) in order to reach this goal. Almost all of the essential features of Confucianism, its emphasis on study, its inclination toward history, can be derived from this fundamental attitude.

For the Taoists, "life" was something completely different. They were wholly under the spell of the second Chinese term created for this idea: **seng > sheng.*[4] For its written form, the oracle priests used the sign "sacrificial bull" which is read in the same way. In the present context, however, it has no assignable meaning (unless one assumes a rather implausible verbal relationship). It is significant that originally the word had an almost exclusively verbal function, meaning "to live," "to give birth," "to be born" (all these variations are possible in a language without grammar). Phonetically and graphically, it is identical with the word **si̯ĕng > hsing*[5] "nature," which was originally written in the same way and later differentiated by the addition of the radical "heart." It did not really denote nature as such (a concept which requires an immense psychological distance from nature to come about at all), but rather the *natura naturans* in every being, indeed in every object, and certainly not merely nature in man, although in Confucian usage it was often and revealingly restricted to this latter meaning. There are also considerable phonetic and graphic similarities to the word **si̯ĕng > hsing*[6] "clan," "family," "clan name," which replaces the radical "heart" with that of "woman" (matriarchal reminiscences?). But it is also possible that old

1. 名 2. 令 3. 鳴 4. 生 5. 性 6. 姓

Confucian scholars described it as related (as in the *Ch'un-ch'iu fan-lu* of the second century B.C.)[77] in analogy to the established relationship between *ming* "life," and *ming* "personal name." The early Taoists were concerned with this quasi-faceless concept of life which merely denoted the life *force.* A deeply rooted conviction that—given the existence of time—the loss of form was possible at any moment, and an equally firm belief that substance, the life force, could not be lost, a notion superficially reminiscent of the physical law of the preservation of energy, led them to see the path to immortality in the voluntary surrender of form. The elimination of all personal characteristics, the complete identification with a nature whose namelessness was no accident, the "forgetting" which they never tired of preaching[78] (a concept both linguistically and graphically related to "losing" and "dying" in Chinese), was for them only a loss of what was superficial, a reduction of the personality to the truly inalienable. The life of the "true men leaves no traces (which are fundamentally nothing but violations of nature, tracks in the grass); their deeds are not passed down to posterity."[79]

DREAM AND DEATH IN *CHUANG-TZU*

As the Taoist definition of life had differed substantially from the Confucian, so did their definition of happiness. For the Confucians simply adopted the traditional conception which was rather naive, its differentiations notwithstanding. In the book *Chuang-tzu,* we find the following passage concerning this matter:

> Does perfect happiness exist on earth, or not? Are there people who enjoy life, or not? If there are such people, what do they do, what do they desire? What do they avoid, where do they find peace? What do they accept, what do they reject? What do they love, what do they hate? What the world values is riches, honor, advanced age and kindness; what it delights in is a life of ease, good food, splendid garments, beautiful women, and music. . . . [But from the point of view of physical existence, that is nonsense:] the rich who toil to accumulate more money than they can ever spend, don't they go too far from the point of view of physical existence? And the officials who turn night into day in their effort to accomplish something, are they not moving along a false path, from the point of view of physical existence? And since man is inevitably born to grief, does it not mean prolonged grief if he should have the misfortune to live a long life, his senses dulled? Is that not [also] a mistake from the point of view of physical existence? . . . When I look at what the world does, and where people nowadays believe they can find happiness, I am not sure that that is true happiness. The happiness of these ordinary people seems to consist in slavishly imitating the majority, as if this were their only choice. And yet they all believe they are happy. I cannot decide whether that is happiness or not. Is there such a thing as happiness? I believe that true joy consists in not-doing, [precisely in] what the world considers great unhappiness. Thus we have the old saying: "Perfect happiness is the absence of happiness, perfect glory is the absence of glory."[80]

The decisive test for this attitude toward the happiness of this world is always death. There are some sections in *Chuang-tzu* which reveal a truly majestic stand vis-a-vis this terror of all terrors. As literature, they are impressive and belong to the best that has been written in Chinese. There is an uninterrupted account describing two small groups of Taoist eccentrics in turn. The way they came together may have provided a model for early Taoist communities. The first section reads as follows:

> Four men said to each other: "Whoever can make not-doing the head, life the body, and death the buttocks, and has recognized that death and life form a single body, he shall be our friend." The four looked at each other, laughed, and became friends forthwith. After a while, one of them, Tzu-yü, fell ill, and another, Tzu-ssu, went to visit him. "Truly, the creator is great," said the sick one. "Look what he has done to me. My back is so crooked that my entrails lie on top; my cheeks are level with my navel, my shoulders are higher than my neck, and my hair grows downward. All my physical functions are in a state of confusion. And yet I have my spiritual balance." He dragged himself to a well where he could see himself, and exclaimed: "How terrible what the creator has done to me!"—"Are you afraid?" Tzu-ssu asked. "No," replied Tzu-yü, "what do I have to fear? Soon I will be dissolved. My left shoulder will become a cock announcing the morning, my right shoulder a cross bow with which I can hunt ducks to eat. My buttocks will serve as a pair of wheels, and with my soul for a horse to pull them, I will drive along in my own chariot. So what need would I have for any other vehicle? I was given life because it was my time, and now I take leave of it according to the same law. Content with the natural sequence of these events, I am touched neither by joy nor by grief. I am simply hanging in the air, as they said in antiquity, incapable of freeing myself, tied by the threads of things. But it has always been true that things have less power than heaven [in the long run]—why then should I be afraid [of returning to the creator]?" After some more time had passed, another of the four, Tzu-lai, fell ill and lay there fighting for breath, while his family stood around him weeping. Tzu-li, the fourth of the friends, went to visit him. "Away, away," he shouted at the wife and children. "You are delaying his disintegration!" Resting easily against the gate, he then said to his friend: "Truly, the creator is great! I would like to know what he will make of you, and where he will send you. Do you think he will make a rat liver (the Chinese believed that rats had no liver) or a snake shoulder of you?" "A good son must go where his parents send him," Tzu-lai replied. "And [the primordial forces] Yin and Yang are the parents of man. If they suggest I die, and I rebel against it, that merely means that I have no piety—how could one reproach them for that? Imagine that the metal, boiling away in the crucible, wanted to splash, and exclaim: 'Make me into a Mo-yeh sword.' Surely the founder would consider it a wretched metal. Now, if I, in my shape that repels men, were to say [to the creator]: 'Turn me into a man, nothing other than a man!' Then the creator would surely also cast me away as an unfortunate creature. If we look on heaven and earth as a single crucible, and on the creator as the founder, would there be any place I could not go? When it is time, I will fall asleep, and when the right time comes, I will wake up again."[81]

The second part of this passage, a parallel construction, introduces Confucius and his group of disciples, as repeatedly happens in the book *Chuang-tzu.* The contrast between the two conceptions of life is illuminated even more clearly here:

> Tzu Sang-hu, Meng Tzu-fan and Tzu Ch'in-chang said to each other: "Who can be, and yet not be? Who can act and yet not act? Who can ascend to heaven and roam through the clouds, pass beyond the limits of space, and forget existence forever and eternally without end?" The three looked at each other and laughed, and, since no one objected, they became friends. After a while, Tzu Sang-hu died. Confucius heard about it before he was buried and sent [his disciple] Tzu-kung to participate in the rites of mourning. But he [only] found that of the [two friends of the dead], one was singing a song while the other was accompanying him on a drum. The verses were: "Oh, come back to us, Sang-hu,/come back to us, Sang-hu,/you have already returned to your true form,/while we still live here as men, alas!/" [Indignantly,] Tzu-kung rushed into [the chamber of the dead] and said: "How can one sing in the presence of a dead person! Is that propriety?" The two men looked at each other, laughed, and said: "What does that fellow know about propriety?" When Tzu-kung returned to Confucius and asked him what this meant, . . . Confucius said: "These people move outside of the laws of life, I move within them. Inside and outside do not touch each other, and I made a mistake sending you there for the mourning rites. Even with the creator, they deal as with an [ordinary] person, and walk in the same atmosphere as heaven and earth. They look upon life as a huge excrescence from which death frees them. Yet they do not know where they were before they were born, nor where they will be after their death. Although they acknowledge the difference between the elements, they insist on the unity of all things. They ignore their passions, they do not use their eyes and ears. With eternity stretching out behind and in front of them, they acknowledge neither beginning nor end. They roam about far from the dust and dirt of mortals, and walk in spheres of not-doing. Why should they trouble with the conventions of this world and concern themselves with what others think of them?"[82]

Yet the resemblance between the two stories is only apparent. On closer inspection, one discovers a really enormous difference which can be shown all the more clearly because of the superficial parallels between them. In the first story, nothing exists beyond the world. Even the "creator" (the word might also be translated as "the creative principle" since Chinese here cannot differentiate between a personal and a neuter noun) is merely the formative power imbedded in nature. Death is a kind of dreamless sleep, a mere transition to a new life, a life constantly renewed in this process and therefore eternal. In the second story, on the other hand, death is described as the transition from one existence to another, the purification of the imperfect human form. As a result, it becomes much better, more "authentic;" death is the liberation from the chains of this world and the flight into another, higher one above the clouds. The equality with animal and tree, with the "ten thousand creatures," is replaced by the equality with spirits. Viewed from this perspective, human life can be nothing more than an "excrescence."

It is very probable that the second story is of considerably more recent date although it directly follows the first in the *textus receptus.* But perhaps the heroic acceptance of death found in the first story had always contained the seed of a hope that the hereafter would not bring the same, but something better than the life lived heretofore. For to accept such heroism joyfully surely went beyond the strength of most, since it involved not merely a renunciation of this world, but the metamorphosis into the "shoulder of the snake," i.e. into pure nothingness. Chuang-tzu's encounter with the skull forms a sort of bridge between the two conceptions. It is a macabre scene, somewhat reminiscent of "Hamlet," and also often represented in paintings in China:

> One day Chuang-tzu saw a skull, whitened by the sun, but still well preserved. Poking it with his riding whip, he said: "Were you once a citizen who lost his reason because of his greed for life, and thus got yourself into this state? Or a statesman who was executed by sword and axe when his country went down? Or a rascal who left his parents and family nothing but disgrace? Or a beggar who perished in hunger and cold? Or did you get this far after having reached an advanced age in the course of nature?" After these words, he took the skull, placed it under his head as a pillow, and fell asleep. During the night, he dreamed that the skull appeared to him and said: "Sir, you spoke almost as well as an advocate. But your words referred only to life among men, and the concerns of mortals. Nothing of that sort exists in death. Do you wish to hear about it?" And when Chuang-tzu replied that he did, the skull continued: "In death, there are no rulers above and no subjects below. The course of the four seasons is unknown, our life is eternal. Even a king among men can experience no greater happiness than is ours." Chuang-tzu was not yet wholly convinced and asked: "If, with the help of the creator, I could restore your body to you, renew your bones and your flesh, and take you back to your parents, your wife and children and old friends, would you not gladly accept my offer?" The skull opened its eyes wide, furrowed its brows, and said: "Why should I throw away a happiness greater than a king's to once again thrust myself into the troubles and anxieties of mankind?"[83]

For the first time, we also encounter here an evident reference to a particular quality of the ideal world which later came to play an increasingly important role: the absence of rulers and subjects.[84] The book *Chuang-tzu* also contains a number of stories of a similar trend. An example would be the anecdote about the holy emperor Yao whose offer to pass his empire on to them met only horrified rejections by the various hermits to whom he made it.[85] But the reasons here were rather an extreme individualism and the conviction that politics was generally dirty business. In Lao-tzu also, it is not government as such that is condemned, but only the government of ambitious men bent on accomplishing things. Extended passages of the *Tao-te-ching* searchingly discuss how such a form of government can be avoided. The model of the anarchical state, on the other hand, cannot be found prior to the report of the skull from the world of the dead.

Just as the motif of the alliance of three or four sages against death exists in more than one version, there is also a second if much shorter account of this narrative about the skull. It shows a very significant shift in conception. The experience is attributed to the historically unverifiable Taoist philosopher Lieh-tzu:[86] "While on a journey, Lieh-tzu sat eating along the side of the road when he discovered a skull one hundred years old. He plucked a blade of grass, pointed it at the skull, and said: 'Only you and I know that there is never such a thing as life, and never such a thing as death. Are you free of worries? Am I truly glad to be alive?' "[87]

Something becomes recognizable here that goes even further than the discovery of another world as we found it in the second version of the story telling of the union of the three men, namely a curious effect of this discovery on the attitude toward this world. For the oracle priests and the Confucians, spirits formed part of this world when they were acknowledged at all. This is obvious from the advice "to stay away from them." But here, in a somewhat later Taoist belief, this world and the next are rigorously separated. But because the beyond was sometimes considered the "real" or at least the better world, a sense of unreality began to tinge attitudes toward the Here and Now. In an infinite mirroring of real unreality and unreal reality, all things began to lose their contours and thus their indubitable, tangible reality. The many parables of the book *Chuang-tzu* point in this direction. They bring out the relativity of all convictions, as in the curious conversation about the small fish playing in the water and the question whether they are really enjoying themselves or not; or in those passages where dream and reality are experimentally substituted for each other.[88] In those cases, it is the dream, unknown to the "true men" as we have seen, that is adduced as proof of a possible complementary existence in another world: "Chuang-tzu told this story: 'Once I dreamt that I was a butterfly, a butterfly flitting here and there according to the desires butterflies have. All I knew were my joys as a butterfly and I had no idea of my human characteristics. Suddenly I woke up. There I was, lying on the ground, and myself again. Now I no longer know: was I really a man who dreamt he was a butterfly, or am I perhaps a butterfly that dreams at this moment that it is a man. And yet there is surely a difference between man and butterfly. It is called metamorphosis.' "[89]

Quite apart from the dream which was surely chosen with care, metamorphosis was of special concern to the Taoists. The butterfly which passes through several of them is a particularly striking symbol of it. It is a metamorphosis, however, which is intended to conceptually transcend the changes in nature and thus to overcome the terror of death. To point to the flickering uncertainty in all apparent reality merely serves the purpose of forcing man into a higher, eternal reality. We have seen hints that this did not prevent many from getting stuck in the first heaven which was no less threatened by unreality. The book *Chuang-tzu* contains another passage where life is discussed as a dream. It is a conversation between Ch'ü Ch'iao, allegedly a disciple of Confucius, and Chang Wu-tzu, a legendary sage of antiquity. After Chü asks him about some Taoist definitions of the "sage" which Confucius rejected, Chang Wu-tzu instructs him as follows:

> [The saint succeeds] in having his place next to the sun and the moon and to squeeze the universe under his arm [only] if he makes it a harmonious whole, if he raises [fertile] chaos [to a principle] and worships the lowly placed. Ordinary men may excel in their profession, but the "sage" is foolish and obstinate. He partakes of the [change] of millennia and perfects simplicity in unity. For him, the ten thousand things are of a natural rightness and thus they yield plenitude. How am I to know that joy in life is not mere illusion? How am I to know that he who is afraid of death does not resemble a child that has lost his parents and can no longer find a home? . . . How am I to know that the dead do not feel remorse for having once been so attached to life? He who dreams of a banquet must [sometimes] weep the morning after. He who dreams of weeping, [sometimes] awakens the next morning just in time to join a merry hunting party. While he dreams, he does not know he is dreaming . . . only when he awakens does he know that he has dreamt. But there is also the great awakening *(ta-chiao),* and then we see that [everything] here is nothing but a great dream. Of course, the fools believe that they are already awake and think they know precisely who is prince, and who is shepherd. What foolishness! Confucius and you, both of you are dreams, and I, who tell you this, am also a dream. Such speeches as I am making now are still called ruse and deception. But in ten thousand years, a great sage will come who will decipher them, he will come before the sun sets.[90]

A messianic hope could easily be read into the last sentence were it not that the prophecy has intentionally been transposed into the atemporal realm by its contradictory temporal indication. Simply waiting for this salvation thus becomes meaningless. Early Taoism did not conceive of happiness as the salvation of a large human community, to be attained for the many by the efforts of a single person, but rather as the personal liberation of many individuals through a natural power present in them all. The early Taoist ideal state, leading an unconscious existence in a multitude of individual villages, is simply an image of this. One of the most important sources of Taoist teaching about a world that is whole is thus a passionate individualism. But this response to the ever-increasing regimentation of life in Confucian and Mohist conceptions was an individualism that found its fulfillment in the abandonment of the self.

4 / THE GOLDEN NOW AND THE DISCOVERY OF THE FUTURE

HEDONISM AND INDIVIDUALISM

But in conjunction with some lateral branches of Confucianism, the individualistic and naturalistic component of Taoism gave rise to entirely different conceptions concerning the realization of an ideal world which constituted the diametric opposite of both Taoist and Confucian ideas. It is fascinating how Confucianism and Taoism, which appeared irreconcilable, again drew closer to each other in what were precisely their most extreme forms. In this convergence, both completely lost sight of their real aims.

In the numerous polemics against the Taoists found in Mencius, the Taoist ideas are never directly identified with the teachings of Chuang-tzu or Lao-tzu, but with those of another, younger philosopher, Yang Chu, who probably lived in the fourth century B.C. He and Mo Ti are the two heretics whom Mencius attacks. No authentic writings by Yang Chu have come down to us. There are merely some sayings which give only a very approximate idea of his teaching. But a Taoist collection of texts, ascribed to the previously mentioned philosopher Lieh-tzu, but which probably was not put together before the second century A.D. and perhaps even much later (fourth century),[91] contains a rather long chapter where sayings passed on in his school are brought together. That they thus became part of the Taoist corpus and were accepted by them without opposition shows that Mencius did not simply construct this connection by an unfair lumping together of the exaggerated opinions of a nonconformist with those of the Taoists. On the contrary, the teachings of Yang Chu actually represented an essential component of Taoism, and in the view of reputable scholars (Chan Wing-tsit, and to some extent also Feng Yu-lan),[92] their origin dates back even further than classical Taoism itself.

It is likely that Yang Chu was the author of the frequently documented slogan which consisted in the provocative phrase: "I would not give a single hair of my head even if I could save the entire empire (or the whole world) by doing so." The customary definition of Yang Chu as a "hedonist," an "individualist," or even an "anarchist" thus undoubtedly has a certain justification. But the aggressive element which—as in all slogans—appears to be the most important aspect, dissolves at once when one studies the basis for the pronouncement in the book *Lieh-tzu.* It is wholly Taoist:

> Ch'in-tzu asked Yang Chu: "Would you give a single hair of your body if you could thereby save the entire world?" "One cannot save the world with a hair," Yang Chu answered. "But let us suppose," Ch'in-tzu pressed him, "that it could actually be saved in this way?" Yang Chu did not answer. Ch'in-tzu walked away and turned to Yang Chu's disciple Meng Sun-yang. "You don't understand what our teacher means," Meng said. "May I explain it to you? Would you let your skin be scratched if you were given ten thousand gold pieces for it?" "Certainly," Ch'in-tzu replied. "And would you let one of your limbs be cut off if you were given a state in exchange?" Ch'in-tzu did not answer. After a while, Meng Sun-yang said: "Of course, a single hair is less than the skin, and the skin is less than a limb. But all that is involved here is a question of more or less. A hair is merely the ten thousandth part of the body, but why should this part be considered insignificant?"[93]

The core of the argument is not primarily the rejection of state and society but the value assigned to life as an all-pervasive force. This can also be inferred from the name this school gave itself: "preservation of life" *(ch'üan-sheng).* This force has been conferred on the individual in a definite way and is to be protected against all infringements. This opinion is also expressed by the sages in *Chuang-tzu.* But a small though decisive shift in accent becomes noticeable in the spiritual attitude toward death which constantly threatens the happiness of life. The four friends Tzu-yu, Tzu-ssu, Tzu-lai and Tzu-li bypassed the problem by ignoring it: for them, death was a change of form, no different from all the other changes in the world. They tried to eradicate the sense of a personal and unique self, a personal and unique time, in order to rid themselves of something that death would inevitably take from them some day. For them, birth, life and death became a single body with head and tail only because their life blended into unity with eternal nature. Yang Chu also looked on death with a mixture of mockery and heroism, but he drew an entirely different consequence from its invincible power. Nothing was further from his mind than to allow a short life to be stamped by the bitter law of death. Instead, he accepted death for what it clearly was: an absolute end, but which for that very reason had neither extension nor dimension. Surprisingly, it suddenly became clear that it therefore had no power. For if he properly understood it, this absolute end gave man a blessed measure of freedom to be used in a life that was given to him, and to him alone. Yet he only retained this freedom as long as he did not make the grotesque, almost inconceivable misjudgment of trying to make precisely that time when he would no longer be living the law governing the time when he was. For this is exactly what Confucians and Taoists alike were striving for; the former, because their entire longing was for a fame that would survive death, the latter because they sought to attain the condition of a "living corpse" (an expression occasionally used by Chuang-tzu)[94] in the midst of a bloody earthly existence. Yang Chu did not seek the fulfillment of life in its prolongation but in its intensification, not in its merging with eternity, but in the realized fullness of the moment. He was the discoverer of the Golden Now:

> "The most advanced age man can attain," Yang Chu said, "is one hundred years, and there is not one among a thousand who reaches it. But let us take such a person: an unconscious childhood and an infirm old age take up about half of it; the time he spends sleeping and lets idly pass while awake, is again half of that; pain and illness, grief and worries, loss and failure, sadness and anxiety, come to half of that. What remains is hardly more than ten years, and of that there is barely one hour of carefree, unclouded enjoyment. What then is one to do in life, and in what is one to take pleasure? There remains beauty, abundance, music, and love. Yet beauty and abundance cannot always be freely enjoyed, nor can music and love. Besides, there are the effects of reward and punishment, of fame and of examples worthy of imitation. During their brief life, people are forever running after vain praise for the sake of a doubtful and meaningless glorification after their death. It is pointless to suppress the senses and to wonder if one's desires are legitimate or not. That way, one senselessly cheats oneself out of the most intense enjoyment of the present and is never master of oneself, not even for a single hour. What is the difference between such a life and that of a criminal in chains? . . . One person dies at the age of ten, another at the age of one hundred. Perfect saints die, and so do dangerous fools. While alive, some were saintly kings, such as Yao and Shun. Once dead, they are molding bones. While alive, some were monsters, such as the tyrants Chieh and Chou. Once dead, they are molding bones. As molding bones, they are equal. Who can tell the difference between them? Let us therefore grasp life's moment—what is the point of worrying about the time after death?"[95]

The ideal man as envisaged by Yang Chu also looked quite different from the Taoist hermits. As occasionally described in Taoist writings, their appearance with uncombed hair, dusty garments full of holes, unkempt beard and a knowing and absent smile, sometimes made them blend so completely with the dusty rocks of the mountains and the sparse brush of a meager vegetation that they seemed to be sliding back into nature while still alive. But this ideal man was just as different from the clean and disciplined Confucian who sought to advance step by step on his way toward propriety and prosperity, charitable and strict toward himself and others. A certain decadence, though in a form which is actually more appropriate to the third century A.D. than the third century B.C., effortlessly fits in with the image of the hedonistic hero as he is described in the book *Lieh-tzu* in the Yang Chu chapter, although that is not to say that these elements were not already implicit in Yang Chu's basic teachings:

> Tuan Mu-shu from Wei, a descendent of the (Confucian) Tzu-kung, inherited a huge fortune from his ancestors. Tens of thousands of gold pieces were piled up in his house. Since he felt unable to discipline himself, he gave rein to his desires.

Whatever people might wish to do, whatever they dreamed up in their pursuit of a merry life, he did. Palaces and terraces, gardens and artificial lakes, food and drink, chariots and garments, music and willing female slaves—all that he owned in as much abundance as the princes of Ch'i and Ch'u. Whatever pleased his fancy, whatever could delight eye, ear and mouth, and even things that could be obtained only in the remotest regions, he had brought as if it had grown within his own four walls. When he traveled, he did not care about the obstacles and dangers of mountains and streams, the length of the roads. He went everywhere as readily as others take a few steps. Day after day, hundreds of guests filled his halls, the fire never went out in his kitchens, in the chambers above the terraces the music never stopped playing. What was left of the food intended for his closest relatives he gave to his clan, what the clan left, he passed out among his neighbors, what they left, he distributed in the entire realm. When he came into his sixties and began to age in body and soul, he retired from his affairs and gave everything away. Within the course of a year, he had given away all his house contained of pearls and jewels, chariots and garments, women and female slaves. He left nothing to his sons and grandsons. And when he finally became ill, there was nothing to buy medicines with, and when he finally died, not a cent was left for his burial. But all the people of the realm had benefited from his kindness, and so they joined together and raised the money to bury him and to return their fortune to his sons and grandsons. Ch'in Ku-li (a disciple of the thrifty Mo Ti), heard about this and said: "Tuan Mu-shu was a fool who disgraced his ancestor [Tzu-kung]." But when Tuan Kan-sheng heard about this, he said: "Tuan Mu-shu was a magnificent fellow. His soul was even greater than that of his ancestor. His way of acting awed the masses, yet he attained true perfection."[96]

From this standpoint of unlimited individual freedom, the world and its striving for happiness does indeed take on a wholly new aspect: the hope for the morrow, the longing for the past, suddenly turn out to be a turning away from life itself, for life finds its fulfillment only in the moment. It is no less a turning away from happiness which can touch man only in the Now. The openness with which Tuan plunged headlong into life to let it penetrate his every pore, the sweep of the pleasure with which he gathered the treasures of the entire world in his house, and roamed the remotest regions, the indulgent magnanimity he showered on relatives, neighbors and all the people in the realm, particularly as he sensed death approaching, all that is of a magnificence compared to which the Confucian zeal and even the Taoist flight from society are merely philistine timidity. Yang Chu's individualism merely seems an uninhibited egoism which begrudges the world a single hair of his head. Actually, he is intent on laying bare the inexhaustible sources of vitality hidden in every individual, and to make them flow again as he incessantly rolls aside the burdens that society and its moral demands never stop imposing on man. His "egoism" does not drive him into isolation, but rather reveals to him the remotest corners of the world and the hearts of all men.

Under these circumstances, it is not surprising that in the writings ascribed to

Yang Chu even the despised last rulers of declining dynasties suddenly appear in a different light. According to the cliché coined by the Chou, these men had to have been fundamentally evil, for otherwise their dynasties could not have lost their heavenly mandate. It is true that the Taoists had always mocked their counterparts, the industrious sage kings. For, like the saintly Yü, taming the Yellow River when it inundated its banks, they "ran the hair off their legs" (it should be remarked parenthetically that this is a typically Confucian rationalization of the fact that the emperor Yü developed from a river god who still appears at a much later date on paintings, showing him with a smooth fishtail like a mermaid's). But they had never gone so far as to defend, let alone glorify, a Chieh or a Chou, the last carousing, blood-stained kings of the Hsia and Shang dynasties. But the "hedonists" violated this taboo as well:

> Yang Chu said: "All the good imaginable is said about the [two sage emperors] Shun and Yü, and about the duke of Chou and Master Confucius, everything bad about the kings Chieh and Chou. But Shun had to plow south of the Yellow River and make containers near the Thunder swamp. He could not take a moment's rest, he did not enjoy delicious food, he lacked his parents' love, and his brothers and sisters did not feel kindly toward him either. . . . He died in misery and grief: he was the most unfortunate and hapless of men. . . . Yü directed all his efforts to the reclamation of land. When a son was born to him, he had no time for him. When he passed by his own house he could not spare a moment to go inside. His whole body was shriveled, he had callouses and swellings on his hands and feet. He died in misery and grief: he was the most plagued and anxious of men. . . . The duke of Chou had to withdraw (from the capital) and spend three years in the East because evil rumors were spread about him. He was obliged to execute his older brothers and to exile his younger ones. . . . He died in misery and distress: he was the most threatened and disquieted among men. Confucius was almost killed by a tree that was being cut down without his knowing it, he had to flee from the state of Wei, he failed in the states of Shang and Chou, he was prevented from leaving the states of Ch'en and Ts'ai; in his home state, he suffered injustice at the hands of the head of the Chi family. . . . He died in misery and grief and he was driven from place to place like no other man. . . . The tyrant Chieh, on the other hand, inherited the wealth of many generations, and sat on the throne, highly honored. He was clever enough to keep the mass of his subjects away from himself. The terror he spread brought fear and trembling to all that lived in the lands encircled by the four Oceans. He gave rein to his pleasures and followed his every inclination to the end. Reveling, he died. He was the happiest and freest of men. The tyrant Chou also inherited the wealth of many generations and sat on the throne. The terror he spread knew no limits and no one went against his will. He indulged his passions in the harem, and pursued his desires throughout the long nights, nor did he let them be soured by ritual or a sense of propriety. Reveling, he approached his end. He was the freest and least inhibited of men. During their life, the two monsters had the satisfaction of being able to indulge their lusts. It is true that they were called fools and fiends after their death, but in reality they missed nothing because of that. They do not hear the insults since nothing distinguishes them now from

a shriveled tree stump or a clod of earth. Good things are said nowadays about those four sages, that is true. But their life was bitter to the very end, and they walked the path to death like everyone else."[97]

Although presumably not written down until much later, these insouciant words may well have been formulated during Yang Chu's lifetime. The thought expressed here breached barriers which certainly had been considered impassable as late as the fourth century. In the political arena, these ideas did indeed have a much more provocative, explosive effect than in the private sphere where they were meant to have their impact. When one takes a closer look, it becomes apparent that the conviction underlying these words was not confined to the "hedonists," but shared not only by the Taoists, but even by a fully recognized movement within Confucianism. It was the conviction that all morality was not only unnatural, but actually violated nature, for it necessarily and constantly inhibited the desires of the individual and thus deformed his real nature, his real life (in Chinese, there is hardly any difference between these two concepts here, as we have seen). An artistically cut and carved jade vessel or a tamed horse, for example, both involve changes of form. It is only when one asks whether such changes should be called cultivation or coercion that opinions diverge. They depend on the value attributed to this nature. In the comparison between the somewhat bloodless, overworked and moralizing sages, and florid tyrants, bursting with vitality as they commit their crimes, Yang Chu unhesitatingly takes the side of these villains because there was so much more life in their actions. But there were those Confucians who shuddered not just at the alleged misdeeds of these rulers. It was precisely the pure, untrammeled vitality of their acts which sent shudders down their spine. They felt they must fear the irruption of a bare-toothed animality into the narrowly hedged, laboriously constructed and so easily damaged sphere of human civilization. The most consequential thinker within this Confucian branch was Hsün-tzu, whose name we encountered first when we considered the reciprocal relations between music and joy.[98]

HSÜN-TZU AND ORDER THROUGH RITUAL

Hsün-tzu (?298–238 B.C.), probably one of the most profound and most consistent philosophers China has produced, was the declared opponent of Mencius within Confucianism. That not his teachings but those of the latter were declared canonical in the eleventh century A.D., and that Mencius had also previously been honored as Confucius's true successor, merely testifies to a certain insincerity in Confucianism. For in the course of time, Confucianism actually inclined increasingly toward the conceptions of Hsün-tzu. Paradoxically, this was especially true after Mencius was officially enthroned. An officially promoted Confucianism subsequently left as little room for his quasi-mystical notion of a salubrious force pulsating through all beings *(hao-jan chih ch'i)* and which the individual could again become part of, as it did for the high esteem in which the people were held by this man.[99] For the rulers of large states who either strove to acquire power over even larger ones, or indeed over the empire as a whole, or for those who were merely making efforts in that direction, Hsün-tzu's promises were certainly much more interesting than Mencius's admonishments to share everything with the people. Hsün-tzu announced quite simply that nature, and more particularly human nature, was evil. "The nature of man is evil; what is good in him, is artificial,"[100] he wrote, for, as far as we know, he was the first unquestionably historical figure among Chinese philosophers to have written down his thoughts himself. He thus intensely mistrusted this "nature" *(hsing)* which both conceptually and linguistically had originally been identical with the Taoist concept of "life" *(sheng)*. It was "artificial" *(wei)* for him, a term which can just as readily be translated as "false" or "unnatural," for its original meaning is both "affected" and "made" (in the sense of "manufactured"). He believed that the good is not present as a seed in the creations of nature but brought into the world in a second, purely human act of creation, and in a struggle against nature by the "sages" (whose existence is thus viewed as having the same axiomatic character as that of the cosmos). "Ritual" was the means by which they tamed nature, tamed the beast in man, and wrested oases of culture and historicity from the unending cycle of the seasons with its blind and brutal sequence of life and death. For Confucius, ritual still had had the function of utilizing age-old magical and religious practices such as sacrifices and the cult of the dead, which had actually lost their meaning when living man had become the center of the world view. By conferring a new, humanistic dimension on them, ritual was to infuse them with new meaning. But for Hsün-tzu, ritual became something considerably more important. It was not merely an expression of "humanity," but the tool which made possible the very creation of humanity against the will of nature, the carving knife, as it were, by which the image of man could first be cut from the resistant, raw wood.

This conception also had a decisive influence on Hsün-tzu's idea of the happiness of man and the nature of the ideal state, for as a Confucian he always thought in social terms. In Confucius, we previously encountered a curious form of "equality" when he spoke about the modesty that might be inculcated in the people through ritual. This "equality" now loses the somewhat nebulous quality it had had in the earlier philosopher and takes on clear outlines. For Hsün-tzu, the secret of a felicitous world order consists in the introduction and preservation of clearly defined social barriers between men which make it possible for everyone to receive his share *equally*—though it must be added that this share is very *unequal:* "The sage kings," we read, "hated disorder and therefore established the rules of ritual and justice, so that the people might be divided into the classes of the rich and the poor, the nobility and the commoners, thus checking each other. This is the guiding principle for the fertilization of the world. In the classical *Book of Records* it says: 'they are equal (*t'ung*) only to the extent that they are all *un*equal.' That is precisely what I mean by it."[101]

In a chapter of his work, entitled "A Wealthy State" (or "The Enrichment of the State"), Hsün-tzu goes into considerable detail about the reasons for this conviction. It is a carefully structured speech, somewhat reminiscent of certain chapters of the book *Mo Ti.* In reality, however, it is directed against this philosopher, perhaps precisely because they are not so very different from Hsün-tzu in certain respects, although their premises have nothing in common with his:

> The ten thousand creatures live under the same *(t'ung)* sky, and yet have different shapes. They have no real purpose, and yet are of use to man: that is the structure (*shu,* actually "number") [given them by nature]. Men of all social stations live together, they are equal *(t'ung)* in their desires, yet vary in their methods; they are equal in their passions, yet different in their intelligence: that is their nature-given vitality *(sheng).* In the fact *that* they can do something, the intelligent and the stupid are equal, but in *what* they can do, they differ. One must remember equality, yet also be aware of difference, for if the people are allowed to act as it pleases them without [anywhere] coming up against displeasure, if one gives rein to its desires without setting [any] limit, it becomes confused and can no longer take delight in anything. When that happens, the intelligent can no longer come to power. When they can no longer come to power, success and renown can no longer have any effect, and when they can no longer have any effect, nothing is left to which the mass can be bound, and if it no longer can be bound to anything, the positions of prince and subject no longer exist. Then, no princes are left to govern the subjects, the superior are no longer there to govern the inferior. Misfortune would sprout all over the realm only because desires were given rein. The things men desire and hate are the same, but [precisely because of that], there are many who desire and few of the things desired, and since they are few, people begin to quarrel. Therefore hundreds of different kinds of skill have to be developed before even a single person can be kept alive, but [that person] does not have the ability to pursue two such skills at the same time. Since no one can occupy two offices simultaneously, and men suffer when they live in isolation and without helping each other, they form a society. But if they do not divide [into groups], they begin to quarrel. Misery is evil, quarreling a misfortune. There is only one possibility of avoiding both: a clear division of society. [Otherwise,] the strong tyrannize the weak, the intelligent frighten the stupid, the inferior resist the superior, and the young mock the old. . . . When that is the case, the old and the weak experience the misfortune of not being cared for, and the strong the calamity of murderous struggle.[102]

Hsün-tzu then describes how the measures of an intelligent ruler can create an ideal government:

> To make a state content, one must be moderate in one's own consumption, and generous toward the people: that is the best way of garnering the surplus of the country. If one brings about moderation through ritual, and the government is generous toward the people, the people will enjoy abundance. If the people are treated generously, they will grow; if they grow, the fields, being properly cultivated, will yield a rich harvest, and if they yield a rich harvest by being properly cultivated,

their fruit will grow a hundredfold. If the superior follow this rule and gather the wealth of the country, and the inferior follow the ritual and are moderate in their consumption, the surplus will pile up and form hills and mountains, so that no space will be left to hoard it unless one sets fire to it from time to time. . . . But ritual means that high and low have their place, that there be a difference between old and young, and a relation between important and unimportant. That is the reason that the Son of Heaven, the feudal princes, the high dignitaries, and the officers have the clothing appropriate to their station. Virtue finds its expression in position, position its expression in salary, and salary its justification in the task allotted. From officer upward, people have to be educated by ritual and music to become moderate, but the simple people must be educated by laws and paragraphs. Thus [the leaders] measure the land and create the state, they calculate benefits and discipline the people, they determine the strength of men, and distribute the work and see to it that the people always do their work, that work is always profitable, and that the profit suffices to nourish the people. . . . Those endowed with physical strength are thus the helpers of the "virtuous" [ruler]. It is only through the physical strength of the people *(po-hsing)* that he achieves success [everywhere]. Because it forms a society, he attains harmony, because it is capable, he acquires wealth, because it is steady, he achieves peace, and he lives long because it attains an advanced age. Father and son cannot help loving each other, older and younger brothers cannot help obeying each other, nor men and women making each other happy. Children are raised without misery, and the aged are fed. And it will be as the proverb says: "Heaven and earth have created it, the sages have perfected it."[103]

Very much in opposition to Mo Ti, who is directly attacked in this chapter, and although he stresses moderation, Hsün-tzu's ideal state is in no way defined by a parsimonious Puritanism. On the contrary, following the model of the old kings, the right ruler sees to it that the "ears, eyes and mouths (of his people) are stuffed"[104] with all imaginable kinds of intoxicating music, the dazzling brilliance of colors, and sumptuous food. Of course, he also takes care that those at the head of the state obtain a particularly generous share of all these things, so that their splendor and dignity might be enhanced. It is only in this way, as Hsün-tzu emphasizes, that the "ten thousand creatures come to have their good purpose"[105] which mere nature did not give them. Life under the old kings who knew how to bring all this about was thus truly paradisiacal for the members of society:

The old kings saw to it that people did not suffer heat strokes in summer and the cold of winter; that, when speed was called for, their strength was not taxed; and that when there was a chance to let up, this did not mean that they let the right moment pass by. Thus, everything was seen to, and successes were achieved, so that both the highly placed and the lowly were rich, and the people loved its superiors. The people arrived as in a flowing stream, enjoyed the presence [of kings] and felt about them as they had about father and mother, and they were happy even when ordered to die on the field of battle. . . . The earlier kings created a clear ritual and a clear law so that all might be of one mind. They induced loyalty and fidelity, so

> that all loved each other; they honored the sages and assigned tasks to the able so that a hierarchy might arise. They invented gowns for the nobility and ceremonies to instill respect. Work was imposed on the people as the times demanded, and they easily shaped its responsibilities to make all men equal *(ch'i)* and to help all of them. They took care of the old and the young [among the people] just as defenseless children are looked after. Since this was so, vice and heresy did not spread, robbers and thieves did not appear. Whoever [could] benefit from civilization did his best.[106]

But this splendid political order is not confined to antiquity. Time and again, Hsün-tzu interspersed his talk with many remarks intended to prove that countries where it had become a reality perhaps already existed. Since China was divided into a number of individual states during his lifetime, this did not seem an altogether remote possibility. He therefore suggested criteria that would enable even an outside observer to distinguish between such a well-run state and a poorly administered one. Perhaps such clues were of particular importance to the "wandering scholars" who roamed all over the country from the sixth to the third century B.C.

> Whether a state is ordered or not can already be seen when one crosses its borders. . . . When the farmers show pleasure in their fields, when the officers remain calm though the fighting is dangerous, when the lower officials love the law, when solemn rites are observed at court and the nobility and the ministers negotiate harmoniously with each other, it is a well-ordered state. If an inspection of the court shows that the nobles are the wisest, if an inspection of the corps of officials shows those who govern to be the most capable, and if an inspection of the entertainments shows that those responsible for them are men of the highest integrity, then an enlightened prince governs there.[107]

This world was stabilized by fixed social differences, free of unrest, and therefore happy, in Hsün-tzu's view. It is striking that within it, the one necessarily unstable, constantly shifting line separating groups, i.e. those of the young and the old, should not have been given special importance. This may seem surprising at first glance since the various Confucian writings on ritual dealing intensively with "piety" were strongly influenced by Hsün-tzu, as we have already suggested. Indeed, some of them derive directly from his work. This is also true of a number of chapters of the *Classic of Filial Piety (Hsiao-ching)*,[108] which was probably given its definitive formulation in the second century B.C. In this work, filial piety experiences a genuine apotheosis. It is extolled as so central that it almost supersedes "humanity" and becomes the source of all other virtues. But what is really interesting here is this: it can easily be shown that the Confucians, following Mencius, did not generally stress filial love as a fundamental principle of the social order until all other basic values (particularly the feudal system and the "law" of the Legalists, both of which still play an undisputed role in Hsün-tzu), had totally lost their hold. Precisely because it was rooted in nature and could be preserved intact throughout the intellectual chaos into which China's most productive philosophical century plunged about one hundred years after Hsün-tzu's death, filial love was the only concept which offered the fundament of a new order. In Hsün-tzu's work, however, the all too "natural" priority of the old over the young is no absolute, but merely a relative value. It derives simply from their greater knowledge and, to exaggerate somewhat, their greater temporal distance from birth and thus also from what is elemental and evil. For "man is indubitably vile at birth."[109] Otherwise, the aged occupied the same plane as minors in Hsün-tzu's ideal state. They are groups within society which may lay claim to the support of the strong, but beyond that they cannot ask for more than a sort of formal respect. A (possibly apocryphal) chapter (added only in the second century B.C.) of the book *Hsün-tzu,* entitled "The Way of the Child" *(Tzu-tao),* surprisingly contains almost nothing but anecdotes which confirm the right of children to be disobedient. They are introduced by a remark which no longer sounds really Confucian, as that term is commonly understood, but which is revealing for that very reason. It proves that much more was implicit in Confucianism than could later fully develop:

> To observe piety within the house, and brotherly love outside of it, that is the small path of man. To show obedience to those above, and sincerity to those below, that is man's middle path. To follow the "Way," and not the prince, to follow righteousness and not the father, that is man's great path. For truly: only when his striving has been satisfied by ritual, only when his words are used according to fixed categories, only then is the "Way" of the Confucian *(Ju)* complete. Even a [sage emperor] Shun could not add anything to this. There are three cases where the pious son does not obey the commands [of his parents]: 1. If his parents would incur danger were he to follow their command, but would remain in tranquillity if he disobeys. If the pious son does not obey their command [under these circumstances], he does his duty. 2. If his parents were to be disgraced if he obeyed their command, but were to gain fame if he fails to do so—if the pious son does not obey their command [under these circumstances], he is in the right. 3. If his parents were to conduct themselves like animals were he to obey their command, but act in a civilized manner if he fails to do so—if the pious son does not obey their command [under these circumstances], he is respectful. Therefore: if it were permissible to obey them, and he fails to do so, he is not [the right kind of] son. If it were not permissible to obey them, and he obeyed them nonetheless, he is derelict. Only when he clearly understands the lawful meaning of obedience and non-obedience and is able to exercise caution in his acts by observing respect and reverence, loyalty and honesty, custom and decency, it may be said about him that he has the "Great piety." This is precisely what is meant when a tradition states: "to follow the 'Way' and not the prince, to follow righteousness and not the father."[110]

These nearly revolutionary maxims are noteworthy because they show the gradual detachment, the developing autonomy of virtues which in Confucius still clearly derived from man and human relations. The "Way" *(tao)* and "righteousness" become concepts which have a value in themselves and impose on men a form of action which tends to counter his spontaneous human feelings. For emotionally speaking, man tends to take the side of his parents and his family, whatever the right or wrong of the matter, and this is precisely what constitutes the point of departure of Mencius's teaching concerning the goodness of human nature. Hsün-tzu, however, mistrusts this instinctive, innate "goodness" profoundly and tries to show in this chapter about the right to contradict that love within the family may even be downright bad and thus cannot form the basis of a natural morality. Much more abstract, colder, clearer concepts deriving from an entirely different sphere—the "Way," and particularly ritual—are the ideals through which man can be extricated from a nature that pulls him downward.

No more "Confucian" but just as consistent is Hsün-tzu's suggestion that one should not follow the teachings of the earliest "sage kings" but those of the later ones. Of course, this demand is directed not only against Mo Ti's and the Taoists' tendency to reach back ever further into the past in their search for support for this or that new theory, and to attribute at will significant anecdotes to figures of remotest antiquity about whom up to that time barely the names were reliably passed down, thus beating the Confucians at their own game. Hsün-tzu also seems to have recognized how difficult all intellectual and political decisions became in his own time if excessive reliance were placed on more or less shadowy models since in many respects the present had its own problems. Thus he wrote:

> The "Way" of men cannot be without differentiations. Among these, none is more significant than social differentiations, and among these none more significant than those effected through ritual, and among these none more significant than those invented by the sage kings. But there were hundreds of sage kings—which ones should we adopt as models? We have the following rule [for these difficulties]: "when a civilization becomes too old, it grows tired; when a good family has become too old, the succession of generations is disrupted; and when those who have to supervise law and order exaggerate the ritual, it becomes insubstantial." And this is the reason [we have] a further rule: "if you wish to see the tracks of the sage kings, look where they are freshest, and you will find the ones left by the later kings." These later kings were the rulers of the entire empire. To discard them, and to make remotest antiquity one's "Way" instead is the same as discarding one's own prince and serving a foreign one instead. And therefore [we have a third] rule: "if you wish to see the thousand years, look at today, if you wish to understand the millionfold, then look at the one or the two, if you wish to understand earlier ages, look at the 'Way' of the Chou, and if you wish to understand the 'Way' of the Chou, look at the rulers that were honored by the people of that period." And therefore [the last rule also applies], which states: "through what is near, one understands what is far away, through the one, one understands the ten thousandfold, through what is tiny one understands what radiates [far]." This is what I mean by it.[111]

In this not wholly avowed yet clearly recognizable emphasis placed on salvation in the present, we find a surprising affinity between Hsün-tzu's teaching and what is in all other respects the wholly different and even opposite teaching of Yang

Chu. And yet this is not the only parallel. As the sentences quoted above show once again, Hsün-tzu's mistrust of nature also expressed itself in an equally great mistrust of the "mass"—which included both large numbers and, in politics, the people in its totality—matched by a confidence in the blessings the individual can bring to the world. Of course, this individual is not someone devoted to his pleasure and who indulges his egoism, but the good ruler. To make possible the realization of the ideal state he describes requires the work of certain sages of antiquity; to actually bring it into existence requires certain eminent rulers who rise above the mass and impose on its recalcitrance but to its benefit their own will, which is based on "ritual." Yang Chu's teaching was wholly devoid of political ambition. The provocative transgressions of all accepted orders notwithstanding, it was therefore irrelevant in the social sphere. Although he may not have been wholly aware of it, Hsün-tzu's teaching, on the other hand, contained an enormous explosive force. For it required merely a tiny shift in concepts to turn what still seemed a fundamentally rather conservative ideology into a much more aggressive one with clear totalitarian characteristics. As such, it came to oppose all traditional teachings and brought a fundamental change to China's intellectual landscape in a brief, but enormously vehement and momentous rule.

THE LEGALISTS AND ORDER THROUGH LAW

It would seem that the feeling that times had changed, that consequently a government according to the old models could only increase the chaos, had already spread before Hsün-tzu appeared. It is typical, however, that this sense did not become dominant in the central states of what was China at that time—states with an old culture such as Chin, Ch'i and Lu, for example, and which, to use a bold comparison, constituted the Greece and Italy of old China—but rather in the border states of Ch'u in the South and Ch'in in the West. Originally, they had had the status of colonies, but in the course of time, and as always happens in history, they grew more powerful than the old, centrally located dominant states because they could extend their borders at will. The fact that the entire cultural tradition had been passed on to them in a very diluted form was something they turned to their advantage. Making a virtue of necessity, they attempted something new where the old seemed so clearly to fail.

Among the states which "were better off" in this way, the state of Ch'in, which was ethnically probably still permeated with "proto-Turkish" and "proto-Tibetan" elements, made the decisive break with antiquity by detaching itself not merely from the model of the old states but from the model of the old ideals of statecraft generally. It may well be that Hsün-tzu's teaching was already influenced by this turning away, that it was a last minute attempt to incorporate this much more efficient ideology into Confucianism. But at a time which had passed through so much intellectual juggling and was pressing for a radical solution even at the price of catastrophe, this attempt was doomed.

According to tradition, Shang Yang (died 338 B.C.) was the first philosopher and politician to establish wholly new maxims. The son of a concubine of the (not very powerful) king of Wei, he was related to the most aristocratic families. He was trained as an educator of princes and allegedly had a long-standing, special interest in penal law. When the minister responsible for him was dying, he is said to have advised the king to either take this dangerously intelligent young man as councillor, or to execute him immediately.[112] Because the king did neither, Shang Yang followed the stream of countless knights and scholars who, each with a different skill, were traveling from court to court at the time to acquire money and property. Finally, he came to Ch'in. Legend reports that he was first granted three audiences there during which he gave the customary, Confucian advice. The result was that the prince of Ch'in fell asleep. It was not until the fourth audience when Shang Yang suddenly expounded entirely new ideas which no longer stuck to models but were aimed at discarding them that the prince became so enthralled that he did not even notice that in his excitement Shang Yang was touching the prince's mat with his knees. After an audience which allegedly lasted several days, Shang Yang was asked what he had done to be so successful. He answered: "When I told the prince of the 'Way' of the old emperors and kings, he said: 'That takes a long time, and is a distant ideal. But I cannot wait!' . . . But when I told him how to make a state powerful, he became enthusiastic."[113] This encounter, which led to Shang Yang's appointment as minister, is reported in the biography which also reproduces the speeches with which he defended himself against protesting Confucians:

> He who proves himself an extraordinary person by his deeds is rejected by the world; he who has independent ideas is hated by the mass. The stupid don't even understand something that happened long ago; the wise understand it before it develops. One cannot discuss the origins of a thing with the people, but at most share the pleasure they take in its fortunate accomplishment. He who studies the highest 'virtue' will deviate from popular conceptions. He who wants to accomplish a great deed will not ask the mass for advice. For that reason, a sage will not take antiquity as his model when he can strengthen the state in this way, and if he can thus benefit the state, he will not follow customary ritual. . . . [The founders of the dynasty] King T'ang and King Wu achieved their victories precisely because they did not follow antiquity, while the Hsia and the Shang dynasties declined, precisely because they retained their ritual.[114]

This scepticism toward antiquity is stressed again and again in the collection of texts *Shang-chün-shu,* which bears Shang Yang's name *(The Book of the Prince Shang),* yet was certainly not composed by him but comes from the tradition of his school which called itself the school of the "Legalists" *(Fa-chia).* The following utterly straightforward comment is an example: "The 'Way' of the sage consists neither in imitating the past nor in following the present, but in acting as the times demand."[115] These "times" unquestionably refer to the future, even if it is not called by that name but rather merely alluded to by the omission of past and present, or circumscribed in some other manner, as in these words: "the sage understands a thing even before it has developed." The miraculous means by which Shang Yang believed he could best do justice to these budding developments was the "law," i.e. the penal law, for that was all that was meant by this concept *(fa)*. For him, "law"[116] has an absolutely independent value. It appears as a kind of extension of natural law, indispensable for the welfare of humanity as a whole, although it is created entirely by one person and, if only apparently, for just one individual: by and for the ruler at the top. Through this new conception, all traditional values were stood on their head. Piety, brotherly love, wisdom, honesty and even loyalty became crimes which merely interfered unduly with the all-pervasive demands of the state and the ruler.

The order everything was subjected to was the order of the military. In Shang Yang's system, soldiers occupied the highest rank or, more accurately, the most important place. For equality before the law up to and including the crown prince, an equality which paid no attention to any past merit and therefore also immediately dissolved the old, traditional groupings of the nobility, was one of Shang Yang's fundamental principles. In still another, at first glance rather surprising fashion, the law turned out to be a kind of leveling principle: for while the number of offenses threatened with punishment was considerable, punishment itself varied little. Almost all crimes were punished by death. Only the method of execution and its possible extension to relatives changed from case to case. Even the most inconsequential mistakes carried corporal punishment of a truly barbaric severity. And yet it is precisely in giving the reasons for these measures that Shang Yang's argument turns a surprising somersault, revealing one of the central ideas of Legalism. It is true that Legalism as such was soon to be condemned. Yet this idea continued to have its effect and can be shown to have been an important component among the principles of Chinese government through the centuries: "If the punishments are so strict," we read in the book *Shang-chün-shu*, "that they even extend to the entire family, people will not dare to try and see how far they can go, and if they do not try, the punishments will no longer be necessary . . . and no one will be punished anymore."[117]

This motif of the self-cancellation of a means driven to excess appears time and again in the book *Shang Yang*. Of course, the means itself does not wholly disappear, but merely passes into another kind of aggregate where it no longer actually changes the world but has a merely potential effect on it. This motif constitutes not only the basis of the merciless penal law but also inspired all other forms of violence which later were to distinguish the state of Ch'in: "If one wants to abolish war," Shang Yang says, "war may be used toward that end. If murder is to be abolished by murdering, murdering is a permissible means, and if one wishes to abolish punishment by punishment, the most severe punishments are permitted."[118]

According to tradition, an exemplary order came to prevail in Ch'in just a few years after the introduction of these laws. When, in view of this success, Shang

Yang's former opponents changed their mind and announced their agreement, Shang Yang had them exiled as "rebels," for even their agreement showed that degree of criticism which was tantamount to an infraction of the law in this legalistic paradise, which is described in this manner:

> The people were divided into groups of five and ten members which checked up on each other and were punished together. . . . Both the highly placed and the lowly shared basic tasks such as ploughing and weaving. Those who produced large amounts of grain or silk were dispensed from forced labor, while those who profited from the work of others or became impoverished because of laziness, were made slaves. . . . Only ten years later, the people of Ch'in were overjoyed. Things lost on the streets were no longer picked up and kept, and there were no robbers left in the mountains. Families could maintain themselves by their own effort, and the people lived in abundance. They were brave while fighting for the state, and timid in private quarrels. Thus the Great Order *(ta-chih)* prevailed both in the country and in the cities.[119]

In the calm of its merely potential effectiveness that prevailed once the "Great Order" had been fully implemented, a Taoist element unmistakably emerges. For the not-acting *(wu-wei)* the ruler is to learn from nature is one of the most essential conceptions of the Taoists concerning government in an ideal world. Although he was one of its most significant representatives and also gave it its name with his idolatry of the "law," the legalistic school did not derive its ideas entirely from Shang Yang but also from two philosophers, Shen Tao and Shen Pu-hai, who clearly inclined toward pure Taoism. Only a few meager fragments of their writings have been preserved, however. Not much more can be gathered from them than that Shen Pu-hai attributed to the methods of government *(shu),* and Shen Tao to the hierarchical "positions" *(shih)* in the state an autonomous, almost magical effect.[120] It is likely that the school of Kuan Chung (died in 645 B.C.) also exerted an influence. Its writings, ascribed to Kuan Chung himself (although it is demonstrable that they cannot have originated until centuries after his death), contain some chapters concerning government through "law."[121] But it is only with Han Fei-tzu (died in 233 B.C.), a philosopher with Confucian training and not by mere chance a direct disciple of Hsün-tzu, that these various components coalesced into a unified system. Han Fei-tzu was the theoretician of Legalism, as his fellow disciple under Hsün-tzu, the later all-powerful chancellor in Ch'in, Li Ssu (died in 208 B.C.)[122], was its practitioner. Han Fei-tzu's life ended tragically. He himself was caught in the wheels of the system he had so zealously helped create. For, acting from jealousy, Li Ssu had him thrown into prison and forced him to commit suicide when he appeared in Ch'in to proclaim his teaching which up to that time he had only disseminated in written form, having allegedly been a stutterer. A little more than a century earlier, Shang Yang had been overtaken by a similar fate. After the death of the prince of Ch'in to whom he had first proclaimed his teaching, he saw himself embroiled in a net of intrigues and tried to escape and go underground. Tradition reports that due to the increased authority of Ch'in in the entire empire and its systematic, perfectly functioning practice of spying and informing, he was unsuccessful in the attempt. He was finally caught and quartered.

In the writings of Han Fei-tzu, Hsün-tzu's influence is still clearly perceivable. With a certain doggedness, he develops the implications of his teacher's thesis concerning the evil of human nature. Like a distant echo, one still hears certain notes which remind one of Hsün-tzu's critique of the natural virtues Mencius had championed, and whose most important seedbed was to be the family. But for Han Fei-tzu, they were nothing more than "lice and parasites" on the body politic:

> Ha, in a strictly run household there are no recalcitrant servants, but a "tender mother" has spoiled children! That is enough for me to know that authority and "position" can curb violence but that rebellion is not prevented by "virtue" and magnanimity. Ha, when a sage governs the state, he does not count on the people to do what is beneficial to him. Instead, he sees to it that their utilization can do him no harm. If he only relied on those that are well intentioned toward him, he could not find one dozen. But if he uses them in such a way that they can do him no harm, he can employ all the people in the entire state in the same manner *(ch'i)*. . . . Therefore he works with the law, and not with "virtue." It is exactly as if one were to rely only on those arrows which had grown straight all by themselves—in a hundred generations, one still would not have a single arrow. Or as if one were to rely only on pieces of wood growing perfectly round [for making wheels]—in a thousand generations, one still would not have a single wheel! . . . Not to rely on tools for the straightening and bending of wood, but to rely on its growing straight or round by itself is hardly something a good carpenter would appreciate. Not to rely on rewarding and punishing the people, but on its being naturally good will be appreciated no more by an enlightened ruler. Why? Because the law must admit of no exception, and because there is more than just *one* [kind] of person to be governed. Therefore the prince who has "methods" will not adjust his actions to those who happen to be good, but will take the way that is determined by what is true in *every* case.[123]

For Han Fei-tzu, the naturally grown patriarchal order of the family was not to be replaced by the principle of order of the cultic and court ceremonial which Hsün-tzu had seen as the basis of society. Like Shang Yang, he is thinking of the order of the military. In an ideal way, this order combines equality and inequality: uniforms and officers' insignia. It was Han Fei-tzu's avowed purpose to organize the entire people according to an order wholly instituted by man, though certainly not humanitarian. Such a system would not permit the escape into a so-called higher order which would be subject neither to man nor the sanctions of the state. He consequently urged that the army be strengthened, but this was not the principal objective. The contrast becomes quite apparent in the following anecdote told by him:

A man from Lu [the home state of Confucius], went to war for his ruler. He fought in three battles and fled in all three. When Confucius asked him about the reason for his cowardice, the man answered: "I have an old father. If I die, no one will be left to take care of him." Because of this answer, Confucius considered him a son full of piety, praised him and presented him as an example . . . and since that time, the people of Lu have never failed to surrender or run away the moment they engaged in battle.[124]

The emphasis on the military goes hand in hand with a pronounced anti-intellectualism which does not wholly derive from such an attitude, to be sure, but results equally from a deep-seated mistrust of all pure theory. This mistrust also has an age-old, occasionally vigorously erupting tradition in China, and forms a kind of contrast to the empty moralizing of the innumerable literati concerned with the care of their long fingernails. "Nowadays, all the people in the empire talk about political order," Han Fei-tzu writes.

But although every family owns copies of the writings of Shang Yang and Kuan Chung about the "law," the states become poorer and poorer. The reason is simply that too many talk a lot about tilling the soil, but only a few actually take plow in hand. Everyone within the state also thinks he knows something about strategy. But although every family owns copies of the writings of Sun Wu and Wu Ch'i, the armies keep getting weaker, simply because too many prattle about the art of war, and too few put on their armor. Therefore the enlightened ruler uses the physical strength of men, but does not listen to what they say. . . . That is also the reason literature does not exist in the state of an enlightened ruler. Only the law is taught. Nor do we find the traditional sayings of the sage kings. The functionaries of the state are the only teachers. Nor is anyone esteemed because he uses his sword to act in his own interest. Only the execution [of rebels] is considered bravery. Thus it happens that the people inside the borders of the state always follow the law when they talk, always have worthy objectives when they act, and excel nowhere but in the army when they seek recognition. Because of all this, the state is rich in times of peace, and the army is strong in times of war.[125]

MIXED FORMS OF LEGALISM

With these maxims, traceable to a radicalized Confucianism bearing the stamp of Hsün-tzu, Han Fei-tzu also moves very close to the Taoists. It may be mentioned in passing that this shows once again that the walls which a later period erected between the two world views are quite artificial. This may perhaps be due in part to a desire to make people forget that Legalism had for a time been the connecting link between the two. In the *Tao-te-ching*, for example, there is a section alongside of which Han Fei-tzu's thought almost looks like the practical application of an idea which already existed in principle:

When one stops looking for "sages," there will no longer be jealousy among people, and when one stops hoarding goods that are hard to come by, robbers will disappear.

> When people no longer see things that arouse their desires, their hearts will remain peaceful and discerning. Therefore the sage rules by emptying their hearts and filling their bellies, by weakening their mind and strengthening their muscles, and always takes care that the people remain ignorant and without desire. He also brings it about that those who do have knowledge do not dare interfere. Through this quiescent activity, all things are accomplished.[126]

The "non-action" of the ruler is also praised by Han Fei-tzu as one of the most important characteristics of the genuine, successful king. Just as in Shang Yang the law disappears from the sphere of its actualization by virtue of its excessive severity, the ruler disappears in Han Fei because of his inordinate control achieved through this very same law: once the law has been established, it works by itself. The ruler can, indeed he must, renounce all "his knowledge and skill so as not to lose the eternal principle of his rule." "Looking as if he were drunk," he listens to the report of his minister. He frees himself from all inclinations or aversions and "makes his empty heart the abode of the 'Way' *(tao).*" "He bolts the doors of the palace" and finally becomes something "divine *(shen)* . . . like Heaven and earth."[127] The phase described here represents a kind of statecraft that is almost completely Taoist. A reflection of it also falls on the ideal state of Han Fei-tzu as defined in a chapter of his work. Although the authenticity of this section is occasionally questioned, the words used here have a much less realistic tone than those of the more sober Shang Yang:

> In the age of the highest peace *(chih-an)*[128], the law lies on the land like morning dew. Simplicity and plainness have not disappeared. Men feel no hatred in their hearts, and words of dispute are not heard. Chariots and horses are not ruined on roads leading into the distance, flags and banners remain orderly [even] in large marshes, the ten thousand fold people do not lose their lives fighting robbers, brave warriors do not acquire immortality [by giving orders] with flags and pennants, eminent men are not mentioned by name in writings and books. No inscriptions are found on bowls and vessels [of bronze], the annals remain empty. Therefore the saying: "No benefit is more constant than simplicity; no happiness more constant than peace."[129]

In spite of the amazing similarity between this "simple life" of the Taoists and that of the Legalists, there is all the difference in the world in the methods used to attain this condition. Because their views concerning the direction of human civilization conflicted, this divergence was only natural. For the Taoists, paradise was situated in the precultural phase of a period preceding all historicity, and which merged with eternity. While the Legalists also believed in the existence of ideal conditions in antiquity, there was in principle no ideal age as such. Rather, the breakthrough to the ideal could be achieved at any moment. But this was precisely the reason why the manner of its realization was not tied to the demands of yesterday but to those of tomorrow. It is true that they saw the condition of nonaction as a distant ideal, but they certainly did not believe that it could be assured by nonaction, as the Taoists did. Taoist passivity meant waiting until things straightened themselves of their own accord, until the wounds inflicted on mankind by civilization would heal of themselves. This tendency toward passivity is something the Taoists shared with the Confucianism of Mencius, perhaps, but certainly not with Hsün-tzu and Han Fei-tzu.

In this connection, a matter previously touched upon is instructive.[130] What was the role "waiting" played in the various systems of thought, the waiting for the realization of paradise? As we have seen, the prince of Ch'in fell asleep when Shang Yang first told him of the principles of the old kings, and remarked that "he could not wait." And the book *Han Fei-tzu* is in fact full of anecdotes which pillory the passive hope for a happiness that is supposed to fall from heaven. The best known among them is the following: "A man from Sung was once ploughing a field which had a tree trunk in the middle. He saw a rabbit crashing against this trunk at full speed. It broke its neck and fell down dead. The man threw down his plough and from then on did nothing more than observe this trunk, hoping that a second rabbit would appear. He did not catch another one, however, but was only laughed at by all the people in the land."[131]

In Mencius, whose thought is quite similar to that of the Taoists in this respect, waiting has a completely different, clearly positive meaning. He also tells a story about a man from Sung—the state in the South which represents a kind of Chinese Schilda.* His stupidity, however, was not that he expected too much, but too little: "A man from Sung was sad because his rice was not growing rapidly enough. So he pulled it up, shoot by shoot. He came home utterly exhausted, and said: 'I am really tired today. I helped the rice grow.' His son ran out into the field and saw that all the shoots were lying on the ground, withered."[132]

These two stories are also almost symbolic of the divergent courses taken by Legalism on the one hand, and Confucianism and Taoism on the other. With an energy previously unknown in China, the state of Ch'in swept away the musty old feudal states a few years after Han Fei-tzu's death (between 230 and 221 B.C.), and created a polity which hardly contained a single institution that was not fundamentally new. Many legends exist about a book burning which, if it did not actually occur as some modern scholars believe, is certainly an invention of genius. It was an effort to extinguish the past which was now considered a great hindrance. Allegedly, the only classic to escape proscription was the *Book of Changes* because it was oriented toward the future. The powerful ruler of Ch'in who accomplished all this—a man of uncertain origin, the son of a concubine and of a man of possibly non-Chinese origin, perhaps a wholesale merchant admitted at court—boldly called himself the "First Divine" *(shih huang-ti)*.[133] He thus usurped a title which heretofore had been bestowed exclusively on "deified," i.e.

*In German folklore, the people of Schilda habitually engage in obviously foolish undertakings. (Translator's note.)

deceased rulers of antiquity. It was also an attempt to signal the advent of an entirely new dynasty whose measure was to be eternity. One must admire the energy of this man who could deal with an alleged daily workload of one hundred twenty pounds of records written on bamboo slips. And during the mere twelve years he ruled the entire empire, he brought about a breathtaking transformation of China. By setting up provinces, standardizing the system of writing, of weights and measures, by building roads and issuing a thousand other orders, he created the first unified empire which, though severely criticized, remained an unavowed model. But he did not bring an "age of the greatest peace" which, in the opinion of the Legalists, should really have followed this hectic process of transformation. He did not wait, he lost no time. Yet finally he had to recognize that while he might begin a great undertaking, he would not also be able to complete it. His death was kept secret for weeks. Yet only a year passed before a rebellion erupted in which his son, the "Second Divine," perished together with the dynasty. Neither Confucians nor Taoists had ever had anything to offer that could have compared with the vigor displayed by the Legalists. But it was they who survived, and thus found in themselves the proof of a common conviction which had a tautological quality: nothing has a longer life than the old, and nothing is more shortlived than the new.

Throughout the course of his life, Shih Huang-ti suffered from an almost morbid fear of death. Perhaps he sensed to what extent this enormous, incomplete achievement depended on his own person. He therefore saw himself surrounded by swarms of magicians who promised that their art would assure him eternal life. When he heard rumors that far out at sea off China's east coast there were three islands—P'eng-lai, Fang-chang and Ying-chou[134]—where immortals led a happy, never-ending life, he sent the magician Hsü Fu with a group of boys and girls intended as a present to explore these islands and to bring back from them the elixir of immortality: "When he returned without anything," the historian reports,

> Hsü Fu invented an excuse and said: "I saw a great god in the sea who said to me: 'Are you the envoy of the western emperor?' When I affirmed this and he asked me what I wanted, I said: 'I wish to ask you for the medicine that prolongs life.' 'But the gifts the king of Ch'in gave you to take along,' the god answered, 'are scanty. In exchange, you may look at the medicine, but you cannot take it with you!' Thereupon he dismissed us and bade us go southeast, and we reached [the island of] P'eng-lai. I saw the gate of the Chih-ch'eng palace. A messenger [of the ruler of the island] was standing there. He was of the color of bronze, with the body of a dragon. The light sent forth by it illumined the entire sky. I greeted him twice, and asked what gifts I would have to bring [to obtain the medicine]. 'If you bring us the sons and daughters of the best families, and craftsmen of every description, you will be given the medicine.' Ch'in Shih Huang-ti was overjoyed at this report, had three thousand boys and girls collected, and turned them over to Hsü Fu along

> with seeds of the five kinds of grain, and craftsmen with a wide variety of skills. Hsü Fu set sail and finally found a calm, fertile land. There he settled, made himself king, and never returned."[135]

Only a few days before his death, while on a tour of inspection in the east of the empire, Shih Huang-ti is said to have scanned the horizon along the sea coast, looking for Hsü Fu. One night he dreamt of the sea god and shot with his cross bow at a large fish which had interfered with Hsü Fu's undertaking, as he explained to the magicians accompanying him.[136] These escapades did nothing to delay his death; if anything, they hastened its arrival. But in the poetic heightening given them by the historian, they take on a tone of tragic, almost Shakespearean grandeur. They portray the all-powerful ruler as a fool, absurdly chasing a paltry happiness, waging a ludicrous struggle for mere survival.

The short rule of Shih Huang-ti, the first self-appointed and, in some respects, the most magnificent emperor in Chinese history, had a decisive but double-edged influence on the reality and the ideals of that country. On the one hand, almost all the important institutions which were after all the results of a definite attitude, were taken over in their entirety. But his legalistic ideals of statecraft were generally condemned. This probably unavoidable, yet lame compromise was subsequently especially harmful to Confucianism and deprived it of a good measure of the spiritual freedom it had had originally and which could only be based on integrity. What was particularly damaging was the stigma of Legalism which came to attach itself to everything new. On the other hand, innumerable legalistic elements began to permeate ideologies which had superficial connections with antiquity. Not until this century, when European influence had made the 'new' an all-too-uncritically accepted mark of quality, were there intellectuals daring enough to call attention to the positive aspects of Legalism. That they did not do so without a shudder is both clearly noticeable and readily comprehensible. One of them was Lin Yü-t'ang (born in 1895). Still burning with revolutionary ardor at the time, he wrote the following sentences in the article "Han Fei as a Cure for Modern China," published in 1931:

> Briefly, we may say, therefore, there were two opposing conceptions of government in Han Fei's times as well as in our own times, the Confucian conception of government by gentlemen, and the legalist conception of government by law rather than by persons. . . . I need hardly say that the first is the traditional view and the second the western view. . . . As Han Fei says, we should not expect people to be good, but should make it impossible for them to be bad . . . If Han Fei were living today, he would have said: "What we should do today is to hasten to assume [officials] to be crooks and say to them, 'We will not exhort you to the path of righteousness, and we will not erect *pailou* in your honor in case you turn out to be gentlemen, but in case you turn out to be crooks, we will send you to prison.' " . . . He hated the Confucianists of his day and called them a pack of gabbling fools, which might fittingly be applied to so many of our "long-gowned patriots" today.

> . . . Han Fei believed that the law should be supreme, that all people should be equal before the law and that this law should be applied in place of personal preferences and connections. . . . Han Fei's idea was to have a system so rigidly applied that it would not require any "talented persons" but could be run by any average individual. . . . The king [also] should do nothing, because he saw the kings couldn't do anything in any case, as the average run of kings goes. . . . The system should run of itself. That in essence is the theory of the do-nothingism concerning the king.[137]

Behind all the praise, however, one clearly notices that here also Legalism is understood merely as a "cure" for China. What was being admired was a devil. Legalism never really lost the mark of Cain.

II

ON THE BOUNDARIES OF THIS WORLD

(ca. 200 B.C.–A.D. 300)

1 / THE PAST AS FUTURE

RENEWED FUSION OF CULTURE AND NATURE, PAST AND PRESENT

After the experiment with the new had ended in chaos, exhaustion and disgrace, a sober and sobered China once again took its destiny in hand. The Han dynasty (206 B.C.–220 A.D.) found itself in a spiritual climate wholly different from what had prevailed prior to the Ch'in, although this was not recognized at first or, perhaps more accurately, it was deliberately ignored. No longer was a decision awaited with burning longing as had once been the case. A decision had been made. What counted now was to work it out, to answer for it to a sort of national consciousness. In a curious, though psychologically understandable form, action was taken in the political sphere to combine the unified state and its provinces with the concept of the feudal empire of the Chou period. This was done by introducing fiefs which lay like islands in the empire and were never very long-lived. Similarly, an effort was made to provide a Confucian basis for legalistic concepts. It seemed most plausible to have recourse to Hsün-tzu's teachings for this purpose. (In many respects, the latter had in fact furnished the basis for Legalism.) In this way, at least the terrain of Confucianism did not have to be abandoned. On the other hand, Hsün-tzu was too closely tied to Legalism through his disciple Han Fei-tzu for people not to hesitate to openly represent his views as the new ideals. The compromise eventually settled on consisted in stressing and further developing the ritual books. Very heterogeneous material was incorporated in them. But due to the simple fact that, purely thematically, it seemed to constitute a surface unity, it could also be given internal coherence. In addition to many texts which clearly derived from the school of Hsün-tzu, although his name was not mentioned, other texts were introduced which were intended to demonstrate that the Confucian attitude had grown like a thing in nature, as had been maintained by the school of Mencius. As mentioned previously, the bridge here was the notion of family love as rooted in nature. By an almost unnoticeable shift in the argument, the presumably much less "natural" love of children for their parents, "piety" *(hsiao),* was given priority over the (most nearly "natural") love of parents for their offspring (for which a special term was not even created). This shows the extent to which these ideas were influenced by Hsün-tzu. In any event, the impression could thus be conveyed that the largely legalistic ideal of a perfect political order where all of life took its precisely regulated course derived not solely from the severe injunctions of the law or cold ritual but from human nature as well.

The best example of this mode of thought is a paragraph in the most important compendium of rituals, the *Li-chi (Book of Rites).* Under the title "Great Learning" *(Ta-hsüeh),* this work was raised to the level of a classic in its own right in the twelfth century, and many commentaries were written on it, its shortness notwithstanding.[1] In a chain of arguments, the peace of the state was based here on order in the family which was based in turn on the order of the individual self, the individual "heart," and individual thought. State and family thus come to form a totality, but this structure was bipolar. Precisely because the state was based on the family, it could exercise a certain influence on the form taken by the latter. The ideal order into which such a state passes as the result of such governmental measures based on morality and ritual hardly differs from that of the Legalists. In the biography of Confucius found in the historical work *Shih-chi (Historical Records),* the success of his brief (and probably legendary) activity as minister in his home state of Lu is described in words almost identical with those we could read in the same historical work concerning the result of Shang Yang's activity in Ch'in[2]: "Three months after Confucius had assumed the government of the state [Lu], even cattle dealers no longer cheated others by demanding excessive prices; men and women walked along different sides of the road, and objects lost on the streets were no longer picked up. Strangers came from the four directions of heaven, but when they arrived in the towns, they never found it necessary to turn to the police, for they were treated as if they were in their own country."[3]

But a considerably more detailed and more crucial description of the ideal Confucian model of the state saw the light of day at about the same time in a voluminous work. Characteristically, it was again closely connected with ritual, and indeed even constituted one of the traditional compendia of rites, the *Chou-li (The Rites of the Chou Dynasty).*[4] Not only the ritual but the entire governmental apparatus of the Chou dynasty, from the king on down to the state employees working in the orchards, and the duties of all of these individuals, are described in the most minute detail in this book. There can thus be no doubt that these accounts are not inventions but are based on oral, and perhaps partly also on written tradition, for the names of many offices can not only be found in bronze inscriptions from the Chou dynasty, but even in bone inscriptions. Yet it is equally certain that this exemplary order, which here characterizes the entire governmental apparatus, the care taken to harmonize the various functions and their rigorously integrated structure could neither have developed by themselves, nor functioned properly with such perfection and almost confusing differentiation. Rather, what is described here is a state as it *ought to* look in the opinion of the Confucians. Especially in this book, the Confucian idea of the coincidence of past and future, of the identity of the past and future ideals, where change but not genuine development are recognized, becomes particularly striking. Already during the Han period, the *Chou-li* may well have seemed anachronistic. Yet it was and remained an undisputed theoretical model, perhaps precisely because it seemed so unreal. That merely served to increase its appeal as a utopian ideal. That its commands were not merely taken as remote fantasies, but that an occasional attempt was made to realize them, is proven quite convincingly by the Han dynasty.

The Confucians changed the spiritual rule of the "law" of the Legalists back to a rule of "ritual"; psychologically, this shift already contained the idea of a return, of the renewal of immortal principles as it had emerged previously at the beginning of the Chou in the ideology which proclaimed that the "heavenly mandate" was passed on from one ruling family to the next. But precisely as a result of the bold attempt of the Ch'in to create something truly new, this thought was decisively extended. For this attempt could no longer be represented as a gradual "decline" because, in contradistinction to the earlier "precedents" of the Hsia and the Shang dynasties, it had been the *very first* ruler that had been the worst monster. Nonetheless, great efforts were made to endow his weakly son, the "Second Divine," *(Erh-shih Huang-ti),* who was already losing his grip on the empire, with all the epithets of the cruel, "last ruler." The old concept of a mere alternation of decline and reform was therefore suddenly replaced by the concept of a sequence of old-new-old. But because the new could not be accorded its proper place without making the return of the old appear absurd, it became necessary to pretend that this sequence was one of morally neutral states of equal value. It is only logical that the "Earlier Han dynasty" (206 B.C.–A.D. 6) thus became the time of the invention of cycles in the Chinese philosophy of history. This was the only possible answer to the disquieting challenge posed by the emergence of the new to all nonlegalistic world views, and especially to Confucianism. By accommodating the new within a cyclical sequence, it was domesticated in a sense, and deprived of its dangerous explosive force. Admittedly, this meant that the existence of qualitatively different historical periods had to be acknowledged (which certainly had not been true of the concept of a mandate passed on from one dynasty to the next). It did not mean, however, that the new was accorded a priority of whatever sort over the old. The new in the cycle was newer than the old immediately preceding it, but was also older. And precisely because it was still older, its claim to a return to power could be justified. The new thus became renewal, revolution restoration.

Cycles have always been used in the recording of time. It is something that is suggested by the recurrence of the seasons; all calendars are based on them. Specifically Chinese was the sexagenary cycle which developed from the combination of a decimal and a duodenary cycle where the former was in a manner of speaking based on a human (fingers of the hand), the latter on a cosmic (months) elementary number. Its constant use for the designation of days is already found on the oracle bones. Similarly, the isolation of five elements (earth, wood, metal, fire, water) and their differentiated ring-shaped arrangement (enumerated here in the "order of victory" following their mutual conquest) can be found long before the beginning of the Han period. It is alleged that their inventor was the philosopher Tsou Yen (third century B. C.).[5] This is naturally even more true of other cycles one was always aware of, such as day and night, the course of the year with its four seasons and, in a way, the alternation of life and death as well. While it was only during the Han period that a connection was established between these cycles and historical periods, that event was so decisive that the experience of time, and particularly the attitude toward the future, were fundamentally changed. This idea that history not only could but necessarily had to repeat itself according to a pattern laid down from the very beginning had barely been accepted when historiography became in a sense a branch of the investigation of the future (as had happened once before, if in a different fashion, during the Shang dynasty). For an attempt was made to find a historical period to match every example provided by the theory and to document this correlation by the enumeration of certain phenomena. At the same time, such phenomena were sought out in the present in order to assign it its proper place and to be thus in a position to predict events.[6]

In the doctrine of the transmission of the heavenly mandate, there had already existed certain phenomena which were interpreted as the signs of a beginning, a flourishing or a declining dynasty. But they had been confined to certain good or evil acts of the ruler. People believed that they knew that such acts would either result in the approval of heaven and thus the transfer or the retention of the mandate, or provoke its displeasure and therefore its withdrawal. But during the Han period, a special "language" of the silent heaven was beginning to be discovered. It no longer tended to express itself in the language of the people and its right to revolution, as had been the case in Mencius, but in the language of nature. History books were suddenly filled with reports about miraculous celestial or terrestrial phenomena which were assigned a particular significance and usually meant that the ruler was being either encouraged or admonished. Of course, reports of this sort concerning comets, earthquakes, mountain slides, hail storms and similar events had been provided in earlier chronicles. Similarly, the vague feeling that some of them at least had a more profound significance can be shown to have existed at an early time. What was new was their systematization, and especially the opinion that they were not mere reactions of heaven to the way the ruler governed, but were frequently devoid of moral overtones. This was the case when they announced by certain signs the dawn of a new dynasty destined to rule under a different element. The ruler (and therefore mankind as a whole) was no longer wholly the master of his own fate. Even when his conduct was exemplary, his time could have run out and an era might end. Historical development no longer followed the laws of men as much as it did those of nature.

It is true that this reorientation did not come about by itself but was manipulated, at least in its application to individual cases. For just as, during the Shang period, the oracle priests had engaged in politics on their own while interpreting the oracles, this same possibility offered itself to that stratum of court officials that was charged with recording these omens. Among them were the astrologers and makers of calendars called *Shih,* who had gradually pushed themselves into the foreground during the Chou period and, exercising a kind of double function, were active as historians as well. Today, the word *shih* means primarily "history" or "historian." That they were careless with the truth not only in their interpretation of omens but also in the recording of them can be proven, for reports about ominous celestial phenomena exist and can be checked. They are recorded in historical works, but many of the comets, for example, that are mentioned there, cannot have existed.[7]

How much this doctrine changed the historical sense, how profoundly the balance shifted from the decisions of the rulers to the workings of supra-human natural forces in the shaping of history, can be inferred from the introduction of the "reign titles" used in chronology, for there is a close connection between it and this anxious search for a confirmation of one's own actions by natural phenomena. Up to the third Han emperor Wen-ti (governed 179–156 B.C.), the year of accession of each ruler coincided with the beginning of a new period, and the years were counted from that point forward (". . . in the nth year of prince X"). But in 163 B.C., a "reign title" (*Hou-yüan* "later primordial beginning") was announced for the first time. It replaced accession as the basis for chronology (". . . in the nth year of the year title X"). In A.D. 1368, the founding year of the Ming dynasty, (1368–1644), a change in climate became apparent. Internally, it had been prepared for during the Sung (960–1280), while the external impetus had been provided by the Mongol dynasty (1280–1368). Prior to 1368, the reign titles had varied and been chosen according to a number of criteria (yet the omens continued to be among the most important). Sometimes they changed repeatedly (up to fourteen times) during the rule of one and the same emperor. This meant that a change of emperor certainly represented a significant, but not the only significant historical break (no reign title was ever retained after the death of an emperor). After 1368, however, the reign titles were changed only with the accession of a new emperor. Practically, this was tantamount to a return to the old chronological method. This system remained in force until the empire collapsed in 1911. The republic, in any event, gave itself a title which could not be changed without a change in system (*Min-kuo,* "People's State," "Republic"). It remained in force after 1949. Surprisingly enough, the mainland did not replace it by a new one but by the introduction of western chronology.

The interest in the future, dressed in scientific garb, put its stamp not only on the entire Han period, but also on the subsequent three or four centuries. Nor was the observation, description and interpretation of omens the only form it took. In the course of time, a gigantic literature came into being. Its exclusive purpose was the exploration of future ages. The *ch'an-shu (Books of Prognostication)* formed one branch of it. Allegedly, they originated when holy creatures revealed two mystical diagrams, the *Ho-t'u* (Yellow River Map) and the *Lo-shu* ("Writings from the Lo River"). In the course of time, a whole stream of documents resulted, many of which contained the word "map" *(t'u)* in the title and therefore were probably also based on diagrams. It was natural that a connection should be established between them and the old, traditional text of divination, the *Book of Changes.* But this latter document also constituted the point of departure for another group of texts which were brought together under the name of *wei* ("woof," in contrast to *ching* "warp," the metaphoric expression for "[Confucian] classics").[8] These supplements to the *Book of Changes,* but also to all other classics, were claimed to be not just commentaries but descriptions of truth from another perspective. For this reason, they were not, in principle, oriented exclusively toward the future but interpreted the more sober documents to which they referred in a more colorful, frequently more fantastic manner which included the unreal, as yet unrealized future as an element. In any event, both kinds of texts soon merged in a single type and appeared as *ch'an-wei* books in old catalogues under a single heading. For centuries, and not unlike the bone oracles, they not merely predicted events but probably helped shape them. For, whether consciously or not, their every word also attempted to influence the decisions of the ruler. It was only at a relatively late date that the emperors apparently began to feel the chains placed on them in this subtle fashion, and to defend themselves against them. These books were first proscribed in A.D. 460, and again in 510. In a large-scale and seemingly successful action, they were collected for a third time in 605, and apparently destroyed. For after that date, the tradition dwindled more and more. Fragments of it were rediscovered only in the most recent past when interest in the apparently so meager testimonials of a form of Chinese thought directed toward the future began to intensify.[9]

TUNG CHUNG-SHU AND HISTORICAL CYCLES

Other products of prognostication could be mentioned. There are the "prophetic" childrens' rhymes babbled in the streets, mostly carefully launched among the people by political groups and which from the Han period onward repeatedly played a role in political disputes.[10] But it is the writings of a scholar, Tung Chung-shu (about 179–104 B.C.), whose dominant concern was not really prediction, that had the most profound effect. In his principal work, the *Ch'un-ch'iu fan-lu* ("Luxuriant Dew of the Spring and Autumn Annals")[11], he attempts a justification of the Han dynasty by a curious interpretation of the *Spring and Autumn Annals (Ch'un-ch'iu)* ascribed to Confucius. Actually, this work is an extremely dry and insignificant chronicle about Confucius's home state of Lu.

But at a later time, other Confucians believed they could discern in it profound secrets in coded form. Tung Chung-shu was the first to systematize the close connection between the world of nature and that of man, between events in heaven and on earth. The very complex way in which the various ontologies of the end of the Chou period, especially the theories of the Yin-Yang and the five elements, but also older numerological speculations are woven together, filled out and integrated in an organic unity, is a work of genius. With it, he laid the foundations for all later pseudo-scientific explanations of the world, indeed for all scientific efforts of traditional China generally. Precisely because it was assumed that heaven, man and earth were linked, "scientific" thought also had a profound effect on the philosophy of history. Thus Tung Chung-shu invented a whole system of interlocking cycles in order to explain the succession of dynasties. In fact, he succeeded in squaring the circle, i.e. through the argument on different levels he himself had been the first to introduce, he managed to make understandable why the Han dynasty, although different from all those that had preceded it, could yet consider itself their legitimate successor. Toward the end of the first chapter of his work, he explains his conception of the nature of dynastic change and thus of the nature of historical change in general, in the following words: "[The founder of a new dynasty] must move his residence to a new place, find a new name for his rule, change the beginning of the calendar and the color of the garments in order to do justice to the will of heaven and to clearly express his own election. As regards the great bonds such as human relations, morality, government, education, customs and language, everything remains what it was. Why should it be changed? A [true] king therefore changes the names of institutions, but actually leaves the principles *(tao)* intact."[12]

All the various cycles which enter into play when dynastic change occurs and which must be observed by the new ruler function in a way which excludes genuine development: "There are things the king [of a new dynasty] may not change at all. There are some which he must reintroduce after a two-phase [cycle], others after a three-phase [cycle], some after a four phase [cycle], others after a five-phase [cycle], and finally, some after a nine-phase [cycle]."[13]

Yin and Yang, of course, furnish the model for the two-phase cycle, the trinity of heaven-man-earth the model for the three-phase cycle, the four seasons that for the four-phase cycle, the five elements for the five-phase cycle, and the nine sage kings of antiquity for the nine-phase cycle. The latter are mentioned directly following the passage quoted. Assigning a place to the dynasty according to the five elements became the method most commonly used. Not having been invented by Tung Chung-shu alone, it existed in a great number of variations with each party citing natural phenomena from history to support its view.[14] Whether the Han governed under the element "earth," as Tung Shung-shu believed, or the element "fire," as others held, was a question arousing particularly keen disagreement. How certain dynasties were to be correlated with certain elements continued to be a topic of discussion even after the Han period, while the other cycles receded somewhat into the background although they continued to have a subliminal effect.

The two-phase cycle was based on the idea of an alternating emergence of "simplicity" *(chih)* and "refinement" *(wen),* the period preceding the Hsia dynasty being correlated with "simplicity," the Hsia dynasty with "refinement," the Shang dynasty with "simplicity" once again, the Chou dynasty with "refinement," etc. This two-phase cycle is most closely connected with the four-phase cycle, which is nothing more than the autonomy of the four phases just mentioned. For alongside the *chih-wen* cycle, Tung Chung-shu set up a concurrent Shang-Hsia-chih-wen cycle representing spring-summer-autumn-winter. Here, "Shang" and "Hsia" no longer referred to the corresponding dynasties, but only to certain conditions. According to this cycle, the pre-Hsia period corresponded to the *Shang* phase, the Hsia period to the *Hsia* phase, the Shang period to the *chih* phase, and the Chou period to the *wen* phase. The *Ch'un-ch'iu fan-lu* gives certain instructions concerning the customs to be observed in these various ages. While they tell us little about the intellectual climate to be expected during these periods, they do indicate that during the *Shang* and *chih* periods ("spring" and "autumn") which are related to each other, a greater measure of strictness prevails: when the son attains majority, it is his father who gives him his name; bride and groom must sit on separate mats; husband and wife are buried in separate graves. In contrast, a special mildness becomes noticeable during the *Hsia* and *wen* periods ("summer" and "winter"): it is the mother who names, bride and groom may sit together, couples are buried in the same grave.[15]

No details are given concerning the nine-phase cycle, probably for the simple reason that it had run its full course only once, in remote antiquity. For the three-phase cycle, however, Tung Chung-shu provided two different interpretations: the first assigns to the three alternating periods the qualities of "loyalty" *(chung),* "respect" *(ching)* and "refinement" *(wen),* and then integrates the three dynasties, Hsia, Shang and Chou, in this scheme. The quality of "refinement," which had also been represented in the two- and four-phase cycles, marks the Chou dynasty here also. It follows that this dynasty is characterized by "refinement" according to all three cycles mentioned so far. In the interpretation of this cycle, which Tung Chung-shu introduces by the name "Three Teachings" *(san-chiao),* he also quotes a saying of Confucius's contained in the *Lun-yü.* After considering the peculiarities of the three oldest dynasties, Confucius is supposed to have remarked: "Whatever dynasties may follow the Chou dynasty, the characteristics they will have during the next one hundred generations can already be recognized now."[16] More interesting still is the second three-phase cycle of the "Three Systems" *(san-t'ung)* or the "Three Beginnings" *(san-cheng).* Again, the first three dynasties are assigned their place in this system and examined with reference to their year of inception (*cheng*, actually "erect," has the meaning "beginning" in connection with expressions used in the calendar as, for example, in *cheng-yüeh* "first month"). Because all three dynasties began their rule at a different time during the year, this determined when the dynasty following the Chou dynasty, and all other subsequent dynasties, would begin theirs. At the same time, a connection was established between this cycle and the three basic colors, black, white and red. In addition to particular constellations of stars and growth characteristics in nature, certain ceremonies were to be in force during each of these ages which succeeded each other in a ring-shaped pattern. The ceremonies were to reveal their character most clearly in the choice of colors. In the "black" age, the robes, the tassels on the hats of officials, the emperor's carriages, the horses, the seal ribbons, the banners and sacrificial animals would be black. All this would be white in the white age, red in the red age.[17]

THE BEGINNINGS OF TELEOLOGICAL THOUGHT AND THE "GREAT EQUALITY"

It is a striking characteristic of the cycles introduced by Tung Chung-shu that all of them (with the exception of the irrelevant nine-phase cycle) begin a new revolution at the end of the Chou period. Theoretically, of course, none of them has a beginning properly so-called, although we find the following unmistakable comment regarding the last cycle: "The black system comes first."[18] Naturally, this is no accident but proves that the fundamental idea according to which everything new is somehow also something old could coexist with a feeling that some periods could be more intensive in their production of the new, than others. The jump from the end of a cycle back to its beginning was clearly considered a more profound change than a change within the period of a single cycle. As if by chance, the end of the Chou period coincided with the end of a number of cyclical periods, and this made it possible to advance a seemingly scientific explanation of the tremendous upheaval. But this mode of thought also contained the first seeds of a less cyclical sense of history. For if it is unconsciously conceded that individual cycles undergo certain "compressions," and that these can become more pronounced when cycles are combined, the move toward a conception of history working with such centers of compression has at least been prepared. For Tung Chung-shu, however, this center of compression was not so much the Han dynasty as the span of Confucius's life when the Chou dynasty was leading a merely shadowy existence and could therefore be considered to have reached the end of its time. This period was therefore restylized as a turning point of universal events, although this was not done by Tung himself but by various later philosophers belonging to his tradition. But the beginnings of this trend can be found in the *Ch'un-ch'iu fan-lu.* For Tung Chung-shu points out that the periods described by Confucius in the *Spring and Autumn Annals* could be divided into "Three Epochs" each of them consisting of three, four and five reigns of the rulers of Lu, and that he had consciously chosen different expressions for each of them:

> The period he experienced personally comprised 61 years (541–480 B.C.), the period he heard about through [oral] tradition comprised 85 years (626–542 B.C.), and the period about which he knew only through a [written] tradition comprised 96 years (722–627 B.C.). Concerning the events in which he participated, he used veiled language, concerning those of which he knew through oral tradition; he allowed compassion to prevail when bad things [were reported]; and, finally, concerning matters he knew about only through the written tradition, he did away with all compassion [and reported the entire truth]. Thus he acted wholly in accord with his feelings.[19]

According to this theory then, descriptions of the historical past by Confucius differed, and the difference was a function of its remoteness from him. This made it plausible to conclude that it was not merely *described* differently by him but that it was essentially different *in fact.* While this idea does not appear in Tung Chung-shu, there is a barely veiled reference that Confucius had been a "ruler without a throne." The world having rejected him, he ruled on the plane of the intellect by writing the *Spring and Autumn Annals* which, as Mencius reported, "frightened" all the princes of the realm.[20] The accession of prince Yin of Lu, with which the annals begin, happened to coincide with the time of year the Hsia dynasty had chosen as the beginning of its reign. According to the cyclical theory of the "Three Beginnings," this could only mean that with this year, 722 B.C., and after the completion of the Hsia-Shang-Chou (black-white-red) cycle, a new "black" dynasty had started in Lu which signaled its inception with the appearance of Confucius in the realm of the intellect. Tung Chung-shu probably conceived of the Han dynasty with its Confucian orientation as perfecting a "Confucian" era which had begun with the *Spring and Autumn Annals.* In its course, and after an extended period of spiritual preparation, Confucius's principles concerning a new epoch would finally also be realized on the political plane.

Because Tung Chung-shu's conception is cyclical in spite of certain modifications, there is no room for an assured paradise at the end of all development. In contradistinction to all the other ideal conceptions of man and society dealt with so far, the remorseless law of incessant transformation prevails also in this sphere, according to Tung. Yet a very lively description of an ideal world can be found in his writings as well. For though it is true that the qualities governing the alternating periods might constantly change as in a seasonal cycle, there was nonetheless, provided one adapted oneself just as constantly, something that survived all change. This was the possibility of an ever-vibrant ideal world that was internally stable in spite of all its transformations. Another new element in Tung Chung-shu's paradise is that nature becomes part of this state of happiness among men. We search in vain for such a notion in the Confucian-legalistic models. In the Taoist models, on the other hand, nature is so powerful that it makes man disappear. In Tung's paradise, events in nature and the world of men are interlocked in a complex mechanism, the investigation of which was his entire endeavor. A balance is created between these two spheres, and it is consistent that the concerted action of heaven, earth and man should bring forth a harmony which creates "supernatural" conditions. As in the ideal world of the Taoists, there is the intimate contact with wind and rain, with plants and animals. In contradistinction to them, however, this contact is infused with an elevated human morality. It resembles the ideal world of the Legalists in the strict mechanism of the laws, but these laws do not represent a value above man, as is the case with them. Instead, man occupies a mediating position between heaven and earth, between spirit and matter. Particularly as king or emperor, he thus holds in his hands the key to the happiness of the entire universe:

> If the king is of the right kind, the primordial forces (Yin and Yang) are in harmonious relation to each other. Wind and rain come at the right time, auspicious constellations appear, and the Yellow Dragon descends. . . . When the five sage emperors and the three sage kings governed, no one dared take the attitude of a "prince" or of a "people" [that was ruled]. . . . The tenth was raised for taxes, teaching was done with love, and orders were given with loyalty. The ancients were honored, relatives had feelings of kinship for each other, and showed respect to those worthy of it. The people were not robbed of their time and not used for compulsory labor for more than three days a year. Since families were given all they needed, the grief born of excessive hopes or furious disappointment did not exist, nor were there problems in the relations between the strong and the weak. People did not engage in libel or theft, and were not filled with jealousy and hatred. They cultivated virtue and praised kindness. They walked about, their hair hanging loose, and patting their bellies. The desire for riches and positions of honor was unknown, but men were ashamed of evil deeds and did not think of committing crimes. Fathers had no occasion to weep for their sons, nor older for younger brothers. Poisonous insects did not bite, wild animals did not attack other creatures, and evil beasts harmed no one. That was also why sweet nectar dripped from heaven; the red grass of happiness grew [which sprouts a leaf every day for the first fifteen days of every month and loses one during each of the fifteen last days, thus serving as a calendar]; crystal-clear springs gushed forth, wind and rain came at the proper time, the blessed corn [with several ears on a single stalk] thrived, and phoenix and unicorn were not afraid to approach the outlying districts of towns. The prisons were empty, and although the [only] punishment was the marking [of the delinquents'] garments, the people did not transgress. Even the barbarians from the [most distant] points of the compass, whose speech had to be translated by two interpreters, appeared at court. The sentiments of the people were plain and unaffected, sacrifices were offered to heaven and earth, and mountain and river [spirits] were remembered at the proper time. The sacrificial rite *Feng* was held on the T'ai-shan mountain, and the sacrificial rite *Shan* on the Liang-fu mountain. The "radiant hall" was built where sacrifices were offered to the preceding holy rulers to assure the ancestors' entry into heaven. The feudal lords of the entire realm came to participate as their office demanded. As tribute, they brought the fruits of the earth. They first went into the ancestral temple of the kings, straightened their hats and put on the most

splendid garments. Only then did they appear for an audience. Gratitude for the grace bestowed on them and requital for the gift of life were uppermost in their minds as they paid their respects.[21]

Described as situated in the past, yet always attainable with proper adaptation, this ideal world was placed into another temporal connection by a group of scholars who largely shared the textual tradition with Tung Chung-shu. Like Tung's, it was a school which followed a certain interpretation of the *Spring and Autumn Annals* contained in the *Kung-yang-chuan* commentary. This work allegedly goes back to a nephew and disciple of Confucius, Kung-yang-Kao, but actually was not written before the Han period.[22] On the very first pages, and along with comments on entries for the first year of prince Yin of Lu, we find the reference to the "Three epochs" into which Confucius's description of the past is divided, as mentioned above. Unlike Tung Chung-shu, however, a Confucian called Ho Hsiu (A.D. 129–182) took this remark as the basis for what was no longer a cyclical but rather a linear and teleological view of history. In a secondary commentary on the *Kung-yang-chuan* (since the Han period, intellectual disputes among both Confucians and Taoists were largely carried out in "commentaries"), he began by designating the first period as that of the great-great-grandfather and of the great-grandfather of Confucius, the second as that of his grandfather and the third as that of his father and of Confucius himself. But then he suddenly established a parallel between their succession and a continuing civilizing influence originating in Lu and spreading over the world:

> Concerning the epoch about which he knew through the written tradition, he showed how order began to arise in the midst of confusion and chaos, and thus he concentrated his mind on the most essential. That was the reason he considered his own state of Lu as the inside, and even the rest of China *(Chu-Hsia)* as the outside. He wanted first to establish the best [order] inside, and only subsequently went about extending this order to the outside. [Concerning the outside,] he wrote about important matters but omitted what was minor. . . . Thus he reported fruitless governmental conferences held inside [for example], but did not report such conferences when they occurred outside. Concerning the epoch about which he heard by oral tradition, he showed how this order gradually turned into peace. [Now] he viewed all of China as inside and only the states of the barbarians as something external. He also reported fruitless governmental conferences that took place outside of his own state. . . . Concerning the epoch of which he had personal experience, he revealed that the order had reached the "Highest Peace" *(tai-p'ing).* The barbarians themselves became members of the hierarchy of officials, the entire world, distant and nearby, great and small, had become one. Thus he concentrated still more and became concerned with the refinement of order everywhere. This was the reason why he thought highly of humanity and righteousness and found fault with [deceitful] personal names of two characters.[23]

In connection with a discussion of the tax system of the Chou period contained in the *Kung-yang-chuan,* Ho Hsiu expressed himself in considerable detail about the nature of this so mysteriously unfolding "order" which was to usher in the epoch of "Highest Peace." His thoughts are evidently influenced by Mencius's "well field system" and Hsün-tzu's ideal state. Yet they also reveal some other, rather interesting developments. The entire argument is based on what strikes the reader as a very modern idea, i.e. that the happiness of mankind is primarily determined by the economic order:

> Ha, when hunger and cold attack [a country], even [the sage kings] Yao and Shun and all their civilizing endeavors cannot prevent robbers from appearing on the open fields. And when the rich and the poor oppose each other, even [the lawgiver of the sage emperor Shun] Kao Yao, and all his laws, cannot prevent the strong from suppressing the weak. Therefore the sages created the well field and thus distributed [the land] according to the number of mouths. Together, a man and a woman are given 100 mou of arable land to feed father and mother, wife and children. Five mouths form one family. The public field [which they cultivate in addition], comprises 10 mou which is the reason we speak of a taxation of one in ten. There are 2½ mou to each "manor." Generally speaking, a field unit thus consists of 112½ mou, eight families together cultivate 900 mou and form a "well unit"; that is the reason one speaks of "well fields." The "manors" lie in the center; they belong to the nobility. The public fields adjoin them directly; they are respected as [the property] of the state. The private fields lie outside. They belong to the simple people as private property. The "well field system" is significant [in five ways]: 1. It prevents the loss of fertility of the land. 2. It prevents [unnecessary] expenditures for individual families. 3. It unifies *(t'ung)* customs and usages. 4. Technical achievements complement each other *(ho)*. 5. It offers the possibility for the reciprocal exchange *(t'ung)* of commercial goods. It follows that the "well fields" also become places of commerce. Therefore the colloquial language also calls them "market wells." The sowing of a single kind of crop is avoided to afford protection against natural catastrophes. The people also avoid letting trees grow on the fields to prevent damage to the grain. Mulberry trees [for the breeding of silk worms] are planted around the "manors," as are various kinds of trees for timber. Five kinds of fowl are kept, and two kinds of animals are raised for fattening. Pumpkins are grown along the edges of the fields. The women devote themselves to the breeding of silk worms, and to weaving. The old may dress in silk and eat meat. The dead are given a grave. The members of a family of more than five mouths are called supernumerary and receive 25 mou each. Ten well field units together equip a chariot. When they allocate land, the well field supervisors distinguish carefully whether fields lie on high or low ground, are good or bad. Three distinctions are made: a first-rate field, which can be cultivated every year; a second-rate field which can be cultivated only every other year; and a third-rate field which can be cultivated only once in three years. Not just a chosen few may enjoy the fertile, productive fields, nor are there just a few that suffer because their fields are meager and produce nothing. This is the reason all fields and dwellings are exchanged once every three years. Thus fortunes are equally distributed *(chün)*, equal amounts *(p'ing)* of physical strength [are called for], and the burdens of war are determined justly. This is called balancing *(chün)* the strength of the people and strengthening the families

in the state. Corresponding to the *"Lu"* (a group of ten well field units) [in the country], there is the "Li" [in the towns]. It consists of 80 households, and 8 households (corresponding to a well field unit) form one "block." In the center of the "block" is the school. Among the old, those of highest virtue are chosen; they are called "fathers." Those who have proven the winners in debates and the strongest in competitions are made Li leaders. They are all given twice as much land [as the ordinary population] and are allowed to ride a horse. The "fathers" have the rank of a *San-lao* or a *Hsiao-ti,* the *Li* leaders the rank of an unennobled lower court official. In spring and summer, the people move out to the fields, and return to the towns in fall and winter. In the spring, during the time the fields are prepared, the "fathers" and the *"Li* leaders" open the gates in the morning and then sit down on the flatroof. Those who have overslept or want to leave too late are not let out, and no one is let back in who comes without firewood. When the harvest is done, all remain at home. The *Li* leaders encourage people to weave and plait, and the men and the women of the same block work until late at night. That is why the men do one and one-half times the work of the women during the three winter months. When men or women are angry about something, they go [out into the street] together and present [their grievances] in the form of songs. When they are hungry, they sing before eating; when they are downcast, they sing of their distress. Men of sixty and women of fifty who do not have children are fed and clothed at government expense. It is their task to collect the songs [that are sung on the street]. From the country, these songs are then sent on to the district town, and from there to the capital where they are performed for the Son of Heaven. Thus the ruler need not even pass through the gates of his palace to hear of all the suffering in the empire, nor does he have to come down from his throne room to know what occurs in the four directions of heaven. In the tenth month, [at the start of winter,] the "fathers" start teaching in the schools. [Beginning at the] age of eight, [the children] are given "small lessons," [beginning at the] age of fifteen, [they receive] "great lessons." Those who excel are turned over to the community school; those who excel there pass on to the district school; and those who excel in the latter go on to the state school where they are given "small lessons" on a higher level. Every year, the princes report the names of those who do exceptionally well in this last school to the Son of Heaven so that they can receive the "great lessons." Those who take the lead once again are given the title "perfect scholars" *(tsao-shih),* and whose conduct and ability are of the same quality compete in archery. Only those who are successful here join the corps of court officials. Thus the scholar can advance through his talents and abilities, and the prince can choose his officials after their capacities have been tested. Of a three-year yield, one year's harvest is stored; of a nine-year yield, one-third is retained, and of a thirty-year yield, a ten-year yield is put into the granaries. Even when inundations occur as during the time of Yao, or droughts as during the time of Shun, the people do not even come close to misery, and there is no one within the Four Oceans who does not do his task joyfully. Therefore it is said [about such a period]: "Songs of praise resound [all over the empire]."[24]

A number of the characteristics of this marvelously ordered society, indeed precisely the most important ones, are not reminiscent of Confucian or Taoist teaching, of course, but of that of the "socialist" Mo Ti. Thrift and industriousness are part of it, as is the care of the aged and needy (also stressed by Hsün-tzu), and finally the possibility to inform the ruler through the well-organized help of his subjects. He hears about everything in the empire without having to leave his palace. This connection with Mohist ideas can be further documented by the fact that Ho Hsiu's previously mentioned conception of "Three epochs" already appears in the writings of the Mohist school, although in a somewhat shadowy form. Here also, these epochs follow an ascending line. According to this theory, conditions thus do not deteriorate in the course of history, but continue to improve gradually so that their perfection in the present, or at least the future, may be counted upon. It would therefore seem that the "left wing" of Confucianism, from which Mohism had once developed, was reintegrated in Confucianism during the Han period when the school of Mo Ti declined. But it made a somewhat strange appearance there, and in its terminology (but only there) it occasionally approached the egalitarian and individualistic Taoism which was also to the "left" of Confucianism. This is particularly true of an exceptionally influential chapter of the ritual classic *Li-chi,* which contains descriptions of an ideal state deriving in part from Hsün-tzu, in part from Mo Ti. Only because it is contrasted with the description of a much deteriorated stage situated in the present, and makes critical comments about the founders of the dynasties who were usually also attacked by the Taoists, is this document tinged by an alien Taoist nuance:

> At one time, Confucius participated in the sacrificial rites held [in Lu] toward the end of the year. Afterwards, he walked to a look-out tower [with his disciples] and sighed profoundly [as he surveyed the land]. He sighed about the state of Lu. Yen Yen, a disciple, was standing at his side, and asked him: "Why did you sigh?" Confucius answered: "I was thinking of the time when the Great Way *(ta-tao)* prevailed and the three [past] dynasties were flourishing, [a time] which I [will] not live to see again, but carry in my heart as a desire.[25] When the Great Way prevailed, the entire empire was 'public.' The most virtuous were chosen, the most competent were given offices, the truth was spoken and harmony cultivated. Therefore people did not only treat their own parents as parents, and not just their own children as children. They saw to it that the aged found a place where they could die [in peace], that adults found a place where they could work, and that the young could grow up [without interference]. Widowers and widows, orphans and the childless and also the sick were all fed [by the community]. All men had steady work, all women a stable home. They hated simply throwing away useful things, but this does not mean they hoarded. They hated being unable to make use of their special abilities, but this does not mean that they only looked to their own advantage. Therefore [selfish] plans could not be carried out. Robbery and upheaval did not occur, and consequently the outer gates did not have to be locked. This is called the 'Great Equality' *(ta-t'ung).* But today, where the 'Great Way' is already in decline, the entire empire has become a family affair. People treat only their own parents as parents and their own children as children, useful things and energies are commit-

ted only to further their own purposes. [The appointment] of 'important people' and hereditary succession are becoming a 'ritual,' walls are put up and ditches dug for 'security.' Ritual and righteousness become the guide for the sincerity between ruler and subject, the truthfulness between father and son, the harmony between the older and the younger brother, the concord between man and wife, the elaboration of laws, the distribution of land and the value placed on courage and knowledge: [every] achievement becomes something selfish. Therefore [selfish] plans develop, and the use of armed force increases. That is why [the old emperors] Yü and T'ang and the Chou rulers Wen, Wu Ch'eng-wang and Chou-kung were praised. . . . It is called the 'small peace' *(hsiao-k'ang).*"[26]

The reversal of the temporal sequence found in Ho Hsiu, who had placed Confucius in the time of the "Highest Peace," can be justified logically only by assigning two contradictory qualities to Confucius's life span: that of a complete decline which, while not set forth in the *Li-chi* passage quoted above, might be thought of as a situation necessarily following the dubious "small peace" of the beginnings of dynasties. The second is that of the "Highest Peace" or the "Great Equality" which becomes recognizable as a seed of new hope at the very moment the total collapse of all order occurs. Such a "great" cycle, describing the decline of external order and the simultaneous and parallel development of an *idea* of internal order on the one hand, and the reversal of this development during Confucius's life and the subsequent, gradual realization and spread of this idea of order in the real world on the other, has not been directly described in any old Chinese text. At most, one can discover a weak allusion in the words "not again" (*wei,* identical with "not yet")[27] which point toward the future and are put into Confucius's mouth in the sentence: ". . . a time I will not live to see again." Or, quite generally, such a reference can be found in the reflection that all of the ideal images derived from the past could have no other meaning except to serve the future as models for a new realization. Nonetheless, the fact remains that the many, infinitely turning cycles of Tung Chung-shu found no counterpart in an equally clearly developed unique cycle leading from an ideal, timeless eternity through a grievous temporality back to an equally ideal, atemporal eternity. What can be documented in Confucianism are merely partial aspects of such a cycle. But it would seem somewhat hazardous to infer from them that a whole exists.

One of the most important of these aspects is a phenomenon that can be observed as early as the end of the Chou period (fourth/third century B.C.): the piling up of the terms "great" *(ta),* "highest" *(t'ai, chih),* "real" *(chen),* "eternal" *(ch'ang),* when they precede certain basic philosophical concepts such as "way," *(tao),* "virtue" *(te),* "man" *(jen),* "order" *(chih),* "peace" *(p'ing),* and "equality" *(t'ung).* This practice is not confined to Confucianism and shows that these concepts had lost their force through overuse, and consequently required intensification. More important, there was an effort to penetrate the veil created by a variety of views that nearly canceled each other out, and to arrive at an absolute system of values which would have eternal validity, no longer subject to the relativity, the wear and tear of time. That the search for the "authentic," a term which can be used to translate all of these concepts of intensification, involved an unconscious yet frequently quite decisive revaluation; that consequently the "new" was not infrequently hidden behind the "eternal" is certain, particularly since the "new" as an idea had totally lost its persuasiveness after the disaster of the Ch'in dynasty. But if the "new" could only be imagined as the "eternal," the fatal consequence was that the idea of gradual progress (and also the idea of revolution) could never win out in the end. The notion of a "goal of history," as it had been intimated in Ho Hsiu's commentary and the *Li-yün* chapter of the *Li-chi,* took a distant second place as compared with the really old idea of what might be called a standing movement, which also constitutes the basis of Chung-shu's cyclical theory. It is true that Tung's ideal realm lacked the rigidity which ordinarily affects many paradises, since it required a constantly renewed, mutual adaptation of the three fundamental factors in the world: heaven, man and earth. But because salvation was to lie in this constant adaptation, because it was possible *at any time* and not merely at a specific moment, the temporal aspect again lost importance. And the mystical and religious expectation of a great redemption of society still hidden in the future, a hope which seems to have budded among some of Tung's disciples, soon began to fade again.

NEW TEXT SCHOOL AND OLD TEXT SCHOOL

The religious trend in the Confucianism of the earlier Han period, which also expressed itself in the spread of many legends that came to be woven about the life of Confucius as a half divine, uncrowned king, also quickly provoked a counter movement with distinctly political motifs. For after careful preparation Wang Mang, a member of the empress' clan, usurped the throne by a coup d'etat in 9 A.D., and founded a dynasty which was given the name of *Hsin* (and never recognized by official historiography).[28] With burning zeal, this man initiated a reform of China or, more precisely, a restoration of the Chou dynasty, which was interpreted by him in a very definite, quite willful and certainly not wholly unselfish manner. For in contradistinction to the religious Confucianism of the *Kung-yang-chuan* school, for which Confucius, and *only* Confucius, occupied the center of the world, he had recourse to a doctrine first documented in Mencius, and according to which a restoration of the empire would be brought about every five hundred years by a savior of the realm.[29] It was only natural that a man ordering a portrait showing him striking the pose of the prince of Chou should consider himself that savior. It is fairly certain that he forged Confucian writings for his purpose, relying on the help of the scholar Liu Hsin (ca.46 B.C.–A.D. 23), a man who was devoted to him. He presented a number of books which had supposedly been discovered toward the end of the second century B.C. when Confucius's house had been torn down, were written in the "old script" *(ku-wen),* and therefore alleged to have been composed prior to the ominous book-burning by Ch'in Shih Huang-ti.[30] In his political measures, he followed the half-utopian descriptions of the state apparatus found in the *Rites of Chou* (on the basis of which he also wanted to eliminate the private ownership of land, for example) down to their most minute detail and, quite consistently, placed an eminent value on the omina connected with Tung Chung-shu's cyclical theory. Even today, the place to be assigned to Wang Mang as a historical figure is a matter of dispute. Judgments range from Hu Shih's glorification of him as an idealistic social revolutionary whose downfall was wholly the result of intrigues, to the view of H. H. Dubbs, the American sinologist, that he was an unscrupulous adventurer who finally succumbed to megalomania, paranoia and blood thirstiness.[31] In any event, and official calumny notwithstanding, his influence on the further development of Confucian ideals must have been considerable. For when his regime was finally overthrown in 25 A.D. and the ("later") Han dynasty was restored, the "Old Text School" with its this-worldly and historical orientation continued to exist as such; indeed, in the course of time, it prevailed over the religiously-oriented "New Text School" (*chin-wen,* actually "present text school"). A further proof of the continuing efficacy of certain of Wang Mang's measures is the injunction forbidding personal names consisting of several components, which was obeyed down to the middle of the fourth century. Apparently, this order became so characteristic of a well-run state that we even encounter it outside of any relevant context in the description of the epoch of the "Highest Peace" given by Ho Hsiu.

The Confucians of the latter part of the nineteenth century felt that the victory of this sober version of a Confucianism without orientation toward an ultimate goal, manifesting itself in the success of the "Old Text School" as it would once again at a later date in the triumph of Sung Confucianism, was to be blamed not only for the stagnation of Confucianism but of that of all Chinese culture during the last eight hundred years. Confronted with western world views that were all teleological whatever differences might exist among them, they felt —perhaps not wholly without reason—that the absence of a religion hoping for a transformation of the world also implied the absence of any sort of belief in progress. The most important advocate of this view was the famous scholar and politician K'ang Yu-wei (1858–1927). During the "One hundred days reform," in 1898, he joined with the young and inexperienced emperor Kuang-hsü in the vain effort to make China into a modern state without wholly abandoning tradition. This was a last-minute attempt.[32] Working with a great number of students, he engaged in zealous, almost hectic research into classical Chinese literature during the eighties and nineties. He attempted to unearth an earlier version of Confucianism which he believed had been insidiously suppressed by Wang Mang and Liu Hsin, and which had been possessed of the same propulsive force as Christianity. In his book *Hsin-hsüeh wei-ching k'ao* (*A Study Concerning the Forgery of Classics by the Scholars of the Hsin Dynasty,* 1891), he declared almost all Confucian classics to be forgeries by Liu Hsin and his father Liu Hsiang, the only exceptions being the *Li-chi* passage previously quoted, the

Kung-yang-chuan commentary, and the books *Meng-tzu* and *Hsün-tzu*. In a later book, *K'ung-tzu kai-chih k'ao (A Study about Confucius as a Reformer),* he introduced Confucius in the garb of a religious and social revolutionary.[33] He felt absolutely certain that Confucian thought had originally presented Confucius as the center of history, thus dividing the span of human civilization into two halves, and assigning to Confucius a place analogous to that of Christ in the thought of the Christian West. There had been a period of gradual degeneration, a kind of protracted fall of man, and a period of gradual redemption through the teachings of Confucius. As described in Ho Hsiu's commentary, these teachings would spread over the entire world in the course of time. K'ang Yu-wei was also the first to introduce a chronology dating from Confucius's birth, a method that was adopted by many Chinese scholars of his generation. Ch'en Huan-chang (1881–1931), for example, who wrote in English, made this new interpretation of Confucius known in the West.[34] Yet K'ang's bold modifications of the text attempted almost the very thing for which he had previously blamed Liu Hsin: i.e. a reformulation of Confucianism by ideas extrinsic to it. As happens to many reformers, he only succeeded in the first part of his chosen task, the destruction of the traditional system, which was traditional Confucianism in his case, but he failed in erecting a new one. Because it had begun to doubt the validity of Confucian norms in view of their readily apparent failure in the modern world, the generation of young intellectuals following K'ang Yu-wei assumed that not only the Confucianism of the "Old Text School," but Confucianism as a whole, had become antiquated. However great the enthusiasm that greeted his books as testimonials against the ruling Confucianism may have been, they received scant attention as a possible foundation for a new Chinese religion that could accept the challenge of Christianity. Turning Confucianism into a "myth" while undertaking to unmask as "forgeries" the very texts that were both most popular and best known, and thus to rebuild Confucianism as a religion, was doomed from the very beginning. Hu Shih (who belonged to this younger generation although he also, if for entirely different reasons, tried to discover dynamic aspects in Confucianism), made the sarcastic comment that the effect was tantamount to staging *Hamlet* without the Prince of Denmark.[35] The intellectuals, most of whom had received their education in Japan or the West, had different ideas of the ideal age toward which the world was to move.

In their clearly Marxist reflections on the philosophy of history which originated in the twenties and follow what is at times an almost maniacal habit of dividing Chinese history into periods, we find echoes of the cyclical doctrines of Tung Chung-shu, although these did not envisage an end of history. The concept of the alternating rule of "simplicity" and "refinement" during certain periods, for example, seems to have provided the basis for a theory deriving from the observation that extended, calm epochs in Chinese history were always introduced by very vigorous, very imaginative times of short duration. Examples are the Han dynasty, preceded by the Ch'in, the T'ang dynasty (618–906) preceded by the Sui (589–618), the Sung dynasty (960–1280) preceded by the Later Chou (951–960), and the Ming dynasty (1386–1644) preceded by an earlier rule which, while overlapping with this dynasty, was nonetheless clearly distinct from the later, "real" phase. Time and again, periods of alien rule and disruption intervened between these double periods. They may be called times of "confusion," and it is consequently not difficult to rediscover the traditional circular pattern of the "Three Epochs" here.[36] No less a figure than the philosopher Feng Yu-lan also attempted to revive Tung Chung-shu's color sequence of black, white and red, by adducing modern examples. In his *A Short History of Chinese Philosophy* written in English in 1948, the remark quoted below escapes him. While he attempts to attenuate it by the sentence immediately following ("of course, this is only coincidence"), it is clear that he did not want this thought to go unexpressed: "It is interesting that in modern times, colors have also been used to denote varying systems of social organization, and that they are the same three as those of Tung Chung-shu. Thus, following his theory, we might say that Fascism represents the Black Reign, Capitalism the White Reign, and Communism the Red Reign."[37]

Shining distantly on the horizon, the great, ultimate goal of Republican China between 1912 and 1949 continued to be the concept of an age of "Great Equality," which had been rediscovered by K'ang Yu-wei. It is a tragic fact that this conception became outdated at the very moment it took hold as an ideal. Undoubtedly, it also had a decisive influence on the writings of Sun Yat-sen (1866–1925), the "Father of the Chinese Republic," and therefore also made its appearance in the national hymn of Republican China still sung on Formosa today. Even in the People's Republic it was recognized as the symbol of a hope for socialist redemption which is rooted in Chinese thought, and was never extinguished. This can be seen, for example, in the introduction to a collection of original "utopian" texts which appeared in 1959 under the title, *Texts on "Utopian" Ideas in China (Chung-kuo ta-t'ung ssu-hsiang tzu-liao).*[38] In this introduction, the editors give their reasons for the decision not to use the customary foreign word *Wu-t'o* to translate the term "utopian," although it is an excellent transliteration since it not only reproduces the sound but also the concept ("something without foundation") by its two characters. Instead, they chose *Ta-t'ung,* and point out that the *Ta-t'ung* idea serves best to group together all the precursors of the communist movement in China. To be sure, the men who undertook the attempt to once again connect the new with the old were later very much blamed for it.[39] Yet such an effort is all too understandable in a people which may not have believed in an "origin and goal of history," but was more firmly convinced than any other of a meaning inhering in history, and in the course of millennia never tired of trying to fathom it. It is consequently not surprising that connections were established between all the new, foreign philosophies of history and the old familiar ones, even when this was done unconsciously or secretly or, as in the case of Feng Yu-lan, with half a smile.

2 / *THE COUNTRIES AT THE END OF THE WORLD*

NORTH AND SOUTH AS SYMBOL AND MODEL

Fundamentally changed conceptions of both time and space resulted from two factors: the brutal onslaught of the Ch'in regime, and the classification mania of the Han dynasty which imitated its predecessor in so many respects. Because of the unification of the empire and its division into provinces, the sense of intimacy due to the smallness of a single state gave place overnight to the feeling that one was living in a gigantic dominion governed by a distant capital, and which continued to expand as its foreign policy became more vigorous. For while toward the end of the Chou dynasty early in the third century B.C., only the northern part of what is today China's heartland had become Chinese, the following two centuries witnessed the conquest of large parts of Turkestan in the west, an area that extended close to the eastern rim of the Roman empire. North Korea to the east and North Vietnam to the south had also been occupied. Except for Tibet, China had thus attained a size which corresponded to its present sphere of influence. Reports about countries lying beyond these far-flung borders came from all points of the compass, particularly from the West, about which the envoy Chang Ch'ien sent the first detailed report in 125 B.C. This tempestuous development had two apparently contradictory yet actually complementary effects: an oppressive constriction of the space available to the individual, and an enormous expansion of the realm of the imagination. In the descriptions of the early Taoists, civilization appears time and again as an island-like area of confusion, embedded in the infinite space of an unconscious, happy nature. Though beginning to spread dangerously, it can never prevent escape into the wilderness. During the later Chou dynasty, the freedom of the population to move and settle elsewhere was difficult to curtail, and it is this circumstance that constituted the solid basis for this notion. The discussions of princes and their councillors at the time frequently focused on the possibility of enticing a foreign people to settle, or at least on measures designed to prevent emigration. It had not only been Mencius who had viewed the urge of a people to turn its back on a state as the most reliable indication that its government was bad. But since the time of the Ch'in dynasty, this situation had abruptly and fundamentally changed. Because the unified state was huge, it made emigration impossible. Through the expansion and unification of the area under government control, the relationship between civilization and wilderness had been reversed. Civilization was no longer an island in the wilderness. Instead, there were only a few islands of wilderness left within civilization. The "mountains and marshes" so frequently celebrated in song became areas of retreat, reservations for all those who refused to adapt to civilization, and this included both the formerly dangerous indigenous population, and the Taoist hermit. At the same time, the thoughts of all those caught in this civilization as in a noose traveled to its outer limits. They still existed, of course, but had been pushed further outward after having once been so easy to cross when men sought to escape the constraints of society. The conviction that more beautiful and happier countries lay beyond those borders merged with old mythologies and new eyewitness accounts, and resulted in the most curious conceptions of the world outside the Chinese sphere of power. During the Han period, Tsou Yen was therefore believed when he taught that China constituted only 1/81 part of the entire world—a view which could not have been held or even discussed in the Earlier Chou period. The *Classic of the Mountains and the Seas (Shan-hai-ching)* with its fantastic descriptions of the lands on the edges of the world and their curious inhabitants came to be written at this time. As can be inferred from quotations that have come down to us, these accounts also played an important role in the apocryphal supplements to the Confucian classics.[40]

The mountains to the west and the oceans to the east were indeed the furthest points where the diffusion of Chinese civilization, rejoiced in by the Confucians and Ho Hsiu, bemoaned by the Taoists, finally had to stop. More convincingly and earlier than any others, these limits thus became the gates of paradise. Beyond the moving infinity of an ocean that drew the eye into the distance, beyond the mysterious labyrinth of mountains and gorges and their confusing echo, men felt they could hear the whispering of another eternal world which soundlessly eluded the brutal clutches of civilization. Even before the cultural space began to expand, there were rumors of abodes of happiness and immortality allegedly situated in the extreme west and the extreme east of the empire. In the K'un-lun Mountains on the borders of Tibet, the "Queen Mother of the West," *(Hsi-wang-mu)* was said to rule a fairyland, and far out at sea, off the eastern shores of China, there was the land of the "isles of the blessed" where the first emperor of the Ch'in had sent his expedition. But it was not until the Han period that these conceptions came fully alive, most strongly perhaps under the emperor Wu-ti (governed 140–86 B.C.), a man as powerful as he was devoted to magic, and who assembled a whole staff of magicians at his court. Countries whose legendary treasures might contribute to the glory of China and the wealth of its emperor seemed to be burgeoning in all the corners of the world. Modern researchers have therefore probably been justified in thinking that many campaigns of conquest waged during the Han period had their cause in this joy of discovery. Among the precious objects sought, there was one in particular which had already mocked Ch'in Shih Huang-ti: the elixir of immortality.

It is true that in the older accounts of distant and miraculous lands, there appeared at first only those conditions which had previously been thought to prevail in remote times. The shift from the temporal to the spatial plane made sense because the journey to the edges of civilization, which had been undertaken with increasing frequency since the Ch'in dynasty, really came to the same thing as a journey into the past. Initially, the descriptions thus had a genuine symbolic content, were thoroughly moralistic, and in no sense wild fantasies. In the earliest of these stories which we find in the book *Chuang-tzu,* the country described still has an allegorical quality. At least that is the view of the philosopher who tells of it, although his listener no longer shares it. He is a prince who cannot understand how he can travel to another country without boat and chariot, merely by a change in attitude:

> I-liao of Shih-nan (a member of the royal house of Ch'u who was influenced by the Taoists) visited the duke of Lu. . . . (After the duke had told him with some concern that in spite of all his efforts on behalf of the state he was unable to shake off his misery, I-liao compared him to the foxes and leopards which are hunted only for their beautiful skin and are killed in spite of all their wariness.) "Now then," I-liao continued, "isn't it true that the state of Lu is also nothing but the beautiful skin of Your Majesty? I wish you would cut it off your body to cleanse your heart, to free yourself of your desires, and to walk in open fields where men cannot be found. In the southern state of Yüeh, there is a fief called 'the land of established virtue' *(Chien-te kuo).* The people there are stupid and simple. They have little private property, and hardly any desires. They are familiar with work, but know nothing of thrift. They enjoy giving, but do not demand gratitude *(pao).* They do not know when 'righteousness' is called for, or when to observe 'ritual.' They conduct themselves like savages or mad people, yet they follow certain important rules. During their lifetime, they know how to please each other; and they know how to bury the dead. If only you would leave your state, give up your customs and live in consonance with the 'Way.' " "Alas," the duke said, "the way there is long and dangerous, so many mountains and rivers have to be crossed. What should I do without boat or chariot?" The master of Shih-nan answered: "If you stop insisting on your haughty ceremonials and stop sticking to your position as if you were glued to it, then that will be your chariot." "Alas," the duke said, "the way there is dark and long, and I have no one to accompany me; whom shall I take as companion? And how could I reach my goal without provisions?" The master of Shih-nan answered: "If you spend very little, and have very few desires, you will have all you need, even if you do not have provisions. You will ford the rivers and drift on the seas, you will look into the distance and no longer know where the end may be. All your companions will accompany you no further than the coast, and then return. You, however, will go into the distance from there. For he who hampers others is chained, he who is hampered by others is sad, which is the reason why Yao neither

hampered others nor was hampered by them. I wish I could undo your chains, put away your sadness, and be the only one to accompany you to the Great Land of No One *(Ta-mo chih kuo).*"[41]

In later descriptions of paradises and miraculous lands, there is nothing to equal the illimitable dignity and gentle melancholy of this account of a happy land that can be reached by only one path. The tone is characteristic of Chuang-tzu, and sounds like a poetic description of the inevitable loneliness of old age and death. Later narratives are more sober, more scientific, more in consonance with the practical thinking of a "duke of Lu." This applies even to the relevant sections in the book *Lieh-tzu,* although they also never wholly lack a more profound, ethical meaning. But perhaps they tell us all the more about the world here and now, the integration of the Chinese state and its society into a universe of opposites and relativities. In one chapter, the words used to describe the "Middle Kingdom" in the focal position it occupies both geographically and morally are chosen so skillfully that it is difficult to decide whether they convey praise or are critical of China. This passage is also interesting because in this self-representation China appears as it preferred to see itself throughout its history, and down to the most recent past: as a country where nature ordained the interplay and balance of extreme opposites:

In the southernmost corner of the western pole lies a land that extends no one knows how far. It is called the Ku-mang land. There the forces of *Yin* and *Yang* do not meet, and therefore the contrast between cold and warm does not exist. Sun and moon do not shine, and thus there is no difference between night and day. The people do not eat, and do not wear garments, but sleep almost all the time. They wake up only once every fifty days. They think that what goes on in dreams is real, and take for appearance what they see when awake. The Middle Kingdom lies amidst the Four Oceans, to the north and south of the Yellow River and to the east and west of the Great Mountain *(t'ai-shan)* in an area far greater than a thousand square miles. Dark and light are clearly separated, and thus day follows night. Among the people, some are clever, others stupid. Nature thrives, the arts and the crafts are highly developed. The prince and the people face each other, morality and righteousness support each other. It is impossible to enumerate all that people do and talk about there. Waking and sleeping alternate. What is done while awake is considered real, what is seen in dreams, appearance. In the northernmost corner of the east pole lies a land called Fu-lo. It is always hot there, sun and moon shine [constantly] with a glaring light. The earth does not produce good grain so that the people have to nourish themselves with roots and fruits from the trees. They do not know cooked food. They are hard and cruel by nature. The strong oppress the weak, only the victor is honored, and justice is disregarded. Most of the time, the people run around doing things; they rest little. They are always awake, and never sleep.[42]

The two fantasy lands bordering on China are not paradises, to be sure,[43] but rather realms of a preexistence characterized by the absence of *Yin* and *Yang* in one case, and an excessive existence caused by the simultaneous appearance of both, in the other. The one is a realm of darkness, peace and sleep, the other of brightness, dispute and wakefulness. But here it can already be seen that Lieh-tzu's sympathy goes to the Ku-mang land, preexistence rather than excessive existence, and this is demonstrably characteristic of Taoism from the very beginning. The genuinely paradisiacal lands are therefore more like the Ku-mang land. Almost always that typical mildness and lack of differentiation prevails in them which we encountered previously in descriptions of paradisiacal epochs. Not only in Taoism, but also in other Chinese world views, even including Confucianism, preexistence was indeed always considered an ideal, because this phase *prior* to the polarization of the fundamental forces can hardly be distinguished from the stage of balance *between* those same forces. In Taoism as in Confucianism, on the other hand, the Fu-lo realm with its hectic industriousness, where the grain does not thrive and disputes govern life, is clearly evil and closer to the conception of hell than of heaven. This connection emerges clearly in the following story about Huang-ti, the "Yellow Emperor," the first sage ruler. It tells how Huang-ti tried to order the realm, and then continues with the description of the following event:

> Once, the Yellow Emperor was sleeping in broad daylight. He dreamt that he was taking a walk in the kingdom of Hua-hsü, a country that lies even further west than the westernmost continent Yen-chou, and to the north of the northernmost continent T'ai-chou, and I do not know how many thousand or ten thousand miles from China. Neither ship nor chariot will do for the journey. One can only travel there in one's mind. Neither rulers nor elders exist in this country; everything functions by itself. The people have neither wishes nor desires; they own everything naturally. They know neither the joy of living nor the distaste for death; consequently, there is no such thing as premature death. The know neither the love of self, nor the detachment from others; therefore neither affection nor hatred exist for them. They do not turn away from others or rebel, nor do they turn toward others and obey; thus profit and loss have no existence for them. They have nothing they love, or to which they are attached, nothing they fear or shy away from. They go into water without drowning, they go into fire without being burnt. When they are beaten, they suffer neither wounds nor pain, and the bites [of insects] cause neither burning nor itching. They climb into emptiness as others step on firm ground, and sleep in space as in a bed. Clouds do not veil their sight, peals of thunder do not confuse their hearing, beauty and ugliness do not delude their senses, mountains and valleys do not impede their movement. For they move only in spirit. When the Yellow Emperor awoke, he had understood, and found himself. . . . And after 28 years, the highest order *(ta-chih)* prevailed in the empire, almost as in the land Hua-hsü, and when Huang-ti died, the people wept for him for two hundred years, without ceasing.[44]

Yü, a later sage emperor mentioned previously, also seems to have come to this mysterious land, as did King Mu (governed 1001–946 B.C., according to tradition), an undoubtedly historical figure though shrouded in legend. The description of the country is again contained in the book *Lieh-tzu* and accompanies the report of their travels. It represents a somewhat later phase in the development of conceptions of ideal countries. The writing loses its allegorical character more and more, it becomes increasingly objective and detailed, it no longer describes events in a dream, but concrete reality which becomes all the more fantastic as a result. The abolition of social differentiation moves progressively into the foreground. We have not only the equality between ruler and subjects as it first appeared in Chuang-tzu and the just quoted section from the *Lieh-tzu*, but also the equality of young and old, men and women:

> Once, when emperor Yü was taming the waters, he lost his way. By mistake, he found himself in a land on the northern coast of the northern sea, I don't know how many thousand or ten thousand miles from the continent of Ch'in (China). The land was called "Northend"; no one knows where its borders are. Wind and rain, frost and thaw are unknown there. Birds or animals, insects or fish do not live there, and grass or trees do not grow. The territory is completely level in all directions, but surrounded by high mountains. Exactly in the center of the country lies a mountain called "urn's neck" *(Hu-ling)*; it is shaped like a jug. On its top, there is a circular opening named "cave of abundance." Water gushes forth from it. It is referred to as "spirit font." Its fragrance is more intoxicating than that of orchids and pepper, its taste stronger than that of wine and sweet cider. This one source divides into four streams which flow down the mountain and through the entire country, leaving not a single corner without water. The climate is mild, and diseases are therefore unknown. The people are gentle in their manners, and follow their nature without disputes or quarrels. They are obedient and have supple bodies, are neither proud nor afraid. The old and the young live together, they have equal rights, there is neither ruler nor subjects. Men and women mix as they wish, there are no professional matchmakers, and betrothal gifts are not given. They live on the banks of the streams which supply their food. They neither plough nor harvest, and since the climate is warm, they do not weave and wear no garments. They die when they are one hundred years old, there is no illness, no premature death. They are of great fertility, know only joy and delights, and are ignorant of sickliness and old age, mourning and bitterness. Making music is a beloved custom. They hold each other by their hands, and take turns singing all day long until evening. When they are hungry and tired, they drink from the "spirit font," and immediately their bodies and minds are restored to harmony and balance. If they drink excessively, they become inebriated, and sleep uninterruptedly for ten days. When they bathe in the "spirit font," their skin recovers its tautness and smoothness, and the sweet fragrance lasts for ten days. King Mu of Chou [also] came through this country on his voyage north. For three years, he forgot to return home. When he had finally returned to his palace, he longed to be back in this country. He became so restless that he could not come to his senses. He no longer had wine or meat served, and stopped asking for his wives and servants. Several months passed until he was his old self again.[45]

EAST AND WEST AS PLACES OF REFUGE AND IMMORTALITY

It is certainly not by chance that this paradise was placed in the extreme north of China, for a conception taken from Indian sources and certainly known when this text was written also situates paradise in the northernmost regions.[46] Besides, the area in the northeast was the center of Taoist scholarship during the Han period. Here, the former fiefdom of Ch'i was located, and that state stands as *pars pro toto* for "China" in the section just quoted. In many academies there, scholars searched not only for wisdom in the conduct of life, but were primarily interested in prolonging it. However, it was the West and the East that were the classical compass points for paradise, as mentioned before. According to legend, King Mu of Chou was the first to discover the paradise of Hsi-wang-mu, the "Queen Mother of the West," in the course of his (historical) journey to the north and west just referred to. Originally, in transcription, the term *Hsi-wang-mu* seems to have designated nothing more exotic than a small state in the west of China. By chance, a sign meaning "mother" was chosen for its final syllable *mu (*məg> məu).* But later, the imagination seized on this sign, turning the place into a personal name, the "Queen Mother," and this in turn came to designate the fairy land ruled by her.[47] Since the beginning of the Han period, legends about this country in the K'un-lun massif had begun to multiply. The version found in Lieh-tzu, on the other hand, still largely resembles the sober comments in the old history texts *Mu t'ien-tzu chuan (Biography of the Son of Heaven Mu)* and *Chu-shu chi-nien (Bamboo Annals).* In lapidary style, they merely note that King Mu paid a visit to the ruler of that country: "The king climbed the peak of K'un-lun to see the castle of the Lord of the Yellow Earth. . . . Then he was the guest of the Queen Mother of the West, who regaled him on the Jasper lake. She sang a song for the king, and he joined her. It was a very affecting song. Then he also saw the spot where the sun sets. . . . And he said: 'Alas, I do not cultivate virtue, and only care about my pleasures. Posterity will reproach me for this.' "[48]

Here, the direction in which the conceptions were developing is already discernible. The realm of Hsi-wang-mu never became a paradisiacally ordered country but was and remained a kind of citadel of happiness in a very aristocratic and elite sense. The court of the "Queen Mother" with its innumerable servants reflected the imperial court. Only the regents of this empire enjoyed full happiness, although all others possessed something of importance, namely immortality, which those dwelling in the paradise of the north had been able to relinquish without sorrow. A relatively early report contained in a collection of texts ascribed to the Taoist philosopher Huai-nan-tzu (i.e. Liu An, 179–122 B.C.) points in this direction:

> The mountains "Hanging Garden," "Cool Wind," and "Enclosed Park of Paulownias" lie in K'un-lun city; they make up its parks. The ponds in these parks are fed by a yellow water which, having traversed three of them, flows back to its source. It is referred to as "cinnabar water"; those who drink it become immortal. . . . The three peaks tower above each other. When one climbs the first, called "Cool Wind," one [also] becomes immortal. When one climbs the second, which is twice as high and called "Hanging Garden," one becomes a spirit endowed with magic powers *(ling)* and can command the wind and the rain. When one has climbed the third, which is again twice as high [and is called "Enclosed Park of Paulownias,"] one can ascend directly to heaven and become a divine spirit *(shen),* for one then finds oneself in the palace of the highest emperor of heaven *(ta-ti).*[49]

It was immortality, and especially the peaches of immortality also said to ripen in the gardens of K'un-lun according to later reports, that time and again stirred interest in expeditions to this country so difficult to discover. They could be brought back, and sometimes stolen, as was reported in early legends influenced by mythology, ever new variations of which continue to be told down to the present. Life in the mountain palaces of the "Queen Mother," on the other hand, was less attractive. It was not a happiness one could really long for, unless one was a king oneself. Thus the realm of the "Queen Mother" became a reservoir of the most diverse, scattered mythological fragments, but not a place of promise whose ideals also had meaning for this world.

This also applied, if less markedly, to the three islands of the blessed off the east coast of China. The names of these three islands, P'eng-lai ("proliferating weeds"), Fang-chang ("square fathom"), and Ying-chou ("ocean continent") may also have been quite ordinary place names originally.[50] Yet all three contain a sign which suggests a supernatural element: *lai* is part of the name of the legendary sage Lao-lai-tzu, whose biography blended with Lao-tzu's from the very beginning. *Fang* means not only "square" but also "magic," and *ying* does not designate an ordinary ocean but the island-less ocean that encircles all land. But with the inclusion of all kinds of variants (instead of "square fathom," reference was also made to "square urn" *fang-hu,* and the three islands were spoken of as the "Three Urns" *san-hu,* both of which in turn are reminiscent of the "urn-neck mountain" *hu-ling* in the northern paradise), they soon came to represent the essence of happiness. The historical work *Shih-chi,* to which we owe the account of the disappointed hopes of the First Emperor of the Ch'in dynasty, discusses these islands very seriously in another passage. This shows that all the transparent deceptions of the magicians at the court of the Ch'in notwithstanding, the existence of these islands was not altogether discounted:

> In the time of Prince Wei (governed 378–343 B.C.), Hsüan (governed 342–324) and King Chao (governed 311–279) of Yen, people were first sent out to sea to search for the three spirit mountains P'eng-lai, Fang-chang and Ying-chou, which allegedly lay in the Po-hai sea. They are not far distant from the habitations of men. The only problem is that at the very moment they have almost been reached, the ship

is [usually] seized by a wind and carried off. Once there were [sailors] who approached very close. [They saw that] only "immortals" *(hsien-jen)* lived on the islands, and that they had found the elixir of eternal life. All creatures there, birds and animals, are of the clearest white, and the palaces and gates of the purest gold and silver. [The sailors] had not yet landed, but saw all this in the cloudy distance. When they thought they had actually reached the shore, the three spirit mountains sank into the sea, and a wind blowing toward them swept the boat off its course. They never again reached that place.[51]

While these paradisiacal islands appear as a sort of mirage in the realistic yet also cautious report of the historian, the book *Lieh-tzu* transposes them into a purely mythological space where many other miraculous moments also determine events. Actually, the description is devoid of significance. Its profounder meaning derives merely from the fact that as part of a more extensive argument (omitted here), it serves as a colorful symbol of the relativity of all orders of magnitude:

Countless thousands of miles to the east of the Po-hai sea, there is a great depression which is really a bottomless abyss. It is called the "Big Grave." All the waters of the earth and the streams of the Milky Way flow into it, yet its depth does not change. In its center, there once were five mountains: T'ai-yü ("Great Chariot"), Yüan-chiao ("Rounded Peak"), Fang-hu, Ying-chou and P'eng-lai. These mountains were 30,000 miles high. On each of their peaks, there was a level area of nine thousand square miles. The mountains were 70,000 miles apart, and yet they were considered neighbors. Up there, one saw nothing but gold and precious stones. Birds and animals shone in a splendid white, trees of pearls and corals formed dense woods, all the flowers were fragrant, and the fruits sweet. Eating them brought freedom from old age and death. Nothing but goddesses and immortals lived there. Day and night, they flew in countless numbers to visit each other. But the roots of the five mountains were loose and thus they constantly rose and fell with the flood and the waves and were never at rest. The immortals were much annoyed about this and reported it to the "Master." The "Master" began to fear that the islands might be swept to the western pole and thus be lost to the immortals as a dwelling place. He therefore ordered the spirit named "Bounds of Origin" to bring fifteen giant turtles which were to bear the mountains on their head, taking three turns of 60,000 years each. Thus the five mountains recovered a firm foundation and stopped moving. But there was a giant who lived in the "Realm of the Dragon Prince." Taking only a few steps, he came to the five mountains. Using a fishing rod just once, he caught six of the turtles, put them on his back, returned to his country and roasted the shells for the oracles they might yield. Thus the two mountains "Great Chariot" and "Rounded Peak" drifted to the North Pole and sank into the sea there. [Only the three others remained.] Thousands upon thousands of immortals thus became homeless.[52]

The five hundred years following the Han dynasty were a time of burning religious zeal in Chinese history. There was a proliferation of reports about the islands of the blessed surrounding the inhabited world. They already show clear traces of Indian influence, which may also be assumed in the story just quoted, at least as regards the motif of the turtles supporting the mountains. The great world ocean which encircled the "nine continents," according to general belief, seemed dotted with these places of pure happiness. In part, the chains and circles they formed also suggest the stations of the course of the sun. More and more frequently, their size and geographic position also were described with painstaking accuracy,[53] and it would actually not be difficult to draw a map of all these islands, or of the mountains of the blessed. For the concepts merge here because the islands were also viewed as mountains, as the terminology indicates. In contrast to previous practice, however, the dimensions took on ever more astronomical proportions. Already the closest islands were hundreds of thousands of miles away, and could therefore not be reached by anyone who was not himself one of the genii or immortals who could wing his way to these places of delight.

But as the number of these islands of the blessed increased, the descriptions of conditions there became progressively flatter and devoid of content. With the names of the original islands, such as P'eng-lai, as titles, a growing number of accounts appeared that lacked almost all feeling and were artlessly strung together without any attempt to integrate them in a new unity. These descriptions are thus nothing more than debris, consisting of mythologies, fairy tales and philosophical or pseudo-scientific theorems. While they do create an interest in what may be called archaeological investigation, they can no longer be considered genuine intellectual structures. In many cases, we are no longer dealing with accounts of paradises but rather the presentation of perfectly ordinary countries with a familiar apparatus of rulers and officials: "The customs of the inhabitants resemble those of the people of Wu (the southeastern coastal region of China)," it says somewhat laconically in one such report, for example. "Otherwise everything is the same as in the Middle Kingdom."[54] In most cases, these islands merely came to serve as a sort of geographical designation for China, (as had already been true of Lieh-tzu's Ku-mang and Fu-lo empires) or as the popular demonstration of a scientific doctrine. An example of this would be the presentation of the five paradises of the four directions of heaven and the center, easily recognizable as the realms of the five elements, judging by the materials and colors dominant in them (yellow, green, white, red and black). Generally speaking, all that still reminds the reader of the paradisiacal is the painstakingly precise description of the means for gaining immortality, for these countries were never without them. But although new medications such as the "grass of immortality," or a paste made from the decoction of the horns of sacred rhinoceri were added, they also sank to the level of sterile clichés, and nowhere surpass the vigorous image of the stream gushing forth from the mountain top. Indeed, in most instances, they are but weak imitations. Instead of a central, all-nourishing stream of life, we encounter small rivulets conveying their blessings, but they are overwhelmed by a thousand other curiosities and usually introduced with these dry words: ". . . also, there is a source named . . . he who drinks its water becomes immortal."[55]

In contrast to this inflation of earthly paradises, which increasingly resulted from the indirect influence of Buddhism, it is remarkable that descriptions of heavenly paradises are rare. A number of reasons may be responsible. It is possible that the openness of heaven offered the imagination less of a chance to conceive of real countries there, although their existence had been a staple element of popular belief since the Han period. It was easier to be fascinated by the thought of walking through mountains of clouds than to take up residence in cloud castles. On the other hand, the mist-enveloped paradisiacal mountain peaks functioned as a heavenly sphere which had the additional advantage of being rooted in this world. The sacred mountain mentioned in *Huai-nan-tzu* is a good example, for it allegedly rose into heaven, thus forming a kind of bridge between it and earth.

A little later, the Milky Way was also conceived as a similar connecting link, for it was viewed as a kind of continuation of the sea into heaven. The *Report About All Sorts of Miraculous Things (Po-wu-chih)* by the poet and scholar Chang Hua (232–300), for example, maintained in a lapidary manner that "Heaven and earth are connected on all four sides by the waters of the oceans,"[56] and then attempted to support this view with the following story:

> Old reports already mention a passage from the Milky Way to the sea. [According to accounts] of more recent date, people who lived on the islands in the ocean [are actually said to have been able], year after year, and always in the eighth month, to use floats drifting in the water to establish such a connection, provided they did not miss the right moment. Once, especially daring men erected a high structure on one of these huge floats, loaded large amounts of provisions, and thus set out on a voyage. . . . For more than ten days, they could still see the distant stars, the sun, the moon and the planets [clearly distinct from each other], but then [large stars] appeared in such confusing numbers that they could no longer be counted. After another ten days, they came to a place which looked [like an island]. It had walls and fortifications. [Further inland] houses and palaces rose majestically, and inside the castles floating in the distance, one could make out weaving women. [Finally] the sailors encountered a man who was leading a calf by a rope to the quay of the island to water it there. When he saw them, he asked in consternation: "By which route did you get here?" They introduced themselves and told how they had made the plan for their voyage. Then they inquired where they were. "Just go back home," was the answer, "and ask [the magician] Yen Chün-p'ing from the district of Shu, and you will find out." The sailors decided not to go ashore, but immediately returned so as not to exceed the period [of the eighth month, the only time during which the passage between heaven and earth is possible]. Later, when they came to Shu, they asked [the magician Yen] Chün-p'ing, and he said: "[Yes,] on such and such a date, an alien star entered the constellation of the Herdsman." And when the date was calculated, it turned out to be precisely the moment these daring men had penetrated across the Milky Way.[57]

One of the rare early passages where not only a realm above the clouds, but also the space *beyond* heaven is described, can also be found in *Lieh-tzu.* Once again, it is King Mu of Chou, that great wanderer between the worlds, who is granted this superhuman experience. *Lieh-tzu* reports that King Mu had a much admired magician at his court, who made such great demands that, to satisfy him, the king had to empty all his treasuries and build him a palace called "Palace of the Middle Heaven." The most beautiful girls moved in, the best food was served, the most precious garments were brought. But all of this barely came up to the expectations the magician had of a pleasant life. "After a few days," the report continues,

> the magician invited the king to travel with him. The king held onto the magician's sleeve, and thus they moved upward, directly into heaven. Finally they stopped, having reached the magician's castle. It was built of silver and gold, with ornaments of pearl and jade. It towered above the clouds and the rain, it was impossible to see what it rested on, it appeared to be piled-up clouds. What the senses perceived was wholly different from what is customary in the world of men. The king thought that he was bodily in the purple depth of an ethereal city, surrounded by the music of the spheres, where the great emperor of Heaven lives. When he glanced down, he saw his castles and summer homes, tiny like mounds of earth and piles of straw. Thus he lingered for a few decades, and thought no more of his empire. Finally, the magician again invited him to continue their travels. At the place where they now arrived, sun and moon above, and the rivers and oceans below, could no longer be seen. The figures of light which appeared were so dazzling that the king was blinded; nor could he hear the sounds that rushed in upon him because his ears were deafened. He almost fainted and nearly lost consciousness, so that he asked the magician to let him return. The magician cast a spell and the king felt as if he were falling into the void. When he came to, he was sitting at the same place as before, the servants waiting on him were the same, and when he looked down, he found that his goblet was still full, and the food still warm. The king asked what had happened. Those surrounding him said: "Your Majesty has been sitting silently for a while." At this moment, the king lost his mind and did not recover until three months later. He then asked the magician, who said: "Your Majesty, I wandered with you in spirit, why bother moving the body? The place where we were, how could it be less real than your castle; or the region to which we traveled less real than your garden? You, of course, are used to permanent conditions and mistrust appearances which only last a moment. But the highest forms of metamorphosis and [the extremes] between slow and fast, how can they be wholly grasped [conceptually]?"[58]

THE FEAR OF HEAVEN AND THE ATTACHMENT TO EARTH

Conceptions of heaven are revelatory because in contrast to all the paradises situated on earth, heaven is everywhere experienced—whether consciously or not—as the most elemental space of the beyond, of transcendence. Other than life in paradises, which could be discovered or recovered, life in heaven demanded a wholly different kind of existence. It was symbolized by "flying," the only form of movement nature has denied man. The role assigned to heaven as a place of happiness in the tales and legends of China therefore reflects very clearly and in a popular form the changing value philosophy accorded the transcendent generally. In the later sections of the *Chuang-tzu* text, which tell of the sages that "walk in the spheres of not-acting beyond the dust and dirt of mortals," or of the happy life after death, there is an understanding of something truly otherworldly not yet to be found anywhere in the early *Chuang-tzu* chapters. But the Chinese mind seems clearly oriented toward this world, and it is therefore only during a short transitional period that it could bear this divergence of two worlds. For it was precisely in its *description* of paradises that it undertook to reintegrate paradises in this world. Their transformation from a no longer conceivable, transcendent dream image to an almost embarrassingly real, geographically specifiable place can clearly be traced through all its transitional forms. As previously suggested, it is true that heaven escaped this curious fate of becoming an object of colonization, measurement and planning. But this was not the reason it remained an unassailable sphere of the supernatural. Rather, it was simply forgotten because it was less suited for this purpose than the more tangible islands and mountains. Innumerable times, the legends of the saints describe the heavenly hosts, dressed in splendid garments, descending to earth to the sounds of the music of the spheres. They evidently come from above. Similarly, the sages who have attained immortality not infrequently ascend "in broad daylight" from high mountains to the ether. But only in the rarest cases does it become wholly clear whether heaven is really their home, or whether they are not merely traveling through the air to shorten the long distance between the faraway but this-worldly paradises, and the continents inhabited by men.[59]

In the oldest period, conceptions of the beyond began by naively identifying it with this world. Toward the end of the Chou period, there arose an intimation of something truly transcendent, particularly in connection with death. A further differentiation finally occurred during the Han dynasty, where a kind of synthesis was created by once again assigning the transcendent a place in this world. A very impressive illustration of this progressive shift can be seen in the gradual change in burial gifts: beginning with real human beings, animals and articles of use during the pre-Shang period where writing was unknown, and containers with symbolic import during the Shang and Early Chou periods, the road led back during the Han period, as it were. Here, copies and models of all those things were used which had once actually been placed into the grave, i.e. representations of men, animals and articles of use made of clay. Also, things were now added which could never have been placed into a grave in their actual form, such as houses and gardens. Besides, the grave itself became a house, carefully built in stone, and decorated with friezes, reliefs and paintings. Innumerable graves of this kind were constructed during the first four centuries A.D. They were stuffed full with clay statues reminiscent of toys and which were still made during the T'ang period in a more refined form (T'ang horses).[60] They show how close the beyond was felt to be. The world of heavenly paradises had very this-worldly desires. It was other-worldly only in the sense that every wish, every thought in this world of pure spirit quite automatically became reality.

And yet, there was also an intensive effort to join heaven to earth, although it could not be imagined as vividly as the miraculous lands here below. This can be inferred from the development of an idea which became central to all Taoist conceptions of paradise, the idea of the "immortal." The Chinese term, *hsien,* went through a very interesting development at the beginning and end of which it is represented by two wholly different characters. Phonetically, the word is related to, indeed practically identical with, a word having the meaning "to rise," "to rise into the air." In the script, the only difference between them was that originally the term which later came to mean "immortal" was written with the additional radical "human being." As is also proven by the earliest texts in which it appears, the word thus meant a person who can fly, a fantastic winged human being, who was also occasionally imagined as completely covered with feathers, but was not initially endowed with any special intellectual qualities.[61] Only when the existence of a beyond was first sensed in the fourth and third centuries B.C., and the beyond again lost its status as a distinct sphere one or two centuries later, did the *hsien,* the flying immortals, become significant key figures, i.e. messengers of two worlds, not unlike our angels. The essential difference lay in the fact that in China it was increasingly believed that men also could become *hsien* and thus transcend this world in two ways: by conquering gravity, and by conquering death.[62]

This hope was not confined to the scholarly community, but put its stamp on an entire age (second–fourth century A.D.), and continued to make itself felt for centuries more, nor has it really altogether vanished today. In a sense, Taoism had thus traced a circular path, for the desire to preserve life had been one of its earliest roots.[63] Physiological techniques, already present in a rudimentary form in Lao-tzu and Chuang-tzu, now made a powerful reappearance in Taoism: fasting and breathing exercises, sometimes also sexual practices were meant to make the body "light," and could readily be combined with the older conviction that at the time of his death, man divides into two souls, a transitory body soul *(p'o),* and an imperishable spirit soul *(hun).* On the other hand, the impression left by the amoral ethical teachings of philosophical Taoism was too profound to permit men to return to a purely formal doctrine. Here also, the result was a synthesis. Two reasons had occasionally been given for Taoist physical practices: to recover from certain illnesses, and to enter paradise as a *hsien.* To attain each of these objectives, it was believed that a two-fold effort was required: the performance of certain exercises, but also a particular cast of mind as exemplified by the classical figures of philosophical Taoism. This meant a turning away from the world, and the preservation of vitality in solitude. The later written form of the word *hsien* took account of this new, more ethically founded view of the "immortal." That it ultimately prevailed may also have been due in part to the fact that it was easier to write, and expressed its meaning in a visually more striking form. It consisted simply of the two characters for "man" and "mountain." It thus had an attractive double meaning, referring not only to the man who sought solitude in the mountains, but also to the person who found a happy home on one of the paradisiacal mountains or island peaks.

Even where the legends evidently report ascensions to heaven, the extent to which the gravitational pull of the earth gradually overtook the "immortals," the degree to which their flight through the clouds became a walk across mountains, is easily recognizable. Ascensions were less and less often presented as the transition to a wholly different mode of being, but rather as a kind of voyage into another country. Similar to the palace of the "Queen Mother of the West," such countries had only one characteristic that was desirable and valuable beyond all doubt, and that was immortality. Very typical in this connection are the stories telling of the eagerness of many *hsien* to take along into the new world the greatest possible number of objects for their personal use. There is even the case of an "immortal" who was accompanied by his entire family and household goods as he ascended to heaven,[64] a naive parallel to the previously mentioned custom of placing models of all the things the dead had come to cherish during their lifetime into the grave with them. To free oneself from all the ties of this world, to take one's leave from all the companions left on the shore before the great ocean was crossed, was no longer the essential element in gaining blessedness, but more nearly the opposite: the attainment of immortality, the promise of everlasting life, but precisely a life on earth or, at least, a life *as it had been lived on earth.* The mistrust of conditions in heaven emerges quite clearly in the biographies of some immortals: one feels a comprehensible fear of an existence in the spiritually rarefied atmosphere above the clouds, where the multiplicity of saintly figures gradually developed into a "hierarchy" in the truest sense of that word, and began to bear a depressing similarity to relations of domination on earth. Thus we find the following account about one of these (naturally wholly legendary) immortals in a collection of biographies:

> "Master Whitestone" was a disciple of "Old Middle-Yellow." When P'eng-tsu appeared, he was already more than two thousand years old. He had decided not to strive to ascend to heaven but instead simply not to die, so that he might not miss out on the joys of this world. Among the methods he tried, he did not hesitate to assign first place to sexual practices and [the extraction] of gold-juice medicine [for the making of gold]. . . . He ate meat [without qualms], drank wine, and also used cereals. He could travel three to four hundred miles in a day. He looked like a forty-year old. . . . When P'eng-tsu asked him: "Why don't you drink the elixir which will enable you to ascend to heaven?" he answered: "Do you think I would enjoy the same pleasures in heaven that I enjoy among men? All that would do would be to rid me of the worry that I might die before having attained great age. But on the other hand, there would be multitudes of the most Venerable in heaven, to whom I would have to show respect. Things would be even worse than they are among men." Because he neither tried to ascend to heaven and to become an

immortality official, nor to make a name for himself in this world, his contemporaries called him a secret immortal.[65]

The existence of such "secret immortals," for the Taoist imagination knew of more than just "Master Whitestone," enriched the Taoist vocabulary by a concept which is really a contradiction in itself. Yet actually it merely restates the development which had already been apparent in the two written versions of the word *hsien:* the discovery of the "immortal on earth" *(ti-hsien)* as contrasted to the "immortal in heaven" *(t'ien-hsien).*[66] The holy men of this world gave symbolic expression to the voluntary renunciation of transcendence, a renunciation that did not lack a tragic element. For it was based on a certain insincerity which weakened Taoism internally just as much as the previously mentioned, no less insincere combination of the contradictory ideals of "humanity" and Legalism had weakened later Confucianism. Taoism attempted to combine the temporal, finite happiness of this world with the atemporal, eternal happiness of the beyond, of heaven, and thus maneuvered itself into a position where imprecise and evasive thinking was soon followed by deliberate deception, pure hocus-pocus, and confusing hallucination.

The fashion of compiling biographies had been imitated from Confucianism. But these collections did not contain biographies of ordinary people whose life, as in the case of Confucianism, had a distinct beginning, an equally distinct end, and a clear effect on society. Precisely at the moment where they became interesting for a Taoism that properly understood itself, these individuals were leading a life whose biography made about as much sense as the biography of a ray of sunlight or a waterfall. This shows how distorted these conceptions had already become. The Confucian and the old Taoist views of life entered a bizarre union and created first the dubious ideal of a saint living by and for himself, and for ever-increasing periods, in the caverns of mountains. Looking like a young man, he only occasionally mingled with mortals whom he astounded by performing a variety of magical tricks.[67] That such a life was really *no* life at all perhaps did not dawn on the superstitious crowd, but certainly soon became clear to the educated. Like "Master Whitestone," they were no longer willing to renounce the pleasures of this world for the difficult life of solitude, and also mistrusted all reports concerning splendid worlds in the beyond. All that counted for them was the life here and now. Death was no longer a mysterious transition but shrank to a kind of illness people thought could be cured like any other.

From this fundamental attitude, alchemy developed. It constituted the final rebuff to the beyond, since men now even hoped they might find the elixir of immortality in this world. Up to this point, it had indisputably been the greatest good of paradise and provided the impetus for the expeditions undertaken by Ch'in Shih Huang-ti and emperor Wu-ti of the Han dynasty. The secularization of Taoism was consequently not confined to "Vulgarized Taoism" where saints, personified ideas and natural forces soon began to form a gigantic pantheon. It was also present in the apparently strictly scientific search of alchemy. Beginning in the third century A.D., its theoretical truth became an article of faith among many, otherwise sober Chinese scholars. The conquest of death as the evil of all evils, and the attainment of happiness implicit in it, had thus undergone an astonishing metamorphosis in Taoism. The spiritual victory over death by its heroic acceptance was replaced by a material victory through chemical elimination. The Chinese philosopher in whose doctrine all of these ideas came together as in a burning glass was Ko Hung (284–363).[68] In the "esoteric" part of his principal work *Pao-p'u-tzu,* he only discusses alchemy; but in the "exoteric" part he describes the ideal conduct of the saint in the world. In contrast to the early Taoists, his attitude toward society is no longer uncompromisingly hostile. He merely recommends moderation and caution, and even portrays the hermit on the mountains as a man whose indirect labor for the redemption of society becomes all the more effective for that very reason. He is a kind of unofficial official, whose sphere of competence is the *wilderness.* Ko Hung is the author of a number of the earliest collections of biographies of "immortals," including the biography from which we quoted the remarks about "Master Whitestone."[69] He thus made his peace with this world in the scientific, the social and the historical sphere, and the Taoist doctrine of salvation lost its disturbing supernatural element.

This Taoism, which not merely affirmed the world here and now, but apparently loved it so much that it could no longer abandon it, and therefore concentrated all its energy on the struggle of the individual against death, infused new meaning into many mythical figures also honored by Confucianism. This is particularly true of Huang-ti, the "Yellow Emperor," who merged with Lao-tzu in a single divinity *(Huang-lao),* which was destined soon to occupy a central place in popular Taoism. P'eng-tsu, a legendary Methuselah, who is already mentioned in the oldest Confucian texts and whom we encountered in "Master Whitestone's" biography, is another figure. Precisely because he was said to have lived hundreds of years, but not to have enjoyed eternal life, because life, in other words, had obviously been prolonged but not transformed into a different condition, he may be considered a precursor of this new or, more accurately, renewed form of Taoism. The legends that began to be woven about him at his time are indeed very revealing. They show once again the incisive skepticism directed at the other-worldly existence of a heavenly "immortal," and that it was almost held in less esteem than life on earth, although the priority of the former was conceded without envy. In the collection of biographies of immortals ascribed to Ko Hung and quoted previously in connection with "Master Whitestone," we find the following rather interesting sections in a report on the life of P'eng-tsu:

> P'eng-tsu said: "Of the genuine 'immortals,' some ascend to the clouds with their body erect, and fly about there without wings; some ride on vapor, being drawn by dragons up to the steps of Heaven; some change into animals and birds, and roam

the blue clouds; some dive into the depth of rivers and oceans, or flutter to the peaks of famous mountains; some eat the original essence or the grass of immortality; some mingle with men without being noticed; some hide so that no one sees them. Curious bones grow on their heads, and peculiar hair on their bodies. They all love what is profound and simple, and disregard the ordinary or fashionable. Such men have been granted eternal life without death, but have [first] relinquished all human feeling, and stayed away from pomp and pleasure. They resemble the sparrow that has changed into a shell, or the pheasant turned into a sea serpent. They have lost their original nature and are animated by an alien life force. Stupid as I am, I have not come to the point where I desire that sort of thing for my own person. He who merely wants to enter the 'Way' (like myself), eats sweet, well-tasting food, dresses in light, pretty garments, gives his sexual desires their due, and also accepts official and honorary positions. His bones are hard and firm, his face content and healthy. He ages without becoming sickly. Living among others, he prolongs his years, thus enjoying extended life in human society. Cold and warmth, wind and mist cannot harm him, ghosts and spirits dare not approach him, the five weapons and the hundred insects cannot hurt him, displeasure and joy, slander and praise do not touch him. For all these reasons, he may be held in high esteem. If he takes care of himself, man's vitality can bring him to an age of 120 years, even if he knows no magical means. If he does not become that old, he has somehow damaged his life force intentionally. If he has the merest inkling of the 'Way,' he can become 240 years old, and if he knows a little more, 480 years. Should he make the fullest possible use of his intellectual powers, he need not die at all. But this still does not make him [a genuine] 'immortal.' For the Way of the cultivation of long life simply means that life must never be injured. One feels warm in winter, and cool in summer, and never loses the harmony inhering in the four seasons. In this way, one adapts one's body. In dark chambers, one delights in women, and does not allow the confusion of desire to arise: thus one's vitality is given scope. As for chariots and uniforms, power and influence, one knows when it is enough, and has no desires beyond that point. Thus one gathers one's will. One takes the eight tones and the five colors to delight eye and ear. Thus one guides one's heart. All those who attempted to live a long life but did not succeed in observing these rules, quickly and unexpectedly suffered misfortune. The greatest men of antiquity feared that their less gifted successors might not know how such matters are undertaken, and that they might not find their way back, once the flow [of physical pleasure] ceases. Therefore they plugged the sources to begin with. Thus the custom developed that the greatest sages slept in their bed without a woman, and that the average scholars at least used a separate blanket, swallowed hundreds of drugs, and also thought the ideal was to sleep alone. It is true, [of course,] that it is the five tones which make people deaf, and that it is the five kinds of taste which dull the palate. But if one is moderate in developing one's justifiable inclinations, and succeeds in freeing oneself of one's inhibitions, this will not shorten one's life span, but increase it. All of these things can be compared to fire and water: only their excessive use is harmful. . . . Immoderate desires and powerful memories harm man, joy and suffering harm man, pleasure that knows no bounds, and anger that does not abate harm man, restless wishes harm man, sexual repression harms man—there are all kinds of things which harm man. Isn't it nonsense to always caution only against eroticism? Man and woman create each other, as heaven and earth create each other. When vitality and the life fluid are guided and nourished, man will not lose his balance. Heaven and earth practice the union of love; for this reason, they are without limits. If man surrenders the path of loving union, he can be certain that he will only harm himself. But if he can avoid all harmful influences and learn the art of love, he will attain the path of immortality. During the day, heaven and earth separate, at night they come together. Three hundred sixty-five times a year they mingle with each other and exchange their fluids in complete harmony. Therefore they can bring forth the ten thousand creatures without becoming tired. If man can pattern his conduct after them, he can live eternally."[70]

The high value attributed here to unrestrained sexual activity by P'eng-tsu made him the official founder of the Taoist sexual practices we have repeatedly referred to. But as is probably true all over the world where suggestions of this sort are the fruit of hard scholarly work, these practices were based on incredibly complicated, painstaking instructions which certainly convey no impression of laxity and are weighted down by various abstract reflections. Central among them is the often unscrupulous desire to multiply the male, spiritual and "heavenly" immortal *Yang* element at the expense of the female partner.[71] Yet what is attributed to P'eng-tsu here and reflects a relatively early tradition nonetheless implies an attitude which has little or nothing in common with the later tradition discussed here. His teaching addressed itself to the harmonious fulfillment of erotic desires, unrestricted by moral laws. Through this imitation of "heaven and earth," man was not only to live a long life but also to experience joy. The above passage and its connection with P'eng-tsu is of particular importance because descriptions of the conditions of human happiness in almost all Chinese sources are sober, almost prudish, and omit the erotic (the only possible exception are some texts in the book *Lieh-tzu,* but they may have been written as late as the third century, and owe their existence to foreign influences). In the passage discussed here, there is a suggestion that the joys of love are perhaps among those things one is afraid of not finding in a world beyond.

To the disappointment of the Taoists, sexual exercises, dietary practices and breathing techniques could no more banish death than alchemy. The answer to the question whether eternal life was ultimately to be found in heaven or on earth thus simply expressed very concrete attitudes toward life here and now. Innumerable explanations were designed to account for the fact that not a single Taoist master had ever demonstrably attained the goal of immortality, and this despite all efforts and the alleged solution of all theoretical problems. In popular legends, it is always cases of infinitesimal negligence or the machinations of all-powerful, jealous spirits that topple the promisingly bubbling cauldron of the alchemist, or cause the body—just beginning to levitate after indefatigable fasting—to slump heavily back to earth.[72] Ko Hung[73] was not alone among scholars when he conjectured that it was not just the drug but ethics also which might be a determining factor in the attainment of immortality, or that certain "contaminations" kept vitiating the prescriptions. In any event, it was only in the rarest cases involving real historical Taoist personalities that the fact of their death could be obscured. Very occasionally, there was the consoling belief that they had merely gone to the mountains to continue leading an undisturbed existence, being seen only now and then in the course of centuries by travelers to whom they confided their true name. The only remaining possibility was thus a daring intellectual leap: death itself had to be proclaimed as the conquest of death. But not in the magnificent metaphorical sense envisaged by the sages in the book *Chuang-tzu*, but in a much triter, more literal way. The term chosen, "detachment from the body," or, perhaps better, "detachment from the transitoriness of the body" *(Shih-chieh)*, expresses the idea clearly. Dying was understood as a necessary transformation if eternal life was to be attained. This concept emerges for the first time in a passage of the *History of the Later Han Dynasty (Hou-Han-shu)*, written in the third century A.D., and is commented on as follows: " 'detachment from the corpse' means that one takes on the appearance of a corpse before one ascends to heaven as an 'immortal,' in order to accomplish thereby the detachment from this world and the transformation."[74] A later text adds the following more precise indications: " 'Detachment from the corpse' means presenting one's body as apparently dead. . . . When the body of a dead person looks as if it were alive, when the feet are not colorless, the skin not wrinkled, and the sparkle of the eye not dimmed, precisely as if it were still alive . . . if the dead person then returns to life after death, or makes his body disappear before it is buried so that only his clothing remains in the coffin, but his body dissolves; or if his hair falls out and his body drifts away—in all these cases one speaks of 'detachment from the corpse.' "[75]

Innumerable legends illustrate such events. During burial, the coffin suddenly becomes light as a feather. When it is opened, it is discovered that the saint has risen to heaven unnoticed. Only his garment remains. It is the chrysalis left behind as the butterfly flutters away. Such reports became *Topoi* in the biographies of saints.[76] This meant that Taoism tried to preserve individual life at the very moment it renounced the transcendence of death by the ordinary person through its integration within the larger life of nature. It thus surrendered its central thought, and lost itself as a result. Similar to the frequent descriptions and spatial localizations of paradises, the thesis of the liberation from death by death through the "detachment from the corpse" had concretized old Taoist ideas which had once been symbols. But simultaneously, these ideas were transposed to an immeasurably lower level. As a result, they lost their meaning, at least for the educated. For a while, Taoism could still fascinate some scholars by alchemy, which represented a wholly new, enticing experience. But later, they also were disappointed and turned away. As the Taoist paradises were dragged into this world from distant skies and the remote corners of the earth, they suddenly turned to dust. A wave of nihilism swept over some generations of disillusioned intellectuals, while the ideal conceptions, having been domesticated, took root among the people and began their push toward implementation. All this happened at a time when the entire country was shaken by terrible uprisings, devastated by murderous wars, finally collapsed under the attack of foreign peoples, and sank into chaos.[77]

3 / *REBELLION AND PEACE*

FUSION OF TAOIST AND MOHIST IDEALS

Yet conceptions of the ideal were not only projected into fantastic countries at the edges of the world, to be concretized later and then reintegrated into the world, thus taking on an unbelievable, fairy-tale quality. Already at a very early date, they were also amalgamated with realistic reports concerning distant lands. In spite of occasional superficial similarities, it can be shown that what was originally involved here were more realistic, more politically-oriented forms of ideal conceptions than those we have just considered. Initially, conditions in the distant lands of the Taoists were wholly other-worldly and situated in a space beyond society which became increasingly remote as the sphere of influence of that society extended. They were not really metaphors but rather descriptions of conditions also found inside the self. Something of this sort is already suggested in the previously mentioned journey of King Mu to the realms beyond heaven. It becomes more explicit in later Taoist legends, where the journey to remote lands of happiness becomes a voyage through one's own body, one's own soul.[78] But the connection between ideal conceptions and descriptions of remote regions could also be based on genuine reports which offered a credible alternative to the prevailing social system without also involving the negation of the social order in general. In contrast to those just mentioned, they were thus initially this-worldly and were therefore at first combined with Mohist and Legalist rather than Taoist ideas. Only gradually did Taoism come to take over and then lead the opposition to Confucianism, at least in name. But it was only after the free-floating ideas of other schools had penetrated a Taoism that had become tolerant and now saw Confucianism as its only enemy that such strictly-speaking absurd phenomena as Taoist rebellions, or even Taoist states, became possible. They developed political programs, but the genuinely Taoist element in them was minor. False to its very core, this worldly form of Taoism moved increasingly into the foreground during the Han period and finally manifested itself in the founding of a Taoist church in the second century A.D. whose rigorous organization bore clearly Mohist characteristics.[79] It is in this cast that Taoism finally survived, while its "purer," other-worldly form dissolved into "nothingness," or found a new home in Buddhism. Taoism, which had always been in retreat, took on an aggressive character at that time, and its hidden role in all movements of revolt also increased. During the first few centuries A.D., however, we still encounter a variety of mixed forms, presenting combinations of this-worldly and other-worldly Taoism. Later, this became increasingly rare. In the description of distant, ideal countries there is, on the one hand, the attempt to assign paradises a specific geographic location (as we have noted). On the other, we find an effort to lend paradisiacal attributes to countries that really existed. For a long time, the idea of the "island" as a place of happiness seemed the ideal compromise. While situated on earth, it was yet adequately detached from it. But as the world began to shrink still further, an even more ideal place was discovered. It was the "cave," or better, the world, the "heaven" *beyond* the cave. For the "cave" was even closer to earth than the island. Like the latter, it could also be connected with the idea of the "mountain," that old place of refuge for the Taoists. Yet it was also other-worldly and, being much more difficult to discover, its magic could not as easily be lost as that of the island.

To find the right place for the ideals of "this-worldly" Taoism, it is necessary to first go back to the older, unmixed sources. The most astonishing document in this connection is a description of the land "Great Ch'in" *(Ta-Ch'in)* in the official *History of the Later Han Dynasty (Hou-Han-shu).* Geographically, this country can be readily identified as the Roman Empire, as was done by Chinese scholars since early times. The significant passages of this account read as follows:

> The area of the Ta-Ch'in empire comprises several thousand square miles with more than 400 cities and some ten smaller dependent states. Cities and fortifications there are built of stone, even the postal stations are firmly constructed of brick. . . . The capital has a circumference of more than 100 miles. In its center lie five palaces, each ten miles away from the next. All buildings have columns of mountain crystal, the same material they use for their dishes. The king of the country moves to a different palace every day to hear what is new. Five days complete a round. He sees to it that his chariot is always followed by a man carrying a bag in his hand. When someone comes to present a case, he notes the matter on a slip of paper which he then places into the bag. As soon as the king arrives at the palace of the day, he has the bag opened, studies the individual cases, and finds out what is true and what is false. In every palace, a large number of officials and archives are at his disposal. In addition, there are 36 generals *(chiang),* all of whom participate in councils of state. But to help him, the king does not rely exclusively on career officials but also on a group of carefully chosen sages. When natural catastrophes or unusual phenomena occur, or when wind and rain do not come at the proper time, the king immediately dismisses them and replaces them with others. But the men who are thus removed from their offices consider their dismissal as extremely agreeable and do not harbor the slightest grudge. As regards its size and uniform order *(p'ing cheng),* the people of that country are on the same level as the Middle

Kingdom. For this reason, the country is called Ta-Ch'in. . . . The character of the people there is one of exceptional honesty: on the market, two different prices do not exist, grain and other foodstuffs are always cheap. The country has riches in abundance. When envoys from neighboring countries come to the borders, they travel on postal horses to the royal capital. Upon their arrival, they are given gold and silver as presents. Their king had always wanted to establish ambassadorial relations with the Han Chinese, but the Parthians wanted [to continue] trading Chinese silk with [the Romans]. They therefore closed their borders and permitted no one to pass. In the 9th year of the reign title "diffused splendor" under the emperor Huan-ti (A.D. 166), however, the king of Ta-Ch'in sent Antonius an ambassador via Jih-nan. . . . This established contact for the first time. According to other reports, "light water" and quicksands[80] are said to extend to the west of this country almost reaching the abode of the "Queen Mother of the West," not far from the place where the sun dips into the earth. . . . According to still other reports, [the people in Ta-Ch'in are said to have a great many commercial routes]. Every ten miles, there is a postal station where horses are changed; every thirty miles there is an inn. Robbers do not exist and therefore there is no police, only wild animals, tigers and lions, which block the path of travelers and do damage. One is immediately devoured by them unless one joins a caravan of more than one hundred men, and carries weapons. According to another source, there is a "flying bridge," several hundred miles long, [in this country]. Crossing it, one supposedly reaches [the continent] north of the ocean.[81]

This account is revealing in several respects. Although it is found together with descriptions of a number of other countries and states omitted here and which, some imaginative elaborations apart, are demonstrably historical, the admiration expressed in this passage is striking. It is obvious that the scholars who collected news about this country from travelers' stories also tried to hold a mirror up to China—much as the Jesuits and later the philosophers of the Enlightenment did with their idealized image of China in eighteenth-century Europe. In later official dynastic histories, which ordinarily reprint the report of the *History of the Later Han Dynasty* almost verbatim, this tendency, present in the description from the very outset, becomes even more pronounced. The fairy tale-like insertions in the report of *Hou-Han-shu* which tell us that the country lies close to the point where the sun sets, i.e. less "centrally," are explicitly rejected with the remark that sun, moon and stars move across the sky just as they do in China.[82] Furthermore, it is also stated that the coastline in the west follows the same direction as the coast line of China, including the characteristic Shantung peninsula projecting into the Po-hai Ocean.[83] Ta-Ch'in is thus a China whose sides have been switched and which stretches westward. That this is intentional is most persuasively evidenced by the name given the country. The self-designation of the population which decides the name in all other countries has here been cast aside in favor of another name which clearly refers back to China. The dynastic name Ch'in, by which China became well known to the peoples in central and western Asia during the short but powerful reign of Ch'in Shih Huang-ti, is probably also the term from which our word "China" derives. With the addition of "great" *(ta),* a particle we have previously come across and which served the purpose of idealization during the declining Chou and beginning Han periods, it became the term for a country that appeared to represent a "different," a better China to a certain social class. Allowing for the fact that Ch'in evoked the "West," it is certainly no accident that this was done by recourse to the Legalist self-designation of China, a step which could only be a thorn in the side of the Confucians. It emphasized the different nature of the social order (which, characteristically, was also based on "generals"). Yet it seemed appropriate as a model for China, nonetheless.

The Han dynasty declined in a protracted agony extending through the entire second and the beginning of the third century A.D. This was brought about by continuing struggles among the various groups of a newly arisen nobility. The eunuchs also joined in this conflict. At that time, it was actually in the west, not far from the ancestral territory of the old Ch'in dynasty, that a small, "Taoist"-governed state was established. It survived for several decades and adopted many of the ideals of "Great Ch'in." It was situated in what is today Shensi province, and flourished between 186 and 216 A.D. Its founder, Chang Lu, traced his teaching back to Chang (Tao-)ling (?34–?156), the first Taoist "pope," who in turn is considered a descendant of Chang Liang (died in 189 B.C.), a high official of the founding period of the Han dynasty, who figures in the first, historically absolutely reliable reports of Taoist practices designed to prolong life.[84] As with Chang (Tao-)ling, the essence of Chang Lu's teaching was the combination of physical well-being and morality in a very conspicuous way. He preached that all diseases were sent by spirits as retribution for evil deeds, and that they could consequently be cured by a remorseful confession which had to be embedded in a larger ceremonial. For cures of this kind, Chang Lu demanded five pecks of rice. This custom gave this politico-religious sect its name. It entered history as "The Way of the Five Pecks of Rice" *(Wu-tou-mi).*

The gradual transformation of the enthusiastic disciples of a miracle healer into the population of a new state—a not atypical phenomenon that recurred in later, politico-religious movements—gave rise to a number of organizational forms vividly reminiscent of both the ideals of the Mohist school and the ideal image of "Great Ch'in" just described. The Mohist component is manifest in the belief in spirits—also promoted by Mo Ti for practical reasons—the disciplined, military rather than bureaucratic administration by "teachers" and sacrificial priests, the nonetheless pacific attitude and, most importantly, the "socialist" public institutions. Among these latter, the "community homes" should be mentioned. They seem to have constituted a kind of center of public life. Foreigners could eat there free of charge. Food was placed in front of these houses, and people could take as much as they pleased. The curious punishments which were not meted out until three warnings had been given also served the public weal. They consisted of the imposition of construction work on public roads, and specified the distance, such as one hundred steps, for example, over which this labor had to be carried out. From time to time the sacrificial priests also called on people to "confess" *(tzu-yin),* where participants made known their mistakes and then voluntarily reported for work on road construction.[85]

The connection between all these institutions and the ideal of "Great Ch'in" is really indirect, but nonetheless clear. It is closest in some identically sounding terms for administrative units and in the description of the inns at the postal stations of "Great Ch'in" in a version of the official *History of the Three Kingdoms (San-kuo-chih),*[86] where the "community houses" can easily be recognized in these inns. But the indirect connection is much more sophisticated. For in the description of "Great Ch'in," we have an account of the other half of Mo Ti's ideal state, one half of which had already been realized by Chang Lu. This includes the information constantly supplied the emperor by the collection of songs and "rumors" on the streets, and an elective monarchy. Citing the example of the earliest holy emperors, Mo Ti had advocated this institution in opposition to Confucian hereditary monarchy, which was based on the idea of the family.

We have already encountered the curious combination of Mohist and Taoist thought in the ideal conception of the state in Ho Hsiu's sketch and in the *Li-yün* chapter of the *Li-chi.*[87] It is most evident in some sections of the book *Spring and Autumn of Lü Pu-wei (Lü-shih ch'un-ch'iu).* Interestingly enough, this work is attributed to Ch'in Shih Huang-ti's illegitimate father, but actually consists of texts of the fourth century B.C. and later, and may be considered a reservoir of the most diverse Taoist mixed forms. In a passage consisting of a string of anecdotes testifying to Mohist influence, elective monarchy is justified in the following terms: "[The sage emperor] Yao had ten sons, and yet he gave [the empire] to none of them but to [the sage emperor] Shun. Shun had nine sons, and yet he gave [the empire] to none of them, but to [the sage emperor] Yü. That was 'public spirit at its best' *(chih kung).*"[88]

In the selection of officials also, the welfare of the community, not personal connections, determine who is the right man for the right office. This principle is glorified in an anecdote which follows directly the section just quoted:

> Prince P'ing of Chin asked Ch'i Huang-yang: "I have no one to head the Nan-yang district; who could fill this post?" "Hsieh Hu could," Ch'i answered. "Isn't he your arch enemy?" Prince P'ing asked [in astonishment]. Ch'i said: "Your Majesty asked who might fill the post, and not who my arch enemy is." "Very well," Prince P'ing said. He appointed Hsieh Hu, and the people in the country praised him for his choice. Some time later, the prince again asked Ch'i for advice. "I need a colonel for the army of the state. Who would be best qualified?" "Ch'i Wu would," was the answer. "But isn't that your son?" asked Prince P'ing. "Your Majesty asked me who could fill the post, not who my son is." "Very well," Prince P'ing said. He also appointed Ch'i Wu, and the people praised his choice. When Confucius heard about this, he exclaimed: "Truly, the councils of Ch'i Huang-yang were marvelous. When he recommended someone outside his family, he did not even pass over his

> arch enemy, and when he recommended someone within his family, not even his own son. It can truly be said of Ch'i that he had 'public spirit.' "[89]

The following story where Confucius can no longer be the star witness, but the hero is quite openly introduced as a Mohist, makes the point still more incisively:

> Among the Mohists there was a "great man" *(chü-tzu)* by the name of Fu T'uan, who lived in Ch'in. When his only son committed a murder, King Hui of Ch'in said to him: "You are quite an old man and have no other sons. I have therefore ordered that no execution will take place. I request that you obey me in this matter." Fu T'uan replied: "Master Mo made the law: 'He who kills someone, dies; he who injures someone, is given physical punishment. This is done to prevent murder and injury.' Now, the highest justice of the state lies in the prevention of murder and injury. Even though Your Majesty has done me a favor by setting aside the execution, I cannot but obey Mo Ti's law." And he did not obey the king but killed his son himself. A son is something that is the personal property of a person. Since he sacrificed what was his property to make "highest justice" prevail, one can say of this "great man" that he had "public spirit."[90]

"Public spirit" *(kung)*—an expression that originally meant "prince" but already at an early date took on the more general meaning of "governmental," "of the state,"—is glorified here in a way that already carries a nuance of Legalism. It is therefore probably no accident that this anecdote relates events occurring in Ch'in. And yet, the puritanical strictness of this "great man," as the functionaries of the Mo Ti school called themselves, reveals an attitude that may well have been similar to what animated the sacrificial priests of the "Five Pecks of Rice Taoists" when they called upon others to examine their conscience. The purely Taoist rationale for what was originally the fundamental Mohist virtue of "public spirit," and which was rediscovered by a this-worldly Taoism, is thus not absent from the *Spring and Autumn of Lü Pu-wei.* The first statement connects with Lao-tzu's *Tao-te-ching,* where the impersonality, indeed the "inhumanity" of heaven and earth is discussed in Chapter 5.[91] The second is simply put in the mouth of the "Yellow Emperor" who, as previously mentioned, became increasingly important during the Han period as the personification of a Taoism intent on prolonging life, and finally merged with Lao-tzu in the figure of the god Huang-lao: "Heaven does not cover from personal motives, the earth does not bear from personal motives, the sun and the moon do not shine from personal motives, the four seasons do not create from personal motives. . . . Therefore the Yellow Emperor said: 'Excess (literally 'double') of sounds (music), of colors (sexuality), of garments, of fragrances, of the pleasures of the palate, and of dwelling places shall be forbidden.' "[92]

This warning against excess again plays an important role among the "Five Pecks of Rice Taoists." Those, for example, who ate more of the food placed in the "community houses" than was necessary to satisfy their hunger had to expect that the all-knowing spirits would visit illnesses upon them.[93] For "public spirit" was not merely the all-pervasive principle of society, but also the principle of nature. This is again made clear in the following passage from the *Lü-shih ch'un-ch'iu:*

> The sage kings of the early age always considered public spirit as the most important thing in government. When public spirit prevails, the world is at peace *(p'ing):* Peace derives from public spirit. . . . The world does not belong to a single individual, but belongs to the world. Yin and Yang in their harmony do not prefer a single species, the sweet dew and the rain coming at the right time do not give priority to any one creature. Therefore the ruler of the tenthousand fold people must not favor any one person. . . . A man from the state of Ching once lost his bow. He did not go looking for it, but merely said: "A man from Ching lost it, and a man from Ching will find it. Why bother looking for it?" When Confucius heard about this, he said: "If he had omitted the word 'Ching,' he would have been right." But when Lao-tzu heard [the two remarks], he said: "Only if he had also omitted the word 'man' would he have been [really] right." Thus Lao-tzu expressed the highest form of public spirit *(chih-kung).*[94]

"HIGHEST PEACE" AND MILITARY EQUALITY

The concept of "public spirit" *(kung)* is developed with so much temperament in the book *Spring and Autumn of Lü Pu-wei* that there is some justification for having called the work the starting point of a "socialist" tradition in China.[95] It bears an interesting relation to the concept of "equality." In the *Li-yün* chapter of the *Li-chi,* where a Confucian tinge is noticeable, the two terms are used interchangeably. Because what is really a Mohist term, *kung,* is stressed at the expense of the Taoist colored *t'ung,* the Mohist component emerges more clearly than in the glorification of the age of the "Great Equality" in a text which is Confucian *de jure.* Yet the *Lü-shih ch'un-ch'iu* is usually considered a Taoist text. Still more important in this connection, however, is the reference to another concept which also played an indirect role in the account of the ideal given in the *Li-yün* chapter, the concept of "peace." For it will be remembered that the stage described there after the age of "Great Equality" was called the period of the "Small Peace" *(hsiao-k'ang).* Admittedly, the ideal condition where the "public spirit" is raised to a principle of government is not called by the name of "small" peace, but of peace generally. Nor is this kind of peace rendered by the concept *k'ang,* which has the connotation of "health," but by the concept *p'ing,* whose basic meaning is "level," "equally high." In this key concept (which appears in the *Lü-shih ch'un-ch'iu* in another passage dealing with the almost magical effect of music where it is provided with the epithet "highest" or "great" *t'ai*), two fundamental themes coincide. Whatever its stamp or nuance, and this includes Legalism which primarily paid homage to the "Great Order," peace and equality are the two motifs that Chinese thought invariably associated with the idea of an ideal society. In the concept *t'ai-p'ing*, the "Highest Peace," used by the most strongly conflicting intellectual currents in the course of Chinese history, there is discernible the shadowy shape of an idea concerning a kind of entropy in nature and society which would automatically lead to universal peace by the elimination of all inequalities (naturally, opinions regarding its form differed widely).

It is presumably also in the just-mentioned passage in the *Lü-shih ch'un-ch'iu* that the concept *t'ai-p'ing* makes its first appearance,[96] for a section in *Chuang-tzu* where *t'ai p'ing* is also mentioned has all the earmarks of a text from the Han period which was added later.[97] In the Ch'in dynasty, on the other hand, the idea of the "Higher Peace" had apparently already become general knowledge. On a marker which Ch'in Shih Huang-ti had put up in 210 B.C., in any event, the expression already appears with its full meaning and, characteristically, as a term whose sense parallels "rules that make equal": ". . . men rejoice in rules that make equal, they congratulate each other on the preservation of the Highest Peace."[98] The repeatedly quoted historical work *Shih-chi*, which gives the inscription, also confers the qualities of "Highest Peace" on the age of the five sage emperors (although, perhaps intentionally, it renders the term "highest" by a variant).[99] Around the middle of the second century B.C. when this book was written, a great many philosophers and politicians were already attempting to monopolize this concept: Tung Chung-shu, for example, used it in the description of the mild natural phenomena occurring in a well-governed empire:

> During the time of "Highest Peace," the wind never becomes a storm; it merely opens the capsules and scatters the seed. The rain does not gouge the soil but merely dampens the leaves and wets the roots. Thunder terrifies no one but merely commands and stirs people to act. Lightning blinds no one, but merely shines and shows things in radiant brightness. The vaporous dew does not hinder sight, but merely brings some dampness and lies lightly [on the leaves]. Snow does not block the hills, but merely covers sadness and disperses poisons. The clouds appear in all five colors, and bring blessing. Rain falls [only] for three days, yet fecundates everything. The dew forms into pearls and provides juices. [For] when the saint above holds the reins of government in his hands, Yin and Yang are in harmony, and the wind and the rain come at their proper time.[100]

Certain periods of rule, especially that of the emperor Wen-ti (governed 179–156 B.C.) were declared periods of "Highest Peace" by the historians even if the atmospheric phenomena noted by Tung Chung-shu did not occur. The sceptical philosopher Wang Ch'ung (927–91) viewed them as a wholly unnecessary mystification of the *T'ai-p'ing* condition, which could only be socially defined.[101] Yet the attainment of ideal conditions on earth continued to be associated with favorable weather, for it is a fact that happiness (which depends in part on material factors) is not really conceivable without it. Due to this frequent and often rather superficial use, the concept naturally lost precision.

Already during the Han period, it frequently meant no more than "abundant harvest," as had been Tung Chung-shu's usage.[102]

But in addition to the established powers of government, very rebellious forces also used the term "Highest Peace" as the ideal to be achieved by their movements. While the conservatives were more concerned with the "peace" component, the revolutionaries were interested in the aspect of equality. That the term "peace," *p'ing* retained its connection with the original idea "level," is proven most conclusively in the description of the "Northend" land in *Lieh-tzu.* Here, not only social equality prevails, but "the territory is also completely level in all four directions." It was situated to the "north of the Ch'i country," i.e. to the north of that province which was not merely a center of Taoism generally, but a center of that very form of Taoism which had made the problem of "equality" its special concern. All this shows the close connection between egalitarian desires in Taoism, and the concept of "Highest Peace." This is not to say, of course, that the revolutionaries were not interested in "peace," but for them peace was not defined merely by calm, but also by equality. Without the latter, peace was merely a deceptive quiescence to them. Thus they expected struggle to create the presuppositions for genuine, i.e. the "Highest Peace."

These considerations lie in back of one of the greatest popular rebellions of the older China, the rebellion of the "Yellow Turbans," which erupted in the region of what had been the state of Ch'in, in 184 A.D.[103] The uprising of these wild bands, which wore the color yellow to honor the divinity of the Yellow Emperor, could be quickly suppressed, but led to the final collapse of the Han dynasty. Its leader was Chang Chio. He was thus a member of the Chang family which had maintained a particularly close contact with Taoism dating back to Chang Liang's time, and extending to the present day. Like Chang Lu somewhat later, he had gathered about him a huge band of followers by using uncommon methods of healing. His ready success is ascribable to a time when natural catastrophes and pestilences raged throughout the country and often drove the population away from their homes. He called his method of healing the "Way of the Highest Peace" *(t'ai-p'ing-tao).* It was purely magical and not associated with a particular social morality, as was true of Chang Lu, yet bore a clear relationship to the ideal state of "Great-Ch'in." It is known that Chang Chio organized his bands in purely military fashion under thirty-six generals carrying the title *fang.* Further subdivisions were headed by "great" and "small" generals *(ta-fang, hsiao-fang).* On himself, he conferred the title "Heavenly Prince General," and on his two brothers the titles "Prince General of Earth" and "Prince General of Men."

In this military organization of the "Yellow Turbans," we can observe a phenomenon which countless later instances proved to be the most important characteristic of Chinese popular movements. Interestingly enough, its basis was not so much the particularly militant posture of whatever world views might lie in back of them, but rather the invariant fundamental attitude of an always identical opponent, i.e. Confucianism. For in China only Legalism had military tendencies from the very beginning, while the Mohist tradition was ambivalent. Actually, it was really anti-militaristic, against "wars of aggression." Only because it wanted to fight "wars of aggression" by increased defensive measures did the warlike element play a certain indirect role. It is only natural that the quietist and individualist ideals of Taoism originally implied an even lesser degree of militarism. Only when it partially renounced its desire to escape from the world and inadvertently moved close first to Legalism and later to Mohism did the latent militaristic elements of the two doctrines it absorbed intensify. But, as mentioned before, the real reason was clearly the common rejection of an unshakably civilian Confucianism. Something had to be found that would counterbalance the Confucian model of society which used the family as its base and thus provided an example of the combination of equality and inequality that was difficult to improve upon. The small band of the aged provided the apex, the mass of the young the base of the pyramid. Due to the passage of time, there took place a constant flow from below to above, making yesterday's young the old of tomorrow. The only alternative to this hierarchical order was (and still is) the order of the military, although in a sense conditions here are inverted. Among men whose equality seems to manifest itself in their uniform (even if it consists of a yellow turban wrapped around the head, as in the case of the "Yellow Turbans"), it is not the older but the stronger that is the natural leader (and this may well mean the younger). The upward movement within the hierarchy is not so much a question of time, of the ability to wait, as it is one of personal achievement and activity. The difficulty always was and continues to be that "an empire can be conquered on horseback, but cannot be governed from it" (as a politician formulated it after the founding of the Han dynasty).[104] It therefore happened regularly in popular movements that the principle of military organization was gradually forgotten after victory had been won. The warriors with their rough customs were only too inclined to give up their real aims once they had reached their immediate goal, the seizure of power. Usually they soon came to feel that their dress and weapons were absurdly anachronistic once peace had been secured. Willy-nilly, they switched to a civilian principle of order which promised a permanence of power and a calm rule in their old age, something the military did not provide.

Of course, most popular rebellions were defeated long before they had a chance to implement their concept of governmental structure. While Chang Lu had been able to govern his state for thirty years before he was defeated by the legendary and invincible general Ts'ao Ts'ao (155–220), Chang Chio's revolt was crushed in the year it erupted, although it had been prepared for a long time. Chang Chio had chosen this year because it initiated a new sexagenary cycle in the naming of years. Contrary to his hopes, however, it did not bring a new beginning, but only his own end.

In the historical works which passed through the hands of the Confucians, of course, we find only imprecise references to his real plan of action and, with the exception of those noted, hardly any remarks concerning his political program.[105] But although it is not complete, a work belonging to the Taoist tradition and composed in Ch'i has come down to us. It seems to contain the teachings of the "Yellow Turbans" in addition to many later documents of "Vulgarized Taoism." In any event, its title *Classic of the Highest Peace (T'ai-p'ing-ching)*[106] suggests this. It has also been documented that a book with this title played an important role among the "Yellow Turbans," although this does not mean too much, for already under the rule of the Emperor Ch'eng-ti (governed 32–7 B.C.) a book with a similar (longer) title had been turned in at the court and rejected as heretical, a procedure which was repeated under Emperor Shun-ti (governed 126–144). Yet the work, as we have it today, and in spite of its heterogeneous contents and alien formal aspects traceable to Buddhism (particularly the dialogues between teacher and disciples not known in pre-Buddhist China in this form) belongs to the few early sources which convey at least an approximate idea of the conceptual framework of the popular leaders. For this reason, it became the object of a good deal of Asian research during the last twenty years. Particularly noteworthy among these investigations are those carried out in present-day China.[107] To what extent these ideals may have prepared those of contemporary China is a question that tended to be answered affirmatively up to 1965, and usually negatively after that date. It is actually possible to adduce arguments on both sides. For on the one hand, a great number of documents point to an eschatological picture of the world, to the expectation of a renewal of society through the intervention of heaven, which would send envoys to change the course of history. On the other, the expected ideal condition has a hierarchical structure which merely eliminates the old class oppositions to posit new ones. Since an emperor would also continue to rule, things begin to look quite familiar on closer inspection. The suspicion of contemporary Chinese scholars that crafty Confucian officials were the real authors of the *T'ai-p'ing-ching* and then proceeded to attribute it to the unsuspecting, rebellious peasants in order to give the popular movement a conservative turn from the very beginning, is therefore as justified as the sober judgment of a western sinologist: "To my personal disappointment it turns out . . . , that the *T'ai-p'ing-ching* is anything other than 'revolutionary' in the modern sense of that word. In its way, its loyalty to the emperor is total. He is a kind of unique superman and forms the hub of the universe, just as he did in Tung Chung-shu."[108]

This characterization does indeed go to the heart of the problem. It is not necessary to assume that the *Classic of the Highest Peace* represents a Confucian fabrication. Yet it must be admitted that the direction taken since Tsou Yen and Tung Chung-shu, where the distinctions between man and nature were obscured by explaining historical events scientifically and natural phenomena as human, had penetrated so deeply into Taoism that it lost much of its former flexibility. The tendency to always see a uniformly functioning organism in the cosmos, in society, and in history, and the associated, pernicious compulsion to incessantly weave a network of correspondences which not only failed to result in new insights but actually prevented them, also turned conceptions of an ideal state into frozen clichés. These clichés necessarily had a similarity with those of the Confucians, because the "scientific" basis of both was the same. It was the duality of Yin and Yang, the trinity of heaven, earth and man, the fivefold nature of earth, wood, metal, fire and water, and similar rigid models. This is the reason the *T'ai-p'ing-ching* contains far fewer descriptions of an ideal world than one might at first expect. One of the most fruitful can be found in the answer of a master to the naive question of a group of disciples concerning the real value of Taoist writings of the kind represented by the *T'ai-p'ing-ching:*

> "Since [you], the heavenly master *(t'ien-shih),* are about to leave, and it is not certain when you will return, we should like to ask one or two more questions in order to resolve our doubts." "Go on, speak up quickly. I have gone to a lot of trouble all day long, as it is. What things do you want to inquire about?" "We should like to ask something regarding the Taoist texts which you, illumined master *(ming-shih),* have given us disciples. What we are about to say may appear immodest and irrelevant. But if we do not ask the question now, we will not know the answer in all eternity." "Speak up, don't restrain yourself!" "Are you then, illumined master, prepared to instruct us stupid disciples?" "Yes, of course." "Now then, what is the value of the Taoist texts that you have given us latterly?" "Really, your stupidity is excessive! Do you mean to say that my Tao can be weighed? Yes? You want the price of everything I explained to you in order to enlighten you, and give you a profound insight into the values of the heavenly Tao? Now, if I had given you one thousand pounds of gold instead of all this so that you might use it on behalf of the state, would you then be able to give heaven and earth a joyful heart and bring it about by the alignment of Yin and Yang that natural catastrophes and bad omens disappear, that the rulers [like divine] emperors and kings attain a high age, and that the government enters the phase of the 'Highest Peace?' (*T'ai-p'ing; shang-p'ing,* according to a variant reading.) If I had given you ten thousand precious stones so that you might invest them for the state, or hoard them as valuables in order thus to possess 'worldly treasures,' do you think that you could then bring it about that the fluids of the 'Great Harmony' *(t'ai-ho)* reveal themselves in all the six directions of heaven, that auspicious omens appear everywhere, and that the barbarian tribes retreat ten thousand miles without doing any damage? But with the means of the 'Way' I gave you, you can bring it about that a divine ruler *(ti-wang)* brings a joyful mood to heaven and earth, that the band of ministers roundabout is content, that pure joy prevails even among worms and flies, that the barbarian tribes submit, that auspicious omens appear everywhere, that natural catastrophes and accidents stop altogether, that vitality increases everywhere in the land and the people become extremely old. If you can be charitable and kind with circumspection and thoughtfully put my writings into deeds, you will find an echo everywhere, even if you only grasp what is most essential. It will be as if laws were taken seriously or customs followed, and no one will wish to dissociate himself from you. You will accomplish great things, . . . I have spoken in the name of Heaven, and have not deceived you. If, with the help of the heavenly law, you now help a

ruler who is virtuous, if you bring it about that he does not suffer harm but goes about joyful all his days, what price can one put on that? Have you stupid fellows understood, or not?" "We have." "Well, then, in that case I will explain something else to you. Of all the love, kindness and pleasure a man can experience in this world, nothing is more beautiful than the love of a woman. If it is granted him, and the two have a child together, they are fused in a single heart in the child, which is truly the most pleasing thing love and kindness can give, and this will always be a bond between them. Now, even if you could make a present of ten thousand men to a state, all of whom were joyful and happy so that whoever saw them forgot that he himself ages, would you then perhaps bring peace between heaven and earth which is like the love between a man and a woman, would you bring joy and conciliation to the ten thousand states, and bring it about that a joyful echo resounds in the eight distant regions, and the 'Highest Peace' descends on the world? My 'Way' can still the infinite Heaven above and bring the infinite earth below to surrender. There would be no one in the eight regions of Heaven that would not come running joyfully to submit, none even among the rebellious who would not feel overcome by this shaping of virtue, and who would not try to find a place for himself. Can you discover in your innermost self whether a 'price' has any meaning here? If you wish to repay the delight of having understood the mind of Heaven, which has become yours through the great blessed gift of Heaven, hurry to repay it with my writings. Even if you could succeed through the deceptions of magic to pile up the greatest treasures so that they would form real columns under the sky, Heaven would not rejoice because you would not yet have found the real heart of Heaven. If you wish to find the heart of Heaven, think from morning till night about the words in my writings, and as soon as you have discovered their meaning, you will have found the heart of Heaven. What should be the price for this? Therefore: if you make a present of one thousand gold pieces to a state, that has less value than a single important word from these writings, with which one can govern. And if you give ten thousand precious stones to a state, that is worth less than when you bring it two great sages. Ha, with the valuable 'Way' of important words and great sages, one can bring it about that the divine ruler sleeps peacefully on his pillow, and yet preserves order, that he spreads the greatest joy and yet brings about the 'Highest Peace,' that he eliminates natural catastrophes and [bad] mutations, and brings calm to the world. That is what the mysterious 'Way' of important words and great sages brings about. What price should this have? Therefore: the holy and wise divine rulers of antiquity never had insufficient money or possessions, yet always worried that they might lack scholars, and worried that the great sages did not come hurrying to them, and that the people might not gather around them. . . . But when you reflect carefully on these writings, the great sages will come by themselves, and together with them you will help a ruler govern. On the one morning where you will counsel with him, the people will come streaming into the capital as on the morning of a market day. The ten thousand creatures will come in throngs, as will all the treasures men try to find all over the world. If you can put my writings into deeds, Heaven and earth will be transformed into brightness, the sun, the moon and the stars will double their radiance, the splendor will penetrate as far as the eight corners of the sky and will also be seen by the four barbarian tribes, who will come joyfully without exception, and submit. Sages and scholars will emerge everywhere, and never withdraw again; weapons and armor will be thrown away, people will let their arms hang by their sides and only put them together for greetings, but no longer use them to hurt one another. Thinking alike, *(t'ung),* people will only do good, and all will delight the divine ruler. That is what my writings can bring about. So what shall be their price? Do you finally understand? Therefore: the saints and sages of antiquity cared only about the profound knowledge of the values of the 'Way' and of the 'Peace' *(p'ing)* of the fluids. Therefore they did not simply appear to bring harmony to earth, but only joined a ruler who really possessed 'virtue,' . . . therefore they honored the 'Way' and highly esteemed 'virtue.' But the stupid people think that the deceptions of magic are something real, and therefore Heaven does not send down writings, and saints and sages place themselves at no one's disposal. That is what I want to say. Therefore, pay heed. My words are no deception, pay heed to my 'Way.' If someone carries around valuables, precious stones, and gold pieces, to do something with them, he will still be sitting upright in the darkness and watch them and will not bring himself to fall asleep. If that is true where only a few valuables are at stake, what should one say if it is a question of secret diagrams and books which pass on those treasures of Heaven with whose help one can bring peace to Heaven and earth, to the six endpoints and the eight distant regions? Therefore, when you leave, be doubly careful!" "Yes, yes." "Spirit messengers from Heaven *(t'ien shen-li)* will always be sitting next to my writings to guard them. Therefore, pay great attention to them." "Yes, yes." "My writings will always be followed by a spirit messenger of three-fold illumination, who will observe them with his radiant glance." "Yes, yes." "For my writings are the heart of Heaven, its real meaning. Try to think carefully about that as you fathom all these subtle things." "Yes, yes." When you have managed to obey my words, I will reveal other things to you, which you have not seen as yet." "Yes, yes." "What has left my mouth and entered your ears you must not tell everyone, but only a virtuous ruler. When such a divine ruler grasps these teachings, the entire empire will submit to him, spirits and spiritual powers will help him govern through you. Of themselves, men will consider him the best, and not a single day will have passed after he takes command, and they will already adapt themselves to him of their own accord." "Yes, yes. The six of us disciples, however stupid and limited we may be, will certainly not speak carelessly and break the command of silence. But now, since we have all said 'yes,' to the revelations of the divine Heaven concerning the 'Way' and 'virtue' as you have conveyed them to us, and have said 'yes' to the valuable tools a divine ruler will use to take measures which will remain in force for ten thousand times ten thousand years, will you also reveal to us all the esoteric matters without passing anything over in silence? If we should really be privileged humbly to receive all these strict doctrines and secret commands, we would not dare say anything about them." "Yes. But if I now present to you thoughts of the divine Heaven, it is on the condition that you will reveal everything when the time has come, and not dare keep back something for yourselves. But if you cannot reveal it, you should not dare misuse your knowledge for evil deeds. The deeds of Heaven and earth all have their established order. If, after examining whether the time has come, you make known my revelation, what is right will have an everlasting effect and the state will attain the Great Happiness, and there will be no danger. Therefore do not follow a 'small person,' but only a divine ruler. The order of the divine ruler consists in this, that his heart is always the same as that of Heaven and earth. That is the reason he can do things here, while the 'small man' can accomplish nothing. Therefore superior persons consider it their duty to follow such a divine individual."[109]

TAOIST MESSIANISM

It is really necessary to expose oneself to connected sections of this *Classic of the Highest Peace* to sense the entirely different climate which gave rise to them. The language is much more relaxed, but has a curious urgency for that very reason. In contrast to all the quotations we have examined heretofore, the persons speaking now are not detached philosophers but religious leaders who also wanted to be political leaders. An air of conspiracy hovers over all of this. But it is a conspiracy which still accepts traditional ideas concerning the changeover from one dynasty to the next. The passing on of a book by a mysterious person sent from Heaven as the first indication of an imminent dynastic change has a tradition which can be traced back to the beginning of the Han dynasty at least, and was closely connected with Taoism in particular. The previously mentioned ancestor of the first Taoist pope, Chang Liang, for example, was given a book about military strategy by an old man who called himself "Master of the Yellow Stone."[110] This allegedly happened at a time when the Ch'in dynasty was still flourishing. The book had the title, *Strategy of the T'ai-kung (T'ai-kung ping-fa),* and the advice it contained is supposed to have contributed to bringing the first Han emperor to power. The "Master of the Yellow Stone" revealed himself as a manifestation of the element earth, which is the element under which, according to a widely accepted, older belief, the Han dynasty governed. The words he is said to have spoken when he passed on the book, and according to which he, Chang Liang, would help a "divine" *(ti)* king assume the government, bear an astonishing resemblance to the prophecies which are also at the center of the initiation in the section of the *T'ai-p'ing-ching* quoted above. Besides, the connection with military ideas becomes apparent there also in a twofold manner. For the book of the "Master of the Yellow Stone" is not merely a work about military strategy. The personality to whose tradition the book is assigned by its title, T'ai-kung (Wang),[111] the teacher of the founder of the Chou dynasty, King Wen, was himself very much of a warrior. The stories which came to be told about him show him as a figure that differed considerably from the mild Confucian ideal image most clearly represented by his counterpart, the "duke of Chou." T'ai-kung Wang is severe and implacable, he represents the type of councillor *prior* to the seizure of power, and therefore understands struggle and punishment. Nor does he fear a fiery catastrophe for he sees a new, better society arising from its ashes.

In its fundamental ideas, the conceptions of popular Taoism hardly differed from those of a Confucianism for the educated, as represented by Tung Chung-shu, for example. They also can be traced back to the conviction that the heavenly mandate is periodically transferred from one ruling family to another; that such a change of rulers manifests itself not only in society but also in nature, and that a new order has to be preceded by a period of decline and chaos. There was a difference in emphasis, however. For Confucianism, these transitional periods were exceptions. It was important to return as quickly as possible to "normal," peaceful times. But for the Taoists, they were the most important phases of human history, times when the wall separating this world and the beyond became transparent, when heavenly emissaries peopled the world and where it was precisely from the most profound misfortune and the most destructive struggle that the "Highest Peace" might be born. Differing in this respect from the Confucians, they did not see the rule of the "Highest Peace" as simply the rise of a new dynasty, but rather as the dawn of a mystical order where the new ruler established harmony between nature and society. He would establish a "heavenly government," and be supported by a staff of sages whose function was determined with precision. Mankind would become a "child" of heaven and earth, the fruit of their mutual love.

The next, the decisive step consisted in connecting this divine spark arising from the loving contact of heaven and earth, and which made the trinity of heaven, earth and man into a kind of divine family, with the name of Lao-tzu. The first unquestionable documentation of this development is provided by an inscription dating from the year A.D. 165. It is the famous "Lao-tzu inscription" *(Lao-tzu ming)* of a Taoist minister, Pien, from the fief of Ch'en.[112] Here Lao-tzu is praised as a figure "which lived before Heaven and earth," "was connected to the fluid of primeval chaos," and descended time and again "to be a teacher to sages."[113] In the previously mentioned book by the Taoist Ko Hung, *Biographies of Gods and Immortals* which was written at least one or two centuries later, this thought already appears in a developed form. A list of thirteen "councillors" is presented who—like T'ai-kung and Chang Liang—and apparently independently of each other—assisted the founders of dynasties. In reality, however, they were nothing other than the manifestation of Lao-tzu who had been made over into a divine force and saw to the periodic renewal of the world in this form.[114]

During the three centuries following the collapse of the Han dynasty, Taoism saw its expectations become reality, for the period did indeed seem one of endlessly prolonged chaos and transition. The empire disintegrated progressively, small dynasties which mostly only ruled a fraction of the country and were often supported by non-Chinese tribes that had invaded the north and the west, followed each other in rapid succession. As if under a spell, the expectation of the ever more uprooted, increasingly miserable masses was directed toward the future, which surely could not fail to bring salvation after the countless disappointments it had endured. Undoubtedly under the influence of foreign religions, particularly Buddhism and Manicheanism, the first genuinely messianic conceptions arose. The later sections of the *Classic of the Highest Peace* abound in mysterious promises. There is one chapter where the cycle of the ages according to Tung Chung-shu's principle of the "Three Systems" *(San-t'ung)* is briefly recalled, and then a group of disciples asks the "master" for the name and origin of the expected redeemer. Besides some enigmatic hints concerning the principal dates of a life that still lay in the future (presented in cyclical signs and thus not unambiguously fixed), the name of Li Yao-ching is given.[115] According to traditional belief, Lao-tzu himself had had the family name of Li. The personal name Yao-ching simply means "radiating splendor." According to other documents, however, this reincarnation of Lao-tzu was to bear the name of Li Hung (*hung* means "far").[116] It is obvious that all these revelations did not have much content. They merely led the various rebel leaders to choose appropriate names and to observe certain dates for initiating actions, so that they might correspond to known prophecies (a practice which had already been followed by Chang Chio). Rebels who had the perfectly ordinary name of Li Hung (which is about as original as the American "John Smith," since Li is demonstrably the most frequent family name and the word *hung* was also often used as a personal name) appear time and again in Chinese history. Generally speaking, the family name of Li was a considerable asset to a revolutionary during the period extending from the second to the seventh century A.D., which was so strongly marked by popular Taoism. The founders of the T'ang dynasty (618–906), which was the first to unify China for an extended period, bore the family name of Li and derived considerable benefit from the hope of the people that they would bring peace to the empire because Lao-tzu was incarnate in them.

It was consequently not the desire for greater social equality that caused the fanaticism at the core of all the religious and political uprisings of the people. The greed and egoism of the ruler, denounced time and again in the *T'ai-p'ing-ching*, are primarily viewed as an offense against nature which impedes the eternal flow of gifts sent to men by heaven and earth. What fired the rebelling masses much more was really a positive feeling: the mystical conviction of their own election, which gave them the illusion of invulnerability, and resulted in their frequently becoming all too easy a prey for the troops of the government. Thus the "Yellow Turbans," for example, were unarmed at first. In any event, the *T'ai-p'ing-ching* refers in many passages to "seed people" *(chung-min)*, which are granted a "long life" *(ch'ang-sheng)*. It states that they would emerge unscathed from the unavoidable decimation of the population, and thus provide the seed for a new people in a new time.[117]

We can only guess at the ineffable disappointment which time and again must have seized the bands of ordinary citizens when, deluded by their naive belief, they were cut down one after the other in their fierce struggles with the coldly calculating, much more sober authorities, or with other competing groups that only cared about power politics. In the despair of their final hour, they never failed to be consoled by the pale hope of a redeeming paradise far from this remorseless world. Thus we have two legendary reports concerning the unexplained death of Chang Lu, the leader of the Taoist state. According to one of them,[118] he is said to have died in 217. But when his grave was opened in 259, he is alleged to have lain in his coffin wholly intact. This was interpreted as a sign that he had died only in the sense intended by the doctrine of the "detachment from the corpse,"[119] but had actually entered paradise. According to a second report,[120] Chang Lu ascended directly to heaven in 243, in front of many witnesses. During the uprising of a later rebel, Sun Hsiu, which occurred in 301 and can be placed in the same tradition as those of the "Yellow Turbans," mysterious councillors were involved. It goes without saying that their efforts had no results. They wore feather garments to demonstrate that they had come flying from the paradises of the immortals.[121] And one of Sun Hsiu's descendents, the rebel Sun T'ai, is said not to have been beheaded in 389, as historical works report, but to have fled with his immortal soul to the isles of the blessed.[122] Finally, Sun T'ai's nephew, Sun En, unleashed a powerful rebellion one year later but was utterly defeated in 402, and used the island of Yü-chou off the east coast of China as a base for his operations. Both phonetically and sometimes graphically, the name Yü-chou has been identified as one of the three islands of the blessed. After his last, crushing defeat, he and his closest friends and wives, more than one hundred people altogether, are said to have jumped into the water. Popular belief has it that he returned to the islands of the blessed as a water sprite.[123]

This list could be extended indefinitely. It shows that in a kind of devout, childlike belief, the Chinese people shared the dislike of many other nations for seeing its heroes die. Instead, it moved them to a different world from which a return seemed possible, and to which hopes could be attached. In Chinese popular uprisings, this element of the supernatural is thus one of the most important and characteristic features. The idea of a rebellion was frequently prepared for years, even for decades, in a sort of supernatural space to which only the members of the respective secret societies had access. Unless the timetable was upset by betrayal, this idea ignited events in the world at a definite, numerologically-determined moment. In case of failure, it fizzled and retreated into the supernatural realm, there to await another opportunity. All governmental measures notwithstanding, the tradition of secret societies, which dates back to the "Yellow Turbans," was never wholly interrupted. It suggests that the rebellions, and the conceptions lying in back of them, did not consist of isolated actions or ever newly emerging ideologies, but that they form part of a long tradition. During extended stretches of Chinese history, this tradition merely disappears underground, in catacombs as it were, and thus escapes our observation. This dark side of the Chinese, always suppressed by a sober and enlightened Confucianism which yet could never wholly destroy it, is present in the subliminal hope for an uncertain future and always reasserted itself in times of misery. It is as important in the shaping of the Chinese character as that aspect which is fully visible and involves the incessant exploration of a secure past. During quiet times, of course, this normal everyday regains the upper hand with the same regularity. So far, hardly any texts concerning this current in Chinese history have been translated. To be conscious of it is important not only for a balanced consideration of traditional China's conceptions of the ideal, but at least equally for a just evaluation of such conceptions in contemporary China.[124] It has been said that "the name of Chang Chio defines the beginning of a historical sequence that only finds its successful conclusion with Mao Tse-tung."[125] Whether or not this is really true will be answered in various ways. But the opinion at least deserves that the question be raised.

III

ENTHRALLED BY THE BEYOND (ca. 300 – 1000)

1 / *FREEDOM AND ANARCHY*

THE ABSENCE OF PRINCES AS THE IDEAL OF HERMITS AND REBELS

It is a curious though perhaps not entirely uncommon phenomenon that almost at the very time when popular uprisings with what were fundamentally still very hierarchical social ideals began to convulse the country, the opposite happened in the upper stratum of society. Here, what was clearly anarchistic thought was gaining currency. While "Vulgarized Taoism" increasingly assimilated Mohist and Legalist motifs which gave it a solid organization and therefore political strength, Taoism, as we encountered it in Chuang-tzu and Lao-tzu, tended to be cultivated in the esoteric circles of the educated and underwent a characteristic transformation in the process. For an attempt was made to apply Taoist teachings to society, although these teachings had originally rejected it in its entirety. But without the structural elements of Mohism and Legalism, which Vulgarized Taoism had integrated into its system to provide internal support, the transfer could only lead to a genuinely utopian, anarchistic model which, for that reason, never attained particular political effectiveness.

In Taoist jargon, anarchism is called the "doctrine of the absence of princes" *(wu-chün-lun).* The question whether a "state without a ruler" could exist or not was never posed by Chinese philosophers. Rather, anarchism had indisputable validity as a form of social life which had been realized in at least two instances: in earliest antiquity, and in the barbarian countries surrounding China. As we have seen, the Taoists held that there had been two additional domains: the realm of the dead and the countries at the ends of the world.[1] These latter, however, can be omitted from consideration here where what is involved is the direct application of the concept of an ideal, anarchistic state to political reality. The point where anarchism is assigned its place in a kind of history of the creation is most clearly defined in a commentary on the *Book of Changes* dating from the Han period. There it says unmistakably:

> After Heaven and earth had been created, there were the ten thousand creatures. After the ten thousand creatures had come into existence, there were the two sexes, male and female. After the two sexes, male and female, had come into existence, there was man and wife. After man and wife had come into existence, there was father and son. After father and son had come into existence, there was prince and subject. After prince and subject had evolved, there were relationships of superior and inferior. And after the relationships of superior and inferior had arisen, ritual and righteousness found their starting point.[2]

This description does not yet contain a value judgment. The disciples of Chuang-tzu and Lao-tzu would also have assented to this sequence, but they would have viewed the development as a decline, not as progress. In the books *Chuang-tzu, Tao-te-ching* and *Lieh-tzu,* there are numerous passages which express this quite clearly. The idea, however, that quite primitive, "barbarian" social systems also had structures of domination, and that these were generally quite rigorous, was something that occurred to neither of the two parties. It is interesting that a negative classification of anarchism, strongly reminiscent of Hsün-tzu's diction, is provided in the repeatedly mentioned collection of texts, *Spring and Autumn Annals of Lü Pu-wei,* which is ordinarily classified as "Taoist," and was admittedly influenced by Mohist and Legalist writings. It expressly characterizes the original anarchic condition as "misery" or "misfortune" and thus takes the side of Confucians, Mohists and Legalists in this respect:

> Princes did not yet exist in remotest antiquity. People lived together in herds and groups, they knew their mother, but not their father. Names designating relationships, or concepts for above and below, old and young, did not exist. Nor did they know the various forms of politeness, the advantages of clothing and dwellings, or the use of tools, means of transport, or protective structures. That was the misery of a time without princes. . . . To the east of Fei-pin (in Korea), . . . to the south of the Yang and Han rivers . . . , to the west of the river Li . . . and to the north of the wild goose gate . . . there were many peoples without princes. Among these tribes without princes in the four regions of the sky, men lived like wild animals. The young gave orders to the old, the old feared those who were in the flower of their years. The strong were considered saintly, the brutal and arrogant worthy of respect. Day and night, they harmed each other without resting for a single hour, until they had finally extirpated each other completely.[3]

The passage is noteworthy in that the place of anarchy in the sense previously suggested is also localized geographically: the reference is to the barbarians along the edges of Chinese civilization. By equating "order" and the area of Chinese domination on the one hand, and "anarchy" and the barbarian countries on the other, it made evident sense to view the enlargement of the Chinese area of domination as a diffusion of "order" itself, and thus as a kind of further development of creation generally. This opinion, which came very close to being a Chinese cultural messianism, had been developing with ever-increasing clarity since the third and second centuries B.C. We encountered it before in our consideration of the teachings of the *Kung-yang-chuan* school.[4] In older Confucianism, on the other hand, it is apparently absent. What we find there instead is a much simpler national sentiment which still makes a distinction between the principle of "order" and the concept "China," and in any event assigns it a lower place. Confucius's much-quoted saying in the *Lun-yü:* "When the I- and the Ti-barbarians have a ruler, they still are not worth as much as the Chinese *(Chu-hsia)* when they have lost theirs"[5], proves this adequately enough. It also shows, however, how much people suffered already during Confucius's times from the fact that relations of domination in China itself were less clear than among the barbarians. A certain defiance is present in these words, and the hope that this condition might be no more than a transition cannot be ignored.

Conversely (and as it does everywhere else), anarchism took its arguments precisely from the many instances of glaring failure of the established order. As before in the Taoism of a Chuang-tzu or a Lao-tzu, it was the result of a sudden switch from the criticism of many bad individual rulers to a criticism of the principle of rule itself. The central issue of all discussions was always the question concerning the qualities a ruler had to have. The very majestic-sounding observation of Confucius that "the superior person is no 'tool,' that he has no aptitudes,"[6] naturally provoked as much contradiction as Mencius's remark that a certain group of men was simply predestined to rule, and predestined to nothing else, and this by an unverifiable decision of heaven.[7] The answer of the disciples of the "School of Agriculture" was really quite moderate, but internally inconsistent for that very reason. Their demand that the ruler take the plough into his own hands and prepare his own breakfast certainly did not question the position of ruler as such. They were merely concerned with noting that the ruler be able to do *more* than the subject, that he first show that he could earn a living like any other citizen, and then prove his ability to head a government. It had been relatively easy for Mencius to reduce this demand *ad absurdum* by implicitly defining governing as a profession which could no more be practiced on the side than any other. Yet it was felt that the demands of the "School of Agriculture" had a certain justification. It was in part due to its influence that the ploughing of the emperor as a public occasion, and the weaving of the empress, developed into a ceremonial that was taken seriously. Its importance is also stressed in various passages in the work, *Spring and Autumn of Lü Pu-wei,* where the "School of Agriculture" is mentioned.[8] But it became a mere ceremonial, which did not mean that the demands of the agriculturists were taken seriously, but that their danger was recognized and blunted by this stylization. Beginning in the first century A.D., when the empire gradually lapsed into the same condition of a total disintegration of public order as had prevailed for the first time in the fourth and third centuries B.C., it was only natural that it should once again be asked from what particular abilities rulers derived their position of power. But the tone of this question was already much more aggressive than in Mencius's conversations, although the authors often deliberately placed the discussion into this long-gone period. Thus the book *Lieh-tzu,* for example, reports a conversation between the representative of a group of hermits who had gathered around the Taoist hermit Po-feng-tzu, and the philosopher Teng Hsi-tzu, considered the forefather of the Legalists:

"Do you know," Teng Hsi-tzu said to Po-feng-tzu, "the difference between the way parents are fed and cared for by their sons, and the way dogs are kept? Animals such as dogs and pigs, for example, are kept by men, they cannot manage for themselves. Since it is man's effort that keeps these creatures alive, he can use them for his purposes. But if people like you run around well nourished and well dressed, it is only the rulers of the state that you have to thank for it. The way you live together [pell-mell], old and young, like animals in stables and kitchens, how do you differ from dogs and pigs?" Po-feng did not answer, but one of his disciples stepped forward and said: "Mister scholar, have you not heard anything about the skilled workers here in Ch'i and Lu? Some are good at working in clay and wood, others in metal and leather. Some are good singers or musicians, or good scribes and diviners. Some are skilled in the arts of war, others in temple service. There are crowds of talented people. Only they cannot assign duties to each other, nor order each other about. [But] those who assign them duties [for that reason] certainly do not have their knowledge, and those who tell them what to do, do not have their abilities. It is only through the knowledge and skills [they do not have] that they become what they are. So the truth of the matter is that it is *we* who maintain the rulers of the state and [not the other way around]. That being so, what are you so conceited about?"[9]

What were originally the wholly different presuppositions of the disciples of the "School of Agriculture" and of the Taoists meet on common ground in this argument. Teng Hsi-tzu still reproaches the group of hermits in the customary anti-Taoist manner by saying that they live like wild animals. A genuine Taoist could only answer by remaining silent, because in the Taoist world view this was not a reproach, but praise. But the answer of the anonymous disciple comes from a wholly different direction which shows the traces of the "School of Agriculture." What he sees as a hierarchy standing on its head, he puts back on its feet by talking about a community where achievement counts. Here also, of course, there is all the difference in the world between a reversal of rank and the total equality of all places within an order, such as many Taoists envisioned it. But there can be no doubt that an inversion of the social pyramid prepared egalitarian and later also anarchistic ideal conceptions, and that not infrequently they went hand in hand.

Juan Chi (210–263) was the first philosopher to sketch the lineaments of the kind of state to be created here on earth. Its ruler was not merely to be an anonymous individual as earlier Taoist writings had repeatedly set forth; rather, there was to be no ruler at all. He was one of those wild, fiery figures that galvanized the restless third century A.D. However much they may have been mere epigones when seen from Chuang-tzu's vantage point, it is nonetheless true that their bold thought rejected all conventions and penetrated to the very limits of human existential possibilities.[10] In the fictitious biography of *Master Great-Man (Ta-jen hsien-sheng chuan),* he represents a mysterious person who is as old as the universe, and in whom he presumably wants to see himself. Ten thousand miles are a mere step for this man, one thousand years seem a morning, and the past of the sage emperors Yao and Shun is as close to him as his outstretched hand. With his existence, still more with his words, he confounds not only the thesis of the necessity of orders of domination within society, but also the value of the very concept "prince" as it is stressed in the term for the Confucian ideal man, the "superior person" (*chün-tzu,* actually son of a prince) on the one hand, and was negated in the term for "absence of princes" *(wu-chün)* on the other. Indeed, he goes so far as to assign merely relative importance to the special position occupied by heaven vis-a-vis all other creatures, a position which had been undisputed up to that time, and had been generally used to justify the rule of the "superior" over the "inferior." To document this, the first sentence of the most important commentary on the *Book of Changes (Ta-chuan* or *Hsi-tz'u-chuan)* suffices, being the most characteristic example: "Heaven is high, the earth is low, and this already defines the creative and the receptive. High and low are thus determined, and thereby high and low positions are fixed."[11] Juan Chi was therefore only consistent when he has his "Master Great-Man" begin at the very bottom in his argument against all models of domination. For otherwise his anarchistic thought always ran the risk of being refuted by the claim that it went against nature, which clearly implied that its implementation in the social sphere was also impossible. Having first paid the proper respect to the towering qualities of "Master Great-Man," Juan Chi writes in his fictitious biography:

> One day someone sent a letter to "Master Great-Man" which stated: "Among the values of this world *(t'ien-hsia),* none is more precious than the 'son of a prince' *(chün-tzu):* his garments have their reliable color, his gestures their firm rules, his words their fixed law, and his actions their defined order. . . . In this way misfortune is kept away and good fortune is attracted; in this way, one aspires to hardness and gives firmness to one's self. That is the high goal which a true scholar, a 'son of a prince,' can attain. Neither in the past nor in our time has man ever deviated from these beautiful [ideals] of action. You, however, have wildly growing hair, live in a place encircled by the sea, and are nothing like a 'son of a prince.' I fear the world will sigh over you and reprimand you. But if the way is ridiculed by the world and the self has no base from which to attain to self [realization], that may be called disgraceful. Since, in addition, you live in a frugal, miserable place, and yet are mocked by the plain people, I believe that you did not make the right choice." "Master Great-Man" sighed deeply, raised himself above clouds and rainbow, traveled to the author, and gave him his answer: "How could one call reasonable what you said just now," he asked. " 'Master Great-Man' acquired his form at the same time as the creator, and his life at the same time as heaven and earth. He is far-ranging and moves through the world unshackled; in harmony with the 'Way' he accomplishes everything, he transforms himself with it, dissolves himself and

gathers himself. Nothing about his shape is constant. His knowledge of the laws of Heaven and of the limits of the earth is innate, and the revelations of the floating ether and the perfections of light embrace him. What is truly solid and eternal about heaven and earth is incomprehensible for ordinary men. Perhaps I should explain it to you: Once there was a time when Heaven was below, and the earth above. Thus, at that time, everything stood on its head, and nothing was calm and secure. Why then should unchanging criteria not be abandoned, why should one continue to cling to 'eternal' values? If [at that time] Heaven formed the base, and the earth turned [above it], if the mountains were abysses and the rivers towered, if clouds splashed and thunder trembled, if the six directions of Heaven lost their meaning, would you still want to pick a certain spot on earth to walk about there [in an orderly manner], sometimes running, sometimes walking, as if choreographed? The raven of the sun flies above the dust [of this world], the wren plays among climbing plants: great and small have no points of contact. How do you know what impression your 'son of a prince' will make on me? Besides, the Hsia dynasty was recently[12] destroyed by the Shang dynasty, and the Chou dynasty, which followed it, had to pass the mandate in turn to [the ruling family of the Han dynasty, the] Liu. The splendid capitals became piles of rubble, the magnificent residences ruins. Men come and pass away in a moment's time and [even] eons and ages follow each other [in rapid succession]: nothing lasts. What others once called their own is now your miserable abode, and who will own it in the future and in distant eternity? Therefore the Master *(chu-jen)* does not pick a [permanent] place to live, he makes no preparations to govern. Sun and moon provide him his calendar, Yin and Yang the seasons. Other than that, why should he chain his ample feelings to what surrounds him, or be tied down to a single hour? With the clouds, he comes from the East, and rides westward with the wind. In harmony with Yin, he preserves the feminine within himself, and carried by Yang he develops his masculine element. What he wants, he attains, what his wishes command, he does, and all things remain inexhaustible for him. Why should he be unable to find self-realization; why should he be afraid of being derived by the people of this world? When heaven and earth separated from each other long ago, and the ten thousand creatures acquired their existence, the great felt at ease in nature, and the small content with their form. The [female] Yin concealed its fluid, the [male] Yang revealed its essence. Deprivation was not avoided, nor advantage fought over. Dispersing things was not experienced as loss, nor collecting them as gain. [Premature] death was not experienced as early death, [a long] life not as advanced age. Good fortune was not experienced as good, nor misfortune as evil. All did the tasks assigned to them, and abided by their fate. The intelligent did not [try to] gain the upper hand through their cleverness, the simple were not taken advantage of because of their stupidity, the weak [did] not [have to be] afraid of oppression, and the strong did not attempt to make full use of their powers. For princes did not exist *(wu chün),* and thus all creatures were ranged in their solid order: subjects did not exist *(wu ch'en),* and thus the ten thousand events all had their meaning. Because they preserved their self, cultivated their nature, did not offend against ordained fate, but only conducted themselves as nature had made them, they could live a long life. . . . Therefore it can truly be said: when there are no superior persons, the inferior need not worry.

When there are no rich people, the poor need not quarrel with each other, and everyone finds a sufficiency within himself. If there is nothing which will make him experience profound love, and he no longer tends elsewhere, he will not feel that death and misfortune are evil. When no marvelous sound is created, the ear will not be tempted to listen; when no provocative color can be seen, the eye will not be prompted to look. But when the ear is not tempted, and the eye is still, nothing will be left to confuse the mind. That was the 'highest abeyance' of the early ages. . . . But the rituals and laws of your 'son of a prince' are really only the means by which moral decline and banditry, disorder and danger, death and doom are brought about. Is it not a terrible misunderstanding when you let yourself be spellbound by them in the belief that they of all things are the 'Way,' from 'whose beautiful [ideals of] action no one has ever departed?' "[13]

It is true that the rejection of every kind of system of domination still has a rather individualistic, playful character in Juan Chi. The dimensions of "Master Great-Man" are so huge that he does not fit into the small world of men. From his encompassing perspective—it might be argued—perhaps even the best rulers would appear pathetic. Yet even he could offer no real deliverance from the injustice and suffering among men except the escape from the here and now, grandiose though this flight undoubtedly was. Essentially, he simply took up the theme of the previously mentioned sages in the book *Chuang-tzu,* who ran away when emperor Yao wanted to bequeath the empire to them. Even before Juan Chi wrote the biography of his superman, the lives of these saints had come to be lovingly painted in ever more fantastic colors. About one of them, Hsü Yu, it was reported that he not only rejected the offer, but afterwards washed out his ears; another, Ch'o Fu, who lived in a nest in a tree, was even said to have refused to ford the river in which Hsü Yu had just washed his ears.[14]

Time and again these droll fellows also appear as ideal figures in the works of the Taoist Ko Hung, though in a very characteristic modification. They no longer question the hierarchically-structured world as a matter of principle. Rather, they warn against an excessive valuation of it, and attempt to make clear that an unshackled life in nature has to be preserved as a correlate to the life molded by society. It is true that Ko Hung did not go so far as to deny the right to exist to those who found their happiness in becoming one with the world, like "Master Great-Man." But he recognized how close this extreme attitude came to quietly abandoning to Confucianism the sphere of the here and now. Thus he discovered the value of compromise, and therefore also considered himself the philosopher in whom Confucianism and Taoism merged. As regards this world, moderation (*chih-tsu,* literally "knowledge of what suffices") became his motto, and it had a temporal as well as a geographic import. For it meant that only part of human life should be devoted to public tasks, and that civilization should only be brought to part of the empire. The "mountains and marshes" became a kind of wildlife preserve where the hermit would do his work as a nonappointed official

We thus have a neat division of the world into three spheres. The first has become shadowy; it is that of the supernatural. The second is a sphere that has been allowed to remain in its original state; it is "natural." The third is that of social reality. All of them have an equal right to exist, though their value is not the same. The ideal man must pass through all three. This division is the reason we also find a chapter in the work of Ko Hung, where he unexpectedly launches a sharp attack against anarchism. To apply the standards of the supernatural to the things of this world seemed fundamentally improper to him. Because the flying "immortals" knew how to overcome the principle underlying the distinction between above and below which was implied in the existence of gravity, they perhaps enjoyed freedom from any sort of "authority." But this was not true for ordinary, earthbound mortals. In a controversy he authored but alleged to have had with the philosopher Pao Ching-yen,[15] Ko Hung expressed his disagreement with anarchistic Taoism, a kind of leftist deviationism vis-a-vis official Taoism, which preached "moderation," established churches, practiced alchemy, and had become part of the "establishment." Pao Ching-yen, on the other hand, was intent on redeeming the world by the proclamation of anarchism and the first to portray the nature of revolution in impressive images. Its purpose was no longer merely the overthrow of the evil ruler, but the overthrow of all forms of domination. Yet nowhere can we discover anything precise about this philosopher. We are certain only of his family name, for the personal name Ching-yen may be due to a corruption of the text.[16] All we can be reasonably sure of is that the anarchist tradition was cultivated in the family of Ko Hung's parents-in-law, which was also close to Taoism. (Ko Hung was married to a born Pao.) This tradition found expression in various writings which, as with Juan Chi, frequently took the form of debates. In any event, the formal similarity to the controversy in Juan Chi's biography, "Master Great-Man," cannot be ignored. In his debate with Ko Hung, the anarchist Pao argues as follows:

> The Confucians maintain: "Heaven once created the countless people, and placed rulers above it." Is that perhaps supposed to mean that the sublime Heaven actually made great speeches at the time, and expressed such intentions? No, what happened was simply this: the strong suppressed the weak until the weak submitted to them; the clever outsmarted the stupid, until the stupid served them. And it was only after they had submitted that the "Way" of princes and ministers developed. It was only when it had begun serving them that the energies of the poor were manipulated. . . . The azure sky has nothing to do with this whatever. . . . That the bark is peeled off the cinnamon tree, that sap is collected from the mountain pine, is not what these trees want. That pheasants are plucked and the kingfisher torn to pieces is not the wish of these birds. . . . The seeds of fraud and cunning lie in acting against nature, when such action is based on violence. . . . That the healthy nose [of bulls] is pierced and the unfettered legs [of horses] tied together does not correspond to the idea that the lives of the ten thousand creatures are to unfold equally. By imposing forced labor on the people, one obtains the means to pay officials. The greater the revenues of the aristocrats, the greater the misery of

the people. . . . In remote antiquity, princes and ministers did not exist. Wells were dug for drinking, and fields tilled for nourishment. At sunrise, the people went out to work; at sunset they came home to rest. Movement was free and without restriction, and desires did not go unfulfilled. Competition and planning were unknown, and as were honor and disgrace. There were no roads and paths in the mountains, nor were swamps crossed by bridges or boats. Because rivers and valleys could not be crossed, wars of conquest between states did not occur. Because officers and soldiers did not form armies, people did not attack each other. Nor did anyone steal the eggs from [birds'] nests high up on trees, or drain the deep waters of ponds [to catch fish]. Male and female phoenix came down together on houses to rest, and dragons and [other auspicious] scaly animals roamed the gardens in throngs. It was not dangerous to step on hungry tigers or to touch poisonous snakes with one's hand. When people waded through swamps, waterfowl did not fly up, nor were foxes and rabbits frightened when people penetrated into the forests. Greed for power and profit had not yet budded in the hearts of men, and therefore unhappiness and confusion did not arise. Shields and spears were not yet in use, nor walls constructed or ditches dug. In mystical equality *(hsüan-t'ung),* the ten thousand creatures forgot each other in the "Way," epidemics and pestilences did not spread, and the people became very old as a result. Pure and innocent as they were, men had no cunning in their hearts. They felt at ease when they could simply eat their fill, and walked about stroking their stomach. It would have been impossible to multiply taxes to bleed the people, or to introduce strict punishments to trap it. But when the gradual decline entered its final phase, cleverness came into use and cunning was born. When the "Way" and "virtue" declined, the superior and the inferior were assigned their fixed station. Rules of ascent and descent, of demotion and promotion were created in confusing multiplicity. . . . Stagnating in perverse sensual pleasure, people rebelled against the root of the great origin. Every day, the bonds to their ancestors became weaker, and they turned their back on natural simplicity. When the sages are honored, the people fight for name and renown! When treasures are valued, robbers and thieves make their appearance. If one sees what is desirable, the true, honest heart becomes confused, greed for power and profit parade about, and the path to extortion and robbery is opened. Shiny, sharp weapons are forged, and the misery of martial ventures is bred. People fear only that the crossbow might not be taut enough, the armor solid enough, the spear sharp enough, the shield thick enough. And yet, they could all be thrown away if suppression and violence would stop. Therefore it can be said: Who could make a scepter without destroying the pure, uncarved jade, who could choose humanity and righteousness without rejecting the "Way" and "virtue"? Let us take fellows like [the evil kings] Chieh and Chou, who burned people alive . . . and committed all kinds of horror till they dropped from exhaustion. . . . Suppose all these tyrants had been perfectly ordinary men of the people, would they have been able, in spite of their cruel and extravagant disposition, to live their life to the full? No, they only could give rein to their cruelty and pursue their desires without restraint, butchering the world, because they were princes. Therefore they could act as they pleased. But when princes and ministers have once established themselves, the anger of the masses grows day by day. They feel the urge to shake their fists, tied down and chained though they be, and to bemoan their labor in dirt and misery, until the prince finally seeks refuge in the hall of the temple of the ancestors, trembling with fear, and the hundred noble families, flushed and excited, fall into affliction and danger. To try to discipline the masses now by punishment or to calm them by ritual is like first opening a fountain splashing toward heaven or letting a river of unfathomable depth flood its banks, and then attempting to close it with a clump of earth or to dam it up with a flat hand.[17]

FREEDOM, THE ROMANTICISM OF NATURE, AND MADNESS

The account of the ideal age that knew no princes can of course readily be traced back to accounts we already found in Chuang-tzu and Lao-tzu. All the characteristics of a life in nature recur: the intimate familiarity, indeed the "equality" between man and animal, the absence of roads and bridges. At the same time, however, an element deriving from Tung Chung-shu slips in: phoenixes and dragons bustle about in a world transfigured by its lack of domination. As a kind of placet of nature, these animals normally suggest a good age. More patently even than the old Taoists, the anarchist Pao makes the decision to do without "unnatural" class distinctions. This decision not only leads him back to the bosom of nature and makes him happy there, but also brings happiness to nature in its entirety. But precisely because of this twofold tie to nature—the Taoist and the Confucian—a thought which represented the genuinely new element in the discourse of the anarchist Pao could not properly unfold, and that was the idea of freedom within a social context. The claim to freedom founded in "nature," and which the masses, "shaking their fists in their chains," were allegedly bringing forward, showed itself to be considerably more susceptible of attack than might at first have appeared. In his counterargument (not quoted here), and where he naturally does not give the philosopher Pao a real chance, Ko Hung can easily prove that not only the world of nature as originally created, but also the world of men made by the sages does indeed imply a hierarchy. Without retreating to a supernatural space like "Master Great-Man," Pao cannot simply sweep these objections aside and arrogate to himself a fantastic knowledge of unheard-of early structures of the cosmos. In the end, he is thus obliged to admit that nature is "unfree" when seen from the perspective of society, and that man is consequently naturally unfree within it.

In China as elsewhere, the reciprocal relations between happiness, freedom and nature are generally especially revealing for the evaluation of conceptions of the ideal in the social sphere. What first strikes one as most surprising is a fact already discovered by Max Weber.[18] Chinese does not really have a term for "freedom," or perhaps better and more fairly, it has no old term which would also have represented freedom *in* society in a single character. There was a word combination, however, which characteristically surfaced first in the second century A.D., but was used only in a narrow area and not rediscovered until the very recent past. Its use as a slogan came about at a time when an equivalent for the western concept of freedom had to be found. This is the word *tzu-yu,* which can be translated literally as "self-initiating." This expression appears, for example, in an indirect allusion in Juan Chi in the previously quoted, naive letter of the unknown individual who quarrels with "Master Great-Man." The sentence: "the self has no base from which to attain to self-realization" *(shen wu yu tzu ta),*[19] is meant to make clear that the writer has no idea of a freedom directed wholly toward the attainment of self-realization by its own efforts. But already at an early period, this concept was evidently connected not only with the experience of a spiritual and mystical freedom, but also with a very concrete, not to say brutal, independence. In what is probably the earliest passage where this concept appears, reference is made to the successes of a political party after its victory over a competing group: "It now occupied the key positions, and had authority, wealth and 'freedom.' "[20] "Freedom" thus tended to have an unpleasant tinge in China from the very beginning. Not without justification, it evoked the idea of a lack of restraint because, surprisingly, it had not been discovered among the suppressed and disinherited, but in the ruling milieu. The absurd consequence was that at the very moment the rebellious masses adopted fundamentally astonishingly conservative ideas of order, as we noted, the members of a slowly degenerating leadership class proclaimed the ideal of freedom. But in so doing, and with the exception of an ever-decreasing number of Taoists like the anarchist Pao, who never went beyond the notion of an uncivilized life, they did not mean the liberation of those that were really suppressed, but very selfishly thought of their own emancipation from the fixed rules of morality and ritual which Confucianism still imposed on them.

The concept of "nature" is very much older than this highly specific expression for "freedom," and yet it is connected with it in a very conspicuous manner. The old concept *hsing,* which we encountered while considering the ideas of "life" in China, had designated only the nature of a creature, a tree, an animal, a human being or a group such as humanity, but not nature in its totality. To the extent people were aware of it at all, they, and especially the Taoists, called it "Tao" (Way). But this made it impossible to contrast nature and civilization. Still, this contrast was naturally perceived by all philosophical movements. Indeed, it was actually almost always at the center of discussion, yet nonetheless not recognized as such for a long time. For just as the Confucians on the one side (and in this respect they were joined by the Mohists and the Legalists) were willing to acknowledge nature only as "non-civilization," the Taoists conversely recognized civilization only as "non-nature." The "humanity" of the Confucians and the *Tao* of the Taoists represented irreconcilable opposites in their claim to totality. But when during the second century A.D. and after, a kind of division of the world set in, both sides suddenly began to discover "nature" as a kind of correlate of civilization. All at once, descriptions of nature found their way into literature.

The joys of walking, the beauties of mountains and rivers were discovered, and a spirit of romantic empathy for events in nature began to stir. It can be shown that this was even true of descriptions of paradise, particularly those written in the form of poems (Ts'ao Chih, etc.).[21] It was no accident that this occurred at a time of the worst political catastrophes where with increasing frequency invasions by foreign warrior bands drove the population from their homes, causing panic, mass flight, and heavy losses. In this escapism, which had been prepared by both internal and external events, and which was only apparently purely Taoist, it was precisely Taoism which gradually lost its real center. For when it surrendered its original claim that nature had absolute priority over civilization, this proved much more consequential than the converse compromise did for Confucianism. The latter had never considered nature a disease, as the Taoists had civilization, but had rather viewed it more neutrally, as a sort of untapped raw material. Thus it was easier for the Confucians to remain loyal to their principles. By contrast, and without really being aware of it, the Taoists slipped into a kind of intellectual despair at a time their world view appeared to be flourishing, and there was no longer any way to lead them out of it. This development was actually prefigured in the etymology of the concept "nature," in the sense discussed here. The expression *tzu-jan,* to be translated literally as "being thus of itself," is encountered first in the *Tao-te-ching.* There it designates the irreducible internal structure of the *Tao:* "Man has the earth as his law *(fa),* earth has heaven as its law, heaven has the 'Way' as its law, and the 'Way' has as its law in 'what is thus of itself.' "[22] This freedom from every kind of law except as prescribed by one's self was thus originally a special characteristic which applied only to the *Tao* itself. But gradually, it was also conceded to heaven and earth,[23] and finally, and to a certain degree, to all things existing in "free" nature.[24] The concept *tzu-jan,* which had depreciated considerably as a result of this development, could ultimately be equated with nature itself. At this point, we observe the convergence with the concept *tzu-yu* "freedom," such as the Taoists discovered it in the second and third centuries A.D. The imitation of life in nature was no longer the only route to the perfection of the personality in the "Way." That perfection could be brought about more directly by the imitation of the way of life of the *Tao* itself, which went hand in hand with it. For the Tao was precisely defined by the fact that it only had itself for its law. The element "self" *(tzu),* present both in the concept "nature" and in the concept "freedom," is not there by chance, but simply makes clear that only the recognition of the self in all expressions and actions of life is the decisive characteristic of all "naturalness" and "freedom," both of which are attributes of nature and the *Tao,* as they are of the ideal man. This identification emerges everywhere in the relevant literature of the period, although the idea of freedom is only very rarely rendered directly by *tzu-yu.* But the words used in its place are no less clear: they all derive from a conceptual field grouped around the idea of "letting oneself go."[25]

While the liberation of the people from all forms of rule as envisaged by the anarchist Pao did not emerge as a goal until relatively late, and was quickly forgotten when it did, the emancipation of the upper class from the conventions of society through a life in nature became an increasingly fashionable wish. Idylls replaced ideals. Slightly snobbish scholars, suddenly weary of civilization, thought they were discovering forgotten paradises in a nature which was of course decked out with all imaginable comfort for men of their class. The rustic flavor of country life inspired them with the enthusiasm so typical of the mentality of the town dweller living far away from nature. One of their earliest representatives was Chung-ch'ang T'ung (?179–219). His essay "Desire for Joy" *(Lo-chih-lun)* allows us to infer with great clarity the direction Taoism was taking:

> The place where we want to live must have good fields and a big house on a slope, affording a view of a river. It must be surrounded by artificial brooks and ponds, with lots of bamboo and trees. Thrashing floor and vegetable garden should be out front, an orchard in back. There should be enough chariots and boats so that one can avoid the trouble of walking or wading through water, and a sufficient number of servants so one need not trouble oneself with demeaning work. The best dishes will be available for one's parents. Wife and children will do no heavy work. Friends dropping in for a visit will be served wine and refreshments. If the season is beautiful or a holiday is being celebrated, a lamb or suckling pig may also be roasted for them. One can roam about in the fields and gardens, the woods are a good spot for exercise, the clear waters can be used for bathing, the fresh breeze drawn into the lungs. Swimming carps may be caught, or high-flying wild geese shot. A prayer can be sung at the foot of the rain altar, one can return to the great hall singing. High spirits may be calmed in the women's chambers, one can meditate on the mysterious emptiness in Lao-tzu, or attempt to harmonize one's vital powers by breathing exercises to become a "perfected one" *(chih-jen).* With one or two experienced companions, one can discuss the "Way," interpret books and inquire into the two forces, heaven and earth, above and below, men as well as phenomena. The strings of the lute may be plucked in accompaniment to the tender song "The Southwind," or a wistful melody may be sung in the pure mode. Thus all that is worldly can be transcended: one can reflect on all things between heaven and earth from a higher vantage point. The demands of the present are neglected, life becomes eternal. Coming to heaven, one enters a sphere beyond space and time. Why then should one aspire to being received by kings and emperors?[26]

In a poem by the same author, the desire for self-fulfillment without the vexing interference of society is coupled with a contempt of that society as expressed in the last sentence above, and even a certain hostility toward civilization. But the contempt is not so pronounced as to be revolutionary in tone, nor does the hostility go beyond an almost plaintive, passive reflection:

> The Great Way is simple/yet few know its origin/follow your desires without recrimination,/adapt to things without praising them.//
>
> Torturing, fatiguing, boring thoughts have been laboriously turned this way and that since time immemorial./What is the point of such thoughts?/The highest value lies only in the self.//
>
> I confide my pain to Heaven,/and bury my sadness in the earth./Full of disgust, I cast away the Five classics,/and destroy and disavow my songs and my odes.//
>
> The writings of the Hundred Philosophers are unclear and pathetic,/I would really like to burn them./My desires reach high above the hills,/and my thoughts extend far across the oceans.//
>
> The primordial breath is my skiff,/the gentle breeze my rudder,/I float in greatest purity/and take my delight in the entire cosmos.//[27]

In this late phase of philosophical Taoism, the negative, destructive elements latent in it from the beginning surface ever more clearly. The discovery of human freedom almost becomes the discovery of the dissolution of the self. But in the very brief transitional phase during the first half of the third century, when an autumnal intimation of imminent disaster touched wide circles of the intelligentsia, there were also some philosophers that attained a lightning insight into the greatness of the person and the unconditional quality of human happiness. The classical simplicity of their statements has hardly ever been attained again. All ideals having some connection with the ideal of childlikeness became the object of an enthusiastic, and finally of an excessive glorification. Already in the *Tao-te-ching,* that quality had been portrayed as the source of all happiness, and even the anarchist Pao had described it as typical of an anarchistic age where "men behave like children, . . . comparable to sucklings and babes, in whom cleverness and intelligence have not yet awakened."[28] The most impressive passages can once again be found in the book *Lieh-tzu.* One describes the happiness of oblivion and the disintegration of that happiness in the form of an almost devilish recovery which reads like the violent destruction of innocence, as if the patient had been coerced to eat of the tree of the knowledge of good and evil:

> Hua-tzu from Yang-li in [the state of] Sung became ill with forgetfulness in his middle age. What he received in the morning, he had forgotten in the evening; what he had given in the evening, he had forgotten the next morning. When away from home, he forgot to walk; at home, he forgot to sit down. Today, he no longer knew what had happened before, later, he could not remember what had happened today. The entire family felt unhappy because of this. Diviners were brought in to consult oracles, but the answer was silence. Magicians were requested to come. They recited their prayers, but their spells did no good. And physicians were called to try their art, yet the illness persisted. But in [the state of] Lu,[29] there was a scholar who offered to heal the sickness. Hua-tzu's relations were ready to give him half their fortune, and asked for his cure. The scholar told them: "We are certainly not

dealing with something that can be inquired into by oracles, changed by prayers, or cured with medicine or acupuncture. I shall try to change his mind, to change his interests, perhaps he will become better." He tried the following: he undressed the invalid—who then asked for clothing. He starved him—and the invalid asked for food. He locked him up in darkness—and was asked for light. Then the scholar from Lu was pleased, and said to the son of the sick man: "The sickness can be cured. But my cure is a secret which I may reveal to no one. Send away all those standing about and leave me alone with the patient for seven days." He was obeyed, and no one knew what the scholar was doing to the invalid. And indeed, when the appointed time had passed, the illness of many years had disappeared overnight. But when Hua-tzu had recovered, he became very angry. He turned his wife out of the house, beat his son, picked up a spear and chased the scholar out of Lu. The people of Sung took hold of him and asked him why he was acting in this way. Hua-tzu replied: "Before, I was sunk in forgetfulness, and therefore without bounds. I did not even notice if there was such a thing as Heaven and earth, or not. But now I have suddenly become conscious and all that has happened to me during these two or three decades in the way of happiness and unhappiness, profit and loss, sadness and joy, love and hatred, stirs again and confuses me with a thousand entanglements. I fear that the happiness and unhappiness, the profit and loss, the sadness and joy, the love and the hatred the future may still hold for me will confuse my heart. If I could only recover that forgetfulness for a brief moment."[30]

The motif of the illness, which is not really illness but natural health, and whose "cure" is therefore tantamount to infection, infection, that is, with the pernicious seeds of a world entangled in social interests, recurs in *Lieh-tzu.* It is present in the following anecdote where the relationship between saintliness and madness is set forth:

Lung Shu said to the physician Wen Chih: "Your art is considerable. Can you also cure my illness?" "I am at your disposal," Wen Chih answered, "but first describe the symptoms of the illness." Lung Shu said: "I consider it neither an honor to be praised by the people at home, nor a disgrace when the entire state reproaches me. Profit does not delight me, loss does not sadden me. For me, life is like death, wealth like poverty, man like the pig, I like anyone else. I live in my house as in an inn, and look on my own country as if it were a foreign, barbarian land. Suffering like this, neither titles nor reward can spur me one, nor punishment and fines keep me from doing anything whatever. Flowering and decline, profit and loss, cannot change me, joy and sadness cannot affect me. Therefore I am too unskilled to serve the prince, to deal with relations and friends, to communicate with wife and children, to give orders to servants and laborers. What kind of illness is this, and how can it be cured?" Wen Chih told Lung Shu to turn his back to the light while he stepped back and looked at Lung Shu against it. Finally, he said: "Well, I see your heart. One spot is completely empty, you are almost a saint. Six holes in your heart run together, only the seventh is stopped up. Is that perhaps the reason you believe the wisdom of a saint is an illness? My weak art cannot cure you."[31]

INDIFFERENCE, INTOXICATION AND GENIUS

The group of the "Seven Sages of the Bamboo Grove" *(Chu-lin ch'i-hsien)* was made up of philosophers who lived in the first half of the third century. They tried to find happiness and perfection in the indifference toward all the conventions of society. The group had an enormous influence on Chinese conceptions of the ideal human being. One of its most brilliant representatives was Juan Chi, who laid the foundations for the anarchism of a Pao, as we have seen. Even greater, however, is the importance of the scholar Hsi K'ang (223–262), on whose estate the men used to gather.[32] One of his most famous essays is entitled "The Cultivation of Life" *(Yang-sheng lun).* Like so many Chinese philosophers, he showed a curious persistence in investigating the possibility of escaping old age and death. At first glance, it may seem that he merely repeated the age-old maxim already proclaimed by Lao-tzu, and especially Chuang-tzu. But when one looks more closely, considerable differences become apparent. A veritable crisscross of doubts spreads like a thin net over the ostensibly so positively stated doctrine of human immortality. The disquieting observation that no one had ever demonstrably encountered an immortal was answered by masses of proofs. But there was also another sense in which traditional Taoist thought appeared in a new light. Chuang-tzu had tried to lead man back to the idea that equality with all the creatures of nature had vanquished death. That idea now gave way to an ideal of indifference which differed from resignation only by forestalling it through an act of voluntary renunciation: "Pure and empty, calm and peaceful, [the sage] reduces his personal needs and wishes," we read in the essay.

> Knowing full well that fame and position harm his "virtue," he remains indifferent and wholly unattached. It is not that he still harbors such desires and violently represses them. [No,] he simply knows that luxuriant fragrances harm [human] nature; therefore, he avoids them and pays no more attention to them. It is not that he still desires them and then curbs those desires. [No,] he keeps these things outside, so that his heart cannot remain enchained. Only spirit and breath, clear and white as flowers, find their dwelling place within him. Being empty, he knows neither worry nor misfortune. Being calm, he is neither anxious nor fearful. He maintains [this condition] through the "One," and nourishes it through the "Harmonious," so that his harmonious order grows day by day until he is [finally] united with the "Great Obedience" *(ta-shun).* Only then does he let himself be soaked through by magic mushrooms, wetted thoroughly by sweet springs, dried by the morning sun, lulled by the five strings [of the lute]. In not-doing he finds himself, his body becomes mystical, his heart darkly mysterious. He forgets joy, and can therefore become joyful, he loses his life, and can thereby preserve his body.[33]

This ideal of a sage without desires is permeated by paradox; indeed, it sets out to create them. Unlike the sages in *Chuang-tzu,* this man does not leave society. He has no greater interest than the preservation of his own self, yet wishes to forget it at the same time. It is an ideal that was violently attacked by Hsiang

Hsiu, a friend of Hsi K'ang. Hsiang Hsiu, a Confucian and an official, was not hostile toward Taoism, but interested in somehow incorporating it in Confucianism (as many Taoists, proceeding inversely, also tried to do). But while he appreciated its artistic aspects, he was dissatisfied with Hsi K'ang's mystification of life. For him, "to forget joy so as to become joyful" was not a thought where the contradiction forces the intellect to understand the truth on a higher level, but a contradiction pure and simple. In his reply (*Nan Yang-sheng lun* "Criticisms of the Text Concerning the Cultivation of Life"), his conflicting viewpoint finds clear expression:

> What brings joy in life comes from mutual contact in sympathy and love which the nature of Heaven gave man in his relations to what surrounds him. Peaceful, amenable women make his heart joyous, renown and splendor quicken his ambition. He eats rich food to develop the five senses within himself, and lets music and passion take possession of him so that his inborn nature and vitality may develop. . . . If, on the other hand, someone merely stares at his own shadow, if he sits there like a corpse, has only trees and stones for neighbors, and tortures himself, figuratively speaking, with moxibustion without really being ill, imposes silence on himself without being indisposed, only eats vegetables without being in mourning, locks himself in without being guilty, and chases the void in his search for happiness without having the success his efforts would merit, I have to say about this way of "nourishing life" that I have never heard of that sort of thing being called reasonable. Therefore, [even] a [Ssu-ma] Hsian-ju has said: "If one tries everything within one's power to prolong life [just] to escape death, that will not bring joy, even if one should survive ten thousand generations." That means: if one turns away from one's feelings and denies one's nature, one abandons the basis of Heavenly nature. What is a long life without joy compared with a short but joyful one?"[34]

In a very wordy reply consisting of eight sections, Hsi K'ang elaborated once again on the two opposing attitudes toward life which undoubtedly have divided mankind from the very beginning. The questions concerning a career in society, and the place of the ruler, are touched upon. But characteristically, they are answered not from the perspective of anarchism, but from that of an indifference toward such irrelevant matters generally, an outlook which is clearly recognizable even in the "anarchist" Juan Chi. Although Hsi K'ang was nonetheless repeatedly reported to the authorities for his anarchistic views, became involved in an intrigue, was finally put on trial on this pretext and executed at the age of thirty-nine, he actually expressly admitted the fundamental necessity of a government, though with the reservation that he felt obliged to recommend the same indifference to the rulers as he did to the governed. Generally speaking, however, Hsi K'ang's reply to the objections raised by Hsiang Hsiu is rather weak. When reproached for sacrificing joy in life for the sake of its preservation, he answers with the suggestion that this also results in the simultaneous deliverance from suffering. But at the same time, he also mentions the supernatural delights to be derived from elixirs of life alluded to in the "magical mushrooms" of his first essay. The alchemic component which later was to become dominant in Ko Hung is already detectable here. Like Hsi K'ang, Ko hoped to attain long life and happiness by a combination of internal and external means. It is difficult to state definitively to what extent the pleasures described here may be due directly to the use of drugs; the possibility cannot be rejected out of hand.

The individualistic aspect of this Taoism which the aristocracy discovered prevented a genuine unfolding of the traces of political anarchism it contained. Yet it accomplished something even more astonishing by deflecting "socialist" tendencies which had already been formed at an early date by the influx of Mohist thought. A key document in this context is Hsi K'ang's essay on the "Liberation from the Selfish" *(Shih-ssu lun).* The virtue of "public spirit" *(kung),* which had played such an important role in the writings of Lü Pu-wei and later been put into practice in Taoist organizations[35] as previously mentioned, was here miraculously transformed into a wholly individualistic attitude by Hsi K'ang. A bridge was provided by reinterpreting the role of one of the most fundamental human acts, namely confession, which had been accorded considerable social significance in Taoist communities. Among the believers gathering around Chang (Tao)-ling, the founder of the Taoist church, the public confession of sins was one of the fundamental premises for the deliverance from illness and misfortune. It became an established institution with him, as it did with Chang Lu, the founder of the state of the "Five Pecks of Rice Taoists."[36] The confessions were not secret but very public acts, and were used time and again in later popular movements as the most effective means of suppressing the selfish hybris of the individual and preserving his feeling that he was merely a member of the community. In Hsi K'ang's interpretation, however, this concept *kung* "communal" becomes something wholly different in its opposition to *ssu* "selfish." Indeed, it almost turns into its opposite, i.e. a form of expression of that indifference toward the world which Hsi K'ang took to be the basis for the redemption of man: "I was asked once," he writes at the end of one of his essays,

> whether Ti-wu Lun, famous in antiquity for his honesty, had been selfish, since the following saying of his has been passed down: "Once, when the son of my older brother fell ill, I ran to look after him ten times in the course of a single evening [to show my compassion], but slept marvelously well afterwards. But when my own son was ill, I did not look in on him during an entire morning. At night, however, I did not close an eye [because I was really concerned]." I answered: "Certainly not, Ti-wu Lun was not selfish." Selfishness has its [real] name in not-saying, "public spirit" has its [real] designation in saying everything. The good has its substance in not being stingy, the bad is weighed down by holding something back. Now, Ti-wu revealed his feelings without reservation, irrespective of whether they were right or wrong. So he was *not* selfish, although it was wrong that he ran [to his sick nephew just because he wanted] to boast [of his piety to his older brother]. And it was also wrong that it was only when his own son was ill [that he could not sleep]. That one is not selfish even when one makes mistakes lies in the will to hold nothing

> back. Of course, he who holds nothing back in his speech is not to be equated with someone who ignores all bounds. On the other hand, the person who always withholds something in his speech cannot be lumped together with someone who does not talk at all. Therefore the following applies: it is wrong to be always stingy, it is right to hold nothing back. When one has attained what is right by no longer holding back anything, when the will no longer sees anything to aspire to, when the heart no longer thirsts after something to be desired, when one has thus penetrated to the sentiments of the great "Way" *(ta-tao),* and allows only nature *(tzu-jan)* to move one, the possibility of making mistakes is wholly excluded. When one embraces the One and holds nothing back, one is selfless. Thus to have reached the two noble goals, selflessness and flawlessness, is the highest beauty. But he who [still] makes mistakes, but can be frank about them, is better than the one who practices the selfishness of not speaking out by hiding his feelings when he has made mistakes, and thereby commits the really important error. If Ti-wu made a mistake but was able to reveal it, one cannot say of him that he did not act "communally" *(kung).* For although what he revealed was a mistake, one cannot say of him that he held something back. Calling someone selfish simply because he makes a mistake is definitely due to a false belief. That is the principle of "public spirit" and "selfishness."[37]

The teaching of Hsi K'ang and his friends who shared his beliefs was undoubtedly filled with a high ethos that had its roots in his desire for the natural perfecting of the self. Admittedly, the "Seven Sages of the Bamboo Grove" delighted in eccentric behavior. But they were also highly educated men with thoroughly developed artistic sensibilities. Certainly, very outstanding human qualities were required to sustain the ambivalent existence led by the "Seven Sages" and their disciples. While Hsi K'ang was active as an official and certainly had a hand in politics, he also worked indefatigably in essays and poems to create the image of a new man. At times, he presented it as a self-portrait, and just as often as the picture of the "sage in society." This new, truly curious sage of his is no longer the hermit in the mountains, but the abysmally lazy, indolent, utterly disorderly, yet also nature- and art-loving, witty and quick-witted *official.* Although not without some difficulty, one can still see, peering out from behind him, the Taoist-legalist figure of the ruler, sitting on his throne "as though drunk."[38] Yet it could easily happen that this outer shell of a sage transcending the anxieties of the world by his genius should be equated with his real nature. And it was tempting to obtain certain exculpation from any and every conceivable transgression of law, custom and convention by being unburdened of the weight of guilt through public confession; indeed to look for that exculpation incessantly so as to experience purification, that fascinating alternation of filth and purity. How easily freedom could thus turn into licentiousness, lack of prejudice into frivolity, and mystical detachment into dypsomania. Perhaps Hsi K'ang did not have a clear consciousness of all this. Yet the sentence that one need not immediately "ignore all bounds" gives food for thought.

Even among the "Seven Sages," we encounter men who gradually came to believe that the infraction of the external norms of society constituted a step in the direction of the liberation of man, which would somehow necessarily bring his inner freedom with it. This trend toward superficiality going hand in hand with an enormous loss of substance of the entire intellectual base of this movement took on increasingly catastrophic forms during the two generations following the "Seven Sages." Most characteristic was the increasing importance of wine. In marked contrast to the sages of older Taoism, the "Sages of the Bamboo Grove," and still more their epigones, could no longer be thought of without a bottle of wine in their hand, a pose that might be called an iconographic characteristic (metaphorically speaking). The official collapsing with glazed eyes behind his desk, who uses his offices primarily for drinking bouts, and makes his acceptance of a position in the provinces depend upon the quality of the wine cellar, became a kind of ideal figure to be applauded and admired. Of course, there were innumerable other ways taboos could be broken. Society could be shocked by long hair and negligent dress, those eternally unchanging signs of man's closeness to nature, of the sense of being an exile within civilization. This is equally true of the provocative nakedness and the use of wine in what can only be called nudist clubs, where they became the expression of the freedom of genius.[39] This new attitude was most convincingly expressed in the changed descriptions of the lands of paradise. The paradises of the earlier Taoist philosophers became paradises of drunkenness. The classical example comes from the somewhat later philosopher and poet Wang Chi (585–644).[40] Not without justification, he looked upon himself as a descendent of the eccentric, dissolute sages such as Juan Chi,[41] to whom he specifically points as a representative citizen in his description of the "Land of the Drunk":

> The "Land of the Drunk" *(tsui-chih kuo)* lies I don't know how many miles away from the Middle Kingdom. It has the sweep of the desert. There are no shores, no mountains or cliffs. Its climate is harmonious and mild *(ho-p'ing)* everywhere, the contrast of light and darkness, of cold and heat is unknown. Its customs correspond to [the principle of] "Great Equality" *(ta-t'ung).* There are neither towns nor settlements. People there have the most highly developed intellects, being strangers to love and hatred, joy and anger. They sip the wind and drink the dew, and abstain from the Five Cereals. Their sleep is dreamless, their walk leisurely. They live among fishes, crabs, birds and animals, and have no idea what ships and chariots, weapons and implements are good for. In the past, the "Yellow Emperor"[42] once succeeded in reaching the capital [of this country]. When he returned, it dawned on him that he had come close to losing his empire [through bustle], because a [simple] government which uses knotted cords [for its correspondence instead of documents] already represents a stage of decay. During the time of the sage kings Yao and Shun, sacrifices were already celebrated with thousands of kettles and hundreds of jugs. Therefore, the Ku-yeh-spirit man *(shen-jen)* tried to find the way [into that country]. It is true that he got no further than the borders, but he spent the rest of his life in the "Highest Peace" *(t'ai-p'ing).* Later, when [the virtuous dynastic founders] Yü and T'ang issued their laws, and ritual became ever more

confused and music more multiform as a result, the borders of the "Land of the Drunk" [gradually] closed over the course of some ten generations. When the ministers [of these kings], Hsi and Ho, [failed in their systematization of the] calendar, resigned their positions and fled, hoping to reach that country, they could no longer find the road, and died on the way. Since that time, there has been no peace in the empire. Even if the last grandchildren of Yü and T'ang, [the tyrants] Chieh and Chou, furiously climbed up a mountain of grape husks eight thousand steps high [which they left behind after their banquets], and looked far south from there [as from a throne], they never so much as caught a glimpse of the "Land of the Drunk." But when king Wu, [the actual founder of the Chou dynasty], later imposed his will on the world, he ordered the duke of Chou to create the office of a master of the wine, including the appropriate supervisory officials for the five different qualities of wine. Also, he enlarged the land under his rule by 7000 miles so that it almost bordered on the "Land of the Drunk." That was the only reason punishments became unnecessary over a forty-year period. But when [this system] degenerated [into the reign of terror of the evil kings] Yu and Li, and things became even worse with the advent of the Ch'in and Han dynasties, the empire fell into confusion. Thus relations with the "Land of the Drunk" were cut off [for good]. Some of the subjects [of these depraved regimes] however, who had received the true teaching *(tao),* secretly made off and found their way there: Juan Chi, T'ao Yüan-ming, and about a dozen others traveled together to the "Land of the Drunk" went into hiding, and never returned. When they died, they were also buried there. [Since that time,] the Middle Kingdom has honored them as the "immortals of wine" *(chiu-hsien).* Yes indeed! Is the way of life of the "Land of the Drunk" not like that of the Hua-hsü empire? How else could one account for this purity and this calm? I had the good fortune to be able to travel there myself once. That is the reason I wrote this report.[43]

A still more profound, more complex insight into the way of thought of that period is provided by an uncommonly fascinating collection of anecdotes entitled, *New Words from the Conversations of the Time (Shih-shuo hsin-yü).*[44] Its stories usually deal with specific situations. They contain not only witty aperçus of an ambiguity often incomprehensible for the contemporary reader, but also many abstruse, amusingly imaginative acts which in some respects almost have the quality of "happenings." The book is divided by subject matter, but arranged chronologically within each chapter. The entries give an impressive insight into the flowering and decline of certain forms of behavior born of a spirit of freedom. The lonely individual in *Lieh-tzu,* who thought he was mad because the chains of society did not press down on him, has turned into a countless multitude believing itself both raving mad and extravagant. There is a very revealing anecdote in the *Shih-shuo hsin-yü,* according to which one of the "Seven Sages" protested desperately when a young relative presented himself to him as a new disciple, determined to become a genius.[45] Yet not even the sage could stay the advent of the new fashion. The incessant wars, which had been partly responsible for this disintegration, resulted in profound poverty. And these pranks of an ingenious age, inspired partly by high spirits, partly by a nihilistic despair, soon came to a stop. What failed to develop was the idea of freedom within society. It remained confined to a narrow segment of the upper class. Cut off from real problems, it was soon ridden to death. What was left was the old, depressingly familiar opposition of nature, wilderness, and freedom, on the one hand, and civilization, order and lack of freedom, on the other. To find happiness in some rapprochement thus seemed a continuing impossibility.

2 / REDEMPTION IN THE PARADISE OF THE WEST

THE TRANSFORMATION OF THE REGIONS OF HAPPINESS BY BUDDHISM

The cynics of genius just discussed consciously attempted to stay away from the plebeian sphere of politics, yet lived at its expense. In their so-called "pure conversations" *(ch'ing-t'an),*[46] an element becomes increasingly recognizable that would soon absorb the nihilism and pessimism in back of this thought, and turn it into something positive in its way, and that was Buddhism. Despair and doubt, disappointment and cynicism, the terminal aspects of an age of this-worldly orientation that had begun with Confucius, became quite naturally the points of departure of an era wholly rooted in the religious, and that was to last almost as long. Unnoticed, the end became a new beginning, and what had started as a swan song turned into an overture.

The first traces of Buddhism in China[47] go back at least as far as the first century A.D. Oddly enough, however, many years went by before the educated Chinese became aware of the fact that Buddhism was not a variant of Taoism, but something radically different. There are several reasons why what was distinct in Buddhism remained obscure for a long time. For one thing, its origin in the West certainly was not felt to be foreign. For according to legend, Lao-tzu had disappeared in the mountains of the West after having turned his *Tao-te-ching* over to a sentry on a mountain pass. The work was his last will and testament. It was in the West that one of the oldest Taoist paradises, the land of the "Queen Mother of the West" was situated. Later also, many Taoists stuck to the theory that Buddha was none other than Lao-tzu who, having left China, had proclaimed his teaching in India. Besides, there was the social attitude of the Buddhists. Scholars who tended to see the world and society as one and the same thing could not easily distinguish with the requisite clarity between the pessimistic rejection of all being in Buddhism, and the fundamentally optimistic rejection of society by the Taoists, who placed their trust in nature. For superficially, the defensive reaction of Buddhists and Taoists against the demands of state and society was almost the same. There was the additional fact that the enormous conceptual apparatus used by Buddhism was not transliterated at first (which meant that foreign words were left standing). Being conceptual, the Chinese system of writing was indeed ill-suited for such a task. Instead, an attempt was made to really translate every term. But all that was available for this purpose was the strictly-speaking rather simple vocabulary of traditional Chinese philosophy, which could not compare with the incredibly richer and more complex Buddhist terminology. Certain serious misunderstandings consequently arose at the very outset. It is true that they were corrected later, but in theory only. Practically speaking, these errors could never be wholly made good because they had entered consciousness too deeply and too early. For the first time, it became unmistakably evident that the much-admired assimilative power of Chinese was really due to an incapacity of the language, and particularly the system of writing, to take over foreign systems of thought without falsifying them. All ideologies which penetrated China from the outside came to grief because a conceptual system of writing did not allow a single foreign word to be smuggled into the vocabulary without forever remaining identifiable as an alien element. Foreign terms either had to be "translated," which meant that they had to be assimilated (usually simplified), or they were forever saddled with the stigma of the exotic in the full meaning of that term. Where a national movement of whatever nature was involved, this fact became their doom.

One of the early, most momentous misunderstandings resulting from the acceptance of Buddhism was due to the erroneous equation of the Buddhist and Chinese concepts of the soul. For in the Buddhist view, the "soul" (although, or precisely because it does not really exist) is one of the most essential constitutive elements of the illusion of individual existence, and also the reason for the continued movement of the wheel of life in reincarnations.[48] Originally, this did not mean a soul passing through various transfigurations, for this would again have implied the existence of a "self." What was envisaged was a kind of karma whirl, a vital impulse propagating itself, which can most readily be compared to a wave in physics. This Buddhist concept was translated by the Chinese word *shen* "soul." According to old Chinese belief, this soul was an imperishable part of man. But after death, it was reabsorbed into the world soul (at a later time, it was also called *hun* to distinguish it from the transitory "body soul" *p'o*). What resulted was more than just this misunderstanding. Because philosophical Buddhism not only rejected the concept of a soul, but proposed to destroy these karma whirls, a problematics immediately arose which was foreign to it, and that was the question concerning the immortality of this newly discovered soul, whose discovery was a misunderstanding.[49] This question provided a direct connection with the great theme which had always preoccupied Taoism so intensely and on a variety of levels, i.e. the preservation of life.

Confucianism and Taoism had changed sides once before in the quarrel about a life after death and the immortality of the individual. Originally, Confucianism had built its entire cult on the principle of ancestor worship. The continued life of the spirits of the ancestors was thus axiomatic. But gradually it moved away from this early, more naive concept, and tended increasingly to see everything religious, including the belief in surviving souls, as a metaphor. What had been religious preoccupations were shunted to the esthetic and moral sphere. Conversely, Taoism had begun by preaching that the individual should surrender his individuality while still alive, since the fact of death made it impossible to save it. But later, it turned more and more to the task of finding ways of preserving individual life, and of making man an immortal, spiritual being.

The opposition between Taoism and Confucianism had thus persisted, although their respective positions had shifted. A similar shift now occurred vis-a-vis Buddhism. Paradoxically, it was not so much the grandiose attempt to put an end to the world in space and time, but rather a concept exploding all traditional views that fascinated most intellects when they compared it with Confucianism (and also with Taoism). For it envisaged a world of incomprehensibly enormous dimensions where, across equally enormous temporal and spatial distances, all creatures were connected in all directions by the threads of karma. Precisely due to the erroneous belief that the soul passed through a number of existences, it seemed that the individual lives of all these creatures were set on a course that was nothing short of majestic, for it had begun eons ago and led through all the forms of creation. What was central in Buddhism paled before the profound impression these conceptions of enormous magnitudes, mostly traceable to Brahmin influences, made on the Chinese mind, accustomed as it was to "human," historical dimensions. The notion of a wholly personal retribution continuing to be effective through an endless chain of rebirths gave Buddhism a mighty impetus as a religion. That this should be so in China is readily comprehensible, for ethics had always been more important than speculation in that country.[50] The following two texts give a good insight into this new consciousness. The first of them was written by the monk Hui-lin in 431. He rejected the idea of the immortality of the "soul," but allows his adversary to state his position, and it is that argument which is quoted below. The second passage is by the Buddhist Tsung Ping (375–443), written in 433. Because it attacks Hui-lin's treatise, it accords more or less with the view of the latter's opponent:

> The teachings of the duke of Chou and Confucius may suffice for a single life, but they fail to consider the endless chain of causalities which comes into being with every existence and is relevant to future lives. In their opinion, the piling up of good deeds brings happiness which will last down to children and grandchildren, while repeated misdeeds bring punishments which result in further misfortune for the nearest relatives. All they could promise was glory and riches, all they could threaten was extreme poverty. They did not know what they could not see or hear. All that was very nebulous to them; one can only feel sorry for them. Sakyamuni, however, turned his attention to the infinite karma, removed the dangers which block our path like a double fence [on our way to nirvana], and calmed the beating of our

heart. His breadth of illumination was such that the universe in all its greatness could not fill it. The possibility of deliverance he created by his mildness transcends the powers of cultivation of all [other] beings [on earth]. He describes the various kinds of hell so that people might become fearful of their punishments, and the Heavens so that they might look with hope to the delights awaiting them. He showed them nirvana, which will be their permanent condition, and let them climb the *dkarmakaya* [the doctrine of salvation], to broaden their horizon. His mysterious transformations comprehend the entire cosmos, his light radiates everywhere. Already in the earliest times, saints with the greatest illumination soared upward, but those with second-rate knowledge [merely] hopped about fluttering, and did not attain it. How can one grasp the dimensions of a spacious house from the perspective [of a man] sitting in a well![51]

Life is not completed in a single life span, it cannot but pass on its impulses. If the chain of life is traced back into the past, one does not come to a beginning, and if one follows it into the future, one generation follows the next, and no end is ever found. . . . Because of this limitlessness of space, this infinity of time, man walks in the chain [of incarnations] and extends himself in them. [Even before,] there was no doubt that we [merely] inhabit the continent of Ch'ih-hsien within the eight poles.[52] Now we are told that there are three thousand suns and moons in the sky, that twelve thousand worlds are distributed [in space], that there are as many eons as there are grains of sand in the Ganges river. . . . A single hair and the ocean in which it floats can be more readily compared than the [Confucian] rules about social relations, [tiny as they are,] and the [Buddhist] "Great Learning." Words cannot define that difference. . . . People say: "How distant, how dark is the time before the 'Yellow Emperor!' " But seen from the perspective of the "Heavenly Way," all that happened only yesterday. The *Book of Documents* is said to know about antiquity, yet it reaches no further back than to the time of a Yao and Shun, and the contents of the *Spring and Autumn Annals* gives us no more than reports about [the time of] the kings. Not to mention the *Books of Rites* and the *Book of Music* about good manners and propriety, the *Book of Songs* and the *Book of Changes* for entertainment and edification! Now that the three thousand suns and moons shine in their splendor in an endless universe, and let the chain of 12,000 words be seen clearly, we become conscious that everything the duke of Chou and Confucius put on paper merely corresponds to the inarticulate cry of dwarf states for a savior. [As in the fairy tale, they live on the two horns of a snake and fight with each other], but none of this suffices to solve [the problems of] even a single life. As regards problems going beyond this, [these sages] left matters as they had found them, and did not express themselves at all. If I am wrong, how is it that they are so verbose about physical existence and so silent about the life of the soul after death? "Climb the Meng mountain, and [the state of] Lu will appear small to you; climb the T'ai-shan mountain, and the whole world will appear small to you,"—this proverb well characterizes the narrow limits of these [men].[53]

Through this explosive expansion of the living space, reality here and now shrank to something pathetically small. It also had a profound influence on the various conceptions of the ideal conditions for the individual and society. The

Golden Times of antiquity suddenly seemed as questionable as the paradises on the edges of the world, for in the context of the gigantic dimensions of this new cosmos, both were separated from reality by only a few moments, a few inches. They seemed to have come too close for genuine, eternal salvation to be expected from them. Even more decisive was the fact that the meaning of happiness in Buddhism differed substantially from that in indigenous Chinese systems of thought. Buddhism did not deny the existence of a great variety of temporally limited experiences of joy. But the central tenet of its doctrine was the conviction that there was no such thing as absolute, lasting happiness in life, and this belief was not surrendered by a single one of the many sects which arose at a later time. This iron law applied not only to men and animals, but even to godlike beings of a higher order. All existence on whatever plane was poisoned by unhappiness from the very start; sooner or later, it would inevitably assert its dominance. Only nirvana offered deliverance from this curse of all existence. But any idea, description or definition of this condition was impossible in principle. While it was not "nothingness," it necessarily lacked all polarities, delimitation or differentiation. This conviction resulted not only in a turning away from the world, but from happiness itself. For every form of happiness contained new suffering; worse still, it merely veiled the only true knowledge of the all-pervasiveness of suffering, distracted man from the path of salvation, and implied a decline even where it had developed from a good karma. It represented a life lived on previously accumulated capital. Even the heavens and paradises, painted in the most glowing colors for its believers by Buddhism, were not free of this taint. They were temporally limited paradises and their questionable value was recognized and discussed within that religion. In the treatise written in 431, for example, Hui-lin gives the following answer to his opponent, whose paean on the felicity expected in Buddhist paradises we just quoted:

> [Some Buddhists] pretend that there are paradises in order to influence creatures to the good. Would it not be better to persuade them by righteousness, and thus to lead them to the Way *(tao)?* . . . When you praise the happiness of nirvana, you merely induce laziness. When you describe the wonders of *dkarmakaya,* you merely stimulate curiosity. The obvious desires [for worldly pleasures] have not even been put to rest, yet [new desires] for advantages in foreign lands already arise. Although you say that the Buddha has no desires, it is precisely in his name that the creatures are confirmed in theirs. [What nonsense.] Although you wish to save the people from its blindness, you permanently instill the bad habit of chasing after benefits. If you do that, how can you hope to purify the spirit and to lead it back to the "Way?"[54]

Thus it came about that detachment from the world and mistrust of the possibility of realizing happiness on earth put their stamp on the intellectual life down to the tenth and eleventh centuries. It is true that this did not manifest itself in an abatement of the pursuit of the pleasures of this world. It would be more correct to say that the reverse was the case. The religious age of Buddhism in China was a period of continuous struggle, lively cultural exchanges between nations and across continents and, last but not least, the unfolding of a mature and cosmopolitan splendor such as China had never seen before and was never to attain again.[55] But it was precisely in this intensity and flexibility that the ever-present conviction of the transitoriness of all glory, of the tragic element in life as revealed by Buddhism manifested itself. The world was no longer as solidly constructed and imperishable as it had once appeared to all Chinese philosophers, however widely they might have diverged in other respects. Not only the extinction of the self, but also that of the entire universe, where man's abode was now no more than a grain of dust, seemed ineluctable. Indeed, such extinction actually represented the ultimate goal of all human endeavor. It was this spiritual certainty, which spread beyond the actual disciples of Buddhism to many scholars and large sections of the people, that revealed the new pessimistic attitude much more concretely than the incredible proliferation of monasticism which gradually became an important (and not always positive) economic and political factor.

It is obvious that this intellectual climate was not propitious to the creation of models for an ideal social order. It was not worth the effort to construct emergency solutions for a world doomed to inevitable suffering, for they could not have the eternal validity indispensable to any ideal. What was the use of an exemplary political system or of a happy life in a setting where it was commonly held that the monk who had freed himself from the obligations and pleasures state and family might offer was closest to ultimate salvation? It was a world where, as stubborn Confucians often complained, fanaticism did not stop short of self-mutilation if this would ensure salvation. Thus hope turned from this calamitous vale of tears to the beyond. Strictly speaking, the heavens and paradises described by Buddhism did not differ in principle from this world, yet the bliss and length of life promised for most of these places were so tempting that it was not always necessary to look beyond them. Another factor was the doctrine concerning Bodhisattvas. While difficult to defend on theoretical grounds, it found enthusiastic acceptance, especially in Mahayana Buddhism, which played the decisive role in East Asia. These figures were those Buddhas who had renounced nirvana in order to help others achieve salvation. The best known among them was Avalokitesvara, the helper who looks in all directions. Beginning in the seventh century, he was gradually transformed into a female figure in China. The Kuan-yin, as it was called, has been represented countless times in impressive paintings and statues since that period, and is curiously reminiscent of Christian representations of the Mother of God. As with all other Bodhisattvas, the popular imagination conceived of Avalokitesvara as enthroned in Heaven-like intermediate realms. These in turn conferred an increased value on other paradises, and justified the longing for them, particularly since some of them were presented as outer halls of nirvana.

Yet even without particularly stressing their value and justifying it theoretically, the heavens and paradises of Buddhism overwhelmed the Chinese simply by the exuberant descriptions given of them. Their mere number, which might vary considerably from case to case, and which encouraged the imagination to conceive of an increasingly complete happiness, had something intoxicating about it. While early Taoist paradises, let alone the ideal descriptions of Confucians and Legalists, had always had something very simple about them and been socially oriented, the ideas coming from India confronted the Chinese with an imaginative power that burst all bounds. The detailed enumeration of treasures whose very names were unknown proved so confusing that they surrendered unconditionally to this magic. The much richer, even exuberant, if sometimes turgid Indian imagination remorselessly reduced the old, somehow more solidly constructed, yet also almost touchingly homespun Chinese paradises to insignificant trifles. That the Indian paradises were much more shadowy, all but fatiguing in their endless repetitiveness, and almost cold in their sterile schematism, was not of much consequence at first. Precisely because they could not serve as models for the here and now, and contrasted in this respect with the earlier Chinese conceptions of the ideal, they had that degree of remoteness which could assure those who turned their back on this world that the vexations and problems of life on earth would not catch up with them.

THE PARADISE OF THE WEST

The most famous of all Buddhist paradises, actually a whole complex of them, is Sukhavati, the "Paradise of the West," ruled by Amitabha, an earlier, legendary Buddha, the "Buddha of Infinite Light," who is not identical with the historical Buddha Sakyamuni. This land of happiness is verbosely described and discussed in countless texts.[56] The oldest one known in China, and the most influential, is the "Greater *Sukhavati-vyuha* Sutra," which was translated into Chinese as early as A.D. 252, and given the title *Ta wu-liang-shou ching* ("Great Sutra of Infinite life"). It contains a detailed description whose tenor will be suggested to some extent by the following quotation:

> The Buddha has not disappeared, nor has he not yet appeared. He, the holy one, is living now, having reached the highest stage of knowledge. . . . He lives in the western sphere, in the land of Buddha. Its distance from this world is 100,000 *niyutas* of *kotis*[57] of Buddha lands, in a world called Sukhavati. His name is Amitabha, the Tathagata, the holy and perfectly illumined one. He is surrounded by innumerable Bodhisattvas, worshipped by infinitely many sravakas, and in possession of the infinite perfection of the Buddha land. The light [radiating from him] is immeasurable, one can hardly say where its limits are. . . . At each end [of this land], in the south, the west and the north, the zenith and the nadir, at all these ends there are 100,000 *niyutas* of *kotis* of Buddha lands, as numerous as the grains of sand in the Ganges. They also are all illuminated by the light of this Bhagavat Amitabha. . . . This world . . . blossoms and is rich, a good place to live, fertile,

lovely, and full of gods and men. There is no hell there, nor animals or realms of the spirits of the dead, nor bodies of Asuras, nor [human beings] born at the wrong time. . . . This world is redolent with the most various, sweet fragrances. It is rich in the most diverse flowers and fruit, adorned with trees of precious stones. Swarms of many different, sweetly chirping birds live there, which were especially created by Tathagata. . . . There are golden trees made of gold, silver trees of silver . . . beryl-colored trees of beryllium . . . and trees . . . made of [all imaginable combinations of precious stones]. . . . There are lotus blossoms with a circumference of half a *yojana*,[58] [and bigger,] consisting of pure precious stone. And from everyone of these precious stones emanate 36 times 100,000 *kotis* of rays of light, and from each of these rays of light there emerge 36 times 100,000 *kotis* of Buddhas with gold-colored bodies. They have the 32 marks of the great man. They go to teach the law in the immeasurable and innumerable worlds of the East. . . . In this Buddha land, there are no dark mountains, not even mountains of jewels, nor Sumeru mountains. This Buddha land is level in all directions,[59] lovely like the palm of the hand, with regions full of precious stones and treasures of all kinds. . . . In this land, the most various rivers flow, some with a width of one *yojana*,[60] others 20, 30, 40 or 50 *yojanas* wide, and sometimes reaching a depth of 12 *yojanas*. All of these rivers refreshen the spirit. Their water has many sweet fragrances. Bunches of flowers decorated with all imaginable jewels float along on it, and their rustling is full of sweet music. This heavenly music comes from instruments consisting of 100,000 *kotis* of parts, and is played by the most expert musicians. On the banks of these rivers, there grows a great variety of trees made of gems, with the most magnificent blossoms, leaves and branches that hang down [into the water]. When the creatures dwelling on the river banks wish to delight in heavenly joys, the water of the rivers rises up to their ankles the moment they enter it, if they so desire. Or it rises to their knees, if that is what pleases them, or to their hips or ears, and heavenly joy envelops them. If they want the water cold, it becomes cold; it becomes hot when they so desire, or both hot and cold if that is their wish. . . . In this world, there are no signs of sin, misfortune, distress, sadness and mortality. No sound of pain, not even the sound of a feeling that is neither pain nor joy, exists there. . . . The creatures of this world do not eat coarse food. Whatever they wish to eat is granted them as if it were brought to them, and their bodies and spirits delight in it. They do not even have to put [the food] into their mouth. And if, having eaten, they should crave various fragrances, the entire Buddha land is filled with them. . . . And if they desire musical instruments, flags, umbrellas, coats, powder, ointments or wreaths, the entire Buddha land is filled with these things. . . . And if they desire ornaments for the head, the ears, the neck, or armbands or rings for their ankles, they can see that the entire Buddha land shines with them. And if they desire a palace painted in different colors and with ornaments, of a given height and width, provided with a hundred or a thousand gates with all imaginable jewels, it is precisely such palaces that come into view. . . . In this world, the difference between gods and men does not exist, except perhaps in the sense that one still has to use this terminology when speaking an ordinary, imperfect language. . . . Concepts such as fire, sun, moon, planets, constellations or fixed stars or [the opposite], darkness, are never mentioned in this land. Except for the Tathagata in his conversations,

> nobody mentions day or night. All the creatures that were, are, or will be born in this land will only speak the truth until they enter nirvana. All the Bodhisattvas who were, are, or will be born in this land will only have this one birth and will then attain to the highest knowledge. . . . All the creatures in this Buddha land have no conception of property. All who walk through this land feel neither joy nor pain. When they move, it is not because they are prompted by any particular desire, nor do they feel desire as they move about. They do not think of any other creatures. . . . They have no concept of other creatures, no concept of a self, no concept of inequality, dispute, quarrel or animosity. Full of equanimity and benevolent, tender, loving, strong, useful, serious, firm, clear thoughts, full of conceptions directed toward the practice of order and the wisdom of the beyond, they have attained to a knowledge which is of great assistance in thinking, and may be compared to an ocean of knowledge, a Meru mountain of knowledge. . . . Thus they are intelligent in the investigation of all things, familiar with the knowledge concerning the end of movement of all things, for they even recognize what is no longer visible. They are not concerned with anything, not attached to anything, free of anxiety, of grief, of attachment to anything whatever, of impurity. . . . The light of their wisdom and the splendor, purity and beauty of their knowledge surpass the light of sun and moon. . . . In the patience with which they suffer the good and the evil deeds of men, they resemble the earth; they resemble the water as they clean and wash away the stains of sin; as they burn away the calamity of pride, they resemble the ether; they are like lotus blossoms because they are not defiled by anything in the entire world; they resemble the great clouds during the rainy period as they proclaim the law.[61]

As it is described here, the "Paradise of the West" played an eminent role in the "Pure Land Sect" which gradually evolved during the second half of the third century and had a particular attraction for the uneducated masses. Imprisoned in the misery of the everyday, large numbers of simple believers placed their final, glowing hopes on this blessed country which not only promised bliss but, beyond that and counter to all Buddhist logic, the direct transition to nirvana. Many artists were inspired by the image of this paradise. Painters covered devotional grottos and temples with the colorful representations of this splendid place,[62] poets described it in their verse. Because of its roots in the people, the "Pure Land Sect" survived more successfully than others the counterattack of Confucianism which began in the ninth century and was primarily aimed at the reconquest of the educated. During more recent times, it consequently became one of the strongest components in the modern, organized church of Buddhism, not only in China, but in Japan as well.[63] It was not so much the individual qualities of this ideal country as it was projected into space that lent wings to the popular imagination and even endowed it with political efficacy in secret societies. Rather, it was the hope it could stir in the hearts of men as an ideal. For however huge the spaces may have been that were first disclosed in the descriptions from India, however profound the awe in face of this almost unreal eternity, the practical sense of the Chinese finally tended to humanize the cosmic dimensions, and thus to deflect some of the rays of the infinite light of the beyond onto the world inhabited by men. Under Chinese influence, paradise became smaller, but more realistic and more readily comprehensible in a social sense. A very early document shows this quite nicely. The monk Chih Tun (314–366), a significant figure who was responsible in part for the momentous fusion of Taoism and Buddhism, and may almost as justifiably be called a Taoist as a Buddhist (he wrote an important commentary on the book *Chuang-tzu*), left a written confession in which he stated it as his goal to be reincarnated in the "Paradise of the West."[64] Although it is naturally quite brief, he also gives a description of the paradise itself. Its terms are very characteristic of the changes or shifts in accent that could occur in accounts of paradise in a Chinese milieu:

> In the West lies a country called An-yang ("cultivation of peace").[65] The way to it is long, very long, takes countless turns, and passes constantly through sand. No one can reach its borders without help, and unless one hurries, how could one ever attain the speed necessary to get there? The Buddha who rules that country is called Amitabha. In our language, its name is "Land of Eternal Life." Kings *(wu wang)*, laws, classes or ranks of nobility are unknown. The Buddha is considered the only master, the proclamation of the "Three Vehicles" the only doctrine. Boys and girls are born from lotus blossoms, and therefore not defiled by the maternal womb. Inns and houses, palaces and halls are all decorated with the seven treasures. Everywhere, ready to be plucked and as if they had grown naturally, the most beautiful things hang from the trees. They are finer than human craftsmen can make. Gardens and parks, pools and ponds shine in marvelous splendor. All that flies and lives in the water exists in natural abundance in streams, lakes and marshes. Up to the time of their death, men live in the company of animals, following their real nature without interference. The entrances to houses are not barred by gates. In the coral woods, the sound of precious stones raises the spirit to heavenly serenity, while dark mists settle as flutes play. As the chalices near the dwellings sway in a divine wind, their fresh sweet dew turns into a strong wine. The fragrance of orchids calls forth virtue, until the aroma is wafted in all directions. Sacred music responds to the stirrings of the spirit until it resembles the roll of thunder. Clouds, born of a swamp of wisdom, hang down until the greatest clarity results. Education and scholarship are imbibed until they express themselves in precious words. "True men" immerse themselves in dark principles until they have shed all that is playful. The void is crossed on the Five Bridges until one enters Non-being. And in Prajna, one approaches knowledge until one has left the darkness of ignorance.[66]

Without ado, the Buddhist paradise has been transformed again into a Taoist one. It is no longer the "land of infinite light," but the "land of infinite *life.*" The trees of jewels, which the sober Chinese did not really know what to do with, have moved into the background, as have the splendid palaces. The marshes and waters, on the other hand, swarm with all sorts of edible creatures—a downright inconceivable notion for a Buddhist—and the heavy wine of the gods invites inebriation, a conceit that is equally inimical to Buddhism. For as we have seen, intoxication and mystic ecstasy are reconcilable in Taoism, and were not infrequently almost identified with each other at a later time. For the Buddhist, on the other hand, the key to salvation was not the warm, unconscious return to the prehuman condition of the innocent, life-giving creature, but instead the cold, even icy insight into the hopelessly tragic situation of all being to which life and suffering are always given conjointly. It is therefore no accident that animals of any description are absent from the "land of infinite light." It is also for this reason that the Buddhists drank tea, not wine. Its acceptance all over Asia coincided almost exactly with the introduction of Buddhism in China. It does not lend wings to the mind, but sharpens it and tends to emphasize rather than to break down what separates men. It is not esthetically inferior to wine, but probably superior, and therefore gave rise to a whole literature which dealt entirely with the various kinds of tea, of water, and methods of preparation. The latter were subsequently stylized as the "tea ceremony" and took on a cult-like character.[67] The Taoist influence in Chih Tun's description of paradise becomes quite unmistakable where he speaks of the life of men in the company of animals, since it had been one of the important aims of Buddhism to establish a distinction between the two. This was not due to any antipathy, but to the belief that animals and even gods were denied the ability to understand the connection between life and suffering. No wonder that Chih Tun introduces a thoroughly Taoist concept toward the end, i.e. the concept of the "true man," the ideal man who has entered the cycle of nature instead of having detached himself from it, a figure that had already occupied the center of discussion in Chuang-tzu.

Surprisingly, we even find some Confucian clichés in the description, such as the absence of outer gates, an epithet applied to a country without thieves, comparable to the topos about the objects lost on the street that remain lying there. The value placed on "education and scholarship" expressed in one sentence and, more generally, the stylistic form where the virtues of this paradise are listed in strict parallel clauses in the final passage, point in the same direction. Even where the tenor is clearly anti-Confucian, as in the very opening with its praise of anarchic conditions, it is manifest that the thoughts of the Chinese author are much more strongly directed toward the social sphere in what is a typically Confucian manner than had been the case in the Indian model.

This may also be the reason why it was Maitreya and not Amitabha among the non-historical Buddhas that first became popular. In Buddhist conceptions, Maitreya was a future Buddha, one "who had not yet appeared." According to some schools, his birth lay in the remote future while others, more important in our context, thought his advent might occur at any time. Maitreya's residence was the Tusita heaven, a place reserved for all those Buddhas who had only one more round to absolve on earth to free themselves of the last traces of karma. For this reason, he had also been visited by the historical Buddha Sakyamuni before he found his final (i.e. historical) reincarnation. Like the "Western Paradise," the Tusita heaven was therefore also the place to which all believers longed to go. Yet its importance was decidedly inferior to that of the "Western Paradise" because altogether different associations were connected with Maitreya. With his paradise, Amitabha promised salvation from the suffering of this world by pledging to bring those who believed and confided in him into his realm. The thoughts connected with this were escapist through and through, other-worldly, and in no way directed toward the improvement of this earth. In the case of Maitreya, things were altogether different. However long delayed his arrival might be, he was a figure that did not distance himself from the here and now, but approached it irresistibly like a shining star. Although it can hardly be justified by original Buddhist teaching, it is yet psychologically understandable that he therefore became a world redeemer in the eyes of the believers. For he would not merely proclaim the teaching like the historical Buddha, but simultaneously and at a single stroke free the world of misery and injustice and create conditions of undiluted joy and happiness in it. Those Taoist expectations of salvation which had crystalized earlier in the *T'ai-p'ing-ching,* or come into existence under Buddhist influence, could readily identify with this hope. The splendor of the worship of Amitabha began to outstrip the Maitreya cult from the middle of the seventh century on.[68] Ultimately, this may have been due in part to the gentle direction of the state, which had recovered its power during the T'ang dynasty (618–906). For a Buddhism that turned its back on this world may have seemed more acceptable than one that took an interest in it. Yet Maitreya continued to play an exceptionally important role in the secret societies. He became a symbolic figure for these important but not easily identifiable undercurrents in Chinese society which attracted all those that were dissatisfied with a world administered and planned in the Confucian image.

After the victory of Confucianism over Buddhism, which became increasingly apparent toward the end of the first millennium A.D., Maitreya reappeared in an entirely different form. This was certainly no mere chance, but indicative of the danger Confucianism saw in a personified belief in a better, wholly reordered future, for its interest lay in a stabilization of order and the stabilization of the present. During the Sung period (960–1280), Maitreya suddenly emerged as the laughing "Pot-bellied Buddha." Representations of this figure in all sorts of material have swamped East Asia ever since, and even today blemish Chinese art and curio shops. Consciously or not, the hope for a better future had taken a new direction. Under the influence of Confucianism, it had become less threatening to the existing hierarchy, and therefore did not have to fear the light of day. For the once august figure of Maitreya, its unfathomable eyes turned toward an eternal future, and promising the dawn of a new, universal law, is very unlike this new Maitreya, who embodies something much less complex, namely the confident good spirits that come from a full belly. A grandiose banality had been created which indirectly interpreted all the unhappiness and misery of this world as a kind of insufficiency. Although this may not have been entirely false for a naive consciousness, it also meant that the Maitreya cult had been stripped of its revolutionary sting. The clumsy, good-natured "Doppelgänger" was a terrible philistine and thus gave the best possible aid in the struggle against the ascetic, genuine Maitreya. Not infrequently, he guaranteed that those who really starved could not manage to look beyond their stomach, however empty it might be.

THE LAND OF UTTARAKURU

The very earthly character of the Chinese is probably also the reason that it was not only Buddhist paradises that took on a different form in their new environment. Conceptions of such places that were not part of the Buddhist tradition but had come into China at the same time as that religion (or perhaps even earlier) also became very popular. By and large, they derived from the Brahmin tradition which was less indifferent to the concerns of this world. They were situated on earth and could offer tangible pleasure which people other than saints could enjoy. For it is the exclusivity of almost all religious paradises that so alienates the ordinary sensibility. The earliest of all such places, which served as model for innumerable others, partly formed the conceptions of the "Paradise of the West," and influenced the descriptions of ideal lands in the book *Lieh-tzu*, was the country of Uttarakuru to the north of the world mountain Meru. Reports about it can already be found in the *Ramayana* and the *Mahabharata*, i.e. as early as the fourth century B.C. They passed not only eastward, but also westward where both Pindar and Herodotus described Uttarakuru as the land of the Hyperboreans, the inhabitants of the extreme north.[69] Certain motifs strongly reminiscent of Uttarakuru can be found in the philosophical texts of the *Huai-nan-tzu*, and the *Lü-shih ch'un-ch'iu*, documents dating back to the second century B.C. and earlier, and also in the previously mentioned, half-legendary geographical treatise *Shan-hai-ching*, although these connections have not been proven beyond all doubt.[70] In any event, we have here an incredibly fascinating, highly complex network of mythologies that spread over all of Eurasia, and perhaps even further. Because these mythologies differ to some degree from people to people, interesting insights into markedly divergent mentalities become possible. If the reports concerning certain southern peoples, the Wu and the Tieh in the *Shan-hai-ching*, actually have Uttarakuru as their model for example, China again seems characterized by a remarkable restraint. In the *Ramayana*, the entire country literally overflows with gold, sapphires and lapis lazuli, and the beds of the countless rivers do not consist of sand but of pearls and jewels. The corresponding passage in the *Shan-hai-ching* merely stresses the abundance of jade, iron, silver and cinnabar (the basic substance of Taoist alchemy). While in the former work the trees bear any and all imaginable treasures on their branches, the music of the spheres rings in the air and men attain a well-nigh infinite age, the Chinese book merely states that the inhabitants are clothed and fed without having to plough and weave, that they are entertained by the dance and songs of the magical birds Luan and Feng, and that all their wishes are fulfilled.[71] Even when their imagination takes them into dream worlds, the Chinese retain a sober sense of reality and a profound dislike of luxury and waste.

Early in the seventh century, the monk Dharmagupta brought out a translation which was incorporated in the Buddhist canon. The description of the land Uttarakuru it contained was a version which, in a certain sense, took a middle course between the two extremes. It thus quite clearly accommodated Chinese taste, yet did not deviate too markedly from the luxuriant utopias of the earliest accounts. The success of this mixture is evidenced by the fact that even at a time when Buddhism had been almost completely dislodged among the upper classes, the description of this blessed country still found an audience. Thus the scholar Huan Chou-hsing (1611–1680) made a number of excerpts and concluded each with a poem of his own invention where he expressed his enthusiasm.[72] The modern writer Lin Yü-t'ang found these excerpts interesting enough to translate them in his book *The Importance of Understanding,* and presented them to his western readers as a typical example of Chinese thought.[73] The following translation does not use this selection, for it only gives passages interesting to the Chinese which are brought together toward the end and describe social conditions. Instead, an attempt is made here to give a somewhat broader overview of the original text. It is subdivided into a rather large number of individual sections, each of which begins with the exclamation: "Listen, you monks," (omitted here):

> Infinitely tall mountains rise above the continent of Uttarakuru. A great variety of trees grows among them. Their luxuriant foliage exudes the most diverse, intoxicating fragrances. Everywhere, different kinds of grass grow. They are purple and green in color, yielding and elastic like peacock feathers. . . . All kinds of birds sing, their voices are charming, their sounds strange and lovely. Many different rivers flow between the mountains. Branching out, they all come down [from the heights] in hundreds of courses and only then gradually become calm. They flow neither too rapidly nor too slowly, and do not form waves. Their banks are not high, the rivers themselves are shallow and therefore easy to wade through. Their water is of a crystalline clarity and covered with various blossoms. Their width is half a day's journey, yet they are equally deep everywhere. . . . The country is most carefully maintained throughout. There are no thorny bushes, no abysses, no impenetrable forests, no swamp holes, no latrines, no excrement, no filth, no ruins and no debris. . . . If the people of Uttarakuru feel the need to evacuate, the earth opens below them, and afterwards closes up again so that everything looks exactly as before[74]. . . . Everything is as clean as if it were made of gold and silver. The climate is neither too hot nor too cold, the seasons are in harmony with each other, the earth is always fertile. The green grass grows thickly, as do the different kinds of forest, and branches and leaves surpass each other in luxuriant strength and also bear blossoms and fruit. Then there is also a kind of tree called "dwelling of peace." All of these trees are six *krosa* tall.[75] Their leaves are arranged in several closely packed, ascending layers like the straw on the roof of a house. Consequently, rain cannot penetrate and all the people there can live underneath them. There are also all kinds of fragrance trees which are also six *krosa* tall, and sometimes smaller—five, four, three, two and one *krosa* tall. The smallest are half a *krosa* tall. . . . Then there

are trees called Po-so. Their sizes are the same. They produce all imaginable kinds of garments by themselves, which hang from their branches. Then there are other kinds of trees where ornaments . . . jewels . . . and all sorts of implements grow, and also trees which produce a variety of musical instruments. In this country, rice grows by itself. Ploughing and sowing are unnecessary. Everything is of a sparkling cleanliness . . . shells and refuse do not lie around anywhere. If a cooked meal is to be prepared, all kinds of fruit exist for that purpose, which are called *Tun-ch'ih*. A kettle is heated with a "fire pearl," wood or coal are not required. Because the "fire pearl" radiates heat, one can warm whatever one wishes to eat or drink. When the food has been cooked, the "fire pearl" goes out. . . . Four lakes, lying in the four cardinal directions, encircle this country. Anavatapta is their common name. To travel across them requires fifty days. Their water is cool and gentle, of a sweet lightness and fragrant clarity. . . . On all four sides, they are bordered by seven varieties of To-lo-hsing trees which give off a lovely, multicolored glow, and are made of the seven precious materials, gold, silver, crystal, beryllium, red pearls, diamonds, and agate. . . . All the flowers growing on the lakes have the circumference of chariot wheels. . . . The stalks of the lotus flowers are as thick as the hub of a wheel. When they are broken off, a juice flows from them which looks like milk, has a marvelous taste, and the fragrance of honey. . . . At midnight, a great, heavy cloud always rises from the Anavatapta lakes. It spreads over the entire country, envelops all the seas and mountains, and finally discharges a miraculous rain. It is like cow's milk, and leaves four *chih* of water which is completely absorbed by the soil on which it falls. None of the water flows away. Just after midnight, the rain stops, the cloud disappears, and the sky is clear once more. A wind rises from the oceans, it blows sweetly and strongly, and is fresh and soft. Wherever it blows, it brings contentedness and joy. . . . Selfishness, rulers, or police are unknown *(wu-wo, wu-chu)*. . . . When the people of Uttarakuru bathe in one of the four miraculous rivers flowing through the country, or wish to swim to enjoy themselves, they simply go to the banks, undress, leave their clothing on the beach, step into boats and move out into the water. There they bathe and play in the waves for as long as they enjoy themselves. When they return to the beach, they all pick up the garments lying nearest them and in the order of their arrival. They dress and wander off without looking for their own clothes. Why? Because the people of Uttarakuru pay no attention to what does and does not belong to them. . . . Their hair is of a purplish blue, and they are uniformly eight *chih* tall. They also all look alike, both in body and face, and there is not the slightest difference by which one might tell them apart. They all walk about well dressed, no one is naked or half-dressed. . . . Kinship relations are uniformly ordered, prejudices do not exist. Their teeth are always perfectly straight, with no gaps, no irregularities, of a miraculous beauty in their glowing whiteness and a coloration reminiscent of light jade, lovely in its radiance. . . . When they have prepared a meal and wish to eat, they put down dishes, look for a place, and sit down. If others come to share their meal, they give them something to eat also. Food never gives out, for as long as people are sitting about eating, the dishes are always full. . . . After they have finished their meal, they feel physically strengthened in every way. Weakness, decline do not exist. They retain an unchanging freshness and do not know aging or change. For the food gives them such energy that their appearance and strength remain untouched, and they never have occasion to complain about weakness. When the men and women of Uttarakuru want to unite in love, they only obey their hearts and show their desire by casting glances at each other. When a girl recognizes the feelings of a man in this way, she immediately accompanies him, and thus they walk together under the miracle trees. But if the woman the man has chosen is his mother, aunt, older or younger sister, or some other relative (which cannot be readily established since they all look alike), the branches of the miracle trees look like those of ordinary trees. No gifts hang down from them, but their leaves immediately fade and turn yellow, fall down and no longer afford protection. Nor do they continue to blossom or bear fruit, and beds no longer grow on them. But if it is not his mother, aunt, older or younger sister, then all kinds of beautiful things hang down from the branches: bed covers, clusters of leaves of white jade, blossoms and fruit of the greatest splendor. Hundreds, thousands of different things are produced by them for the two humans, including beds and mattresses so that they can come together as soon as they are below the trees, and make each other happy to their hearts' content. Among the people of Uttarakuru, the children remain in the womb for just seven days, they are born on the eighth. Whether it be a boy or a girl, the mother puts the child at the place where the four great roads of the country cross, leaves it to its own devices, and walks away. People coming from all directions pass there, and when they see boys or girls sitting at that place, they feel compassion and a desire to nourish them. They place their finger into the childrens' mouth. From its tip, and all by itself, sweet milk immediately flows with which they feed them and keep them alive. After the children have been fed in this way for seven days, they are fully grown and look precisely like adults. Not even by their size can they be told apart. Men and women join their respective groups and wander away with them. Thus the entire country becomes in truth one single family! The life span is of uniform length for all the people of Uttarakuru. No one dies prematurely in his middle age, every one lives out his years, all become quite old. . . . They live for one thousand years, no more and no less. When someone is about to die, no one mourns or weeps during his final hour. His body is simply picked up, taken to the crossing of the four great roads, and allowed to lie there. The people then walk off. . . . Now a bird called *Yu-ch'eng-chia-mo* comes flying quickly from a tall mountain, seizes the dead by the hair and carries the body away, letting it fall down on one of the continents at the four corners of the country. Of the four realms at the four ends of the world, the land of Uttarakuru in the north is the best and most miraculous, the highest and the most eminent.[76]

In this paradise, certain things already alluded to in earlier Taoist descriptions of ideal places leap to the eye. Most important is the motif of the absence of rulers, mentioned first as a peculiarity of the realm of the dead by Chuang-tzu, and repeated frequently since. The anarchism, however, is not designated by the Taoist, terminologically clearly anti-Confucian expression *wu-chün* "absence of princes," where the rejection of the Confucian ideal man, the "son of a prince" *(chün-tzu)* who is conceivable only within a hierarchy, finds its indirect expression. What is used here is the somewhat more neutral Buddhist equivalent *wu-chu* "absence of rulers." The anarchistic state of this country is noteworthy because it is more strongly articulated than in other Buddhist paradises. For the "Paradise of the West," the most popular among them, is ruled, albeit in a very sublime way, by the Buddha Amitabha. The fact that "kings, laws, classes and ranks of nobility" no longer exist there points less to the absolute equality of all than it does to the equality before the Buddha, a kind of equality before God, which is something altogether different. In Uttarakuru, on the other hand, we find not merely a true absence of rulers. With remarkable consistency all those premises are present which insure that absence for all time to come. The equality of all the inhabitants of this country, their "lack of self," is driven to the ultimate point: they are all equally tall, and can therefore exchange their clothes without trouble; they also look entirely alike. According to older Indian sources, they all have square faces, just as the country itself is square. Also, they all die at precisely the same age. Furthermore, the hierarchy of age has disappeared, since youth lasts only seven days in a life of a thousand years, and the process of aging does not occur. Yet it is precisely this hierarchy which constitutes the basic model for all hierarchies in China. The total abolition of the family—undoubtedly breathtaking for the Chinese of that period—is shown by the fact that the raising of children becomes in a sense the task of the community, that burials are executed without piety, that members of a family do not know each other at all and can thus be preserved from incest only by the reactions of nature. The incest taboo is actually all that remains of the family system.

With this single exception, freedom in the erotic sphere is unlimited. Understandably, this gift is normally rather restricted in Buddhist paradises, and must therefore be especially emphasized. The "Lesser Vehicle" *(Hinayana),* a school more strongly influenced by pre-Buddhist Indian religions, and which also includes the legend of the Hyperboreans, has fantastic universal rulers, the "Wheel-Kings" *(Cakravarti),* who differ from the inhabitants of Uttarakuru because they can attain to the knowledge that life is full of suffering. They are granted the pleasures of love. And to a certain extent, this is also true of the many-layered paradises of the "Gods" (consisting ordinarily of twenty-eight steps). But there, love becomes more spiritual with each ascending step. Indeed, the form it takes becomes the very criterion for the elevation of the respective heaven. This parallels the life span which stretches from five hundred god years, where one day corresponds to fifty human years, to thousands of eons. Thus genuine sexual contact is still preserved in the lowest of the heavens but is replaced by a touching of hands in the next higher ones. In those higher still, all that remains is a smile or a mere glance, until finally all such desire dies altogether in the uppermost regions.[77] The paradises of the "Great Vehicle" were more sublimated to begin with, as we have noted. Although a reflection of Brahmin conceptions of happiness is still detectable in them, they represent a less adulterated fruit of Buddhist longings. In any event, the joys of love existed neither in the "Paradise of the West" nor in the "Paradise of the East" under the Buddha Bhaisajya, which never played a prominent role in East Asia due to its geographical location, however. The simple reason was that no one entered them as a woman. However strongly the sense may be stimulated and satisfied by the view and enjoyment of countless treasures—although the abundance of jewels in their cold, crystalline splendor almost seems to symbolize a certain distance from life—the enjoyment of love is wholly denied them. Yet it is in love that the joy of life and its perpetuation find their most elemental expression.

Although of different origins and the objects of ever-renewed attempts at a systematic ordering which yet failed to wholly reconcile them with each other, these various heavens and paradises almost certainly fused in a homogeneous whole where the popular imagination hoped to find the largest possible choice of blissful conditions. What remained in any event was undoubtedly the vague feeling that one encountered an ocean of time and space beyond this world where all human orders of magnitude lost their meaning. China, accustomed to modest conceptions of happiness up to this time, "acknowledged her crushing defeat" (as Hu Shih once noted somewhat sarcastically[78]) when confronted with this immense cosmos of heavens (and hells), this inconceivable infinity in time and space. But as we noted before when studying the first transformations of the "Paradise of the West," the realistic spirit of the Chinese rebelled against this excessive stretching of all dimensions. Probably much more strongly than the people of India, it became conscious of the fact that these superhuman proportions also entailed a certain permissiveness invading all rules of conduct. For if salvation in nirvana was so far distant, it could easily stop having any interest whatever. Similarly, the gigantic, labyrinthine paradises lost ever more of their attractiveness as the naive and excessively wordy accounts lent them an increasingly supernatural cast. It is only normal that the educated should have shown the greatest reserve vis-à-vis these excesses. This was most evident in the early phase of Buddhism in China, up to about 450, when the doctrine was still largely misunderstood and confused with Taoism. It was equally clear in the late phase, after 650 approximately, when those forms of belief which meanwhile had been most strongly exposed to indigenous Chinese thinking began to become dominant—and this meant Taoism once again. Its enthusiastic reception notwithstanding, Buddhism necessarily remained foreign to China. During the dawn and dusk of this world view, it was precisely what were essentially fundamental Chinese conceptions that occasionally took on particularly defined contours.

THE ELIMINATION OF TIME AND THE BUDDHISM OF MEDITATION

A new concept of time, developed within a tradition of Chinese Buddhism and as the indirect result of the dialogue with Indian Buddhism became one of the most momentous new discoveries. Almost exactly during those years when Tsung

Ping expressed himself so enthusiastically about the infinity of the eons, the monk Seng-chao (384–414) formulated a doctrine which had the total abolition of time as its core. At least as much of a Taoist as he was a Buddhist, he had understood as in a flash of illumination that all phenomena are firmly tied to units of time. This included the Dharmas, those small, atom-like elements whose diverse concretions form the world of existence. Movement and change, which generate the sense of time, are nothing but an illusion due to the fact that an identity in time is erroneously attributed to all those things that appear to be subject to movement and change. But the moment one becomes aware that every phase of movement and change rests firmly and immovably within its unit of time, the apparently flowing movement resolves into a kind of film strip with an infinite series of motionless images standing next to each other in complete equivalence. Only because observation is imperfect does the illusion of movement occur. What is fundamentally the purely accidental point of view of the Now conjures up a sort of temporal perspective which can give rise to the absurd notion of forward development or a return to the past. Seng-chao attempts to express this insight:

> It is generally considered a self-evident premise that birth and life alternate, that winter and summer follow each other, that some things flow along and move [in our world]. For me, things are wholly different. Why? In the *Fang-kuang*[79] it says: "There is no *Dharma* that comes or goes, there is no *Dharma* that changes its position." When we look more closely, we find that the act of "non-movement" does not mean "the giving up of movement in the striving for rest," but undoubtedly "rest within all movement." Therefore [one can say]: Even if [things] move, they are yet always at rest. They do not stop moving to come to rest. And even when they are at rest, they do not abandon motion. It follows that movement and rest have never been two fundamentally different forms of existence, but that they merely appear different because we are deluded. . . . In the *Chung-kuan*,[80] it says: "[When people] look at a place and know of a man [getting ready to] walk there, this man is [in reality] no longer the same when he gets to that place. . . . The reason people talk of movement is that past [things] do not enter the present. They infer that movement [exists], but not rest. . . . But if past things do not come, how can present things go away? What follows? When we look in the past for things past, [we observe] that they are [there] forever. But when we look for them in the present, [we observe] that they are never present. That they cannot be found in the Now makes clear that they do not come [into the present]. That they remain forever in the past shows that they do not leave [the past]. . . . Therefore it is evident that there are no connections between things [across periods of time]. Since such connections are totally impossible, how can there be things that move? This means that even storms that uproot mountains are really calm; that rushing rivers do not flow; that the hot air dancing over the lakes in the spring is not in motion; that the sun and moon do not revolve in their orbits. . . . Those who maintain that the body a person has in his youth and in his old age is the same and that the substance lasts throughout a life of one hundred years, observe only that the years pass, but fail to see that the body follows them. This becomes clear in the following story

of the Brahmin who had left his family and came back with his hair turned white. When his neighbors recognized him, they called out: "The man who once left us is still alive?" But the Brahmin answered: "I resemble him, but am no longer the same!" . . . That is the reason why the good karma of the Buddha retains its effectiveness for thousands of generations, and why the doctrine remains unshaken after hundreds of eons. Therefore it is said: "When a mountain is piled up, the first basket of earth is the beginning of the end, . . . and when one travels, the first step is the beginning of the arrival."[81]

This clearly observable collapse of the temporal component as foreign systems of thought are adopted is a typical, recurrent phenomenon in Chinese intellectual history. Whether it was the past or the future that was stressed, there always existed a certain tendency to efface the lines of demarcation between temporal dimensions and to recover what was genuinely Chinese in the breadth and presence that resulted. Buddhism undoubtedly aroused and nourished sentiments that were characterized by waiting and hoping. Indeed, from 250–600, when during an uncommonly turbulent and restless time several dynasties repeatedly rose and fell within a single human life span, such sentiments may occasionally have been dominant. Generally speaking, however, the conviction gradually returned that hope lay wholly in what may be called the timeless Now.

As regards Buddhism, this view manifested itself not only in Seng-chao's concept of time, but almost simultaneously and more directly in the dispute over the question whether salvation in nirvana could be equated with enlightenment. And could this enlightenment, which was the same as salvation, only be attained in an extended process of cognition, marked by self-denial and successive reincarnations, or might if not also, or perhaps rather, consist in a lightning-like intuition of the truth? The Chinese Buddhist monk Tao-sheng (ca. 360–434) was the first to voice this revolutionary opinion. His observation that "a good deed does not deserve a reward," is consistent with that position. In a treatise entitled *Pien-tsung-lun* ("A Discussion of Essentials") by Hsieh Ling-yün (385–433), Tao-sheng's thesis is described in some detail as a "new doctrine."[82] Interestingly enough, we find it connected with a theory where the contrasting national character of Indians and Chinese serves to explain that the two halves of the highest Buddhist truth had to mature in two hemispheres before they were finally synthesized by Tao-sheng. For although it was undeniable that the doctrine itself had originated in India, it could be perfected only in China's intellectual climate where it was understood that the element of time played no role. This great developmental leap is explained by Hsieh Ling-yün:

The differences between the two world views in India and in China are the expression of varying geographical determinants, a function of the landscape and its inhabitants. Roughly speaking, one can say that they reflect the national character. The Chinese, for example, have a special gift for direct, intuitive insight into the truth *(li),* but find it difficult to acquire something gradually through learning. Therefore they reject the notion of gradual learning, but are receptive to the

> thought of some single Ultimate *(i-chi).* Conversely, foreigners have a special talent for acquiring something gradually through learning, but find it very difficult to seize the truth immediately and intuitively. Therefore they reject the thought of a lightning-like apprehension and open themselves to gradual enlightenment. Although gradual enlightenment can accomplish something, it remains in the dark because truth can only be seized suddenly. Although knowledge lies in the "single Ultimate," it has nothing to do with the hopes that attach to gradual learning. The Chinese are right when they say that truth cannot be grasped gradually, but are mistaken when they believe that the path toward it may not also include learning. Foreigners are right when they say that understanding the truth also involves learning, but are mistaken in their opinion that the path to it is gradual. Thus the two nations resemble each other as regards their principles concerning the truth, but differ in their application of them.[83]

This doctrine of a lightning-like intuition which brings ultimate salvation with it, was perhaps China's most essential contribution to the development of Buddhism. It was so essential, in fact, that it almost unhinged Buddhism itself, since it made possible a "Buddhist" attitude which could dispense with an explicit formulation of fundamental Buddhist truths. For it need not be pointed out that this enlightenment could only occur in what may be called an extra-logical space where time and space, and consequently all reflection, abruptly collapsed. All intellectual efforts centering on Buddhist doctrine, their sophisticated, infinitely reflected formulae designed to annihilate reality in thought, all the good works and all meditation exercises paled to insignificance by comparison. They became propaedeutic games without genuine significance. The true lightning stroke of insight which suddenly brings the world to a stop for the illuminate came from a wholly different direction. Any encounter, any experience could trigger it. A single loose stone shifted in the prison wall by the blindly, continuously groping hand of a person in search of salvation made the entire wall collapse, whatever its height. Behind it, existence lost its spell, and even the meaningfulness of Buddhist teaching disintegrated. The thoughts of Seng-chao and Tao-sheng came to full flowering in the school of the "Buddhism of Meditation" (Chinese *Ch'an*, Japanese *Zen*). According to tradition, it was not founded until 520 by Bodhidharma, although its beginnings with their marked Taoist coloration date back to the second century.[84] It is true that the so-called northern school, which developed within it around the middle of the seventh century, retained the idea of gradual knowledge. But it could maintain itself for only a short time against the main current which expressly rejected this notion. At this moment, however, a wholly new form of Buddhist experience arose which differed substantially from all other Buddhist schools. For although the monasteries continued to be centers of religious work in the Buddhism of meditation also, the line separating monks and laymen was much less marked since the letter of the doctrine now had a merely subordinate significance. Ch'an attitudes could be much more readily integrated into the everyday life of the ordinary, well-educated person who had no connection whatever with monastic life. Conversely, extensive hiking and physical work were also part of the techniques used by the monasteries to induce ultimate enlightenment, for they multiplied impressions coming from the outside world and thus the occasions for triggering the decisive event. Such practices led the Ch'an monks back into society to a much greater degree than was the case with other schools. It is true, nonetheless, that in Ch'an Buddhism also the encounter with a master in dialogue remained the most important method in the pursuit of enlightenment. But what was expected here was not so much some doctrine or insight, but rather a kind of spiritual blow which would penetrate to the very marrow of the disciple's personality and effect his complete transformation. Although these liberating shocks (which allegedly were also induced by a blow with a stick or an unexpected act of the master) were, of course, carefully adjusted to the individual case, many of these illuminating dialogues with the curious name "public cases" (Chinese *Kung-an,* Japanese *Koan*) were reported in Buddhist documents.[85] Here are some examples:

> Monk: "I, your disciple, am thoroughly ill. Please heal me!" Master: "I will not heal you." Monk: "Why will you not heal me?" Master: "So that you might neither live nor die."
>
> Monk: "What did patriarch Lu mean to suggest by sitting with his face turned toward the rock?" The master covered his ears with his hands.
>
> Monk: "An old sage once said: 'No one has ever fallen on the ground without getting up again.' What does 'fall' mean here?" Master: "The fact is simply stated." Monk: "And what does 'get up' mean?" Master: "Get up."
>
> Monk: "How can one express silence?" Master: "I don't want to express it here." Monk: "Where do you want to express it?" Master: "Last night, around midnight, I lost three pennies near my bed."
>
> Monk: "What sort of people sink time and again into the sea of life and death?" Master: "The second month." Monk: "Don't they try to free themselves?" Master: "Yes, but there is no way out." Monk: "When they are free, what sort of people will receive them?" Master: "Prisoners."
>
> Monk: "What is the most profound meaning of the laws of the Buddha?" Master: "To fill all streams and valleys."
>
> Monk: "Everytime one has a question, one feels confused in one's mind. Why?" Master: "Kill, kill."[86]

To decipher these *Kung-an* phrases is as difficult as the interpretation of the Taoist-tinged anecdotes in the *Shih-shuo hsin-yü* collection. For the answers of the masters are not simply nonsense, but complex verbal compositions where a reply is given but simultaneously destroyed in order to create in the disciple that consciousness of emptiness which must precede insight. In the last dialogue, for example, the exclamation "kill, kill," seems to contain the demand to cut all ties which become apparent precisely in the act of asking questions. But the brutal formulation also suggests that this cutting of ties is not a wholly passive process. There are certain similarities in language between the *Kung-an* phrases and the *Shih-shuo hsin-yü*[87] which would seem to be more than superficial. The shadowy contours of a continuing tradition exist. Having soon lost their base as Taoism remained stationary and reverted to religion and pseudo-science, the final developments of late philosophical Taoism with their nihilistic aspect were absorbed and developed by Buddhism. The "pure conversation" became a sort of "empty dialogue."

Still more important perhaps was another gift Taoism bequeathed to the Buddhism of meditation: the experience of nature. In a world view such as Buddhism, which is pessimistic to its very core, it is actually surprising that such a daring link could be established. In the accounts of paradise Buddhism brought from India, we could note a curiously artificial quality, something almost dead. One of the reasons for this is surely the total absence of animals. Being creatures of a lower order, it was hardly possible for them to inhabit a Buddhist paradise, although this did not prevent Chih Tun from smuggling them into his version of the "Western Paradise." Zen Buddhism also introduced the experience of nature into the otherwise abstract doctrine from the Far West, although in a much more sublime form. Since the second century, at the very moment they discovered it, the Taoists had no longer seen nature as wholly "natural," no longer as the wilderness it once had been, but rather as a large garden. For the Ch'an Buddhists, who started from this idea, nature became incomparably more spiritualized. They were not attracted by the seething life in the endless cycle of birth and death, but by the atemporal idea, constantly blurred by the multiplicity of movement, yet rising behind it in inexhaustible calm, yet promising to emerge in a clear and immutable glow only when the flickering of the visible word was extinguished. Here, Tao-sheng's insight into the irreality of all movement suddenly acquired a surprisingly concrete meaning: Tao-sheng's abolished time became the measure of time in meditation, the mark that insight had been achieved. The closeness of these concepts, the degree to which their realization meant the experience of greatest bliss for the Ch'an Buddhists, is suggested by some sentences by a monk very close to Taoism, Te-ch'ing (his monk's name was Han-shan, sixteenth century). They occur in a letter addressed to a friend:

> When I was young, I once read the sentences (in Seng-chao) that "even storms that uproot mountains are really calm, that rushing rivers do not flow, that the hot air dancing over the lakes in the spring is not in motion, and that the sun and the moon do not revolve in their orbits."[88] For long years, I doubted these words. But then I once spent a winter in P'u-fan with Master Miao-feng. We were preparing a new edition of the works of Seng-chao, and I was reading the proofs. When I came to these sentences, the insight into their meaning suddenly came over me like an illumination. My joy was unbounded. I jumped up and prostrated myself before the image of the Buddha. Yet, miraculously, my body remained immobile. I raised the curtain and stepped out to have a look around. A gust of wind shook the trees in

> the garden, and falling leaves were whirling about in the air. But in my imagination, not a single leaf was moving, and I knew then that the storm that uproots mountains is truly entirely calm.[89]

Naturally, it is impossible to describe the real content of such mystical experiences, or the happiness felt in them. Consequently, they are not too frequent in literature. Even when they are recounted within the highly personal framework of a letter, as is the case here, they always seem a bit banal. The significant accounts of this sort were therefore not rendered in language, but in images. The strongest impression of the spirituality of the Ch'an monks does not derive from their writings, but their paintings. It is especially in the modest, ideal landscapes composed in a variety of hues of China ink that we recognize their paradises. They are wholly different from the earlier, highly-colored representations of the Buddhist "Paradise of the West" or the Taoist "Islands of the Blessed," both of which were frequently done in the robust blue-green style. For even when they show the most intense movement, there is something restrained, remote and wintry about them, just as the concepts "ice" and "cold" as ciphers for "calm" passed from late Taoism to Buddhism. They are not representations, but metaphors. They do not show an object, but reveal a condition of detached insight where a curiously transformed reality is reflected. The goal was not a joyful paradise or a liberating nature, but simply this insight. Even the naive legends of the saints took this wholly different sensibility into account. In them, the Ch'an monks do not ascend to heaven like the Taoist saints, or hasten into paradise like the Buddhas and Bodhisattvas. But some of them are said to have disappeared in their own paintings as they wandered through the mountains and valleys of their landscapes of cognition.[90]

3 / THE WORLD BEHIND THE CAVES

TYPES OF TAOIST PARADISES

The influence of Taoism, always and everywhere in evidence when we consider Buddhism in China, does not mean that Taoism tried to prevail over Buddhism, or that it determined the actual nature of this religious age during the middle six or seven centuries of the first millennium A.D. The reverse is more nearly true. Buddhism had become the dominant world view to such an extent that it could afford not only to fight Taoism but actually to engage it, and thus to largely absorb it. In all direct confrontations, when solid arguments and not irrational motives decided the issue, Taoism came off second best. The public discussions held at the court between representatives of both religions, and which frequently recurred at a later time, are a case in point. Sometimes, it seemed as if Taoism could only survive as the result of occasional coincidences. There was the fact, for example, that the ruling family of the T'ang dynasty bore Lao-tzu's family name. Actually, of course, conditions were considerably more complex. For the incontestable superiority of its imaginative sweep, the range of its perspectives on time and space, and the internal logic of its thought processes were all factors that not only gave Buddhism an advantage, they also hurt it. To assume that so carefully constructed and highly differentiated an intellectual edifice would inevitably, in all places and at all times, gain greater acceptance than a comparatively simple, perhaps even naive one such as Taoism would certainly be an error. The opposite was the case. It was always in danger of being branded as too abstract, too intellectual, and as non-Chinese besides, and such charges were not unjustified. One need not agree with the modern Chinese writer and politician Wu Chih-hui (1864–1954) who, in a kind of holy wrath, dismissed all indigenous Chinese philosophy as the harmless gossip of clumsy peasants who begin pondering things during the quiet time of year when the sun, standing low above a wintry horizon, warms their backs.[91] Yet it must be admitted that Chinese philosophy tends not merely toward the practical, but also the simple. And this tendency asserted itself time and again (and today is no exception), when foreign world views were taken over. It is consequently no accident that the two most successful versions of Buddhism in China, Amitabha and Ch'an Buddhism, should in a sense be simplifications where—and this is an additional and important factor—the element of time has been eliminated.

The strength of Taoism thus consisted in its very simplicity. It is true that under the influence of Buddhism, time and space were extended here also to no inconsiderable degree. But they remained surveyable. This was especially true of the paradises. The enormous dimensions, the unconquerable distances typical of Buddhist paradises may have lent wings to the imagination, but they also had something discouraging about them. The only access they seemed to offer man was a lucky "reincarnation," but it would necessarily be preceded by the terror of death. At an earlier time (perhaps already under the influence of Buddhism), the view had also occasionally been held among Taoists that no one could enter paradise without such a complete transformation. It certainly stands in back of the doctrine of the "detachment from the corpse." But here, death is clearly defined as merely apparent, for in spite of a sort of rebirth, the continuity of the "old" life is not broken. Whether the transition from one sphere to the next was described as a voyage or a flight into paradise, it assumed an eminently important role in Taoism. In Buddhism, on the other hand, it played none whatever. For the paradises were situated in such remote regions that a voyage there necessarily transcended the imagination, even if it could be undertaken on angel's wings. But in addition, they did not represent a final goal, as in Taoism, but were themselves merely a transitional stage.

As a result of Buddhist influence, attitudes toward paradises thus necessarily became increasingly complex in Taoism. At first, paradise had simply been the endless region of non-civilization, encircling civilization like a ring, escape into which had been relatively easy. Later, when civilization had spread as far as was possible—to the ocean in the east and the mountains in the west—paradise was discovered on the islands in the sea and on the peaks of mountains in the direction of Tibet. This mode of looking at things may have been due to western influence, and represented a decisive turning point, since it now was no longer civilization but paradisiacal, untouched nature which took on an island-like character. The subsequent attempt to describe these places of happiness in some detail, and to increase their number in competition with Buddhism, resulted in two conflicting trends. On the one hand, the imagination gained in concreteness to the point where the accounts became quasi-geographical in character, although ample use was made of mythology and legend. At the same time, however, these paradises proved to be increasingly unsatisfactory and implausible. At least the educated therefore recognized them for what they were: mere intellectual structures where disappointment in the world as it was merged with unfulfilled and unrealizable desires.

In a given instance, it is naturally difficult to distinguish between the more concrete and the more dreamlike Taoist versions. Yet a relatively reliable index does exist by which the predominance of the one or the other component can be determined. The more static the description, the more clearly it portrays an ideal place independently of any human beings attempting to reach or discover it, the more closely it resembles speculative geographic accounts. Its uselessness as a model for any kind of real human society increases correspondingly. For the previously mentioned enumeration of marvels allegedly present in these paradises had hardly any relation to reality, not even an inverse one. In the contrasting case, the element of movement, i.e. the approach to paradise, can only be conveyed through shifts in sentiment, the increased yearning or the curiosity of foreign visitors. The vision of paradise then becomes a personal experience, and the question whether it belongs to the sphere of reality or that of the dream really loses its relevance.

Beginning in the second century B.C., a specific genre of "geographic" accounts of paradise developed. The very detail of its unrealistic descriptions tends to paralyze the imagination. The genre reached its zenith sometime in the fourth century A.D. As examples, five short, relatively late reports have been chosen. They convey a particularly typical impression of this really terribly dry literature.[92] The first four come from a work, *Record of the Ten Continents (or Islands) in the Oceans (Hai-nei shih-chou chi),* while the last is part of a legendary biography of the "Queen Mother of the West" *(Hsi-wang-mu chuan).* All of them allegedly date from the second century B.C., but were probably written in the fourth–fifth century A.D.

> Ying-chou, a country of 4,000 square miles, is situated in the eastern sea. Its west coast lies 700,000 miles from the district of Kuci-chi. The "divine plant" and the "grass of immortality" grow there. Rocks of jade more than a thousand fathoms tall can also be found. The bubbling springs taste like wine, and have a sweet fragrance. They are called "jade cider springs." Just a few cupfuls soon make one completely drunk, but the water has the power of conferring long life. Many immortals live on the island. Their customs resemble those of the people from Wu, and the mountains and rivers are no different from what we find in China.

> Sheng-chou ("Island of Life") lies in the northeastern part of the eastern sea, 170,000 miles on the far side of P'eng-lai. It comprises 2,500 square miles; its west coast lies at a distance of 230,000 from China. Some ten thousand immortals live there. The climate is pleasantly mild, herbs and grasses grow throughout the year. Because excessive cold or heat are unknown, the creatures living there have no need to worry about food. There are many mountains and rivers; besides, the "divine plant" grows there, as do all kinds of immortality herbs. The water on the entire continent tastes like sweet buttermilk. It is a very choice continent.

> The island of Fang-chang ("Square Fathom") lies in the very center of the eastern sea. Its four coasts in the west, south, east and north form a precise square whose sides are 5,000 miles long. The island is the preferred dwelling place of dragons. Palaces of gold, jade and crystal can be found there. They are the places of government of the "three heavenly supervisors" *(San t'ien ssu-ming).* All those

immortals that do not wish to ascend to heaven move to this continent, and receive the "primordial-beginning-life-certificate." There are several hundred thousand of them. They plough the fields and plant the immortality plant, surveying the land down to a hundredth *mou,* as if they were cultivating rice. There are also jade rocks, and among the springs, there are the life-giving "nine founts." The princesses who are married to the rulers of the country command the water sprites, dragons, sea serpents, whales, and all other marine creatures living in the *Yin* fluid.

Ch'ang-chou ("Long Life Island"), also called "Green Hill," is a country in the southeastern part of the southern sea. It is square, each side measures 5,000 miles, and it lies 250,000 miles away from China. It has an abundance of mountains and rivers, and many tall trees, some having a circumference of 2,000 fathoms. Since the entire island is covered by forests, it has been given the by-name "Green Hill." Besides, the "immortality plant," the "soul plant," the "sweet dew" and the "jade blossom plant" grow there. No miracle plant exists that cannot be found here. There are also wind mountains from whose caves storms blow. In their interior, a constant rumbling of thunder can be heard. Finally, there are purple palaces. It is a country which the heavenly-true immortality maidens wander through.[93]

The palaces which are the residence of the "Queen Mother of the West"[94] lie to the west of the turtle-and-spring-mountains. The capital of her empire consists of the K'un-lun park and the Far-wind-gardens. It is surrounded by a wall that is 1,000 miles long, and has twelve jade towers. It is embellished by gates decorated in red, halls glowing like emeralds, and dark castles that are nine stories high and have chambers for the nobility decorated with purple and halcyon feathers. To the left, it is encircled by the Jasper lake, to the right by the halcyon river. Below the massif, there is a "light-water" ocean on nine levels where the waves are 10,000 fathoms high, so that access is impossible without a "chariot with winged wheels." The "Gate of Jade," as it is called, rises up to the sky, and the "Green Terrace" is lost from sight in the clouds. Under the projecting roofs with their blue jewels, in the chambers with their red purple, there are rows of silken tents. They are decorated with precious stones diffusing such a radiance in all directions that one might think they were standing in the bright light of the moon. Servant girls wearing head-dresses with colorful patterns and tigerstriped belts are posted there, ready to offer their services, while "feather-lads" with precious umbrellas stand about in the sunlight moving their feather fans. Below these palaces and the steps and balustrades leading up to them, the trees form a bright ring, and the forests are like red-pillared halls. The sky is blue over ten thousand distances, and the jade green of the trees shimmers over a thousand distances. There is no breeze, yet divine Aeolian harps play, wind chimes ring out without being touched, and everywhere the most charming, magical music can be heard.[95]

Although there are many lyrical interpolations, especially in the last of these five examples, these accounts which continued to be popular down to modern times were usually written in prose, and that is in keeping with their generally somewhat prosaic character. Occasionally, as in the description of the island of Fang-chang, a Confucian view of life makes an embarrassing intrusion. A strict authority governs that country, and the "immortals" are obliged to grow the plant of immortality by the sweat of their brow on the land assigned to them, a conceit which must be unique in its grotesque philistinism.

THE JOURNEY AS AN EXPERIENCE OF HAPPINESS

The "dreamlike" descriptions of paradise are incomparably more poetic. Not infrequently, it is not the paradises themselves but the longing for them that is the subject. Here also, a specific literary genre gradually developed. This occurred sometime in the second century B.C., at the very moment when we observe the beginnings of the geography of paradises. There are even instances where works of either genre are attributed to the same author. An example would be the scholar Kuo P'u (276–324) who is considered the author or at least the principal commentator of the previously mentioned *Classic of Mountains and Oceans* and also of a number of poems which have the longing for paradise as their content.[96] The generic term for lyrical compositions of this type was "Wandering Immortals" *(yu-hsien),* a concept where especially the term *yu,* "to wander" is interesting for its ambiguity. For it refers both to aimless wandering, roaming about, vagabondage, and also to leisurely, recreative strolling, which has no aim other than itself. In contrast to the Taoists, the Confucians always felt negatively about both meanings. If "wandering" as a mode of life was voluntary, it militated against the person that preferred it; if involuntary, against the period that forced him into it. "Leisure," "swimming," (especially in Taoist literature, it is not the radical for "walking" but that for "water" which is used. This is intentional. It gives the character the meaning of "swimming," "playing.") was not really consonant with the Confucian concept of a life of duty. On the other hand, however, *yu* could also refer to the genuine "journey" to a specific destination. But even this meaning of the concept encountered a certain scepticism on the part of Confucians. While it is true that the "journey" could evoke the welcome assumption of an official position in the provinces or, at a later time, the adventure of the state examinations in the capital, distant journeys, particularly to uncivilized areas, let alone to foreign countries, suggested war, exile, removal from office, or even flight. Not only movement itself, but also the encounter with the other, the new, which is of the very essence of a journey, was profoundly disquieting to Confucianism. The exhortation: "Stay at home and earn an honest living," could easily have been formulated by Confucians. Conversely, the glorification of a "Long March" would have been incomprehensible to them.

It is therefore no accident that the journey to faraway places, and the lament about the misery of the present are closely connected in Chinese literature from the very beginning. This is also true of religious poetry, where the goal of the journey is not the discovery of a distant land, but of heaven or paradise. The sorrow may be of two kinds. In one case, it may not set in until man has returned to his own world, after he has come back to earth. According to Lieh-tzu, it was this sadness that afflicted the emperor Yü when he returned from the Northend country. It was also experienced by the shaman of Ch'u after her encounter with the god in the clouds, as described in the *Elegies of Ch'u.* But it may also be the reason that prompts man to leave his world, and to escape into a world beyond. Indeed, this is undoubtedly the older motif. The classical example is to be found in the first, most famous and probably also earliest among the *Elegies of Ch'u.* It is attributed to the Chinese national hero Ch'ü Yüan, the half-legendary minister and poet of King Huai of Ch'u (fourth century B.C.). Having lost his post through intrigues, Ch'ü Yüan allegedly wandered aimlessly through the country, a lonely and deserted man, and finally committed suicide by drowning himself in a southern tributary of the Yangtzu river. Actually, it is here that we find the earliest link between water—primarily the water of the Yangtzu river —and the removal into a supernatural world, a connection we encounter time and again in curious forms on the by-ways of Chinese intellectual history. The elegy, however, does not describe Ch'ü Yüan's desperate leap into the water, but a melancholy journey to heaven. Following the course of the sun on a chariot drawn by dragons, he travels to famous mythical places. But a final fulfillment is denied him. He finds all the heavens closed, and is also disappointed in all love encounters. The rather extended elegy, consisting of 187 long lines, is entitled "Encountering Sorrow" *(Li-sao),*[97] and is difficult to translate because of its rich, frequently allusive style. The following lines give an approximate idea of the sequence of images, and they convey an impression of the stylistic force and color of this curiously southern poetic style:

> I knelt on my outspread skirts and poured my plaint out,/And the righteousness within me was clearly manifest./I yoked a team of jade dragons to a phoenix-figured car/ And waited for the wind to come, to soar up on my journey.//
>
> In the morning I started on my way from Ts'ang-wu;/In the evening I came to the Garden of Paradise./I wanted to stay a while in those fairy precincts,/But the swift-moving sun was dipping to the west./I ordered Hsi-ho to stay the sun-steeds' gallop,/To stand over Yen-tzŭ mountain and not go in./Long, long had been my road and far, far was the journey:/ I would go up and down to seek my heart's desire.//
>
> I watered my dragon steeds at the Pool of Heaven,/And tied the reins up to the Fu-sang tree./ I broke a sprig of the Jo-tree to strike the sun with:/I wanted to roam a little for enjoyment./I sent Wang Shu ahead to ride before me;/The Wind God went behind as my outrider;/The Bird of Heaven gave notice of my comings;/And the Thunder God told me when all was not ready.//
>
> I caused my phoenixes to mount on their pinions/And fly ever onward by night and by day/The whirlwinds gathered and came out to meet me,/Leading clouds and rainbows, to give me welcome./In wild confusion, now joined and now parted,/ Upwards and downwards rushed the glittering train./I asked Heaven's porter to open up for me;/But he leant across Heaven's gate and eyed me churlishly.//

> The day was getting dark and drawing to its close./Knotting orchids, I waited in indecision./The muddy, impure world, so undiscriminating,/Seeks always to hide beauty, out of jealousy./I decided when morning came to cross the White Water,/ And climbed the peak of Lang Feng, and there tied up my steeds./Then I looked about me and suddenly burst out weeping, Because on that high hill there was no fair lady.//
>
> I thought to amuse myself here, in the House of Spring,/And broke off a jasper branch to add to my girdle./Before the jasper flowers had shed their bright petals/I would look for a maiden below to give it to./And so I made Feng Lung ride off on a cloud/To seek out the dwelling-place of the lady Fu-fei./I took off my belt as a pledge of my suit to her,/And ordered Chien Hsiu to be the go-between.//
>
> Many were the hurried meetings and partings with her:/All will and caprices, she was hard to woo./In the evenings she went to lodge at the Ch'iung-shih Mountain;/ In the mornings she washed her hair in the Wei-p'an stream.//
> With proud disdain she guarded her beauty,/Passing each day in idle, wanton pleasures./Though fair she may be, she lacks all seemliness:/Come! I'll have none of her; let us search elsewhere!//
>
> I looked all around over the earth's four quarters,/Circling the heavens till at last I alighted./I gazed on a jade tower's glittering splendour/And spied the lovely daughter of the Lord of Sung./I sent off the magpie to pay my court to her,/But the magpie told me that my suit had gone amiss./The magpie flew off with noisy chatterings:/I hate him for an idle, knavish fellow.//
>
> My mind was irresolute and wavering;/I wanted to go, and yet I could not./Already the phoenix had taken his present,/And I feared that Kao Hsin would get there before me./I wanted to go far away, but had nowhere to go to;/I longed for a little sport and amusement:/And I thought that before they were wedded to Shao K'ang,/I would stay with the Lord of Yü's two princesses.//
>
> But my pleader was weak and my matchmaker stupid,/And I feared that this suit, too, would not be successful:/For the world is impure and envious of the able,/And eager to hide men's good and make much of their ill./Deep in the palace, unapproachable,/The wise king slumbers and will not be awakened;/And the thoughts in my breast must all go unuttered./How can I bear to endure this for ever?//
>
> Enough! There are no true men in the state: no one to understand me./Why should I cleave to the city of my birth?/Since none is worthy to work with in making good government,/I will go and join P'eng Hsien in the place where he abides.//[98]

Already at an early date, the elegy "Encountering Sorrow" was frequently imitated. Beginning during the Han period, i.e. the early second century B.C., these imitations degenerated into a kind of fad where the theme of lament over the inadequacy of the world was repeated to the point of tedium. This is one of the many examples in Chinese literature which shows that quantity does not always change into quality but may also quite easily suppress and stifle whatever quality was originally there. One of the earlier and consequently much more original elegies, whose tone resembles that of Ch'ü Yüan, is entitled "The Nine Arguments" *(Chiu-pien).* It too was reportedly composed by a minister of the state of Ch'u, Sung Yü, who is said to have suffered the same fate as Ch'ü Yüan at a somewhat later time under King Ch'ing-hsiang (ruled 298–265 B.C.). The quality of this elegy, which was also incorporated in the collection of the "Elegies of Ch'u," is apparent in the independence which characterizes it in spite of all its similarity with its literary model. The difference from the *Li-sao* consists in the fact that the journey to heaven takes up much less space than the lament over the world. More importantly, it does not again become the occasion for a new lament, as is the case with Ch'ü Yüan. The *Li-sao* ends with an expression of fatigue, disappointment, indeed despair, the *Chiu-pien* with an exuberant, thoroughly hopeful journey to heaven:

> In singleness of heart, I wished only to be loyal;/ But the jealous kept me apart and stood in my way.//
>
> Just grant me my worthless body and let me go away,/To set my wandering spirit soaring amidst the clouds;/To ride the circling vapours of primordial ether,/Racing the myriad hosts of spirits;/Bright rainbows darting swiftly in the traces,/I pass through the thick throngs of the powers of air;/On my left goes the Scarlet Bird with beating of wings;/On my right the Green Dragon with undulating coils;//
>
> The Lord of Thunder with rumblings brings up the rear;/The rushing Wind God leads the way;/In front, the light coaches, creaking as they go;/Behind, the waggons, slowly trundling./We bear cloud banners that flap in the wind./A train of squadroned horsemen follow, file on file./My plans are firmly fixed and cannot now be altered:/I will press forward and make them prosper./Blessed with rich favours from the Lord of Heaven,/I shall return to see my lord free from all harm.//[99]

Thematically, the poems about the "Wandering Immortals," which had their greatest flowering in the third and fourth centuries, are most closely related to the descriptions of an ascension to heaven written by Sung Yü and Ch'ü Yüan. They borrowed many motifs from them, particularly the experience of flight. Of course, certain differences cannot be overlooked. They are not only stylistic in nature (generally speaking, the *Yu-hsien* lyric follows a completely different rhythm), but also pertain to content. In the *Elegies of Ch'u,* the return to earth is never entirely omitted (although it may be in sadness, as with the Shamans and Ch'ü Yüan, or in triumph, as with Sung Yü). The world is never abandoned for good and in principle, but only left for a limited time in a typically Confucian manner. The "Immortals," on the other hand, bid the earth and society quite unmistakably an eternal farewell in their poems, and thereby stress the Taoist motif not yet in evidence in the *Elegies of Ch'u.* Their domain is not of this world, they do not place their hopes in an improvement of conditions during their absence, but rather in the happiness which will be theirs in the paradises beyond. But the idea of transcendence, which maintained itself more stubbornly in this lyric poetry than in the pseudo-scientific descriptions of paradise, had a dreamlike component from the very beginning. The transition from this world to another is not experienced as an objective, but a subjective reality. For this reason, it could absorb motifs which were neither political nor religious in nature, such as erotic desires, for example. It is true that they already play an essential role in Ch'ü Yüan's ascension, but in the course of time they also passed increasingly into Taoist conceptions of paradise, and thus into *Yu-hsien* lyric poetry. More and more frequently, we come across "immortality"- or "Jade-maidens" *(yü-nü)* in the paradises and the processions of Taoist saints rushing through the air. They captured the imagination to such an extent that from the fourth century on, all those expressions which had been coined for the immortals and their domain took on an erotic tinge which the language has retained down to our time. Examples of this are the term "immortal" *(hsien)* itself, but also all those concepts grouped around the complex "light," "flying," and "clouds."

What expresses itself here is that Taoism boldly sidestepped a conflict with which all conceptions of paradise, not only those of the Chinese, had always had to come to terms, be it overtly or covertly: the essence of this-worldly happiness, physical and spiritual love, does not seem to belong in heaven, and this not merely because it conflicts with the idea of "purity," which is also integral to all paradises. For love forms an inextricable part of the network of familial and social ties which usually are its direct result. In the earlier Taoist writings, the sages occasionally lived with their families, as is shown by the passage in *Chuang-tzu,* which reports that Chuang-tzu was good-humoredly humming as he received some visitors after the death of his wife. He had seen through and overcome the petty self-centeredness of his initial, spontaneous sadness. But this example also shows the Taoist tendency toward a detachment of the self from all ties of love in order to attain to the great freedom of the hermit, who can completely shake off such worldly burdens and ascend to heaven. This conflict becomes overt in the words of master P'eng-tsu, who renounced entering heaven under such conditions, and founded the community of those "secret" immortals who spurned the heavenly paradise altogether. Of course, to the extent that they were remote islands and mountains, the "earthly paradises" also were open only to flying immortals. That they were filled with seductive maidens who received the immortals with open arms in their role as naive servants and companions or goddesses, and thus lent these places of happiness an additional charm, may well be traceable to Buddhist influence, albeit of a very indirect kind. For precisely because the joys of love were unknown in the Buddhist paradises, as previously mentioned (which thus differed from the basically non-Buddhist land of Uttarakuru), they suffered from a weakness which Taoism could exploit. Just like all other Sutras dealing with this question, the famous *Saddharma-Pundarika* Sutra, which became well known in China after its first translation by Dharmagupta in the third century, proclaimed with lapidary severity that "no women lived in the 'Paradise of the West,' that consequently intercourse between the sexes was wholly unknown, and that children were born in lotus blossoms."[100] In its competition with Buddhism, Taoism did not overlook this lack in Buddhist paradises, a certain antipathy against the female generally, which had never been an aspect of Taoism. For from the very beginning, during the time when the *Tao-te-ching* had established a connection between the Tao and a kind of "eternal feminine," Taoism had tended instead to emphasize as particularly valuable all "feminine" qualities, such as the "soft," the "yielding," the "passive," the "earthly," and the "lying underneath." Consequently, it could integrate the erotic element into its system of thought much more easily than Buddhism. This is undoubtedly one of the most fundamental reasons that the power of Taoism remained secure even during those centuries when Buddhism attained the zenith of its spiritual dominion in China and enjoyed an almost total predominance.

In more recent Chinese literary criticism, most notably by the scholar Chu Kuang-ch'ien,[101] attempts have been made to show that there were three kinds of *Yu-hsien* literature. First, the literature of escapism and protest, for which Ch'ü Yüan and the poetry of the following writers, some of whom have been mentioned previously in another connection, are allegedly typical: Juan Chi, Hsi K'ang, and T'ao Ch'ien. Secondly, there are the genuinely Taoist and religious works, in which especially poets such as Chang Hua, Kuo P'u, and Ts'ao T'ang expressed their mystical visions. Thirdly, there is the romantic and erotic verse, allegedly first composed by Sung Yü, and subsequently by Ts'ao Chih, Fu Hsüan, and Pao Chao, all of whom continued the former's tradition. This classification is valuable because it sets forth the three main currents which are fundamental to any study of the airy fantasies of the paradises. As the founder of a tradition of truly religious works, Chuang-tzu should not be omitted in this context, however, although he did not write lyric poetry, of course. On the other hand, it is a fundamentally questionable undertaking to establish such lines of tradition, although studies of this kind have always (and indeed for too long), been assiduously produced in China. For they inevitably sacrifice the individuality of an author to a classificatory schema by ignoring what is ambivalent and complex and constitutes the human personality. For this reason, they never get beyond what may be called a one-dimensional view. In any event, a glance at the various *Yu-hsien* poems shows that the three elements were almost always intimately fused, although it is true that the romantic aspect came to dominate the mystic and religious in the course of time, while the escapist remained a constant, at least as background.

Two pieces indicate the two important phases the poetry about journeys to paradise passed through after it had been given its original form in the *Elegies of Ch'u.* The first is a relatively early composition by the poet Ts'ao Chih (third century); the other a very much later one by the Buddhist monk Kuan-hsiu (ninth century), who inclined so strongly toward Taoism that he has been justifiably referred to as "syncretistic."[102] Ts'ao Chih's poem, entitled "Journey to the Faraway" *(Yüan-yu),* undoubtedly has a romantic tinge, yet is suffused by the naive seriousness which touches us so intimately in Ch'ü Yüan's elegy. Kuan-hsiu, on the other hand, indicates the distance he has to his subject in the very title of his poem. Both by the term "dream," and the content itself, his "Dream of a Journey to the Immortals" *(Meng yu-hsien)* makes its irreality quite clear. An ironic distance permits him to conclude his description with an amusing jest which may be said to awaken the reader (and the poet) from his dream, and cause the paradise to dissolve into something unreal. This is a literary artifice not unknown in Buddhist literature.

Journey to the Faraway

Journey to the faraway, the four oceans in front of me!/I look down and see the tall waves/gigantic fish, like crooked hills,/move toward the waves, one behind the other.//

Spirit turtles are carrying the Fan-chang island on their heads./Its high peaks rise to majestic heights./Immortals flutter along the edges of the island./Jade maidens play on the slopes of the mountains.//

Pollen, the color of red jade, stills their hunger./They raise their head and drink the morning dew./The K'un-lun mountain is our true home/the Middle Kingdom China is not our father's house.//

I will hurry to the "Father of the East."[103]/In a single leap, I cross the desert with its quicksands./With resounding wings, I dance in the storm of the seasons,/and sing my songs with a jubilant voice in the clear air.//

Inscriptions on metal and stone, however permanent they may seem, will some day pass away./Thus I would rather shine as do the sun and the moon,/and become as old as heaven and earth./Even a force of ten thousand chariots could not be stronger.//[104]

Dream of a Journey to the Immortals

In a dream, I came to a mountain in the middle of the ocean,/and entered a palace of white silver./I encountered a Taoist sage,/who called himself Li Pa-po.//[105]

Three or four immortality maidens/in garments the color of lapis lazuli,/held balls in their hands, iridescent like moons/to toss them at the golden peaches.//

The country was glistening white and without any dust./Thus I walked on, and came to the shore of a lake transparent as a precious stone./From below the luxuriantly growing long-life trees, a white dragon crept out/to sniff at the alien human being.//

The palaces and halls, towering high above each other, were lost from sight in a purple haze./Water in five colors rippled in gold-bordered courses over a sand of jade./The gatekeepers and immortality maidens slept peacefully side by side,/but when I wanted to secretly pluck a peach from the crooked tree, I suddenly fell, and almost broke my neck.//[106]

In a particular kind of conception of paradise, which developed independently of the *Yu-hsien* lyric poetry and somewhat after its flowering, yet was undoubtedly influenced by it, a touch of the romantically unreal also makes itself felt. It deals with imaginative accounts of castles and fairy palaces on the moon. Ever since antiquity, of course, the moon and all other heavenly bodies including the sun had been peopled by legendary figures. Indeed, there is an early myth which creates an especially close connection between the moon and paradise. Heng O, the spouse of the mythic archer Hou I, who was said to have shot out of the sky nine of the original ten suns that were scorching the earth, stole the immortality plant that had just been given her lord and master by the "Queen Mother of the West." With it, she fled to the moon, and remained there, while Hou I, vainly attempting to pursue her, later chose the sun for his abode.[107] But the actual transformation of this cold place of exile into a sort of outlying palace of the residence of the "Queen Mother of the West" did not occur until the eighth century, perhaps even under the influence of western ideas which had come to China together with Buddhism.[108] At the same time, the moon was discovered as a worthwhile goal of adventurous travels through the air, a new rocky island of the blessed, swimming in the ether. The belief in this so clearly visible yet unattainable fairy land has cast its spell over men, and found expression in poems, prose pieces, and even in novels ever since. It is thc paradisiacal realm of dreams that has survived down to the modern period, and has most completely retained its integrity and vividness.[109] Legend connects its exploration with a heavenly journey of the emperor Hsüan-tsung (governed 713–751), who ruled during the heyday of the T'ang dynasty. An early report dating from the T'ang period, which represents the basic version of the legend and shows curious parallels to the heavenly journey of the Chou king Mu, reads as follows:

> In the sixth year of the reign title "commencing primordial origin" (718), the emperor Hsün-tsung celebrated the moon festival with the "Heavenly Master" Shen and the Taoist Master Hung Tu-k'o.[110] When evening came, the "Heavenly Master" performed an act of magic by which all three journeyed to the moon on a cloud. At first, they passed through a gigantic gate. Behind it, they saw a number of flying and floating palaces, glowing with precious stones, and swaying incessantly up and down. An icy wind caused them some difficulty, and a misty rain soaked through all their garments. After a while, they suddenly saw a palace loom up ahead of them. A plaque with the following inscription was attached to it: "Palace of the far-flung frost and the clear void." The soldiers standing guard by the portal made an awe-inspiring impression. They had glistening white swords. From a distance, they looked as if made of ice and snow. The three men stood still for a while near the palace, unable to enter. But then the "Heavenly Master" led the emperor upwards. Their bodies were floating now as if they were stepping on mist or vapor. Below them, they saw the royal city, looking like a mountain landscape. They sensed the pure fragrance of incense, and when they again looked down, they had the impression that an area with rocks of glass was stretching out for some ten thousand miles ahead of them. With the greatest ease, immortals and Taoist masters were floating along on clouds or riding cranes among these rocks. But when the three mustered the courage to advance a few steps further, they felt an icy-blue glow and a cold splendor overcome them with such vehemence that they became dizzy. The

cold was so intense that they could not take another step. Below them, they now noticed some twelve moon goddesses *(su-o)* in white, shining garments frolicking about on the backs of white Luan birds, dancing and laughing in the shade of giant cinnamon trees near the palace mountain. A great many melodies of great clarity and beauty could be heard. The emperor had an inborn, profound feeling for music; he enjoyed the spectacle enthusiastically and felt a perfect happiness. But soon the "Heavenly Master" urged their return, and thus the three of them rushed back to earth as though carried by a whirlwind. When the emperor recovered his senses, he felt as if he had awakened from a heady dream *(tsui-chung meng)*. The following evening, he expressed the desire to take another journey to that place. But the "Heavenly Master" smiled, excused himself and said that that was impossible. But the emperor could not keep from thinking about the moon ladies, and the way they had danced, flying in the wind, their sleeves and capes buoyant. So he started composing and wrote the melody for the dance, "Cloud Garment and Feather Dress." From antiquity down to the present, there has never been anything purer or more beautiful.[111]

In spite of its vividness, this very early description suggests that its creators had no genuine belief in their own words. They tell a charming fairy tale, which was obviously primarily intended to explain the origin of a new, "heavenly" dance melody. It therefore has nothing in common with a naive belief in miracles or the fundamental seriousness that sustains Ch'ü Yüan's rhapsodies. Too much had happened for the mountainous island paradises to be revitalized by the incorporation of a new sphere whose crystalline iciness could perhaps represent the ideal of purity, but not that of a relaxed life of ease. Because the moon seemed to have come palpably close for any observer, and myth had woven countless tales about it, the imagination was at least as much hampered as it was inspired. For it was difficult to rid the moon of a glassy, colorless quality. It remained a star of myth and dream, not really one of fervent hope.

THE CAVE AS REBIRTH

As the paradises in heaven, on mountains and islands, and even on the moon began to lose their paradisiacal character in excessively "scientific" descriptions, or their credibility because accounts were too much like dreams, an entirely new idea of paradise that was much less susceptible to attack than the earlier ones developed in Taoism. A significant increase in travel was a contributing factor. Traffic was moving westward along the mountains, and eastward on the sea lanes opened by the Arabs. What arose now was the belief in the existence of ideal places reportedly lying hidden behind mysterious caves. The discovery of these worlds did more than disclose a sphere which had somehow been accidentally overlooked up to this time. What found expression here was a shift in thought similar to the one we could observe when the characters for the concept "immortal" *(hsien)* were switched. While in the latter case, the declining belief in a transcendent reality had become apparent through the substitution of the element "mountain" for the old "flying," the change now was due to a movement which actually brought the paradises closer to the real world. In a sense, only a few steps rather than vast, not easily traversible spaces now separated them from the Here and Now. Basically, they formed part of the sphere inhabited by ordinary men, they surrounded them on all sides, just as the wilderness had in the past. Appearances to the contrary notwithstanding, they did not merely constitute oases within nature, preserved by a fortunate accident within what the Taoists considered the destructive expansion of civilization. Rather, they broadened out into a gigantic space which once again turned the human world into what it had been from the very beginning in the Taoist view, i.e. a wretched island in the midst of a world of the blessed. This thought emerges even more clearly when we consider that in the case of the paradise caves, the transition from one sphere to the other demanded only a form of movement which was naturally man's, i.e. locomotion on earth. For the "flying," or at least the "swimming" necessary to reach the islands of the blessed or, in most instances, the paradise mountains protected by "deserts of quicksand" *(liu-sha)* did not have that quality. The fundamentally optimistic this-worldliness, the love of life which always and everywhere distinguished the Taoists and characterized their conceptions of paradise, is nowhere more clearly evidenced. They only fled the world because society drove them away. It was their entire endeavor to lead the world back to its natural condition of innocence, or to preserve at least the largest possible areas from the encroachment of civilization. They had no desire to abandon it like a sinking ship.

The classic and probably also the oldest passage about the paradise behind a cave can be found in the work of the famous poet T'ao Ch'ien (better known by his second name T'ao Yüan-ming, 372–427).[112] In keeping with the spirit of the age, the essay describing this paradise shows Taoist and Confucian motifs intertwined. For it has not just a geographic but, surprisingly, also a historical dimension. The idea of the garden where the peaches of immortality ripen is tied to that of the golden age of the Chou dynasty, which gradually disintegrated until it was finally irretrievably lost with the advent of the Ch'in dynasty:

> At the time of the Chin dynasty, during the period of rule called "Highest Primordial Beginning" (376–396), a fisherman once rowed his boat up a river without paying close attention to the distance he was covering. He suddenly saw himself surrounded by a forest of peach trees. After a few hundred paces, the banks moved closer and closer, until nothing but peach trees were standing on all sides. Fragrant herbs grew there in heady abundance, and a confusing rain of petals scattered over him. The fisherman, very much surprised, continued rowing to discover where the forest might end. He finally found that he had stopped at precisely the spot where the source of the river [on which he had traveled] gushed forth. He found himself facing a mountain with a small hollow behind which he thought he noticed a thin ray of light. Leaving his boat, he entered the cave. At first, it was so narrow that

a person could barely pass. But after he had pushed forward some ten paces, it suddenly widened and became light as day. He saw an extensive plain with clean and orderly houses and gardens, beautiful fields, charming lakes, and bamboo and mulberry trees growing on it. Paths led through the landscape, and the crowing of cocks and the barking of dogs could be heard. In the midst of all this, he noticed some men and women hurrying back and forth, tilling the fields. They were dressed the same as people on the outside. The old had yellowish white hair, the young wore theirs tied in pigtails. They all seemed to enjoy life without a care in the world. But when they noticed the fisherman, they were rather startled. They asked him where he had come from, and he readily told them everything. They invited him into their houses, brought wine, and killed a chicken for him. When it became known in the village that a stranger had arrived, all the people gathered and overwhelmed him with questions. Concerning themselves, they said that their ancestors had come to this remote region with wife and child, as had all the other villagers, when the evil time of the Ch'in dynasty had begun, and that they had never left their hiding place since. Thus the connection with those on the outside had gradually come to an end. They asked what dynasty was now ruling. They knew nothing of the Han dynasty, and had never heard of the Wei or Chin dynasties.[113] While the fisherman told them everything in order, they all sighed and were deeply moved. Late arrivals also invited the fisherman into their houses one after the other, and gave him wine and food. After he had spent some days there, he finally bade them farewell. With their last words, they admonished him: "Do not tell those outside anything about us." He walked back through the cave and found his boat where he had left it. Returning by the same route, he carefully memorized the various landmarks, and reported to the district commander the moment he had returned to the district capital, telling him about his adventure. The commander immediately ordered some men to explore the way to the cave, using the landmarks as guides. But the troop lost its way and could not find the route the fisherman had traveled [to the land behind the cave].[114]

T'ao Ch'ien himself added a poem to his story where he expresses his yearning for that ideal, bucolically peaceful country in moving words, thus writing something rather similar to the *Yu-hsien* lyric poetry. Key phrases such as "cocks and dogs whose sounds one hears in the distance" or simply "village"[115] are reminiscent of the *Tao-te-ching,* but the Taoist element emerges much more clearly in the poem. Following his example, many scholars of a later period engaged in melancholy reflections over the lost paradise behind the peach font. Among them, there were not only Taoists but also many pronounced Confucians such as Han Yü (768–824).[116] More than any other word, the term "peach font" *(t'ao-yüan)* or "peach blossom font" *(t'ao hua-yüan)* has come to denote the very essence of paradise in China. For regardless of their intellectual orientation, people were reminded of the peaches of immortality because the name of this paradise contains the element "peach," and evoked the sense of an unalloyed happiness, of a world that was whole and unthreatened.

Furthermore, the term "cave" had something special about it. Its Chinese meaning does not wholly coincide with that in western languages. The Chinese sign is written with the radical "water" on the left, and thus first suggests "flowing." Actually, the word often has the meaning "flowing rapidly" in early texts. When it is read *tung* (from **d'ung*> *d'ung*),[1] the sound permits us to assign it to a word family which includes concepts such as *t'ung* (from **t'ung*> *t'ung*),[2] "to pass through," "to connect," "to have a connection with," or *t'ung* (from **d'ung*> *d'ung*),[3] "pipe," which has the same sound; indeed probably even the word for "equal," *t'ung* (from **d'ung*> *d'ung*),[4] which we have encountered repeatedly, as in the ideal of the "Great Equality," for example. In the character for "cave," it constitutes the other, so-called "phonetic" component (on the right).[117] For the concept "equal" also did not so much bring to mind the idea of a static identity, but that of a reciprocal adaptation based on an exchange. In Chinese, the word "cave" therefore did not really evoke the association of "grotto," i.e. a closed vault in a rock or the ground, which might serve as a tempoary hiding place, but rather that of a "passage," a "transition." It was not the darkness of the cave that attracted attention, but rather the light of day shimmering far away at its end, and which promised a new world. Nor is it probably too fanciful to interpret this push through a tight passage toward the light so impressively recounted in T'ao Ch'ien's story and in many later ones as the archtype of a "rebirth" in a non-Buddhist sense, indeed a sense which ran altogether counter to the Buddhist view (and therefore could not be appropriated by Buddhism), a liberating rebirth into a life wholly of this world. Entry into this earthly paradise did not call for the "superman" who leaves earth on luminous wings, but the "new man," who dug his way back through the womb of mother earth and thus actually returned to the condition of the old, the original "true man" *(chen-jen),*[118] as the Taoists called him.

The "cave" thus unquestionably became the most Taoist of all Chinese paradises. This was so true that in Taoism the term "cave" immediately evoked a blissful condition and was therefore used in countless Taoist concepts, including book titles.[119] "Cave-heaven" *(tung-t'ien)* became the expression most commonly used for this kind of paradise. Precisely because it is really self-contradictory, it shows how strongly the desire to bring heaven down to earth was alive in this concept. Reports of visits to these hidden spheres are not infrequently inserted into the biographies of historical personalities.[120] The following two passages are rather typical examples:

> During the period of transition from the Shu-(Han) (221–264) to the Chin dynasty (265–419), a group of hungry men armed with bows and arrows once made their way into the "White Tiger Mountains"[121] in order to hunt there and thus keep body and soul together. They startled a herd of deer which scattered in all directions, so that the animals had to be pursued individually. One of the men saw a stag [he was following] disappear between two rocks just wide enough apart for a

1. 洞 2. 通 3. 筒 4. 同 [illegible]

man to pass through. He crept through the passage in pursuit of the animal. After some ten paces, he [suddenly] noticed a gigantic city with many successive market-places, wells and gates, but the stag had disappeared. He walked on to one of the markets, and asked someone what place this was. "This is 'Little Ch'eng t'u,"[122] the person answered, "ordinary people are not allowed here. It would be a good thing if you did not stay." [Following this advice,] the man slipped back out of the cave, but paid attention to the way there. He reported his adventure to the commandant-in-chief Liu Ch'üan, who sent some men along with him [to explore]. But they could not find the passage again."[123]

Near the Tung-t'ing ("Cave-Hall") mountain, there is a "soul-cave" *(ling-tung).* Passing through it, one has the constant impression of seeing a light up ahead. A strange fragrance fills the area, and the springs and rocks shine in a curious light. A man collecting medicinal herbs and minerals once penetrated deeply into the cave. After having marched some ten miles, he suddenly saw a land of supernatural beauty, with a clear blue sky, shining pinkish clouds, fragrant flowers, densely growing willows, towers the color of cinnabar, pavillions of red jade,[124] and far-flung palaces. He then noticed a group of girls clad in rainbow-colored garments with faces of so delicate a glow and such seductive bodies as could not be found among ordinary mortals. They approached the herb gatherer, offered him a ruby-red drink and a jade-colored juice, and took him to a house of jasper. There, they entertained him a while with flute and lute music. Although the herb gatherer naturally felt a strong urge to get to know the maidens a little better, he thought of his children and suppressed his desires. He therefore went back through the cave, being guided all the way by a light moving rapidly ahead of him. Finally, having become terribly hungry and thirsty, he got back to his village. He noticed that buildings and people were all quite different from what he remembered. When he made inquiries in his own house, all he encountered were descendents of the ninth generation. And when he asked them, they said: "Once upon a time, an ancestor of ours did not return when he had gone to gather herbs on the Tung-(t'ing) mountain. That was some 300 years ago. His family asked all over the neighborhood at the time, but no one could say where he had gone."[125]

As more such stories were told, there was of course a corresponding increase in the number of strange worlds people believed lay hidden behind the walls of rock. For the various descriptions naturally differed considerably from each other, and could be reduced to a common denominator only if one imagined a multitude of different paradises of this sort lying behind the caves, an idea which strongly stimulated the imagination. In many cultures, men dream the same dreams (the country of "Frau Holle" or the "Schlaraffenland,"* both of which are accessible only through hollows—a well in one case, a hole eaten through rice pap in the other). And in China as elsewhere, fairy tales soon picked up these motifs and developed them. In this process, as in the two stories just quoted, the profound meaning still present in T'ao Ch'ien gradually dissolved. Soon, the worlds behind

*Reference here is to German fairy tales. (Translator's note.)

the caves were no longer real paradises, but often simply foreign countries, although the tendency to see them as realms of a high order persisted, generally speaking.

A cavernous domain which could hardly be more typically Chinese also belongs to this group of semi-paradises. It is associated with the previously mentioned poet and polyhistor Chang Hua, who also played a role in *Yu-hsien* lyric poetry. It represents an inexhaustible library which can be used to explore all the detail of history. This scholar's Eldorado is all the more striking because it is a fact that sinological research does owe almost all of its original sources (except for stone, bronze and bone inscriptions) from the period predating the tenth century to a gigantic library which had been built into the walls of a kind of cave temple in Tun-huang (East Turkestan), and which was not discovered until early in this century when a partition collapsed by chance:

> Chang Hua, also called Mao-hsien, a scholar of comprehensive knowledge and great gifts as a writer, once traveled to the area of Chien-an[126] for professional reasons. As he was taking a walk through the grottos there, he encountered a man who asked him how many books he had read. "Among those which came out during the last twenty years, there are probably some that have not passed through my hands. But I have certainly worked through all the literature published before that period." He continued talking to the stranger and quickly felt more and more attracted by him. On their walk, they finally came to a large rock in which a gate suddenly appeared. The stranger unlocked it and showed Chang Hua the way. They had hardly walked a few paces, when another world opened up in front of them. It had its own sky, its own earth, palaces and houses, mountains and hills. The stranger led Chang Hua into a house where Chang saw many books spread out, whole shelves full. "Here you can find the documents of all of history," the stranger explained. They now went into a second house, and the stranger said: "Here you can find the local chronicles of the ten thousand countries." It turned out that the rarest books of various sorts were stored in every house. There was one house, however, which was especially tall, and secured with great care. Two dogs were guarding it. Chang Hua asked what was special about it, and was told: "Here, the cinnabar books of the 'Golden Truth and the seven crystals' from the purple archives of the jade capital are stored. They are all secret documents in purple characters." He then pointed to the two dogs, and said: "These are [really] two dragons." After Chang Hua had rapidly surveyed the documents stored in the various buildings, it became clear to him that they consisted entirely of sources predating the Han period. Of most of them, such as the documents belonging to the group "Three Graves" and "Nine Hills," he had never heard.[127] But there were also other works such as the documents of the state of Ch'u, or the *Spring and Autumn Annals* of the state of Lu, present in their entirety. Chang Hua was beyond himself with joy and immediately wanted to take lodgings for some ten days. But the stranger just laughed and said: "You must be a little mad. Is this the kind of place where one can take lodgings?" And he instructed a young servant to take Chang Hua back. "What is the name of this country?" was Chang Hua's final question. "Lang-huan land of happiness," was the answer. Chang Hua had barely stepped outside the gate when it closed

again of its own accord. When he turned around, he could see nothing but various kinds of grass and climbing plants forming a network over the rock. Even the moss covering the stone had grown back together. No break was visible anywhere. For a long time, Chang Hua touched the rock again and again. Finally, he looked up at it, made a profound bow, and walked away. The book *Po-wu-chih (Records about Various Matters),*[128] which he wrote later, originally contained much of the material he had seen in the Lang-huan country. But unfortunately, these passages were struck by imperial edict.[129]

THE PARADISE BELOW GROUND AND THE SHIFT IN TIME

In the course of time, the stories about cave countries proliferated to such an extent that the imagination began to visualize the earth as a porous, sponge-like structure. Mysterious fissures, doors, shafts and channels connected it in all directions with other worlds. Those lying on the surface were soon complemented by others where these far-flung, unknown spaces were conceived as subterranean regions. They thus represented the precise opposite of heaven, the oldest and yet least adequately described abode of the blessed. The location of paradises in the interior of the earth, however, encountered considerable resistance on the part of the popular imagination, for that region was already occupied by the realm of the dead.

Especially among a people that has always simply buried its dead, the conviction that they inhabit the "nether world" is so utterly natural that it can hardly come as a surprise that this belief should already be present in the earliest Chinese texts. It is at least as old as the idea of the divinization of the respected ancestors in heaven. The much more complex idea that presumably resulted from the combination of these two, and according to which man divides into an ascending spiritual, and a descending physical soul at the time of his death, did not develop prior to the end of the Chou period. The earliest term for the lower regions is "yellow source" *(huang-ch'üan).* It occurs in the previously mentioned old chronicle *Tso-chuan.*[130] The context makes it quite clear that this meant a subterranean place that had water flowing through it. During the Han period at the latest, the concept "Nine Sources" came into use for that reason (apparently in analogy to the "Nine Continents" allegedly making up the world). Both concepts were value-free at first; they hardly say anything about the fate of the souls dwelling in this underworld. Nor does the older literature give details about this matter, and this is quite logical, for only those spiritual elements ascending to heaven were thought of as surviving, not the material elements that sank back to earth. It was only due to Buddhist influence which introduced a new, clearly negative concept, the "earth-prison" *(ti-yü),* that the image of a "hell" in the lower regions developed as a dim place of judgment. It soon acquired all the characteristics of a bureaucracy, and also those of the corruption and cruelty all too familiar in the real world.[131] During the following period, both Buddhism and Taoism displayed an unending zeal in describing these infernos (an activity whose pedagogical value in the "education" of the people is still endorsed today, even by Confucians). A terrifying many-layered structure of hell was created; compared to it, the many heavens and paradises, including the most exuberant Buddhist ones, pale in every respect.[132] A frequently quoted Chinese proverb tells us that paradises have "no inhabitants." In hell, on the other hand, there was an abundance of sinners of every description. They were first filtered through a juridical machinery, and then tortured by devilish hangmen, the pain inflicted varying with their crimes. If one was inclined to take seriously the penal code in force in hell as it was published time and again in popular literature, one had to conclude that punishment was meted out with barbaric severity.[133] Even when the naive believer could see himself directly threatened, the imagination was obviously titillated more by the description of horrors than thrilled by accounts of happiness.

It was really Buddhism that made the interior of the earth a "devilish" place, and this seems to have enabled Taoism to finally also discover paradises down below. In any event, beginning in the fifth century, there was an increase in information concerning certain mysterious lakes below whose surfaces palaces were allegedly discovered and the sounds of music heard,[134] holes or thin places in the ground where fluids of miraculous potency or other materials surfaced, or individuals occasionally disappeared who told stories of an unknown world after their return.[135] Surprisingly, these men never saw acquaintances from their daily life on their visits to these paradises down below, nor did they ever meet historical personalities that had passed away, for that was precisely the rule in the no less frequent visits to hell. Because this was also true of the Taoist paradise islands (but not of the non-Taoist ascensions to heaven which were clearly intended as visits to certain divinized ancestors), and because the Chinese have always had an intense historical consciousness, this phenomenon can only be explained by a deliberate omission of the historical on the part of writers of Taoist orientation. For the clinging to individuality was irreconcilable with the idea that the Taoist saint became part of nature. It is also for this reason that the Kyffhäuser motif cannot be found in descriptions of cave paradises. As noted previously,[136] the belief that one and the same personality, i.e. Lao-tzu, would periodically return to save the world, was not foreign to Taoism. But nowhere do we encounter the concept of a historical figure awaiting his return like a seed in the interior of the earth. The figures that people the paradises behind the caves lead an ahistorical existence, since the utopia they embody had been realized. This is already true in T'ao Ch'ien. Their happiness is indeed directly derived from this ahistoricity. Only those who have lost their individuality can join them, so that even a person once famous on earth is no longer recognizable as such. One of the most colorful reports about a paradise in the interior of the earth—albeit of a systematizing character and therefore of a relatively late date—is contained in a collection of miracle stories by the scholar Cheng Huan-ku (first half of the ninth century). The most important motifs are present here in a particularly attractive form:

In the first year of the period of rule called "Divine Dragon" (705 A.D.), a very wealthy man called Yin Yin-k'o lived in the district of Chu-shan, of the prefecture Fang-chou.[137] He wanted to have a well dug behind his estate. But while drilling had been going on for two years and to a depth of more than one thousand feet, water had not been found. Yet he did not give up. When another month and more had been spent drilling, the workers thought they suddenly heard the crowing of cocks, the barking of dogs, and the chirping of sparrows coming from the hole. When they had drilled a few additional feet, they apparently cut through the lateral wall of a rocky cavern. One worker had himself lowered into the hole to examine the matter. [Having arrived at the spot and] penetrated some ten feet sideways, he did not at first notice anything special. But he continued, groping his way along the wall, and suddenly saw the reflections of daylight. Moving along in the hollow, he observed with some surprise that it led directly to the peak of a mountain which he could reach by climbing down. When he finally straightened up, he found that he was in a different world with its own sun, its own moon and its own earth. At his side, and stretching out over tens of thousands of feet, he saw thousands of peaks and ten thousand rivers. Everything made a magical impression. All the rocks were of emerald or rock crystal, and palaces of gold and silver lay among the mountain peaks and rivers. Huge trees, their trunks knotty like bamboo, but with leaves like banana clusters, rose to a considerable height, and purple flowers as large as rice bowls were blooming everywhere. Colorful butterflies the size of fans fluttered back and forth among them, while birds as large as cranes and of diverse colors sat on the branches of the trees, beating their wings. A spring of mirror-like clarity came gushing forth from every mountain peak, and another spring of a milk-white hue poured water into the valley. After the worker had gradually walked down the mountain, he came to a place with a towering palace gate. He was about to enter to seek information, but as he was approaching, he noticed a plaque attached to the gate. It bore the following inscription: "Palace of the heavenly cinnamon-tree-mountain." Two men, clearly surprised, came rushing out of the two small guard-houses flanking the gate. They were a little more than five feet tall, had boyish faces the color of jade, and were dressed in garments which appeared light enough to have been made of white mist and grey-green smoke. Their lips were red, their teeth of a shining whiteness, and their hair looked as if it consisted of silken threads of a shining blue. They wore golden helmets, but had no shoes on their feet. They looked at the worker and asked: "How did you get here?" He told them his entire story from beginning to end. Before he had finished, several dozen men came through the gate and exclaimed: "What sort of dark, dirty vapor is spreading here?" And they violently reproached the gatekeepers. Trembling with fear, the latter reported: "Here is a worker from the outside world who came here by mistake. We were just interrogating him, that is the reason we have not yet made our report." At this very moment, there appeared a man clad in a dark red garment, and brought this order: "The gatekeepers are to treat the stranger with all appropriate politeness." The worker bowed and thanked them, while the gatekeepers told him: "Now that you are here, why don't you go for a stroll and look around awhile? Afterwards, you can return home." "A moment ago I would not have dared make such a request," the worker answered. "But if you will really give me your permission, I would like to take this opportunity, and consent with pleasure." Thereupon, the gatekeepers passed a jade tablet inside the palace on which they requested permission for their proposal. It was returned in no time at all, giving them the permission requested. The gatekeepers now took the worker to a mountain top and told him to wash himself carefully in one of the clear springs, and also to clean his clothes in it. Then they led him to one of the white springs and ordered him to rinse his mouth with its water. The water tasted marvelous and sweet as milk. After the worker had had a few handfuls, he felt as though drunk and completely satisfied. The gatekeepers then took him back down the mountain. Whenever they passed a palace, he could only step up to the gate but was not allowed to enter anywhere. In this way, half a day had passed before they came to the foot of the mountain where the capital of the country lay. All the palaces and houses were of gold, silver, alabaster and jade. A tablet of nephrite glittered above the tower of the gate. It bore the following inscription: "State of the steps to the immortals." "What kind of a state is this?" the worker asked. "Only immortals live here," was the reply. "Those who have just become immortal are taken to this country. After they have spent 700,000 days here, they can enter the heavens or the paradises such as the 'Jade capital,' the 'P'eng-lai-islands,' the 'K'un-lun-gardens,' or the 'Ku-yeh-land.' Only then do they become real immortals. The official business in the palaces with its stamps, authenticating officials, seals and uniforms, proceeds with great speed, as if of its own accord." "If this is a land of immortals," the worker continued asking, "what is the relationship between my own country and this land of the underworld?" The gatekeepers answered: "This land of ours is the uppermost land of immortality in the nether world. Above your country, which means in Heaven, there is another land which has the very same name as ours and does not differ from it in any detail." Having given this explanation, they told him: "But now you have to return home." All of them now ascended the mountain he had come down from after his arrival. Then they advised him to drink once again from the white spring. As the worker was marching toward the mountain top, and wanted to search for the cave through which he had come down, they told him: "Although only a short time has passed since your arrival here, a few dozen years have gone by in the world of men. If you try to climb back up through the old opening, you will hardly succeed. Wait until we have asked for the key to the gate of Heaven, so that we can accompany you home from there." The worker bowed and thanked them, and a moment later the gatekeepers already had a golden seal and an inscribed jade tablet in their hands. They now conducted the worker along a bypath until they reached a gigantic gate which looked like a city gate. Some men were squatting on the ground nearby, guarding it. After the two gatekeepers had shown them the gold seal and the jade tablet, the gate was opened. Accompanied by the gatekeepers, the worker had no sooner entered the gate tower than he felt storm-tossed clouds rising. As they carried him off, he could no longer see, but he did hear the words of the gatekeepers who called out to him: "When you get back, give our best regards to the 'True count of the Red Region.' "[138] A moment later the clouds scattered, and the worker found himself in a cave on the top of Ku-hsing mountain, some thirty miles north of the prefecture of Fang-chou. After having emerged from the cave,

> and returned to his native village, he inquired about the house of his employer Yin Yin-k'o. But the people answered him: "He lived three or four generations ago." And they knew nothing about the well, or anything connected with it. Thus the worker made his way back there by himself, but all he discovered was a huge hollow. It was the spot where the well had once been drilled and gradually collapsed. It was the seventh year of the governmental period "chaste primordial beginning" (791 A.D.). The worker inquired about his family, but could discover nothing about any member of it. He now lost all interest in a life among men, turned to fasting, and wandered about aimlessly. A few years later, someone ran into him near the "Cockscomb mountain" in Chien-ko. No one knows what became of him afterwards.[139]

One of the frequently recurring motifs in this and many other stories is the shift in time in the encounter with the eternity of paradise. Several western literatures have made us familiar with it, for it plays an important role in the "Mönch von Heisterbach" and also in "Rip van Winkle," where the cave motif is also present. It is interesting that time does not always begin to rush while man stays in the beyond; it may also come to a nearly complete stop, as was the case during the visits to heaven by King Mu and the emperor Hsüan-tsung, and in many other stories. One has the impression that there is a certain logic in the contraction of time during journeys through heaven, and in its expansion when the interior of the earth is visited.[140] Whatever the nature of the shift, however, quite a few of the stories that include it have a Buddhist tinge. This is consistent with the equations Buddhism established time and again between "human years" and "divine years," and the varying gradations of both. Yet this motif of a temporal shift is not necessarily wholly due to Buddhist inspiration. What seems to be involved here is an experience encountered in a variety of ecstatic states resulting either from mystical trance, or a trance-like state induced by artificial means. In opposition to the historically conscious Confucians, the Taoists and Buddhists both knew this breaking away from the flow of time. But for the Confucians, the intoxication accompanying the loss of a sense of time was tantamount to total moral collapse. They put their faith in the old story from the Chou period about the "superior man of Chi" who predicted catastrophe for the state because the king and all his councillors had forgotten the date after a huge drinking bout and therefore sought advice from him, the only sober person left.[141] The Confucians were always keenly aware of the degree to which the other-worldly and atemporal threatens any world, however solidly anchored in reality it may appear to be, and this is true even when the other-worldly is unreal and utopian.

But the systematization of paradises, which is also apparent in the story quoted above, is certainly traceable to Buddhist influence. It is not so much the division into three planes—heaven, earth, and underworld—which is perfectly natural, but rather the precise sequence of paradises where the subterranean paradise just described, for example, represents a kind of preparation for the real abode of the blessed in heaven. This is very much like the Sukhavati paradise, which also represents a mere transitional zone from which one passes into nirvana. Nor is it unlike the Christian millennium in this respect, and the hopes that attach to it. Certain characteristics of the subterranean realm, especially the houses of precious stones, also point to Buddhist (although already strongly sinicized) models. Another book from the same century, the *Yu-yang tsa-tsu,* even starts off its exceptionally schematic listing of the paradises inside and outside the three spheres with the unmistakable assertion: "The heavens within the three spheres listed by the Taoists are numerically identical with those of the Buddhists. Only their names are different."[142]

But precisely as the attempt to assign their proper place to the cave paradises gained ground, the same sobriety which had dominated earlier accounts of the island paradises soon returned. In both cases, writers became entirely preoccupied with doing justice to certain numerological values regarding the location of these paradises, and with affecting the greatest realism in their descriptions. While anecdotes about visits to cave paradises, and descriptive passages not tied to a particular frame became increasingly attractive for speculative theories, and could more readily be integrated in a comprehensive, pseudo-scientific world view, they were also transformed into contentless, inordinately dry enumerations. As the *Yu-yang tsa-tsu* shows, this tendency was already apparent during the T'ang period. But in the following centuries, it became ever more pronounced, until the minute descriptions of precious stones and other miracles of nature they allegedly had to offer resulted in a total loss of the paradisiacal in these caves. Occasionally, the extensive worlds to which they had once led contracted to what they may have been in the very beginning: bizarre stalactite caves, whose strange beauty might delight the eye when seen by torchlight, but which could hardly evoke a deep desire to live forever in this cold splendor. In later accounts of paradises, it is often only the names of the various places that have survived. But even they do not provide the imagination with a clue, since their purpose was not to stimulate it, but rather to create an abstract grid.[143] The *Report Concerning the Cave Heavens and Lands of Happiness in Famous Mountains (Ming-shan tung-t'ien fu-ti chi)* by Tu Kuang-t'ing (850–933) for example, is a work which satisfied these demands. Here, ten "cave heavens" and thirty-six "small cave heavens" are listed by name. Apparently, the "lands of happiness" *(fu-ti),* of which the book-paradise seen by Chang Hua is one, are ranked as "small" cave paradises.[144] However, the Taoist count which finally prevailed looked a little different: It listed sixteen large "cave heavens" and thirty-six small ones. In addition, there were seventy-two "lands of happiness."[145] Yet despite this misguided scholarly zeal, the feeling, particularly powerful among simple folk, that worlds of lively activity lay hidden behind the quiet mountainsides, could not be wholly destroyed. Like the islands behind the infinite oceans, they constituted unconquerable places of refuge for a hope which had confidence that the contemporary world also could be improved.

Beginning in the ninth century, the tendency to look at paradises soberly increased. In contrast to their Buddhist-inspired gradation and systematization, what is apparent here is a slow change in the spirit of the times, which was also destined to spell the doom of Buddhism. The religious age was approaching its end. Born in the second century, at the beginning of a period of political catastrophes and recurring disintegration that lasted to the end of the sixth century, it reached its zenith during the first half of the T'ang dynasty (618–906) under the protection of a powerful state. Not only Buddhism, but in a sense all other religions as well, had enjoyed triumphs. However vigorously they may have fought each other occasionally, this was as true of indigenous Taoism as of many other foreign religions such as Manichaeism, small though the number of their adherents may have been. It was an era with a well organized governmental machinery, and during the apogee of the T'ang dynasty, it produced both unparalleled military success and cultural growth. Yet even during this time, the hopes and desires of both the overwhelming majority of the people and the educated elite were directed to the religious and other-worldly, not toward politics and secular affairs. This can readily be inferred from the intensive preoccupation with Buddhist and Taoist paradises during this period. Before, and as late as the first and second centuries A.D., conceptions of political ideals had claimed the undivided attention of the scholarly world. Now they played only a subordinate role. "Happiness" was understood as the never-ending happiness of the individual. But only religion could promise such absoluteness. In the course of the individualistic and nihilistic movements of the second and third centuries, the hope for a common happiness in society had been lost, and had not really revived under the scepter of Buddhism. Consequently, even a wholly concrete ideal of society such as T'ao Ch'ien describes had to be presented in the form of a "paradise." However limited their applicability to reality may be; however pronounced their fairy-tale quality, descriptions of paradises have enormous importance for that reason. For they reflect not merely the visions of happiness of the Chinese in a particular historical period, but also those of the uneducated, "unenlightened" Chinese during the many subsequent centuries, and indeed down to our own time. The image of friendly, chubby-faced immortals flying about on clouds, of seductive maidens with jade-like skin, or of paradisiacal guards with boyish faces, shaped the naive conception of happiness much more profoundly than all the socio-political theories ever could. This is proved by the millions of cheap and tasteless representations which can be seen even today in all those parts of Asia where Chinese immigrants live. These images, where Buddhist and Taoist traditions fuse, are kept alive by the theater, for it is here that the immortals coming from their paradises have always had their place. But popular literature, which always swarmed with saints, also contributed its share. Today, this role has largely been taken over by the movies and television plays, which are produced in great numbers in Hong Kong and on Taiwan. Most of the incessantly repeated motifs of supernatural and happy worlds can be traced back to fantasies which came into being during the T'ang period and the era of disunity preceding it. They found a place in the hearts of the people after a Confucian reaction had put them out of circulation among the educated.

IV

THE DUST OF REALITY
(ca. 1000 – 1800)

1 / LOYALTY AND HERESY

THE VICTORY OF CONFUCIANISM AND THE SHRINKAGE OF THE WORLD

One of the most significant characteristics of the religious age had been its cosmopolitanism. Although it cannot be said to have created it, Buddhism had nonetheless made a major contribution to this development. For the openness toward the world which enriched the Chinese imagination to such an enormous degree and gave it an idea of the dimensions of the world was not just the effect of an intellectual penetration, but equally the result of a long-lasting military invasion which had swept across the northern part of China in wave after wave, beginning in the second century. Buddhism thus had periods of efflorescence prior to the T'ang dynasty. They occurred under systems of domination that were headed by non-Chinese conquerors, such as the Toba, for example, under whose Wei dynasty (386–534) Buddhist monumental sculpture attained its apogee. But even during the T'ang period, which is justifiably considered a Chinese dynasty, the non-Chinese element was very marked. The ruling family Li descended from a line related to the Turks, and the maritime trade of the Arabs also brought numerous foreigners into the country from the southern ports. Among these, there was a not inconsiderable number of Buddhists from India, although a great many had also immigrated along this route and by land across central Asia at an earlier time. Most of the foreigners, however, were to be found among army commanders, and this was all the more consequential because the military enjoyed considerable prestige at that time. For as the result of a curious mechanism, periods of intense religious life in China were also invariably periods of marked military activity. It is here that the dangers of comopolitanism were most apparent. They had been perfectly evident in the conquests by foreign peoples prior to the seventh century. During the T'ang dynasty, they manifested themselves in the constant efforts of the generals, who were often fighting far away in foreign lands, to make themselves independent. In 755, the military governor An Lu-shan (693–757), a man of Sogdian origin, started a rebellion which revealed the whole extent of this dilemma. It is true that he was finally defeated, though not before a great deal of the T'ang civilization had been brought to ruin. But this victory was again achieved with the help of foreign auxiliaries, the Uigurs, who became an important political factor after this, and could also assure their religion, Manichaeism, a privileged and highly protected position.

It is not surprising that such conditions should gradually have given rise to a movement which saw the real danger to the survival of the nation in this ready acceptance of alien cultural influences, and considered it even more threatening than the frequent tactical and weapons superiority, particularly in cavalry combat. What is surprising is that this reaction became vehement only at so late a stage, and that the evident reciprocal relation between the introduction of Buddhism and the disintegration of the country was not immediately and clearly recognized. The pluralism of views which, from the second to the ninth century, had been responsible for a similar or perhaps even greater degree of intellectual vitality than had characterized the Chou period, was unquestionably caused in part by Buddhism. But it was precisely Buddhism which brought a certain inner instability that weakened the very core of the empire. And this was true even though it remained united during the first one and one-half centuries of the T'ang dynasty, and penetrated far westward in the course of military expeditions. Because their historiography was uniform, the Confucians may be considered responsible for having preserved an unbroken national self-identification, from which China's long life in history derives. Yet even they took a long time to become aware of these connections. Although occasional persecutions of Buddhists had occurred since the fifth century, and their rationale had included a nationalist element even at an early date, persecutions did not become annihilations until the "Old-style Movement" *(Ku-wen)*—a nominally purely cultural, yet actually intensely political organization—succeeded in giving a theoretical formulation to the problem concerning the superiority of the "Chinese" over the "non-Chinese." In the destructive persecution of Buddhists in 844/845, 40,000 temples and 4,600 monasteries are said to have been laid waste. Yet it was not really a single, admittedly terrible blow such as this that cost Buddhism its role of intellectual leadership, but rather the persistence with which it was fought after this time, occasional periods of pro-Buddhist sentiment notwithstanding.[1]

All this indicates a profound change in the intellectual climate, and amounted to more than a mere shift of accent away from the ideas of Buddhism and Taoism and toward those of Confucianism. What was really behind all this was a pervasive turning away from pluralism in all its forms. Beginning in the ninth century, a curious striving toward spiritual unification that gradually extended in concentric circles and with ever greater intensity, began to take hold of widening cultural and political circles. It seemed that at first the state was barely affected. The T'ang dynasty disintegrated gradually because of armed conflicts between opposing forces during the second half of its reign, forces it had tolerated and even cultivated during the first half. It was also a time where rapidly changing systems of power dominated the empire successively during a good half century ("Five Dynasties" 907–960). In spite of all this, the belief that a uniform intellectual concept had to inform all imaginable strata, and that a multiplicity of world views could not exist side by side, had struck deep roots and gradually but irresistibly won out in almost all areas. This idea had its first and most beautiful bloom during the Sung dynasty (960–1280), the most Confucian of all ages. Yet when it became ever more firmly entrenched after the Mongolian interval, it spelled the doom of the very Confucianism that had called it into life. For it deprived it of an inner dialectic which had always been its characteristic, its external cohesiveness notwithstanding. This hardening was followed by petrifaction, and by total destruction in the nineteenth and twentieth centuries, since now every attempt to be flexible necessarily had to end in ruin.

The leader of the "Old-style Movement," which constituted the beginning phase of the eight-century-long development sketched here in rough outline, was Han Yü (768–824).[2] He was certainly anything but a petrified intellect. Even more important than his famous writings against Buddhism,[3] where he did not even hesitate to criticize an emperor for being excessively friendly toward religion —an attack which nearly cost him his head—was his essay "Concerning the Origin of the 'Way' (Tao)" *(Yüan-tao).*[4] For the first time, we discover here the consistent exposition of the idea that only one doctrine, the Confucian, contained the message appropriate to the civilized world (which he naturally equated with the Chinese). However much it had tried to preserve its distinctiveness, Taoism had allowed itself to be enriched by Buddhism. In a very skillful tactical maneuver, it was now denounced along with Buddhism as "degenerate" and "alien." It was thus directly attacked by a force from which before it had had nothing worse to fear than indirect attacks. I am referring to the threat of nationalism. To the extent that Confucianism had been skillful enough to suggest that what was "really" Chinese manifested itself in the "order" of the state, whose diffusion from a centrally located "Middle Kingdom" to the "barbarians" on the outside[5] brought happiness with it, the Taoists, who denied this "order" any good qualities whatever, had always been in danger of being counted among the "barbarians." For it was a fact that "their" regions had always been the edges of civilization where the barbarians also dwelled. But the situation did not become really awkward until the "barbarians" abandoned a position which made them appear as "potential Chinese," as a kind of "heathen children," and emerged from their spiritual passivity by way of Buddhism. For now they began to represent a "counter-culture" rather than merely a (Not-)yet-culture. Among the barbarians, the Taoists naturally cut a much worse figure (however unfair this equation might be, it was not undeserved). For if they could be reproached with simply having turned their back on civilization, this was something altogether different from being blamed for having switched from the Chinese side to the side of *another,* non-Chinese civilization.

Of course, all of this only related to the psychological element, not to the substance of the matter. For beginning with Han Yü, Confucianism denied all existence to whatever could not be accommodated within a doctrine that had become somewhat more encompassing than the original teaching, for it now included ontology and cosmogony. What did not fit was superstition, which meant that it was not a naive, as yet undeveloped belief, but one that had degenerated. In the eleventh and twelfth centuries, as Confucianism increasingly won out over both Taoism and Buddhism, this tendency became ever more marked. In the so-called Neo-Confucianism, which developed during this period and derived from Han Yü, many Buddhist elements compatible with a secular explanation of the world were absorbed without difficulty. But a decided, very characteristic modification occurred where the this-worldly, the human and the social again reasserted themselves. It is typical, for example, that the notion of the world periods *(kalpa)* was taken over by Neo-Confucianism (Shao Yung, 1011–1077), but that the cosmic temporal dimensions (1 *kalpa* = 432,000,000 years) were replaced by human ones. They were human not only in the sense that they were much shorter, having a duration of 129,000 years (which was still quite long enough), but also that their relation to human life was changed. For the number results from equating the "double hour" of the "cosmic year" (12 hours × 360 days = 4,320 hours) with thirty years, the span of a human generation.[6]

Many analogous examples could be quoted. They all suggest that the conversion of Buddhist inspirations, which were not infrequently grafted onto *I-ching* speculations from the Han period, brought it about that in purely quantitative terms, the world picture shrank to a fraction of the size it had in Buddhism. But the qualitative shrinkage was even more consequential. Due to the ever more persistent effort to describe Confucianism as the only, central path of truth, compared with which all other thought at best paled to imperfect reflections of these truths if it did not sink into nothingness, the thinking of the educated became disturbingly one-dimensional. The man who perfected this intellectual structure of monolithic severity was Chu Hsi (1130–1200),[7] undoubtedly one of the greatest scholars of Chinese history, but also the man more responsible than any other for an intellectual rigidity which became ever more apparent in the course of time. Before him, Neo-Confucianism had already had a paralyzing strength which had successfully resisted the bold attempts at reform of men such as Wang An-shih (1021–1086),[8] and which might have given China's history a wholly different direction. Chu Hsi's activity now severely restricted the possibility of alternate forms of thought in all important areas. This tendency can be gleaned from various innovations he originated. Historiography furnishes an example. Basing himself on the preliminary studies of another pronounced Neo-Confucian, Ssu-ma Kuang (1019–1086), he compiled a work where the purely annalistic presentation of history became dominant.[9] To be sure, "official" historiography, where every dynasty was treated as a self-contained, individual unit, continued to be written. But it was assigned second place, and this was certainly no accident. For we know from the works of Chu Hsi, particularly his polemical correspondence with the philosopher Ch'en Liang (1143–1194),[10] that he believed he could discover a meaning in the history of the direct, en bloc realization of an eternal, immutable universal moral principle which he called "Way" (Tao). Given such premises, the idea of historical development could not arise, still less that of a dialectical relationship between various competing political systems. Chu Hsi was so rigorous in this respect that he viewed historical periods where a definite, i.e. the Confucian attitude had not inspired the government, as having existed "contrary" to the "Way," as a kind of lost time. In one of his letters to Ch'en Liang, who tried to save these periods of Chinese history—almost the entire historically documented past—he wrote as follows:

> When you look into the achievements of the founder of the Han dynasty Han Kao-tsu, and those of [the founder of the T'ang dynasty,] T'ai-tsung, you should also look at their motives through a magnifying glass in order to determine whether their principal interest was morality or their own advantage, the principle of honesty or something less honorable. In the case of Han Kao-tsu, the share of selfishness cannot yet be clearly determined, but its existence can hardly be denied. As regards T'ang T'ai-tsung, I would be inclined to believe that his acts were wholly based on personal desires. . . . When his [alleged] righteousness is defended with the suggestion that he managed to found a state which could be held together over an extended period by his heirs, this means that righteousness is defined by success. It is exactly as if one were to praise a hunter because of the large number of his kills without being disgusted by his disregard for the rules of hunting. During the 1500 years from the Han to the beginning of the Sung dynasty . . . there may occasionally have been an era of "Small Peace," but the "Way" which had been passed down by [the legendary kings] Yao and Shun to the kings of the Hsia, Shang and Chou dynasties, and from these to the duke of Chou and Confucius, could no longer prevail for even a single day in this later period. The "Way," which is eternal, actually has nothing to do with human acts. It is something that is pervasive in antiquity and modernity, that exists eternally, and can never be destroyed. Man has attacked it for 1500 years, but been unable to undo it in the end. Where would the so-called wise rulers of the Han- and T'ang-dynasties have taken the strength to promote [its realization]?[11]

The conspicuously round number of 1,500 years, during which Chu Hsi sees the "Way" as lost from history, immediately reminds one of the old tradition of a world renewal to be accomplished every five hundred years by a redeemer, and which Mencius had already alluded to. It is not improbable that Chu Hsi looked upon himself as such a Messiah. What is certain, in any event, is his close spiritual affinity with Mencius, this militant Confucian whose birth predated his by almost precisely one and one-half thousand years. Chu Hsi brought it about that in addition to the Analects *(Lun-yü),* where the sayings of Confucius are collected, and two smaller works *(Ta-hsüeh* and *Chung-yung),* the book Mencius *(Meng-tzu)* also became a new, officially recognized Confucian classic. From the Sung period on, these "Four Books" *(Ssu-shu)* enjoyed an almost greater popularity than the old "Five Classics" *(Wu-ching)* which (due to their greater age) said nothing about Confucianism but derived their dignity merely from the fact that they were said to have passed through the hands of Confucius himself. Although monolithic, Neo-Confucianism did not fail to break up into various schools as time passed. Yet nowhere does its central concern emerge more clearly than in these "Four Books." This applies particularly to conceptions of social ideals. In contradistinction to the ontological and cosmological doctrines, these conceptions may have been influenced by Buddhism in their underlying rationale, but not as regards their content.

The two shorter works within the group of the "Four Books," the *Ta-hsüeh (Great Learning),* and the *Chung-yung (Doctrine of the Mean)* deserve most attention, for unlike the *Lun-yü* and the *Meng-tzu,* they had really always been classics. They are actually two chapters from the *Book of Rites (Li-chi),*[12] which had always belonged to the "Five Classics." By being detached from this group and presented as separate writings, they were accorded a special weight not given any other Confucian document. The tendency toward uniformity—pervasive in Neo-Confucianism—shows up in an important mutation in the *Great Learning.*[13] For this document attempts to suggest a connection between the three spheres, that of the individual, of society, and the world as a whole, which makes the isolation of any single sphere appear impossible. The decisive passages, characterized by a somewhat rigid but indisputably effective form of exposition where the sentences are like links in a chain, and the whole consists of a descending and an ascending movement, betray their origin in the third century. Within a short time, even the least educated Chinese became thoroughly conversant with this text, and most of them adopted these ideas as maxims guiding all thought:

> In their desire to diffuse the shining virtue in all its clarity over the entire world, the ancients first sought to govern their countries well. In their desire to govern their countries well, they first ordered their families. In their desire to order their families, they first refined their own person. In the desire to refine their own person, they first rectified their mind. In the desire to rectify their mind, they first sought sincerity in thought. In the desire for sincerity in thought, they first increased their knowledge. . . . But only if things are examined does knowledge grow. Only when knowledge grows does sincerity arise in thought. Only when sincerity in thought has been attained, is the mind rectified. Only when the mind is rectified does one's own person become refined. Only when one refines one's own person do the families become ordered. Only when the families are ordered are the countries well governed. And only when the countries are well governed is there peace in the world.[14]

Everyone is thus individually responsible for "peace," and, consequently, for happiness in the world. The sentence which directly continues this passage again makes this unmistakably clear: "From the ruler on down to the ordinary person, everyone must recognize the refinement of his own character as the root which, if flawed, will not allow the branches to thrive."[15] The use of the family as a connecting link between the individual and the state is also extremely important.

For in this way, every attempt to contribute directly and by the strength of one's individuality to the happiness of the world is made to appear a hopeless enterprise. It is precisely in this intermediate position that the "family" as such represents an image of the universe. Of course, this idea had already been fully developed during the Chou period at the latest. But in Neo-Confucianism, it was given much greater depth, and portrayed as binding for every individual, not just the ruling class. Philosophical Taoism had originally endeavored to expand the "small self" to the "large self," yet had been primarily concerned with the happiness of the individual, and not differed from Buddhism in that respect, although both naturally claimed to redeem mankind as a whole. But this mankind consisted of nothing but individuals. They had never really been interested in the functioning of the family. In Neo-Confucianism, however, Confucianism propounded happiness within the community with renewed vigor, and this can be interpreted in two ways: the effort may be directed toward perfecting society, indeed the world, and this is unattainable without the perfection of the individual. But it may also be directed toward the perfection of the individual, which has its entire meaning in the contribution it makes toward perfecting society and the world as a whole. What was accomplished on a small scale within the family found expression in the larger dimensions of the state.

This conception of happiness, which centered entirely on society, and permitted neither the individual nor the universe a life of its own (and this latter fact is important), was admittedly not a new idea. Perhaps it was only dimly recognizable in the *Ta-hsüeh.* Strictly speaking, however, it underpins all the cosmological speculations of the Han period, to which the doctrines about the "omina" reacting to historical events owe their existence. Neo-Confucianism differed in two respects. Due to the encounter with Buddhism, the concept of the cosmos had become more complicated. And to a greater degree than before, man and the universe were understood as a real, not merely as a dialectical unity. But it was clearly man that was emphasized, and not the cosmos, as had been true during the Han period. The degree to which the identification of the individual not just with society but also with the entire universe (in an unquestionably Taoist sense) was aspired to may be inferred from a text which the Neo-Confucian Chang Tsai (1021–1077) attached to the west wall of his study, so that its words might spur him on. Soon after it became known, this document, the "Western inscription,"[16] became one of the most celebrated Confucian texts. For more than eight hundred years, it remained a kind of Neo-Confucian confession of faith. Its curiously prayer-like quality is almost reminiscent of the Lord's Prayer:

> Heaven is my Father, the earth my mother, and even a tiny creature such as myself finds an intimate place in their midst. In everything that moves through the universe, I see my own body, and in everything that governs the universe, my own soul. All men are my brethren, and all things my companions. The great ruler is the oldest son of these my parents . . . while on the other hand even those who

> have neither brothers nor children, wives or husbands of their own, still are my brethren in misery. . . . Wealth and honor, benefits and blessings shall enrich my life; poverty and failures, grief and anxiety shall help fulfill it. In my life, I will serve heaven and earth, in death I will find peace.[17]

THE HAPPINESS OF LOYALTY

When one remembers the enthusiasm with which large segments of the Chinese educated classes had welcomed the immeasurable spatio-temporal expansion of the world after becoming acquainted with Buddhism, this simple, readily comprehensible but perhaps excessively modest confession seems like a spiritual retreat to the limited and narrow field of personal experience. But perhaps this development is done greater justice when it is viewed as a concentration, a gathering of the spirit around a permanent center, which seemed most appropriate to the "Middle Kingdom." This idea is suggested by the second of the two small Li-chi chapters, the *Chung-yung,*[18] raised to the status of independent classic by Chu Hsi. The *Doctrine of the Mean* glorified there comprises all those qualities which Neo-Confucianism considered fundamental in the human realm: the unification of all imaginable spheres, the harmonious balance of all contraries, but equally the continued existence of "layers" and differences. These qualities had nothing to do with compromises, the "mean" did not gradually establish itself, it was not conceived as a point resulting from the reciprocal action of contraries, but precisely the opposite: as a center which was a center because it did not shift, because it embodied the immovable measure of all imaginable opposites. As a result, an enormous severity came to govern the entire moral and social sphere. A certain dryness extending all the way to the style itself can also be observed. Although the *Chung-yung* was not created by Neo-Confucianism but merely chosen as commendable, it already offers a good example of this trend:

> What Heaven has granted is called human nature. The fulfillment of this nature is called the "Way." The cultivation of the "Way" is called culture. Even the slightest deviation from the "Way" is impossible. For if it were possible, it would not be the "Way." . . . When feelings such as joy and annoyance, sadness and enthusiasm, have not yet been awakened, it is called "concentration." When these feelings have been awakened and are all balanced in the correct degree, it is called "Harmony." "Concentration" is the great root, "harmony" the long "Way" of all that is in the world. When "concentration" and "harmony" have been realized, Heaven and earth occupy their proper place, and all things are nourished. Confucius says: "The life of the 'superior man' is 'holding to the mean,' the life of the 'small man' is 'resistance against it.'[19] The life of the 'superior man' is a 'holding to the mean' because as a 'superior man' he always stays within the mean. The life of the 'small man' is resistance against it, because as a 'small man' he knows no restraint."[20]

The "keeping within the mean," which distinguishes the Confucian ideal man according to these words, can be most easily described by saying that man constantly achieves the coincidence of his own self with the form of realization innately his, that he does justice to his own, genuine self in every one of his acts, that he always finds himself again within himself. For this concept, the *Chung-yung* uses the word "sincerity" *(ch'eng)*. It is familiar to us from the *Great Learning* as one of the steps on the path toward the attainment of peace in the world. Surprisingly the formulations used even show certain Taoist traits:

> Confucius said: " 'Sincerity' is the way of Heaven, the attainment of sincerity is the way of man.[21] He who possesses sincerity attains what is right without effort, acquires knowledge without thought, and finds his middle in the Way easily and naturally. He is a saint. He who strives for truth and chooses the good, holds fast to 'sincerity.' This demands extensive learning, critical examination, careful thought, clear distinctions and serious action! . . . Only he who possesses unconditional 'sincerity' can fully develop his own nature. Capable of fully developing his own nature, he can develop the nature of others. Capable of developing the nature of others, he can develop the nature of all beings. Capable of developing the nature of all beings, he can help the transforming and nourishing powers of Heaven and earth. Capable of helping the transforming and nourishing powers of Heaven and earth, he can form a trinity with Heaven and earth."[22]

That this "sincerity" constitutes the essence of superhuman as well as human nature, that it is the inner principle of the "Way" that connects all beings in almost mystical fashion, and lets them sink back into the cold night of the denial of the self if they do not share in it, is described in many Neo-Confucian writings. For them, evil is "non-truthfulness" and destruction at one and the same time. In this concept of "sincerity," it is also possible to establish a link to the book *Meng-tzu*, which Chu Hsi had brought into such close relationship with the *Ta-hsüeh* and the *Chung-yung*. In point of fact, this is the first instance in literature of this meaning of "sincerity." It occurs in the passage where Mencius says: "All beings are already perfect in themselves. There is no greater joy than to find oneself in the state of 'sincerity' as one examines oneself."[23] It also seems to be identical with that mysterious "flowing vital force" *(hao-jan chih ch'i)*, whose development Mencius stressed as most important, although he expressed himself only quite vaguely concerning it: "It is difficult to talk about this vital force," he answered the question of a disciple. "It is of the highest greatness and the greatest hardness. When it is nourished by uprightness and not damaged, it fills the space between heaven and earth. It goes together with righteousness and the 'Way.' If they are missing, it languishes. It is something that can only grow through the repeated practice of righteousness, but cannot be taken by storm in a [single] right act."[24]

In "sincerity," which might also be defined as "being true to oneself," we can already discover the traces of another concept which was to have an even more far-reaching importance for Neo-Confucianism, and which can also be traced back to the fundamental concept of the "mean," of "concentration," and "unification," i.e. the concept of "faithfulness" or "loyalty." It is interesting that the Chinese term, *chung* (from **t͜iông> t͜iung*),[1] is very closely related phonetically to the word "middle," "to hit," *chung* (from **t͜iông> t͜iung*).[2] The written sign is also largely the same. In the character for "loyalty," the sign for "middle" (the old form shows a "hit" on a target, marked by small flags) has only the element "heart" added to it (below). "Loyalty to others," as *chung* could perhaps be translated, gradually outstripped "sincerity" in importance. The reason was not only that it played a decisive role in the social and political system, but also because the term enjoyed complete dominance in the intellectual effort concerned with that sphere. The experience of "sincerity," on the other hand, was a more individual matter and had an attractive counterpart in the Buddhist "enlightenment." In any event, following the victory of Neo-Confucianism in the tenth century, "loyalty" became the essential Confucian virtue, almost more important than "humanity," which had always been central in older Confucianism. Only occasionally did it take second place to "piety toward the parents" *(hsiao),* but in contrast to an earlier period, this sentiment was simply considered a special case of loyalty. Thus an initially stabilizing, but later increasingly paralyzing principle prevailed on all levels: in the family, it was the frequently grotesquely exaggerated respect shown "chaste widows," and more generally the hold of the home on women (who had been surprisingly mobile, indeed warlike during the T'ang period), which found eloquent testimony in the practice of binding their feet, which became fashionable at that time.[25] It had its effect on the careers of officials by restricting their service to the period of a single dynasty or even that of a single ruler, after whose termination it was best to leave public life. It also affected foreign policy by proscribing service under non-Chinese heads of state. It is only natural that all these ideals should have been disregarded in countless instances. Indeed, the last-mentioned was, strictly speaking, unrealizable, since foreign dynasties governed for centuries. Yet they enjoyed general recognition. Thus loyalty to a fallen indigenous dynasty during a time of foreign rule, for example, was time and again accorded eminent political importance. This happened for the last time during the rebellions of the nineteenth and early twentieth centuries, which finally brought about the overthrow of the Manchu dynasty.

In the new climate in China created by Neo-Confucianism, all conceptions of the ideal also very quickly took on a different form. The "conquest of the middle" it had accomplished created an intellectual atmosphere which was in principle markedly unfavorable to the development of ideal conceptions. For in China as elsewhere, utopian regions were precisely not located in the "middle," but both spatially and temporally on the extreme periphery of the here and now. As we

---

1. 忠 2. 中

have seen, they always involved the idea of movement, of a journey, of change, not the notion of a pole resting at the center. That conceptions of ideal conditions also always included the realization of the "Highest Peace" in one form or another was something else. For all movements intent on finding this peace not just in a beyond, but on bringing it into this world, were conscious of the fact that they would be unable to attain their objective without a painful transformation of the world, which would entail a period of restlessness, struggle and destruction. But Neo-Confucianism dashed all these hopes for a salvation coming from the outside, as it were. The previously quoted sentence of Mencius that "everything is perfect in itself,"[26] was irreconcilable with the notion of the "new." Men as both individuals and members of society (and thus all of society as well) could but recognize the world in all its reality and identify totally with a destiny that was conceived as wholly social. The "Way" which had been found by the sage kings of antiquity was the only "real" way toward the perfect happiness of both individual and society. Admittedly, Neo-Confucian opinions differed widely concerning the best method of finding it, whether by study or intuition. And already during the Sung period, two schools came into being, a rationalist and an idealist one, of which the latter may be said to have come into the legacy of *Ch'an* Buddhism. But there was never the slightest disagreement about the fact that this "Way" had nothing other-worldly about it, either temporally or spatially. It was always present in both senses of that term.

This conception, so entirely oriented toward this world, made an all-inclusive claim, and represented the exact counterpart of Buddhism in the sense that all existence had a wholly concrete character, while Buddhism had viewed it as altogether unreal. It was a natural consequence that conceptions of paradise could not survive. Their dubious concretization had already occurred at an earlier date, and had finally made them unworthy of belief. Under the Confucians, they were additionally stripped of all the supernatural characteristics they had still retained, and which extended from a variety of means for the prolongation of life to legions of fabulous beasts. Thus they finally merged with the human world. No difference any longer existed between them and the remote countries of the barbarians surrounding China. Therefore they no longer constituted a challenge to the reality of the world as it was, as had undoubtedly been the case before. The dream of countries where men lived in community without finding themselves chained to each other by their dependence, of countries in which the absolute freedom of the hermit was joined to the total security created by the generosity of an abundant nature, was replaced by the description of the smoothly running Confucian state of functionaries. Nowhere does the gradual change in attitude become more conspicuous than in a story from the "Idle Reports from the India-ink Village" *(Mo-chuang man-lu),* written by the scholar Chang Pang-chi (twelfth century),[27] from the Sung period. It gives an account of a voyage to those islands of the blessed off the east coast of China, on which the emperor Shih Huang-ti had still placed all his hopes:

A scholar from Ming-chou by the name of Ch'en—his personal name has been lost—once wanted to journey to the capital in order to take an examination there. The time can no longer be precisely determined. He packed his bags and tried to find accommodations on the ship of a wholesale merchant in Ting-hai, because his family was poor. It was his intention to proceed [northward along the coast] as far as T'ung-chou, and then to travel west from there. A convoy of more than ten ships had gathered for the voyage. One day, when the small fleet was far out at sea, a tremendous storm suddenly arose. The waves were as high as mountains. The order of the ships was broken. They could be seen capsizing everywhere, and disappearing in the water one after the other. Only the ship to which Ch'en had entrusted himself was an exception. Using all their skill, the sailors succeeded in keeping all the sails hoisted, and simply let the vessel drift in the direction of the wind. Yet several times they came close to being buried in the stomachs of the fish. After they had been driven eastward for several days, the storm finally subsided. The men now recognized that in the confusion they had strayed far from their course. They did not know the coast [lying ahead of them], for they had never sailed past it. But suddenly they heard bells ringing and grain being threshed. As they steered in the direction of these sounds and observed [the coastline] more carefully, they noticed that the water was quite agitated at a point where some mountains came close together. They had discovered the mouth of a river. They cast anchor and approached the beach by boat. Mister Ch'en, who was the first to have recovered from the excitement, stepped ashore unaccompanied. He noticed a small path and followed it, full of curiosity. On both sides, marvelous trees and luxuriant bushes were growing, and splendid birds were sitting in them, singing their songs. After having walked some ten miles, he came to an exquisite palace gleaming with gold and green jade. A plaque with the inscription "Palais Heavenly Castle" was attached to it. After Ch'en had looked up and made the appropriate bow, he entered. The large presence chamber lay in a subdued light, and no sound could be heard. But at the far end of the spacious room, he saw an old man with bushy eyebrows and grey hair sitting on a couch as on a throne. His expression was ethereal, and of an exalted emaciation. One had the impression that he was giving instructions, for some three hundred men in white garments and with jet-black caps on their heads had formed a half circle around him. When they noticed the stranger, they were startled, and asked him how he had found his way there. But after Ch'en had told them about his adventure and the storm, they immediately showed great compassion. They prepared a guest room where a canopy of precious brocade was hanging from the ceiling, and served him a meal. All the plates and dishes were of gold and jade, the food and drink shone with a supernatural purity, and the vegetables tasted like the tender shoots of medicinal herbs. They were sweet and very lovely, yet Ch'en could not have said what they were. Finally, the venerable old man also began speaking about himself. "We are all from China," he explained. "We escaped here from the unrest caused by the rebel (Huang) Ch'ao[28] toward the end of the T'ang dynasty. We have no idea what year this is. To what family does the present son of Heaven in China belong? Is Ch'ang-an still the capital?" Ch'en now told them that there had been the period of the "Five Dynasties," which had lasted for more than fifty years after the decline of the T'ang dynasty, but that subsequently calm and order had been restored in the entire empire. He mentioned that the present emperor was of the Chao family, that the dynasty was called "Sung," that the capital was Pien-[liang], that peace had returned to the country between the oceans, that war and unrest had come to an end, and that conditions were like those during the age of the sage kings Yao and Shun. Lost in thought, the old man nodded and sighed fervently. He then ordered two of his disciples to take the guest for a walk through the country. Ch'en used this opportunity to ask his two companions in what region he found himself, and what the name of the old man might be. "We call ourselves 'scholars who have left their position'" *(chu-shih),* the two answered. "We are neither gods nor immortals, but perfectly ordinary people. The venerable old man is the former chancellor of the T'ang dynasty, P'ei Hsiu.[29] We, his disciples, are divided into three grades, consisting of exactly one hundred men each, but we receive our instruction in a group." They now took Ch'en up a mountain from which one could see beyond the summits and peaks. At the very top, they came to a pavillion bearing a tablet with this inscription: "Smiling at the desires of Ch'in," which was meant to express that one could not help smiling about Ch'in Shih Huang-ti having sent Hsü Fu to look for the three island mountains of the immortals and the herb of the gods.[30] The two companions then pointed to a mountain in the far distance. Its peak rose up into the clouds and was covered by white, glittering snow. They said: "That is the island P'eng-lai. All sorts of dragon-like creatures creep about at the foot of the mountain. Therefore all alien beings are afraid of approaching it too closely." After Ch'en had spent a long time in the country of his hosts, he was looking longingly toward the west one day, for he felt homesick. He said nothing about this, but the venerable old man noticed it immediately and told him with a gentle smile: "I daresay you long for your family. Well, it must have been your fate to be permitted to set foot on this ground. Is that a small thing? Yet your attachment to ordinary life does not yet seem wholly severed. You should be aware that once you leave here, you will never be able to return. Since you have come here, however, I will help you get back. But before you leave, take a ship to the island of P'eng-lai, climb the mountain, and have a final look at the region." He then ordered that a ship be made ready. The foot of the island mountain was soon reached. The night was still dark, but almost directly one could see the wheel of the sun rising in fiery splendor from the sea by the mountain. The waves splashed and rustled, gurgled and rose threateningly, then subsided with a clap of thunder. Through a cylinder that was red as fire, and from which the storm was erupting, one looked into the "Great Void" *(t'ai-hsü).* A moment later, it was bright daylight, and many-storied towers and superposed terraces could be recognized. They seemed to float in the colorful distance, towering above the clouds, and were so artfully arranged that no mortal could have constructed them. Yet no one could be seen that might have lived there—everything remained hidden behind the blissful, impenetrable vapor. The "scholars who had left their position" that had accompanied Mister Ch'en on his excursion told him: "In our world *(Chin-shih),* traces of men who found their way here can be detected everywhere. The immortals became weary of it. Therefore, they vaulted still further into the distance beyond the clouds of mist. Only one of the 'eight genii,' Lü Tung-pin,[31] comes here twice a year to stretch out under the firs and listen to the wind rustling in the branches." They now took Mister Ch'en back to the venerable old man. When Ch'en expressly requested permission to return home, the old man said: "I will have you accompanied." Huge ginseng plants grew in the mountains,[32] most of them having human shapes. Ch'en asked for permission to take a few shoots of this herb with him, but the old man replied: "That is something all spirits are after. I fear that you would only suffer misfortune if you had it in your possession on the trip back across the ocean. But the magnificent gold and the beautiful precious stones in the mountains are not to be despised. You may take as much of them as you like." Then the venerable old man repeatedly admonished Mister Ch'en, addressing himself to the development of attitudes and sentiments, the strengthening of the natural powers, the practice of the good, and the defense against evil. Finally, he said: "Be careful once you return among ordinary men. Don't start talking carelessly. If you do, you will suffer the greatest misfortune." And finally: "The real morality of Buddhist teaching has its foundation in the *Leng-yen* Sutra.[33] Take it as your guide in everything." Mister Ch'en bowed twice, and said farewell. He was now ordered to board a ship, and a moment later, he had already landed in the port of Ming-chou. It was during the period of rule "Original Blessing" (1086–1093). But when Ch'en reached the gate of his village, he heard that his wife and children had died. Utterly bewildered, he recognized that he no longer had a place to turn to. Only now did he regret having come back, and wished with all the fibers of his being that he might be able to return to the land he had left. But the way there was barred. Thus he began talking to people about his experiences. But then he fell ill, lost his mind, and died a short time thereafter. What a pity! Once, when I was in Ssu-ming, I met some people from the district who could still remember this story well. I also found out that a certain Shu Hsin-tao had written it down in all its detail at the time. I tried to find the manuscript, but unfortunately did not succeed. Thus I put everything down on paper as it was told to me.[34]

This story by Chang Pang-chi reflects the transformation of the world through the victory of Confucianism with startling clarity. Although fantastic in content, it is told with the total philological precision characteristic of the strict scholar. The simple fairy-tale motifs and their symbolism speak a much more succinct language than complex philosophical writings. The islands of the blessed, once the undisputed refuge of Taoist immortals, have become places where the Confucian life style is practiced. Its ruler is the military governor P'ei Hsiu, who became famous during the T'ang period for his just regime based on Confucian moral principles. He and his three hundred students, who correspond to the three thousand disciples tradition assigns to Confucius, refer to themselves as "scholars who have left their position"; in a manner of speaking, they preserve the by-gone mode of life of the T'ang period. The Confucian hermit did not turn his back on society or abandon it forever, he merely turned away temporarily from a corrupt society and may be compared to a mourner who falls into the kind of passivity that ritual prescribes for the period following the death of a close relative. Of course, the concept had a long tradition which can be traced back to the end of the Chou dynasty. But it was only during the Sung that it was combined with the concept of "loyalism" and became so prominent that it not only overshadowed the ideals of Taoist and Buddhist hermits, but absorbed and thereby transformed them.[35]

The conquest of the Taoist "islands of the blessed," which is symbolized in Chang's story, has curious parallels in historical events which recurred repeatedly long after it was written down. While the "island" and the surrounding "ocean," and "water," more generally, had been the essence of a purely Taoist form of life prior to the Sung period, and had therefore—if only in their thinking—represented a refuge for Taoists after the failure of their uprisings, all these concepts now suddenly became the ideals of the Confucian loyalists. When the Mongols had conquered all of China in 1279, the last Sung pretenders to the crown, the regents and their followers jumped into the sea off the Cantonese coast, and drowned. Toward the close of the Ming dynasty (1368–1644), which had earlier driven out the Mongols, this event recurred in a different form. Of the many "Ming loyalists" who had resisted the approaching Manchus, a certain Cheng Ch'eng-kung ("Koxinga") (1642–1662) could hold out longest. He conquered the island of Taiwan (Formosa), largely occupied up to that time by its original inhabitants (and, after 1624, by Dutch merchants), and there set up a regime loyal to the Mings, which survived until 1681, some nineteen years after his death. Around this time other rebels tried to do the same, but were less successful. Their bases were several small islands off the southeastern coast, which lay in the very same area once believed to have been the region of the paradise islands of P'eng-lai. And it probably does not require mention that in 1949, Taiwan once again played the role of a place of refuge for Confucian loyalists when the communists had achieved victory on the mainland.

THE SUPPRESSION OF RELIGIOUS IDEALS

Concurrent with the transformation of Taoist regions of a "pure," "undefiled" world of nature into Confucian places of a "pure," "undefiled" world of legitimate order, there occurred a change in some important characteristics of these protected areas of retreat. While they had been what may be called Taoist protectorates, it would have been useless to search for historical personalities in them, as previously mentioned. With his reference to P'ei Hsiu, however, Chang deliberately broke with this principle. But the connection to the ordinary world of mortals thus established also introduced the motif of waiting, which distinguishes the eremitism in historically conscious Confucianism from the escapism of atemporal Taoism. The Confucians had been familiar with waiting from the beginning of their existence. They followed the "Way" and therefore were both consistent and justified when they fled from the center, the "Middle Kingdom," whenever the "Way" was no longer discernible there, thus creating a kind of historical vacuum, at least in Chu Hsi's view. But they had always been persuaded that such a condition would not last, and had consequently always been prepared to return to the center to again assume the government. Those who ruled during such a putative historical vacuum or interregnum must certainly have experienced such a possibility as a far from innocuous threat to the spiritual order.

What Confucianism had still been willing to concede to Taoism and Buddhism with the magnanimity of the victor from the Sung period on can also be deduced quite clearly from Chang's account. Although Taoism had earlier turned to the purely cosmological, the Confucian affiliation with that domain is brought out by the experience of the sunrise. Yet the immortals themselves remain "invisible." Their existence is not denied outright, but neither is it asserted. Only Lü Tung-pin, the most popular among the Taoist "Eight Genii," takes on palpable shape, but only because he occasionally visits the Confucian island to "listen to the rustling of the wind in the fir trees," and thus demonstrates a touching allegiance to Confucianism. For if the idea of immortality from a Confucian perspective is symbolized anywhere, it is in these trees. The toughness of their needles, their even, unchanging coloration, suggests an equally unchanging identity. That the motif of a shift in time should be merely alluded to is no more than consistent. The paradise of the loyalists is too this-worldly, too historical, to permit a break in the temporal sequence. In a similar way, even Buddhism ultimately bowed to the Confucian claim to priority. For the *Leng-yen* Sutra, which the ancient P'ei Hsiu praises as the quintessence of Buddhist teaching in a remark that does not form part of any discoverable context, is a famous work of Ch'an Buddhism. As such, it could most easily be reconciled with the conceptions of Neo-Confucianism, for it does not represent a real challenge to it. In a sense, the condition which gradually became reality after the Sung period is already prefigured on the island in Chang's story. It is a kind of trinity of Confucian, Taoist and Buddhist world views. Yet these views are not of equal rank. Confucianism is undisputedly dominant, though willing to make concessions in areas lying outside its sphere of interests.

It adopted this cautious and ultimately wise procedure because it was fully conscious of the potential loss of sympathy it might incur, were it to reject everything supernatural too bluntly. Such moderation can be inferred not just from parables such as the one just discussed, which was written during the flowering of Neo-Confucianism. It is no less evident in philosophical writings from a much later period. In the correspondence of Wang Shou-jen (better known as Wang Yang-ming), (1472–1529),[36] the most significant Neo-Confucian of the Ming period, a man of a stature comparable to Chu Hsi's, but who belonged to the idealist, not the rationalist wing, there is an interesting document where Wang discusses the problem of immortality. He sidesteps the problem of death (and thus the problem of the supernatural) as unwaveringly as the Confucians always had since Confucius's times. The following gives his answer to the letter of an unnamed friend, written in 1508:

You ask if "Immortals" really exist, and demand more precise details. You wrote three times before, and I did not answer you, not because I did not want to, but simply because I know nothing about the matter. . . . When I was eight years old, I took great pleasure in reports [about "Immortals"]." [Yet today,] where I am over thirty, my teeth have already fallen out one by one, some of my hair is grey, and my eyes and ears have become weak. Not infrequently, I find myself confined to bed for a month at a time, and my consumption of medicine rises alarmingly. That's what reality looks like. Nonetheless, even my closest friends believe that I must know something about immortality, and now you too have heard this rumor and press me with your questions. Thus I have no choice but to answer them. But the way things are, I can only do so disconnectedly. It is said that there were some extraordinary men in antiquity who had pure virtue and realized the perfect way. They harmonized the Yin and the Yang within themselves, adapted to the four seasons, and gathered their physical and psychic energies until they could allegedly walk anywhere [in the cosmos] and experience things beyond the pale of the ordinary. It is true that such things have been reported about Kuang Ch'eng-tzu,[37] who is said to have retained an undiminished vitality to the age of 1500 years, and of Li Po-yang (Lao-tzu), who lived throughout the course of the Shang and Chou dynasties, and finally went west through the Han-ku pass in Honan. If these things should really be true, and I were to maintain that they are not, you would assume that I wished to mislead you. . . . Perhaps immortality is a gift of heaven rather than the result of some human effort. At a later time, it was said that Taoists had ascended to heaven, taking their houses along with them, and that they could transform or conjure up things. . . . But these are matters which even Taoists such as Yin Wen-tzu[38] call "magic" and the Buddhists "false beliefs." If I now maintained that they really do occur, you would also assume that I wished to mislead you. Therefore the question whether "Immortals" exist cannot be so simply answered, yet its nature can be understood when one reflects about it for a long time. If you consider it seriously, the answer will reveal itself, but if I were to force the solution on you before you had come to that point, you would not understand it, even if you wished to believe it. Scholars such as myself also have a doctrine about immortality. The philosopher Yen Hui (Confucius's favorite disciple) died when he was a mere 32 years old, yet he is remembered today. . . . If you really want to find out something about immortality, you have to live in the mountain forests for 30 years. If you succeed in perfecting your eyes and ears there, if you harmonize the heart and the will so that your mind becomes clear and pure and free of all that is evil, you will be able to discuss the matter. As things stand, you are still far from the path of immortality. I have spoken disconnectedly; please do not be offended.[39]

Both the agnosticism and the hope for immortality through the fame of the good deed are the enormous intellectual demands discernible behind Wang Shou-jen's words. But even among scholars, it was quite frequently only their rational self that could rise to such a challenge. It was certainly not true of the people which in any event were excluded from the kind of immortality a great name confers. That the rigorous systematization of the Chinese world view also had its drawbacks can be seen at this point. For although a total this-worldliness was only one of its elements, it was the most important one in the creation of conceptions of the ideal. What resulted now was a repression of all "heretical," i.e. specifically religious and other-worldly but also all non-Confucian views and beliefs in the political and social sphere. The consequence was that their visible manifestations, as in the public cult, for example, lost much of their prestige,[40] and that they actually degenerated to some extent. In part, however, they also frequently began to lead a dangerous life underground. Because during the Sung period a state examination had finally become the *sine qua non* of a career, the number of candidates who failed increased enormously. In addition, there were religious leaders of various kinds (not infrequently celebrated as healers),[41] who managed to articulate the suffering of the lower strata. The combination of these two elements often resulted in a highly explosive mixture which could bring the state to the verge of catastrophe. The Confucian authorities were fully conscious of this threat, and attempted to deal with it by a strict supervision of religions and the permanent ban on "superstitious" customs. In a slightly modified form, this tradition has persisted down to the present. But the authorities could never completely suppress these currents. The pluralism of political opinions, a roaming imagination which could not accept this world as the best of all possible worlds, and, most importantly, the hope for something that was simply different and discoverable beyond Confucian conceptions, immobilized in time and space as they were, found ever new and diverse realizations. The internally divided, janus-faced aspect China has always had for the West is thus a reflection of conditions which largely arose during the Sung period. Throughout the T'ang dynasty, civilization had been like a painting of many hues and nuances. In their desire for complete systematization, the Confucians transformed this into a woodcut, a black and white picture of enlightened Confucian belief and popular "superstition." Of course, this disjunction was valid only from a Confucian perspective and for those Europeans whose vision had been molded by it. For any unprejudiced observer willing to take a closer look, both aspects of this image again dissolve into countless nuances.

The "dark" aspect represented by popular religions, the colorful, many-hued "superstitious beliefs," had disquieted and worried Chinese authorities from the end of the second century on, except that up to the Sung period, religious thought had been dominant in both camps, while after that time it had been largely confined to the people, the victims of "superstition." It was especially the form of thought in terms of "world periods" that had come into China with Buddhism, eons whose revolutions allegedly announced themselves by catastrophes, that troubled the government, particularly because this belief was also supported by Manichaeism,[42] albeit in a wholly different form (i.e. as an alternation of the phases of "victory of darkness," "struggle between dark and light," and "victory of light"). The teaching concerning the "future Buddha" Maitreya was equally dangerous, for his appearance promised a new world. As early as 515, a rebellious monk, Fa-ch'ing, proclaimed that "a new Buddha had appeared, so that the old devils had to be eliminated." He even had his followers put fire to Buddhist temples and burn Sutras since they no longer fitted into the new time. One year later, another rebellious group presented a "new Buddha," a nine-year-old boy, whom they took along with them on their wanderings. This sort of thing recurred countless times in the course of the subsequent centuries, as for example during the uprising of Sung Tzu-kuei and the monk Hsiang Hai-ming, his competitor, around 613; during the rebellion of Wang Hui-ku in the first half of the eighth century; or finally the rebellion of Wang Tse in 1047.[43] The organizational form used by the rebellious movements from the beginning was that of the religious brotherhood *(chiao-hui).* In the West, it became known as "secret society," although the term "secret" does not actually occur anywhere in the otherwise very imaginative names these brotherhoods adopted. Nonetheless, this interpretative translation is fully justified here. For although these religious societies did not initially view themselves as "secret," they had no choice but to operate secretly. For in spite of all their differences, their ideals were always predicated on the transitoriness of the present and thus represented a challenge to the state which banned and persecuted them for that reason.[44]

Innumerable secret societies came and went in the course of Chinese history. During extended periods, they covered the country like a net, occasionally constituting almost a sort of shadow government always on the point of seizing power. We shall mention only the two large groups which formed around the Maitreya and the Amitabha (Pure Land) sects respectively. The former (subsequently called *Mi-lieh chiao-hui)* was organized early in the sixth century, the second early in the twelfth under the name *Pai-lien chiao-hui* (White Lotus religious order).[45] Following the trend toward Amitabha Buddhism, the "*Mi-lieh* secret society" was gradually absorbed by the "White Lotus secret society" from the fifteenth century onward. The latter was the power behind many rebellions during the Sung period and even the much later "Boxer" rebellion where this little-known aspect of Chinese society became best known in Europe. Although proscribed and broken up time and again, this gob-like configuration managed to maintain itself for centuries. To no small part, its strength seems to have derived from the proliferating, syncretistic multiplicity of beliefs which gave it a protective anonymity and an unlimited capacity for regeneration, for it must be doubted that it was always the adherents of an identical persuasion that united under the "White Lotus" name throughout the centuries. What seems to have been immortal, however, was the name "White Lotus" itself, which simply evoked the possibility of realizing another, better, and, initially, other-worldly order. What insured cohesion was not so much vague conceptions of an ideal, but certain rituals having their roots in Taoism. Confessions, sexual cults, dietetics (vegetarianism), and the burning of huge amounts of incense would be examples. All of these practices addressed themselves directly to the subconscious.

From the Sung period on, however, the secret societies also propagated what had originally been perfectly orthodox Confucian doctrines, but which were no longer consonant with the program of a Neo-Confucianism spellbound by the idea of "unity." In the new environment, they underwent a mystification, sometimes even a certain coarsening, but their origin can nonetheless be discerned. Of primary importance here is a number of prognostic writings which were consulted in the secret societies, such as the *T'ui-pei-t'u (Chart of Opposing Backs),*[46] allegedly dating from the seventh century. The term "chart" in the title suggests the intent to carry on the Han tradition of books of prognostication *(ch'an-shu),* which had been banned ever more emphatically since 460.[47] It was only natural that these new prognostic texts should immediately incur the same fate, for in them the Han conception of a cyclical alternation of certain reign periods ("dynasties") combined with theories from the *Book of Changes* and western doctrines of world periods in a coherent whole. The form of these prognostic writings[48] is somewhat reminiscent of our Nostradamus. They regularly contain verses (which vary considerably from one edition to the next) and are frequently accompanied by pictures, as in the *T'ui-pei-t'u,* for example. Some were even provided with commentaries which attempted to determine which of the events described in the verses had already occurred, and which were still outstanding. This represented an important piece of information for correctly identifying the present time and the immediate future, which was of course of the greatest interest.[49] Because Neo-Confucianism believed that a single, immutable principle governed all of human history (differing from Han-Confucianism in this respect), the idea that history moved in individual, rising and declining phases was necessarily suspect, particularly when one considers that it had even attempted to substitute an annalistic historiography for a history that progressed through successive dynasties. It thus had to view as even more dangerous a book such as the *T'ui-pei-t'u* whose structure was based on a succession of such alternating individual periods, each of which was represented by a picture. Furthermore, these individual periods moved toward a "Great End," where it remained unclear whether this meant the start of a new cycle (as most of those Han-Confucians firmly believed who had accepted the idea of a "greater" and a "smaller" end), or perhaps rather a genuine "New Beginning," which would become a tribunal sitting in judgment over the entire past. It would seem that the commentators and probably also the authors of the *T'ui-pei-t'u* inclined to the latter view, for the first picture, which remained the same in all editions and represented the sun and the moon, as well as the sayings belonging to it, were generally interpreted as a kind of creation of the world. Nor does any single interpretation attempt to run through all the pictures and sayings (usually there are sixty stations)[50] and their connection with historical events, or to go through them several times. The "Great End" always remains in the future. In addition, it is noteworthy that the various editions differ considerably in their reproduction of the final picture.

Although they were constantly banned, the prognostic writings disseminated by the secret societies continued to have a considerable effect on the population. Even during the period from 1945–1949, when the communist troops fought the Kuo-min-tang party under Chiang Kai-shek, this became apparent once again. A picture of the *T'ui-pei-t'u* showing a grass-covered rock surrounded by water[51] was interpreted as a representation of Chiang Kai-shek (the family name "Chiang" is written with the signific "grass" at the top of the character), surrounded by the rising tide of the "people." This use of the prognostic writings as direct propagandistic support for political goals moves them close to the children's rhymes[52] which had been a favorite device of all revolutionary movements since the Han period, and the manipulation of "omina," which had received such enormous attention, particularly during the last two centuries B.C. Having been a Confucian weapon against rulers tending toward Legalism during Han times, they and the prognostic writings turned into a weapon of the secret societies against the Confucians who had thrown in their lot with the authorities. This development began early during the Sung period and indicates the extent to which Confucianism had drifted toward the "right" in the course of the centuries. But it is possible to go a step further. Even the concept of a "heavenly mandate" passed on from one dynasty to the next—undoubtedly one of the slogans which Confucianism may not have invented but certainly propagated vigorously—was gradually but increasingly exploited by the secret societies, because Neo-Confucianism felt uncomfortable with the very idea of dynastic change. From the Sung period on, such change no longer occurred in China unless either conquest by foreigners or, conversely, the overthrow of foreign rule was the defining element. This meant that the "heavenly mandate" was an irrelevancy (in the case of foreign conquest) or did not require discussion (when foreign rule was overthrown). But the indigenous dynasties rather called on the "barbarians" than admit the loss of the "heavenly mandate."

SECRET SOCIETIES AND THEIR SOCIO-POLITICAL GOALS

The fact that formerly Confucian elements were taken over by the rebellions directed by the secret societies shows that the forces attempting to seize power viewed themselves as potential ruling groups and did not merely have an otherworldly order as their goal. At least the leaders of the various rebellions appear to have manipulated the usually genuine religious beliefs of the people. It seems likely that the alternative they sought was often not so much a fulfillment in a beyond, but rather the reorganization of state and society. The predominantly military power structure characteristic of the majority of rebellious sects suggests this. There are also the titles their leaders assumed. "Heavenly General," for example, represents an interesting mixture of religious and military thinking. The revival of Taoist organizational forms that had first been worked out during the two or three centuries before the penetration of Buddhism—among the "Yellow Turbans" and the "Five Pecks of Rice Taoists," for example—points in the same direction. But like the practice of confession, mentioned above, we do not encounter them in their original form, but with some characteristic modification due to the influence of foreign religions. Unfortunately, almost all reports about popular uprisings passed through the hands of Confucian historians. As a result, our impression of the ideologies in back of the various movements is probably imprecise and may often be distorted. Yet we can form at least a rough idea of their origin. For even allowing for the tendentiousness of Confucian scholars on the one hand, and the poor education, the frequently outspoken anti-intellectual bias and hostility to an unduly detailed presentation of their program on the part of the leaders of uprisings on the other, it is still true that certain terms reveal the tradition to which they belonged. The report about the spiritual heirs of the "Yellow Turbans" and the "Five Pecks of Rice Taoists," who formed the sect of the "devil worshipers and vegetable eaters," is quite typical in this regard. It was written by the Confucian Chuang Chi-yü (thirteenth century)[53]:

> The "devil worshipers and vegetable eaters" forbid their followers to eat meat and to drink wine. They worship neither gods, nor Buddhas, nor ancestors. . . . The dead are buried naked. . . . Some of them got rich after they adopted this faith. The people are too naive, of course, to consider [when they hear about this] that it is only natural to become rich when one neither drinks wine, nor eats meat, and also does without celebrations, sacrifices and burials. Poor, new members of the sect are given small amounts of money for their support by older members. While the individual sums are small, they add up so that [new members] also become rich. When they travel, members are given shelter and food by other members in every place they pass through, even if they do not know each other. They make use of things and persons without distinction, and call themselves "a single family." They talk a lot about their ideal of "being unhampered," with which they try to lure the people. Their leader is called "devil king," his assistants "devil fathers" or "devil mothers" respectively. They very actively solicit new members. On the 1st and the 15th of every month, the members burn incense before the "devil king," and pay 49 gold coins each. These sums are collected by the "devil mothers" and turned over to the "devil king." Thus, a considerable amount is collected every year. Their prayer is the recitation of the "Diamond Sutra,"[54] but since it is their opinion that one may not attain to the truth through its external manifestations, they worship neither gods nor Buddhas. They do worship the sun and the moon, however, since in their view these are real Buddhas. . . . Initially, they rigidly upheld their laws and vows. Since they consider Chang Chio[55] to be the founder of their sect, they dare not pronounce the word *"chio"* even if this should mean death for them. . . . They also say that life is misery, and that therefore one saves a person from misery by killing him. This is called "salvation," and those who "save" lots of people [in this way] are promised eventual Buddhahood. . . . This joy in killing makes them especially dangerous. They also hate the Buddhists, because their ban on killing contradicts their principles.[56]

This description, so inconsistent at first glance, becomes somewhat more comprehensible when one takes a closer look at the curious word "devil" *(mo),* which plays such an important role in the name the sect gave itself. For it seems to derive from the Confucians' deliberate distortion of the word *ma,* which in turn points to Mani, i.e. Manichaeism (and perhaps also Mazdaism).[57] In such a context, the worship of the sun and the moon would also make sense. The Buddhist traits, however, clearly seem to be isolated elements which do not suggest a genuine influence, and this is confirmed by the last sentence. Yet the motif of killing as a deliverance from all evil may derive from Buddhism indirectly, for its pessimism is more in keeping with that religion than with any indigenous Chinese world view. Intimations of it can already be found in some reports from the early years of the fifth century,[58] which discuss the uprising of the Taoist Sun En, who certainly made use of Buddhist ideas. And in the *Kung-an* cases of Ch'an Buddhism, we also came across the expression "kill, kill" in a curious context.[59] In any event, the motif of killing as the most complete deliverance man can bring his fellow man has surfaced again and again since the end of the eleventh century, the time when the sect of the devil worshipers came into being. It happened for the first time during the uprising of Fang La (1120),[60] considered a devil worshiper by some scholars. The motif reappeared with one of the most outstanding rebels of the Ming period, Chang Hsien-chung (died 1649), who saw himself as an envoy of the Taoist divinity, the "Jade Emperor," and made killing his principal occupation. In his case, however, it seems that an atonement or sacrifice motif was also present, for on his famous stone slab of seven "kills" *(Ch'i-sha pei),* which may be said to have stated his program, we read: "Heaven nourishes the people with the Hundred Cereals, but the people do not do a single good deed to serve Heaven. Therefore kill, kill, kill, kill, kill, kill, kill."[61]

But in the rebellion of Fang La just referred to, the religious component actually no longer played the sustaining role it did in the rebellions of the T'ang period. Whatever the cause invoked, it was socio-political elements that disquieted the people and caused it to act in most uprisings from the establishment of the Sung dynasty on. The *Ch'ing-hsi k'ou-kuei* of the scholar Fang Shao (twelfth century)[62] provides a rather vivid account of the intellectual climate at the time Fang La's rebellion erupted. It may be somewhat poeticized, but presumably conveys recurrent aspects of most of these uprisings that were referred to as "peasant rebellions," and have attracted the attention of western and eastern, primarily Chinese, scholars[63] during the last two decades:

> Secretly, Fang La took advantage of the sentiments of people who had had to suffer the inhuman rule of the corrupt minister Chu Mien, and gave alms to the poor and unemployed, and surrounded himself with them. When he could feel certain of their support, he had calves killed, provided wine, and invited more than a hundred, who were considered especially ruthless, to a feast. After a few rounds, he rose from

his seat, and said: "One and the same basic principle applies to both the state and the family. Let us assume that the young [in a family] had to do all the ploughing and weaving, and to slave all year long. But after they had harvested some grain and made some cloth, the old people were to come along and take every thing away from them, squandering it all for their own benefit, remorselessly flogging the young for the slightest act of negligence, and torturing them to death. Would you like that?" "No, certainly not," all of them exclaimed. "Well," Fang La continued, "what is not squandered [by the state] today is lost because it is given [to the northern barbarians] as a present so that [it is our enemies that] get richer and richer. But that does not keep them from pressing against our borders, and now they send you out to fight them. If you cannot drive them back, you can be certain there will be no limits to your punishment, but tribute will continue to be paid. Do you like that?" "How could we," all exclaimed. With tears choking his voice, Fang La continued: "Taxes are numerous and oppressive, the officials take what they please, and agriculture and the weaving of silk do not even yield enough to satisfy the simplest needs. All we have left to make a living is trees: lacquer trees, paper mulberry trees, bamboo, and timber. But even here, all profit is taxed down to the last piece of copper. When Heaven made the people, it appointed the authorities primarily to feed it, yet the terror of exploitation has reached this point. What could be more natural than that Heaven and man are equally indignant? And look at all the treasure being wasted on entertainments, sports, public buildings, temples, armaments, collections of rare stones and plants, and finally the millions of annual tribute in silver and silk to the two barbarian states in the north and west, the Liao and the Hsi-hsia. We, the people of the southeast, are sucked dry to pay for all this. All these presents merely increase the arrogance of the barbarians toward the Middle Kingdom, and make them harass it incessantly. The court pays them tribute because it does not have the courage to stop it, and the ministers even consider it a far-sighted plan intended to avoid border conflicts. It is only we who work all year long year after year, and only our women and children freeze to death and never have enough to eat. How do you feel about this?" "We will do what you say," they all exclaimed angrily. "During the last 30 years, practically all former statemen were either exiled or died. Those who are running things now are a despicable bunch of flatterers. All they know is how to mislead the emperor. If you were to rise up now for justice's sake, there would be a response from all the four directions of Heaven. Within a span of ten days, tens of thousands of men could be won over to our side. . . . We would only have to defend the Yangtzu river as our border, lighten the corvé, and lower taxes, so that the people might enjoy a respite. If that were done, wouldn't everyone tidy his dress and come running to our court? In ten years, we could reunify the empire. The alternative is a senseless death at the hands of corrupt officials. Please consider all this carefully!" "All right," everyone shouted. Fang La now organized his followers, a few thousand of them, and started his revolt with the slogan that [the minister] Chu Mien had to be eliminated. They killed all officials and functionaries they could lay their hands on. Everywhere, the people who were suffering from the oppression of the state responded to Fang La's message with enthusiasm. In a few short days, 100,000 people rallied to his support.[64]

As one analyzes Fang La's speech carefully, one discovers that it already contains the three essential elements which provided the thrust in all uprisings during subsequent centuries and down to our own time, and this independently of any religious factor, which was merely carried along by the impetus. In a sense, all three of them are negative ideals born of misery. First, and quite generally, there is the striving for freedom from an oppressive state, primarily its horrendous taxes and corrupt officials. Secondly, the striving for a measure of local autonomy, evoked here by terms such as "We, the people of the Southeast," or "the Yangtzu river as our border," although this is carefully balanced by the vision of a united, strong empire. And thirdly, the striving for national power and greatness, which will put an end to the humiliations inflicted by the barbarians. At the same time, these three ideals constituted an indirect attack on Confucianism, or at least Neo-Confucianism, even if their propagandists were not always wholly aware of it. For Neo-Confucianism not only completely backed the state, it was also rigorously centralist and pacifist as well. Confucian pacifism merits special attention, for it was not only during the Sung period that this position had created an astonishing military weakness which in turn had led to the policy of tribute payments, a practice Fang La denounced with some justification[65] (although it is true, of course, that this method was less costly than war, except that it did not prevent it in the long run). Besides, this pacifism was also responsible for the relatively ineffectual foreign policy of the indigenous Ming dynasty, which succeeded the Mongols. The far-flung borders claimed by China in our time result from conquests made by the Manchus, who were foreigners. To find China in possession of a comparable territory under an indigenous dynasty, one has to go back to the T'ang period in the seventh century. At that time, it was really Buddhism rather than Confucianism that was the official creed. Confucianism had always tried to weaken the military, and had succeeded in doing so under the indigenous dynasties from the Sung period on. By and large, this meant military weakness and an ineffectual foreign policy. As a result, Confucianism was always embarrassingly vulnerable to attacks by any and every kind of nationalist movement. In a clash of opinions, it was not always possible to assert that a higher "culture" compensated for the obvious humiliation of the nation, particularly when this argument had scarcely any meaning for the opponent (as in the case of the rebellious masses), or when the very superiority of that culture began to be questioned by its proponents, a trend that became increasingly pronounced in the nineteenth century.

But whether they were religious or nationalist in character, or expressed localism, all "peasant uprisings" had as their fundamental cause, their pervasive theme, the shameless exploitation of the people, practiced time and again under the cloak of a patriarchal Confucianism. All other motives might be missing, this one was always there. This is most convincingly demonstrated by the fact that when no other ideals were proclaimed, the radical reversal of all those conditions believed to be unjust became the ideal. The goal of the uprisings that occurred so frequently, particularly during the Ming period, was a more equitable distribution of property (particularly landed property). The form of government that was to accomplish this change was frequently not mentioned at all, or merely alluded to by worn-out clichés such as the "well field system."[66] Wang Hsia-po's uprising in 993 is typical in this regard. He was a man who came from such a low social stratum that he only had a forename, and that name apparently only in its oral form, for the sources use a variety of characters for it. The official history of the Sung dynasty only gives a very dry report of his activity: "Wang Hsiao-po, a man of the people in the district of Ch'ing-ch'eng in Shun-hua gathered masses of people and rebelled by telling them: 'I hate the inequality *(pu-chün)* of rich and poor, and will put a stop to it for your sake.' The crowd following him kept increasing, so that he could finally occupy the district town and ravage the area around P'eng-shan."[67]

The argument of another rebel, Chung Hsiang, proceeded along the same lines, but on a very much higher level. In the twelfth century, when the Sung dynasty waged its frequently catastrophic defensive war against the Yürched in the north, he joined the ranks of those very un-Confucian men who, partly patriots, partly "Robin Hoods," waged a kind of guerilla war behind and between the fronts. Particularly in popular novels, these men were glorified as late as the nineteenth century.[68] The following account by the Confucian historian Hsü Meng-hsin (1124–1205)[69] sounds considerably less enthusiastic, although there were also those Confucians who saw something of value in these patriot-robbers:

> Chung Hsiang from the district of Wu-ling in Ting-chou . . . had the byname "Old Father," which he had chosen himself, but he was also called the "Great Saint from Heaven," for there were rumors that he had direct contact with the gods and heaven and could therefore also free mankind of disease and misery. When he talked secretly to his followers, he used to say: "The law distinguishes between the elegant and the uncouth, the rich and the poor. That is not a good law. When the time has come for me to make the law, the elegant and the uncouth will be on the same level, and the poor will have their share of the wealth." With this kind of talk, he stirred up the poor so that he finally controlled an area of 100 square miles. Their banners flying, the uneducated among the poor came running to his support. There were swarms of people on the streets bringing him presents and visiting him. They called it "the worship of the father" *(pai-yeh).* This went on for more than 20 years. . . . When the Yürched attacked T'an-chou [where Chung Hsiang had taken up quarters], and [the turncoat] K'ung Yen-chou moved into [neighboring] Li-chou, he exploited the fear and terror of the crowds about him, and organized an army within a few days. The entire population of Ting-chou, Li-chou and Ching-chou turned to him. . . . He put fire to public buildings, markets, temples, and the houses of the leading families, killed officials, Confucian scholars, Buddhist and Taoist monks, miracle workers, physicians and diviners, and generally all those who thwarted him in some way or another. The robber soldiers he called "children of the father," the public statutes "heretical laws," the killing of people "the implementation of the law," and the confiscation of fortunes "compensatory justice"

> *(chün-p'ing).* The sick were forbidden to take their medicines, the dead could not be buried properly. People just "worshipped the father," and turned the natural orders upside down. But drunk with joy as they were, they adhered to the "father" in everything they did, and firmly believed that such was heavenly reason. . . . The uprising spread to no less than 19 districts.[70]

One senses here how profoundly shaken a sober Confucian such as Hsü Meng-hsin must have been by this eruption of the soul of the people. To him, it would have looked like mass hysteria. The unconditional, unthinking "worship of the father," a worship that verged on divinization, was no less baffling than the reversal of the "natural orders," a term that refers to the five fundamental, essentially hierarchically structured relationships between ruler and subject, parents and children, husband and wife, elder and younger brother, and friend and friend, within Confucianism. It is not altogether clear to what extent Hsü, a committed Confucian proceeding along the "Way of the Mean" may have been aware that the two extremes of father worship and equality might really be correlatives in spite of their ostensible divergence. For both Confucianism and Taoism had too little familiarity with the curious sense of liberation induced by the "equality before God." Only Buddhism seems to have known this ideal in its paradises where it was often a single Buddha or Bodhisattva that governed as undisputed ruler over entire worlds of equal subjects. One might almost be inclined to believe that the same calm Confucian spirit, which reacted to every enthusiasm of this kind with extreme reserve and frank scepticism, even survives in contemporary China. In 1959, shortly after the establishment of people's communes, an anonymous study group published a selection of texts to illustrate the development of the idea of the "Great Equality" *(ta-t'ung)* over the course of Chinese history. It is curious that Hsü Meng-hsin's account should have been included.[71] After the beginning of the Cultural Revolution, these texts were considered extremely objectionable, for the major Marxist historian, Hou Wai-lu, who had been very much in vogue up to this time and was probably correctly assumed to have been the guiding light of this group, was denounced as an enemy of the people in August, 1966. This book was certainly one of the reasons for this action, for it was said that the implied criticism of such "extremists" was also intended as an attack on Mao Tse-tung himself.[72]

In any event, the total equality of men could never be realized in China except in secret societies run by very strong leaders with military power, and even then only for limited periods. Nonetheless, the old Taoist idea of a wholly anarchistic society living in small village communities persisted as an ideal. In fact, it asserted itself more strongly from the Sung period on, as even among anti-Confucians the religious element became mere trappings. It is interesting that the most perfect model of such an anarchistic, but also rigorously communist state should once again have taken the form of a promised land lying behind a cave. It is true that the process of secularization undergone by the previously mentioned island paradise from the Sung period is also in evidence in this cave paradise from the same period. Almost all supernatural ingredients have been eliminated. Unlike the "island of the loyalists," however, the cave described here was not "conquered" by Confucianism, but remained Taoist through and through. Indeed, it has much more in common with the prototype of the cave paradise in T'ao Ch'ien than with the later T'ang imitations with their superfluity of wonders. That it could only be three *warriors,* masters of Taoist combat techniques and other Taoist arts, that chose it as a final refuge, expresses the spirit of this allegory more clearly than anything else. They are personifications of warlike and religious individuals to whom a newly-born world belongs. The chronicler, a scholar by the name of K'ang Yü-chih (twelfth century),[73] writes in the first person singular:

> During the reign periods "Governmental Harmony" (1111–1118) and "Extended Harmony" (1119–1125), three brothers of the Yang family lived [in my home town]. K'o-shih, K'o-pi and K'o-fu had been diligent students and acquired an exceptional knowledge of divination according to the I-ching. They also had much mantic knowledge and interpreted wind directions, cloud formations, the flight of birds, and horoscopes. They had an even profounder knowledge of strategy, and became famous generals because of it. [One day,] they were returning [from a campaign against the Yürched] near the Yen mountain. On that occasion, they paid a visit to my father, who has since died, and told him the following: "Some years ago, we met a very old man in a mountain range near the "Western capital" [K'ai-feng]. He addressed us like old acquaintances, and was obviously very pleased to see us. He urged us not to accept any public office, but felt we should find a secluded place to live. "But are there places where one can live a life of solitude?" we asked. The old man said: "Do you want to find such a place?" And he led us further into the mountain to a large cave. He entered first, we followed. Gradually, the cave became narrower, until we finally had to crawl along on our bellies. After some 30 or 40 feet, it widened again, and when we had covered another stretch of similar length, it opened onto a country with fields, cocks and dogs, potters' sheds and smithies. What we saw was like a complete village community. As we approached a house, some people came running out to greet us, and said laughingly to the old man: "It has been a long time since we last saw you here." The old man answered: "These gentlemen would like to come and live here. Would you give your permission?" "It is true that our country is large," they answered, "and there are only a few of us living here. Yet we cannot permit any one with ordinary interests to settle. We are sorry, but we cannot allow them to remain." [In spite of this answer, they brought] wine and invited us to share it. It was light and clear, and had a bouquet of a kind unknown in the outside world. Now [some] chicken were killed and a meal prepared. When the festive mood had reached its peak, our hosts suddenly said to us: "Come back as quickly as you can, and stay. If by chance unrest should come to the empire, we will simply block the entrance to the cave with a clump of earth. No one will be able to find us." And they added: "It is true that the people living here come from a great variety of families, but they all have absolute trust in each other, and live together in the most marvelous harmony, incomparably greater even than the harmony you normally find among members of a single family. That is why they can live together without distinctions *(t'ung-*

chü). But we don't like people who cannot reconcile their interests, let alone those who have disputes or quarrels. Now that we have had an opportunity to study your temperament and physiognomy, we can see that you are neither high officials nor famous scholars. And since the old gentleman brought you here, you must be capable men. It is a principle among us that there should be no private property, and that includes clothes and foodstuffs, cattle, silk and hemp. Everything is owned communally. That is also the reason we can all live together without distinction. If you really want to settle here, you must not bring any gold, pearls, brocade, embroideries, or any other valuables. They would be useless here, and only provoke quarrels. It would be best if you came with empty hands." They then pointed to a house, and continued: "The people living there also arrived here just a short time ago. They belonged to a class that normally walks about bedecked in velvet and silk and covered with pearls and jewels. But they burned everything. All we have here is rice, firewood, fish and meat, but those things we have in abundance. We simply count the heads in a family and distribute land for cultivation and the breeding of silk worms accordingly. No one may accept material or food from someone else." We thanked our hosts for their instructions, and promised to take them to heart. Then we were given this warning: "Should you take too long to come to a decision, the entrance to the cave will be blocked." At nightfall, the three of us and the old man slipped back through the cave, and out of the country. Now all of us have decided to renounce all our obligations and to go to this country for the rest of our lives. ["We just came by here, Mr. K'ang, to ask] if you might wish to join us." [But my father declined.] The three Yang brothers returned across the mountain [to their home] on the Lo river, gave away all they owned and had stored in chests and bags, exchanged their silk and brocade for ordinary linen, and thus prepared for life among the people behind the cave. Later, it was heard that K'o-shih, [the oldest of the brothers,] had been seen with a turban on his head and dressed in a sack, selling oracular sayings, while the two younger brothers had allegedly built a house in the mountains and never left it. But when unrest came to the country, as they had expected, they walked to the cave, and since that time nothing further has been heard from them. My deceased father sent someone to the place [in the mountains] where they had built their house, but it had changed owners three times, and no one could say where the brothers had gone. When a peace treaty was concluded with the Yürched during the reign period, "Continuation and Recovery [of the Dynasty"] (1131–1162), which returned our three capital cities to us,[74] I journeyed to the capital to discover what had happened to our old house. A man suddenly appeared and asked: "Doesn't judge K'ang live here?" And he pulled out a letter written by one of the Yang brothers. In it, he inquired very politely how our family was getting along, and then added: "Here, where we live, we have enough to eat and to drink, and can sleep in peace. Nothing ever happens. Why should one strive to become an immortal! It would be wonderful if you could come here!" I gave the messenger this answer to take back: "Our venerable father died in the Hsin-hai year (1131). We are now living in I-hsing, and are waiting for conditions to calm down in the three capital cities. Then we want to return home with our mother. Since you never forgot our venerable father, would you tell us whether you also include us, his remaining children, in your invitation? If so, we would like to come to your

> clear, pure country." But a short time thereafter, the Yürched broke the treaty, and we had to rush back to the area south of the Yangtzu. Since that time, I have been unable to establish contact with the Yang brothers.[75]

THE BIRTH OF NATIONALISM

However great the differences between this fairy tale and the two previously quoted stories, the account of Fang La's conspiracy, and the description of Chung Hsiang's uprising, all three have one element in common, and that is the threat of the non-Chinese enemy in the north, rising like a black thunderstorm in the background. Of course, this danger had threatened China throughout its history. Between the fourth and the sixth centuries, the entire northern half of the empire was lost to foreign, war-like nomadic tribes. But at that time, when the Neo-Confucian concept of "unity" in all political and intellectual spheres had not yet come into existence, the amalgamation of Chinese and "barbarian" cultures had proven less difficult than could be imagined at this later time, and this despite the terrors of war and the mass flight of the population southward during that earlier period. The Confucian ideal of loyalty knew only an either-or. If the latter alternative meant defeat in the struggle against the barbarians, it was a calamity that was all the more deeply felt. The position of the "secret societies" and the previously mentioned patriotic robber bands was much more flexible than this somewhat rigid Confucian view, and had retained much of the earlier attitude toward the barbarians. For one thing, their tactics stressed mobility and thus represented a kind of adaptation to the warfare of the barbarians. More importantly, there was the apparent paradox that while they were ideologically more thoroughly "infected" by foreign beliefs than the Confucians, they could yet wage a much more uncompromising struggle against the invaders. When one reads in the popular novel *The Marsh Heroes,*[76] for example, that the robber bands, whom the Sung had bitterly fought at first, later battled the barbarians from the North with self-sacrificing courage and were publicly praised for this by the emperor—an event apparently based on historical fact—one is involuntarily reminded of the alliance between the troops of Chiang Kai-shek and those of Mao Tse-tung during the defensive war against Japan. Of course, the most decisive among the many differences in these two situations is that China failed to defeat the invaders in the twelfth and thirteenth centuries. Rather, it was more completely conquered than ever before in what at that time was already a three-thousand-year-long history. And this meant the end for motley rebellious groups such as Chung Hsiang's that found themselves in a kind of No-man's land between the area controlled by the central government and that of the foreigners. Other rebels could align themselves with Confucian loyalists and wage war on the foreign occupying power in recurrent uprisings, finally driving it out of the country a little less than one hundred years later.

From a psychological point of view, however, the victory of the barbarians had even greater consequences for the Confucians. When all of northern China including the eastern capital K'ai-feng and the two secondary capitals ("western capital" Lo-yang and "southern capital" Shang-ch'iu) was lost in 1126/1127 to the repeatedly mentioned Yürched, a Tungusic tribe, it might still have been possible to put up with the defeat. For it really only created a state of affairs that had been endured before in the dark centuries between the Han and the T'ang dynasties, and had ultimately been weathered. There had been no complete break in the "Chinese" tradition at that time; it had been carried on in the southern dynasties. The expression "Six Dynasties" *(Liu-ch'ao),* used by Confucian historians to refer to this period, clearly takes account of this belief. For although many more dynasties thought they were governing legitimately between the third and the seventh centuries, and were even felt to merit a history of their own, the official count included only those where the emperor's family could claim Chinese descent. Because the "Crossing of the Yangtzu river to the South" *(Nan-tu)* (1127) had been a fearful event, and the new capital was founded in a much less developed and culturally quite different, much less continentally-oriented southeastern coastal region, it was deeply felt that the end of a Confucian Golden Age had arrived. Too many lives, too many cultural treasures, too many beliefs in national greatness had been lost in the course of this precipitous flight. Yet some assurance could be had in the conviction that the Mandate of Heaven continued to lie with the Middle Kingdom. For if its territory had been reduced, its core had remained free. But when, in 1280, *all* of China was occupied by the Mongols (with whom the Chinese had previously allied themselves agains the Yürched), this meant not merely a political, but also a devastating spiritual catastrophe of greater proportions than had ever been experienced before. For a while, small, isolated groups of loyalists continued the struggle. The most sustained resistance was put up by those fighting on islands in the south. As their ideals gradually waned, they may have clung to the belief that the "real" Chinese rule was being perpetuated in these groups, a sort of government in exile. But in the long run, consolation could only be found in a kind of "inner emigration," sustained in the name of loyalty. Nor was this implausible, since the four-class system of the Mongols (Mongols, non-Chinese auxiliaries, northern Chinese subjected earlier, southern Chinese subjected later) excluded from government all members of the lowest class, and that class included all subjects of the (South) Sung dynasty, which continued to rule in the South after the Yürched conquest. For a century, the Confucians were thus forced into loyalist inactivity. This state seemed to bear a noteworthy resemblance to the temporally limited (three-year) period of mourning and retirement from office consequent on the death of parents, or the faithfulness of the "chaste widow," which extended beyond the husband's death.[77]

The power of government over the entire empire had now passed to a non-Chinese people of conquerors, and it could not really be conceded that they had received the heavenly mandate lawfully. The effect of this event on some Chinese scholars went beyond the sense that they were experiencing a major break in what, from a Confucian perspective, was the "real" and therefore the only meaningful historical development. The mere fact that a foreigner should have been able to become the "Son of Heaven" at all caused some of them to look with profound suspicion on the absolute rule of the emperor as it had been institutionalized by the Neo-Confucians. They did not go so far as to propagate those anarchistic and egalitarian ideals whose intellectual simplicity (which stood in inverse relation to the difficulties of their implementation) had time and again provided the ideology of popular uprisings. But they did revive the "socialist" tradition which Mo Ti, the *Lü'shih ch'un-ch'iu,* and the "School of Agriculture" had repeatedly given expression to during the second half of the first century B.C. The foreign, occasionally brutal rulers alerted them to the abuses a hereditary monarchy entailed. But like these writings, which served as their models, they followed the ancient custom of projecting their ideal of a modest ruler, chosen by the people almost again his will, a sort of "first servant of the state," into the past, not the future. They looked back to the time of the sage kings, whose form of government had allegedly lasted until the legalistic system of Ch'in Shih Huang-ti had put a definitive end to it.

The philosopher Teng Mu (1247–1306), whose life had reached its halfway mark when the Mongolians conquered China, was the most forceful representative of this view. The title of his principal work, *The Lute of Po-ya (Po-ya ch'in),* is an allusion to the story of the musician Po-ya, contained in the *Lü-shih ch'un-ch'iu.*[78] Because his songs were so unusual that only a single connoisseur could appreciate them, he broke his instrument after that man's death, and never played again. Teng Mu thus saw himself as a voice in the wilderness. But in the introduction to his book, he states that he would not tire of playing his song for, unlike Po-ya, he had never yet encountered the person capable of understanding his message, but that in spite of his isolation, he had not abandoned all hope. Yet this message is not really all that unfamiliar:

"In antiquity," he writes in the chapter concerning the "Way of the Ruler" *(chün-tao),*

> kings felt that governing the world was [a heavy responsibility] which they had no choice but to accept. But later, people began to look [on the throne] as an object of personal well-being, and therefore started fighting for possession of the world. In the beginnings of mankind, probably no one was pleased about becoming king. If someone was unlucky enough to win the hearts of the people, he could not really refuse the throne. He could truly say: "I desire nothing from the world, but the world desires me." Have you never heard of the era of "Highest virtue" *(chih-te)?* In those days, [the kings] ate mostly unhusked corn, bean pods, and coarse vegetables. They did not indulge in fancy foods. They wore linen garments during the summer, and deerskin in winter; all men dressed the same. Their palace and the earthen steps leading up to it rose no higher than 3 feet above the ground, and with

its roof of uncut straw, it was anything but luxurious. They received the people in their own apartments, a fact that has become known through the expression: "the emperor inquired personally into the difficulties of the little people." There was no strict dividing line [between ruler and subject]. When emperor Yao wanted to resign in favor of [the hermit] Hsü Yu, the hermit ran away,[79] and when emperor Shun tried the same thing for a farmer from Shih-hu, the farmer fled to the sea and never returned. This shows that the throne had not yet become something elevated. Under such conditions, it could happen that people felt content under a good king, and never tired of him. Their only worry was that he might abdicate some day, and that no one of equal merit might be willing to take his place. Unfortunately, the state of Ch'in later conquered the empire. . . . Ch'in Shih Huang-ti ran through the treasures of the entire world to amuse himself. As a result, the position of the prince became mightier and mightier. He ordered the burning of books, enforced the penal law to the utmost, and had the Great Wall built, 10,000 miles of it. He did all he could to strengthen his rule and position. Yet since that time, the ruler has become ever more lonely. He [constantly] trembles [with fear], like someone who has gold hidden on his person and dreads being attacked from behind. One cannot call that being safe. When Heaven created the people and placed rulers above it, it did not do so for the sake of the ruler, [but for the sake of the people]. The treasures within the four oceans were not intended for the satisfaction of any single individual. Emperors Yao and Shun did not indulge in fine foods or wear elegant garments, nor did they live in magnificent palaces, but Ch'in Shih Huang-ti did all those things. It was not the emperors Yao and Shun that set up barriers between themselves and the people, but Ch'in Shih Huang-ti. Why is it that so many rulers of later generations have praised Yao and Shun in songs and poems, yet conducted themselves no better than Ch'in Shih Huang-ti? A ruler, after all, is not born with four eyes, two mouths, the head of a dragon, and wings, but looks like anyone else. Basically, anyone has the ability to govern. If the ruler claims as his own what people desire, and retains for himself alone what everyone longs for, he teaches the people to steal and deceive by his example. . . . When a king has to be afraid that the people will take the throne away from him, when he has to be protected by soldiers who wear armor and carry bows and arrows, when he has to worry about rebels, the world is really in a sad state. Why should a genuinely saintly king, whom the people loves like a father, always fear that men might rebel, and always be obliged to employ soldiers in armor and with bows and arrows to protect him? Therefore I believe: a ruler who molds himself after the emperors Yao and Shun should make certain that no one in the world finds pleasure in becoming one. [But] if he chooses Ch'in Shih Huang-ti as his model, he need not be surprised if rebels and robbers fight [him] for possession of the throne. Alas, the world constantly changes. A successful rebel is called "emperor;" one who fails is just a "rebel." Liu [Pang] (the founder of the Han dynasty) led an insurrection in Han-chung, and Li [Yüan] (the founder of the T'ang dynasty), who did the same in Chin-yang, [are two historical examples]: Both became legitimate and happy rulers [because they started their uprisings] during times of upheaval. Had they done so during times of order, they would have been nothing but "rebels." How can

> suffering end in this world as long as those at the head of dynasties don't bother solving this problem, as long as the clever take advantage of the simple, and the strong impose their will on the weak?[80]

Some modern scholars have pointed out that the ideal of a ruler whose manner and dress differed in no way from those of the simple man on the street, and who occupied a modest throne with the unanimous consent of the people represented an indirect criticism of the hated Mongolian emperors, whose display of power and splendor was "un-Chinese."[81] There certainly is an element of truth in that view. But the technique of obscuring the real target of the attack works both ways. From the Confucian point of view, the emperor Shih Huang-ti was a semi-barbarian, the offspring of an illicit union, born in the colonial territory of Ch'in, and Teng Mu may well have alluded to the Mongolian rulers in his criticism of that figure. Yet the wording of his attack also exposed a genuine flaw in the smug, Confucian system of government, that "lame compromise" which Confucianism had secretly struck with Legalism after the Ch'in empire was defeated in the second century A.D., as noted above.[82] This criticism became all the more telling when Confucianism once again permitted an amalgamation of its own ideals with those of the rude nomadic rulers after the Mongols had been driven out, and the Chinese Ming dynasty was established (1368–1644). The Mongolian Yüan dynasty was the first to choose what may be called a program rather than a clan or place name as its designation, for Yüan means primordial beginning. And it did mark the beginning of a new epoch in the sense that it added the "brutalization" of the entire social domain to the standardization and constriction of the intellectual sphere effected during the Sung period.[83] But although this unaccustomed brutality was one of the principal reasons uprisings against the ruling house were finally crowned by success (as also happened in the uprisings against the Ch'in), the new rulers did not hesitate to adopt at least some of the rigorous measures of the overturned dynasty. Both times, during the Han and the Ming periods, this was done under the cloak of "Confucianism," which thus prostituted itself to the point of self-destruction.

The previously mentioned alignment of the chronology with the installation of the emperor, which was taken over from the Mongolian period, was a very typical and visible sign of this turn toward Legalism and of the actual divinization of both emperor and state. Of greater import was the draconian punishment of even the most insignificant infringements of the state's claim to total power. Time and again, thousands upon thousands of persons, usually entire clans, were turned over to the executioner in what can only be described as waves of "mopping-up" operations, and mass trials were held to deal with real or imagined attempts at rebellion. Public punishments of officials in their own offices and exceptionally cruel executions dragging on for months became an established procedure. It is not surprising that even one of the most important classics, which the Neo-Confucians themselves had raised to that status, the book *Meng-tzu*

(Mencius), could only appear in expurgated editions. All those passages discussing the rights of the people had to be deleted, particularly those which based the legitimacy of the ruler on the popular will.

That all of this could still be called "Confucian" shows the extent to which Confucianism had become the victim of its willingness to compromise. What is recognizable here is a striving for power at any price. The founder of the Ming dynasty was a former monk who had been a member of the White Lotus secret society and come to power with its help. Yet the dynasty was hardly less totalitarian than the Mongols. The criticism of Teng Mu thus applied as much to this Chinese dynasty as to the non-Chinese dynasty of the Mongols. It will be remembered that doubts about the justifiability of hereditary monarchy, and thus about monarchy generally, had already surfaced in the oldest texts. The sage kings Yao and Shun were said not to have chosen their own, less worthy sons as their successors, but rather the best among the people.[84] While such doubts were never wholly forgotten in China, it was during periods of alien rule that they found a particularly strong echo among both the people and the educated. And foreigners ruled for 355 of the 631 years from the time of China's conquest by the Mongolians (1280) to the collapse of the Manchu dynasty (1911). The latter also finally succumbed to this onslaught that was propelled by a particularly explosive mixture of social and national motifs, and which has retained its effectiveness throughout the world and down to our own times. But with the expulsion of these "old" foreigners from the north, the presence of the "new" foreigners from the west became all the more noticeable. Besides, the new republic soon displayed any number of monarchical traits. As a result, the bitter criticism of Teng Mu—and he was only one among many—continued to be influential in China during the first half of our century and contributed its share to lending China the aspect it wears today, and which disquiets many.

2 / THE "INVESTIGATION OF THINGS"

PHENOMENA OF POLARIZATION WITHIN CONFUCIANISM

The ideal of reducing all conflicting world views, particularly Confucianism, Taoism and Buddhism to a common, i.e. Confucian, denominator, had been propagated from the ninth century A.D. on, and been realized for the first time during the Sung period. All those beliefs which could not be bent to this purpose began to lead an existence of their own. Surviving in spite of their illegality and a certain spiritual erosion, they became increasingly virulent in the social and political arena. But Confucianism itself also suffered far-reaching consequences. As so often happens in history, the victory of a single system did not eliminate the real conflicts, it merely glossed them over. While the senseless and fundamentally dishonest notion that the "Three Teachings" *(san-chiao)* were really only "one," (i.e. Confucian) was being proclaimed more and more insistently from the Sung period on, the very same positions which had once been taken by Confucianism, Taoism and Buddhism and their various Legalist and Mohist admixtures resurfaced *within* Confucianism. All that had changed was that they now manifested themselves as internal rather than external tensions.

All its striving for uniformity notwithstanding, Neo-Confucianism in its fully developed form had never been rigorously monistic, but had also contained elements of dualism. While it developed the concept of a single, quasi-neutral "Great Ultimate" *(t'ai-chi),* the ground of all Being, by recourse to the *I-Ching,* two other concepts which had always played a certain role in philosophy became even more important. It was only in Neo-Confucianism, however, that they came to the fore as a kind of unfolding of the *T'ai-chi.* This also derived from the *I-Ching* (in this case, its *Yin-Yang* theory). The first of these concepts was the "ether" *(ch'i),* with the original meaning of "vapor," a basic, initially amorphous but malleable substance; the second, the eternally immutable "structural principle" *(li),* a term which actually refers to the irregular markings in jade, but which was already used at an early time to mean "structure." All Being was to have arisen from the interaction of these two basic elements, with *ch'i* providing the matter, and *li* the form.[85] But this relatively simple model permitted countless modifications both with respect to the description of its two components and the relative weight they were given. Most Neo-Confucians, for example, equated *li* with *Tao,* "Way," which had lost some of its force and been taken over by Taoists and Buddhists. Those philosophers who assigned greater importance to the "ether" even accorded it absolute priority because they denied that a "structural principle" could exist without a material base. Chang Tsai, who had been the first to "discover" this "ether" and its way of connecting all that exists, had still viewed it as the only ground of Being. He was opposed by those philosophers who considered the material world of forms to be merely a cruder, imperfect copy of a world of pure "structural principles" which might well have existed without its materialization in the "ether." Because the world was good "in principle," it was the "ether" that was responsible for all its imperfections and the existence of evil. To no inconsiderable extent, these theories were inspired by the numerological speculations of Shao Yung which described the functioning of an incorporeal world.[86]

The many nuances that give their specific tone to all those conceptions of the ideal that had developed under Confucian aegis since the Sung period must be seen against this iridescent background. In his monumental life work that extended to all areas of intellectual culture, Chu Hsi had in a sense created new Confucian classics. Divergent interpretations of those few, though still highly ambiguous and short works Chu Hsi had defined as the quintessence of Confucianism, were now advanced. Discussion centered largely around the interpretation of the individual steps leading toward that "Peace in the World" that is described in the "Great Learning."[87] But it was the "investigation of things" that aroused the most intense controversy. For it was this "investigation" which allegedly represented the very core, the essential impetus for a salutary chain reaction that would spread ever further into the outside world and bring it peace. What was at issue was not only the meaning of "investigation," but, more fundamentally, the structure of the relationship obtaining between the "investigating" individual concerned with the "extension of knowledge," and the world in which he found himself. It was Chu Hsi's opinion that the essence, the "nature" *(hsing)* of man consisted of the two components *li* and *ch'i,* that it therefore participated in the great "Principle" of the world and thereby even in the "Supreme Ultimate," but differed from it in complexity. Man had to make the moral effort to achieve an ever more complete adaptation of his "nature" to the "Principle," a process made possible by the "investigation of things." While Chu Hsi was still living, the Neo-Confucian Lu Chiu-yüan (Lu Hsiang-shan) (1139–1193)[88] formed a school which opposed this teaching. It declared that this split in human nature was irrelevant since it characterized all being. Instead, it drew attention to the human individual in his indivisible wholeness, a concept for which it chose the expression "mind" (*hsin,* actually "heart"). Through this shift in accent man is not only indirectly connected with the "ether" and the

"Principle" in many gradations, as Chu Hsi had maintained, but his innermost being, his "mind," in its concrete form is actually identical with being in its totality. Monad-like, the entire universe manifests itself in every individual. In some passages of Lu's work, we thus find the same intimate nexus with the universe which we previously noted in Chang Tsai: all that has changed is that it is now not so much the all-connecting "ether," but the all-connecting "principle" that is stressed (and its dualistic aspect is simply ignored): "The universe is my 'mind,' and my 'mind' is the universe. If a sage were to appear by the Eastern Sea, he would have precisely the same 'mind' and the same 'principle' [as I], and the same would hold true if a sage appeared by the Western Sea or the World oceans in the South and the North. And if a hundred or a thousand generations ago or a hundred or a thousand generations hence sages appear, they also would have precisely the same 'mind' and the same 'principle.' "[89]

The "idealist" branch of Neo-Confucianism founded by Lu Chiu-yüan, and known in China as *Hsin-hsüeh* ("Study of the Mind")[90] could gradually assert itself vis-a-vis the "realist" or "rationalist" school of Chu Hsi (*Li-hsüeh,* "Study of Principle") during the Ming, although Chu Hsi's prestige remained intact. It was more in harmony with the general trend toward unification, being open-minded toward the philosophical and mystical forms of Taoism and Buddhism. The Buddhism of meditation—a combination of Buddhism and Taoism—had influenced the earlier idealist representatives of Neo-Confucianism, and its presence is unmistakable in the work of the most important philosopher of the Ming, Wang Shou-jen (Wang Yang-ming),[91] (whom we mentioned before in a different context). His autobiography, part of his collected works, tells how he first followed Chu Hsi's view and vainly tried to grasp the nature of the highest, all-inclusive "Principle" by a kind of additive "investigation of things" round about him and extending down to the smallest blade of grass. But one night, he was suddenly struck by the insight into the real meaning of the "extension of knowledge through the investigation of things": "Without knowing what he was doing, he shouted [one night] with a loud voice and danced around so that all the servants became alarmed. For the first time, it had occurred to him that one's own nature was enough [to understand] the 'Way' of the sages, and that it was false to search for the 'principle' beyond the self, among outside events and things."[92]

It was in the book *Meng-tzu* (Mencius) that he discovered a concept which had hardly been noticed before and been mentioned only once by Chang Tsai. As "intuitive" (actually "naturally good") knowledge *(liang-chih),* which is man's "without the exercise of thought"[93] because it is a gift he receives at birth, it became the central tenet of his own teaching. For Wang Shou-jen, the investigation of things thus became the calm and withdrawal of meditation, and the extension of knowledge an extension of intuitive knowledge. What occurred here was thus a complete reversal of positions: human knowledge does not depend on things; instead, it is things that depend on this human "intuitive knowledge": "The 'intuitive knowledge' of man [is the same as] the 'intuitive knowledge' of plants and trees, tiles and stones. Is this true only of these [simple] things? [No], even heaven and earth would not be what they are if they did not have man's 'intuitive knowledge.' From the very beginning, heaven, earth and all things formed a single whole with man, whose highest form are the tiny manifestations of spirit and intellect found in the human mind."[94]

Clearly, the line between this position and Ch'an Buddhism is difficult to draw. It is also obvious that this teaching necessarily engendered the most diverse forms of individualism, and finally even led to utterly contradictory interpretations of Master Wang Shou-jen's words themselves. Of the two great schools which considered themselves the heirs of his teaching, one, founded by his disciple Wang Chi (1498–1583), became known as the Lung-hsi school, and merged almost completely with Buddhism. His synthesis of the "Three Teachings" only appeared to be Confucian; actually, it was Buddhist in nature.[95] Another disciple of Wang Shou-jen, Wang Ken (1483–1540), founded the "T'ai-chou" school, so named after his birthplace. The philosopher and historian of philosophy Huang Tsung-hsi (1610–1695), of the early Manchu period, reproached it for its Buddhist tendencies. But actually it continued traditions that were really Chinese.[96] The many offshoots of individualism bore curious flowers at times, and some of its followers are strongly reminiscent of the droll figures of the third and fourth centuries A.D. Li Chih (1527–1602),[97] for example, was not really a Buddhist, but adopted a monk's garb, shaved his head because he wanted to be "free," and lived with two "nuns," who both happened to be daughters of the provincial governor. Finally, at the age of 76, he was put in prison and committed suicide. At the same time, however, we notice in this school the first, very realistic attempts to come to terms with this world. As time passed, they led ever further away from the idealism of Wang Shou-jen. This is already evident in the theses of its founder, Wang Ken, who once again reinterpreted the meaning of the "investigation of things" by working out the basic meaning of the word "investigation" *(ko)*, which originally meant no more than "measuring square" (the character is still written with the signific "wood"). He therefore took the "investigation of things" to be the adaptation of all things to the human measure. The constant corrective action required to achieve this result must be mutual. The "measure" and what is being measured must be reciprocally adjusted:

> Our own self is the measuring square, and the world or the state are the squares to be measured with it. When we apply our measuring square, we should notice that the incorrectness of the squares means that our measuring square is incorrect. We therefore have to correct this measuring square of ours, rather than look for correctness in the squares. Once our measuring square is really correct, the squares to which it is applied will become correct, and once they are correct, we will have completed the task of applying the right measures to things.[98]

Wang Ken thus bridges the gap between the subjectivity of the individual and the external world. Because he deliberately includes the state in the latter, it is not surprising to find proposals in his "Treatise on the Kingly Way" *(Wang-tao lun)* which are very much in line with the quite concrete, if perhaps excessively structured ideal of the state set forth in the old ritual classic *Chou-li (The Rites of Chou).* That his writings give renewed recognition to the old Confucian concept of "Learning," which accords much more with an outward than an inward turn to be pursued in the "investigation of things," points in the same direction. In a "Song of Joy," he even equates pleasure and learning:

> The human mind has its own pleasure/Except that it is bound by selfish motives./ Even intuitive knowledge is aware of these selfish motives,/but after the mind has eliminated them,/it reverts to pleasure./ Pleasure is the state of being brought about by what you learn;/Learning is the process of entering into experience of this kind of pleasure./No pleasure, no learning./ No learning, no pleasure./ By having pleasure you begin to learn,/by learning you have pleasure./ Pleasure *is* learning./ Learning *is* pleasure./ Indeed, what is the greatest pleasure other than Learning?/ What is the greatest learning other than pleasure?/[99]

What is an erotic relationship to knowledge in a platonic sense also shows through in Wang Ken's social teaching, and in modern times earned him a reputation as a "democratic" even a "leftist" philosopher, at least among Wang Shou-jen's followers.[100] Even before he became Wang Shou-jen's disciple, he proclaimed that anyone, even the most ordinary person, could perform the acts of a sage if he were given the opportunity, and attempted to attract the uneducated by a rhetoric tailored to their taste. Thus the following remarkable observation of his has come down to us: "It is conditions that determine learning, it is conditions that constitute the 'Way.' If people have to vegetate in poverty and suffer hunger and cold, they lose what is fundamental and will no longer be able to learn."[101]

The almost egalitarian ideas Wang Ken presented for a reform of the regulations governing the manufacture of salt from the sea[102] and his fantastic costume—allegedly the same as emperor Yao's[103]—move him very close to the leaders of popular rebellions who had so often attracted the masses by a blend of program and masquerade. It seems that it was only his encounter with Wang Shou-jen that caused him to abandon a path which would have led to a transformation of political conditions rather than the conception of philosophical systems. Yet it was due to him that what was really a heterogeneous element found its way into the "Learning of the Mind" school which, gradually gaining in influence, ultimately transformed the whole idealist strain of Confucianism into its opposite.

But even Wang Shou-jen had to deal with philosophers and politicians who may not have shared the egalitarianism of many rebel leaders, but certainly represented those socialist ideas which in China always harked back to the never wholly forgotten teachings of Mo Ti, and even proposed to derive them directly from Neo-Confucianism. This becomes clear in a dialogue contained in Wang Shou-jen's works:

> Some asked: "But Master Ch'eng [Hao (1032–1085),[104] a precursor of the 'Learning of the Mind' school], said that a loving (*jen*) person considers heaven, earth and indeed all creatures as a single body. Why can Mo Ti's 'universal love' *(chien-ai)* not be considered love?" The master answered: "It is extremely difficult to find a good answer to this question. You have to acquire self-knowledge to really understand it. According to its structural principle love is infinitely creative, infinitely growing. But however infinite it may be in its temporal and spatial extent, the effects of its never-ending growth are only gradual. It is like a tree which shows the first signs of growth when the shoot blossoms. The affection *(ai)* between father and son, or between the older and the younger brother is also the first sign of the growth of the human mind, the same as with the tree putting forth a shoot. The feeling of love *(jen)* toward men and of affection for all other creatures developing from this corresponds in a sense to the growth of the trunk, the branches and the leaves. But Mo Ti's 'universal love' has no gradations. It is the same toward father and son, older and younger brother within the family as toward a stranger passing through, and thus destroys its own starting point. If no shoot blossoms first, we know that there is no root, and that therefore that never-ending growth cannot occur. How could that be called love?"[105]

Such was the serious objection against all egalitarian conceptions of the ideal that had been raised even before Wang Shou-jen. For (as everywhere else in the world), they excluded all family relationships except "brotherly love," and thereby introduced a curious coldness into the relations between man and man. The hierarchical Confucian love, growing out of the family, was always in danger of turning into nepotism, corruption and even despotism, but the "universal," Mohist form was just as consistently threatened by the rigidity of anonymous coldness. Among the "five relationships" of Confucianism,[106] we find only one which is not part of a hierarchy, could therefore have served as a bridge between a patriarchal and an egalitarian social order, and combined equal status and human warmth, and that is the relation between friend and friend. To what extent it actually played this role, at least temporarily and in certain areas, would perhaps merit a detailed study.

CLAN COMMUNISM

But another, larger constellation also did full justice to Wang Shou-jen's demands, and was of greater importance to the development of conceptions of the ideal state, and that was clan communism. The scholar Liang Ju-yüan (1527–1579),[107] better known by his pseudonym Ho Hsin-yin, not only advocated but also tried to implement it. Liang was anything but a rebel. In a very perspicacious essay, "Concerning the Theory: Fatherlessness and the Absence of Princes Are Not Identical with Parricide and Regicide" *(Pien wu-fu wu-chün fei shih-fu shih-chün),* he demonstrated that the rejection of hierarchical arrangements espoused by the "followers of Yang Chu" (by whom he meant the Taoists in so far as they were individualists) and the Mohists could not be justified by the argument from nature or the animal kingdom because the element of consciousness was lacking there. Although the mother and its offspring frequently conducted themselves according to the rules of parental and filial love, this no more demonstrated a special virtue on their part than their killing each other (an equally frequent occurrence) would prove criminal intent. Only man has a consciousness of hierarchy and moral obligation, and it is these insights which reveal the person in the father or prince that is murdered. Indeed, they constitute the motive behind the act, which is the usurpation of their place.[108] At least intentionally, Liang Ju-yüan thus did not try to undermine the existing order. On the contrary, he later participated in the suppression of an uprising of the White Lotus secret society in Chungking (1567). Nonetheless, he belonged to the "left" wing of the T'ai-chou school. His teacher Yen Chün (Yen Shan-nung) (first half, sixteenth century)[109] was one of Wang Ken's disciples, and after Liang's violent death, no less a figure than Li Chih, a man who despised society, wrote a commemorative essay on him. The text is not wholly uncritical, but its admiration is undisguised.[110]

Like the other Neo-Confucians of the Ming period, Liang Ju-yüan made the "Great Learning" the basis of his plans for improving the world. But his point of departure was not the "investigation of things" or the "extension of knowledge,"—concepts which had lost some of their force in the meantime—but rather the "ordering of the family." In 1553, he built the "Hall for Gathering in Harmony" *(chü-ho t'ang)* in the Yung-feng district (in what is today Kiangsi province in southcentral China). He proposed that the powerful and far-flung Liang clan set up a kind of family commune with two principal areas of activity, a communal educational system, and the common cultivation of the fields. In the proclamation addressed to the clan, which called for the standardization of education (*Chü-ho shuai-chiao yü-tsu li-yü,* "A Simply Worded Proclamation to the Clan Written by the Head of Communal Instruction in the 'Hall for Gathering in Harmony' "), we read the following:

> "It is true that we have had instruction in the village schools of our clan for many generations, but it is still the case that in some public buildings with a low ceiling, five or six children plod along, or that a few dozen are herded together and thus keep each other from learning anything. The teacher can never be joyful and relaxed in the classroom, nor do the students find any pleasure in the teaching because they are neither joyful nor relaxed. We therefore propose that, beginning today, they gather in the hall of the ancestors. It should be our purpose to create a joyful and relaxed atmosphere during class hours for both teachers and students. If they gather only in the private residences of the leading families of the clan, our sons and younger brothers will only get to know their relatives in those families, and the same would be true if they gathered merely in the houses of those of only moderate means, or the poor. Besides, coming together in a private house cultivates a private mode of thought. Therefore, the gathering in the hall of the ancestors also eradicates privates modes of thought among our sons and younger brothers. But it is not

only among them that such a mode of thought can thus be eradicated. All their fathers and older brothers will also become familiar and friendly with each other, for they will see each other in the morning and evening because of their sons and younger brothers. On the first and fifteenth of every month, they will meet with the twelve teachers from the head of the communal education system on down, and with the head of the hall of ancestors. On this occasion, they will be delighted to hear how their sons and younger brothers outdo each other in good behavior and vie with each other in their studies. During such a pleasant gathering, friendly, loving relations will readily develop. Thus the gathering of the school children in the hall of the ancestors also serves the cultivation of a sense of closeness among the old and those of higher rank. In view of the fact that the school children all go to the same place for their instruction, it would be a considerable hardship if they had to go to their separate homes for every meal, particularly during the summer rains and the winter cold, quite apart from the fact that their fathers and older brothers might worry about them. For that reason, and regardless of whether they live close by or far away, and are rich or poor, we should have them all accompanied to their meals so that they can be supervised on their way and the older relatives need feel no anxiety about them. But if all of them are taken to a common meal, it would make no sense if they were to go home individually to spend the night, left the house early in the morning, and returned late at night, quite apart from the fact that dillying and dallying once they are out of school does not advance their education. Nor could the teachers concentrate as fully on their instruction as they otherwise might. Whether they live close by or far away, are rich or poor, we therefore definitely want them to spend the night in the hall of the ancestors. Idle play will be avoided, and instruction intensified. [Pedagogical problems attending the instruction of the wealthy differ from those encountered in teaching the poor, but all of these difficulties will be solved by this procedure. Special rules for any and all imaginable eventualities, particularly unforeseen occurrences within the individual family, can be drawn up. In each instance, a careful check will determine whether and in what manner they can be applied.] After half a year, children who seem to show a degree of intellectual activity will be tested. They will be assigned a provisional place on a list ranking their performance. After three years, the "small final examination" *(hsiao-ch'eng)* will be given. The list will be revised accordingly, but remain subject to further change. After ten years, the "great final examination" *(ta-ch'eng)* will be given. It is only at this time, and without regard to wealth, that questions concerning the pupil's majority, his marriage, his position in society and his income will be decided in the hall of the ancestors. [Should this system be introduced,] fathers and older brothers would no longer have to worry that [the school] was too small or not close enough, or wonder if they [themselves] were perhaps in too lowly a position and therefore doubt that the course of study was right for their sons and younger brothers. Nor would [the teachers] any longer have to listen to unqualified speeches or ill-founded advice, which only interferes with their activity. There would be no more idlers who, for reasons of their own, stir up the little people to wreak vengeance and settle family matters and disputes by violence. Nor would there be adulterers to talk servant girls into secretly passing sweets and trinkets [to other men's wives]. [Parents] would no longer permit their

> children excessive luxuries or arouse their desire for sweets. Instead, there would be a general rule that all may speak at the same time, that all must be silent at the same time, that all eat and drink at the same time. If all fathers and older brothers could agree to bring up [their sons and younger brothers] in moderation, they would confine their desires to what the family can provide.[111]

The educational system proposed by Liang Ju-yüan embodies elements of the ideal concept the Confucian Ho Hsiu had developed fourteen hundred years earlier,[112] especially the division into three steps. It is also possible, however, that Liang designed this model independently of any earlier examples. It bears a strong resemblance to western school systems, and certain comments such as the complaint about the senselessness of small schools or the misery of overcrowded classrooms could have been made about recent conditions in our own country.

As regards the standardization of the economic system, things are a little different. The plan was set forth in a second publication with the title "Simply Worded Proclamation to the Clan, Written by the Head of the Communal Supply System in the 'Hall for Gathering in Harmony' " *(Chü-ho shuai-yang yü-tsu li-yü).* In this numerologically structured and somewhat rigid plan, the same, characteristically "Chinese" element is detectable that had given all ideal agrarian orders since Mencius's well field system their particular quality:

> In the first months of the year Kuei-ch'ou (1953), our entire clan first gathered in complete harmony. When [the spirit of] this harmonious gathering had taken possession of our hearts, we realized for the first time that the roots [of our existence] are only nourished by what we receive from our ruler. It is true that we have the yield of our fields, but without the ruler and upward lines of communication, the many would defeat the few in the struggle [for property], and we could never protect what we harvest. We can do so today, but would we be in the same position without what the ruler gives us? It is true we possess our body, yet without a ruler and upward lines of communication, the strong would overwhelm the weak, and we could never protect our body from harm. If we can do so today, would that be possible without the emperor's gift to us? We recognized how difficult it is to reciprocate his largesse. Therefore, having created the position of leader of communal education, we decided to also create the office of head of communal supply *(shuai-yang),* to reciprocate the emperor's largesse. And since we recognized how difficult it is to organize a supply system, we decided to create the office of a director of supplies *(wei-yang).* Because further difficulties remained, we decided[113] to create the office of an assistant director *(fu-yang)* of supplies to help in the organizational work. But since we knew how difficult organizational work still was, we assigned four supervisors *(kuan-liang)* of the grain to each of these three top officials, so that we had a total of twelve. These men are charged with responsibility for the harvest of each of the four seasons. Now, a total of 24 grain collectors *(ts'ui-liang)* was added. They are responsible for the harvest between the eight points of the year. Seventy-two grain gatherers *(cheng-liang)* constitute the lowest echelon. Each of them works during a five-day week. After each week, the respective grain gatherer will turn his grain over to the grain collectors of the eight points of the year,[114]

> who in turn will hand these stores on to the grain supervisors of the four seasons when one of the eight points of the year has passed. The latter pass their stores on to the assistant director of supplies when one of the four seasons has ended. The assistant director will turn them over to the director of supplies who will await the dispositions of the head of the communal supply system. If during any five-day week the targeted amount of grain is not brought in, the grain gatherer in question has to report this to the grain collector in charge of his group. This same procedure is followed on all levels, until the report ultimately reaches the head of the communal supply system, who will examine the matter and make a final report to the head of the communal educational system. If a subsequent investigation fails to uncover discrepancies, the authorities will be notified. A minimal adjustment in the taxes to be paid by every single member, and by the entire clan collectively, with everyone contributing his share, will suffice to reciprocate the largesse all receive from above.[115]

This document demonstrates how incredibly cautious Liang had to be in his organizational scheme so as not to incur the displeasure of the authorities. The entire first part of his proclamation concerning "communal supply" (given here in considerably shortened form) amounts to a profound bow to the emperor, and represents the projected organization as if its only purpose were the orderly collection of taxes. Liang's "clan communes" would indeed have simplified tax collection, which would have been in the interest of the government. Since Sung times, more and more huge kinship groups had come into existence. They were made up of thousands of members. This trend had been actively encouraged by the state, for it facilitated the transactions of public business, since in cases of irregularity the government could call the much smaller number of clan elders to account. But the individual officials did not welcome the consolidation of the clans as envisaged by Liang. By levying unofficial taxes *ad libitum* on a defenseless population, they had been able to secure substantial supplementary funds for themselves. But faced by such massive, consolidated groups, they obviously could no longer exercise their "rights" as easily as before. As early as 1559, six years after the creation of the clan communes, they used a bloody incident involving the collection of taxes in the Yung-feng region as a pretext for arresting Liang as a ringleader, although he actually had as little to do with this affair as his group. He was sentenced to death by hanging, then placed into a penal unit but set free a year later because friends intervened on his behalf.[116] The experimental communal educational and economic program, which had started so hopefully if we can judge by reports, thus came to nothing, for he naturally did not receive permission to run his clan as he had before.

His individualistic views concerning the educational process also brought him into conflict with the imperial minister of culture, Chang Chü-cheng[117]. Toward the end of a conversation Liang had with him shortly after his release, he allegedly asked him the difficult question if he, "who was a member of the Imperial University, had really understood the true meaning of the concept 'Great Learning.' " Chang answered: "You always float somewhere above the clouds with your thoughts, but never manage to really take off,"[118] by which he meant to suggest that he considered Liang's plans utopian. Yet Liang probably lost his last chance with his impudent question. On the way home, he said to an acquaintance: "Mr. Chang is undoubtedly at the head of his class, even among the ministers. He will therefore also be at the head of his class when it comes to poisoning the system of instruction, and in the same place when it comes to poisoning me."[119] But this was not to happen until some time later. Because his enemies alleged that he had been involved in an uprising, the government began looking for him in 1573. In 1576, he was finally captured, but refused to kneel before the investigating officer, and told him: "You cannot kill me, for it is Chang Chü-cheng who will do that job." Because of these words, the official had him beaten to death in prison.[120]

Liang Ju-yüan's almost forgotten writings never reappeared after their first publication in 1625. They were collected in Peking in 1960, and edited with supplements. The editor Jung Chao-tsu must have been politically close to Hou Wai-lu,[121] for in his introduction[122] he praised the progressive spirit of this sixteenth century figure. But he also called him an "extremist," and his teaching "utopian." Without intending to do so, he thus sided with the old minister of culture Chang Chü-cheng, at least to an extent. For it was the latter Liang had called his "real" murderer, because he had had to accept his reproach that he was utopian. In reality, Liang's ideas were not utopian, of course, but merely somewhat ahead of their time (which is not always, though frequently, the same thing).

For only a short time after his death, the provocative question concerning the right understanding of the classical "Great Learning" was raised by an ever larger number of intellectuals. Gradually, the somewhat anti-idealist spirit of the T'ai-chou school developed into the "liberation through the revival of antiquity,"[123] as the famous Chinese scholar Liang Ch'i-ch'ao (1873–1929), who saw himself as part of the earlier tradition, has called this movement which began in the seventeenth century. In his view, this Chinese "renaissance" unfolded in five steps between the seventeenth and the nineteenth centuries. In every case, the more modern doctrine was questioned and destroyed by recourse to the one preceding it. The first was the idealist variant of Neo-Confucianism *(Hsin-hsüeh)* with its marked *(ch'an)* Buddhist component as represented by Wang Shou-jen during the Ming. The second was the realist variant of Neo-Confucianism, which had had its flowering during the Sung, particularly under Chu Hsi's aegis. The third was the sober, philological form of late Han and T'ang Confucianism. The fourth the rather more religious Confucianism during the early Han. And the fifth and last was that form of Confucianism which had been proclaimed by its actual founders, Confucius and Mencius. This schema of Liang Ch'i-ch'ao may appear somewhat rigid, yet is largely correct in its assessment of conditions from the founding of the Manchu dynasty on. An enormous intellectual structure with its roots in the past, Confucianism did not collapse all at once. One might say that it was conscientiously dismantled, layer by layer, and from top to bottom, over a span of three centuries. The only reason this process (which seems to be paralleled in our time by the fate of Christianity in the West) did not arouse the attention of outsiders was that everyone of the intellects busily contributing to the destruction of Confucianism was utterly convinced of being a true Confucian not out to destroy, but rather to "uncover" the earlier, "more authentic" stratum. What was interesting in this procedure was that with their increasing age, the sources became ever more fragmentary. As a result, opportunities for arbitrary interpretations multiplied. Paradoxically, age-old teachings could thus much more easily be presented as having contemporary relevance and thereby found a greater audience than others which were barely one hundred years old. It was only when the entire structure had been demolished and scholars were surprised to find themselves confronted by pure nothingness that even those became uncertain who had not hesitated to rewrite Confucianism in their own image, a group which included men such as K'ang Yu-wei. There was a sudden awareness that this admirable effort had neglected the most important thing. For the focus of attention had remained unchanged. It was still the past, when it should have been the future. In this "revival" of the past, the future had not only not been won; the past had also been lost. Because down to our own century, it continued to be the past which the revolutionaries within Confucianism eyed as fixedly as the conversatives, it is not surprising that we can observe a paralyzing melancholy in the literature of the entire generation born during the last quarter of the nineteenth century, and which had its source in the convergence of two contradictory conceptions. There was, first, the conviction stemming from traditional education that any future could only be the reflection of the past, so that any confidence in a future not rooted in that past necessarily appeared as a blind hope, an airy expectation, and really amounted to self-deception. There was, secondly, the ever more clearly emerging fact that the past as an ideal had been destroyed. This brought not only the loss of pride in a long intellectual tradition but also, and with a finality not wholly comprehensible to us, the loss of hope for a spiritual future of whatever kind. Even today, China has not entirely recovered from the shock it suffered in this encounter with nothingness.

THE DOUBT IN CONFUCIAN IDEALS

One of the earliest scholars to signal the beginning phase of this curious, long stretched out suicide of Confucianism was Yen Yüan (1635–1704).[124] It is true that he went beyond the first of the five steps set forth by Liang Ch'i-ch'ao in that he not only rejected Wang Shou-jen's Neo-Confucianism like other famous philosophers of his period (such as Ku Yen-wu [1613–1682], for example[125] or Wang Fu-chih [1619–1692][126]), but also the Neo-Confucianism of Chu Hsi, and therefore Neo-Confucianism in its entirety. In this, he was typical of the "Han

Learning" *(Han-hsüeh),* whose gradual rise vis-a-vis the conservative "Sung Learning" *(Sung-hsüeh)* set the course of the seventeenth and eighteenth centuries. For during this entire time, the real opponents were the old adherents of Neo-Confucianism and the new adherents of "Pre-Neo-Confucianism." Only retrospectively does it become clear that Han Learning became increasingly radical as it moved further into the past and took up a number of new positions. What Yen Yüan vigorously objected to was primarily the endless theorizing of the Neo-Confucians, trapped as they were within their own "mind." The illumination which had made Wang Shou-jen dance with joy one night, the belief that knowledge of one's own nature sufficed for the knowledge of things, seemed grievous illusions to him. In his view, every Neo-Confucian was a Ch'an Buddhist in disguise, especially in southern China.[127] The typical representative of "Sung Learning" struck him, metaphorically speaking, as a "man who has chanced upon a travel guide and has diligently read section after section. Everyone takes him for an expert about the country, although in fact he has not dared take a single step in it."[128] In Yen Yüan and "Han Learning," we thus find the reassertion of the concrete, realistic trait of the Chinese character. "The time and the strength of man are limited," Yen Yüan wrote. "Every day spent reading aloud and discussing things means a day lost for activity in the real world. The more one handles paper and india ink, the less one genuinely experiences life."[129]

Consistent with this position, the "Ether" *(ch'i)* again assumes a dominant role in Yen's ontological speculation, and becomes the prime constituent of the universe, as for Chang Tsai before him. This is also apparent in the interpretation of the "investigation of things," which continued to be discussed. As we know through his disciple Li Kung (1659–1746),[130] Yen meant by this the direct, practical handling of things and the ability to master them in real life, not just reflecting about them.

Tai Chen's philosophy (1724–1777)[131] developed against the same background that gave its stamp to Yen Yüan's pragmatism. By virtue of the breadth of his interests and the precision of his methods, he was the most impressive figure of eighteenth-century China. He was not merely a philosopher, but also a mathematician, astronomer and, last but not least, a philologist. Of course, philology had had an ancient tradition in China, but early in the Manchu dynasty it was given new life by the previously mentioned scholar Ku Yen-wu. For the sober linguistic commentaries on the classics produced during the Han (in addition, of course, to other, rather more interpretative ones) represented the strongest weapon of the adherents of "Han Learning" in their battle against "Sung Learning," whose commentaries were wholly substantive and caught up in a narrow scholasticism. But Tai Chen was the first to be fully conscious of the real implications of philological criticism of the sacred texts. An anecdote recounts that at the early age of ten he acutely embarrassed his teacher when he asked him during the reading of the "Great Learning" how one could be sure that this or other Confucian writings really expressed Confucius's and Mencius's thought.

The teacher could not answer this question, but the problem retained its hold on Tai Chen throughout his life. This may not be reason enough to call him a Chinese "Bultmann," but without the textual criticism he stimulated and which soon began to flower luxuriantly (and to which Sinology owes an enormous debt), Confucianism would never have lost its magic with such alarming rapidity during the decades preceding and following the turn of the century.

That the revolutionary ingredient in Tai Chen's philology is no accident is borne out by his philosophical writings, where the preference for solid fact found another, but congruent expression. One of them reproduces the answer he gave one of his students who had surprised him by inferring from some sayings of his teacher that the previously eulogized "lack of desire" no longer had any value for Tai Chen, that desires were instead an integral part of the "Structural Principle" *(Li)*, which Neo-Confucianism had raised to a level of august purity. This view seemed too bold to the student to be accepted unquestioningly: "Mencius once said," Tai Chen replied,

> that the best way to nourish the mind lay in decreasing desires. He thus spoke only of reducing them because he knew perfectly well that they could not be wholly eradicated. Indeed, there is nothing worse in the life of a man than being unable to realize his desires. To live and to let live is perfectly reconcilable with "humanity." It is only when the realization of one's desires ruthlessly harms the life of others that one has abandoned "humanity." Thus it is unquestionably true that this form of "inhumanity" has its real root in man's desire to live his life to the full. The eradication of that desire would consequently also bring about the eradication of that "inhumanity." But when man has freed himself of all his desires, he will also be utterly indifferent to the misery and the grief of men everywhere (and that is just as bad). To let others live, and not to live oneself, simply violates nature.[132]

"Lack of desire" as the be-all and end-all of wisdom and happiness was ultimately due to the Buddhist influence in Confucianism. But in the balanced attempt to find a middle ground, the argument advanced against it here is Confucian in the best sense of the word. There are probably only a few literary documents where that coldness of the heart which stems directly from the ascetic lack of desire and has surely contributed no less to universal unhappiness than the unchecked, egoistic fulfillment of all desires by men of uninhibited instincts, has been described more precisely, and in fewer words. Elsewhere, Tai Chen did not hesitate to show that his teaching also had political relevance, and frankly criticized the sham morality of government preferred by the rulers of his time:

> In the classic *Book of Rites (Li-chi)* it says: "Men desire food and love." When the sages governed the world, they showed sympathy for the feelings of the people and helped it to realize its desires. In this way, the "methods of governing of the [true] king" evolved. It is generally known that Lao-tzu, Chuang-tzu and the Buddha were unlike the sages, and no one believes what they preached about the lack of desire. But the Sung scholars did believe them and considered

them the equals of the sages. Everyone [of these scholars] felt called upon to demonstrate the opposition between the "principle" and "desires." The result is that rulers nowadays view the old sages' understanding of the feelings of the people and the realization of its desires as frivolous and unspiritual. Nor are they disquieted by their ignorance of the measures the sages took [to realize the people's desires]. When rulers nowadays talk about the "principle," they have no trouble finding cases of unusual probity in the world and to instill feelings of guilt in the people by such examples. The highly placed admonish the simple people by pointing to the "Principle." The old admonish the young by pointing to the "Principle." The nobility admonishes the commoners by pointing to the "Principle." However wrong they may be, it will be felt that they are in the right. Perhaps the simple, the young, the commoners will try to object by also pointing to the "Principle." But however right they may be, it will be felt that they are in the wrong. People of the lower classes therefore will no longer even have the opportunity of presenting their feelings and wishes—although they are the same everywhere—to people of high rank. For the highly placed gag the lower classes with this "Principle" [which allegedly militates against all desires]. In this way, the "sins" of the lowly [necessarily] become infinite. If a man dies through the violence of the law, there will always be people who feel sorry for him. But when he dies from the violence of the "Principle," who will take pity on him?[133]

The bitterness of Tai Chen's words is partly due to a circumstance which had once before, in the case of Teng Mu, precipitated a particularly critical analysis of relationships of domination, and that was the suppression of the empire by foreign conquerors—the Manchus in this instance—who pretended to be more Confucian than Confucius himself in their conduct of the government. To themselves and the Chinese, they attempted to justify their almost three-century long reign (1644–1911) by a kind of transcendent mission which fell to them as they reeducated a morally degenerate people. Of course, the educated Chinese could never brook such an ideology. Yet it is noteworthy that the overwhelming majority of civil servants continued in their posts, which had not been the case under Mongol rule. This suggests that the Manchus' deference to Confucianism, which stood in a certain reciprocal relationship to the subjection of the Chinese under Manchu rule, did not entirely fail of its effect. The dynastic title "Purity" *(Ch'ing)*[134] the Manchus chose clearly betokens that particular form of the Neo-Confucian spirit, full of puritanical rigor and frozen lifelessness, which Tai Chen so passionately branded as truly un-Confucian.

China's desperate position as a national entity may have been a contributing factor in Tai Chen's refusal to restrict himself to pure philosophy (although this is true of most Chinese philosophers). He wanted to see his teachings applied to politics to bring about an improvement, and that could only mean a change. Tai Chen was consequently also the first great propagator of the idea that it was not an abstract world of rigid ideals—as the adherents of the "Principle" in Neo-Confucianism maintained—which had shaped the course of human history, but a push of all being toward improvement, an urge that was discernible in the perpetual transformations of the "Ether." This new belief in historical evolution, which would ultimately always reassert itself and had certainly been axiomatic in the early Confucianism of Mencius and Hsün-tzu, was the only glimmer of hope left to the nationalist intelligentsia. For after it had lost its belief in a fulfillment in the beyond during the Sung, conditions in this world had steadily deteriorated to the point of becoming unbearable. First, the Ming dynasty had instituted a totalitarian regime patterned after the Mongols, and then the Manchu dynasty had added to this system the sting of the alien. The compulsory introduction of the "pigtail"—part of Manchurian nomadic dress and anything but Chinese—was its external symbol.[135] With admirable psychological skill, the Manchu rulers tried to suggest to the Chinese that all this was the "pure" form of an eternal principle. But this was totally unacceptable. Conditions differed too radically from what they had been during the Sung, when the regime had been relatively liberal, and Chinese.

Attempting to find an ideological justification for a hope that was alien to Neo-Confucianism and rested on a spontaneous evolution of human society, various philosophers of the Manchu period moved back in time to the sources of Confucianism, and came upon the religious, strongly future-oriented Confucianism of the Early Han as it had been taught in the tradition centered around the *Kung-yang* school.[136] They were enormously fascinated by the view expressed in various texts of that time that there were qualitatively different historical periods which necessarily alternated and therefore led either to cultural progress or decline. In the course of the eighteenth and nineteenth centuries, an increasing number of scholars came to accept this doctrine which only now really established itself as the "New Text School." What had been a hopelessly clouded sky suddenly seemed to clear over some, if very distant patches; finally, the immobile wheel of history appeared about to turn again. Furthermore, the writings of the "New Text School" also provided the balm for the wounds suffered by nationalist sentiments, for the *Kung-yang* school, especially the scholar Ho Hsiu, had idealized Confucius as a figure whose beneficial teaching would gradually but irresistibly spread over the entire world and thus finally assure China its proper place in its center, since in Confucius it had produced the universal Messiah.

Admittedly, these thoughts only surfaced at a relatively late time when the disintegration of the Neo-Confucian world view could no longer by doubted by anyone. Perhaps it was the scholar Kung Tzu-chen (1792–1841)[137] who first formulated them most clearly and was therefore referred to by some as the "founder" of the "New Text School," although it is actually meaningless to continue speaking of schools in the old Chinese tradition. For what was happening was that individual philosophers merely expressed a widely perceived spirit of the times; they did not have to start an intellectual movement. In those of his writings that have been preserved, Kung Tzu-chen reveals himself as more than a merely theorizing advocate of the view that the form of government must change and improve as the times demand. He also subjected the various institutions governing the Chinese society of his time to forceful, practical criticism. He covered the entire range from the "kowtow" and other anachronistic and partly superstitious elements in court ceremonial to the conduct of state examinations where (and this Kung had experienced personally) it was often helpless examiners that judged the papers by the beauty of the calligraphy alone.[138] He also protested against the barbaric custom of binding women's feet and the altogether inadequate measures to prevent the import of opium. All of these opinions made him one of the forerunners of the "Reform Movement" of the second half of the nineteenth century. That all his protests against the abuses of his time were due to the influence of the *Kung-yang* school manifests itself in those writings where he distinguishes various phases in the development of the relationship between ruler and subjects. For it was only in the "New Text School" that distinctions of this type (which must not be confused with evolutionary theories of cultural history) were first made. In Kung Tzu-chen, the discussion of this development is not restricted to three phases, but considerably more complex:

> Among the men who called the world their own, the greatest were those who made it their task to eliminate all [social] distinctions *(p'ing);* they constituted the "Remote Beginning" *(sui-ch'u).* Those who only wanted to bring peace to the world stood one step lower. A further step down were those who simply wanted to live in peace with the world. [That was] the time of remotest antiquity: the rulers and the people [conducted themselves] like guests at a festive occasion where everyone has donated his share of the wine and may therefore drink his fill. But already during the apogees of the "Three Dynasties" [Hsia, Shang and Chou], it was as if people were sitting around a kettle of soup; the rulers filled a dish as their share, the ministers used a large spoon, the ordinary people a small one. On a still lower step, those with large spoons attacked those with small ones, and vice versa. Down another step, we find the ruler trying to appropriate the entire kettle, and [everyone] among the people wanting it for himself, with the result that it often dried up or toppled over. As long as there was something left in the kettle, the unequal treatment was bad enough, but when its content dried up or it toppled over, it naturally became much worse. So, the person who called the world his own stood up and said: "If I want to restore the condition of the 'Distant Beginning,' I [first] have to take the [entire] content of the kettle and spoon something out [for everyone]. Those who don't have enough will get more." But at that moment, there rose a chorus of voices shouting [for more]. The greater the disproportion between what remained in the kettle and [the demands of] those that believed they did not have enough, the more quickly the government [usually] ended; the smaller it was, the longer it took [for the decline] to set in. For thousands and tens of thousands of years, there has been order and disorder, advance and decline in political life, and they have been governed by precisely this mechanism. The state of mind of individuals is the basis for the mores of the times. But the mores of the times are the basis for the fate of kings. If the individual's state of mind deteriorate, customs

deteriorate, and when that happens, the time has come for the fate of the king to take a turn for the worse. Even if the king does his planning quite egotistically, he must take into account the state of mind of the individual and the customs of the times. But when the wealthy vie with each other in splendor and display while the poor squeeze each other to death; when the poor do not enjoy a moment's rest while the rich are comfortable; when the poor lose more and more while the rich keep piling up treasures; when in some ever more extravagant desires awaken, and in others an ever more burning hatred; when some become more and more arrogant and overbearing in their conduct, and others ever more miserable and pitiful until gradually the most perverse and curious customs arise, bursting forth as though from a hundred springs and impossible to stop, all of this will finally congeal in an ominous vapor which will fill the space between heaven and earth with its darkness. And if this darkness persists for a time, it will necessarily have consequences. Uprisings will erupt, pestilences will spread, the people will no longer have children, no creature will any longer take pleasure in its offspring, man and animal will begin to wail and complain, and the spirits and the gods will decide that a change is due. And all of that will have happened just because in the beginning no one could manage to reconcile the rich and the poor *(pu ch'i).* For if something remains unreconciled on a small scale, it gradually becomes prominent so that something also remains unreconciled on a large scale. But if something remains unreconciled on a large scale, the end of the world is not far off. Alas, if the highly-placed would only properly take hold of the root, and thus shape the future.[139]

The degree to which Kung Tzu-chen made the conceptions of the "New Text School" and their basis in early Han-Confucianism his own can be seen in the last third of the document quoted here. There, the belief in omina[140] which announce the will of Heaven is as pronounced as ever, although it really does not seem to fit in with the thinking of this sober, enlightened spirit. But the curious interrelation of the various branches of Confucianism made it necessary to attempt the conquest of the future by a detour via the earliest past, even if this meant that, at least initially, elements needed to be taken over which appeared still more antiquated than the world view it was necessary to transcend.

3 / *WAITING AND RESIGNATION*

REVOLUTIONARY IMPATIENCE AND THE IMPERTURBABILITY OF THE PHILISTINE

But the rediscovery of the future cannot be wholly equated with the rediscovery of the "New Text School." Long before Kung Tzu-chen, long before even Tai Chen, we can distinguish the first traces of a thought that once again adverted to the virtue of waiting, and thus to the future because it was dissatisfied with the present. In this sense, it may be said to have turned back to Confucianism as well, if to a still earlier form of it. Developing from an opposition which pursued both social and national goals, it had first arisen after the Mongolian conquest of China, and acquired new life during the Manchu dynasty. While the authorities did all in their power to suppress it, its significance was also sometimes overlooked by what were otherwise confirmed Confucians who were not active within it. This is shown by the fact that the political and philosophical writings of Tai Chen, for example, which certainly belong to this hidden tradition, were printed much less frequently and only against the outspoken opposition of a number of scholars, whereas his mathematical and philological writings immediately found a wide public. Nonetheless, this movement survived throughout the Manchu dynasty. Its earliest and most powerful representative during this time was the philosopher Huang Tsung-hsi (1610–1695),[141] (briefly mentioned before in another context), an active "Ming loyalist." More clearly than his contemporary Wang Fu-chih (1619–1692), who has been called the "father of Chinese racism," he saw behind the brutality of an aging system of domination more than the alien grimace of foreign conquerors. He also observed the all-too familiar face of a Confucianism that had degenerated through its connection with Legalism, and was in need of reform. The ingeniously coded title of his principal work, the politico-philosophical *Ming-i tai-fang lu,*[142] usually translated freely as *A Plan for the Prince,* or *Until Dawn,* convincingly demonstrates this. Literally translated, these words mean *Treatise on Waiting for Information Concerning a Route in a Time After the Darkening of the Light.* "Darkening of the Light" *(ming-i)* is also the title of the thirty-sixth hexagram in the *Book of Changes,* which describes a situation where a ruler "of dark nature" governs, so that "the superior man must live with the great mass and veil his light" and "does not eat for three days on his wanderings."[143] The word "light" *(ming)* is also the title of the Ming dynasty ("brilliant," "light"), while the term "darkening" *(i)* has the additional meaning "barbarian." Huang Tsung-hsi's title may therefore also be read: *Treatise on Waiting for Information about a Route During the Time after the Overthrow of the Ming Dynasty by the Barbarians.* The *Ming-i tai-fang lu* makes Huang Tsung-hsi the spiritual successor of Teng Mu. Yet it is not just this wording that is considerably more aggressive, radical and pointed than Teng Mu's equally allusive title, for the content has those same qualities. Of course, in a work written in 1662, when the Manchus had been in the saddle for nearly twenty years, a direct polemic against them was impossible. But in a few sections where the ignominious spread of "laws that are no laws" is discussed, the point of view becomes fairly clear: "From antiquity down to our time, two catastrophes have brought a great change in our civilization. One of them was caused by the Ch'in, the other by the Yüan-Mongol dynasty. After these two catastrophes, nothing is left of the compassionate, amicable and creative forms of government of the early kings."[144]

There can hardly be any doubt that Huang felt a third catastrophe had come when the Manchus assumed power, although he carefully omitted consideration of this question in the important first chapter of his book where he critically examines hereditary monarchy. But when Liang Ch'i-ch'ao published a new edition of the work toward the end of the Manchu dynasty, the restless, youthful intelligentsia that was thirsting for national and political freedom perhaps understood its hidden, two-pronged attack more clearly than could ever have been the case during the author's lifetime. The 250-year old book "burst like a bomb."[145]

> In the beginnings of human life, everyone thought only of himself and only worried about his own advantage. Although there was such a thing as the public benefit *(kung-li),* no one promoted it. And although there was such a thing as public loss *(kung-hai),* no one took measures against it. But then men suddenly appeared who did not just consider profit what benefited their own person, but who attempted to benefit the entire world. And there were people who did not just consider injurious what harmed their own person, but who tried to preserve the whole world from harm. Thus their achievement was a thousand, indeed ten thousand times greater than that of ordinary people. But to work ten or ten thousand times harder without deriving any personal advantage from it is inconsistent with normal human desires. For that reason, there were men in those early times who refused to becomes princes in view of the many difficulties of that position. The hermits Hsü Yu and Wu Kuang are examples. Others took on the task for a time, and then resigned, such as the sage emperors Yao and Shun. . . . The princes of later generations however, were fundamentally different. Since they had the power over benefit and loss, they thought there was nothing wrong in taking all the benefits,

and burdening the people with all the loss. They saw to it that no one any longer dared to think only of himself and his own advantage. Instead, they made their private advantage the common end. At first, they had some qualms, but in time their bad conscience eased. They soon came to consider the world as a huge estate which they had to pass on to their descendants to their perpetual joy and security. Han Kao-tsu, for example, [the founder of the Han dynasty, whom his father had not considered as capable as his older brother Chuang, proudly] asked [him after assuming the government]: "As you look at the land I have acquired, who would you say did better, my brother Chuang or me?" These words reflect the overwhelming selfishness of the princes of later generations. The reason for [this contrast between early and later attitudes] is this: In antiquity, the people were the owner, and the prince the guest. Whatever he achieved during his lifetime was for the sake of his people. But nowadays, the prince is the owner, and the people the guest. Because [of this position] of the prince, the people no longer find peace and quiet anywhere. To attain the goal of the prince, [the creation of a new dynasty,] thousands of lives have to be sacrificed and thousands of families destroyed, so that one man may be happy. But the prince says without a trace of compassion: "I just want to secure these possessions for my descendents." Once he has founded his dynasty, he squeezes the last drop of blood out of the people and uses their sons and daughters for his excesses. He thinks that is perfectly justifiable; in his opinion, it is the profit from his investment. This shows that the greatest evil in the world is princes, and that they are solely responsible for it. If there were no princes, everyone would only think of himself and worry about his own advantage. Is it really possible that rulership was meant to turn out like this? In ancient times, men loved their prince, loved him as their father, and likened him to Heaven, and with rulers such as Yao and Shun, that was no more than right. But today, they hate him like their worst enemy and talk of him as a megalomaniac, and that is also perfectly understandable. Myopic scholars think that the relationship between ruler and subject is inviolable since it has its root in the "Principle." They feel that even [the tyrants] Chieh and Chou should not have been punished [by the founders of the Shang and Chou dynasties, their successors], and thus they invented the story of [the archloyalists, the brothers] Po I and Shu Ch'i,[146] who respected even this tyranny and fled into the wilderness [after the death of the tyrant Chou] in order not to have to live under a new dynasty. These scholars think that the destruction of thousands of human lives is no more serious than the destruction of rats. How can they view the existence of a single ruling family among millions of other families as something so sacred that it alone deserves reverence and preservation? Mencius called [the tyrants] Chieh and Chou megalomaniacs. He was a true sage. But the princes of later generations, having once created the sacred, inviolate institution of the prince, prevented the people from even peeping at them, and considered the text where Mencius critically examines the institution of princes as so embarrassing that they removed the tablet bearing his name from the altar of the sages.[147] Wasn't this done only so that the opinions of myopic scholars might prevail? Well, if it really were the case that the princes of later generations could hand down their [so-called] property in perpetuity, this selfishness would not be so difficult to understand. But once the prince has come to regard the entire world as his personal

> property, why should not everyone else try to take possession of it? Even if he could put this property of his under lock and key, the vigilance of a single person would be no match for the greed of all the rest. It is a fact that the "property" of every single prince will be lost, if not during his own lifetime, then after some generations at the latest, so that his descendents will have to pay for it with their blood. For that reason, there have also been emperors who swore to themselves before their death that they would not be reborn into a family of princes. The [last emperor of the] Ming dynasty, Ch'ung-cheng, said to his sons: "Why were you so unfortunate as to come into this world as members of my family?"[148] How sad, how tragic are these words! If we take a good look at the duties and responsibilities of a [true] king, we will understand why men refused the honor in the days of a Yao and a Shun, and that Hsü Yu or Wu Kuang were no exception, but represented the general view of the people. But if we do not understand his duties and responsibilities every man in the street will [soon] hunger after the position of ruler, and men such as Hsü Yu or Wu Kuang will no longer be found.[149]

The late success of Huang Tsung-hsi's book (which he foresaw, if we can judge by the title) proves how closely the anti-Manchu and the anti-monarchical movements had been linked from the very beginning. Monarchy itself had been discredited because the princes had been foreigners. In complete contrast to Japan, the overthrow of the dynasty therefore left no alternative but the proclamation of the republic. Later, occasional attempts were made to reintroduce the monarchy in one way or another, but even in their externals they had something so anachronistic about them that they aborted.[150] Nor could Confucianism breathe new life into that institution, for although it had undoubtedly always been monarchist, it had become too petrified. The previously mentioned, desperate attempt to recover its living core by stripping it layer by layer, and the ultimate discovery that such a core no longer existed, make this abundantly clear.

The wretched combination of intactness on the surface and an (eventually) unmistakable inner lifelessness in Confucianism was probably the reason that from the Ming on conceptions of the ideal were more and more frequently accompanied by violent criticism of prevailing conditions, a phenomenon that had been much rarer before. The victory of Neo-Confucianism had been accompanied by a constriction of the range of intellectual activity. But this circumstance was now provoking genuine and vigorous opposition, whereas before such opposition had been able to retreat into other dimensions of the spirit. The most impressive examples of this change can be found in the free play of a roaming imagination, which down to T'ang times had been confined and neutralized by the varieties of Taoist and Buddhist religious experience. But when utopian thought among the enlightened scholarly community finally lost its nexus with religious beliefs, it split into two distinct planes, as it were. Interestingly enough, the old motif of the "voyage," which had always been a part of such thinking, was preserved on both of them.

On one of these planes, we have the experience of an ideal state of being in a somewhat abstract form close to *Ch'an* Buddhism: the feeling of happiness arises more from a turning away from the banal commerce among men, than from the striving for a definable goal; more from the awareness of unending change as one aimlessly roams through nature than the attainment of an unchanging ideal condition. A rather impressive testimonial to this attitude is the small Ming period treatise *Ming-liao-tzu (The Travels of Mingliaotzu)* by the scholar T'u Lung (end of the sixteenth century). It was translated by Lin Yü-tang in 1937 in his book *The Importance of Living* and presented as a model of Chinese ways of looking at the world, a "happy, carefree philosophy of living, characterized by love of truth, freedom and vagabondage."[151] The small book describes the travel of a Taoist sage who has become cautious, "a former official," who modestly refers to himself as someone who has not attained the "Way" but merely "loves it, who only asks for rice, not wine," and who visits the "Five Sacred [Confucian] Mountains," but thinks that the voyage to "those regions lying outside the Celestial Empire, like the Himalayas and the Ten Small Islands and Three Big Islands of the China Sea" is impossible, since he is not "provided with a pair of wings." At the end, he contentedly "builds himself a hut in the hills of Szeming and never leaves it again."[152] *The Travels of Mingliaotzu* reads almost like a travesty of the early, stormy journeys to Heaven. A curious weariness has taken hold of the hero, behind his autumnal wisdom lies a desert of indifference and resignation, a sadness that reveals itself only to those who know the fiery élan and the utterly different mood of his models. This kind of utopia is stripped of all revolutionary spirit; except for a stump here or there, its poisonous fangs have been extracted. Its ideals, an amorphous conglomeration of Confucianism, Taoism and Buddhism certainly represented a desirable outlook from the point of view of the government, for it combined the Confucian demand for loyalty with the Taoist love of life and the Buddhist disdain for misery in an admittedly illogical but uncommonly useful blend. The conquest of heaven has been replaced by the pensioner's experience of nature, the man "who builds himself a hut." Curiously enough, it is this astonishingly simple-minded, repugnantly philistine reduction of the kaleidoscopic range of Chinese versions of the ideal life that has become most popular in the West.

On the other plane we find those writings where the imagination, freed from its ties to religion, is anything but submissive, and does not lose itself in the utopian space of a smug self-satisfaction. Instead, it discovers a genuinely new sphere, satire, which is intimately tied to reality, all its apparent irreality notwithstanding. This movement represents the diametric opposite of the trend described above, and found its finest achievement in the novel *Journey to the West (Hsi-yu chi)* by the Ming writer Wu Ch'eng-en (ca. 1506–1582).[153] Probably based in part on non-Chinese motifs from the Mongol period and even earlier, it describes the pilgrimage to India of a group of very different persons. The equable monk Tripitaka, his down-to-earth companion "Pigsy," dedicated to tangible pleasures and solid citizenship, and the restless fighter and rebel, the

Monkey King Sun Wu-k'ung ("Aware-of-Vacuity") play the principal roles. Sun Wu-k'ung, also frequently portrayed on the stage and probably the best loved character in Chinese popular literature,[154] is the hero of the story. He has left a kind of monkey paradise not dissimilar to all other human paradises, because he feels threatened by death and divine omnipotence. His participation in the pilgrimage is a rebellion against the certainty of death, against the hopeless condition of every mortal creature, however happy his life may be. During a journey which takes the company through the most curious countries, it is he who tries to steal the peaches of immortality in heaven. Though bold enough to accept the challenge of the forces of heaven, it is clear that he cannot win the battle, yet he is not wholly vanquished either. His exchanges with his companions (with some exaggeration, Sun Wu-k'ung has been compared with Prometheus, Faust and, perhaps more accurately, with Don Quixote) and his experiences in foreign lands bristle and flash with an irony and a criticism that is directed not only at conditions in his own country, but at Confucian, Taoist and Buddhist world views as well. Of course, these pilgrims are doomed to fail in their search for an ideal country. Gradually, it dawns on them and the reader that heaven cannot even be found in Heaven, a bitter truth which not a few Taoists had already grasped in the fourth century A.D., as we have seen.

THE WONDERLANDS OF LI JU-CHEN

Another fantastic novel, written about 250 years later and even more outspoken in its criticism, takes us not only through the mountains and steppes of the West, but also to the oceans east of China. *Flowers in the Mirror (Ching-hua yüan)* was written by Li Ju-chen (1763–?1830),[155] a scholar with wide interests like many of his contemporaries who yet barely passed the first civil service examination. He sets his story in the reign of the notorious empress Wu of the T'ang dynasty (governed 684–705), who attempted to establish a second Chou dynasty with the help of her clan, but was finally unable to defeat the loyalist forces. The central figure in the book is the scholar T'ang Ao, a man whose career has suffered because of his connection with these forces. He is the father of a girl who has come to earth as the incarnation of the "Fairy of a Hundred Flowers," and whose fate in the spirit realm gives the novel a mythological frame not relevant in our context. Disappointed in the world and hopeful that a prophecy that he would sometime enter the Paradise of the Blessed on P'eng-lai island will be fulfilled, T'ang Ao goes on a long voyage with his brother-in-law, the merchant Lin Chih-yang. On a junk, they visit more than thirty islands and countries. Lin Chih-yang's helmsman, the old To Chiu-kung ("Number Nine"), ironically called "Know-nothing" (Pu-shih) by the sailors because his knowledge is encyclopedic, provides detailed information about them. On a voyage which has certain similarities with *Gulliver's Travels,* many of the countries seen owe their existence to old mythologies or the narrator's delight in spinning tales. But others, such as the "Country of Women" *(Nü-erh kuo),*[156] for example, where women are in charge of the government and keep men in harems, are clearly intended as a bitter criticism of the author's own society. Through the satirical device of making the familiar appear strange, the attack becomes a brilliant success. By mistake, T'ang Ao falls into the hands of these women. To his horror, he has to suffer all the humiliations and pain normally reserved for women, particularly the very realistically described binding of the feet. In certain other countries, T'ang becomes familiar with institutions which represent the total reversal of conditions in his own. Some have a paradisiacal quality to underline how unlike paradise the world really is. Thus we read about the "Land of Sexless People" *(Wu-chi kuo):*

T'ang Ao said, "I have heard that the people of this country do not give birth to children. Can that be true?"

"I have heard that it is so," said old To, "because there is no distinction between men and women among them. I have been here before, and, indeed, the people look like neither men nor women."

"But if they don't give birth to children, shouldn't they have all died out long ago?" asked T'ang Ao.

"No, because their bodies do not corrupt after death, but they come back to life again after a hundred and twenty years. Thus, their numbers neither increase nor decrease. They think of death as sleep and life as a dream, for well they know that all mortal strife ends in a long sleep. Therefore, they don't crave fame and power and personal gain. They know that these things don't last, and that if they succeed in winning them in one life, they will only wake up a hundred and twenty years later to find that they have to struggle for them anew. Needless to say, these people also eschew violence."

"How foolish we must seem to them then," said merchant Lin, "when we don't even come back to life again, and yet struggle so hard for wealth and fame!"

"If you can look at things that way," said T'ang Ao, "all you need do is to place a different value on these very things."

"That's easy to say, and, theoretically, I can see that wealth and fame are of dubious value when we think that life is like a fleeting dream. Yet, when I find myself embroiled in a real situation, it is as though I were crazed, and I cannot help becoming excited and engaging in the struggle and the strife. However, in the future, when I find myself in that state, I should be happy if someone pinched me. Then I would wake up at once and see the futility of it all."

"Ah, but when you are in that state, I am afraid that you would not listen if I tried to remind you of the futility of it all, but on the other hand, would turn around and blame me for interfering!" said old To.

"That's true," said T'ang Ao. "Lust for fame and fortune are like an intoxication. While a man is intoxicated he doesn't realize it. It's only after it is all over that he realizes that everything is like an illusion. If men could realize this all the time, there would be much less trouble on earth, and there would be much happier people too."[157]

Like the Taoists of earlier times, though in a different form, the author attempts here to unmask the senselessness of the pursuit of profit in a fairy tale-like allegory. In the much longer account of the visit to the "Country of Giants" *(Ta-jen kuo),*[158] he seeks to show the dishonesty of Chinese society during his lifetime. Having landed on the coast of this country, T'ang Ao, the merchant Lin and the old To walk up to a hut to inquire about local conditions:

> They were knocking on the door when they saw an old man carrying a jug of wine in one hand, and a pig's head in the other. He walked toward the hut, opened the door and was about to enter. Putting his hands together in greeting, T'ang Ao said: "May I inquire from you, old man, how this hut is called and if there is perhaps a monk here?" "Oh, I beg your pardon," the old man answered, quickly entered the hut to put the wine and the pig's head down, and then came hurrying back out to answer the polite greeting. "Avalokitésvara is worshipped here, and your humble servant is the monk." The merchant Lin could not conceal his surprise. "If you are the monk," he exclaimed, "why is your head not shaved. And since you have obviously brought wine and meat, are there perhaps also nuns who take care of you?" "A nun does live here," the monk answered [calmly], "my wife. There is no one else. My wife and I have been living here since we were young, we keep the candles and incense burning. Originally, we did not know the term 'monk' at all in this country. But after we heard that from Han times on all people in China living in temples and willing to have their head shaved have been called 'monks,' if they were men, and 'nuns' if they were women, we began using the same expressions. . . ." During the conversation that followed, T'ang Ao continued: "I hear that in your country everyone walks on a cloud. Is this cloud born with a person?" "These clouds are born with us," said the old man. "They are not manmade. It is best if one has a rainbow-colored cloud. Yellow is second, and black is the worst." "We have far to travel before returning to our ship," said old To. "If you would be so kind as to point the way, we should be going along." . . . When they found the city, they saw that everything looked much the same as in the Country of Superior Men, except that everyone was walking on clouds of different colors. A beggar went past walking on a rainbow colored cloud. "Isn't that odd," said T'ang Ao, "since the rainbow-colored cloud is supposed to be best, and the black cloud the worst." "And that old fellow at the hut was obviously a monk who had not kept his vows," said Lin. "Yet he, too, had a rainbow-colored cloud." "When I came here before, I was told that the color of one's cloud depends not on whether he is rich or poor, but on the way he conducts himself," said old To. "If a man is open with people, straightforward and honest, he has a rainbow cloud, but if he is secretive and conniving, he walks on a black cloud. The color of one's cloud changes with his temper, and so you may find a rich man walking on a black cloud, and a poor man on a rainbow cloud. However, look! Hardly a soul is walking on a black cloud! The people of this country must all be kind-hearted and good-natured—doubtless, because they would be ashamed to be seen with a black cloud under their feet, and are proud when they can show off a good-colored cloud. This country is called the Country of Giants. People who don't know think that the people are really giants. Actually, it refers to the largeness of their hearts." . . . Suddenly, the pedestrians

> shied to either side of the street, and someone who was obviously an important official swaggered past, wearing a black turban and an elaborate costume. He carried a red umbrella, and had a retinue of subordinates behind and in front of him, who shouted to the people to make way. But the official's cloud was surrounded by a red curtain, so that no one could see it. "I suppose this official doesn't need a carriage to ride in, since he is already walking on a cloud," said T'ang Ao. "But I wonder why he has hidden his cloud behind a curtain?" "Sometimes a man will get an attack of stormy grey cloud," said old To, "because he has done something which conscience tells him is wrong. This man has hidden his grey cloud behind a curtain because he doesn't want people to see it, but of course by hiding it behind a curtain he is only calling attention to it. Luckily, a cloud changes color when a man changes heart, and a man who persistently walks over a dark cloud is ostracized by everyone in this country, and even punished." "Oh, how unfair!" said Lin. "How unfair?" asked T'ang Ao. "How unfair that it is only the people of this country that have clouds under their feet! If everyone in the world had to carry a self-advertisement like this, how wonderful people would be!"[159]

The idea of revealing the innermost feelings of every single person in order to raise the moral level of society in its totality is explicitly formulated here by Li Ju-chen for the first time, although it is done in jest, in keeping with the satiric spirit of the novel. But of all the countries and islands T'ang visits, and all the people he encounters—and this includes the "loyalists" of the endangered T'ang dynasty who had fled for safety from the empress Wu—an episode that recalls what were once the "loyalist Islands" of the Sung—it is not the "Land of Giants" but the "Land of Superior Men" *(Chün-tzu kuo)* which most nearly approaches a genuine paradise, and this not without reason. For it is not the "Giants"—a concept with a slightly Taoist coloration—but the "superior person" that is the opposite of the "small men" from whom T'ang Ao and his companions seek to escape on their voyage:

> The streets appeared to T'ang Ao and old To to be much like those in the Kingdom on Earth, and were full of people buying and selling. Going up to an old man, T'ang Ao inquired whether it was true that to the people of this country, other people's desires always mattered more than one's own. But the old man could not understand what he was talking about. T'ang Ao asked him what was the meaning of "superior men" and again, the old man could not reply. Finally, old To said, "You are asking him to judge his people by the standards of other countries, and therefore asking him questions he cannot answer. He does not know what being a superior person means, because he does not know what it is to be anything else."
>
> When they came to the market, they overheard a soldier talking to a shopkeeper. He was holding something in his hand and saying, "What a lovely thing this is! But you are charging too little for it! How could I deprive you of it? Please do me the favor of making it more costly, so that I may buy it with an easy conscience. If you refuse, it will only mean that you do not consider me your friend."
>
> "I suppose this is an example of what is meant by other people's interest mattering more than one's own," whispered T'ang Ao to old To.

The shopkeeper replied, "You know that we are not allowed to haggle here. All prices are one! I am afraid I shall have to ask you to shop elsewhere if you insist on paying more than the fixed price, for I cannot oblige."

"You are putting me in an extremely difficult position by refusing to charge more," said the soldier. "I should not be kind if I agreed. How dare I take advantage of you?" The shopkeeper still would not give in, so that soldier had no choice but to pay him what was asked, but took only half of what he had paid for, and started to go. But the merchant pressed the rest of the goods on him, and would not let him go until he had taken more than his money's worth. The dispute was finally settled by two passersby, a pair of old men, who said that the soldier should take not less than eighty percent of what he paid for. . . .

After a few steps, they saw another soldier who was trying to buy something. He was telling the merchant, "I asked you the price of this, and you would not tell me, but kept asking me to name my own price. Now I have done so, you tell me it is much too much, so I have lowered it and still you say the price is too high. What shall I do?"

"Truly, I dare not charge too much for my articles, which are inferior in quality to what they sell in other shops and none too fresh, either. How can I think of charging even half of what you want to pay?"

"Really," thought T'ang Ao, "customer and shopkeeper have changed places. Each is saying what the other would say in other countries."

"What are you talking about?' said the soldier. "I recognize the quality of your goods, and they are not inferior at all. How could you think of charging me only half price?"

"I can only charge you half price," replied the merchant, "if you insist on paying more, I am afraid you will have to take your custom elsewhere, for I honestly cannot let you pay so much and feel easy about it." When the soldier saw that this was the highest price the merchant was willing to charge, he paid it, took only a few items of inferior quality, and started to walk away. The merchant hurried after him, saying, "Why are you such a difficult customer? Why do you take so little, do you want me to make a profit from it? I didn't think that you would be so hard to please!"

The soldier said frantically, "I didn't want to take the best quality. I only took the worst, because I would not feel right about it otherwise, since I had paid so little." "But if you only wanted the inferior quality, you should have given me even less money. How can you pay me so much and take so little?"

The soldier did not heed him, and went away. The people on the street thought that he had not given the merchant a fair deal, so he had no course but to come back, and exchange half of what he had taken for goods of the best quality.[160]

In their walk through the capital, T'ang Ao and his friend witness more such conversations which make them think that they have strayed into a world turned upside down. A passionate altruism informs all of human life, and not infrequently occasions the kinds of dispute and even quarrel selfishness engenders in the real world. But the nature of the "Land of Superior Men" only truly reveals itself when they chance upon two scholars who invite them to their house for a talk. Their curiosity about what seem to them absurd conditions in the Middle Kingdom serves to show the visitors by indirection what values are taken for granted in this ideal land, while conversely all Chinese ritual practices, particularly animal sacrifice and mantics, the trial system and the enslavement of women become the target of a withering criticism, for they strike the foreign scholars as barbaric and exotic. Luxury is also questioned as it becomes increasingly evident that the important contrasts between the two countries result from a different evaluation of the achievements of material culture, including the economic system. A preference for swallows' nests, a Chinese delicacy like oysters in the West, is used as the example that most tellingly shows how questionable many Chinese values really are. Shaking their heads in amazement, the foreign scholars observe that in their country only the poorest of the poor put up with this dish since it tastes like wax and only becomes halfway edible when all sort of condiments are added, and that it would seem therefore that the furore about them is nothing but the snobbishness and arrogance of so-called exclusive circles. The conceptual core of all the beliefs found in the "Land of Superior Men" is the ideal of "modesty." Its much broader Chinese equivalent *(jang)* includes all those qualities we refer to as "simplicity," "reserve," "thrift," "altruism," and is developed in a speech of one of the scholars conversing with T'ang Ao and To Chiu-kung:

> I have heard that the common people in your honorable country love luxury and display above all else. They are said to be excessive in everything, be it weddings and burials, food, drink and clothing, or the amounts spent for housing. This means that the rich and highly placed families do not husband their fortune, but deliberately waste money and therefore invite retribution. And isn't this way of doing things much more harmful to the poor, ordinary people if all they do is try to satisfy their momentary desires and thus lose sight of the hunger and cold that may plague them tomorrow? But if a "superior man" who manages his fortune carefully were to take over the leadership of the village party *(hsiang-tang)* and prohibited luxury but took care that every citizen put aside the surplus yield, he would act in consonance with the saying: "Always think of the days of scarcity during the days of abundance, so that you will not long for the days of abundance during times of scarcity." If this could be clearly expressed in proclamations to the people, extravagance might gradually disappear, and everyone return to simplicity and plainness. If that were to happen, one would no longer have to worry whether the people had saved enough. Even an occasional year of famine need not be alarming. If manners are simple and plain, ordinary people can always find a modest sustenance; they will not become vagabonds or take to cheating others. If only few cheat, the desire to rebel will likewise disappear, and measures against it will not be required. And once the urge to rebel is gone, the Highest Peace *(t'ai-p'ing)* will come to the entire realm *(t'ien-hsia)*. This makes it clear that there is a connection between simplicity and plainness, and other things of no small consequence.[161]

The last sentences of this speech are both climax and end of the conversation between T'ang Ao, To Chiu-kung, and the two scholars from the "Land of Superior Men." They are suggestive because the speaker is not merely interested in conditions in the Middle Kingdom, but voices a political opinion of his own. Beyond that, he develops ideas how the "Highest Peace" might be attained throughout the empire, which is really out of context here. But it is precisely where the fictitious citizen of a fictitious country acts out of character that the author's point of view reveals itself. His barely concealed criticism of a China that has lapsed into a merely formal Confucianism shows that the ideal Confucian state portrayed in the "Land of Superior Men" in an occasionally witty and exaggerated form is not that "State of Ritual and Music" the hero at first naively expected, but rather almost the opposite, i.e. a state with a touch of almost puritanical rigor where the insistence that the concerns of others take precedence over one's own wishes verges on fanaticism. This mixture of altruism, thrift and antipathy to ritual permits us to recognize in Li Ju-chen a successor to the persistent if hardly spectacular "socialist" tradition in China which began with Mo Ti and was carried on in the *Ta-t'ung* chapter of the *Li-chi,* the *Lü-shih ch'un-ch'iu,* and the writings of Teng Mu and Huang Tsung-hsi. But what distinguishes him from all these precursors is that touch of resignation which also characterizes the Taoist *Ming-liao-tzu,* when one compares it to earlier Taoist writings. Two hundred years later, this dreamlike weariness thus also settled on a movement which had been among the most active and occasionally even revolutionary during the course of its history. As the title of the book indicates, Huang Tsung-hsi had written his critique of the present with the hope for a better future. That Li Ju-chen set his "Land of Superior Men" in an imaginary realm suggests how remote the hope for the realization of a state patterned after this model had become in the meantime.

Of course, during the two hundred years that separate these two authors, a development had begun which seemed of secondary importance at first, but gradually and increasingly came to dominate all political and intellectual life, and that was the eruption into Asia of the West. When Portugese merchants had first opened up direct maritime traffic with China toward the end of the fifteenth century, and a number of missionaries soon followed them, it may have seemed that this contact would be no more consequential than that established by the overland traffic during the pax Mongolica in the thirteenth and fourteenth centuries. For during that earlier time, western merchants (Marco Polo, 1254–1324) and missionaries (Plano Carpini, Wilhelm von Rubruck) had also traveled in China, correspondence had gone back and forth between the two hemispheres, and yet nothing of consequence for either side had developed. Even about a hundred years later, when Huang Tsung-hsi was born in 1610 (the year the greatest missionary to China, Matteo Ricci, died),[162] it had been impossible to foresee the extent of Europe's future influence on China. The external threat at that time was quite different. Not the Europeans but the Manchus were standing on the borders of the empire, and it was against these foreigners from the Northeast that scholars such as Huang turned the resentment of their wounded national pride when they ascended the dragon throne in 1644. By comparison, the foreigners from the West were a negligible matter. At least initially, the persecutions of Christians which sporadically disquieted the missions were not primarily xenophobic, but tended toward the preservation of internal order. Besides, both indigenous religions such as Taoism and foreign ones which had been spreading in China for hundreds of years, had been equally subject to such persecutions,[163] and therefore only been able to survive in "secret societies."

But around the turn of the eighteenth century, conditions took a fundamentally different course. While the enormously expanded and still increasing strength of the West was not yet directly perceived, the growing political and spiritual weakness of the Manchu regime and of a Confucianism unhappily linked to it was all the more evident. There was not only the humiliating consciousness of being enslaved by a foreign nation and an ideology it had perverted to further its own ends. Many intellectuals, perhaps often without complete awareness, were even more disturbed by the recognition that these two tyrannical enemies were not even particularly vigorous but themselves in a state of internal decay. Contrary to one's expectations, however, this insight did not lead to the obvious conclusion that it would therefore be all the easier to rid oneself of them, but induced instead a widespread apathy which was accepted as fated by both rulers and ruled, and even tended to weave a philosophy out of all of this. Only a few towering intellects, some of whom we have already become acquainted with (Kung Tzu-chen, for example), could free themselves from this curious spell. For too long a time, since the beginning of the Manchu dynasty, or even since the Sung, Confucianism in its various forms had been used as a kind of tranquillizer for both the ordinary people and the intelligentsia. Or perhaps it would be better to say that it had been so misused. When Napoleon made his famous pronouncement about China as a sleeping giant which it would be better not to awaken, he had grasped the spiritual condition of the Middle Kingdom much more clearly than he himself may have suspected. This sleep was not a natural one, however, but a state of anesthesia from which there would be a traumatic awakening.

V

IN THE TWILIGHT
(since ca. 1800)

1 / SLEEP AND THE MESSAGE OF THE HEAVENLY FATHER

ARTIFICIAL PARADISES

In spite of many initiatives, such as the introduction of certain early forms of industry and capitalism, which have only been discovered recently and greedily mined by scholars, the frequently mentioned "torpor" and the concomitant backwardness that immobilized China during the last eight centuries are a phenomenon that cannot be argued away. Interestingly enough, it was not the clinging to unrealistic conceptions but, on the contrary, an almost excessively enlightened and therefore somehow foreshortened sense of reality that had produced that condition. It was precisely during a time of intense religious life, the T'ang, when the most wondrous ideas and fantastic ideals proliferated in almost vertiginous abundance that China was preeminent among civilizations and sought to establish close contacts with all the metropolises on earth. Perhaps it has never been closer to the pulse of history than at that time. But the victory of an enlightened Confucianism during the Sung changed all that. The rejection of the miraculous of faraway regions, distant eons, or even religions, also necessarily truncated all possibilities of intellectual development. The temporal component, simply ignored by the Neo-Confucianism of a Chu Hsi, can only be shut out for a time, after which a disregard of the utopian invites revenge. The gap between an old reality made into dogma and a new reality that first emerges as a shadowy presence from the utopian realm to then become increasingly palpable widens more and more, until finally the threateningly new must be kept at bay if a catastrophic rupture is to be prevented. But such efforts can only bring a short reprieve. Confucianism had maneuvered itself into this position from the Sung on. Realistic though it seemed, it was really fleeing from reality. And while it could banish that reality for a time from its sphere of influence which at first still coincided with the civilized world *(t'ien-hsia),* it was unable to prevent the new with its many utopian lineaments from gathering force beyond its periphery. Exerting an ever-increasing pressure on this closed system, the outside world finally burst in upon it. The violent "opening up" of China by the West during the nineteenth century—a fate that also overtook other East Asian countries which had fallen victim to the same Confucian spell, such as Japan and Korea—was undoubtedly of a repellent brutality and nothing to be proud of. But it came with a certain natural necessity. In this sense, the East was indirectly no less responsible than the West.

Of course, those aspects of western thought Chinese Confucians first became familiar with were hardly of a nature to arouse such fears. The kind of Christianity the intelligent Jesuit missionaries presented as the world view of the West was prudently limited to the most essential ethical elements, and could not fail to impress them as no less enlightened, realistic and rooted in the past than Confucianism itself.[1] This impression was confirmed by the missionaries' intense interest in the natural sciences. Besides, the Chinese response to Christianity as a religion was extremely muted, especially when one compares it to the fervor and enthusiasm with which Buddhism had once been received, and certainly did not disquiet orthodox Confucians. Only a very few, if any, were aware of the explosive force which inhered in the concept of a millennium, common to Christianity and almost all other western systems of thought. Still less could they recognize the curious changes which—while not imaginable apart from Christianity—had yet led away from it, changes which had been under way in European thought since the fifteenth century, and been responsible for both the more flexible form of missionary activity undertaken by the Jesuits, and their much admired knowledge of astronomy, physics, chemistry and geography. In 1607, for example, Li Chih-tsao (died in 1630),[2] a Chinese convert, could quite sincerely present the missionaries as especially devoted followers of Confucius in his introduction to a treatise on Christianity, written by Matteo Ricci. He overlooked not only the complexity of Christianity, but of Confucianism as well. But when after the "Rites Controversy," which turned on the question whether the ancestor cult was to be considered "idol worship," the Dominicans prevailed over the Jesuits around the middle of the eighteenth century, and a more puristic form of the Catholic dogma was put forward, this merely meant that Christianity slipped into the category of popular religions despised as superstition by the intelligentsia, and was immediately blocked by appropriate measures.[3] After this (probably unavoidable) false start, it was difficult to see how a renewal of China under Christian aegis might occur at a later time, a possibility that many in the West still sincerely hoped for in our century.

However effortlessly Confucianism could thus resist Christianity as an alien religion in the eighteenth century, it found it difficult to permanently fill the void created in its own teaching by the elimination of religious components and the displacement of Taoism and Buddhism into a kind of underground. The frustration some intellectuals must have felt as they viewed what had in a sense become a more barren world that was permanently immobilized in a fusion of the present and the past, and had the added disadvantage of not even being secure, but surprisingly appeared to become ever more boring and brittle, could not be overcome so simply. A second, much less deliberate attack by the West, which started before Kung Tzu-chen inspired new hope for a better world by the revival of the religiously tinctured "New Text School," could therefore not be so easily countered. For it was directed at this void, yet differed from Christianity in having no direct connection with any religion since against such intrusions Confucianism had been able to mobilize the resilient defensive mechanisms acquired in its successful struggle against Buddhism. Besides, this attack came from an entirely different direction and was carried by utterly different adversaries who were probably not even aware of the reasons for their success. This time, it was not the missionaries but the merchants who were the enemy. What is referred to here is the enormous import of opium which was organized in India and increased by leaps and bounds during the first half of the nineteenth century in spite of incessant imperial bans (which initially also included tobacco). Particularly in the southern coastal provinces, large numbers became addicts, while the continuing illegal export of silver brought China to the verge of financial ruin. Everything suggests that opium was unknown in China prior to the T'ang, and only used for medicinal purposes thereafter.[4] In 1729, when it was banned for the first time, it had trickled into the country in what were still relatively modest amounts. Two hundred cases weighing 120 English pounds each were registered at that time. But by 1793, import had increased to four thousand cases and by 1834 and during the following years, it amounted to no less than thirty thousand cases annually, i.e. approximately 3.6 million pounds, and this is probably a conservative estimate.[5]

This thralldom of an entire people to the sinister euphoria of drug-induced reveries was probably an event of hitherto unknown scope. However deliberately engineered it may have been by outside forces, it must be viewed from the perspective of China's spiritual condition at the time. For it is a disquieting problem how such large numbers of people could have become addicts within such a very short time, all the laws against the drug notwithstanding. The fact that simultaneously and under the influence of romanticism and its enthusiasm for everything dreamlike, opium also cast its spell over large segments of the European intelligentsia (Coleridge and De Quincey would be examples),[6] does not constitute a sufficient explanation. It would seem that the majority of opium smokers looked to the hallucinations of intoxication as a compensation, a substitute for the flights of the imagination to paradise, experiences which had been denied them after a sober Confucianism had triumphed over Taoism, and especially Buddhism. For that reason, it was not only intellectuals that fell victim to the magic of opium. The frustration gradually induced by the monopoly of Confucianism was also apparent among the lower strata, which had been allowed a certain measure of religion ("Popular Taoism" and "Popular Buddhism") in carefully calculated doses. And even if this deprivation was not consciously experienced, the hope of escape into an accessible utopian space may well have been the reason they turned to drugs.

For the outsider, it is very difficult to obtain an insight into these "artificial paradises" which suddenly opened up in China, for the experience of euphoria which apparently occurs especially during the initial phases of the use of opium cannot easily be reduced to a common denominator. The extensive literature on this topic, from the romantically tinctured reports in the style of De Quincey *(Confessions of an English Opium Eater)* down to the detailed documents written by careful scientists and physicians is not without its internal contradictions. This is so primarily because it is difficult to distinguish between the symptoms that occur when the organism is adequately supplied with opium, and those accompanying withdrawal (or a less than adequate supply). Modern research has nonetheless discovered certain constants in the euphoria of addicts. They show a surprising similarity with Buddhist and also some Taoist experiences of happiness. This is all the more remarkable because the test subjects were not members of any Asian civilization. Were it not for the fact that there are no objective bases for such an assertion, one would almost be inclined to turn things around and view the accounts of detached bliss in Buddhist and Taoist literature as at least partially induced by drugs. A fairly recent study on the common experiences of opium smokers during the initial phase states the following:

> Cares, doubts, fears, tedium and inhibitions sink away and are replaced by a serene self-assurance. . . . The person is now in a state of listless complacent tranquillity. Nothing worries him, nothing moves him; he is at peace with his fellow men because he does not care about them; their sorrows do not move him, their injuries and slights of which he was so conscious now rebound harmlessly off his invulnerable self-esteem. . . . A French addict told his doctor that . . . he felt as though he were plunged in a bath of tepid milk, or in cotton-wool. . . . Addicts even likened their feelings . . . to flying or floating, to an "exquisite don't-care attitude," a Buddha-like calm, an admission to paradise.[7]

The three principal motives underlying the interest in and habituation to opium cited in this book fit in very well with the Chinese mentality as we encountered it in the religious sphere. They are 1) a restless curiosity about, and delight in, the curious; 2) the longing for peace; and 3) "that element in personality which delights in secret rites and hidden fellowships."[8] It is consequently not simply a persistent historical reminiscence when the word "opium" immediately evokes "China." Still less is it pure chance that in our time a revived interest in Buddhist mysticism (Zen, *Ch'an*) so frequently goes hand in hand with a tendency toward the use of drugs.[9] After a sober spirit of the times had closed the route via the spirit, the large-scale attempt to reach paradise by way of the body was in fact first undertaken in China.

But in addition to the similar experiences of happiness found in the descriptions of opium smokers and some East Asian mystics, there is a further parallel which lies on a wholly different plane but is no less significant, and that is the shift in the perception of time. The encounter with the transcendent, the glance into paradise is, as we have seen,[10] frequently connected with a disintegration of time, and this is as true in China as in many other civilizations. But in contrast to space, time is normally a dimension of human experience that cannot be conquered. Time either stood still or began to rush, and a "thousand years became as a day." The opium smoker has very similar experiences. Initially, it is an ecstatic trance, later painful suffering. The classical account of both states can be found in De Quincey:

> Some of these rambles led me to great distances; for an opium-eater is too happy to observe the motion of time. . . . O just, subtle and all-conquering opium! that, to the hearts of rich and poor alike, for the wounds that will never heal, and for the pangs of grief that "tempt the spirit to rebel," bringest an assuaging balm;—eloquent opium! that with thy potent rhetoric stealest away the purposes of wrath, pleadest effectually for relenting pity, and through one night's heavenly sleep callest back to the guilty man visions of his infancy, and hands washed pure from blood. . . .[11]

> The sense of space, and in the end the sense of time, were both powerfully affected. . . . Space swelled. . . . This disturbed me very much less than the vast expansion of time. Sometimes I seemed to have lived for seventy or a hundred years in one night; nay, sometimes had feelings representative of a duration far beyond the limits of human experience.[12]

It was precisely a disrupted relationship to time which especially afflicted China in the nineteenth century, although for a nation this experience was of course qualitatively quite different and cannot be directly compared to the romantically heightened perceptions of an individual. Yet it may not be going too far to at least take note of certain analogies between the experiences of this famous "opium eater" who despaired in the stifling atmosphere of a time that was enveloping him and seemed to have come to a stop, and those of China which had also slipped into a tormenting state of dead time due to the constant identification of present and future with the past, which at first still seemed to promise paradise. Indeed, this analogy was drawn unhesitatingly by modern Chinese writers. The most famous Chinese author of modern times, Lu Hsün (1881–1936), for example, referred to his own study of ancient literature ironically as "my particular way of smoking opium."

A final phenomenon that seems to have been typical not only of the opium smoker but also of China as it vegetated in the nineteenth century is the feeling of exclusion and the connected messianic conviction of the transparency of the innermost causes of the universe, even if time and again there is no sufficient strength to put this seemingly inexhaustible knowledge to practical use:

> The addict . . . often feels no strong affections even for his own family and friends . . . he is as much cut off from them as though he came from another planet. He feels that he is an outcast, a pariah, and he cherishes his solitude and isolation . . . But behind this dark facade which shuts him in from the world, he may be

> cogitating huge plans. Though humanity treats him as an outcast, he feels that he is omnipotent and holds the secrets of the universe; he alone is percipient, sensitive, wise, superior to dull conventional minds. He has penetrated the hidden analogies and associations behind all the phenomenal world, and in his mind he builds vast metaphysical constructions, which will astonish and delight mankind when they are revealed, and plans great empires of power and achievements. . . . The gigantic scaffolding of his projects . . . is (to him) a heaven-aspiring temple with foundations of adamant.[13]

As we shall see, it was precisely in the period of its greatest weakness and isolation, i.e. toward the end of the nineteenth and the beginning of the twentieth centuries, that China actually produced the most fantastic utopian plans not only for the salvation of the empire, but even of the entire world. And a certain, almost arrogant belief that it had the "real," the "more spiritual" culture and wisdom in spite of all the political and intellectual humiliations it suffered luxuriated at that time. Simultaneously, however, the tormenting question concerning the relationship between "knowledge" and "action" was constantly being agitated; how the true "essence" *(t'i)* of human culture which it was believed had been grasped in China, and only in China, could be made to triumph over the clearly differing "application" *(yung)* which the West had so obviously mastered through its technical skill.[14] But the longer the philosophical debate about this question continued, the more the gap between thought and action seemed to widen, as is true of the opium addict caught up in his hallucinations. It became a yawning abyss, and even the most courageous thinkers finally despaired. Thus it was not only the Opium War of 1839 (or, more accurately, the opium wars, which did not really have the form of a single, major conflict but rather a series of disputes which lasted until 1860),[15] which forced China into a long sleep tormented by confused dreams, but rather once again the ineluctable consequence of century-old decisions. In the nineteenth century, however, the West completely missed the unique opportunity of extending a helping hand in the solution of these difficulties. Instead, it profited from a crisis situation. Indeed, it probably never saw that such an opportunity existed. When it was gradually taken during the 1920s, it was by the Communist powers. Their help, though not wholly unselfish either, was extended readily.[16] But what intervention there was occurred under wholly changed presuppositions, and probably much too late. The distrust of all western approaches including the Russian could no longer be overcome and continues even today to make relationships with China disquietingly vulnerable.

HUNG HSIU-CH'ÜAN AND CHRISTIANITY

That the relationship between China and the West was muddled from the moment it began to take on somewhat firmer contours and to become effective not just among the thin stratum of scholars and officials but among the people, is most clearly shown by the Taiping rebellion, which dragged on for a full fifteen years (1850–1864). Not only for this reason, but also because of the numbers involved (and killed: almost twenty million, twice as many as in the First World War), this uprising must be considered one of the greatest in history.[17] No less a figure than Marx recognized clearly and as early as 1853 that this movement was indirectly connected with the curiously morbid, unreal climate that had come to the country together with opium. This was at a time when the Taipings had won their first major successes and thus come into the purview of the West. In an editorial written for the *New York Daily Tribune* (6–14–1853), he wrote as follows: "Just as the Emperor [according to traditional Chinese conceptions] was wont to be considered the father of all China, so his officers were looked upon as sustaining the paternal relation to their respective districts. But this patriarchal authority, the only moral link embracing the vast machinery of the State, has gradually [in the last half century] been corroded by the corruption of those officers, who have made great gains by conniving at opium smuggling. This has occurred principally in the same Southern provinces where the [Taiping] rebellion commenced. It is almost needless to observe that, in the same measure in which opium has obtained the sovereignty over the Chinese, the Emperor and his staff of pedantic mandarins have become dispossessed of their own sovereignty. It would seem as though history had first to make this whole people drunk before it could rouse them out of their hereditary stupidity."[18]

Admittedly, the Taipings owed their ideology neither to opium nor to Christianity alone. The designation they chose for themselves had a long history and derived from the era of "Highest Peace" *(t'ai-p'ing)* proclaimed by them. It shows that they continued that political and religious tradition that had run through Chinese history along hidden channels particularly since the Sung and had absorbed all those intellectual currents that could not make their peace with orthodox Confucian teaching. Its first cells therefore actually had the character of "secret societies" as they had appeared before and were to emerge subsequently on countless occasions with a Buddhist or Taoist coloration. But precisely because their teaching was not based on these old religions but overtly on Christianity, a connection was established between East and West that was the first to find acceptance among large masses of the people.

Of course, the Taipings, who considered themselves Christians of indigenous, Chinese stock, preached anything but pure Christianity. Yet the amalgamation of Christian and Chinese religiosity could hardly have looked any different short of unconditional subjection (which is unhappily what many missionaries had in mind when they thought of "conversion"). Initially, the Taipings were enthusiastically hailed in the West, but soon came to be considered devilish, murderous incendiaries. Their understanding of Christianity was certainly neither more nor less adequate than that of the much-praised Confucian participants in the dialogue with the Jesuits in the seventeenth century, who occasionally converted to Christianity, except that the Taipings' encounter with it occurred on an entirely different plane. It was not that of an enlightened, detached and unfortunately largely estheticizing and uncommitted humanism, but much more genuinely religious and centered around the unshakable faith that God's kingdom could be realized on earth. This belief was certainly more naive in many respects, particularly where it was heavily laden with accretions of superstition. But at the same time, it was much more gripping, particularly in the social sphere. Precisely because the Taipings thought they had discovered what may be called the Archimedian point outside of the world, they were much more strongly resolved to move it. It was this uncompromising application of Christian teachings to society—so characteristically Chinese in its orientation toward action in the real world—and a blind fanaticism which admittedly frequently degenerated and became outrageous, that shocked many originally sympathetic Chinese no less than it did Europeans. The Taipings thus suffered the fate of those who believe they are taking a middle course between two irreconcilably opposed systems: they became the enemies of both. Being Christian and nationalist, i.e. anti-Manchu, they were finally crushed by an alliance of western and Chinese troops. Much that was to have become governmental program thus turned into a Utopia, not because it had initially consisted of nothing but utopian elements but because there was no time to implement it. In certain respects, the Taiping ideals are still alive today. This is all the more surprising when one considers the simple conditions that gave rise to them.

In 1836, a 23-year-old student, Hung Hsiu-ch'üan, visited the port city of Canton to take part in the yearly examinations on the provincial level. He came from a Hakka family and thus belonged to that curious, refugee-like tribe that had immigrated from the North as early as the fifth century. Over the centuries, it had stubbornly clung to its own customs that differed from those of the southern inhabitants. They refused to have the feet of their women bound, and continued speaking their own dialect. Hung failed in the examination, but happened to hear the sermon of an evangelist minister in a church and took along nine Christian tracts on display there. The next year, 1837, he again took the examination, and failed again. This depressed him all the more because his impoverished family had long undergone all kinds of privations to make his study possible. Ashamed and disappointed, he suffered a nervous collapse. For a considerable time, he remained unconscious, stricken by a disease which some modern scientists believe to have been the initial stage of a slowly developing insanity.[19] During this period, he had several visions which gave him the burning conviction that he was the new Messiah of China and the world. This belief was strong enough to enable him to systematically organize a popular movement during the following thirteen years. It erupted in 1850 in the Taiping rebellion. Up to its final defeat in 1864, he maintained himself as its spiritual if not as its actual leader. In a variety of versions, Hung conveyed these important visions where Chinese and Christian conceptions mingle in a rather characteristic manner to his friends. The most extensive of them gives these details:

When the True Lord (Hung Hsiu-ch'üan) was twenty-five years of age (twenty-four according to Western calculation), on the first day of the third moon of the *ting-yu* year (5 April 1837) between 11–1 A.M., he saw numerous angels come down from Heaven to escort him aloft, and also saw children in yellow robes, like large cocks in size, march before him. . . . After a while the True Lord reclining in a sedan chair, accompanied by angels, ascended the broad road leading east. On his arrival at the Gates of Heaven he was welcomed by a bevy of lovely maidens standing by the roadside. Without a glance at them the True Lord went on into Heaven, where he was dazzled by the bright light, so different from the dull light in the world below. He was received by a number of people dressed in dragon-robes and wearing three-cornered hats. An order was given to open the Lord's body and replace old parts with new. Books, too, were placed at his side for him to read. Later the Heavenly Mother came to welcome him, saying: "My son, you are filthy after your descent upon earth. Let your Mother clean you in the river before you are allowed to see your Father."

When his body had been cleaned the Heavenly Mother conducted the Lord to see our Heavenly Father, Supreme Lord and August God, who wore a hat with upturned brim and black dragon-robe, with a heavy golden beard hanging down from the mouth to the belly. His appearance was very imposing; his body extremely tall; his hands on his knees. After kneeling the Lord stood erect on one side.

Our Heavenly Father, Supreme Lord and August God sadly uttered these words: "Have you ascended already? You quite understand this. The people on earth are for the most part heartless. Who on earth is not cherished by Me? Who does not eat My food or wear My clothes? Who does not enjoy My blessings? The myriads of things both in Heaven and on earth are all My work. All clothing and food are bestowed on them by Me. How does it come about that the people on earth, who enjoy My blessings, for the most part belie their true feelings, showing me neither respect nor awe. They are possessed by devils, to whom they offer up the things I have given them, as if it was the devils who had made them. . . .

Our Heavenly Father, Supreme Lord and August God also took the Lord around high Heaven and pointed out the ways in which the devils on earth bewitch the people. . . . The Lord became very angry, and asked our Heavenly Father, Supreme Lord and August God: "Father, as they are so busily engaged in evil, why do you not exterminate them?"

Our Heavenly Father, Supreme Lord and August God spoke unto the Lord: "Not only are there devils on earth, but also in the thirty-third Heaven there are devils attempting to intrude." The Lord replied: "Father, you are so omnipotent that you are able to give them life or death. Why do you allow them to intrude here?" Our Heavenly Father, Supreme Lord and August God said: "Just let them remain at large for a while, and I shall soon suppress them.". . .

He also attributed the evil activities of devils to the wrong teachings of Confucius. Our Heavenly Father, Supreme Lord and August God ordered that three categories of books be put in order, and directed the Lord's attention to them, saying: "This category of books are those I Myself have left behind, while working miracles during My descent upon earth, and these are truly faultless; the other category are those which I Myself dispatched your Elder Brother Christ to leave in the world upon his descent to perform miracles and to sacrifice his life in order to redeem the people from sin; the third category are those left by Confucius, which are the same as you studied on earth, and which are so faulty that even you have been corrupted by his teachings."

Our Heavenly Father, Supreme Lord and August God thus reproached Confucius: "Why do you teach people in such a muddleheaded way that they do not know Me on earth? Is your name, on the other hand, greater than Mine?" At first Confucius tried to argue, but then became tonguetied and speechless.

Our Heavenly Elder Brother Christ also reproached Confucius: "You wrote such bad books for the instruction of people that even My Younger Brother has been corrupted by reading your books." All the angels also blamed him. Hence he secretly fled down from Heaven, intending to join the devils.

Our Heavenly Father, Supreme Lord and August God immediately dispatched the Lord and an angel to pursue Confucius, tie him up and bring him back to our Heavenly Father, Supreme Lord and August God.

Our Heavenly Father, Supreme Lord and August God was exasperated, and ordered an angel to whip him. Confucius begged mercy again and again. After being whipped many times, Confucius kept on begging sorrowfully. Our Heavenly Father, Supreme Lord and August God then thought that his merits might suffice to pay for his faults, and permitted him to enjoy felicity in Heaven and forbade him forever to come down to earth.

Then our Heavenly Father, Supreme Lord and August God commanded the Lord to fight and chase the devils, conferring on him a golden seal and a "snow in the clouds" (the Taipings' secret term for "knife") and ordering him, together with the angels, gradually to drive the devils down from the thirty-third Heaven. . . .

When the Lord became enraged during the fight and wanted to kill the chief devil on the spot, Our Heavenly Father, Supreme Lord and August God, cried out: "No, no, you can only subdue him." The Lord could not understand why.

Our Heavenly Father, Supreme Lord and August God proclaimed: "This snake is an aged male snake, which is able to bewitch people and devour their souls. If you destroy him on the spot many of the souls devoured by him will be lost and this holy place will be polluted. Therefore we must spare his life for the time being." . . .

When the Lord became hungry during the fighting, the Heavenly Mother and little Sisters plucked some "sweet fruits" in high heaven and gave them to the Lord to eat. Their color was dark-yellow, and their taste very fragrant. When the Lord fought with the devil, the Heavenly Mother and little Sisters also lent him a helping hand so that he was always victorious. After his victorious return to high Heaven, our Heavenly Father, Supreme Lord and August God was highly pleased and conferred upon the Lord the title of *T'ai-p'ing t'ien-wang ta-tao chün-wang Ch'üan* (Ch'üan, the Heavenly King of Universal Peace and Sovereign of Fundamental Truth). . . .

The little Sisters in high Heaven also at times kept the Lord company in studying poetry and the classics, and in playing lute, flute, drum and other musical instruments. Feeling extremely happy, the Lord was not willing to return into the world then. But the Heavenly Father, Supreme Lord and August God often spoke to the Lord: "I, the Father, instruct you to study more poetry and classics to serve as a foundation for you later on. Yet you still have to go down into the world; for unless you do so, how could the people on earth be awakened and ascend to Heaven?" The Lord replied: "Yes," but in his heart he did not want to go back to the world. Sometimes when our Heavenly Father, Supreme Lord and August God pressed him too strongly, the Lord could not but descend for several Heavens and return shortly.

Our Heavenly Father, Supreme Lord and August God became so angry that the Lord said to his wife: "Take care of our Son, and stay with the Father, Mother, Elder Brother, Sister-in-law and little Sisters while I descend to earth to perform duties on behalf of the Father and then ascend to Heaven to enjoy felicity together with you." Thus our Heavenly Father, Supreme Lord and August God, the Heavenly Elder Brother Christ and numerous angels saw the Lord depart. . . .

Our Heavenly Father again spoke unto the Lord: "After your return to earth it will be several years before you awake, but do not worry about that. Later a book will be given to you to explain this, and when you learn the truth you will act immediately in accordance with the book so as to avoid mistakes. But when you act accordingly, most people will slander you, insult you, laugh at you and despise you. . . ."

When the Lord bade farewell to our Heavenly Father, Supreme Lord and August God and our Heavenly Elder Brother Christ to go down into the world, he showed signs of fear. Our Heavenly Father, Supreme Lord and August God said to him: "Fear not, you must act with courage. In case of any difficulty, whether on the left, on the right or wherever it may come from, you shall have My aid. What are you afraid of?" . . .

Since the first day of the third moon (5 April 1837) when The Lord had ascended to Heaven, he spent more than forty days there before he returned to earth.[20]

This description of Hung Hsiu-ch'üan's mystic experiences contains the core of the conception Hung had of himself and managed to inculcate in his followers. He saw himself as Christ's younger brother whose work of redemption could only be completed by his appearance. An acquaintance of Hung, Yang Hsiu-ch'ing,[21] who later achieved considerable success as commander-in-chief of the Taiping forces and "East King," was worshipped as the incarnation of the Holy Spirit and third son of God, standing at Hung's side as his helper. Under the "Heavenly Father, the only God," a trinity of his sons (Christ, Hung and Yang) thus came into being. As becomes apparent in the naive account quoted above, this teaching introduced an element that derives from the structure of the family into the conception of heaven and the divinity. It is marked by certain, typically Confucian, or, at least, typically Chinese traits. But there are also many details which are suggestive of Taoism, such as the reference to the girls at the Gate of Heaven, and the invigorating "sweet fruit" (peaches).[22] Both of these features are always present in Taoist descriptions of paradise. This applies equally to the account of the heavenly battle and the allusion to the "book."[23] For more than two centuries, the passing on of a book whose content usually had some connection with military matters had not only formed part of the initiation of an individual, but had also been considered a harbinger of a new age. This belief had struck deep roots, especially in Taoist-tinctured secret societies.

Here borrowings from the beliefs of secret societies, particularly the Ming loyalist "Hung society" *(Hung-men)* or "Triad society' *(San-tien hui)* are evident, however strongly the Taipings may later have denied such connections.[24] The formal influences are even more striking. There is, first, the curious costume by which the Taipings sought to differentiate themselves from the masses, a device used by almost all secret societies when they became openly active politically, if not before. There are many secret societies of which only the name has come down to us, and which referred to their dress, such as the "Red Eyebrows" in the first century B.C., for example, or the second century A.D. "Yellow Turbans."[25] In most cases, such costumes may also have functioned as uniforms which simply served to distinguish friend from foe in encounters with government troops. The red cloth the Taipings and other rebel units wrapped around their head certainly served as such. As for the long hair proudly worn by them in deliberate contrast to all other Chinese, matters are somewhat more complex. For the latter, being enslaved, imitated the dress worn by the Manchus in the steppes by having all their hair shaved except for a pigtail. The long hair, which earned the Taipings the nickname "long-haired bandits" *(ch'ang-mao tsei)* among Manchu loyalists, was a natural symbol of freedom (as it was, if in a wholly different way, for the *jeunesse dorée* of the third and fourth centuries),[26] and they even provided a theoretical foundation to document the value of this fashion. One of their leaders argued that it showed a lack of filial piety to shave the head since the child was already growing abundant hair while still in the mother's womb, and that it was unhealthy besides, for the hair protected the brain and thus made the person clear-headed.[27]

But the connections between the Taipings and earlier or contemporaneous secret societies also manifested themselves in the language used in Taiping documents. Although still based on the classical written language, it is of a particular simplicity like all the proclamations of traditional secret societies, and thus shows certain affinities with the colloquial speech of the "popular novels," with which the Taiping movement, like other popular movements, shared many ideals. The tendency to choose introductory formulae such as "A proverb says . . ." when Confucian or other writings even they could not dispense with were quoted is also typical of the attempt of the Taipings to write with as much popular appeal as possible and to avoid any appearance of ivory tower book learning.[28] They did, however, use word plays in a way which had also long been practiced by rebellious movements. The rhymed riddle or sing-song with a hidden religious or political meaning would be examples. They could easily be given children to sing as counting-out rhymes and served propagandistic purposes or were used as secret passwords. Thus a child allegedly sang the following tune some years before the outbreak of the rebellion:

Three eight and twenty-one
Grain as your delicacy
Man sitting on a piece of ground
Shall be above you people[29]

In the first three lines (which, incidentally, show a surprising similarity to such verses in the *T'ui-pei t'u*[30]), the three components of Hung Hsiu-ch'üan's name are hidden. For when the characters are analyzed graphically in what is an epigraphically incorrect yet constantly recurring method in mantics, we discover the elements "three," "eight," "twenty" and "one" for *Hung.* For *Hsiu,* we get "grain" and "as," and for *Ch'üan* the elements "man," "a" and "ground." But Hung Hsiu-ch'üan went so far as to read such interpretations, however abstruse they might be, into what were the most sacred texts for the Taipings. Thus he writes the following curious commentary on the passage in the New Testament, Matthew 27:40, which mentions the people passing by the cross reviling Christ: "Thou that destroyest the temple, and buildest it in three days, save thyself. If you be the Son of God, come down from the cross":

"Three dots make 'Hung'; three days is thus the 'Hung' Sun. (The character *hung* has three dots as its radical. In Chinese 'day' and 'sun' are the same character, i.e. 'three days' becomes equivalent to 'three suns,' and thus to 'Hung Sun.') The Great Elder Brother issued an edict in a parable saying that the Hung Sun would be the Lord, the same who was to rebuild the destroyed temple of God."[31]

This identification of himself with the sun is also curiously reminiscent of older secret societies, particularly those that were influenced by Mithraism.[32] This worship of fire and light which may be said to constitute the connecting element between the Heavenly Father and his three sons is particularly obvious in Hung's commentary on the sentences in Genesis, which read: "Let there be light." "The Father is Light, the Brother (Christ) is Light; the Lord (Hung Hsiu-ch'üan) is Light."[33] Or in somewhat greater detail in the commentary in Matthew 4:16 with its echo from Zachariah: "The people which sat in darkness saw great light; and to them which sat in the region and shadow of death, light is sprung up":

"God is fire; the Sun is also fire. Thus God and the Sun (i.e. Hung) have both come to us. God is the Holy Ghost and has come together with the Holy Spirit (i.e. the Eastern King) to us. Thus the Holy Ghost descended on the Pentecost and the fire and wind appeared. Fire and wind both come from God, the source of all things. God is fire, so there was the Divine Light. The Great Elder Brother is fire, so he is the Great Light. I Myself am the sun, so I am also the Light."[34]

This curious belief, a mixture of Christian, Chinese and west-Asian religious conceptions that had come to China almost one and one-half millennia before, first spread primarily among the Hakka which were somewhat isolated from the rest of the population. It also found adherents among the Miao tribes, a group of indigenous inhabitants (comparable to the Indians of North America), who made up a relatively large part of the population in Kwangsi province where Hung carried on his missionary activity with special vigor. Due to the gradually developing connection to purely Chinese secret societies, initially predominantly religious motifs were complemented by national and political ones. As a result, the long-planned rebellion could finally become reality in 1850, after several years of preaching and organizing. In their enthusiasm, the elite troops of the rebels went so far as to burn down their own homes to cut off any possibility of retreat.

At first, the uprising followed the pattern established in countless successful and unsuccessful rebellions in China. The closest provincial capital was occupied. After the first, rapidly organized government troops had been repulsed, operations were extended and other groups of rebels that had been fighting independently were amalgamated. On 25 September 1851, Hung proclaimed the "Heavenly Kingdom of Highest Peace" *(T'ai-p'ing t'ien-kuo).* This was a new, theocratic dynasty, as it were. The first component of its title had Chinese origins, the second referred to the Christian "Heavenly Kingdom." After the Taiping army had gradually fought its way eastward through Hunan, Hupei, Kiangsi and Anhwei provinces, it achieved its most spectacular success toward the end of February 1853, when it took Nanking. That city became the "Heavenly Capital" *(t'ien-ching),* and Hung took up residence there. Under the rule of the "East King" Yang, the next three years were a period of consolidation, although constant and not invariably successful battles were waged against government troops. A northern expedition, which advanced to the very gates of Tientsin, was organized to deal with this threat. During this time, most of the reforms planned by the Taipings were worked out and partly, if provisionally, implemented. The decline began when the "East King," who had become too overbearing, was stripped of his power and murdered, and a destructive power struggle occurred among the other chiefs. Although continuing to be the undisputed leader, Hung Hsiu-ch'üan increasingly lost contact with reality and proved unable to master a situation that had begun to drift. This failure possibly caused and certainly hastened the final collapse of the rebellion, because the tactics designed by the enormously capable Taiping general Li Hsiu-ch'eng[35] to resist the government troops could not prevail over Hung's mystical delusions. While it could easily have been avoided, the fall of Nanking thus caused the collapse of the entire movement. After Hung Hsiu-ch'üan had taken poison in the surrounded city on June 1, 1864, thousands upon thousands of Taiping followers were slaughtered in a hopeless struggle. Scattered groups which had been able to escape could not survive as an effective fighting force. The remnants were routed in 1866.

TAIPING ATTEMPTS AT SOCIAL REFORM

As with any new ideology that does not remain purely speculative but has the potential for implementation, a certain discrepancy between theory and practice also developed in the Taiping. This is most apparent where the program becomes utopian (although it is true that the dividing line between reality and utopia is never rigid). In the social sphere, the cornerstone of the movement was undoubtedly the proclamation of the equality of all men. Of course, this ideal was anything but new, having frequently constituted the integrating element of the brotherhood espoused in countless secret societies. It was a brotherhood which even Confucianism, ordinarily hostile to secret societies, recognized in principle. This is as evident in the famous saying attributed to Confucius that "All men within the four seas are brothers,"[36] as it is in Chang Tsai's "Western Inscription"[37] where the point of reference of this brotherhood, i.e. heaven and earth as parents, is identified. But the decisive difference was that the Confucian concept allowed for a hierarchy by distinguishing between elder and younger brother. It thus unwittingly endorsed all forms of hierarchy, while in the secret societies including the Taiping this aspect was simply omitted. The only distinguishing characteristic of the Taiping was that they had arrived at this result by adopting the western, i.e. Christian concept of brother. A rather skillful fusion of the two ideas obviously intended to win adherents among Confucians can be found in a Taiping document which states: "Your bodies were born of your parents, but your souls were born of God. God is our true Father, and is your true Father too. He is even the true Father of all peoples of the ten thousand countries of the whole world. This is why the ancient proverb says: 'The world is a family and all men within the four seas are brothers.' "[38]

In another treatise, this idea of an absolute equality of all men is substantiated in greater detail and illustrated by examples which imply a social program:

> Since we were all born of the same father of souls, why should there be any distinction between you and me or between others and ourselves? When there are clothes, let us wear them together; when there is food, let us enjoy it together. Whenever calamity or sickness befalls anyone, we should get a doctor to attend him and minister to his needs by making medicine for him. As for orphans, either boys or girls, or anyone who has passed the prime of life and is weak and debilitated, let us be all the more careful in attending to their needs, let us bathe them and help them change their clothes. Only thus will it be possible not to lose sight of the ideal of sharing happiness and woe, of sharing the burden of illness and disease. Giving security to the aged and love to the young stems from the Tung Wang's understanding of our Heavenly Father's love for the living and from the magnanimity of the T'ien Wang, who looks upon all as his own brothers.[39]

It is not difficult, of course, to spot a whole string of old clichés in these few sentences: the care of orphans, the old and the sick is something the Confucians had always inscribed on their banners. Other demands that seem more original at first glance, such as the common use of clothing, are probably traceable to the conceptions of the paradisiacal land of Uttarakuru[40] which came to China with Buddhism.

Parallels to older, also largely Confucian ideal conceptions from the well field system of Mencius down to the family communism of Liang Ju-yüan[41] also are conspicuous in the egalitarian rules worked out for the distribution of land, the central problem in all political and ideological disputes in Chinese history. In the "Land System of the Heavenly Dynasty" issued in 1853, we read the following:

> All land shall be classified into nine categories: those which bear, in early and late harvests per year, a yield of 1,200 catties per *mou* shall be considered as superior-superior land; a yield of 1,100 catties, superior-medium land; a yield of 1,000 catties superior-inferior land, . . . [down to] a yield of 400 catties, [which is] inferior-inferior land. . . .
>
> The distribution of land is made according to the size of the family, irrespective of sex, with only the number of persons taken into account. The larger the number, the more land they shall receive; the smaller the number, the less land they shall receive. The lands assigned are of various grades of the nine categories. If there are six persons in the family, three shall receive good land, and three shall receive bad land: half good and half bad. All lands under Heaven shall be farmed jointly by the people under Heaven. If the production of food is too small in one place, then more to another place where it is more abundant. All lands under Heaven shall be accessible in time of abundance or famine. If there is a famine in one area move the surplus from an area where there is abundance to that area, in order to feed the starving. In this way the people under Heaven shall all enjoy the great happiness given by the Heavenly Father, Supreme Lord and August God. Land shall be farmed by all; rice, eaten by all; clothes, worn by all; money, spent by all. There shall be no inequality, and no person shall be without food or fuel.
>
> No matter whether man or woman, everyone over sixteen years of age shall receive land. If there is any land left, those who are fifteen and under shall receive a half share. For instance, a person over sixteen receives one *mou* of the superior-superior category. If a person over sixteen receives three *mou* of the inferior-inferior category, one who is fifteen or under shall receive a half share and thus get one and a half *mou* of the inferior-inferior category.
>
> Everywhere in the empire mulberry trees shall be planted beneath the walls. All women shall raise silkworms, spin cloth and sew dresses. Every family in the empire shall have five hens and two sows, without exception. At the harvest the platoon-chief shall supervise the section-chief in storing away the amount of new grain needed for the twenty-five families and surrendering the rest to the public store-house. The same applies to wheat, beans, nettle-hemp, cloth, silk, chickens, dogs and so on; it applies to money also. For under Heaven all belongs to the great family of the Heavenly Father, Supreme Lord and August God. In the empire none shall have any private property, and everything belongs to God, so that God may dispose of it. In the great family of Heaven every place is equal, and everyone has plenty. This is the edict of the Heavenly Father, Supreme Lord and August God, who especially commanded the T'ai-P'ing True Lord to save the world.
>
> But the platoon-chief shall keep an account of the amount of money and grain, reporting it to the treasurer, disburser and receiver. In every twenty-five families there shall be established a public storehouse and a chapel, where the platoon-chief shall reside. In every twenty-five families all matters, such as marriage and birth celebrations, shall be at the expense of the public storehouse. But they shall be controlled, and prohibited from spending one cash more than the limit.

> In case of marriage a family is given 1,000 cash and 100 catties of grain. In the empire everything shall be uniform. In everything expenses shall be economized lest there should be wars and calamities. . . . In every twenty-five families the services of blacksmiths, carpenters and stonemasons shall be provided by the section-chiefs and privates, during their leisure after farming. All platoon-chiefs shall take charge of affairs among their respective twenty-five families, such as marriage, birth and other celebrations.
>
> Apart from worship of the Heavenly Father, Supreme Lord and August God, all former bad customs [in worshipping] shall be dispensed with. In every twenty-five families all children shall go to the chapel, where the platoon-chief shall preach and read "The Holy Book of the Old Testament," "The Holy Book of the New Testament" and "The Book of Truth (Heaven-) Commanded Edicts."[42] Every sabbath the section-chief shall lead his men and women to the chapel, men on one side and women on the other, preaching and listening to sermons, singing hymns and praying to the Heavenly Father, Supreme Lord and August God.[43]

This curious, still half pseudo-Confucian, already half-Christian-puritanical idyll could of course never be implemented in this form. As the reference to the "platoon-chief" and his assistants shows, this was at least partly due to the fact that even Hung Hsiu-ch'üan could obviously not dispense with a distinct stratification of his following despite the "magnanimity" with which he allegedly looked on all men as his brothers. The institutions he and his closest friends tried to create for this purpose were no less inspired by old, traditional ideal conceptions than the egalitarian demands by which he appealed to the underprivileged population of the southern provinces, except that they were based on order rather than equality. For the administrative and military apparatus of the Taiping was explicitly based on the ideal-typical hierarchy of functionaries which the previously mentioned *Rites of Chou (Chou-li)*[44] had described as allegedly existing during the first millennium B.C., and which had time and again served as a model for political reformers. Similarities become especially apparent when one compares the structure of the official apparatus with official titles and observes that the Taiping quite deliberately copied both structure and elements of terms used to designate officials. A closer look shows, however, that the ideal Chou administration was copied "in name only," and that this was done to make a point, not because there was genuine enthusiasm for it. Officials having titles identical with or similar to those found in the *Chou-li,* for example, had functions altogether different from what the *Rites of Chou* specified. To what extent these discrepancies merely resulted from the circumstance that the Taiping never had the chance to govern during peacetime is a hotly debated question, particularly among Chinese scholars. It is interesting not only because it leads to the further problem how utopian the utopia of the Heavenly Kingdom of the Taiping really was, but also because it once again raises the previously discussed question concerning the relationships between civilian and military leadership in China.[45]

In the highest leadership echelons of the Taiping, which were not organized according to an articulated, preexisting model, the two spheres are not unambiguously distinct. A collection of secret reports published in 1855 for the use of loyalist troops and dealing with the political structure of the Taiping may not be objective, but is largely factual, and gives these details:

> The title of king (which, in addition to the Heavenly King, Hung, was born by the four kings of the four directions of Heaven and a "special king") is the highest rank. It was followed by marquis *(hou)*, chancellor *(ch'eng-hsiang)*, senior secretary *(chien-tien)*, commander *(chih-hui)* and general *(chiang-chün)*. These describe in general the power structure at the court and the central government of the Taiping. In the army, the corps commander *(tsung-chih)* ranks first, followed by corps superintendent *(chien-chün)*, corps general *(chün-shuai)*, colonel *(shih-shuai)*, captain *(lü-shuai)*, and finally lieutenant *(tsu-chang* or *pei-chang)* and sergeant *(liang-ssu-ma)*.[46]

In spite of the division into (civilian) "central administration" and "army," the titles show quite clearly that military and civilian levels were superimposed on each other. It is also noteworthy that army ranks extended much further downward than positions in the civilian administration. De facto, this meant that both merged completely on the lower levels, for the *liang-ssu-ma*, for example, which might be translated as "sergeant" or "non-commissioned officer" in the military hierarchy is none other than the "platoon-chief" who had purely civilian functions in the "Land System of the Heavenly Dynasty." At this point, the Taiping administrative system and the ideal conception of the *Chou-li* show a remarkable similarity. For according to the *Rites of Chou* also, all classifications on the lowest level for ostensibly purely military purposes (as, for example, the rule governing the number of soldiers that had to be furnished by a group of families of a given size) had the clear objective of additionally organizing the population for administrative tasks. The militiaman who cultivated the fields during peacetime or, conversely, took up arms during emergencies as a "citizen soldier" has thus always been a Chinese ideal, and this was as true of the Confucian-influenced *Chou-li* as among the Taiping. But this involved the risk that the balance might tip decisively, and with devastating consequences. On the one hand, Confucian officials who had more and more frequently led armies from the Sung period on might easily be defeated in battle because they were inexperienced. On the other, and particularly in the pre-Sung period, purely military commanders could cause the collapse of the civilian order. Because they were necessarily antagonistic to Confucianism and inevitably engaged in constant campaigns, all secret societies including the Taiping tended to emphasize the military. The "citizen" never had the chance to lay aside his uniform, the militiaman never got around to tilling the fields. Although this was not intentional, what gradually happened among the Taiping was that the soldier became more important than the farmer (which can be inferred from the "demotion" of soldiers to farmers) simply because he was even more indispensable for their survival than the latter. Although Hung Hsiu-chüan personally withdrew from military operations almost completely after the Taiping occupied Nanking in 1863, the increasing emphasis on military affairs was also pronounced among the leadership. To begin with, the "East King," Yang Hsiu-ch'ing, worshipped not only as the Holy Ghost but also as "God's mouthpiece," seized more and more power, so that Hung allegedly endorsed unquestioningly all the decrees he authored. But even after Yang's death, the real power remained in the hands of the generals, although none of them dared provoke a direct confrontation with Hung. But even Hung did not view himself as the King of Peace, but felt he was carrying out the mission entrusted to him by the Heavenly Father and believed in typically Taoist fashion that he was involved in a struggle with demons in a world of the spirit. Yet his followers soon could no longer defend themselves against their very concrete enemies in the real world.[47]

Surprisingly, an indirect connection with the conflict between military and civilian leadership is also discernible in a sphere where the Taiping went far beyond all earlier uprisings without having received any particular impulses from Christianity in the matter, and that was the liberation of women. In evidence in the few documents quoted, the equal status of men and women is a concept that runs like a thread through Taiping ideology. At least initially, it was also often put into practice. The binding of feet was strictly prohibited, women could take public examinations which were conducted according to revised rules (and, incidentally, resulted in 80 percent successful candidates, an incredibly high rate compared to what was the rule up to that time[48]). Women could even enter the army where they formed their own units. The woman who was like an amazon and also had a humanist education, and who seems to make her first appearance here, was of course not altogether unknown in the China of earlier times. As late as the T'ang, she had been a very popular literary subject, an occasion for praise and admiration. It was only after the eleventh century that this ideal, which offered at least a theoretical alternative to the more traditional image of the woman, was proscribed by a frightened Confucianism that had somehow become unsure of its patriarchal values since it saw here a danger to the continued dominance of its truly monstrous prototype born of weakness and brutality, the wife that is crippled and chained to the home. Li Ju-chen had clearly understood this constellation of circumstances and attacked it through irony. The Taiping went further by introducing changes, probably chiefly because the Hakka tradition had preserved many pre-Sung customs, the considerably more emancipated position of women among them. A woman described in an early Chinese history of the Taiping rebellion would have been admired no less during the T'ang and could quite conceivably have lived at that time: "In the Taiping army there was a woman called Hsia San-niang, who became famous under the title 'woman commander.' . . . She was twenty years old, tall, and had long arms, a great warrior on horseback. She could shoot arrows with either hand. When the Taiping took

Chen-chiang, she stormed the walls at the head of several hundred women soldiers and fought more courageously and fiercely than all men. No one could resist her in this battle."[49]

But this rediscovered ideal of a free woman who was also man's physical equal had difficulty maintaining itself for long among the Taiping. Although they officially advocated monogamy (and therefore also abolished eunuchs), the leaders of the rebellion, and Hung more than the rest, kept large harems. And the radical moral laws which provided for a complete segregation of the sexes and even of couples, also amounted primarily to a curtailment of women's rights in practice. Due to this inconsistency, itself a result of selfishness, the liberation of women by the Taiping soon lost much of its glory. Yet its mere proclamation was a beacon that would not soon be extinguished.

The provisions governing the social position of women were incorporated in the first part of the legal code in 1859, during a later phase of the Taiping movement. It consisted of 1) accustoming by customs, 2) methodizing by methods (serving the development of the state), and 3) penalizing by penalties. The first included the struggle against superstition. Especially Hung Hsiu-ch'üan waged this fight with such fanaticism that one is probably justified in seeing in it his frequently proclaimed "War Against the Demons." This iconoclasm occasionally degenerated to the level of vandalism and entailed the destruction of countless works of art in southern China. Although only "objects" were destroyed, these excesses aroused a profound mistrust among large segments of the population which otherwise were not without sympathy for the Taiping. Later, the Confucian authorities found it easy to exploit this reaction. But the penal code as originally drafted was remarkably restrained. While it did provide for the death penalty, it excluded corporal punishment and collective responsibility. Prisoners were to be sent to other provinces (to facilitate the subsequent resocializing process) and used chiefly for road construction, a practice that is curiously reminiscent of the laws in the communities of the "Five Pecks of Rice Taoists" who also had used road construction as a form of rehabilitative punishment.[50] The "methodizing by methods," finally, contains a long catalogue of provisions which can most easily be reduced to the common denominator of "Westernization" or modernization, for they deal with the establishment of banks and insurance companies and the prohibition of alcoholic beverages, apparently traceable to Christian and puritanical influence.

THE KINGDOM OF GOD AND NATIONALISM

Serving as a kind of introduction, we also find here sketchy descriptions of the countries in the distant West. Their naiveté will perhaps seem less surprising when we realize that even the Imperial court of the Manchu only had rather vague notions about Europe and America, and that all reports concerning them were presented to it in a diction which had come into use in the second century

B.C. to deal with curious phenomena. The following comments about Germany are a case in point: "The German nation is composed of more than ten states, independent of each other and nonaggressive. They believe in God the Heavenly Father and Jesus Christ very piously. The people are conservative; the country is not powerful, yet their morals are extremely high. They have also big ships plying for trade between various states and they are trusted by the rulers and officials of various nations. In their management of affairs, they are easily contented as the people do not wish to move about, deeply believe in the August God our Savior, and do not like fighting."[51]

This flattering portrait shows once again how much distance can transfigure. Yet it was certainly not the "not powerful" Germany that served the Taiping as a model, but more probably the powerful United States. While the relevant account does not reveal the desire for emulation that had informed the description of the Roman Empire, "Great-Ch'in,"[52] more than fifteen hundred years earlier, it is of such unreserved admiration and so permeated by many of the old clichés about a Chinese ideal state that one can at least clearly recognize the intent to portray a goal worth striving for:

> The "State of the Flowery Flag" otherwise known as the United States of America, so far as courtesy, faith, wealth and self-sufficiency are concerned, is surpassed by none. Notwithstanding America's strength she does not invade her neighbors. She has gold and silver mines, but invites nationals of other countries to work them. If the nationals of other states have abilities, she registers them and elects them as officials, which shows her broadmindedness. The tenure of the head of state is for a term of five years, and he is paid a limited salary. At the end of each term he has to retire and the "provinces" will elect another. For purposes of administration the "provinces" meet together for discussion, and then present proposals to the head of state for decision. In selecting scholars, electing officials, filling vacancies and discussing matters of vital importance, a date is fixed, when a big chest is placed in the center of the hall. All able-bodied officials and citizens must take part in the voting and put their tickets in the big chest. The more votes a man gets, the more capable is he considered to be; the more discussions there are, the greater justice there is. In that country the lame, the blind, the deaf, the dumb, widowers, widows, the parentless and the friendless have their asylums, where they are trained to learn various trades. Furthermore, the relatives of widowers, widows, the parentless and the friendless all volunteer heartily to take care of them, and are willing to sign agreements for their adoption. Thus there is no beggar in the country, which is attributed to her courtesy, honesty, wealth and self-sufficiency.[53]

It is quite possible that this account goes back in part to information Hung Hsiu-ch'üan obtained from the American missionary Issachar J. Roberts (1802–1871), from whom he received religious instruction during two months in 1847, before the outbreak of the rebellion. Though very favorable, however, it could not establish closer or better relations to the U.S.A. than to other western states which (such as England and France) were less flatteringly reviewed in this action program of the Taiping. A letter Hung allegedly sent to the president of the United States makes clear that the Taiping did not really understand either the West or its political reactions:

"I have heard," one passage reads, "that your country emphasises the importance of the people, that men are considered equal in every respect, that freedom is your fundamental principle and that there are no obstacles in the association of men and women. I am glad to be able to note that your principles are in complete accord with those on which we have founded our dynasty."[54]

Perhaps the very tone was considered somewhat overbearing in the West at that time. In any event, western observers soon reproached the Taiping for their arrogance, and when commercial relations proved more difficult with the Taiping than the official Manchu government, it was not surprising that there should soon have been foreigners who sought to support loyalist troops. The best-known result of this development was the organization of the Ever Victorious Army in 1860. It was made up of Chinese volunteers under western leadership, first Frederick T. Ward, and later General Gordon. While this force contributed considerably to the defeat of the Taiping,[55] it probably did no more than those western troops that denied the Taiping access to Shanghai, for example. The sympathy the Taiping showed the West and its religion was not repaid by it, but only resulted in rendering them despicable in Chinese eyes.

It is also curious that the Taiping did not succeed in making use of the indisputable nationalist, anti-Manchu element in such a fashion as to compensate for the stigma of the alien from which they themselves suffered. The mistake was that under the influence of the "Heavenly King" Hung, who gradually reverted to mysticism, the national idea of a China infinitely superior to the Manchu barbarians was superseded more and more by the conception of an international or, more precisely, a supranational "Kingdom of God." While it is true that this was consonant in certain respect with the old Chinese ideal of the identity of China and the world, it did not awaken the enormous powers inherent in the nationalism and racism that had been steadily growing since Mongol times. The extent to which opportunities for working up sentiments were missed in what was certainly an estimable but (particularly by the Christians) wholly unacknowledged fashion becomes particularly clear when we compare the various versions of a section of the Taiping tract relevant in this context. The 1850 version reads as follows:

"We believe that the empire belongs to the Chinese and not to the Tartars; the food and raiment found therein belong to the Chinese and not to the Tartars; the men and women are subjects and children of the Chinese and not of the Tartars. But alas! Ever since the Ming misgoverned, the Manchus availed themselves of the opportunity to throw China into confusion and deprive the Chinese of their empire; they also robbed them of their food and clothing, as well as oppressed their sons and daughters."[56]

And this is the 1852 version: "We believe that the 'empire' is the Kingdom of God on High *(shang-ti)* and not that of the Tartars; that the food and raiment belong to God on High and not to the Tartars. That the sons and daughters there are are the sons and daughters of God on High, and not those of the Tartars. But alas! Ever since the Ch'ing dynasty of the Manchus spread its poisonous rule, it has thrown China into confusion, deprived it of its empire, its food and its raiment, and suppressed its sons and daughters."[57]

All the "loyalists" as far back as Huang Tsung-hsi, and that is what the nationalists considered themselves to be, had been committed to the Ming dynasty. But that very name disappears, as does the word "China" over extended sections. While it is true that Hung attempted instead to explain the identity of "China" and the "Kingdom of God" in various ways to his followers, this equation could at best fire the initiates; it was not immediately comprehensible to outsiders or those that still had to be won to the cause. On the other hand, the passages where such expectations are to be documented are all the more important for an understanding of the messianic hopes among the Taiping. First, Hung tried to represent China as a kind of chosen land by what may be called a linguistic trick. In one decree, he proclaimed:

> The Heavenly Father decreed from the beginning that the Kingdom of Heaven would be realized in China. Since China (*Chung-hua,* actually "Middle Blossom") was from the beginning the home of the Kingdom of Heaven, it also became the name of the Heavenly Father (Jehovah, in Chinese transcription *Yeh-huo-hua,* which means in translation "Father-Fire-China"). Before the Father descended to earth, China thus belonged to the Father. And yet the barbarian devils have slipped into the Father's Kingdom. That is the reason the Father ordered me to come to destroy them.[58]

The belief that the Heavenly Kingdom could only be found in heaven Hung considered a crude error which he tried to correct time and again, as in a commentary in Matthew 5:19, where the Kingdom of Heaven is mentioned:

> The Heavenly Kingdom is meant to include both Heaven and earth. The Heavenly Kingdom is in Heaven; the Heavenly Kingdom is equally on earth. Both in Heaven and on earth is the Heavenly Kingdom of the Divine Father. Do not imagine that it refers solely to the Heavenly Kingdom in Heaven. Thus the Great Elder Brother formerly issued an edict foretelling the coming of the Heavenly Kingdom soon, meaning that the Heavenly Kingdom would come into being on earth. Today the Heavenly Father and Heavenly Elder Brother descend into the world to establish the Heavenly Kingdom.[59]

That this Heavenly Kingdom was to extend over the entire earth follows indirectly from another passage which states that the Heavenly Father would govern all the ten thousand lands[60] or, perhaps even more clearly, in a proclamation where Hung states: "As a matter of fact, the heavenly kingdom, the heavenly capital, the heavenly court, and the heavenly hall are those over which the Father and the Eldest Brother brought me down to be the Lord, uniting all elements whether up in Heaven, down beneath the earth, or in the human world to be one grand dynasty at all times and in all places."[61]

When the British interpreter Thomas T. Meadows, to whom we are indebted for one of the most detailed descriptions of the intellectual and historical background of the Taiping rebellion, asked the "North King" in 1852 about the actual nature of the "Heavenly King" Hung, he noted the following: "In reply to my inquiries respecting the T'ai-p'ing Wang, the Prince of Peace, the Northern Prince explained in writing that he was the 'True Lord' or Sovereign; that 'the Lord of China is the Lord of the whole world; that he is the second Son of God, and all people in the whole world must obey and follow him.' As I read this without remark, he said, looking at me interrogatively, 'The True Lord is not merely the Lord of China; he is not only our Lord, he is your Lord also.' "[62]

Hung was utterly convinced that Nanking, which he had made the Heavenly Capital, was the "New Jerusalem" promised in the Revelation of St. John. In a commentary on the passage in question (3:12), he wrote: "Now the Great Elder Brother has come. The Heavenly Dynasty represents the temple of God, the Heavenly Father and True Spirit, and that of the Great Elder Brother Christ; and there are carved also the name of God, and that of Christ. The New Jerusalem sent down from Heaven by God the Heavenly Father is the present Heavenly Capital. This is true."[63]

The hopes for the much more realistic condition of "Great Equality" *(ta-t'ung)* —the paradise of a religiously tinctured Confucianism for millennia—receded into insignificance before this Christian conception of a New Jerusalem. The 1852 edition of a Taiping tract still contains the relevant passage from the old ritual classic[64] in the form of a long, uncut quotation and thus shows that the "Great Equality" was one of the goals of the movement. But it was omitted in the 1859 edition.[65] This indicates that here also a gradual drift away from Chinese ideals and a turning toward supranational and Christian ones was under way.

Against this background, Hung saw himself as the world redeemer who appears not once but again and again during certain times to shape the course of the world. Consciously or unconsciously, he thus continued Chinese traditions, for both in Confucianism and Taoism the periodically returning Messiah had long been a firmly established figure.[66] Hung believed he could see earlier stations of his work of salvation in his incarnation as the sun above the rainbow by which God made his covenant with Noah after the flood (although the sun itself is not mentioned in the passage in Genesis), or in his incarnation in the prophet Melchizedek. On the basis of a certain interpretation of Psalm 110:4 and Hebrews 5:6, the latter had sometimes been proclaimed within Christianity as Christ's precursor, indeed as an earlier Messiah. In Hung's commentary on Genesis 9:16, we read: "When the Father established the everlasting covenant, there appeared a rainbow in the sky. This rainbow in the sky was bent so that it looked like a bow. On the curved point was the Great Sun. As I am the Sun, My name is Hung the Great [this is a play on words: the name 'Hung,' the word for 'rainbow' and one of the many words for 'great' are homonyms which are all read *hung* although they are all written with different characters].[67] The Father formerly established this sign proclaiming beforehand the dispatch of the 'Hung' Sun as the Lord."[68]

And in a commentary on Revelation 12:13–16:

> The Great Elder Brother, Myself and the Eastern King, before the beginning of Heaven and earth, were born out of the womb of God's consort, the Heavenly Mother. Later the Father sent the Great Elder Brother to redeem the sins of mankind and enter the womb of Mary to become a man. Thus the Great Elder Brother's edict said that there was the Great Elder Brother before Abraham. Moreover, I Myself can still recall that when, in Heaven, the Father was going to send the Great Elder Brother to be born of the descendants of Abraham, and I thus descended to save Abraham and to bless him. Then I knew that the Father would send Myself to be the Lord on earth. . . . Afterwards I received the Father's command to enter a Mother's womb and come into the world. I Myself then knew that the serpent-devil, the demon Yen-lo[69] would molest Me, and begged the Father for protection so as to avoid harm from him. Later the Father commanded Me to be born of the womb of a second Mother in order to enter the world. I Myself can still remember that, when I entered the womb of this second Mother, the Father made a sign, that is, he clothed the body in sunlight to show that the embryo inside was the Sun. Who knew that the serpent-devil Yen-lo was also aware that this Mother's embryo, I Myself, was especially sent by God to be born into the world to exterminate this serpent? Thus the serpent attempted to swallow this embryo so as to ruin God's work. Who knew that God was omnipotent, and the newborn baby could not be harmed by the snake? I Myself truly bear witness that the former Melchizedek was I Myself. After the Great Elder Brother ascended to Heaven, the baby, clad in sunlight, born of this second Mother, was I Myself. Thus now the Father and Elder Brother descend upon earth and guide Me to be the Lord and exterminate this serpent. Already the beastly serpent is annihilated, and there is Universal Peace under Heaven. This is true.[70]

Concerning a final passage in Revelation (6:12–14), where it states that the sun will become black and the moon as blood and "the stars of heaven fell unto earth" after the opening of the "sixth seal," Hung writes: "I Myself was the Sun; My wife, the Moon. The record that they [the Sun and the Moon] became as dark as blood is a parable to prophesy that we shall descend upon earth to become human beings. Our Heavenly generals and Heavenly soldiers are those stars in Heaven which fell to earth. . . ."[71]

The sun and the moon also play a role in another Taiping document that reports Hung's visions in 1837. While they are not directly presented as incarnations of Hung, they confirm his mission in another, no less interesting way: "In the *ting-yu* year (1837) he (Hung Hsiu-ch'üan) said at the time of his ascension to his elder sister: 'Sister, what do you see in my hands?' 'Nothing,' answered the sister. The Lord declared: 'My left hand holds the sun, and my right hand the moon. Can you not see them?' "[72]

This anecdote is revelatory because the description of the "Lord" carrying the sun and the moon in his hands is surprisingly like the first picture in the previously mentioned prognostic text *T'ui-pei-t'u.* It obviously symbolizes the beginning of the world. The sun and the moon that appear there are presented in most old editions of the text as being held up by a supernatural, gigantic figure in the very manner Hung here lays claim to.[73] The reference to this picture can hardly have been accidental and means that Hung's appearance would initiate a wholly different, new time where the entire world would have to be recreated from top to bottom. No mere "renewal," which would be tantamount to a revival of the old, but a genuine, dewy beginning was allegedly imminent. This conviction of having been sent into the world to give it a changed face, and to have to act in accordance with laws which no longer had anything in common with traditional ones never left Hung; indeed, it tragically led to his last great defeat and death. When the army commander Li Hsiu-ch'eng called on him to evacuate Nanking as it was being surrounded by government troops, he gave this majestic answer: "I came to this world by the saintly order of God and Jesus to be the only True Lord of the ten thousand nations. What do I have to fear? You need send no further memorials. . . . You say we have soldiers. But my heavenly hosts are more numerous than all the drops in the oceans of the world. What do I have to fear?"[74]

But the ensuing, definitive collapse of the Taiping rebellion was horrible. Particularly in the south, it left a country that was devastated over extensive sections. Instead of the "Highest Peace" striven for by the Taiping, the calm of the cemetery descended over the regions they had governed. Moved to almost poetic utterance, a British contemporary wrote: "Wild beasts roamed at large over the land after their departure, and made their dens in the deserted towns. The pheasants' whirr resounded where the hum of busy populations had ceased, and weeds or jungle covered the ground once tilled with patient industry."[75] As is true of almost all eyewitness accounts of the Taiping rebellion, here also the abhorrence at so much senseless destruction quite clearly outweighs any respect for the ideals the Taiping struggled to achieve: "Their presence was an unmitigated scourge, attended by nothing but disaster from beginning to end without the least effort on their part to rebuild what had been destroyed."[76] It is only in historical perspective that events can be seen in proper balance. Behind the damage done to a traditional civilization that was doomed in any event, the unquestionable greatness of the social and political program of the Taiping emerges once again. During the last hundred years, there has been an abundance of accounts of the Taiping rebellion. Although they differ markedly in their judgments, it may be said in general that more recent writers have attempted to do justice to the revolutionary changes attempted by the Taiping as they became reality. Even so, strongly opposing views still exist. The famous, rather conservative Chinese Taiping scholar Jen (Chien) Yu-wen, for example, still wrote quite critically about the agrarian program of the Taiping: "Under this system all the peasants in the empire practically became slaves of the state. The state becomes the all-inclusive landowner, an oppressor and exploiter of peasants. . . . This [the Taiping] land system may embody high ideals . . . but if it is followed, what the peasant gets will be a minimal share of his product. He will not be able to satisfy his needs and to advance his self-cultivation. His ideals will not be implemented and he will sink into everlasting, miserable poverty, wholly excluded from any happiness. He will be the lifelong horse and ox of the state."[77]

Yet some scholars in the People's Republic also expressed themselves critically about the agrarian system. But usually, they also praised its idealistic objectives. On the hundredth anniversary of the founding of the "Heavenly State of Universal Peace," the *Peking People's Daily* remarked editorially (1/11/1951) that the confidence in the West had been unjustified, and especially the distribution of land to large numbers of small proprietors as "utopian" as all earlier peasant uprisings, but that the "heroic spirit" and the "great patriotism" evidenced in their fight "would forever redound to the glory of the Chinese people."[78] The judgment of the historian Fan Wen-lan, who chose this same occasion to celebrate the Taiping as forerunners of Chinese communism, is most enthusiastic:

> The progressive portion of the revolutionary platform of the "Heavenly State of the Highest Peace" has not only been realized today, it has been greatly developed. From the "Land System of the Heavenly Dynasty" to the land reform of the People's Republic, from the election of local officials to the people's democratic dictatorship . . . from the demand for political and economic equality to the realization of this equality, from the naive, anti-feudal civilization to a national and scientific "people's new, democratic civilization"—in every respect, the achievements of the new democratic revolution have far surpassed those of the Taiping revolution. And yet, if we look on the Taiping as the vanguard in our own struggle, they deserve to be everlastingly remembered by the Chinese people for the first impulse they provided.[79]

The varying judgments about the Taiping by historians and politicians not merely reflect fundamentally different orientations on their part, but inconsistencies in the movement itself. Actually, it was both an end and a beginning, Janus-faced, it looked in both directions. No ideology is better suited to serve the researcher as a point of departure for an investigation of countless earlier, religio-political popular uprisings, since so many old ideas, present only in shadowy outline in traditional historical accounts, came together here. This applies especially to eschatological and messianic ideas including their non-Christian components, which can nowhere be traced more clearly. But there is also no ideology which better shows how western beliefs, once adopted, are refracted in the new medium of Chinese spirituality and take on a surprisingly changed coloration. The Taiping rebellion was drowned in blood. Yet Hung Hsiu-ch'üan had been right when he had promised that peals of thunder would usher in a new age for China, an age where the sun would no longer rise in the East, but the West.

2 / *THE VISION OF THE "GREAT EQUALITY"*

THE "REFORMATION" OF CONFUCIANISM

Both spiritually and politically, the Taiping rebellion brought such a fundamentally changed climate that all modern historians of China have tacitly agreed to date the start of modern Chinese history from this extraordinary event. The unrest, however, had revealed symptoms of decay in a Confucianism that had been undermined in the course of the centuries, all outward signs of respect notwithstanding. After the fighting, and even while the rebellion was being crushed, the loyalist forces therefore tended at first to address themselves to this problem, for it was on a Confucian foundation that they proposed to prop up the tottering Manchu throne. But this attempted restoration, which became known as the T'ung-chih reform[80] (reign name *T'ung-chih,* "Return to Order") proved abortive. It did show, however, that its initiator, Tseng Kuo-fan (1811–1872)[81], a man who united the roles of politician, military leader and poet in his person in characteristically Chinese fashion, was perfectly aware that no problems had been solved by the successful repression of the uprising, which was largely his work. In a sense, the problems had just begun. The revival of the dynasty, the "second-half recovery" as the Chinese term *Chung-hsing*—derived from a number of historical precedents—may perhaps be freely translated, was doomed from the very beginning, and that for the simple reason that genuine historical precedents for the situation in which China suddenly found itself did not exist. Oddly enough, and to the extent that they were honestly convinced of its eternal modernity, the adherents of Confucianism saw this almost more clearly than its opponents. With some semblance of reason, Hung Hsiu-ch'üan could still be viewed as a figure in that long sequence of religious rebels that had time and again and for almost two thousand years created difficulties for Chinese authorities. But after the T'ung-chih restoration miscarried toward the end of the nineteenth century, no one could find the precursors of those new prophets of Confucianism who believed they were uncovering its oldest and most authentic layers but actually, if unintentionally, dealt it its death blow.[82] Their ideas of Confucianism and the character of Chinese spirituality were too deeply influenced by western thought. Even when they proclaimed it as their goal to save the real, Confucian "essence" *(t'i)* of China by the adoption of merely formal "applications" *(yung)*[83] borrowed from the West, particularly technology, their systems of thought tended to reflect the reverse: they were not Confucian values in western guise, but western ideas in Confucian garb, and these western ideas were frequently misunderstood and distorted. The many blends of European/American and Chinese ideas, their combination in ever new, not infrequently bizarre configurations ranging from naiveté to human wisdom, admiration to skepticism, resignation to hope, constitute the particular attractiveness of the intellectual history of this half century from about 1885 to 1935. An abrupt, hectic development gave the young and the youngest their opportunity, not without occasionally outdating them during their own lifetime.[84]

Of all the western theories that flooded China during this period, evolutionism and its variants was undoubtedly the most influential: Thomas H. Huxley's *Evolution and Ethics* was translated in 1896 by Yen Fu (1835–1921),[85] who had acquired considerable prestige through his early translations of scientific works. A short time after its appearance, it became "bedside reading for every student" (Hu Shih).[86] This is also true of the Chinese edition of Herbert Spencer's *Study of Sociology,*[87] which came out seven years later. Darwin's works (and the writings of E. H. Haeckel) were not translated until relatively late[88] by the scholar Ma Chün-wu (1881–1940), who had received his education in Germany and Japan. Yet he became even better known than Huxley or Spencer, and this was due to his fundamental idea of the development of species through the survival of the fittest. Social Darwinism was easily comprehensible in its popularized version, and its mixture of a belief in progress, realism and brutality seemed to characterize most adequately the invaders from the West and the gradually increasing danger they posed. It also revealed the key to their power, and ultimately to the methods that might be used to combat it. Obviously, strength was never static, but always dynamic, and the strong individual was not the only one to participate in whatever developments might occur, and thus conquer the future. The mere belief in progress, the orientation toward the future, seemed to confer strength. Even before they became fully conscious of these connections through their reading of western literature, Chinese intellectuals had begun to have an inkling of them. To the degree they wished to remain loyal to their culture—and this was the case for most of them in the early phase—they began to search for equivalents in their own intellectual tradition and were delighted when they discovered the New Text School of religious Confucianism which, having been forgotten for a thousand years, had timidly begun to resurface in the eighteenth century.[89] Here they thought they could find the same dynamic element which had given the West its material superiority. Beyond that, the school seemed to have the advantage of that familiar "humanity" western systems lacked. This fusion of Chinese and western evolutionary ideas now gave birth to the most comprehensive plan for an ideal social system ever to have been produced in China. It did not restrict itself to a single country but attempted to take in the entire world, indeed it even went beyond the world known to us and therefore cannot really be called utopian, for utopias are places for which there is actually no room anywhere.

The author of this bold, colossal painting, this futuristic project, was K'ang Yu-wei (1858–1927),[90] one of the most fascinating and influential figures on the borderline between the old and the new China. Something abrupt, discontinuous marks his career which bisected the no less abrupt path of modern Chinese intellectual history like a diagonal running in the opposite direction, for it was peripheral and ahead of its time in the beginning, and peripheral and outdated at its end. In his autobiography, K'ang writes that he startled his teachers between his twelfth and sixteenth year by rejecting the traditional "eight-legged" essayistic style.[91] As a result, he repeatedly failed examinations. But at the same time, he devoured all books he could lay his hands on, particularly those that gave him some insight into conditions in Europe and America. At the age of twenty-one, he passed through a Buddhist phase, withdrawing to the countryside to meditate. But already a few years later, he took up the study of political and social problems and founded an Anti-foot-binding Society. His scientific career culminated in the late eighties and early nineties. Working furiously, and assisted by a large number of disciples, he attempted at that time to reinterpret Confucianism or to reconstruct it, as he thought. The rediscovered teaching of the New Text School had stirred him as it had no one else. From the few texts he still recognized as authentic, there arose a purified Confucius, a revolutionary and messiah who yet bore certain unmistakably European traits. The step from revolutionizing Confucianism to confucianizing revolution in evidence in K'ang's *Confucius as a Reformer*[92] soon had direct political consequences: the radical westernizing reforms proposed by him and his followers were favorably received by the young emperor Kuang-hsü and led to the well-known Hundred Days' Reform in 1898. But they also brought an immediate reaction from the conservatives. The emperor was interned by the empress dowager and K'ang had to flee to Hong Kong. From there, he attempted to further organize resistance, but failed to regain real political influence. The revolution of 1911, which cost the Manchus the throne, not only took place without him, it actually was a blow to his position. For at variance with his own ideals, he had remained a monarchist and even openly advocated the restoration of the Ch'ing dynasty in 1916. When he died in 1927 at the age of seventy, he had long since become detached from his own time and the world surrounding him.

K'ang Yu-wei's intensive study of the previously mentioned chapter of the ritual classic *Li-chi*,[93] which discusses the progression of society in three steps from "disorder" through "approaching peace" to the "Great Equality" provided the point of departure for his vision of a future, blissful world society. As early as 1884/1885, he wrote a commentary on this chapter *(Li-yün-chu)* where he attempted to give greater precision to the vague description in the text of the era of "Great Equality":

> What does [the reference to] the "Great Way" mean [which supposedly will obtain during the period of "Great Equality"]? It means that the principle of humanity *(jen-li)* [will be permeated] by the highest public spirit *(kung)* [during this era]. The "Great Way" is the way of the "Great Equality" during the era of "Highest Peace" *(t'ai-p'ing).* Compared to this, the splendor of the Three Dynasties [Hsia, Shang and Chou] merely represents the way of the "Small Peace" in a time of "Approaching Peace" *(sheng-p'ing).* . . . [Once] the world [follows] public spirit, the wisest and most capable will be selected to administer the world. Ha, the world and the nation will be things which the human beings of the world and the nation will call their own, for they will not be things owned privately by a single individual or family. Then, the united masses will elect the wisest and most capable and confer offices on them, and no longer permit that these men pass their offices on to their children, grandchildren and brothers. . . . All men will turn over those means of production and the labor [ordinarily] required for the maintenance of their family to common production, and see to it that the old are taken care of, the young raised, the poor dealt with charitably and the sick healed. Since thus only the strong will have to work, men will no longer know the suffering of aging, sickness, loneliness and poverty, customs will become more beautiful, the races will improve, and progress rise to ever higher spheres. . . . Boundaries set by morality will be recognized as limits: although men are stronger, they will know the limits of their power and not be allowed to exceed them. Independence will be inviolate. Although women are weaker, they will make their own, completely autonomous decisions and their suppression will not be permitted. Both sexes will freely conclude their marriage contracts and observe them jointly. . . . When both "ruler" and "state" will have been abolished, all men will be obliged to obtain their sustenance from what is publicly owned and no longer rely on their private property. In consequence, even people with a great deal of private property will divide it and transfer it to public property. Once private property has become useless, why should anyone continue to employ force and deception and thus infringe on honesty and justice? Why should anyone become a robber or rebel and thus ruin himself and his name? When such evil individuals disappear, so will the evil thoughts that go along with such acts. Inside and outside will be the same, a boundary between them will no longer exist. For that reason, the outer gates will no longer be locked, weapons and arms will be unknown. Such is the way of the "Great Equality," which will obtain in the era of "Highest Peace." Men will form a community, they will be peaceful and therefore able to realize the "Great Equality" through their common effort.[94]

This commentary is still quite traditional. At most, there are hints of western ideas (as in the sentence about "progress to ever higher spheres"), but such influence cannot be proven. During the very years he wrote this commentary, however, K'ang also completed the rough draft of a book which he first entitled *Universal Principles of Mankind (Jen-lei kung-li)* and reworked in 1887. According to a statement by his disciple Liang Ch'i-ch'ao,[95] he finished this text in 1902, three years after his political fiasco, in Darjeeling, the extraordinarily beautiful summer residence of the English governor of Bengal, and entitled it the *Book of Great Equality (Ta-t'ung shu).* This work, which appeared in excerpts in 1913 and 1929, but whose complete version was unfortunately not published until 1935 (the late date of publication makes it impossible to determine what changes were made in the 1902 manuscript, if any)[96] contains the quintessence of K'ang's plans for a reordering of the world. Apparently he believed that the less well known they were beforehand, the greater would be their chances for realization. For although much of what he had dreamed had already become reality at the time of his death, he felt that the world was "not yet mature enough" for his thoughts, and therefore resisted both publication and translation into English, although this was reportedly suggested to him not only by the German-American sinologist Friedrich Hirth (1845–1927), but even by the American president Wilson.[97] And yet it is a distinguishing characteristic of the book that it differs from so many other utopias by not situating the ideal world in a historical and geographic vacuum, and by also supplementing its description by detailing the various, necessary transitional stages leading on from the present. Thus the *Book of Great Equality* contains not merely an account calling for implementation, but also a program of action which rests at all points on the previously mentioned, basic model setting forth a society developing in three phases.

The first edition of this rather voluminous work comprises over 450 printed pages of Chinese, which would probably correspond to twice that number in an integral translation into a European language. Its first chapter sets forth the suffering of the world as it is. Its diction has an unmistakably Buddhist coloration, but this is quite superficial because where Buddhism infers from its premise that suffering should lead to the rejection of life and the world, K'ang executes a courageous, unmistakably Confucian counter-maneuver: however magical other heavens may be—and these are heavens he believed to have seen on other stars, as we shall note—he nonetheless committed himself to this vale of misery here below. Like the Bodhisattva, he considered it his duty to improve it.[98] Conscientiously, he divides suffering on earth into thirty-eight types under six main categories: 1) those given with life itself; 2) those caused by natural calamities; 3) those caused by accidents of human life; 4) those imposed by governments; 5) those springing from human feelings; 6) sufferings arising from those things men most esteem. His analysis of these categories results in findings totally different from those of the Buddhists. For him, it is not the wheel of life which causes human suffering, even though the first place on his list is given over to the unhappiness caused by life itself. Rather, it is the labyrinth of the diverse limitations which always and everywhere confine and restrict man:

> As we look at the miseries of life, [we see that] the sources of all suffering lie only in nine boundaries. What are the nine boundaries? The first is called nation-boundaries: [this is] division by territorial frontiers and by tribes. The second is called class-boundaries: [this is] division by noble and base, by pure and impure. The

> third is called race-boundaries: [this is] division by yellow, white, brown and black. The fourth is called sex—(literally "form") boundaries: [this is] the private relationship between father and son, husband and wife, elder and younger brother. The sixth is called occupation-boundaries: [this is] the private ownership of agriculture, industry and commerce. The seventh is called disorder-boundaries: [this is] the existence of unequal, nonuniform dissimilar and unjust laws *(pu p'ing, pu t'ung, pu t'ung, pu kung).* The eighth is called kind-boundaries: this is the existence of a separation between man, and the birds, beasts, insects and fish. The ninth is called suffering-boundaries: [this means] by suffering, giving rise to suffering. The perpetuation [of suffering] is inexhaustible and endless—beyond conception.[99]

This insight becomes the basic pattern of the book. For the nine sections which follow the introductory one deal consecutively (and in spite of some awkward insertions and repetitions from other chapters which merely show that the manuscript had proliferated when it was finally printed) with the elimination of these boundaries which obstruct the all-comprehending "Great Equality." This organization already proves the unlimited optimism behind the book. Mere elimination is to automatically assure a happy world. The order in which the "nine boundaries" are treated is certainly planned, for it indicates the program, the schedule of salvation. This does not mean that one boundary must first be totally eliminated before the next can be tackled, but rather that their gradual elimination will overlap in the various phases, and must be undertaken in this order. This is the reason the demand for the elimination of the first boundaries, those of the state, the privileges of the nobility, racial differences and privileges of property still corresponds to ideals which had generally begun to become reality while K'ang was still living. Liberation is thus already under way, and this could hardly be otherwise in view of K'ang's belief that it would be a long drawnout process as postulated in the ritual classic. In the establishment of the League of Nations, for example, K'ang already saw the first signs of the world state propagated by him. But the elimination of the final boundaries, those between man and animal, for example, or the boundary of suffering between life and death, is lost in distant, truly utopian perspectives still shrouded in mystical darkness even for K'ang himself.

THE WORLD STATE

In view of what may be called a dynamic account of an ideal world where development is treated in three, occasionally overlapping phases according to the ancient pattern of "disorder," "small (or 'approaching') peace" and "Great Equality" (or "Highest Peace"),[100] and which includes a discussion of the ever-present dangers that may threaten them even after their realization, thus causing a relapse into the earlier corruption, it is not altogether easy to sketch an entirely clear, consistent picture of K'ang Yu-wei's realm of "Great Equality." This dynamism contrasts startlingly with so many other utopias which are really much more "genuine" because situated in a lifeless sphere beyond time and space, and it is that quality which endows K'ang's conception with a particular vividness and realism. In his view, the initial step toward overcoming the first boundary, that of the sovereign state, lies in disarmament and the outlawing of war. Here, he did not need the example of western pacifist movements, but could simply go back to the teachings of the ancient philosopher Mo Ti. It was no mere accident that these had been rediscovered during the second half of the Manchu dynasty, for they had always been closely associated with socialist trends (and in no small measure with the idea of the "Great Equality" itself). A table with three columns appended to K'ang's book[101] to clearly show the developmental stages here as in all other spheres indicates that the armed forces and weapons are first to be limited quantitatively, then internationalized, and finally abolished altogether. During the transitional period, and as in a sports arena, the only kinds of combat permitted would be those where "the adversaries can at most injure each other, and take each other prisoner, but would not be allowed to kill each other."[102] The internationalization of the armed forces would in turn prepare the progressive unification of states, which would ultimately be followed by the creation of the world state, facilitated by the prior institutionalization of cooperation in one partial sphere. K'ang apparently believed he had discovered a law of history according to which there existed a tendency toward the formation of ever larger political units, and which he seems to have understood as an exemplification of Darwinian theory:

> Russia has embraced Albania; France has taken Annam and Tunisia; England has swallowed Burma; Japan has joined Kaoli (Korea) and the Liu Ch'ius to itself; all Africa has now been carved up like a melon. . . . The parts becoming joined thus being due to natural selection, the swallowing up by the strong and large and the extermination of the weak and small may then be considered to presage the era of "Great Unity." But [the way in which] Germany and America have established large states [through uniting their small] federated states is a better method of uniting states. [They have] caused all these small and weak states to forget that they have been destroyed [to form a united state]. Some day America will take in [all the states of] the American continent, and Germany will take in all the [states of] Europe. This will hasten the world along the road of the "Great Equality."[103]

Thus the political unification of the world occurs with the inevitability of a natural law. After a certain time, which K'ang calculated to be "about 100 years,"[104] a penultimate stage would be reached where all the "weak and small states will have been destroyed." For this period, K'ang planned to divide the world into "ten continents," *(shih chou),* a concept which had been used since the first century A.D. to designate the areas where both mortals and immortals reside within the "Four Oceans."[105] They would consist of Europe, East Asia, the South Sea, Northern Asia (Siberia), Western Asia (central Asia and India), South America, North America, Central America, Australia and Africa. But these units would only be ephemeral. After the complete unification of the world, a purely mathematical division would be substituted which would leave no room for nationalist egoisms and thus correspond most adequately to the principle of "Great Equality." After the earth has been divided into one hundred degrees of longitude and one hundred degrees of latitude, only the ten thousand fields making up this network will be used to designate countries, as in the case where the place of birth of a person is indicated.[106] Yet these fields *(tu)* do not serve well as administrative units, and that for two reasons. They refer to large areas that are ocean. Also, and this is more problematical, they are not of equal size, for while they all have the same length (approximately four hundred kilometers), their width is identical only near the equator where they are all nearly square. But toward the poles, they become increasingly narrow and turn into cone-shaped strips. Nonetheless, K'ang involved himself in a rather complex calculation of these longitudinal and latitudinal grade regions *(tu-chieh)* which come to constitute the various continents if one degree is assigned the length of four hundred Chinese miles (obviously taken as a median, one Chinese mile = 0.575 k.m., i.e. approximately 230 kilometers). Somewhat offhandedly, K'ang equated this with one hundred English miles (one English mile = 1,609 meters, i.e. ca. 1.61 k.m.), and thus obtained his basic unit. Having found the area of the individual continents in western sources, he then divided it by the area of the grade regions. In a somewhat confused calculation that is also marred by misprints, K'ang arrives at a total of 5,238 grade regions (this addition is wrong; actually, it should be 5,158), distributed over the continents of Asia (1,700), Europe (370), North America (860), South America (650), Africa (1,155) and Australia (423).[107]

The nominal length of these degrees (it is fixed for the degrees of longitude) also furnishes the basis of a uniform, global system of measures: each degree (*tu*, about 400 k.m.) will be divided into 10 *fen* (about 40 k.m.); 100 *li* (about 4 k.m.); 1,000 *liang* (about 400 m.); 10,000 *yin* (about 40 m.); 100,000 *chang* (about 4 m.); 1,000,000 *ch'ih* (about 40 cm.); and 10,000,000 *ts'un* (about 4 cm.).[108] All other units of measurement are to be aligned correspondingly, including money, which will also be based on the decimal system. Standardized measurements had always had a strongly emotional, almost magical value since Ch'in Shih Huang-ti had attempted to document the unification of the empire by introducing them.[109] But a worldwide system of measuring time was an even more important proposal. The calendar year was to be solar, and even in China only a few celebrations from the lunar calendar were to be retained during a transitional period. Finally, time would be counted from the year during which the world state of "Great Equality" would be established, so that all previous dates such as those used by Christians would be expressed in the form "in such and such a year before. . . ."[110] K'ang did not believe that this "year zero" necessarily had to lie in the future since the worldwide desire to abolish war already represented a first step toward a world state. He proposed 1900, the year following the first Hague Conference, as the starting point for counting years during the era of "Great Equality." This year also seemed particularly appropriate to him because the cyclical signs *keng-tzu,* which are assigned to it according to the old Chinese cyclical calculation, are phonetically close to the expression "changed beginning" *(keng-shih)* which he thought of as a kind of new reign title.[111]

K'ang also gave much thought to a uniform world language. In part, this may have been due to the invention of Esperanto in 1887. It was certainly no accident that that language of hope found a surprising echo in China.[112] Like many of his contemporaries, K'ang was grieved because his own country was divided by dialects and only held together precariously by the tie of a common written language that was independent of sound, and had been recommended by Leibniz as the universal language of scholars for that very reason. He criticized national languages for compelling people to waste many years learning them, and even more because they kept alive nationalist sentiments. He therefore proposed that a world language be learned in addition to the mother tongue during the transitional period,[113] while the final phase would see the exclusive use of a universal spoken and written language, to be created after careful scientific studies:

> Spoken and written language should be the same for the whole world. It will not be permitted to have different words and writing. As a means of studying the languages of each locality, a "global ten thousand sounds room" should be constructed. [That is,] a one-hundred-*chang* room will be constructed, round in shape to simulate the earth, and suspended in the air. For every ten *chang,* natives of that part of the earth will be summoned, several per degree. Where there are linguistic differences they will be summoned; where there are no differences, one person will suffice. Having brought together [representatives of] the peoples of the whole world, whether civilized or uncivilized, we will [then] have philosophers who understand music and language join together to study their [languages]. [These philosophers] will select what is the lightest, clearest, roundest, and easiest for the tongue, as the sounds of the new world language. [They] will also select from the world's high and low, clear and turbid sounds those which are most easily understood, and form an alphabet from them. For all material things [names] will be written according to the division and union of their original constituents. For immaterial things the easiest among the old names [used by] the world's nations will be selected. If the Chinese [language] were to be adopted, with the addition of an alphabet, to form the [new world] language, the energy expended would be slight, and much would be gained. [For,] calculating the easiness of languages, China has one term for one thing, one character for one term, and one sound for one character. India and Europe have several terms for one thing, several "characters" for one term, and several sounds for one "character." Therefore, in simplicity of language China exceeds India, Europe and America by several times. . . . However, the vowels of French and Italian are clearest, being quite like the Peking [dialect] but surpassing it. Now when we wish to construct the sounds of the [new world] language we must take those which are purest and most elevated, which are suitable to singing and harmonizing, which are sufficiently beautiful and clear to gratify the soul. Generally

speaking, if most of the sounds of the [new] alphabet are widely taken from the languages prevailing between the fortieth and fiftieth degrees, then they will be most pure and elevated. If we adopt the Chinese terms for things, but give the sounds by means of an alphabet, and write them with a new simple script, then [the new world language] will be extremely simple and fast. . . . The system of the [new] language having been decided upon, if we make up books and send them to the schools, then after several decades the whole world will use the new language. As for the old languages of the various nations, they will be preserved in museums, where they can serve in the researches of antiquarians."[114]

A single language is also a presupposition for the effective functioning of the new world government, elected by representatives of the grade regions who make up the only lower administrative unit, and thus correspond roughly to what are counties today. To avoid the possibility of a cult of personality, the office of prime minister is intentionally omitted. While there will be no world president, provision is made for a number of ministries, namely 1) the ministry of the people (in charge of all public institutions); 2) the ministry of agriculture; 3) the ministry of pasture; 4) the ministry of fisheries; 5) the ministry of mines; 6) the ministry of industry; 7) the ministry of commerce; 8) the ministry of finance; 9) the ministry of development; 10) the ministry of waters (rivers and waterways); 11) the ministry of railroads; 12) the ministry of the post; 13) the ministry of electrical communications; 14) the ministry of ships; 15) the ministry of air; 16) the ministry of health; 17) the ministry of letters; 18) the ministry of encouraging knowledge; 19) the ministry of teaching the way; and 20) the ministry of "Utmost Happiness" (promotion of the arts, museums, etc.). These ministries are supplemented by four conferences *(yüan)* in the public government: 1) conference Yüan meetings of appropriate ministries to confer on particular topics which may arise in connection with the government and its business; 2) Upper House of Parliament composed of one representative elected from each degree area. This body "will deliberate on the world laws and official regulations" and will also control the 3) Lower House of Parliament (merely a recording and communicating office, without representatives); 4) public information Yüan (collects and disseminates information from and to the degree governments and the public government). The governmental apparatus of the degree governments has an analogous organization. There are the same four yüan, except that the Upper House is composed of the most distinguished elders. The ministries 2, 3 and 4 are here subsumed under the Board of Agriculture, and the ministries 11, 12, 13, 14 and 15 are consolidated in a Board of Communication (roads, ships, railroads).[115]

Under such a government, which may make important decisions only after worldwide telephonic consultation of the people, life will be happy. From the very beginning, cities will be built only on the most salubrious sites, primarily islands and mountains. Farmers will no longer live in small villages but in gigantic farming centers. Since transport will be excellent, daily travel to their fields will be no problem. The farming centers will spontaneously become focal points of cultural life. The farm director is elected, and he and his employees will form a kind of local government and be generally in charge of things. In the cities, factories with their directors and administrative staffs will have a function similar to that of the farms in the countryside.[116] Together they are the basic units of the world state. These units or cells are curiously reminiscent of the economic cells in Ho Hsiu's ideal state[117] but also of the "People's Communes" which became a reality in China half a century after K'ang Yu-wei's vision.

THE END OF CLASS, RACE AND FAMILY

K'ang believed that overcoming the boundary of class, the second boundary interposed between man and the blissful condition of "Great Unity," was even more within reach than world government, for he thought that it had already been largely accomplished in one country on earth, the United States. Like Hung Hsiu-ch'üan, he harbored a silent admiration for this nation, which he took to be a symbol not only of the "new" itself, but of the peaceful cooperation of all peoples enjoying equal rights. The American example therefore forms an integral part of his argument for a classless society, and he does not fail to mention its wealth, which seems to form such a gratifyingly just contrast to India and its caste system:

> The coming to birth of all men proceeds from Heaven. All are brothers. [All] are truly equal. How can [men] falsely be divided [according] to standing in society, and be weighed [in the balance] and cast out? Moreover, speaking of it according to the general trend of affairs, wherever there is much class gradation and men are not equal, the people will inevitably be ignorant and miserable, the state will inevitably be weak and disorderly, as India is. Wherever class gradations have been completely swept away and men are equal, the people will inevitably be intelligent and happy, the state will inevitably be prosperous and orderly, as America is. . . . How great is the significance of equality! Hence it is that Confucius, in regard to the world *(t'ien-hsia),* did not speak of governing *(chih),* but spoke of equality *(p'ing)*[118] and in the *Spring and Autumn Annals* [in discussing] the progress of the Three Eras *(san-shih),*[119] he particularly spoke of it in terms of "increasing equality" *(sheng-p'ing)* and "Great Equality" (and thus at the same time of "Highest Peace" *(t'ai-p'ing).*"[120]

In that chapter of his book where he deals with the elimination of a class society, K'ang Yu-wei introduces the subject by mentioning slaves, the lowly masses, and women as the three major underprivileged classes. But he only discusses slaves (and pariahs) in detail because the other two groups are treated separately in his description of the elimination of the family and of racial differences. In his rather startling proposals for setting aside the boundary of race, the third boundary he argues against, K'ang reveals himself as a racist who seeks to conform to the principle of "unity" by attempting to *make* the races equal instead of merely recognizing their equality in their diversity. In the world of "Great Equality" he seems to consider the continued existence of different races as *a priori* unacceptable: "If we wish to join mankind in equality and unity we must begin by making the appearance and bodily characteristics of mankind alike."[121] What he is thinking of, however, is not the uniform mixing of all races but the assimilation and absorption of the "lower" races by the supposedly "higher" ones. His suggestion that "languages between the 40th and 50th degree of latitude," have a particular value, supported in another passage by the belief that all beings give forth lovelier sounds the "higher up" they live (such as birds, for example), an observation equally applicable to those populations living in the "high" degrees of latitude (i.e. more or less in the north) already indicate K'ang's preference for the nordic races, a taste which has a disquieting overtone in our time. And this is all the more surprising since it obliges him to grant the highest place in his hierarchy to the white rather than the yellow race. Although he assumes elsewhere that the two, most noble races, the white *and* the yellow, will continue to coexist, the aim of his eugenics is thus actually the creation of a uniform, white world population. Such an objective poses difficult problems for him:

> At present there are in the world the white race, the yellow race, the brown race, and the black race. Their surface colors are completely different, and their spiritual constitutions are very dissimilar. How can they be smelted? The silver-colored race is spread out over the globe, while the gold-colored race is still more numerous. These two kinds—the yellow and the white—have occupied the whole world. The strength of the white race is assuredly superior, while the yellow race is more numerous and also wiser. But it is an indestructible principle that when [two kinds] join in union they are smelted. I have seen my countrymen who have been a long time in England or Australia and sometimes those living in this country who have skillfully selected their food and drink. . . . When they came back, their faces were as if dyed a deep red, like the Europeans . . . suppose that in addition there were two or three generations of interracial propagation, a certain amount of moving of southerners to the north, and a removing of mountain people to the littoral. Within a hundred years the people of the yellow race all would gradually become white, and in addition these races would have been able naturally to join and smelt. Therefore, before the world of "Great Equality" has been perfected, the yellow people will already have changed completely into white people. . . . Only the two races, brown and black, being so distant in color from the white people, will be really difficult to amalgamate.[122]

In order to accomplish this last, uncommonly difficult though necessary task, K'ang lists a number of methods which, although more intensively carried through, are yet the same he proposed using in the amalgamation of the white and the yellow races, except that here the desired result would require considerably more time. First, there would be the resettlement of the dark peoples in the cooler regions of Canada, Scandinavia, northern Russia and southern South

America.[123] Secondly, relations between dark-skinned and light-skinned peoples would be encouraged and made more attractive by conferring honorary titles on the participants ("persons of humanity," *jen-jen*[124]). Thirdly, by selecting certain foods for dark-skinned people which ordinarily are eaten only by the white-skinned,[125] K'ang hoped that the brown races could be made white within two or three centuries, while the amalgamation of the black would require approximately twice that time, another example of the three-phase process by which the world would be transformed.[126]

The various compulsory, somewhat macabre measures (not quoted here) K'ang intended to impose on all mankind to achieve racial uniformity reflect the very effective methods of traditional Chinese colonialism, which enabled the Chinese to constantly expand their originally tiny territory in the north in the course of their history, predominantly in a southern direction. Since this is a historical fact, it is impossible to understand why it is so often maintained that China never was expansionist or colonialist. This process was regularly accompanied by the disappearance of the dark-skinned indigenous population. It is therefore no accident that K'ang introduces his plan for the amalgamation of the races by a description of this ouster and absorption of the indigenous population of southern China and compares it with the similar fate of the American Indians and the Australian and Polynesian aborigines, and discusses these events in a Darwinist context.[127]

In his view, these occurrences anticipate the proposed merger of the races. The difference between his racism (and Chinese colonialism) and comparable western conceptions is the tendency to promote rather than to avoid the mixing of the supposedly "higher" and "lower" races, and this is undoubtedly based on confidence in the numerical superiority of the Chinese. He expressly rejects the argument that such a mixing of the races might slow down the transformation of the world population into a uniformly white race, or even have the opposite result. The sense of biological inferiority which ultimately underlies the belief in segregation is wholly alien, indeed barely comprehensible to him. Because of this, K'ang's racism takes on a somewhat more humane aspect, the shocking prejudice in his characterization of the black race notwithstanding. Curiously enough, it would seem that what is offensive in racism (and this is equally true of European, but not of Russian, colonialism, which was always inevitably carried on by a minority living far from home) is not so much the parading of a sense of superiority, but rather the insistence on separation. China's oppressive embrace of its weaker neighbors and tribute-paying enemies of non-Chinese stock over the course of millennia was certainly no less deadly than the heartless separation of the races which, as history proves with such terrible clarity, can easily become the preliminary stage of an equally coldblooded extermination of the weaker. But there was at least the gesture of love which perhaps kept alive the illusion of the dying that they were the partners of the overwhelmingly strong. In any event, the desire to create a uniform white race derived from K'ang Yu-wei's sincere conviction that there was no other way of bringing about equality among men:

> That mankind should be equal *(p'ing-teng),* that mankind should be completely unified in the world of "Great Equality" and "Highest Peace" is of course a universal principle. But the inequality of creatures is a fact. Whenever we speak of equality it is necessary that creatures have the capacity to be equal in abilities, knowledge, appearance and bodily characteristics before equality can be effected. If not, then even though it be enforced by state laws, constrained by a ruler's power, and led by universal principles, it still cannot be effected. . . . Thus, with the noble intention of liberating the black slaves, Lincoln [activated] hosts of troops and shed blood to bring this about; and yet to this day the people of America do not admit to the equality of Negroes. They do not permit Negroes to eat with them or to sit with them; they do not permit Negroes to enter first class on ships and trains; they do not permit Negroes to enter hotels . . . because their appearance and color are dissimilar, they are still kept down. . . . If we wish to join mankind in equality and unity, we must begin by [making] the appearance and bodily characteristics of mankind alike. If appearance and bodily characteristics are not alike, then manners and occupations and love cannot of course be the same.[128]

But if in K'ang's opinion the liberation of the enslaved "lower" classes thus ultimately consists in their unavoidable, planned abolition, he becomes a considerably less prejudiced advocate of the realization of natural equality in the liberation of the third underprivileged class, women. In the introduction to the chapter of his book which deals with the "fourth boundary" between men, that of "form," i.e. sex, he writes: "I now have a thing to do: to cry out the natural grievances of the incalculable numbers of women of the past. I now have a great wish: to save the eight hundred million women of my own time from drowning in the sea of suffering. I now have a great desire: to bring the incalculable, inconceivable numbers of women of the future the happiness of equality, complete unity, and independence."[129]

In considerable detail, he relates the suffering of women in the past and present, which seems all the more unjust as the growth of culture is principally due to women who in primitive times, when men were hunting in the wilderness, had the occasion to stay at home and to lay the bases for technological, artistic and philosophical thought and development.[130] We can observe a clearly Taoist, anti-Confucian aspect in K'ang Yu-wei as he elaborates this idea and discusses the relationship between politically weak dynasties (such as the Liu-ch'ao period [220–589]) and concurrent cultural achievements, or those between the Confucian glorification of "loyalty" and the enslavement of women as "chaste widows" or ineffectual "virtuous wives."[131] Not only in China, but everywhere in the world, women lost their freedom under the pressure of a patriarchal society; they were not permitted to marry freely, were kept like prisoners or slaves, subjected to physical punishment such as the binding of feet or the piercing of ears or nose, looked on as useful animals or toys, as the private property of men, and systematically excluded from all education. Here also, K'ang believed that three phases would be required to abolish these injustices which imposed unlimited punishment on women for a "negligible physical difference" *(hsing-t'i shao i).*[132] First, retaliatory repression would be abolished, then there would be social advance, and finally the recognition of women's equality as a matter of course. The situation of women in the coming era of "Great Equality" is sketched in a number of theses. The most important among them sets forth a program which was revolutionary for the China of that time:

> We should first establish girls' schools whose organization will be just the same as boys' schools. Girls graduating from colleges and professional schools will receive degrees. . . . Having completed their studies, they may by election or examination become officials or teachers. . . . In the eyes of the law, women must be permitted the status of independent persons. . . . The European and American custom of taking the husband's surname will be entirely prohibited and changed. . . . In getting married, women will be entirely independent, and will themselves choose their mates. . . . Countries should establish the office of marriage agent, selecting those who are talented and advanced in years to fill it. These persons will at the same time serve as teachers. . . . Early marriages of those who have not yet come of age should be entirely prohibited. . . . Women will be entirely independent in . . . social intercourse. . . . We would strictly forbid the old customs of binding the feet, compressing the waist, piercing the ears, nose and lips to hang ornaments, and of veiling the face and covering the body with a long cloth. . . . Such customs as baring the shoulders and unclothing the body, and dancing with men in the western style are barbarous, and arouse lewd thoughts. . . . Clothing and ornaments should be the same for women and men. . . . When human morality has reached the perfection it will attain in One World, there will be few distinctions which would give rise to barriers between human beings. . . . Regulations should be made for the clothing of men and women to be uniformly the same. In the Era of Complete Peace-and-Equality, all persons will be independent and free: clothing that is unusual will be permitted unless harmful to the public weal, and in everything people may do as they will. Men and women may dress in any way, even in the old style if they wish. However, in public meetings, when formal dress is worn, men and women will all adopt the same style, and may not wear different colors, in order to revert to complete unity. There being no distinctions of form or color, there will of course be no difference in their manner of behavior. . . . All marriages of men and women will be by the personal choice of the parties. Their affections and will in this matter being mutual, they will then form an alliance. [This alliance] will be called an "intimate relations contract" *(chia-hao chih yo).* We will not have the old terms of husband and wife. For, since men and women will be entirely equal and independent, their love contracts will be like treaties of peace between two states. . . . Alliances of men and women should have a time-limit, and may not be life contracts. For all whom we call humans necessarily have natures which are unlike . . . those who are in love never have exactly identical principles in their natures or never have exactly identical ideas or ideals, and it is easy for them to come to consider each other as perverse and peculiar. Therefore, no matter who they are, people can merely vow to be united, but find it very difficult to hold to their union for long. If they are compelled to it, there will inevitably be quarrelling between

> them. They may see each other but not speak; or they may live apart to the end of their lives; or they may hate each other and get divorced, or they may secretly scheme to poison each other. . . . And how can we take the constrained union for life, and thereby [create] suffering and difficulties for human nature? Thus, to compel union is also immoral. If there actually are [couples whose] unions are eternally happy, naturally they will be permitted to renew their contracts repeatedly and cleave to each other till the end of their lives. But [all unions] must be because of the human feelings, and in accordance with [the principle of] freedom. Therefore we cannot but fix a time-limit to the contracts, to enable [the parties] easily to honor them. Then, if they have new loves, it will not be hard to wait for a little while. . . . The length of the marriage period may not exceed one year, and at the shortest it must be one full month. . . . Women who have not gone to school and completed their education . . . cannot be independent. Those who must look to their husbands for support cannot utilize this right of independence. . . . [But even if a woman] is fully prepared in the qualifications of a public citizen, then it is still human nature that she should temporarily be dependent on her husband and receive his support. Now, if we bring about that women seek to gain the rights of independence, to increase their sphere of responsibilities, and to incline toward studies, then human abilities will increase daily.[133]

Of course, the radical liberation of women proclaimed here by K'ang Yu-wei becomes possible only if there is a correspondingly radical modification of the traditional, strictly patriarchal Chinese family. K'ang is therefore consistent when he follows up on his proposals concerning the abolition of the sex boundary by a large chapter which discusses the abolition of the "fifth boundary," the boundary of the family. In a very detailed introduction, he inquires into the role the family played in China as opposed to the West (of which he seems to know only the Anglo-Saxon or, more correctly, the American form). The careful argumentation in this chapter suggests that he took this matter to be the core of his reform. He wants to show that he does not hesitate to renounce all sentimentality, although it is not without a secret regret that he proceeds to demolish this citadel of Chinese society. He appreciates the fact that it is only through a clan system based on Confucian family ethics that China has become the most populous land on earth[134] and reproaches western children for their offensive ingratitude toward their parents, an attitude he takes to be precisely the result of the more emancipated position of women, of the preference accorded the wife over the parents.[135] He believes nonetheless that the small western family has already progressed much further along the road toward "Great Equality" than the large Chinese one because the degree of personal "egoism" *(ssu)* is necessarily a function of family size. Of course, the family as such—and this includes the western type—must be dissolved before the world of "Great Equality" can be established. The fourteen, partly overlapping charges K'ang raises against the family at the close of his introduction can be subsumed under three headings: 1) children born and raised in a family do not have the same opportunities in a purely physical sense because due to lack of control and regulation, both hereditary factors and feeding and care in individual families differ unjustly; 2) this also applies to intellectual development, for among families of greater means it is longer and more intensive than among poorer ones. School attendance plus education in the home can only be a transitional stage in what is here also a three-phase process leading from the "family school" (customary in China for thousands of years) to the future "total school" to be attended by all children from the first to the twentieth year; 3) family selfishness makes it impossible for the state to dispose freely over work force and personal property, and thereby also prevents their use in public projects (road construction, etc.) and those social tasks previously carried on by families (schools, homes for the aged, etc.). But thinking in terms of the family also prevents the growth of a sense of shared responsibility without which the world order of the "Great Equality" cannot be realized.[136] Quite deliberately, K'ang Yu-wei contrasts his own idea with the venerable Neo-Confucian text *The Great Learning (Ta-hsüeh)*[137] which set forth that peace in the world could only be established through the "ordering of the family." Here are some of his statements directed against the family:

> To have the family and yet to wish to reach Complete Peace-and-Equality is to be afloat on a blocked-up stream, in a sealed-off harbor, and yet to wish to reach the open waterway. To wish to attain Complete Peace-and-Equality and yet to have the family is like carrying earth to dredge a stream, or adding wood to put out a fire: the more done, the more the hindrance. Thus, if we wish to attain the beauty of complete equality, independence, and the perfection of [human] nature, it can [be done] only by abolishing the state, only by abolishing the family.[138]

Accordingly, all those tasks previously carried on by the family will be transferred to public institutions for which K'ang worked out a clear plan. From the cradle to the grave, indeed almost beyond it, man was to be subject to the shaping or helping power of the world state which would thus assure eternal equality. Of the twelve institutions available for this purpose, three were to serve nurture, four education, and five the support of the citizens:

> The first is called the human roots institution *(jen-pen yüan)*. All women after becoming pregnant will enter it. Because it is the institution which from the root beginnings of human beings gives education in the womb, I wish to call it the human roots institution. . . . The second is called the public infant-rearing institution *(yü-ying-yüan)*. After a woman has given birth, the infant will be transferred to the infant-rearing institution to be cared for. It will not be necessary for the mother to take care of it. The third is called the public nursery *(huai-yu yüan)*. All babies after the age of three years will be transferred to this institution to be cared for. It will not be necessary for the parents to take care of them. The fourth is called the public primary school *(meng-hsüeh yüan)*. All children after the age of six will enter this institution to be educated. The fifth is called the public elementary school *(hsiao-hsüeh yüan)*. All children from the age of ten to the age of fourteen will be in this institution to be educated. The sixth is called the public middle school *(chung-hsüeh yüan)*. All persons from the age of fifteen to the age of seventeen will

be in this institution to be educated. The seventh is called the public college *(ta-hsüeh yüan).* All persons from the age of eighteen to the age of twenty will be in this institution to be educated. The eighth is called the public hospital *(i-chi yüan).* All persons who are ill will enter this institution. The ninth is called the public institution for the aged *(yang-lao-yüan).* All persons after the age of sixty who are not able to support themselves will enter this institution. The tenth is called the public institution for the poor *(hsü-p'in yüan).* All persons who are poor and have no one on whom to depend will enter this institution. The eleventh is called the public sanatorium *(yang-ping yüan).* All persons with incapacitating ailments will enter this institution. The twelfth is called the public crematorium *(hua-jen yüan).* All persons who have died will enter this institution.[139]

All the public institutions listed in this organizational outline are discussed by K'ang in separate sections, and in some detail. His ideas are naturally most interesting where this description of projected institutions does not derive from eastern or western models of any kind, and where he can therefore give his imagination free rein. The human roots institution is an example. K'ang justifies it in part by reference to instructions on prenatal care found in the old Confucian *Book of Rites (Li-chi),* although these were intended only for the families of princes.[140] Most of the relevant rules have a rather familiar ring. As everywhere else, they are a compound of the requirements of hygiene and superstition. In addition to constant medical supervision, there are the light, cheerful rooms, the exceptionally friendly nurses, choice food, beautiful books and pictures, and edifying music, which is meant to impart a harmonious rhythm to the mother's movements (which can be controlled by girdle ornaments she will wear) and have a beneficial effect on the embryo. To help maintain this harmony, K'ang also pondered regulations governing the mother's sexual activity. Prior to the birth of the child, she may have relations with only one man. Afterwards, during the short period she has to remain in the prenatal home to suckle the child, hygienic reasons may even dictate the substitution of a mechanical man *(chi-ch'i chih nan*[141].) While K'ang did not believe that the difficulties of giving birth would be eliminated by such procedures, he hoped that they might be mitigated some what. Other measures included the rigorous punishment of abortion (one of the few crimes whose spontaneous disappearance he did not feel he could predict), and the introduction of a precisely ordered sequence of honorary titles ("mother" *mu*) and medals for mothers with more than one child.[142] But he thought that the most important feature of the human roots institution would be its influence in shaping the desired uniform race. These institutions were to be located primarily on mountains, in a favorable climate and attractive landscape. They were to be also, and indeed especially, open to the "lower" races to speed up the process by which they would approach the light ones. K'ang felt that the prospects for this were all the more promising because the newborn did not return home with the mother but would spend the first few years of their lives in infant-rearing institutions located in equally favorable climates. This method would also assure that lower-class status could not be passed on. Because surnames were to be abolished with the dissolution of the family, all children would be given only individual personal names which would make it possible to determine the room in which they were born, the human roots institution, the degree region and the date of birth, but not the origin and status of the parents according to a system not explained in detail.

EDUCATION, NURTURE AND PUNISHMENT

The education of the new man in the world of "Great Equality" from kindergarten to college graduation is characterized in K'ang Yu-wei's plans not so much by unusual institutions but rather by the fact that it is universal.[143] In the two lowest grades, up to the eleventh year, the teachers are exclusively women because they are "more patient, more tender, friendlier, and more harmonious." It is only in the two higher grades, between the fifteenth and the twentieth year, that male teachers assume a more prominent role. This is paralleled by the course of education itself. Consisting primarily of physical exercises in kindergarten, it gradually and increasingly concentrates on mastering intellectual tasks involving progressive specialization during the last four or five years. For "in the epoch of 'Great Equality' there will no longer exist any activity for which there is no specialist, and no person who has not enjoyed specialized training."[144] But the unity of theory and practice must never be lost; theoretical study must find its application in the real world. Generally speaking, schools on the upper levels resemble officers' training schools. They house between ten to forty or fifty thousand uniformed students. Under teachers who function like generals and officers, they are subject to a drill "as strict as that in any army."[145]

A similar conception of surprising, nearly calvinist rigor, possibly due to contact with Christian missionaries (the identification of "poor" and "bad" has no other parallel in Chinese social philosophy) is also reflected in the plan for the institutions for the poor which in a sense constitute the continuation or repetition of the period of education for all the weaklings and incompetents of society. According to K'ang's description, they are really nothing other than "workhouses." Just as "shaming the student" *(k'uei-ch'ih)* is mentioned as an effective (and as the only) punishment in the educational process, so those "who are not employed in what they have been trained for and also cannot find employment in more lowly work" are threatened "with the disgrace of the institutions for the poor where they must work hard to earn their support and can no longer consider themselves the equals of the rest of mankind."[146] Those who are sent to these institutions more than once must wear special, "disgraceful" clothing—a rule distantly reminiscent of the old Confucian description of past golden ages when the "marks on clothing constituted the only punishment."[147] The longer and the more frequent the periods for which someone is returned to an institution for the poor, the harder the labor imposed on him. Because the world state of "Great Equality" frees man from existential anxieties, K'ang saw one of the few serious threats in a paralyzing indolence that might spread to ever larger segments of the population.

The other, genuinely social institutions such as hospitals, homes for the aged and sanatoria are open to all at no charge, although they are expensive to equip and maintain. They are the central points for the delivery of medical care to the entire society. Because a daily (!) check-up is mandatory and may have a variety of consequences, physicians occupy a key role. They decide such important matters as the assignment of the incurably ill to island sanatoria, measures for the implementation of generally practiced eugenics (here again there are artificial men to provide sexual outlets for persons with serious hereditary flaws).[148] In hopeless cases, they even decide whether euthanasia "by electricity" may be called for.[149] The homes for the aged are remarkably luxurious. Even in the lowest class, designed for those who cannot show that they have ever contributed to the public welfare, a two-room apartment with a public bath and appropriate services is provided. Those in the middle class (no details are given for the highest class) already have six-room houses. The Confucian element still noticeable here is totally absent from the plans for the crematoria. What remains in these institutions for the disposal of the dead of the complicated mourning ritual Confucianism had established as a kind of extension of piety beyond the grave is only a carefully worked out set of mourning procedures. Normally, the dead are cremated because—apart from practical considerations—"it is more beautiful because in this way the body returns to Heaven."[150] Burial and gravestones with plaques whose size varies with the merit of the individual are reserved for eminent personalities. Generally speaking, both mourning and disposal of the dead should be brief so as to disturb as little as possible the happiness that prevails in the world of "Great Equality." What remains should not be the grief but the edifying recollection of a fulfilled life. The crematoria therefore have an additional function which can only be explained by the tradition of the old Chinese historiographers. They not only dispose of the dead but also compose their biographies and thus record their acts for posterity.

In K'ang's view, the substitution of the world state for the family is also the presupposition for overcoming the sixth boundary between mankind and happiness, the "boundary of livelihood." By this concept, he refers quite generally to the class structure of society and its economic basis. Although the repeatedly mentioned Chinese writer Liang Ch'i-ch'ao, a disciple of K'ang, assures us that the chapter of the *Book of Great Equality* dealing with this question was not written under direct western influence, there are some passages which make it clear that K'ang had some knowledge, however sketchy, of Marxist thought (Socrates and Marx are the only western philosophers mentioned by him by name). The chapter contains such matters as an account of social development in industrial society where "the rich become richer, the poor poorer,"[151] and a warning against the premature introduction of communism, which should not precede the abolition of individual states and families: "For enabling the farmers to obtain equality in subsistence, we may perhaps advocate the methods of communism. But if we have the family, if we have the state, selfishness is then extreme. . . . With such a polity, to hope to carry out communism is like 'wishing to go southwards by turning the shaft northwards.' Not to mention that it could not be carried out during the French Revolution, even America up to the present has likewise been completely unable to carry it out."[152]

Yet his program comprises the same goals as the Communist Manifesto although it is much more detailed and differs significantly by its commitment to spontaneous change rather than world revolution.[153] In the world of "Great Equality," all land, all industry, all banks and commercial enterprises are to become public property. The gradual shift from agricultural to industrial production would correspond to the emergence of an age of "refinement" and the gradual recession of one of "simplicity"[154] as Tung Chung-shu had once described it in his theory of the two-phase cycle.[155] Because certain groups would no longer enjoy economic prerogatives, class distinctions would fade away, and with the disappearance of the private ownership of capital and property exploitation would finally losc its base.

In elaborating these ideas, K'ang again encounters the difficult problem he had previously alluded to in his discussion of the public institution for the poor, and that is human indolence. It is true that there is a passage in his book where he passionately argues against those "who hate the calm of unity and exalt the hurly-burly of competition." He reproaches them for believing that "with competition there is progress, without strife there is retrogression," and says that "those who advocate the theory of competition understand nature but do not understand man."[156] But he can advance no valid counterarguments, and fifty pages further on he himself asks how, in the age of "Great Equality," "where everything will proceed from the public government, if there is no competition, how there can be improvement, how there can be progress? Assuredly, if we sit idly by and permit this deterioration, the damage thereby wrought will also be severe."[157] The remedy K'ang proposes to deal with this implicit danger is again taken from the age-old repertory of honoring or shaming individuals, a technique which had always been preferred by Confucianism, which was unfavorably disposed to punishment as a matter of principle. He therefore devises a complicated system of honorary titles, prizes and decorations intended to sustain the striving for wisdom *(chih)* and love of man *(jen).* Since there is also a hierarchy of elected officials,[158] it does not escape K'ang that all the honors and offices with their accompanying material advantages contain the danger of once again creating a class society. It is particularly from the medical profession that he fears such a development. Since it practices the love of mankind and is therefore most highly respected, the world of "Great Equality" is molded by it to such an extent that it might, in K'ang's words, also be called the "Medical World" *(i shih-chieh).* With some trepidation, he considers the possibility of a "physicians' religion" or a "physicians' party," which would thrust the world just saved back into the stage of confusion—an idea which loses some of its apparent absurdity and even becomes recognizable as disguised polemics when one considers that Sun Yat-sen, the "Father of the Chinese Republic,"[159] a man for whom K'ang had as little sympathy during the last years of his life as he did for the republic itself, began his career as a physician and continued to practice that profession occasionally at a later time. It would be no less threatening, in K'ang's view, if a widely honored "man of wisdom" were to turn into a great religious leader. Only the most careful selection of both living and historical personalities as recipients of honors and respect seems to offer some protection against such dangers (among historical personalities, he called Lao-tzu, Luther and Columbus exemplary, while he considered the "warrior" Bismarck a "bandit").

But the seventh, the "boundary of administrative boundaries," he expected to be an even more effective defense. Reference here is to the unjust laws of his time. In the section devoted to this subject, K'ang maintains first that most laws are either superfluous *a priori* or would become so after the realization of "Great Equality." Among those he considers as having always been unnecessary, he mentions all punishment for sexual offenses. After demonstrating with some irony that strict observance of the countless sexual sanctions imposed by religion would long since have caused man to die out, he demands absolute sexual freedom, including homosexuality, for all adults. While he does make an exception for sodomy, he considers this a perversion resulting wholly from excessive repression.[160] As regards criminal acts of a non-sexual nature, K'ang believes that they will almost entirely disappear at the same moment as the state, the family, class and property. He also thinks that less significant misdemeanors such as negligence in office, impoliteness and rumor-mongering can be eliminated by patient education: "Therefore, in the Age of Complete Peace-and-Equality, there will be no litigation. In the Age of One World, punishments will be discarded. For every one will act as a scholar and a gentleman without being controlled. There, in the Age of Complete Peace-and-Equality, punishments will not be established; there will exist only the rules and regulations of the various official positions and jobs. Though there be negligence of duty and breaking of the regulations, they will not involve punishments under criminal law."[161]

Yet the world of "Great Equality" is not entirely without its order. Just as Han Kao-tsu, the first emperor of the Han dynasty, replaced the catalogue of draconian punishments by three simple prohibitions (against murder, bodily injury and robbery) after his victory over the Legalist Ch'in dynasty in 209 B.C.—an act which was experienced as salvation from utter chaos—K'ang also establishes four fundamental prohibitions which are to remain in force as the only laws after the destruction of all law books, and which he had already briefly sketched out in earlier sections of his book. They forbid 1) laziness; 2) the cult of personality; 3) competition; and 4) abortion. Regarding this last matter, he simply refers to his comments in the section "Human Roots Institutions," and only adds to earlier remarks on laziness in the chapter on institutions for the poor by stating that the obligation to work should also be extended to Buddhist monks and pious hermits. They will be permitted to flee the world only at age forty when they have repaid the twenty years of public nurture by twenty years of work, since "one cannot flee away into the midst of heaven-and-earth,"[162] a rather interesting rejection of the Taoist ideal life. But in advancing his reasons for the third prohibition, he once again deals intensively with the problem of competition. While valid in nature, competition has no value in civilization:

> . . . Darwin propounded the theory of evolution, considering that what is caused by nature *(t'ien)* is [therefore] right. [This] leads men to believe that competition is the great principle [of life]. Whereupon competition—which is the greatest evil to the public existing in the world, past or present—is carried on every day and month; and eminent men all pay their respects to it without shame. With this, the earth becomes a jungle, and all is "blood and iron."[163] . . . Now natural evolution is a thing [which proceeds] without cognition. Human principles are things in which cognition is inherent. The way whereby we can unite men into a group, whereby we [can] completely pacify-and-equalize [them], is to take the basically loving nature [of individual men] and to extend it [to all men]. Thereby we shall "fulfill the Way of Heaven," cooperate with Nature (literally, the Heaven-suited), "abide in perfection," and attain ultimately to One World. Then will the multitudes find their happiness and profit. Should we follow the example of natural evolution, then among all mankind throughout the world the strong will oppress the weak, mutually gobbling each other up, and wars will occur daily, like fighting among quail. But in the end, there will remain only the strongest individual, and then he will simply end up by being eaten by the birds and beasts. . . . Why should we return to the times of Chuang Tzu and Lao Tzu! In the age of "Great Equality," there will be no different kinds [of men], no different states; all will be of the same bodily type, [all] will be compatriots. Competition is inevitable among differing kinds and differing states; [but] among [those of] the same bodily type and [those who are] compatriots it is very injurious. Why should we again sow this evil seed and scatter it throughout the world![164]

In overcoming or, perhaps better, in overcoming and perfecting an iron, natural law that existed before man but can only be transcended by him, and which shows its most unmerciful aspect in the "survival of the fittest," K'ang Yu-wei sees the salvation of the world, not in its dull acceptance. In back of the argument quoted here, and of many other similar passages in the book, there is the lurking fear that even after the realization of the world of "Great Equality," human society, having ascended to unheard-of heights of civilization, may yet relapse through inaction or, conversely, perish by remorseless competition. Thus an already forgotten jungle would return to the regions of a fragile civilization.

But the most serious offense, more than the others a kind of sin against the Holy Ghost of "Great Equality" is the cult of personality (*tu-tsun,* literally "exclusive worship"). Other regulations notwithstanding, it may even be punished by incarceration. K'ang expresses himself clearly on this:

> In the Age of Complete Peace-and-Equality, everyone will be equal. . . . It will be what Confucius described as "seeing a flight of dragons without a leader."[165] . . . For if we were once to have an emperor or ruler, then [we should have] inequality, then would arise quarreling and killing, and we should revert to the Age of Disorder. . . . But if some leaders are idolized, inequalities will gradually return, they will develop into autocratic institutions and slowly lead to strife and murder, until the world relapses into the state of disorder. For that reason, everyone who leads large masses of people and is excessively idolized by them must be vigorously opposed, however enlightened or holy he may be, irrespective of his office or profession, and even if it is the leader of a party. For if someone wishes to become emperor, king, prince or leader in such a time, he sins against the principle of equality and becomes guilty of the most serious breach of morals. For these worst of all crimes, the public council should incarcerate him.[166]

K'ang is not certain, however, if his prohibition can permanently forestall this imminent danger. He paints a gloomy, melancholy picture of the prospects of the world of "Great Equality" should a "great physician" or "great ideological leader" *(ta chiao chu)* assume leadership of the world: "From being a great religious leader, [a man might] become the great emperor of the globe. In this [way] we should have Ch'in Shih Huang-ti[167] all over again with the [consequent] curbing of [human] rights, the use of force, the burning of books, and the burying [alive] of scholars so as to make ignorant the people. Then, [from] the pole of Complete Peace-and-Equality we should return to [the opposite pole of] Disorder. Such a disaster defies description."[168]

WEIGHTLESSNESS AND THE VOYAGE TO THE STARS

Up to this section dealing with the problems of the "seventh boundary," K'ang's book certainly cannot be called utopian. Not only does it claim to discuss probable events, it also talks about specific times and places. The allusion to Ch'in Shih Huang-ti in the last quotation shows that he was unconsciously thinking of China as the point of crystallization of the world of "Great Unity," and remained entirely within the tradition of the Han New Text School, which believed that Confucian culture would gradually and circumspectly move outward and spread over the entire world. But in his description of the overcoming of the eighth boundary, the boundary of "kind," he becomes truly utopian in the sense that he starts off by explaining that this goal, the preservation of the life of all creatures, can at best be approached but never wholly attained. The Buddhist influence in K'ang's thought is unmistakable here, of course, and yet even at this point his argument is predominantly Confucian. For him, love of animals and all living beings is merely an extension of love itself. In line with the earlier thought of Wang Shou-jen,[169] this love is seen to derive from love of kin *(ch'in ch'in)*. During a second stage, it is extended to all men *(jen min)*, and in a third to all living beings *(ai wu)*. It is an unfolding love of which K'ang says with inimitable Chinese sobriety that "it might not equal that of the Buddha, but it has the advantage of being practicable" because it also takes into account the temporal factor.[170] Thus the preservation of animal life is to be incorporated in the program only after all previously described boundaries have been eliminated, and even then this process is set forth in a succession of stages. He first wishes to protect the apes because they are closest to man. Cattle, horses, dogs and cats are next, then birds, and finally fishes and the rest of the "lower" life forms, while plants "which do not feel" are excluded. At the same time, "artificial meat" will be invented (a technique Buddhist monks in China had been working on successfully for centuries) so that the pleasures of meat consumption won't have to be foregone. K'ang never loses sight of the fact that in spite of all of these efforts, it will ultimately be impossible to protect all animal life. This insight compells him to write some sentences which may in a sense be considered programmatic for all "utopian" effort which never accepts compromise but time and again endeavors to realize a pure ideal consciously and fearlessly, although that endeavor is condemned to futility:

> Buddha said to abstain from killing; and yet he daily killed countless living [beings]. Buddha told Ananda to fetch water in his bowl. Ananda said that water contains microbes, [and so] we ought not to take and drink it. Buddha said that what we cannot see, we may drink . . . Buddha's reply was evasive. Or, even if we knew that Buddha did not drink water, yet he could not help but breathe air. When the air is exhaled and inhaled, then living [beings] are killed. Since I cannot retire out of the atmosphere and not inhale them, then how can I be *jen* to living creatures and not kill them? *Jen! Jen!* We shall never be able to perfect [it]. Thus [it was that] Confucius said: "The superior man stays far away from the kitchen."[171] Life! Life! Eternally there must be killing. Therefore Buddha [limited the proscription against killing to exclude] invisible [creatures]. Alas, alas! The production of life is inexhaustible, the Way is likewise inexhaustible (i.e. imperfectible). However, [given] this imperfectibility, [we should] bring [the Way] to [the highest possible] perfection and perfect it.[172]

In the last chapter, K'ang first summarizes the development of human civilization and then goes on to a bold description of the blissful condition in the world of "Great Equality." The magic world of old accounts of paradise and the fantastic creations of a Jules Verne (who was being translated assiduously into Chinese at the time by Liang Ch'i-ch'ao, among others[173]) coalesce in the most curious configurations. Men will live in gigantic, publicly owned, very luxurious buildings. Equally splendid hotels with tens of thousands of rooms equipped with air conditioning, heating and masseurs are at their disposal. A great variety of vehicles make possible a busy, uninterrupted flow of traffic which is typical of the newly developing man whose mobility increases as he becomes more highly perfected and leaves behind his rooted, plant-like existence. In addition to huge automobiles, railroads and "movable houses" on land there will be gigantic, luxurious ships with gardens, while "flying ships" and "flying houses" sail through the air. In the beginning, the principal areas of settlement will still be located on mountain tops, but later they will float on water and finally there will only be airborne dwellings. All services will be performed by machines. Everything can be ordered by phone. Three-dimensional images will decorate the walls and wherever one walks or stands (even in washrooms and lavatories which K'ang believed were of considerable importance as areas of concentration), lovely music will be heard. As time goes on, food will increasingly consist of concentrates and will finally be taken in liquid form because it is healthy and gives long life. Often harmless drugs may be added, with an effect similar to that of hashish or wine. Clothing will be multi-colored and variegated but—except for badges of honor —it will not indicate differences in rank or sex. Everyone will bathe several times daily in scented waters and remove all body hair (a curious reversion to the "falling out of hair" among the Taoist immortals[174] and the shaving of hair among Buddhist monks). Due to the daily medical examination, diseases will disappear. Only injuries and the ailments of old age will require treatment, but soon men will attain an age of one hundred or two hundred, and later perhaps of more than a thousand years. The western religions, specifically Islam and Christianity, will have been forgotten. Islam primarily because of its strict social order, Christianity because its morality enjoins neighborly love and the renunciation of sin, things which will have become a matter of course. And the belief in God will have been replaced by belief in the laws of nature. The teachings of Confucius concerning the evolution of the "Three Ages" as laid down in the *Li-yün* chapter of the ritual classic will alone be valid, but even they will finally disappear when they have accomplished their pedagogic purpose.[175]

In these final sections of his work, K'ang Yu-wei shifts imperceptibly from the rather naive description of external conditions under the "Great Equality" to a new theme, the overcoming of the ninth and greatest barrier to happiness, the "boundary of suffering." This part includes the world view, the statement of beliefs of the New World. K'ang confines himself to a few sentences which do not describe but contain subtle hints. At the end, he refers to "a special book" he says he has written about this mystery. Yet it does become clear that he does not expect this new "non-religious religion" to come in a single birth but during an extended process again consisting of three phases. The first would include the revival of the old, Taoist immortality doctrines, beginning with the alchemical arts of Ko Hung and including the mysteries of the "detachment from the corpse,"[176] since here death itself is transcended. During the second phase, there will be a revaluation of Buddhist doctrines which not only overcome mortality but also man's confinement to earth. The highest spiritual step, however, will only be reached during the final phase:

For One World is the ultimate Law of this world, but the study of immortality, of longevity without death, is even an extension of the ultimate Law of this world. The study of Buddhahood, a state without birth or death, implies not merely a setting apart from the world, but an actual going out of this world; still more, it is a going out of One World. If we go this far, then we abandon the human sphere and enter the sphere of immortals and Buddhas. . . . Therefore after One World there will first be the study of Buddhahood. After the studies of immortality and Buddhahood will come the study of roaming the heavens *(t'ien-yu chih hsüeh).* I have another book on that subject.[177]

This "other book" about "roaming the heavens" is one of the most curious but also most moving mixtures of popular science and philosophical and religious thought. It is the desperate (if unconscious) attempt of a Confucian humanist to save man as the measure of all things in a world where scientific knowledge seems to discover him as an almost accidental being of only relative value, a nearly insignificant correlate of much more autonomous forces, one form among countless others. Actually, the book had already been conceived by K'ang Yu-wei in 1884/1885, when he was twenty-six. But it was not until 1924/1925, two years before his death, that he finished it under the title *Lectures on the Heavens (Chu-t'ien chiang).* It was a time when he had returned to the dreams of his youth.[178] The book betrays a multiplicity of influences. Buddhism, which also constitutes the prelude to the "roaming the heavens" plays as much of a role as the escapism which came to mark K'ang after his political failures. More important still was the study of astronomy to which he had been devoting himself intensively since about 1880, the experience of viewing the stars through a telescope a few years later, his study of Percival Lowell's (1855–1916) thesis of the possible existence of men on Mars, and perhaps the flight in a balloon over Paris in 1904.[179] In a poem he probably wrote immediately after this last event, all these intimately connected motifs are recognizable: "Many are lands of happiness in the heavens /What prosperity on the stars, each a world in itself! /Myriad eons have I passed in the heavens, /Hankering for nothing, bored by nothing, each moment at ease.// But my compassionate heart stirs and cannot be quieted;/ Into earth-prison again I enter, men to save./With deliberation I seek vexations and worries,/Unwilling an immortal in the heavens to be."//[180]

In addition to the Buddhist compassion with man that makes K'ang place the salvation of the world ahead of his own, there are unmistakable echoes of the age-old Shamanist songs of the *Elegies of Ch'u* (particularly in the bipartite form of the composition) where the experience of flying first became central and subsequently inspired the legendary heavenly voyage of the ousted minister Ch'ü Yüan and all his spiritual heirs and the later flights to paradise of the "immortals," who are also explicitly alluded to.[181] But the decisive step by which K'ang infuses a genuinely new element into a tradition that had always been religious and escapist is the startling introduction of the exact science of astronomy, which adds both a modern and a western component that meaningfully complements the wholly Chinese, religious tradition. While the Chinese spirit had always had the tendency to return to solid earth after the brief flights of the imagination into celestial and paradisiacal spaces, it once more gathered an astonishing momentum in K'ang's "roaming the heavens." Incredulous and embarrassed, the Chinese scholarly community, including his former disciples, took note of this curious doctrine which hardly seemed to fit into the twentieth century. And while the young K'ang had been acclaimed as the hero of the Hundred Days' Reform in 1898, and his *Book of "Great Equality"* enthusiastically received (including the small number of chapters that appeared before his death, the introductory one which mentions the voyage through the heavens and the visit to alien stars among them),[182] no one knew what to make of these ideas, although in 1926 K'ang founded an academy devoted to their propagation. It has only been during recent years that western and eastern scholars have become somewhat more aware of them.

It was probably his excessive religious commitment rather than the inadequacy of his scientific knowledge that militated against the success of K'ang's last project for saving the world. For actually he did not subordinate religion to science, but the reverse, even when he seriously maintained that "All founders of religion *(chiao-chu)* were born in ancient times when good telescopes were not available; all their dicta concerning the heavens are invariably erroneous";[183] indeed even when he predicted the dissolution of religion in science, in astronomy, before he had written his "Lectures":

> With the appearance of Copernicus we have come to the knowledge that the earth is but one of the sun's planets; the ancient doctrine of one heaven and one earth is shattered. . . . So numerous are the stars and so big are they that the earth-globe is [in comparison] exceedingly small. How much smaller [than the earth-globe] is one single country or family? . . . Therefore, once a person understands astronomy, all the religions love their meaning. Infinite power and endless joy pertain to complete enlightenment gained through scientific inquiry. . . . The grief and distress of a single family or a single man are no longer worthy of mentioning."[184]

In his "Lectures," however, the "Copernican turning point" becomes the direct basis for a gripping, thoroughly religious experience, namely the discovery of the earth itself as part of the countless heavens:

> In the struggle for existence the weak are the prey of the strong. Therefore founders of the various religions having piety on men and wishing to save them, feigned orders from Heaven and instructed men by means of the divine way—frightening them with hell, enticing them with the kingdom of heaven in which utmost joy prevails. . . . All these were calculated to soothe men's minds and save their souls . . . to remove their anxieties and afflictions, and to point to utmost joy as the final goal. But these do not constitute adequate solutions [of the problem: to apply them] is like carrying rice to treat the starved. . . . This is because these founders of religions did not know that our earth is a planet in the heavens and that we men

> are celestial beings. . . . Looking up at the stars in the Milky Way in the night, we see their glittering brightness; and looking up at Jupiter, Saturn, Mars, Venus, Mercury and the moon, we perceive their sparkling and limpid light. We say that they are in the heavens and admire them from below. . . . We should realize that inhabitants of the stars, looking up at our earth-planet, should see its shining beams, splendid and glorious . . . precisely like what the stars appear to men on earth. . . . Therefore [it is clear that] we men who are born on the earth-planet are at once inhabitants of a planet and denizens of the heavens . . . As soon as we perceive this fact . . . we shall be always happy and utterly joyful.[185]

But what "roaming the heavens" really meant, or how it might be possible to leave the earth behind remained K'ang's secret in spite of the fifteen voluminous notebooks that make up the *Lectures on the Heavens.* Reading the major part of the passages including those quoted here, one gets the impression that he had in mind spiritual voyages rather than real flights to the stars. And yet there are others where he meditates on the speed of light[186] and these seem to suggest that he also thought of real journeys to other planets. His imagination, in any event, rushed far ahead of all this. In one chapter of his book he enumerates 240 layers of Heaven which are ordered in certain groups though each of them individually consists of millions and billions of separate heavens.[187] In a veritable intoxication with numbers, the exorbitant Buddhist picture of the world and paradise returns to life and the shattering of all temporal and spatial limits is again experienced ecstatically as it had been once before, fifteen hundred years earlier, during the initial contact with Buddhism.[188] And this is not incomprehensible when one considers that over a period of hundreds of years, Neo-Confucianism had caused the world to shrink more and more. The nomenclature comes in part from Buddhist and Taoist sources, and in part from his own imagination, while the immensity of the figures derives perhaps from popular scientific treatises.[189] But although he seems to penetrate to ever more remote distances in his rushing flight, K'ang is quite restrained in the descriptions of his heavens and stars. It is not mere chance that the term "heavenly voyage" should make it quite apparent that "roaming the heavens" is the essence of the scientific religion discovered by him, and not the arrival in any determinate regions of happiness in the cosmos, however superior to earthly conceptions of happiness they might be.

K'ang Yu-wei thus emerges as one of those great figures of Chinese intellectual history who saw the ideal of the "voyage" *(yu)*[190] as an alternative to the earthbound rigidity of Confucianism. For it is a symbol of wholly unhampered movement (as of its secondary meaning of "swimming"); indeed, it is a symbol of freedom itself. It is only in this way that we can understand the previously mentioned, curious human settlements in the world of "Great Equality." Being first primarily "hotels," they gradually become "movable houses," "swimming cities," and find their ultimate perfection as "flying houses." They are nothing other than a new conception of the old Taoist dream of "wandering immortals" who only seem to be seeking paradise or heaven, for they have already found it within themselves, yet can sustain it there only as long as they remain unencumbered, unpredictable, free as they move along lonely mountain passes, in the hubbub of market places, or mysteriously emerge on lakes, on fabled islands in the oceans, or the red clouds of evening, and disappear just as mysteriously. An enigmatic "distance" surrounds them and makes them guests everywhere, not because their home is elsewhere but because they are at home only within themselves. The poems K'ang Yu-wei inserted in his *Lectures on the Heavens* and only read to a small group of faithful disciples in the "Academy for Celestial Peregrination" during the last two years of his life are entirely in the spirit of the Yu-hsien lyric poetry,[191] even though these flights through space no longer afford a view of the garden of the "Queen Mother of the West" or the paradise island P'eng-lai, but of the nebula in Andromeda:

> My thoughts are in the Extragalactic Heavens/where are found countless star clusters:/With green light or purple flames each glows and shines./Rolling clouds, glittering and scintillating, illuminate the Universe./ In our Heavens of the Silvery Stream are two hundred million Suns/Forming merely a part of the Starry Orbit./ One hundred sixty thousand heavens like those of the Silvery Stream,/Each a separate domain with its own tributaries./The two poles of our Silvery Stream are separated by a great distance./Each Cluster a Major Sun which begets small suns./Each constitutes a Heaven which whirls and revolves. . . . I admire Messier 51, with a diameter of three hundred thousand light years,/ which really is the Great Sun that begets great suns./The ancestor of our Sun does not rule these Extragalactic Heavens,/Azure and boundless./ I look up and sigh, hoping to roam with the Immortals.[192]

3 / *THE CONFUSION OF IDEALS*

UTOPIAS IN THE CONFLICT BETWEEN EAST AND WEST

The philosopher K'ang Yu-wei has been called the "most important thinker of the closing years of the Manchu dynasty,"[193] and he was unquestionably the most powerful figure in the complex history of "utopian" thought in China. As through a burning glass, the refulgence of old Chinese social and religious ideals is brought together in his personality and, curiously refracted in the medium of a new, scientific spirit, it continues to radiate with undiminished force into the present. It is true that during the course of his life, K'ang detached himself more and more from his time, from political reality at first, and finally from the world itself. It is equally certain that he was felt to be increasingly outdated for that reason, that his visions seemed to suffer from a touch of that sentimentality which so frequently afflicts secularized fairy tales. But standing at a critical juncture between the old and the new, his influence on the shape of all modern Chinese conceptions of the ideal will become apparent to anyone, once he has studied his writings. That this influence usually tends to be hushed up is partly due to K'ang's defense of the monarchy (which actually merely proves that he was a Confucian "loyalist" and failed to live up to his own ideals, preoccupied as he was with his brief political activity). A second reason is the occasionally somewhat naive presentation of his ideas. Yet this innocence and the unshakable, very Chinese optimism that accompanies it show an astonishing inner strength, a quality that also contributes to the fascination of contemporary Chinese thought. An ingenuous attitude toward the problems of our world that do not reveal their full complexity at first glance may testify to a complete lack of wisdom. It may also be wisdom's highest perfection. One cannot help wondering if K'ang's lyrical teaching, the "roaming the Heavens," may not experience a revival in Chinese literature, should that country some day take an even more active part in the conquest of space than it has heretofore.

But K'ang Yu-wei was not the only Chinese philosopher who attempted to describe and thus shape the future early in this century. It was a hectic atmosphere where ever new branches of science and learning proliferated and even amateurs had a share in giving it its specific physiognomy. During the mid-twenties, for example, the pedagogue, politician and journalist Liu Jen-hang ("Liu Yeng-hong") (born ca. 1885),[194] who never became known in the West and has even been wholly forgotten in the East, worked out a plan to save the world which is quite similar to K'ang Yu-wei's. Being considerably younger, it was not a generation, but an entire age that separated him from the latter. Like many intellectuals of his time, he studied in Japan (along with the United States the Mecca of all Chinese revolutionaries and modernists) and therefore knew not only English but Japanese as well. A great deal of western literature which had not yet reached China (and part of which has not even reached it today)[195] had already been translated into that language at the time. Unlike K'ang, who knew no foreign languages, and was still a Confucian humanist and did his thinking within the intellectual context of monarchism, Liu was already a child of a new era. For after several unsuccessful attempts, the Manchu dynasty had been driven from the throne in 1911 and replaced by the republic. Nonetheless, power soon fell into the hands of influential provincial generals, warlords, who plunged China into an extended civil war that only ended with Chiang Kai-shek's victory in 1927. This turbulent epoch was really anachronistic in the sense that it once again repeated the age-old pattern where a warlike interlude between two dynasties divided the country. It was during this time that Liu Jen-hang lived and worked. Since 1924, he had been editor-in-chief of the *China Daily News* in Shanghai, had written a book about *Zen and Health (Ch'an yü k'ang-chien)* and translated an American treatise on yoga. He then wrote his principal work, the *Preliminary Studies Concerning the Great Equality of the East (Tung-fang ta t'ung hsüeh-an).*

The date of publication, 1926, is noteworthy because it predates by nine years the publication of the integral text of K'ang's *Book of Great Equality.* Since even without Liang Ch'i-ch'ao's testimony it would be improbable that K'ang made additions to his manuscript one year before his death by using material from Liu's book, the similarities between the two works suggest that a good deal of the content of the *Book of Great Equality,* including its unpublished parts, must have been known to the Chinese intelligentsia.[196] There had been a general upsurge of interest in utopian ideas, as we can see from the prospectus of the publishing house (which had the appealing name "Heaven of Joy" *Lo-t'ien shu-kuan)* that brought out Liu's book. It contains, among other items, a west-east collection of poems on utopias, two books about Kropotkin, and one on Socrates. This rather revealing grouping also indicates that during the twenties many more western "utopian" works were known in China than had been the case around the turn of the century when K'ang was working on his book. The somewhat feverish climate at the time brought it about that after the unexpected irruption of western technology, which seemed to make possible from one day to the next what had seemed impossible for as long as man could remember, the West (and to an extent Japan as well) was looked on as an inexhaustible source of utopias that had become reality. Feelings that were partly mystical and religious, partly socialist and revolutionary were being awakened. There was a sense of both excitement and uplift. In any event, Liu Jen-hang already listed a number of books written in English or translated into Japanese in his bibliography, from Plato's *Republic* and Thomas More's *Utopia* down to various works by Nietzsche, Kropotkin, Russell and the *History of Utopian Thought* by J.O. Hertzler[197]. This more extensive knowledge also enabled him to present at one point in his book a classification of Utopianism based on content and chronology where he used the following categories: 1) fantasy *(shen-hua):* Buddhist and Christian paradises, Saint-Simon, Tolstoi; 2) mysticism *(hsüan-hsiang):* Lao-tzu, Chuang-tzu, Lieh-tzu, Ch'ü Yüan, Indian mystics, Zeno and the stoics; 3) life in nature *(li-shih,* actually "effort and eating"): legendary Chinese hermits of anarchist stamp, School of Agriculture, T'ao Ch'ien, Yen Yüan; 4) socialist innovation *(she-hui chu-i hsin-kuo chia):* Confucius, Mencius; 5) socialist innovation with emphasis on equality of the sexes *(nan-nü p'ing-ch'üan hsin-kuo chia):* Socrates, Plato, More, Francis Bacon *(New Atlantis),* Thomas Campanella *(Civitas solis),* James Harrington *(Oceana);* 6) more recent utopianism *(chin-shih wu-t'o-pang):* Morelly, F.N. Babeuf, Saint-Simon, Ch. Fourier, E. Cabet, L. Blanc, R. Owen; 7) modern utopianism *(hsin wu-t'o-pang):* E. Bellamy *(Looking Backward),* Th. Hertzka *(Reise nach Freiland),* H.G. Wells *(Modern Utopia).*[198]

Liu was certainly influenced in some measure by the western authors he listed, though he probably had not read most of them but knew them only from Hertzler's study. But he was not primarily concerned with writing a compendium of all existing conceptions of an ideal world, but rather with a compendium of all systems *appropriate to the East.* The very title of his book suggests this, although he hints that these systems might also be suitable for the West. Allegedly, it was in part the mystical appearance of a man in a dream who addressed him with an enigmatic sentence that was difficult to decode and similar in that respect to the children's rhymes[199] that led him to develop a program combining three world views: the Chinese, consisting of Confucian, Taoist, hedonist and Mohist components; the Buddhist; and the Christian. This also entailed the division of the book into six sections and, to a large extent, determined its content. For even more than K'ang Yu-wei, Liu refuses to develop his doctrine in a vacuum, but rather first analyzes these three already existing world views for their "utopian" substance in order then to test their chances for implementation by utilizing a variety of reports about modern developments he received as a scholar and journalist. Because of this procedure, the book turned into a somewhat confusing yet fascinating grab bag of all kinds of information. Its central, most important and coherent section is the "Six Principles of the Doctrine of the New Great Equality" *(Hsin ta-t'ung hsüeh liu kang).*[200] (Judging by an incidental comment made by Liu, this part also appeared separately.) For it was Liu's opinion that the three existing world views had only seen one aspect of the future paradise of "Great Equality" and that it was therefore only through a combination of their separate doctrines that its real nature would become recognizable in its entirety. One of the many tables, as frequent here as in K'ang's book, and which indicate the constantly reappearing preference of the Chinese for clear classification, juxtaposes the contrasting characteristics of the "New" and the "Old Great Unity":

OLD RETROGRESSION	NEW PROGRESS
Primitive communism; emphasis on the spiritual	The world as understood by natural science and emphasis on the material
Propagation of a return to the old	Propagation of progress
Emphasis on the simple, deprecation of everything technological	Respect for the technological and art
Emphasis on a natural morality, trend toward a community of all living creatures (animals)	Emphasis on a new social morality, but also trend toward a community of all living creatures
Nations separated according to those living in the colder and those living in tropical zones	Unified ideal state of the future
Lao-tzu, Chuang-tzu, Christ and Tolstoi highly esteemed	The publication of the thoughts of Kropotkin, William Morris *(The Earthly Paradise),* Russell and others[201]

It is Liu's view that the "New Great Equality" can no more be attained without intermediate steps than the "Old" as outlined in the ritual classic, and on which K'ang Yu-wei had claimed to have based himself. Liu identifies six phases, six "worlds," which will succeed each other over an extended duration, but the length of the individual periods is not specified. Gradually, mankind is to be led into a supernatural land of happiness that will take in the entire universe:

> 1. The world of creatures and things: through the most intensive application of scientific [knowledge], new beings and things will be discovered [with whose help] people will vie with each other in their efforts to subject the world of nature, on land, on the sea, and in the air. 2. The world of the new human race: the science of eugenics will be used to bring together the finest and most handsome men and women. The good will be selected, the bad rejected. 3. The world of feminine culture: the patriarchal order will be suppressed; instead, a new matriarchal culture will be built. Only then will we be in a position to radically exterminate the [human] desire to kill. 4. The world of the arts: the arts will be promoted extensively in order to create a world of beauty and [thereby such] a degree of joy that the earth will become a heavenly place. 5. The world of contact with beings and things in the

heavens: through scientific [knowledge], communication with all stars and planets will be established. This will be an experience like the discovery of America. 6. The world of the practical, personal experience of [Taoist] immortality *(hsien)* and of Buddhahood: people will truly and directly enter the world of the immortals and Buddhas. All people will become immortals and Buddhas and enter into communication with all the ten directions of Heaven throughout the universe.[202]

Although this plan is undeniably similar to K'ang Yu-wei's, it contains certain elements which go beyond K'ang's conception or, at least, add precision to it. Communication with other stars, for example, is no longer something between reality and imagination, but expressly characterized as a success due to natural science. The role of women also differs somewhat. Instead of equality, we encounter a new matriarchy on the threshold to paradise, by which mankind recovers its origins, as it were. It is to the justification of this matriarchy that Liu devotes considerable attention in that part of the book which follows the explanatory outline quoted above. He apparently saw this phase of the redemption of mankind as his most original discovery. Even the explanations concerning the "new mankind"[203] refer almost exclusively to it. Yet the bureaucratic and remorseless notions of a kind of human genetics which even countenances euthanasia would seem to contradict the freedom of life in a matriarchal society. Liu, an enthusiastic proponent of group marriage and free love (it is women who freely choose their partners) believed that the genetic improvement of mankind would occur more or less automatically in a matriarchal order. Plato, Darwin, Nietzsche and Haeckel are all quoted as champion advocates, and fragments from their teaching form a curious whole as he advances his reasons for this belief. Generally speaking, it is obvious that Liu's thought is much more occidental than K'ang's, although it had been his intent to set forth a primarily "eastern" path toward the attainment of happiness. The plan of his book obliges him to discuss the various old utopias, paradises and conceptions of the ideal of the East in some detail, yet his "new" world of "Great Equality" is really much more strongly influenced by western than by eastern thought, as his table shows. To simplify somewhat, one might say that everything that is new in his work is also western. Liu himself was perfectly aware of this correspondence. He therefore juxtaposed the contrasting qualities and ideals of China and the West in a special table. This listing is important because it assembles all those clichés about the differences between eastern and western culture that had crystallized in the course of time in both China and America. It is significant also because this rigid juxtaposition seems to reduce Asiatic and Chinese conceptions of the ideal (and, analogously, western conceptions) to a profile which is largely determined by its correlate. In other words, a genuine realization of the entire sphere of the ideal by China or the East alone turns out to be no longer imaginable, given the bipartition of Liu's system (just as this is equally true of the West taken by itself). True salvation can only lie in a combination of the characteristics of *both* hemispheres, which amounts to a *coincidentia oppositorum,* as becomes apparent in the following listing:

CHINA	THE WEST
Application of the principle of the "middle"	Application of the principle of extremes
Gentleness and education highly esteemed	Struggle and power highly esteemed
Use of the natural strength of men and animals	Use of machines
High esteem for the family in matters of morality	Independence in government; the arts and sciences highly esteemed
Emphasis on the family in matters of morality	Emphasis on individualism in moral matters
Unity as pervasive principle in history	Differentiation as pervasive principle in history
Standardization of culture among various peoples and neglect of national boundaries	Strictly observed boundaries between various peoples
Relatively short coastlines	Extended coastlines
Love of the old; emphasis on regressive cultural elements	Respect for the new, emphasis on progressive cultural elements
Similarity with an old man	Similarity with a young, vigorous man
Similarity with a monk	Similarity with a knight
Wearing of a long, solemn garment; willingness to be modest and give way	Wearing of barbarian clothes with short train; ready to fight
Constant talk about morality	Always carrying stick in hand
Like a family of the aristocracy that has seen better days	Like a newly-rising proletarian family
Untrained in securing a living, and in political affairs	Sophisticated in the use of money, in managing people, and in political affairs
Of parochial decency	Of predatory violence
Does not leave his home	Loves far away places

Despotism develops precisely because people are ready to surrender their rights and withdraw	Precisely because people like to fight each other and know their rights as individuals, egalitarian tendencies develop
Because people content themselves with the traditional and well-known, only proven, tested doctrines are examined	Because there is a willingness to take risks, new methods derived from practical experience are constantly devised
People are used to disgrace, and as a consequence fatalism, astrology, physiognomy, oracles and monasticism flourish	People know human rights, men and women are equal, poor and rich are of the same rank, and revolution can therefore break out
People are respected for coming to terms with grief by an inner effort	Those who advertise their grief are respected
Because people come to terms psychologically with their grief, the liberal arts flourish	Because grief is not kept hidden, the law and the natural sciences flourish
Many vegetable dishes with a simple and unobtrusive aroma	Many meat dishes with intense, strong aroma
Because they have much leisure, people lose themselves in indolence	By always keeping busy, people train body and mind
Commerce is primarily overland, and inconvenient	Commerce is primarily coastal and maritime, and highly developed
Moderation of desires is glorified, and simplicity is highly regarded	Expectations and desires are glorified, one attempts to acquire as much as possible through work, and ostentation is highly regarded
Culture consists in mortifying the soul with moral doctrines	Culture consists in taking one's fill of things
Education, refinement, humaneness and honesty are highly regarded	Cleverness, strength, legal rights and profits are highly regarded
Much empty reflection about apparently certain but actually false doctrines; defective scientific knowledge, [yet] pursuit of wisdom	Much systematic, almost hair-splitting research, yet inability to arrive at definitive solutions

Many saints and sages, but also many false "superior men"	Many heroes, but also many real bandits
A culture formed of gentle education	A culture formed by the vehemence of strength
Similarity with the [gently] decaying family [as described in the novel] *The Dream of the Red Chamber*	Similarity with the courageous, noble and patriotic band of robbers described in the novel *The Marsh Heroes*
Pleasure in smoking opium	Pleasure in wine and heated discussion
Wholly enthralled by the beauties of ritual and convention	Effort directed toward concrete realization and practical application
In novels, the plot frequently ends [with the transformation of the principal characters] into immortals and Buddhas	In novels, the plot frequently ends with the suicide of the principal characters
The solution lies in quiet extinction or illusionary magic	The solution consists in the happy end or a heroic act
Feminine by nature, people respect the *Yin,* the soft, maternal, the chthonic *(tz'u)*	Masculine by nature, people respect the *Yang,* the hard, the heroic, the dynamic *(chien)*
The female principle *(k'un)* realizes itself here, therefore it forms the rear guard and achieves perfection	The male principle *(ch'ien)* pushes forward; therefore it forms the vanguard, but [finally] perishes [nonetheless][204]

The extent to which interests and ideals shifted during the twenty-five years that lie between the utopias of Liu Jen-hang and K'ang Yu-wei is nowhere shown more clearly than by the introduction of this list into the discussion about the "New" world of "Great Equality." For K'ang, the concept of the "Land under Heaven" *(t'ien-hsia),* which referred to both the Chinese empire and the inhabited world as a whole, had still been largely inviolate. In his project, China's salvation coincides as a matter of course with that of the entire world. For however extensively western technical achievements might be utilized, that salvation originated in a "Middle Kingdom" which still viewed itself as the indisputable representative of mankind. In Liu's conception, on the other hand, China's most pressing problem was no longer the salvation of the world, but its own, since it had been obliged to learn to see itself as one country among many. China no longer stood at the head of mankind, but had fallen back to the "rear," and it had become abundantly clear to everyone that its need for salvation was greater than any other country's. What appears at first glance as a moderate, reasonable and tolerant restructuring of the new ideal world from western and eastern components proves upon more careful examination to be the outcome of a painful struggle between Liu's love for the poetry of traditional Chinese culture and his admiration for the power of alien, western, technological civilization.

Because ultimately epigonic, Liu's plan for a "New Great Equality" perhaps never really created much interest and was soon entirely forgotten. It does, however, have one undeniable merit. It throws a strong light on the seemingly hopeless dead end into which the Chinese intelligentsia had been driven by its violent contact with the West. Liu attempted to bypass this situation by an ideal which would have blended Chinese and western culture. But this was a profoundly paradoxical effort. Although important in the growth of "utopian" thought in China, his conception was only one facet of the entire complex of problems that had been the subject of a continuous intellectual debate since the 1870s, and which even today cannot be said to have been altogether resolved. Only as we proceed to consider it in somewhat greater detail and become aware of its connection with an even more important and pervasive motif in Chinese intellectual history will this juxtaposition of contrary western and Chinese traits in Liu's sketch take on meaning. And some light will be shed on the seemingly senseless acts that periodically recur in modern China.

POLARITIES BETWEEN "INNER" AND "OUTER," "KNOWLEDGE" AND "ACTION"

Beginning with the closing years of the nineteenth century at the latest, China became increasingly aware of a dilemma which it really shared with all non-western, and particularly with the so-called underdeveloped nations. It was not so much its confrontation with the West and the resulting disintegration of the sinocentric world view but rather the fact that the nationalism due to the disappearance of that world view, a nationalism whose foundations had been laid by the Mongol conquest, took two different, conflicting and mutually exclusive paths. One the one hand, nationalism demanded that what was traditionally Chinese be protected against the irruption of alien western civilization. On the other, it turned out that this defense was possible only if this alien, western civilization was adopted, "at least" in the area of technology. In the desperate attempt to resolve this aporia, an age-old dichotomy in Chinese thought suddenly resurfaced, namely the opposition between knowledge and action, an often painfully experienced cleavage identifiable in all Chinese systems designed to improve the world. This problematics may appear somewhat trite at first glance, and yet it is actually the central theme which was articulated during various periods and in various forms and underlies all preoccupation with ideal man, ideal society and an ideal world. For the Chinese spirit has only very rarely been concerned with merely establishing an ideal. Its pragmatism almost always obliged it to also envisage its implementation, thus adding a historical dimension to what is fundamentally the atemporality of utopia. This is ultimately the way we have to understand the description of the various "phases" separating the present, imperfect world from the ideal, future state as we find them in K'ang Yu-wei (three interlocking periods) or the six-phase scheme of Liu Jen-hang. They represent steps from reality to a beyond, from temporality to eternity, comparable to the rungs of a ladder leading from earth to heaven. Countless earlier Chinese philosophers had struggled with this problem, especially Confucians of various hues. They represent the "pragmatic" Chinese mind most clearly because while they differed from the Taoists and Buddhists in refusing to contemptuously renounce the world and society, they were equally unwilling to wholly abandon the sphere of pure imagination where the former felt especially at home. To bridge the gap between knowledge and action, to reconcile them rather than to sharpen their opposition was precisely the goal of the Confucians, though not at the price of obliterating a polarity which may have been agonizing at times but had also been enormously fruitful at others. For it could ultimately be traced back to an even more fundamental opposition which we have encountered in a variety of guises in our discussion of Chinese conceptions of the ideal, and that is the antithesis between the concepts "inner" and "outer."[205]

If one were to adopt Chinese practice and provide a schematic overview of all those central, paired opposites deriving from them, the following table would result:

INNER	OUTER
Man's natural disposition *(hsing)*	Acquired characteristics; all that has been "made" *(wei)*
Nature	Culture
Spontaneity, life	Order, law
Simplicity *(chih)*	Refinement *(wen)*
Atemporality	Historicity
Sudden illumination	Gradual illumination, learning
Retreat into the self; tranquillity	Activity, liveliness
Self, individual	Society
Knowledge *(chih)*	Doing, acting *(hsing)*
Ideal, "utopia"	Reality
[Structural] principle *(li)*	Ether *(ch'i)*
Idea, "word" *(ming)*	Realization *(shih)*
"Virtue" *(te)*	Power *(wei)*, talent *(ts'ai)*

Loyalty	Adaptation
Essence *(t'i)*	Mode of conduct, application, practice *(yung)*

If the disputes that have taken place in China about the ideals mankind should follow are considered from this point of view, we discover that Mencius's and Hsün-tzu's contradictory answers to the question whether man was good or evil "by nature,"[206] are surprisingly closely connected with the dispute among Buddhists whether illumination is a slow process or a momentary event,[207] or with the argument of the Neo-Confucians concerning the priority of "Principle" or "ether."[208] The actual multiplicity of solutions and doctrines came about in part because these antitheses, even when elaborated in some detail (as, for example, in the contrast between sudden and gradual illumination), were largely purely formal patterns which came to differ significantly as they were fleshed out. In addition, syntheses could vary considerably, and they were the actual goal, of course, since all exemplifications of "inner" and "outer" are ultimately aspects of one and the same thing, a fact implicit in the terms themselves. There always existed a variety of transitions from the absolute denial of a given contradiction or the claim that the thesis already contained the antithesis as an integral element down to the impartial recognition of both opposites and the sincere attempt to synthesize them. Both absolute denial and equal recognition tended to function as limiting values, for all those philosophers who pretended to take either of these positions usually did so in a conscious or unconscious effort to obscure their real stand.

How far they were prepared to extend the applicability of one of the opposing concepts at the expense of the other usually provides a clue to the real position of the respective disputants. If we take the contrasting pair "knowledge/action" as an example, we note that Mencius praises the joys of "sincerity" *(ch'eng)* which, according to him, come from the reciprocal adaptation of knowledge and action.[209] And Wang Shou-jen, who thought he had discovered all knowledge within himself, proclaimed that "knowledge is the beginning of practice, doing is the completion of knowing."[210] Yet both clearly belong to that wing which placed primary emphasis on the "inner." The opposite is true of Hsün-tzu, although he also (if with a qualification that shows greater frankness) assigned an important place to "knowledge" when he said: "Not to hear of something is not as good as to hear about it; to hear about it is not as good as to witness it; to witness it is not as good as to 'know' it; and to 'know' it is not as good as to act upon it."[211] For some, "knowledge" could extend far into the sphere of "action" and refer to theoretical knowledge as well as practical experience, ethical convictions and belief and even the resulting will to act. Conversely, there were those for whom "action" included almost all areas of "knowledge": all thinking, all creating of ideas, all making of judgments, which were simply defined as "actions of the mind."[212]

But the most interesting divergencies resulted when the attempt was made to add to what may be called the established schema of paired opposites other sets of such opposites that existed independently of the former, for the basically neutral dialectical relationship of the two contrasting groups of values thereby suddenly appeared in a new light. This was particularly true when this new, surreptitiously introduced set of paired opposites did not have the same value and thus immediately shifted the balance (a result that was always intended). The earliest example of such an attempt is Mencius's identification of the contrast "natural endowment"/"acquired characteristics" with that of "good" and "bad" (in a social sense). Hsün-tzu made the opposite identification and this counter-attack made the scholarly community aware of the "inner"/"outer" dichotomy. A completely different, but formally comparable addition of an alien set of paired opposites to the familiar schema was the identification of the contrast "sudden" and "gradual" illumination (which was perfectly legitimate and natural) with "Chinese" and "western" (or Indian) thought introduced by the monk Hsieh Ling-yün in the fifth century.[213] A third example is the addition of the antinomy "difficult" (and therefore of greater value)/"easy." Limited originally to the pair "knowledge"/"action," it can already be documented in the pronouncement of a minister quoted in the classical *Book of Records* who allegedly said: "Knowledge is not difficult, but action is."[214]

It was (and in a sense continues to be) precisely these three interpretations of the old model of paired opposites which dominate the conflict of opinions in twentieth-century China. The opposition "China"/"West," still relatively marginal in Hsieh Ling-yün, became increasingly central and much more threatening since what was now involved was no longer a remote, passive India but the modern, aggressive West. Only one, closely connected, new polarity may have been more consequential, and that was the opposition between "old" and "modern." One only has to compare the two tables from Liu Jen-hang's book on the "Old" and the "New Great Equality" and the characteristics of Chinese and western culture with our table listing "inner" and "outer" traits to see how deliberately paired, originally independent opposites are conjoined there. But Liu's schema represents only a momentary phase of the long, constantly changing discussion of this thematics in modern China in which not only all philosophers but also all politicians participated (although men were frequently both at that time). And often, when they were unable to change their minds rapidly enough in the turbulent stream of opinions, they changed overnight "from a menacing sea monster to an old museum piece,"[215] as Hu Shih once remarked sarcastically about K'ang Yu-wei.

The first to explicitly propose a bipartition of ideals to save China, and to suggest that the "Chinese" (i.e. Confucian) world view furnish the "essence" *(t'i)* and western technology the "application" *(yung)* was the scholar, politician and viceroy Chang Chih-tung (1837–1909). Since the turn of the century, his influence had been enormous.[216] In 1898, he published his *Exhortation to Study (Ch'üan hsüeh p'ien).*[217] It was divided into two parts, one of which only contained proposals for a Confucian reform, while the second made rather far-reaching suggestions for the westernization of the country (trips abroad, technical schools, translations of western books, development of the daily press and the railroads, and similar matters). It was enthusiastically received as a manual by the reformers under K'ang Yu-wei in 1898, for they hoped to use it for rallying all traditionalists and innovators. But after the Hundred Days' Reform had ended in violence, Chang suddenly and demonstratively parted company with the reformers and even sent a telegram to the arch-conservative empress dowager expressly demanding the execution of the principal figures of this "rebellion." Some of them were actually put to death (the "Six Martyrs of the Reform Movement").[218] This attitude was inconsistent, to say the least, for it revealed that Chang Chih-tung's solution was dishonest and contrived in its attempt to reconcile the mutually exclusive opposites "Old China"/"Modern West" by recourse to the formula "inner"/"outer," for they lacked a common basis. Like every advocate of a lame compromise, Chang incurred the hostility of both sides, although it is true that his theoretical model did much to stimulate discussion and clarify issues. In the general indignation at his attempt to dialectically interpret the contradiction between a traditional, "spiritual" China and a modern, "technological" West, the antitheses now came clearly into view.

Those who believed[219] that the Chinese tradition alone sufficed to meet the internal and external requirements of a future culture for both China and the entire world were divided into two camps. There was K'ang Yu-wei and his disciples and precursors (Liao P'ing 1852–1932[220]) who wanted to unearth all those dynamic elements of Confucianism (New Text School) which would provide an independent ideological basis even for a modern, technological world that would nonetheless continue to be "Chinese." This was to be accomplished by a "Reformation"; in 1901, Liang Ch'i-ch'ao explicitly referred to K'ang Yu-wei as the "Martin Luther of Confucianism."[221] This group saw itself confronted by the ultraconservatives who were really more consistent than K'ang. They also considered the "Chinese" as the decisive factor for the internal as well as the external aspects of any conceivable culture. Beyond that, they vigorously rejected any manipulation of traditional doctrines by surreptitious borrowings from the West, something K'ang and many following him had undoubtedly been guilty of in countless instances, however widely their doctrines differed in their details. Some of the members of this group were highly-educated Confucians such as Wo-jen, for example, (died 1871), a man of Mongolian origin. Like K'ang, he had discovered the first traces of a dynamic, "western" mode of thought in early Chinese history, but had come to a conclusion directly opposite to K'ang's. He felt that China had abandoned this dangerous path quite deliberately and at a much earlier time, and would therefore be ill-advised to return to it, thus committing a mistake that had been avoided before.[222] On a much lower plane, the group also included a majority of members of secret societies that were both Buddhist-Taoist and nationalist in character, men who, far into the twentieth century, were still dreaming of a return to paradises filled with magic gardens, their hills of gold and jewels, and towering mountains of rice and noodles.[223] Marked by xenophobia and contradictory goals and beliefs, these groups entered into a temporary alliance in the Boxer rebellion which was supported and perhaps steered by a clique surrounding the xenophobic prince Tuan (Tsai-i), a favorite of the empress dowager. In their unsuspecting and naive belief that even western artillery could do them no harm, these rebels may be seen as a symbol of the ineluctable bankruptcy of this stubborn conviction.[224]

There was thus a loose confederation of philosophers, politicians and popular leaders who sought to preserve the central place of Chinese culture in the modern world. Like the repeatedly mentioned scholar Feng Yu-lan,[225] these men came to rank among the most brilliant personalities of Chinese history, precisely because their task could not be accomplished unless they accepted the challenge of the West and did not simply close themselves off like the last-mentioned group. A counterforce developed only relatively late. The demand to ruthlessly eradicate the "essence" of one's own tradition, to surrender the seemingly so indisputable claim to shape the "inside" with its logical nexus to the concept of the "Middle Kingdom" if they wished to participate in a new, modern world was so enormous that even the most extreme reformers, all of whom derived either directly or indirectly from K'ang Yu-wei's school, hesitated for a long time before making this final break. It seemed too dismaying to suddenly see oneself on the periphery of world events, too disgraceful to begin again from the beginning after a four-thousand-year-long history, to have to learn the alphabet all over again in one's old age, as it were. Before this final step could be taken, before all the old gods could be tumbled from their altars, a certain detachment from the motherland was necessary, a distance which students had acquired in their early years in Japan, America or Europe, young men who had almost come to feel at home abroad. Of even greater weight, perhaps, would be a truly unbearable national humiliation which would overshadow any other kind of disgrace. Because their efforts were primarily directed toward the ouster of the Manchu rulers and finally crowned by success in 1911, the revolutionary movements could not at first see their real enemy. A more or less conscious inferiority complex vis-a-vis the West, which was considered superior even on the moral plane, prevented even the boldest for a number of years from engaging it on its own terrain, deprived as they were of the support of a familiar Confucianism. But the First World War brought utter moral discredit on the entire West, yet failed to make it renounce the rights it had arrogated to itself. At the same time, the flames of the October Revolution were heralding the coming of a new age. It was these two events that created among the young Chinese intellectuals that explosive mixture of a last hope and a flickering despair that exploded in the Literary Revolution of the Fourth of May[226] (there had been warning signs since 1916). A relatively minor occasion—the transfer of former German rights in northeastern China to Japan stipulated in the Treaty of Versailles—sufficed to turn a student protest against this arrangement into a gigantic political movement which proclaimed in a holy wrath that "action" had only become "difficult" because the "knowledge" Confucianism had to offer was leading its believers astray. It was a false, mendacious knowledge which no longer prepared for action, as Hsün-tzu had once demanded, but deliberately sabotaged it. Only the genuine, clearly grasped modern western knowledge could provide the strength required to take a long overdue action, to shake off the western yoke once and for all.

The May Fourth Movement was tantamount to a landslide of enormous dimensions in China's intellectual landscape. Many younger intellectuals who had still wrestled with the ever more complex and implausible problems of "essence" and "practice" enthusiastically changed sides, as Liang Ch'i-ch'ao, who had laid the foundations for this development, had done many years before. With fanatic zeal, they went about tearing down the traditional value system once and for all. But apart from this fundamental iconoclasm, their phalanx soon proved as brittle as had been the line-up of the arch traditionalists or conservatives who had put their trust in China's heritage. For even though "praxis" was an uncontested neutral value when it referred to the natural sciences and technology, the "essence" which was really at stake here was confusingly polymorphous, even when the attempt was made to take it over wholesale from the West. Many vexing problems which had presumably been disposed of returned by the back door in a different, western garb. The conflict between idealist and materialist, voluntarist and pragmatic doctrines of western stamp simply replaced the opposition between "knowledge" and "action," "principle" and "ether."[227] There was, besides, the painful if constantly repressed recognition that psychological reasons would necessarily make the creation of a Chinese world view, constructed wholly of western values, as hopeless an undertaking in the long run as philosophical reasons would that of a modern world view derived from Chinese conceptions. Many originally enthusiastic followers began to feel a kind of nostalgia for the conservative, so much more "Chinese" camp where the once sacred concept "old" had not yet become a term of insult, just as conversely many had previously rushed from there into the modernist camp because they had been impatient, patriotic or eager for action.

It is against this iridescent background that the equally iridescent conceptions of the ideal in modern China must be seen if one wishes to understand their real meaning and function. It is often extremely difficult to determine this function, for many conceptions lack the inner logic which had assigned its place to all thought about the realization of happiness in the stream of China's intellectual development up to K'ang Yu-wei. Instead of a steady succession, we find simultaneity, a seething confusion in the sprouting "utopian" ideas where a frequently uninhibited eclecticism and an occasionally almost admirable dilettantism assembled ideas from all times and places in ephemeral, usually quickly fading systems of thought. Gone was the tranquil radiance of a few paradises which had once steadily lighted the way for those setting out from the darkness of reality. What now appeared everywhere along the nighttime horizon were flickering wills-o'-the-wisp which confused but did not guide. Yet it is also true that many conceptions of the ideal took on substance, a paradox which is merely apparent. For on the whole, there had been astonishing outward progress in China's march from the middle ages into a world of greater freedom, though not of greater order, during the first decades of our century. A wholly other-worldly element reminiscent of old conceptions of paradise is still in evidence among a number of reformers and revolutionaries such as Liu Jen-hang. But this was only at the blurred, infinitely distant end of a long path whose initial stages—those that could be expressed as political programs—already lay in an almost tangible, ideal world.

SUN YAT-SEN'S SYNTHESIS

One of the key figures for understanding the ideals of this period between ca. 1900 and 1930 is the founder of the Chinese Republic, Sun Yat-sen (1866–1925).[228] The reason for this is not that he himself advanced particularly utopian ideas. It would be more accurate to say that his doctrines show how different theories, each of which taken individually might perhaps be called utopian, could coalesce in a very concrete action program and function as vectors within it. It is true that his conceptions were repeatedly modified in the course of his life, but this also is typical. He organized the national revolution against the Manchu regime in an atmosphere where secret societies still played an important role. The first president of the republic, he gave up that office after a mere three months because the ideas of his *Three People's Principles (san min chu-i)* could not be carried out. And when he died, he had placed all his hopes on the Communist world revolution and the aid of the Soviet Union. Because the radicalization of his thought was gradual and passed through many intermediate phases, he can even today be claimed as a spokesman by Chinese of widely divergent persuasions. And his political credo, the *Three People's Principles*[229] had been framed in such a way as to allow the most diverse interpretations. His own definition of them reads as follows:

> The *Three People's Principles* consist of the People's Nationalism *(min-tsu)*, the People's Sovereignty *(min-ch'üan)*, and the People's Livelihood *(min-sheng)*. The first principle means that all people of the world are equal, and that no race may ever be suppressed and enslaved by another as the Manchus did when they came into China and usurped the government for over 260 years. When the Han race (i.e. the Chinese) finally rose up and drove them from the throne, this was the implementation of the Principle of the People's National Revolution *(min-tsu ko-ming chu-i)*. The Principle of the People's Sovereignty means that all men are equal and together form a large family, and that a few may never suppress the many. For all men have the same natural human rights. One must not set up princes and rulers and thus create slaves and subjects. The Principle of the People's Livelihood means that the poor and the rich are of identical rank, and that the rich may not

> suppress and enslave the poor. Only the Principle of the People's Livelihood was realized by someone some decades ago, and that was Hung Hsiu-ch'üan. In his Heavenly State of Universal Peace, there was a rule that all those who may be called workers controlled the state and that all goods were public property. This was in every sense the implementation of the Principle of an economic revolution *(ching-chi ko-ming ch-i),* or of Russian communism today.[230]

As the last sentence indicates, this definition of the "Three Fundamental Principles" dates from the time shortly before Sun's death when he once again interpreted this basic doctrine in some detail (1922). But the original concept goes back to a much earlier period predating the revolution of 1911. It is therefore not surprising that Sun's own changing interpretations found expression in differing translations in the West. Terms such as "people's independence," "people's rule," and "people's prosperity" or, even more freely, "national independence," "democracy," and "socialism" have been used also.[231] After 1912, Sun was obliged to abandon the limelight of politics more and more, and one has the impression that he struggled to give a more precise expression to his doctrine or attempted at least to make it more comprehensible and attractive to a wider public. In 1918, he published the introduction to the first part of his principal work, *A Program of National Reconstruction (Chien-kuo fang-lüeh)*[232] which deals with "psychological reconstruction." Here, he bitterly complains that wide circles considered his Three Principles "a utopia."[233] Surprisingly, he takes the reason for this to be the fact that people were constantly repeating the statement of that old minister in the *Book of Records* according to which "it was easy to know, but difficult to act." But actually the opposite was true: not action, but knowledge was hard. If action was difficult, this was only because there was not as yet enough proper knowledge. Becoming accustomed to the new, *seemingly* utopian thinking constituted the real hurdle that had to be taken even if the "enemies intent on the destruction of the spirit" constantly raised it anew.[234] But once this intellectual obstacle had been overcome, the realization of his plans would follow automatically.

That Sun attempted time and again to avoid the propagation of genuinely utopian models is a fact. He recognized that happiness for both the individual and society could be found only along the narrow ridge between the two end points of all social utopias, those of absolute freedom and absolute order. These became really utopian only when the one resulted from the destruction of the other. In a speech given in 1921, he said:

> In the history of politics, we can observe two currents: freedom and order, which . . . must be balanced like . . . the centrifugal and centripetal forces in physics. If freedom is too encompassing, there is the danger that it will degenerate into anarchy. If order becomes dominant, there is the danger of dictatorship. . . . The history of China, which . . . begins with the so-called "Golden Age" shows the continuous movement of freedom toward dictatorship. This contrasts with Europe, where dictatorship gradually became freedom. Our nation had enjoyed freedom for

> too long; it became tired of it and destroyed it. Ambitious emperors and kings took advantage of this opportunity to seize unlimited power, and in this way the dictatorship of the Ch'in and Han dynasties began. . . . In olden times, the Chinese nation was completely free, and no one interfered with the Chinese peasant as he peacefully tilled the soil. With his motto "order through inaction," Lao-tzu gave expression to this conception of the freedom of the people although the latter, being free, were completely unaware of it. . . . It is therefore comprehensible that Europe should reproach the Chinese nation with having no idea of freedom whatever.[235] The Europeans did not enjoy a full measure of freedom and therefore struggled to achieve it. The Chinese, on the other hand enjoyed unlimited freedom and did not know the concept of freedom for that very reason. . . . While freedom and its most extreme form, anarchy, were therefore never much directly referred to in China, Europe has suddenly shown great interest in theories of anarchism in recent times, because they are relatively new there. . . . But it makes a ridiculous impression when one hears about Chinese students who study these anarchist theories and make propaganda for them merely because they do not want to appear backward, and regardless of whether they have really understood them or not. For indirectly, anarchist theories were known in China several thousand years ago, and created considerable interest—or is one going to maintain that the doctrines of Buddhism and Taoism are something other than anarchism?[236]

While Sun thus made freedom as such one of the cardinal elements in his system of the *Three Principles* and believed he could discover a sort of covert tradition of freedom in Chinese history, he decisively rejects all anarchistic tendencies. His neither entirely correct nor wholly false identification of anarchism and Taoism-Buddhism shows that he considered this doctrine irrational wishful thinking. His criticism of Marxism, of course, had a different complexion, although the communist movement in China initially developed under the influence of anarchistic ideas. During his last years, he was quite clearly intent on harmonizing the third of his Three Principles, that of the People's Livelihood, with Marxism. To do so, he had to call all divergencies merely methodological. At the same time, the *Principle of the People's Livelihood* appears as the theoretical basis common to all socialist political systems. Conversely, it is also proclaimed as the best possible realization of all socialist theories. In his notes for the lecture series in 1924, he wrote about this matter in the following terms:

> The terms "socialism" and "communism" are now used synonymously in the West. Although their methods may vary, socialism is often used to describe both theories. In using the term "Principle of Livelihood" instead of "socialism" my prime purpose is to strike at the root of the social problem and to reveal its real nature, also to make it possible for people to understand the term as soon as they hear it. Is the Principle of Livelihood really different from socialism? . . . Is socialism really a phase of the *Min-sheng* Principle, or is the Principle of Livelihood a phase of socialism? The first exponents of socialism were mostly moralists and . . . utopian; they hoped to build an ideally peaceful and happy world in which there would be no more human suffering, but they did not think at all of any concrete methods

> by which suffering was to be removed. Then came Marx. He devoted his wisdom and intellect, his learning and his experience, to a thoroughgoing study of these questions. . . . The principle upon which he proceeded was absolute respect for facts rather than for ideals. After Marx, the socialist movement divided into two groups—the utopian socialists and the scientific socialists. Scientific socialists advocated the use of scientific methods in solving social problems. . . . Marx, in his investigation of the social problem, emphasized the material side. In dealing with material forces you inevitably come first to the question of production. . . . The large-scale production in modern times is made possible by labor and machinery, by the cooperation of capital and machinery together with the employment of labor. The benefits of large-scale production are reaped largely by the capitalists themselves; the workers enjoy but a small fraction of the benefits. Consequently the interests of capitalists and of the workers are constantly clashing and when no solution of the difficulty is found, a class war breaks out. Marx held the view that class war was not something which had only followed the industrial revolution; all past history is a story of class struggle—between masters and slaves, between landlords and serfs, between nobles and common people; in a word, between all kinds of oppressors and oppressed. Only when the social revolution was completely successful, would these warring classes be no more. It is evident from this that Marx considered class war essential to social progress, the driving force, in fact, of social progress. He made class war the cause and social progress the effect. But, if most of the economic interests of society can be harmonized, the majority of people will benefit and society will progress. . . . From ancient times until now man has exerted his energies in order to maintain his existence. And mankind's struggle for continuous existence has been the reason for society's unceasing development, the law of social progress. Class war is not the cause of social progress: it is a disease developed in the course of social progress. The cause of the disease is the inability to subsist, and the result of the disease is war. What Marx gained through his studies of social problems was a knowledge of diseases in the course of social progress. Therefore, Marx can only be called a social pathologist. Marx, in his study of social problems, found only one of the diseases of society; he did not discover the law of social progress and the central force in history. His assumption that class struggle is a cause of social progress puts effect before cause. . . . I make distinction between communism and the *Min-sheng* principle in this way; communism is an ideal of livelihood, while the *Min-sheng* principle is practical communism. There is no real difference between the two principles—Communism and *Min-sheng,* the difference lies in the methods by which they are applied.[237]

Following as it does upon the preceding, clear analysis, the somewhat forced, rather illogical statement that communism and the "Principle of the People's Livelihood" are fundamentally the same thing cannot gloss over the fact that Sun Yat-sen himself had discovered an important difference between the two, and that was the differing evaluation of the class struggle. Certainly Sun's whole temperament originally made him prefer the spontaneous, gradual development of social relations toward an ideal goal that would abolish all conflict to a violent struggle between the classes. It seems that it was only in the very last months of his life that he came to feel that in the mild climate of such thinking, the revolutionary spirit would ultimately weaken, and he considered that spirit indispensable if change was to occur. With some resignation, he said in a speech in 1923:

> Up until now we have had our base and our friends primarily abroad. Within the country, our influence has been almost zero. . . . The time has therefore come to have our party, the Kuo-min-tang, base itself on another power which does not come from the outside but works within: the consent of the masses to the idea of revolution. . . . Let us admit it: the Chinese people are not sympathetic to the idea of revolution. This is why up to the present day, the revolutionary movement has remained a brook without a source, a tree without roots. . . . If the idea of revolution is to win out, it must be through political enlightenment. It is useless to try to impose it by force of arms.[238]

It is only under the weight of a certain despair that Sun became convinced that a social revolution could not be carried out without a class struggle and that he shifted to the communist side. In one of his last proclamations, he definitively identified his "Principle of the People's Livelihood" with the objectives of the communist party. But at the same time, and as if to create a balance, he also identified it with those of a revolutionary Confucianism such as K'ang Yu-wei had preached it:

> To wish to solve the social question in China is tantamount to pursuing the same goal as other countries: it is the wish that the peoples of all countries might attain peace and happiness and no longer suffer from the unequal distribution of capital and the means of production. But if we pursue this goal of liberating them from their suffering, we must also desire communism. Therefore we can no longer say that communism and the "Principle of the People's Livelihood" are two different things. Our Three Principles of the People mean government "of the people, by the people, and for the people"—that is, a state belonging to all the people, a government controlled by all the people, and the rights and benefits for the enjoyment of all the people. If this is true, the people will not only have a share in state production, but they will have a share in everything. When the people share everything in the state, then will we truly reach the goal of the *Min-sheng* principle which is Confucius's hope of a "great commonwealth."[239]

Sun Yat-sen's last-minute attempt to weld together the two extremes in the spiritual and political development of the China of the twenties—reformed Confucianism and communism—by simply ignoring their inherent antagonisms, was undoubtedly well meant. Perhaps it was even the appropriate course for a person who was the "Father of the Fatherland" and therefore felt obliged to do justice to more than just one political persuasion. But he could not even temporarily patch up the deep rift that had split the young Chinese intelligentsia, let alone close it. The development of the *Kuo-min-tang* ("National People's Party," KMT), which had been created by Sun and existed officially since the proclamation of the republic, was symptomatic of this situation. Between 1924 and 1926, it sought to collaborate closely with the Chinese Communist Party (*Kung-chan-tang,* CCP), founded officially in 1921. But in this process, it slipped more and more into the hands of groups with a communist orientation. Finally, in the spring of 1927, and by an act of violence resulting in the death of thousands of communists and left-wing socialists, the previously outmaneuvered right wing of the party under the leadership of the president of the powerful military academy at Whampoa, Chiang Kai-shek, seized control and turned the party into what became an increasingly conservative force. And this in spite of the fact that the divergencies which went back to the time before the turn of the century were not primarily those between a "conservative" and a "progressive" movement, but rather between one basing itself exclusively on Chinese, and another relying wholly on western values, as we have shown. Although with an ineluctable logic, it was only as a secondary phenomenon that one of these movements was carried progressively toward the right, the other toward the left. The followers of the pro-Chinese party, representatives of a variety of points of view since they also did not reject a modernization with western elements out of hand, had been educated primarily in China itself. The followers of the radically pro-western party, on the other hand, who, at least initially, created an impression of greater cohesiveness precisely because of their radicalism, had mostly studied abroad. The more extremist they were, the further away from China they had gone. Those still relatively moderate had studied in Japan (approximately ten thousand of them in 1906), while the most radical had gone to Europe, chiefly to France (about six hundred in 1906). It would seem that their critical attitude toward traditional China was not wholly due to the foreign environment. For the Imperial Manchu government had been naive enough to believe that it could rid itself of its most radical students by sending them to Europe to study.[240]

THE NEW ANARCHISM AND THE "GREAT EQUALITY THROUGH MACHINES"

In the search for the origins of Chinese ideal conceptions of man and society in the twentieth century as they partly expressed themselves in Sun Yat-sen, the traces lead us to the "radicals" and therefore, surprisingly, back to Europe, to Paris. Since 1902, a group of Chinese students abroad, inspired by Bakunin, Kropotkin and Reclus, had begun forming an anarchist cell which surfaced in 1907[241] with the periodical *Hsin Shih-chi (New Century).* Until 1910, 110 issues of this magazine appeared. The ideas of these anarchists clustered around a layer of classical and Chinese (including Taoist) education, theories of social Darwinism, and a fundamental libertarianism. One of the most colorful personalities of modern Chinese intellectual history, Wu Chih-hui (1864–1954)[242] became the leader of the group. Educated in Japan, he had fled China in 1903 because of an inflammatory article he had written while working as a journalist in Shanghai. In England in 1904, he had made friends with Sun Yat-sen, who at that time was seeking support almost everywhere in the world for his anti-monarchist and anti-Manchu revolution. More to be obliging than from real conviction, Wu had become a member of Sun's "Alliance" *(T'ung-meng-hui)*, the forerunner of the KMT, in 1905, and had gone to Paris in 1906. In an article written during his stay in Paris, he was already singing the praises of anarchism:

> The name anarchy is the most auspicious in the world. . . . [With anarchy] each country can do away with national boundaries . . . each will give up all the different and numerous languages and adopt a common tongue; the governmentless state uses seventy or eighty percent of its total effort to impart the ethics of nongovernment. The result is that anarchy is inevitable. Anarchy will have its "ethics" but no "laws." One will have "From each according to his ability," but cannot call that "duty"; one will have "to each according to his need," but cannot call that "right." When everyone "voluntarily places himself in the realm of truth and equity" and when there is no longer the state of "the ruler and the ruled," then there is true anarchy.[243]

Quoting Sun, one might say that the Taoists and Buddhists, and certainly men such as Pao Ching-yen and Juan Chi[244] had already been rapturously hopeful that anarchy might bring salvation as they conceived it. What was distinctive about Wu was the unrestrained admiration he felt for everything European. He resembled his Chinese anarchist friends who had fallen in love with France itself, the country of the French Revolution and the Paris Commune, and continued to express this love decades later through various externals such as the wearing of berets, for example (and this is also true of leftist Chinese today, who continue this tradition). Concerned more with the ideal of physical cleanliness, he scouted the Chinese as dirty and morally degenerate and believed the Europeans had attained "the highest degree of illumination and morality."[245] To him, the superiority of their culture seemed to rest on the very qualities most of his Chinese contemporaries rejected as "unspiritual": the materialist world view and the invention of technology. In an often humorous but seriously intended and deliberately naive history of the creation, he ascribes the origin of the universe to a "black thing" *(Hun-t'un)*, a being that had already appeared in early Chinese mythology, and which one day exploded into millions of selves. He said that the "metaphysical ghost" who wrote this legend had already been "baptized by science" since he had proposed to show that the universe was created spontaneously and without a creator.[246] Wu assumes that man developed in the course of an evolutionary process stretching over a million years. Its inherent tendency and increasing rapidity guarantee that an ideal anarchist state will come into being at some time in the future, although this does not mean that the danger of a universal catastrophe has been banished. Interestingly enough, Wu believed that the path of human society could not be understood as simple moral growth, but rather as a progressive polarization of good and evil:

> As regards kindness, the men of the past do not approach those of today, and the men of today will in turn be inferior in this respect to those of the future. But in their evil, the men of the past [also] do not match those of today, and those living today will again not equal those of the future. For the power of knowledge can as easily bring progress in good as progress in evil. This explains why the world will never attain perfection, although it is [constantly] moving in that direction. For when good men forget this rule and become weary of the world, they thereby initiate retrogression [which annihilates all achievement].[247]

This concern that the ideal world might be lost after, or shortly before, its realization is an important motif that repeatedly recurs among Chinese utopians. It represents the discovery that there is also a historical dimension *within* utopias which corresponds to the no less frequent articulation of the various stages leading *up to* their attainment. Yet this worry did not keep Wu Chih-hui from giving a vivid description of the world of the future as he imagined it. His sparkling humor, his tendency to play tricks on his audience while presenting the most weighty matters, his brilliant style, robust imagery and an imagination occasionally reminiscent of Chuang-tzu sometimes make it difficult to say whether he really believed in his conceptions, at least when he elaborated specific details. What was really important to him in essays such as the "Attainment of the Great Equality by Machines" *(Chi-ch'i tsu-chin ta-t'ung shuo)*[248] was the juxtaposition of the illusionary quality of the age-old, traditional Chinese conceptions of the ideal advanced by Taoists and Buddhists which ultimately merely amounted to a return to the primitivism of past phases of human development, and the solidly founded, truly forward-looking conceptions of a pervasively technicized world. For there, happiness would for the first time become attainable not just by reducing desires or a more equitable distribution of wealth, as before, but directly, through increased production. Thus it becomes understandable that this extraordinarily vigorous young man, this "white-haired youth" *(pai-fa ch'ing-nien)* as he was called up to the end, a man whom a Chinese ambassador in Paris had once called admiringly the Voltaire, Zola, Montesquieu and Jules Verne of East Asia all rolled into one person[249] should have urged that all Chinese classics "be thrown into the latrine for thirty years"[250] and also have portrayed in glowing colors the benefits of a classless machine age where all factories would be run by working students:

> Once worker-students have sketched out their plans and projects and systematized them in curricula, the knowledge of the workers will also increase, so that the collectively owned factory can replace the capitalist one, and the socialism of professional associations can be realized without revolution and the shedding of blood. Every day, steel girders will be cast in tens of thousands of molds, and cement

> manufactured in tens of thousands of kilns. Precision instruments will fill the depots, and there will be an abundance of furniture and durable goods of wood and steel in the warehouses. Every 30 miles, sumptuous, richly endowed universities will rise before the eye. Every twenty miles, costly and beautiful, splendid and spacious libraries and museums will arrest the attention of the passers-by. A lever will be pressed, and mountains of clouds will pile up over an area of 1000 *mou;* at the opening of a single switch, snow will be stacked in 10,000 layers, [and thus the weather will be controlled]. All men will have been educated to be thrifty, and to consume no more than is necessary. The result will be that they will only have to work two hours a day.[251] . . . Therefore, of the twenty-two hours left in the day, eight could be used for sleep, six for amusement, eight for study and inventive efforts which require concentration of the mind. . . . When the time comes that each can take according to his need, everyone would have an exalted, pure and exemplary character; . . . the whole world will not have one place that is deserted, dirty or decrepit. It will be like a huge park. When this time is reached, man will have a head, because of the overuse of his brain, as big as a five pound melon, while his body will be small and delicate (because all his needs of communication will be taken care of by machines). This is not an idealization of utopia. There is already some evidence of its realization in countries which possess better and more skillful machines. Such a state of affairs is naturally the contribution of machinery.[252]

With a membership of some thirty persons toward the end, this group of Chinese anarchists certainly made considerable efforts to take the first steps leading to the social order sketched here. The students subjected themselves to a strict discipline, did not drink, smoke or gamble, and worked almost without exception in factories. While insisting on individuality, it was their hope that this would be one of the smallest cells from which the world society as proclaimed in their journal *New Century* (1907) would arise: "The individual is the basic social unit. He joins with others in a village community, which in turn joins with other such communities to form a country. The world society will finally be created when all the countries of the world will have joined together. The right kind of society thus makes possible the free association of individuals, mutual aid, shared happiness and joy for all, and freedom from all coercive supervision by a few: such is the goal of anarchism."[253]

Yet the Paris group was perfectly aware that there was no successful model that had ever existed anywhere or at any time, least of all in China, that might serve to attain this goal. As Wu Chi-hui's very brusque attitude in this respect indicates, they also did not make the slightest overtures to nationalist Chinese. They insisted on their plan to bring about what had never existed before, to take all or nothing, even if this entailed the reproach that they were utopians, or did not love their country. In a reply to letters sent in by readers, the editors of the *New Century* wrote as follows:

The reason China could not keep pace with the rest of the world was that it always emphasized the old, and neglected the new. The West has made progress because it took the opposite attitude. . . . [Even today], we Chinese are inclined to act as if China had long since achieved the same things as the West. Thus we say, for example, that China already experienced imperialism a long time ago under the Mongols . . . and developed nationalism a long time ago under the "Yellow Emperor.". . . that Lao-tzu is the founder of anarchism, Mo Ti the first advocate of neighborly love, and finally that communism was practiced in China ages ago under the name of the "well field system."[254] Alas! Genuinely new knowledge is not born by chance. It comes at a particular moment, when the conditions for its realization are right. One cannot simply single out a statement from the ancients and maintain that they had already foreseen everything. . . . There are countless things which modern man cannot predict. How much less can we expect that from the ancients.[255]

The charge that the Chinese and all other anarchists were engaged in the paradoxical effort of using terror to usher in the age of eternal peace, and wanted to fight militarism by armed might also led to many exchanges. Their answer drew on the well-known distinction between "military might by which the ruling group stake the lives and money of others in order to preserve their rule and that of the state" and "revolutionary assassination as the sacrifice of the individual to eliminate the enemies of humanity, thereby extending the common rights of the world."[256] In a sense, the anarchist does not live in this world but in a kind of world beyond this one where murder and suicide coincide in a single act designed to do away with this poorly constructed world, and to eliminate the anarchist into the bargain, since it is only logical that he cannot remain in a world that is not yet the same as his ideal, his "utopian" metaworld. From this perspective, a reproach addressed to the traditional, though frequently no less anarchistic Chinese students in Japan by the Paris group acquires profound meaning! They said that when their efforts to realize the ideal were sabotaged by outside forces, their protest still took the traditional form of escapist suicide rather than that of suicidal assassination. Escapist suicide had found its most perfect expression in Ch'ü-Yüan's leap into the water[257] (and Wu Chih-hui himself attempted such a suicide in 1902. While traveling from Canton to Japan, he jumped into the sea after a bitter discussion with a more conservative Chinese politician).[258] In contrast, suicidal assassination not only saved one's own self, but also improved the world:

If you fellows really see in death the answer to things, why do you not follow in the footsteps of the Russian Terrorist Party by killing one or two thieves of mankind as the price of death. Whether one plunges into the sea or is decapitated (as an assassin), both are the same death. But they are different in their impact. Whereas one has no impact and the person merely dies as a courageous man, the other has a great impact, especially upon the Chinese official class. For the fear of death is one of the special characteristics of Chinese officials. In sum, in this twentieth

> century, (the century of world revolution),[259] if there is the possibility of eliminating even one thief of mankind and thereby decreasing a portion of dictatorial power, then the year of the great Chinese revolution will be one day closer.[260]

THE BALANCE OF HUMAN ABILITIES AND DEATH AS SALVATION

Those addressed here were primarily an anarchist group of Chinese students which had established itself in Tokyo shortly after the Paris cell had been founded, and which collaborated closely with the Japanese anarchist Kotoku Shusui (1871–1911),[261] who had returned from the United States in 1906 and was later executed. The ideas expressed in their short-lived periodical, *Natural Justice (T'ien-i pao)* (1907/1908), and *Balance (Heng-pao)* (1908) and occasionally even reprinted in the *New Century,* differed from those of the Paris group for, in marked contrast to Wu Chih-hui, they also wanted to do justice to the old Chinese anarchist tradition. The Tokyo group felt, for example, that the ideals of "indifference" and "non-interference" which they believed Confucianism and Taoism shared to a certain degree might provide an excellent basis for anarchism in China. They also searched for a Chinese model for their revolutionary innovations in the administrative reforms carried out according to the *Rites of Chou (Chou-li)* by the "usurper" Wang Mang, or even based themselves directly on the teachings of Hsü Hsing and Pao Ching-yen.[262] This is not to say that they overlooked the relevant western literature which was available to them in Japan in many translations.[263] More than the Paris group, however, they went back to the more "classical" European sources, and tried to discover connections between them and the Chinese tradition. Liu Shih-p'ei (1884–1919),[264] for example, the editor-in-chief of *Natural Justice,* believed he could see restatements of Kung Tzu-chen's[265] theses and of those of the half-legendary representative of the School of Agriculture, Hsü Hsing[266] in Rousseau's *Discours sur l'origine et les fondements de l'inégalité parmi les hommes* (1754) and the *Contrat social* (1762). The picture of a future ideal world drawn by Liu Shih-p'ei for his anarchist friends in Tokyo was strongly influenced by the teachings of Hsü Hsing, and generally much more Chinese than Wu Chih-hui, for example. Yet however great its similarity to other anarchist utopias, it differed conspicuously in one respect, and that was the curious division of labor it foresaw in the new society. In Liu's "Theory Advocating Balanced Ability in Human Beings" *(Jen-lei chün-li shuo),* we witness the emergence of a thesis that was present as an undercurrent in many old Chinese social teachings: the conviction that there was something profoundly unhealthy in the specialization of the work process which seems indispensable in a rationalized economy (this may be rooted in a "peasant mentality"); that "the king should himself prepare his breakfast and his supper," as Hsü Hsing's slogan had urged, and that intellectual work and physical labor should never be totally separated from each other. It was an ideal which came closest to the life style of the worker-students. In the journal *Natural Justice,* Liu Shih-p'ei gives a detailed description of a future community organized according to these principles. It goes beyond Hsü Hsing's demands and attempts, apparently quite deliberately, to overcome those inconsistencies of his which Mencius had once uncovered:

> The theory of "balanced ability" means a policy to train each individual to acquire various kinds of technique. Inequality emanates from man being dependent upon and employed by another. If one is employed by another, he will necessarily be under restraint and control, which will hinder real independence. To secure independence it is essential for man not to lean against others nor to be employed by others. . . . In order to carry out this theory it is first necessary to do away with the conventional society and the national borders. The theory aims to establish villages with a population of one thousand. Each village should provide homes for the aged and children, in which infants less than five years old and the aged over fifty have to be accommodated. Children from six to ten must learn from the aged letters common to all nations, since a common language will be created after abolition of national borders. Youths from the age of eleven to twenty have to learn from the elders practical technology, spending half a day in general studies and the other half in manufacturing. From twenty-one man must be engaged in work, the kinds of which vary according to the age. At the age of twenty-one man has to labor in road construction, at twenty-two in mining and lumbering, from twenty-three to thirty in producing ironware, chinaware, and other miscellaneous goods, and from thirty-one to thirty-six in weaving, spinning and tailoring. His engagement in agriculture must be limited to sixteen years from twenty-one to thirty-six. Since machinery will be employed, agricultural labor will be reduced to several weeks per year. During the farming season road construction and other labor should be suspended. After farming man can choose any kind of labor for the rest of the day. In that case he is allowed to rest after two hours of work. From thirty-seven to forty he engages himself in cooking, from forty-six to fifty in technology and medicine, and after fifty he enters the protective institute and there devotes himself to nursery and education of the children.[267]

A further characteristic of the Chinese anarchist group in Tokyo not apparent in this plan but which emerged at the same time is the special emphasis on the role women will play in ushering in the new society envisaged here. The journal *Natural Justice* no longer merely discussed a revolution *for* Chinese women—for this had been a recurrent motif since Li Ju-chen[268] at least—but rather a revolution *by* Chinese women. A readily apparent reason for this was the eminent influence of Liu Shih-p'ei's wife, Ho Chen, who was sometimes even more devoted in her editorial work than Liu himself. More importantly, there was the example of the French and even more the Russian anarchists who demonstrated the special possibilities open to women in terroristic assassination attempts. This aspect became dominant when the anarchist group in Tokyo began to take its lead from contemporary western anarchists, as Paris had demanded, and turned the existential weariness rampant among the Chinese students in Japan into suicidal impulses to act. Thus Ho Chen announced during a meeting in 1907 that in their opinion the revolution would proceed by three stages: 1) a stage of political discussion; 2) of political action; 3) of political assassination. And Chang Chi, one of the three principal leaders of the Tokyo group next to the Liu couple went so far as to say: "In my opinion, anarchism is by no means a lofty idea. The highest idea is to extinguish all mankind." This would be carried out in five simultaneous steps: the extinction of all governments, villages, human beings, mass society and the world.[269] This theory, which he presented as the "five nihils" *(wu-wu)* forms a macabre parallel to the program of the Ming rebel Chang Hsien-chung, who also believed he had discovered mass murder, the "seven kills" *(ch'i-sha)* as the only efficacious redemption of mankind.[270]

But it was precisely this rapid radicalization among the members of the Chinese anarchist group in Tokyo that prevented them from fully working out their ideas. Although the Japanese police naturally took action primarily against Japanese anarchists, the Chinese group also felt its pressure, and began to disintegrate as early as 1908. The Liu couple betrayed its own cause by going underground in 1908 in Shanghai and allowing itself to be bribed by the governor of Kiangsu and Kiangnan to spy on subversive organizations,[271] while Chang Chi fled to Paris from which he did not return until 1911, after the success of the revolution. Although it was not accepted, he is remembered for a suggestion he made in that same year to the newly established republican government. He proposed that Ch'ung-ming island off the mouth of the Yangtze River be set up "as an experimental area for world anarchism."[272] These were the same islands which almost two and a half millennia ago the Chinese had taken to be the dwelling places of the immortals, P'eng lai, Fang chang and Ying chou, the isles of the blessed.

The establishment of the republic gave the Chinese anarchists their first opportunity to become active in their own country. Because they had been isolated while abroad, the atmosphere in which the republic had been founded had had something excitingly unreal for them, but this now changed. No attempt was made to eradicate the touch of cosmopolitanism which had intensified to an almost suicidal hatred of their own culture among the Paris group. But an effort was made to fuse the western and cosmopolitan with the autochthonous Chinese. Unexpectedly, this opened up the seductive possibility of representing China as the vanguard of world revolution because in that country eastern and western culture allegedly formed a whole. A new journal which became the organ of anarchism in China, the *People's Voice (Min-sheng)*, originally *Hui-ming-lu, The Voice of the Cock Crowing in the Dark,* founded by the "Heart Society" *(Hsin-she)* in Canton in 1913, expressed this attitude in its make-up. Not only its name *(La Voce del Popolo)*— as, for that matter, the name of the Paris journal *New Century (La Tempoj Novaj)*—but also most of the articles were printed in both Chinese and Esperanto. In the first issue, which begins with a kind of anarchist manifesto ("Deklaracio"), the diffusion of Esperanto became an important part of the proposed action program. Liu Ssu-fu ("Shih-fu"),[273] who had composed it and was really the guiding spirit of this publication from beginning to end, a fascinating figure, almost constantly in flight up until 1915, tubercular and consumed by his dedication, formulated the goals as follows:

> Today, the common people in the empire are deprived of all of their happiness by brutal suppression and have sunk into such suffering and misery, filth and disgrace, that it cannot be expressed in words. If one inquires after the causes, it becomes apparent that the present organization of society is incapable of doing anything for the masses. If we therefore wish to free the people of their misery, we can do so only by radically eliminating the brutal suppression of the present society through a world revolution, and by replacing it by a new society which will be better, legitimate, and follow true principles. Only then will it be possible to say that the simple people have truly found the happiness of freedom. . . . Our principal concerns therefore are: communism, opposition to militarism, syndicalism, opposition to the ideologies of religion and the family, vegetarianism, standardization of all langauges and the "Great Equality" of all nations. To this should be added the newly discovered natural sciences, which can become a source of an easier life and progress of humanity. It is also an urgent matter that a "World Language Office" be founded since all languages can be standardized by Esperanto. A world language is therefore to be introduced in China.[274] Also, a true picture of Chinese society is to be propagated in the world. Once the world language and Chinese have coalesced in a unified literary form, translations from the one into the other have been made, and the texts have become accessible in both versions, eastern and western culture will fuse more intimately every day. Then it will also be possible to direct the attention of the simple people of the East Asian continent to the sacred cause of socialist world revolution which should be accomplished side by side with the lower classes of the entire world. China is a gigantic country indeed. There will be no lack of men of profound insight and large views who will assist us with their advice in this task.[275]

About a year later, Liu Ssu-fu was in a position to formulate this proclamation in greater detail in an address to the "comrades in Shanghai," and to present a complete program of "anarcho-communism" *(wu-cheng-fu kung-chan chu-i)* in fourteen paragraphs:

> 1. All important means of production such as land, mines, factories, agricultural implements, machines etc., will without exception become public property. This will put an end to the private power of the capitalists. At the same time, money will be abolished. 2. Even after all important means of production have become public property, such means may be used at will, provided they serve individual needs only. 3. There will no longer be the distinction between the class of the capitalists and the working class. All men must only engage in productive work and everyone will judge for himself what is most consonant with his own nature and what his physical strength can accomplish, and freely choose his activity accordingly. There will be no compulsion of any sort, or quotas. 4. All the products of work such as food, clothing, buildings and everything else are also owned in common by society, and everyone will be free to take what he wishes. In this way, all men will

> enjoy a happiness common to all. 5. There will be no government of any kind. The entire apparatus of administrative regulations will be totally done away with. 6. There will be no army, police, or prisons. 7. Laws and paragraphs will be abolished. 8. Freely organized public assemblies of various kinds will be held. It will be their task to improve working conditions in the different branches of productive activity, and to direct production to benefit the masses. These public assemblies, both simple and complex, will consist exclusively of the workers of the respective sector. Directors or officials will be excluded. When a position is entrusted to someone, care will be taken that real work is involved and that it is not merely the sort of position which enables the appointee to interfere with the rights of others. Nor will there be any statutes or laws for these assemblies which might limit the freedom of people. 9. Marriage regulations will be abolished. All men and women will be free to associate as they please. For pregnant women or those nursing infants, public care centers will be established. The children born there will subsequently be attended in public nurseries. 10. All children from the sixth to the 20th or 25th year will be given instruction. The finest education will be given to both boys and girls. After finishing school, all men and women will work to the age of 45 or 50. After that time, they will be taken care of in public institutions for the aged. All those suffering from diseases or other ailments will be cured in public hospitals. 12. All religions and beliefs and the commands and prohibitions based on them which contravene human freedom will be abolished. In their place, the natural morality of "mutual aid" will be introduced so that freedom may attain its highest perfection. 13. Working time for all will not exceed two to four hours daily. The rest of the time will be spent studying the natural sciences, for this will contribute to the progress of society. There will also be time for recreation through art and sports so that everyone can increase his intellectual and physical powers. 14. For purposes of instruction in the school, an international language serving general requirements will be used which will gradually supplant the different spoken and written languages of the various nations. In this way, the borders between far and near, East and West, will soon be abolished.[276]

Liu Ssu-fu's paradise shows remarkable similarities not only with Wu Chih-hui's, but also with those of K'ang Yu-wei and Liu Jen-hang. But although the colors in this portrayal may be glowing, the same can hardly be said of the living conditions the Chinese anarchists of all schools imposed on themselves ever more remorselessly in the course of time. The severity of their discipline was only partly due to the external pressure they were not infrequently subject to, perpetually hunted as they were because they were forever planning sabotage and assassinations (the pages following the above quotation give a taste of this). More responsible for what strikes the reader as a puritanical quality was a curious elitist morality which gave them the strength they needed to endure the isolation their chosen life imposed on them. It also complied with the profoundly Chinese norms of simplicity, frugality and strictness which from the very first had entered into almost all Chinese conceptions of the ideal, even the paradises.[277] Already the Paris anarchist group had laid down rather rigorous moral rules for its members. But among those who gathered around the fanatical Liu Ssu-fu, they became increasingly a central ideological tenet. Their influence on other and even some opposition movements was much stronger than that of the genuinely anarchistic ideas. The "twelve basic rules" for members of the "Heart Society"[278] were distributed in tens of thousands of fliers by the anarchists. Their goal was to be prepared for in this fashion, but the strong impression these leaflets made on large segments of the population was not due to any desire for anarchy but on the contrary to the fact that people were choking in filth, corruption and chaos, and longed for cleanliness and order. Paradoxically, the longest-lasting legacy of the anarchist movement in China was the severe moral code. Its traces can be shown in isolated instances in both the extreme moral demands of the KMT party during the early thirties, and those of the communists during that same period. Indeed, even today they are clearly recognizable everywhere on the mainland, although non-anarchists could of course subscribe to only some of these demands: 1) No eating of meat. 2) No drinking of liquor. 3) No smoking. 4) No use of servants. 5) No marriage. 6) No use of a family name. 7) No acceptance of government office. 8) No riding in sedan chairs or rickshaws. 9) No acceptance of parliamentary seats. 10) No joining of political parties. 11) No joining of an army or navy. 12) No acceptance of religion.[279]

VILLAGE IDYLL, PHILOSOPHY OF LIFE AND NATIONALISM

But the Chinese anarchist movement, which had revived so many age-old social utopias under new labels, disintegrated imperceptibly yet irresistibly, and gave rise to movements of an entirely different nature. Wu Chih-hui once remarked that Liu Ssu-fu's short life—always threatened by tuberculosis and finally its victim—served like something of a symbol of this process. When he died in 1915, the circle around him scattered in all directions, although here and there new anarchist movements flared up briefly. But there can be no doubt that it was precisely this dispersal of anarchist thought which assured it a much broader effect than could have resulted from the continued existence of an actual focal point. It is true, nonetheless, that the pure ideals advocated by the anarchists gradually volatilized in the diverse amalgams they became part of. Under the influence of the puritanical ethic, the anarchist organization in Paris developed into "The Society for Frugal Study in France" *(Liu-Fa chien-hsüeh hui)* and later, during the First World War, when France made up its shortage of workers by employing tens of thousands of Chinese with many worker-students among them, "The Association for Diligent Work and Frugal Study" *(Ch'in-kung chien-hsüeh hui)* came into being. It included preparatory seminars in China itself. One of them, in Peking, was attended by the young Mao Tse-tung in 1918. The great war in the West was the explosion of many repressed tensions and conflicts. But this inferno of destruction also deprived many fervent movements such as the anarchist of their inner meaning and as a result, the association of anarchist Chinese students in Europe returned to what it had originally been: an association of worker-students who had to make their way under the most difficult conditions if they were to pay for their studies abroad. And while they did not give up their political commitments for that reason, their poverty severely restricted their freedom of movement. In 1921, the last of them were forcibly removed from France.[280]

The Tokyo anarchist group had been much more short-lived and less cohesive, yet more closely linked to their own country. Because of this, their thinking influenced discussion in China during the twenties and early thirties in a variety of curiously refracted ways. One idea which sparked interest was the notion of organizing all of society in "villages," which had already been suggested in Liu Shih-p'ei's "theory of balanced ability." As of 1918 approximately, and under the leadership of the scholar Mushanokoji Saneatsu (born in 1885), this idea gave rise in Japan to the "New Village Movement" *(Atarashiki mura),* which, inspired by Tolstoi and Kropotkin, established kibbutz-like autarchic communities sustained by a voluntary communism.[281] The movement immediately spread from the Japanese sphere of influence in northeastern China to the mainland *(Hsin-ts'un chi-hua).* Because it had eliminated the troublesome, aggressive and terrorist components from anarchist philosophy, it stimulated a lively discussion that was carried on in the leading modern journals *New Youth (Hsin Ch'ing-nien)* and *New Tide (Hsin ch'ao,* "The Renaissance") shortly after the Literary Revolution of the Fourth of May in 1919. Hu Shih, a Dewey disciple, who placed his trust in "Mr. Science" and "Mr. Democracy" took a rather sceptical view of this movement since he saw in it only a romanticized escapism in modern dress. But among intellectuals such as Ts'ai Yüan-p'ei (1867–1940), the principal organizer of the "Society for Frugal Study in France" and the president of Peking National University during the time of the Literary Revolution, whose philosophy combined anarcho-socialist and esthetic ideas similar to Liu Jen-hang's vision of a "World of the Arts," it was received enthusiastically.[282] This was equally true of the later co-founder of the CCP, Ch'en Tu-hsiu (1879–1942), the famous writer Lu Hsün (actually Chou Shu-jen [1881–1936]) and his brother Chou Tso-jen (born in 1885), who had personally inspected the "new villages" in Tokyo, Hiuga and Ueno in the summer of 1919 and reported on them in the journal *New Youth.*[283] Liu Jen-hang was probably also a follower of this movement, for he specifically called his classification of utopias a "Historical Survey of the Development of the New Village Idea" and closed it with the exclamation: "Long life to the comrades of the New Village Movement in the entire world!"[284]

Yet the example of Liu Jen-hang (who was perhaps even related to Shih p'ei; both of them came from Kiangsu) also shows the ambivalence of anarchism in China. It ran the gamut from the most vehement rejection of religion to religious rapture, from the destruction of the entire world in a single fiery conflagration to the peaceful idyll of pastoral contemplativeness. Thus Hu Shih's scepticism toward this new variant was quite justified in many respects. For more quickly than all the others, he discovered that it was at this very point that anarchism began to turn from an extremely progressive, realistic, iconoclastic, technologically-oriented ideology hospitable to outside (or, more precisely, western) influences into its precise opposite through a relatively minor shift in emphasis, i.e. into an ideology which was turned toward the past, was mystical, clung to all "old values" and therefore also to the Old China, and viewed western civilization with mistrust. Liu Jen-hang still stands on the line separating the two extremes. In his juxtaposition of the "Old" and the "New Great Equality" he clearly gives preference to the "New," but with William Morris and Kropotkin he surreptitiously introduces idols that tended to point toward Arcadia rather than a new world. And this impression is strengthened when one reads in other sections of his book that he affirmed his allegiance not only to Kropotkin, but also to H. G. Wells and Tolstoi as the "three great prophets of the "Great Equality' between East and West."[285]

But at the time he wrote this, most of the intellectuals of anarchist lineage were already facing each other along clearly defined positions which could no longer be bridged by compromise. There were, to mention only the two most important poles, communists such as Mao Tse-tung, who said about his stay in Peking in 1918: "My interest in politics continued to increase, and my mind turned more and more radical. . . . But just now I was still confused, looking for a road, as we say. I read some pamphlets on anarchy, and was much influenced by them. With a student named Chu Hsün-pei, who used to visit me, I often discussed anarchism and its possibilities in China. At that time I favored many of its proposals."[286]

On the other side, we find conservative scholars such as Liang Sou-ming (Liang Shu-ming, born 1893),[287] who passed through a Buddhist and a Neo-Confucian (Wang Shou-jen) phase and then gave a series of lectures during the early twenties where he theorized that all of mankind (and individual man) passed through three successive phases of attitudes: aggression, harmonious balance, and renunciation, the West representing the first, China the second, and India the third. Under the influence of Nietzsche, William James, Dewey, Kropotkin, Bergson and Eucken, the West was about to approach the phase in which China found itself. At some time in the future, both China and the West would move toward the Buddhist-Hindu ideal.[288] The more aware Liang Sou-ming subsequently became that this idea was an illusion, the more he became convinced that the *élan vital,* i.e. action from natural spontaneity, was not a discovery of the European philosophy of life, but an age-old Chinese principle of life, and that it ran counter to western thought. For the "mechanized" city was the mode of life characteristic of western civilization, while the "village," being close to nature, expressed the essence of Chinese culture (to some extent, these reflections owed their origin to the impression the suicide of his conservative father, who drowned himself in a lake near Peking, made on him). Liang went beyond the accusation that this Chinese village culture was being threatened by western urbanization. He drew the consequences from his views and resigned from his teaching position at the university in 1924. After several unsuccessful attempts to found an institution which would be based on the closest collaboration between students and professors and the "inspiring dialogue" between them, he set up village cooperatives, first in Honan province (1930), then in Shantung (1931–1937) through a "Rural Reconstruction Research Institute" *(Shan-tung hsiang-ts'un chien-she yen-chiu-yüan).* Here, "peasant schools" *(Hsiang-nung hsüeh-hsiao)* would become the organizational centers for self-government and social reform.[289] His program stated: "With small-scale cooperative organizations joined to form large-scale cooperative federations, we can provide society with a general economic plan according to consumption and production, omitting the objective of profit. This is precisely to have an aspect of government grow out of the movement of cooperatives into the field of economics. The unification of politics and economics must take place like this in a natural way."[290]

It was an irony of fate that Liang Sou-ming's experiment should have been undone by the Japanese invasion in 1937. Although it was indirectly influenced by the "New Village Movement," it had much older, autochthonous Chinese models. Most influential, of course, was the well field system that had been described more than two thousand years earlier in the book of Mencius. Since the end of the nineteenth century, a long line of famous scholars had been discussing the problem whether this economic and political conception had ever really worked.[291] Answers varied. But as in the old accounts, the well fields were portrayed as village units, a network which evenly covered the entire country. The cities were not seen as centers exerting a shaping influence on the character of the villages; the opposite was more nearly the case: the towns appeared as conglomerations of villages.[292] However radical a socialist, communist or anarchist idea might be, it had something curiously familiar, pleasantly intimate about it within the context of the village. For the concept "rural community" *(hsiang)* had always been identical with that of "home." And the idea of autarchic, communistically-administered village communities was profoundly familiar not only because of the Confucian well field system, but also from the simple Taoist paradises with their bucolic security where "cocks crowed and dogs barked."[293] A New World arising from the villages could therefore immediately and much more readily be recognized as a Chinese paradise than one developing from the cities, as the West promised it. For the Chinese mentality, the very design of the modern western metropolis necessarily had to appear as a self-created hell, as Lin Yü-t'ang once dramatically described it.[294] The degree to which the village community, organized according to the well field system, was viewed as the only truly Chinese answer to the social question by perfectly progressive Chinese from the earliest beginnings of the modern period—a view which even later surfaced sporadically—is most convincingly demonstrated by the following fact. Shortly after the founding of the *T'ung-meng hui,* the previously mentioned precursor organization of the KMT in Tokyo, the decorative double cross of the character *ch'ing,* "well," was almost chosen as the emblem of the new revolutionary flag. It was only by a hairbreadth decision that Sun Yat-sen pushed through the adoption of the "white sun in the blue sky," which is still the nationalist flag today.[295] Whether it was admitted or not, it remains true that even three decades later, the discussion concerning the best way to save China still took place on two planes. One continued to search not only for the most effective, but also the most "Chinese" way. In cases of conflict, the leftists invariably preferred the more effective, the rightists the more Chinese solution.

During the long stormy period between the establishment of the republic in 1911 and the victory of the communists in 1949, it was in the great discussion concerning the evaluation of the philosophy of life that was initiated in 1923 by a young student of Liang Ch'i-ch'ao, Chang Chün-mai (actually Chang Chia-sen, "Carsun Chang," 1886–1968[296]) that this conflict became most visible. Chang had studied in Japan at Waseda University, a citadel of the "New Village Movement," and also in Berlin. In 1918–1919, he had accompanied a semiofficial Chinese group of observers under Liang Ch'i-ch'ao to the peace conference at Versailles, and used this opportunity to visit Bergson and Eucken. They confirmed his growing mistrust of western values, particularly scientific thought, as they had Liang's. In a series of lectures, he now sought to go back to the ultimately undiscoverable causes of life to which only "intuition" could give access. They became the basis of a new, Chinese metaphysics, which fused Bergson, Eucken and Wang Shou-jen. Chang argued that what were precise solutions in a scientific sense could only be found for problems in the natural sciences, not for human problems which were subject to an entirely different law, the law of life, and could only be dealt with by entirely different methods which had not been unknown to traditional Chinese philosophy. The violent response of the respected geologist Ting Wen-chiang ("V. K. Ting" 1888–1936) initiated a controversy that went on for years. Among many others, Hu Shih also participated as a defender of "science" against metaphysics and religion, and formulated a kind of credo of the "scientifically" thinking philosopher.[297]

Although the majority of Chinese intellectuals undoubtedly took sides against Chang Chün-mai, his attack was significant for two reasons. After Chinese humanism had long been fighting what were defensive battles at best, Chang restored the awareness that happiness was ultimately an intensely personal matter; that while man lived by bread, bread alone was not enough. He thus took up arms against an increasingly broader alliance of scholars that believed that the world could only be saved by the introduction of a more just social order and increased production. With the philosophy of life as formulated in China and presented by Chang, not only Neo-Confucian but also Taoist and Buddhist ideals, whose very character was a-social if not anti-social in wide areas, were given a new lease. Life in nature, at the source of life, took on a new value (which Liang Sou-ming had also striven for). So did the unreflective pleasure in all sensory experience, for which Chinese philosophy had always felt a particular affinity. The other side, from "leftists" to liberals, reacted with bitterness, and this is no less comprehensible. For it was not unjustified in suspecting that a totalitarian state authority might arise behind the nebulous life of a nature that was declared unknowable *a priori.* This had happened more than once in China, although the phenomenon is not confined to that country. And such an authority might lay claim to a total freedom from all restraints since it represented a "nature" and a "humanity" whose impenetrability was axiomatic.

This concern was all the better founded since the second component of Chang's doctrine also addressed itself to an irrational complex, namely nationalism. To emphasize "life" as the truly decisive principle for human well-being implied the shift to a plane where China had every reason to feel secure, for it was precisely this preoccupation (and social ethics) that its philosophy had always stressed. Seen from this point of view, the almost total absence of logic, for example, this typically western and normally much envied link between philosophy and technology no longer appeared as a lack, but rather as the expression of a remarkable inner consistency. The natural sciences were relegated to second place where they could once again be understood as instances of "application" according to the old schema of "inner" and "outer." As Bergson, Eucken and Driesch assured it, China could once more look upon itself as mankind's teacher of humanity, as it had done throughout the course of its history. And Bertrand Russell, whose lecture trip in 1920/1921 had found an enormous echo in China,[298] concurred, if for entirely different reasons. It is therefore almost certainly no accident that the word "life" also figured in the "New Life" movement inaugurated by Chiang Kai-shek in 1934. Nationalist and rightist, it was intended to counterbalance communist ideology although, being rather puritanical and intent on the preservation of order and cleanliness, it had hardly anything in common with Chang Chün-mai's ideals.[299] But the expression "life" evoked the nationalist Chinese, predominantly Confucian scale of values, just as the term "new" evoked the socialist. To represent the latter was also a concern of the KMT, if one is to judge by official statements.

THE IDEAL OF TEPIDITY AND THE HOPE FOR THE GREAT DICTATOR

However precarious and vacillating the basis of China's new self-confidence may have been, it nonetheless soon found interpreters who carried its wisdom into the world as if it were a message of salvation. Having become unsure in its naive, nineteenth-century belief in a progress which had once also dazzled China, and sceptical toward its own, only seemingly well-founded order, much of the intelligentsia in the West was discovering that traditional Chinese philosophy was a seemingly unscathed expression of a world that was still whole, and this at the very moment when in China itself a final effort was being made to save it with whatever strength remained. In Germany, the work of the respected scholar Richard Wilhelm (1873–1930) falls into this category. Having gone to China as a Protestant missionary only to return from there as its apostle and to translate a wealth of Chinese classics until the end of the twenties, he created a corpus which not only in its choice of texts but also in its somewhat idealizing tone has shaped the view of China of the German public down to the present day.[300]

The influence of the repeatedly quoted Chinese writer Lin Yü-t'ang ("Lin Yutang") (born 1895) was incomparably greater, because it affected primarily the Anglo-Saxon world. His background shows some (though of course not entirely consistent) parallels with Wilhelm's. He came from a very strict, Christian Chinese family of ministers, was first trained for that career, and therefore systematically kept away from the Chinese tradition. As a result, it was only at a relatively advanced age, and after having turned away from Christianity, that he could discover his own culture from a predominantly western perspective, and thus acquire the detachment necessary to describe it. His brilliant essays, improvisations of enormous skill, sparkling wit, versatility and nimbleness also reveal something else, however. For one thing, it was not only from the distance but also from the angle of the westerner that he saw his own country. Perhaps because of this, his accounts of Chinese wisdom stressed a certain aspect of the Chinese utopians, those eternal seekers after happiness, which had only crystallized under the continued pressure of Neo-Confucianism since the fifteenth and sixteenth centuries. It is that mixture, those not easily unraveled strands of ultimate wisdom, philistinism, resignation and humor where the loss of all ideals could in turn become a new norm and which, from the Sung on, had found its incarnation in the laughing 'pot-bellied' Buddha.[301]

It is revealing that the majority of Chinese thinkers rediscovered through his translations in both West and East belonged to the sixteenth and seventeenth centuries. In his writings, Lin emphasizes again and again that "all human happiness is sensuous happiness,"[302] that "the end of living is the true enjoyment of it,"[303] that the "Lost Paradise" is a fiction,[304] and that "the Chinese are a hard-boiled lot. There is no nonsense about them: they do not live in order to die, as the Christians pretend to do, nor do they seek for a Utopia on earth, as many seers of the West do. They just want to order this life on earth, which they know to be full of pain and sorrow, so that they may work peaceably, endure nobly, and live happily."[305] In a scale where the intensity of four key qualities is assigned a value ranging from one to four, and which includes realism (R), dreams (or idealism) (D), a sense of humor (H) and sensitivity (S) as he takes them to be represented among the various nations, he therefore logically arrives at the formula $R_4D_1H_3S_3$ for the Chinese (as compared to $R_3D_3H_2S_2$ for America, $R_3D_2H_2S_1$ for England, $R_2D_3H_3S_3$ for France, $R_2D_4H_1S_1$ for Russia, and $R_3D_4H_1S_2$ for Germany). In contrast to Russia and Germany, China is accorded a maximum of humor (H_4 is conceded to no nation) and a minimum of dreams (ideals, utopias, images of desire).[306] The "almost-right," the "nearly-ideal" for which Chinese has the wonderful, nearly untranslatable expression *ch'a-pu-to* becomes for Lin not only the quintessence of Chinese wisdom,[307] but almost the essential core of life itself. In view of what, in contemporary terminology, we may call the programming of all life functions on the one hand, and the obvious closeness to death of all seekers of the absolute on the other, perhaps such an idea should not be rejected out of hand even if wisdom and banality seem inextricably intertwined in it. A work by the relatively unknown poet Li Mi-an (? sixteenth century), "The Half-and-Half Song," seems to him the "best philosophy, because it is the most human"[308]:

> By far the greater half have I seen through/This floating life—Ah, there's a magic word—/This "half"—so rich in implications./ It bids us taste the joy of more than wc/Can ever own. Halfway in life is man's/Best state, when slackened pace allows him ease;/A wide world lies halfway 'twixt heaven and earth;/To live halfway between the town and land,/Have farms halfway between the streams and hills;/Be half-a-scholar, and half-a-squire, and half/In business; half as gentry live,/And half related to the common folk;/And have a house that's half genteel, half plain,/Half elegantly furnished and half bare;/Dresses and gowns that are half old, half new,/ And food half epicure's, half simple fare;/Have servants not too clever, not too dull;/A wife who's not too simple, nor too smart—/So then, at heart, I feel I'm half a Buddha,/And almost half a Taoist fairy blest./One half myself to Father Heaven I/Return; the other half to children leave—/Half thinking how for my posterity/To plan and provide, and yet half minding how/To answer God when the body's laid at rest./He is most wisely drunk who is half drunk;/And flowers in half-bloom look their prettiest;/As boats at half-sail sail the steadiest,/And horses held at half-slack reins trot best./Who half too much has, adds anxiety,/But half too little, adds possession's zest./Since life's of sweet and bitter compounded,/Who tastes but half is wise and cleverest.[309]

The many other passages from Chinese literature Lin Yü-t'ang quotes as signposts along the way toward the discovery of the small happiness of the everyday also bear the mark of this curiously tepid "half-and-half": the "thirty-three happy moments" of the scholar Chin Sheng-t'an (seventeenth century), for example, trivial events like rain and thunder after a sultry summer day, or the pleasure of cutting a bright green watermelon[310]; the "nine blessings" in the life of the retired official Ting Hsiung-fei (seventeenth century) such as having a wife who loves reading and writing or his inability to understand chess, an enumeration of things of this sort which another scholar comments and balances by a listing of their opposites: "I am happy that I have no wife who loves to bother with reading and writing." . . . "I love to play chess or watch others playing in silence."[311] Somewhat more profound, yet steeped in that irony which leaves all things indeterminate, is the fable about the poet Chang Ch'ao (seventeenth century) who adopts the style of Chuang-tzu or Lieh-tzu to tell about a hypochondriac who rejects all the pleasures of this world which a well-intentioned friend proposes as remedies for this condition—gambling, riding, government service, literary composition, wine, long journeys—until they begin talking about the attainment of immortality, and he immediately recovers.[312] The whole thing is a metaphor for man's constant suffering because he must die, a condition which only illusion can mitigate for a while.

At first glance, Lin Yü-tang's essays seem to concern themselves primarily with the value of leisure, the "art of sitting on chairs," or the common sense of Chinese dress.[313] As one reads them more closely, however, one begins to sense with an increasing, oppressive insistence that this rippling lightheartedness, this soothing indifference toward the dark side of human life, is not born of naiveté but of the long, painful experience of the Chinese people. It is, as Lin writes, "a form of self-protection, developed in the same manner as the tortoise develops its shell."[314] Lin's principal work, the *Importance of Living* really becomes a book on the importance of surviving, for the voluntary renunciation of ideals and paradises, however utopian they might be, did not come easily to China, as a glance at its spiritual past or its present condition shows so clearly. It was an attitude which developed only gradually from the tenth century on, and under the ever-increasing influence of an all-too unquestioningly accepted Confucianism which was misused by the state besides. The book is not so much a demonstration of the Chinese conviction that it is important to live, but rather that one must survive. Certainly Lin Yü-t'ang was intensely aware of this. How else can one understand those eruptions where he suddenly questions the value of what he had praised so highly as the steadiness of China in earlier passages. The following quotation, the closing lines of an essay on "Chinese Realism and Humor," written toward the end of 1930, are an example:

> And so the merry old China marches on, unhampered by banditry, or by the fear of communists, or by the invasion of imperialists. The placid life flows on serene and unperturbed. It is a serenity that has an element of old rascality in it. It is the wicked, shrewd and cynical laugh of an old man who has seen the world and who is beyond both hope and disappointment. Life is too short to make an over-serious business out of it. It is the hollow reverberant laugh of old China, at the touch of whose breath, every flower of enthusiasm and hope must wither and die.[315]

And how else is one to understand passages such as the epilogue of his book *My Country and My People,* written in 1935, long before the war with Japan and the subsequent moral collapse. Speaking figuratively, one might say that Lin's ordinarily relaxed features suddenly seem to become taut as his normally mild voice begins to quiver with passion under the impact of impotent despair and adventist longing:

> It seems the race cannot adjust itself to a new world, with healthier, more aggressive people all around and demanding a new ethics to suit the new tempo of life. . . . The nation frisks and frets, and alternates between megalomania and melancholia, and easily becomes hysterical. This is especially observable in the more

articulate, I dare not say more intelligent, class, . . . Some of these scholars are ashamed of our own country, of our farmers and coolies, and of our own customs and language and arts and literature, and would like to cover China up with a huge shroud as if it were a stinking carcass, and allow foreigners to see only white-collared, English-speaking Chinese like themselves, whereas the common people merely suffer and carry on. . . . Some advocate salvation by learning the use of machine-guns, another by frugality and the wearing of sandals, another by dancing and wholesale introduction of western life, another by selling and buying national goods, another by physical culture through good old boxing, another by learning Esperanto, another by saying Buddhist masses, another by reintroducing the Confucian classics in school, another by "throwing the classics into the toilet for thirty years."[316] To hear them discussing the salvation of the country would be like listening to a council of quack doctors at a patient's deathbed. It would be humorous if it were not so pathetic. . . . Man, it seems, has been more sinned against then sinning in China. For I remember Sung Chiang and the host of good souls who turned bandits in the end of the Northern Sung Dynasty.[317] . . . And I remember how every great poet expressed his contempt for society by taking to wine and nature, how Ch'üan in a rage jumped into the Hsiang River[318] and Li Po fell overboard in attempting to reach for the reflection of the moon;[319] . . . how even great and upright Confucians who retained a sense of right and wrong always ended in official banishment. . . . I remember how in times of national misrule and disorder the good scholars were hounded and their wives and children and distant relatives were murdered *en masse*, as during the beginning of the Manchu Dynasty. . . . Then I look over the modern times and see how the good men, as in all countries, have abstained from politics; how Wang Kuo-wei jumped into the lake of the Summer Palace, and K'ang Yu-wei spent the last years of his life in lonely pride, and how Lusin shut himself up in dark and unmitigated despair until the call for the literary revolution came, and how Chang T'aiyen is today shutting himself up in Soochow, and how Hu Shih the student of Dewey and influenced by a more progressive outlook, is pragmatizing and patching up the sores of the people, without great enthusiasm, but still unwilling to give up and turn China to the dogs —Hu Shih who, in a moment of prophetic fury, cried out, "If China does not perish, God is blind!" These are the good men of China who cannot help the country, for man has sinned against man, and the bad men have sinned against the good men, and the good men need a simple cotton gown for disguise. Yet there are other good men, not only five, not only fifty, but millions of them suffering and carrying on, unsung and unheard of. The thought wrings pity from the onlooker that there should be so many good men and not a leader half the size of a Gandhi, that in China individually men are more mature, but politically and nationally we are as mere children. . . . At last I thought of the Great Executioner and the moment I saw him in my vision, I knew he would save China. Here comes the Savior, he with the great sword that would only obey Dame Justice's command, and that no one else could pull out of its place without her bidding, the sword that was drowned in a lake centuries ago. . . . The Great Executioner comes, and pulls that sword out of the deep, and he is preceded by drumboys in blue uniform, and trumpeteers in yellow uniform.[320] Dum-Dum-Dum! the procession comes, and the trumpeteers in yellow uniform proclaim the rule of the law.[321] Dum-Dum-Dum! the procession comes from the country, approaching the town and down the main streets, and at the distant rumble of the drums and the sight of the banner, with Dame Justice sitting in state, and the Great Executioner with the gleaming sword by her side, the people cheer, but the mayor and the town councillors run away higgledy-piggledy and hide themselves. For behold, there the Savior comes! The Great Executioner nails the banner of Justice on the city wall, and makes every one of them bow before it as they pass. And a notice is posted all over the city that whosoever says he is above the law and refuses to bow before the banner will be beheaded and his head will be thrown into the lake where the sword was sunk for so many hundreds of years. And he goes into the city temple and throws out their goddesses, whose names are Face, Fate and Favor, and converts it into a House of Justice.[322] To this place he herds together the priests and councillors who ruled the city under the goddesses' names, and with the great sword he chops off their heads and commands that they be thrown, together with their goddesses, into the lake. . . . And of those whose heads the Great Executioner chops off great is the number, many of them from distinguished families, and the lake is dyed red with their blood of iniquity. And, strange to say, in three days the relatives of the distinguished families who have robbed and betrayed the people behave like noble gentlemen, and the people are at least let alone to live in peace and security and the city prospers. . . . That time will come . . . that process is already at work, invisible, penetrating the upper and lower social strata, and as inevitable as dawn. For a time yet there will still be ugliness and pain, but after a while there will be calm and beauty and simplicity, the calm and beauty and simplicity which distinguished old China. But more than that, there will be justice, too. To that people of the Land of Justice, we of the present generation shall seem but like children of the twilight.[323]

4 / *THE NEW EMPIRE AND THE SALVATION OF THE WORLD*

THE BEGINNINGS OF CHINESE MARXISM

When Lin Yü-t'ang published this seemingly fantastic description of the dawn of a new Chinese era, he was probably not aware how soon this vision would become reality, at least in its outward dimensions. And he anticipated even less through what forces and under what conditions this would occur. Perhaps he was still too much a victim of the illusion that modern China was governed only by "those ghostly scholars who wave ghostly fans and believe in the importance of living with the utmost tranquillity," and thus forgot the "vigor and violence of the Chinese mind at its best, grappling with human problems like naked wrestlers."[324] Lin no longer believed in revolutions. In the China of 1935, the "familiar boom of guns and the racket of fusillades . . . seemed more and more like firecrackers in the next street, and I learned it was only Mr. Yang celebrating his assumption of a new post."[325] And yet, his image of the "Savior with the great sword," the Executioner who would lead a procession "from the country, approaching the town," may have looked to some like a picture of the victory of Mao Tse-tung and the soldiers of the People's Liberation Army which, after decades of fighting in the countryside, would celebrate its greatest triumphs in 1949 when it occupied the towns. And these triumphs profoundly impressed western observers as well, precisely because of the curious contrast between city and country as it emerged most clearly when Peking was taken.[326] A perfectly prosaic event, the march of the troops into the city transformed itself into a solemn, festive procession with acrobats and groups of dancers, and was celebrated as a transition from one sphere to another, and this not just in a spatial but also in a temporal sense. For it was hailed as the beginning of a new era where finally, and after long delay, the ideal would gain admittance in the real world.

The earliest form of the Chinese communist movement grew out of the same, curious, almost unreal atmosphere in which anarchism had so quickly flowered and faded before. In both cases, this was a function of the psychological (and often also physical) distance from their own culture. Indeed, in many respects, the roots of these two movements are so inextricably intertwined that it becomes difficult to separate them. After a kind of intellectual calm during the decade from 1907 to 1917, which contrasted oddly with the convulsion of the national revolution (1911) and the outbreak of the First World War, the most diverse associations and organizations which at first still favored anarchist ideals gave birth to groups which studied Marxism and socialism extensively. This phenomenon not only paralleled European developments but also took place in Europe itself. Chinese students abroad and imported Chinese workers, and many who were both, had a special role to play. The reason for this was not only that they had come under the influence of "left radical" ideals while abroad, but also because as "left radicals," and this is what most of them were, they could be active and free of the restraints their own country imposed on them. Interestingly enough, the extraterritorial and colonial territories of the colonial powers on Chinese soil (Shanghai, Hong-Kong, Macao, etc.) frequently provided similar opportunities. Had there been no such areas of immunity, the communist movement in China could hardly have arisen, or would at least have been considerably slowed down.

The influence emanating from that group of Chinese students and workers in France who after 1918 returned to China in large numbers and organized further student exchanges with France was the most enduring. The previously mentioned "Association for Diligent Work and Frugal Study" which prepared students for their stay abroad, particularly in France, spontaneously developed into an organization where increasingly students interested in Marxism could come together. They took the place of those who had formerly been influenced by anarchism. The connections between anarchists and Marxists during the early phase, before 1919 or thereabouts, have been documented repeatedly. We have not only the previously quoted comment of Mao Tse-tung, but also some dates from the life of the first head of the CCP, Ch'en Tu-hsiu, which indicate that he collaborated with Chang Chi and others in the publication of a revolutionary paper in Shanghai in 1903, and that in 1906 he taught at the same university as Liu Shih-p'ei, in Anhui province. Finally, there is the circumstance that the first Marxist texts (excerpts from the *Communist Manifesto*) appeared in 1908 in the anarchist journal, *Natural Justice.*[327] But here also, it was the May Fourth Movement of 1919 which brought the decisive turn, the breakthrough of a somehow changed, more incisive and more sober thought. It created a wide interest in all social questions, but it was an interest that had freed itself of all those elements of childlike naiveté which had been so typical of the anarchists. Admittedly, it was also purged of most utopian elements which had once given Chinese anarchism its particular fervor and color.

Retrospectively, one may say that the founding of the CCP in 1921 was the most important result of this process of maturation. After the restlessness of puberty that was the May Fourth Movement, it propelled the new China into adulthood where a greater realism began to blend with a certain dogmatism and lack of humor. These occurrences are shrouded in a kind of primeval mist of history, so that even today it is not entirely clear in what month the party was founded (whether May or July) nor how many, and what (seven or fifteen) persons participated.[328] What is striking, in any event, is how few of them were left at the end. Twenty years later, when the CCP took over in China, about half of them had gone over to the KMT, and of the remainder, the majority had either been excluded from the party or been executed by the enemies of the CCP. It is more noteworthy still that the founding of the party did not mean the beginning of the study of Marxism. Nor did it, on the other hand, represent a definite end to the growth of widely diverging Marxist systems of thought which had come out of the most variegated "proto-communist" study groups before 1920, but primarily a break in an organizational sense. For although divergent opinions continued to clash, the mere existence of the party now provided a forum where disagreements could be aired and critically evaluated. At the same time, and purely as concentrated power, it represented a value worth fighting for. Not unlike developments after the establishment of a "church" or, in the sciences, after that of a "school," every controversy among communists in China took on a twofold aspect, as is true in politics everywhere: it no longer exclusively pursued the conversion of "infidels," but also that of "believers." For without the anointment of orthodoxy which only the existence of a party made possible, every ideology, however "true," suddenly lost all value and effectiveness. In this sense, the founding of the CCP put a stop to the completely unhampered discussion of Marxist problems in the widest sense precisely because it documented the breakthrough of this mode of thought. In the same way, though in a larger framework, the May Fourth Movement had ended the reception of western thought (which, for that reason, and to this day, is conspicuously confined to that of the nineteenth century). The playful if occasionally almost chaotic exchange of opinions was followed by a strict order based on a single and, at least theoretically, pervasive point of view. But it is also true that this introduction of a "perspective" entailed a constriction of the field of vision.

Yet intra-party disputes retained sufficient scope to permit conflicting ideas to survive side by side, and this elasticity also benefited those whose views changed in the course of time. In many instances, the disagreements that found expression here were the same as those that had also emerged before in the long development of Marxism via Engels, Lenin, Trotsky and Stalin. Some of them were settled by *ex cathedra* judgments, while others were left undecided. But these antagonisms interfered with others that had arisen as socialist ideas were being transplanted to the alien, Chinese milieu, although this did not become entirely clear to the communists who were less interested than the right-wing nationalists in the preservation of national characteristics. Normally, the intelligentsia read the Marxist classics in translation, but the form of expression chosen by the translators evoked associations that differed significantly from those of the original western texts. A process thus repeated itself which had occurred once before, when Buddhism had come to China. A different language and culture brought it about that the new doctrine from the West was either not understood at all, or understood "differently," not to say incorrectly. (For only a few specialists could work their way through the jungle of transliterated "foreign words.") Whether the change that necessarily resulted from the transplantation into an alien intellectual milieu should be understood as deviation and false belief or as "creative development" is less a question of truth than of orthodoxy. It is very difficult to resolve because when the "renewed" new teaching returns to its place of origin (as, for example, when Maoism was imported into Europe), the same unconscious yet asymmetrical misunderstandings consequent on the changed cultural background may arise once more, so that in the end it is not the old, but again a completely new teaching that may confront us.

THE WILL TO ACT AND THE REVOLUTIONARY ROLE OF THE VILLAGE

An impressive example of this gradual merging of Marxist and autochthonous Chinese traditions in the solution of fundamental questions that surfaced time and again, and concerned the temporal dimension and the social milieu in which the happiness of mankind would be attained is the system of Li Ta-chao (1888–1927), next to Ch'en Tu-hsiu the most important early Chinese Marxist. He came from northern China (Hopei), studied first in Tientsin and then, between 1913 and 1916, at Waseda University in Japan. After his return, he first collaborated with the rather conservative Progressive Party *(Chin-pu-tang)* which was working for constitutional monarchy, and to which Liang Ch'i-ch'ao also belonged. But already a year later, he joined the circle around the editors of the journal *New Youth* in Shanghai. In 1918, he was appointed head librarian of Peking National University. Mao Tse-tung came to Peking at about the same time and was employed under him as assistant librarian. Together, they founded a very loosely knit "Marxist Study Society" which met in the library on free evenings. A year later, this group became the more ambitious "Socialist Study Society," and finally, after several further intermediate steps, and through the initiative of the Comintern representative Gregori Voitinsky, the CCP.[329] In a series of theoretical controversies the first of which he engaged in as early as 1919 with Hu Shih,[330] Li Ta-chao molded the CCP more and more in his own image. But this did not prevent him from supporting cooperation with the KMT as had been recommended by the Comintern since 1922, and from joining the KMT (and thus the government) in 1924 as the only communist member of the five-member presidium of the First National Congress. After the ties between the CCP and the KMT were broken and leftist extremists were persecuted as a result, Li returned to direct revolutionary agitation in 1925 and therefore had to seek refuge in the Soviet Russian embassy in Peking in 1926. Almost exactly one year later, when the Warlord Chang Tso-lin attacked the embassy, he was arrested and executed.

Even today, Li Ta-chao is still worshipped as a communist martyr in China. His interpretation of Marxism reflects in many respects his pre-Marxist convictions which had been decisively shaped by Bergson's philosophy of life, and consequently did not require an abrupt break with the fundamental orientation of traditional Chinese philosophy. Originally, he had believed in a "tide of great reality" *(ta-shih tsai)* flowing through all being like a single stream of life and keeping it in movement. But this movement always carried a dialectical element within it and was consequently not directed toward a fixed goal but self-contained, as it were. This conception resulted in a particular view of time and history. In his famous essay "Now" *(Chin),* printed in *New Youth* in 1918, he developed his conception of a kind of quiescent movement in history: "All historical phenomena are always revolving and always changing and at the same time they still forever remain indestructible phenomena in the universe." The present, which is understood as the reservoir of all past and future moments, is the corresponding element: "Unlimited 'pasts' all find their resting place in the 'present' and unlimited 'futures' all originate in the 'present.' "[331] It is not difficult to recognize here the "one-dimensional" concept of time which had already been known in earliest China and resulted from the dialectics of the fundamental forces, the Yin and the Yang, as described in the *Book of Changes* and its commentaries. It also had caused the infinitely small "now" to expand into an infinitely large "now" that absorbed the entire future and the entire past within itself. With his strong emphasis on the Here and Now, which can be traced in all of Li Ta-chao's doctrines even after he became a thoroughgoing Marxist, he thus did not take a non-Chinese, let alone an anti-Chinese direction. At most, it was an anti-Confucian one, but even this only to the extent that he attacked Confucian utopianism, particularly the mirage of a Confucian Golden Age, against which even modern Confucian scholars, principally Ku Chieh-kang (born in 1893),[332] have polemicized. Remaining committed to the "Great Reality" and in opposition to all genuine utopians who expected salvation from what was most remote in time and space, in which they sought to immerse themselves, or whose "arrival" they expected, Li could see the key to man's happiness only in the "Now," since it alone offered the possibility for action.

As a consequence of this position, Li Ta-chao encountered a much discussed but never entirely resolved problem in Marxism (and probably this problem was not resolvable due to its dialectical character): the opposition between determinism and activism. In his early years, Marx had tended to stress man's free decision as the essential factor in history and had seen it against the background of alienation and the growth of consciousness. In his later work, he had given greater weight to laws deriving from socio-economic conditions. In contrast, the Chinese intellectuals, and among them again primarily the leftists, had been intrigued by the iron law Marx believed he had discovered in history. It seemed to be superimposed on what had originally been taken to be the no less iron law of the survival of the fittest as formulated by Darwin. Even better, it appeared to transcend it by predicting that the seemingly impregnable West in its capitalist-imperialist form would collapse of its own weight. With the First World War, this disintegration had entered its initial phase. After all, there were numerous precedents for such historical laws in the Chinese tradition itself, beginning with Tung Chung-shu's various cycles, and down to the no longer cyclical but linear "Three Epochs"[333] which had sustained hope for a spontaneous upward development of human society in the New Text School, and still inspired K'ang Yu-wei. China had been thrust into modern times. As long as it experienced itself as hopelessly inferior to the West, it could find a certain consolation in such fixed, historical laws, for they seemed to promise both the inevitable decline of the capitalist West, and also the irresistible advance of a humiliated China. It is in this light that one has to see the incessant efforts of Chinese scholars since the beginning of this century to divide their long history into "periods." Some sought to discover a specific, inherent pattern, while others searched for equivalents of the various phases through which history had passed in the Marxist view (primitive communism, slave society, feudal society, bourgeoisie, and capitalism). Both of these schools were at least indirectly influenced by Marxism. Yet it is also true that their concern, whether implicit or not, was with China's salvation rather than that of the world as a whole.[334]

But from the early twenties on, this rather mechanistic view of history was gradually supplemented in Marxist circles by a voluntaristic one. According to this conception, salvation was no longer to depend on the passive trust in autonomously operating universal social laws, but on action born of a higher consciousness. Two causes may have been responsible for this shift in accent. One was the weakening of the West and the resulting change in the balance of power that now favored a previously utterly impotent China. There was also the insight that even during the twenties, China's mode of production was still "Asiatic." If the Marxist socio-economic historical mechanism was the exclusive determinant, there was little hope that the ideal world of communism would become accessible in the foreseeable future (and certainly not at the same time as, let alone earlier than, for the envied western industrialized nations). Since China was more interested in this than in anything else, an exceptional effort would have to be made to overcome its backwardness.[335] The belief that this need not be pointless even if the necessary economic presuppositions were lacking derived from the fact that according to Marxist doctrine, it was not only economic conditions but also a particular form of consciousness on the part of the masses that was required for a transformation of society. Even if all the presuppositions for a revolution were given, in other words, that would be of no avail unless there were people ready to make use of them.[336] With some boldness, this last sentence could be turned around: to bring about those social changes that would "inevitably" follow from economic conditions required not only consciousness. Instead, "consciousness" seemed strong enough under certain conditions to *create* social changes *and* their economic presuppositions at one and the same time.[337] In this reasoning, a correlation of extreme significance for modern China may be observed. There is the sensational Marxist insight that human history actually obeys scientific laws and can therefore be predicted as reliably as, say, the path of planets. This was the dream of all Chinese historians, for they had originally been astronomers, as we have seen. However paradoxical it may appear, this view suddenly found its counterpart in the notion that these natural historical laws, which seemed to negate man's free will, were subject to that will in turn. The total determination of human society by historical "laws of nature" was thus followed by the "miracle" of a consciousness that could move mountains, as it were, and thus invalidate these same natural laws.

All of Li Ta-chao's arguments tended in this voluntarist-activist direction. For he was admittedly enthusiastic because "with Marx' materialist conception of history the study of history had been raised to the same position as that of the natural sciences" and therefore after "Scientific socialism has taken as its basis the materialist conception of history . . . it has discovered the necessary laws of history. On the basis of these laws, it has advocated the social necessity of socialism. From this it can be said that a socialist society, no matter whether men want it or not . . . is a command of history."[338] But he also, and much more emphatically, condemned the view that one need do no more than wait for the spontaneous transformation of society: "There are some people who misinterpret the materialist view of history by saying that social progress depends only on natural material changes. They therefore disregard human activity and sit around waiting for the arrival of the new situation. . . . This is an especially great error because the influence of the materialist conception of history on human life is precisely the opposite."[338a]

In a letter Li wrote to a friend in 1921, he went on to say that it was not the degree of development of a given country that decided whether it was about to enter a new phase of society, but rather the degree of development of the most advanced nations, for they had an indirect influence on those that were socially backward. What was important was not the monotonous repetition of all phases of development but the rapidity with which shortcuts were taken:

> If one asks whether or not the economic conditions of present-day China are prepared for the realization of socialism, it is first necessary to ask whether or not present-day world economic conditions are tending toward the realization of socialism, because the Chinese economic situation really cannot be considered apart from the international economy. The contemporary world economy is already moving from capitalism to socialism, and although China itself has not yet undergone a process of capitalist economic development such as occurred in Europe, America, and Japan, the common people [of China] still indirectly suffer from capitalist economic oppression in a way that is even more bitter than the direct capitalist oppression suffered by the working classes of the various [capitalist] nations. Al-

> though within China the relations between capital and labor still have not developed into a very great problem, the position of the Chinese people in the world economy and in the ever-growing storm of the labor movement has already been established, and it is really impossible to think of preserving the capitalist system either in theory or practice. If we again look at the international position of China today, [we see] that others have already passed from free competition to the necessary socialist-cooperative position, while we today are just at the point that the others have started from and are following in their footsteps. Others have reached maturity, while we are still juveniles; others have walked a thousand *li,* while we are still taking the first step. Under these kinds of conditions, if we want to continue to exist and adapt ourselves to the common life [of the world], I fear that we will be unable to succeed unless we take double steps and unite into a socially cooperative organization. Therefore, if we want to develop industry in China, we must organize a government made up purely of producers in order to eliminate the exploiting classes within the country, to resist world capitalism, and to follow [the path of] industrialization organized upon a socialist basis.[339]

Already the first part of this quotation indicates Li Ta-chao's view that the Chinese people had an exceptional role to play in the Marxist concept because its oppression by the capitalist system was even more "bitter" than that of the other nations of the world. In another passage, he attempted to characterize the Chinese people in their totality as a "proletarian nation,"[340] which was simply intended to suggest that it was therefore ready for the revolution of the proletariat which would introduce the age of communism. He supported this interpretation with the thesis that it was not so much the different stages of the class struggle (which Sun Yat-sen had also dismissed as a symptom of disease whose significance had been overestimated), but rather the various stages of "mutual aid" in society that provided the measure for the degree of development. This concept came from Kropotkin and had been picked up by Li during his student days in Japan. Through its use, he succeeded in eliminating social Darwinism, a theory which was discouraging to a weak China and even seemed to lead a ghostly existence behind the idea of the class struggle. He also placed China in a position where it could act, for it was a principle that could be put into practice immediately. Hesitation and delay because external conditions were not propitious could thus be avoided:

> Most of the preceding discussions about natural evolution centered about [the problem of] the survival of the fittest and [advocated that] the weak are the prey of the strong and that one ought to sacrifice the weak for one's own existence and happiness. . . . Now we know that these discussions were greatly mistaken [because] biological progress does not arise from struggle but from mutual aid. If humanity wishes to strive to exist and if it wishes happiness and prosperity, then it must have mutual friendship and ought not to rely upon force for mutual extermination."[341] . . . This spirit of mutual aid, this ethic, this social ability, is able to cause human progress. Moreover, with human progress the content [of this spirit] develops greatly. . . . Because the ethics of men has been a powerful social ability since the

most ancient period of human life, there has developed in the human heart a voice of authority that down to the present day still echoes in our own hearts. It has a mysterious quality that is not due to the stimulus of the outside world, nor is it a matter of advantage or disadvantage; [rather] it is a naturally produced authority. Its mysterious nature is similar to the mystery of sex, the mystery of mother love, and the mystery of sacrifice.[342]

As one reads the last sentences, one is tempted to believe that just as Marx had once put Hegel "on his feet," Li Ta-chao now went about putting Marx on his head. But actually these thoughts, which are vividly reminiscent of Mencius and his notion of "sincerity"[343] simply show how readily even a very modern Chinese thinker unconsciously recurred to the old "inner"/"outer" dichotomy and simultaneously to an idealist orientation, the moment the national element came into play. For as though of their own accord, a number of qualities began to cluster around the initial opposition of "Now" and "Not-now" (i.e. utopian, idealized past). Some of these, such as human consciousness, mutual aid with its "natural" origin and the atemporality of an infinite present could easily be subsumed under the category "inner" (and this meant "China"). Others, such as technological and economic progress, "artificial" class struggle (because present neither in primitive communism nor in the final communist society), and a temporally clearly definable gradation of social development could be ranged under the concept "outer" (i.e. foreign countries). Only "knowledge," "ideal," "utopia" on the one side, and "action" and "reality" on the other have switched sides as compared to the old schema.[344] The distant, the truly unattainable utopia and empty knowledge are now assigned to the "outer," while in the "inner," in China, we have the "action" that defines reality. But precisely in this switch, in this attribution of the will to act to the more fundamental "inner," Li Ta-chao clearly saw the essence of the materialism which seemed to give China its opportunity in the national sphere as well. Truth, for him, was: In the beginning was the deed.

Li's glorification of the village and rural milieu, clearly so much more part of the Chinese "inner," his downgrading of the city atmosphere, harmonized with this conception. In a proclamation addressed to the youth of his country, he wrote: "My young friends who are idle in the cities! You should know that while the cities have a great many evils, the villages have a great many happinesses. The dark aspects of life in the cities are many; the bright aspects of life in the villages are many. City life is virtually the life of the devil, whereas village life is a wholly human life. The air of the city is filthy, whereas the village air is clear."[345]

The high value placed on the rural milieu betrays the influence of the "New Village Movement" which Li Ta-chao had come to know as a student at Waseda University. It had direct political consequences. In 1919, he called on the revolutionary Marxist students to seek increased contact with the peasants in the countryside, and not to let themselves be wholly taken up by theories in the cities:

> We should not drift about in the cities and become cultured vagrants existing outside of working society. We ourselves ought to go to the villages . . . and take up hoes and plows and become companions of the toiling peasants. . . . It should be known that the term "dignity of labor" is certainly not applicable to those people who talk but don't do a bit of physical work. Those intellectuals who eat but do not work ought to be eliminated together with the capitalists. The condition of China today is that the cities and the villages have been made into two opposite poles and have almost become two different worlds. The village people have not the slightest relation with the problems that develop in the cities and the spread of culture. Generally the city people are wholly unconcerned with life in the villages and are completely unaware of their conditions. . . . The peasants, who are in close daily contact with the world of nature, come naturally to believe in humanism. By working together with them, not only can we informally influence them and spread culture, but also the cultural tools that are produced in the cities, such as publications, will necessarily follow in the footsteps of the youth and enter the countryside. In periods of agricultural slack we ought to come to the cities to study, and in times when the peasants are busy, we ought to work in the fields . . . then the atmosphere of culture will merge together with the shadows of the trees and smoke of the village chimneys, and those quiet, depressed old villages will become transformed into lively, active new villages. The great unity of the new villages will be our "Young China."[346]

The more apparent it gradually became that the proletarian revolution in China (and for China) would not be carried out by the workers but the peasants —and the bloody suppression of the strike of railroad workers on the Peking-Hankau line in 1923 might have been considered an ominous sign of this—the more Li Ta-chao became interested in organizing the peasantry, especially during the last year of his life. Almost necessarily, this went hand in hand with the increased emphasis on China as a "proletarian nation." In a speech in 1924, he amplified this idea by suggesting that there was a front of proletarian races which would have to constitute itself in opposition to the front of white oppressors, although fundamentally he hoped that a future, intermediate creation of three great federations (Asia, Europe, America) would some day lead to the establishment of a world state.[347] In this speech (which has come down to us only through the notes taken by a member of the audience), Li quoted some shockingly racist passages from Gobineau's *Essai sur l'inégalité des races humaines* and Putnam Weale's *The Contest of Colours,* and then continued: "The white peoples see themselves as the pioneers of culture in the world; they place themselves in a superior position and look down on other races as inferior. Because of this, the race question has become a class question and the races, on a world scale, have come to confront each other as classes . . . the struggle between the white and colored races will occur simultaneously with the class struggle."[348]

In one of his last writings, a commentary on his own translation of Marx' essay on "Revolution in China and Europe," he therefore also sees China as the leader of the coming proletarian world revolution:

> The manifestation of China's role is daily becoming more obvious, and the tendency for the Chinese revolution to urge on the world revolution is increasing day by day. . . . According to the courtesy of "gifts ought to be exchanged," disorder should be transported from China to Europe and all the imperialist states. If the imperialists intervene in the movement of the Chinese masses, then, as Marx so well put it, this will only cause the Chinese revolutionary movement to become increasingly militant and hasten to end the commercial enterprises of the powers in China. . . . Now at the same time that the Chinese national revolutionary movement has spread throughout the whole country, the English workers have called an unprecedented strike of a million men . . . is this not the phenomenon of China returning to the West the violence that has been brought to us by the "order" imposed by the armies and warships of the English bourgeoisie? Is not the Chinese revolution the spark that will set off the land mine already planted in the overproduction of the European economic system? Is this not about to produce a gigantic explosion? In the revolution that is imminent, this historic fact will be proved.[349]

That in spite of its technological backwardness, indeed precisely because of that backwardness, China would necessarily become one of the "proletarian nations" whose leadership it would assume with equal necessity because its size was so superior, and that it would thereby recover its hereditary place in the center of the world was a conviction that animated not only Li Ta-chao but also countless other Chinese communists. Marxism had been discovered in the West, yet did not bear its mark, but presented itself as a "scientific," neutral system. But in its Chinese version, it could also do justice to nationalist sentiments because it emphasized the rural and the agricultural and the associated Chinese sense of superiority in the sphere of "humanity." This constellation had something fascinating for all "leftist intellectuals." The two components which had always been closely associated in the old "socialist" Chinese tradition from Teng Mu on,[350] socialism and nationalism, could here combine harmoniously once again. More than that, the fusion of a "scientific" knowledge concerning certain historical laws, and the dignity an emphasis on the continuing existence of the simply human or, more precisely, of human initiative, conferred on this insight seemed to give rise to a new form of socialism and communism which would ultimately bring salvation not only to China, but to the entire world because it did not succumb to the temptation of remaining merely theoretical.

THE CONVERSATION BETWEEN MARX AND CONFUCIUS AND THE REVOLUTIONARY ROLE OF THE CITY

This motif can even be sensed behind an amusing story written at about the same time (1925) by the Marxist scholar Kuo Mo-jo (born 1892).[351] Kuo Mo-jo, a personal friend of Mao Tse-tung and today the president of the Academy of Sciences in Peking, is an uncommonly versatile and talented individual. After studying medicine in Japan, he made a name for himself as philologist, historian, writer, literary critic and translator (especially of Goethe's works, including *Faust*). In this story, Marx is shown visiting Confucius and his closest disciples as they are sitting together in a temple, about to partake of the dishes offered them during the autumn sacrifice. The imaginary dialogue between Marx and Confucius is not intended to be merely humorous. It also presents a serious confrontation of Confucian and Marxist conceptions of the ideal and their interconnections as they were being discussed at the time. The sketch ends on a humorous note as the superiority of Chinese practice over western theorizing is outlined in a few strokes:

> On the second day after the autumn sacrifice, around the middle of the tenth month, on a day when Confucius had gathered in the Memorial temple in Shanghai with his favorite disciples Yen Hui, Tzu-lu and Tzu-kung[352] in order to feast on the pig's head, cold though it had become in the meanwhile, four young, elegantly dressed businessmen suddenly carried a red-lacquered sedan chair directly into the temple. Tzu-lu was the first to see them. Uncontrollably, his hair rose straight up on his head and thrust his hat upward, that's how angry he was about this improper behavior. He hurled his chopsticks down on the table and was about to jump up to confront the strangers when Confucius restrained him and said: "You are more tempestuous than I, but don't see the way things are."[353] Tzu-lu had to calm down, and then Confucius ordered Tzu-kung to go down into the hall and receive the arrivals. The red-lacquered sedan chair had been placed on the ground directly in front of the hall. A European, his face red as a lobster and wearing a beard that covered the entire lower half of his face, climbed out. Tzu-kung first welcomed him and then led him inside. The four bearers followed, and in the large reception hall, the five guests and the four hosts advanced toward each other. After Confucius had introduced himself and inquired after the names of his guests, it turned out that the bearded man with the red face was called Karl Marx. Recently, this name had become so well known that even Confucius had heard it mentioned. . . . When he heard who had come to visit him, he could not suppress his emotion and delight, and called out: "Ah, ah, that friends should come to one from afar, is this not after all delightful?[354] Mr. Marx, your journey here must have been troublesome, really troublesome. May I have the pleasure of learning something from you, now that you have come to my lowly temple?" Without further formality, Marx now began speaking, but all that came out of his mouth were sounds like the croaking of the southern barbarians. The bearers of the sedan chair had to interpret so that Confucius could understand, just as his words had to be translated for Marx. Marx said: "I especially made this trip to be instructed by you. Our doctrine has already reached your Middle Kingdom, and I had actually hoped that it would be put into practice here. But a short while ago, some people told me that my teaching did not accord with your system of thought, and that there would therefore be no chance of its being applied here since the Middle Kingdom is dominated by your system. So I made this journey to contact you directly and to inquire from you what your system of thought really is, whether it is true that it does not accord with mine, and how it differs, should that be the case. I sincerely hope that you can give me

precise answers to these three questions. Confucius now explained that his teaching had been formulated at a time when there had been no natural sciences and no logic, and that it therefore was not sufficiently systematic to be formulated in a few theses. He therefore requested that Mr. Marx expound his own thinking. Marx was surprised to learn that up to this moment all that was known of his teaching in China were newspaper articles based on indirect knowledge and hearsay, none of his books having been translated into Chinese in its entirety. This being so, he expressed his willingness to give a brief summary of his doctrine. "My doctrine," he said, "takes a positive view of the world and human life, by which I mean that I do not consider the universe and life as something 'empty' or 'non-existent,' nor as something 'sinful' or 'bad.' Since we live in this world, we should get to know it. Only when that decision has been made can we attain the greatest joy and happiness and adapt the world to the requirements of our existence. . . . In this respect, I differ from most believers and metaphysicians. But I would like to ask you about this point. What are your views on these matters? Do they accord with mine? For if our points of departure differ, our paths will utterly diverge, and there will be no point in pursuing our discussion." Marx had barely finished when Tzu-lu burst out: "Yes, our master is a man who also stressed that life should be useful and joyful. What he emphasized most were the needs of the people. That's why he said: 'The greatest virtue of heaven and earth is life.' "[355] "Indeed," Confucius remarked, and then continued. "As regards our fundamental orientation, we agree completely. Except when you propose molding the world here and now to the needs of our existence, what kind of a world are you thinking of that can be adapted to our needs and enable us to attain the greatest joy and happiness in our life?" "You are asking about my ideal world? Excellent, excellent! Your questions are very good indeed!" Marx had suddenly jumped up with excitement, a curiously warm, friendly light was shimmering in his eyes. Stroking his wide beard with both hands, he went on: "Because I developed a materialist doctrine, most people take me for a kind of animal or at least someone who only understands eating and drinking, but has no ideals. The truth is that I have a very high, very distant ideal world, exactly as you expressed it in your question. Actually, I am afraid that I may be the idealist with the highest ideals history ever produced. For one thing, my ideal world postulates that myriads of people live harmoniously as if they were a single person, and that they develop their talents in freedom and equality; that all men be able to do their best without hope for reward; that everyone gets what he needs to live without suffering from the misery of hunger and cold: such would be the communist society of which it is said: 'Everyone does what he can, everyone takes what he needs.' Wouldn't it be heaven on earth if this society became reality?" "It certainly would," Confucius exclaimed. For in spite of all his dignity, he was so enthusiastic, he could not help clapping his hands. "This ideal society of yours, and my world of Great Equality accord completely, without our having expressly agreed on it beforehand. Let me have your permission to recite a section from an old essay of mine," (and he recited the entire section on the age of "Great Equality" as it is written in the ritual classic).[356] His voice was solemn as he quoted his favorite essay, and when he came to the two sentences, "People hate throwing away useful things, but this does not mean that they are hoarders. They hate being unable to develop their particular abilities, but this does not mean that they only act on their own behalf," he also nodded his head to the rhythm of his words so that one might have thought he was hypnotizing himself. But Marx had become utterly silent and did not look as if he could see anything of consequence in this part of Confucius's work. "Stop right there," he called out, forcefully breaking in on the monotonous flow of language. "My ideals are not the same as those of a few mad visionaries. My ideal is no castle in Spain, and it cannot be reached in a single leap. The first thing we have to learn from history is that the means of production can be gradually increased and improved and, secondly, that these gradually increased and improved means found their way into the hands of a few and, thirdly, that the class struggle will not allow us a single day's rest if society is to emerge from the disease of poverty and misery." "Ah, yes." Confucius, still utterly under the spell of his own words, had not yet returned to full consciousness, but continued nodding his head approvingly. "I myself once said: 'One should not be concerned if the people have little, but be concerned if what they have is unevenly distributed. One should not be concerned if they are poor, but if they have no peace!' "[357] "No, no," Marx exclaimed. "I can see now that our views diverge totally. As far as I am concerned, I worry just as much that people have little as I do about the fact that what they have is not evenly distributed. Beyond that, I worry as much about their being poor as I do that they have no peace. You have to learn to understand that if there is too little, there can be no even distribution, and that poverty is the root of peacelessness. That's the reason I object to the means of production being privately owned. But in addition, I not only object to everything that inhibits the increase and improvement of the means of production, but try to speed up their development as much as possible. . . . Only when the increase in the means of production has reached a certain point will there be a basis for the common enjoyment of wealth by all, only then will men be able to develop their abilities and natural talents peacefully, harmoniously, and without selfishness. It hardly needs pointing out that the driving force here will be the proletariat or, differently expressed, those who succeed in abolishing the private ownership of the means of production. The forces making for this development will first arise within individual countries. As time goes on, the movement will become international as well. . . . Only when that point has been reached will human life attain the highest degree of happiness. My ideal therefore comprises a series of quite distinct steps leading up to it, and it can be convincingly shown that this can gradually be realized." "Quite, quite." Confucius was still nodding approval. "I myself once said: 'When the people have multiplied, I will enrich them. When they have been enriched, I will instruct them.'[358] And as a method of governing, I proposed: If there is sufficient food, and sufficient weapons for defense, the people will become confident."[359] And he quoted other passages, some his own, others from the classics, and even some from the famous economist Kuan Chung. He did all this to demonstrate that feeding the people and taming the wealthy merchants had already been the necessary prerequisite for peace in ancient China, except that under the primitive conditions in those days, that cause could only be advanced by thrift, not by increased production. But in any event he would have to advocate such a method even today: "As long as people generally do not have enough to eat, one must not permit a few to eat sharkfins." "That's certainly true," Marx now sighed, deeply moved as he heard this sentence. "I would never have dreamed that an old comrade such as yourself actually lived in the distant East two thousand years ago. Our views are really precisely the same. I don't understand people who say that our two systems of thought don't accord with each other, that my system does not agree with the national character of your Middle Kingdom, and that it therefore could find no support here." Suddenly, Confucius sighed deeply. His sigh was so profound and so sustained that the resignation which had been accumulating in his heart for two thousand years and more could pour forth all at once. He sighed again, and finally said: "And now, what can we do to realize your ideal? I myself have been sitting here for two thousand years, chewing my cold pig's head." "What," Marx exclaimed, 'do you mean to say that the Chinese are incapable of realizing your ideal?" "If one preaches enough, perhaps," Confucius answered with some embarrassment. 'But we have to understand that your disciples must not agitate against mine, and vice versa." "Agreed. Well, in that case—" "What?" "In that case, I can go back home to my wife." If Confucius really were as ethereal as he seems to the Neo-Confucians, he would have had to start thundering loudly at this moment and accuse Marx that he was no better than an animal if he could think of his wife under these circumstances. But since the sage does not inhibit human emotions which cannot be suppressed, and our Confucius is a sage, he not only failed to reprimand Marx, he even addressed him with heightened interest: "You have a wife, Mr. Marx?" "Why not? Philosophically, we see eye to eye; besides, my wife is quite good looking." What a lack of manners on Marx' part, to praise his wife for being every bit as ideal as his teaching! But Confucius sighed again when he discovered this smugness, and said: "All men have a wife, only I have none!"[360] Tzu-kung, who had been itching to make a contribution for quite a while, now seized the opportunity and interjected quickly: "Within the four seas, all women are the wives of the superior man. Why need you be concerned, Master, that you have none?"[361] So, in the final analysis, the powerful orator Tzu-kung was the only one among all those who were not ashamed of being Confucians that altered the well-known saying of his Master and thus turned it into something humorous.Marx, who did not grasp the deeper connections, however, assumed, after a further question, that Confucius believed in liberal divorce laws. He also sensed that this fellow Confucius had some other thoughts at the back of his mind. But Confucius immediately turned back to him, and said: "Treat with the reverence due to age the elders in your own family so that the elders in the families of others shall be similarly treated; treat with the kindness due to youth the young in your own family, so that the young in the families of others shall be similarly treated.[362] Treat with love the woman in your own family, so that the women in the families of others shall be similarly treated. And thus, I love your wife." When Marx heard these words, he shouted out loud with indignation. "What? Mr. K'ung number two![363] I only advocate the socialization of the means of production. But you seem to advocate that of women. Your system of thought is even more dangerous than mine! I don't have the courage to provoke you further." And with that, he hastily called out to the four respectable businessmen who carried his sedan chair, fleeing head over heels as if he had lost a battle. He must have been afraid that his wife—faraway in distant Europe—was going to be socialized by Confucius then and there. After

> the master and his three disciples had seen the large sedan chair disappear behind the western outer gate, Yen Hui, who had been sitting there like a dumbbell from beginning to end, finally commented: "For one word, a man is often deemed to be wise; for one word, he is often deemed to be foolish.[364] But today, Master, you were not the master of yore. What was the point of those strange words?" Confucius laughed amusedly and said: "I was only joking and having fun when I said those things." Now all of them laughed loudly. Then they sat back down at the table and continued chewing away at their cold pig's head.[365]

When one analyzes it carefully, this complex, suggestive story is more than a sarcastic version of a confrontation between Marxism and Confucianism. In Confucian texts, Yen Hui always plays the role of the disciple who relies on supernatural illumination rather than acquired knowledge. When he contrasts the "Master of today" with the "Master of yore" and the words for which he will be considered "wise" (not defined in detail) and those for which he would be considered "unwise" there seems to be the suggestion that Kuo Mo-jo intentionally represents Confucius as expressing two divergent attitudes: that of an old Confucianism that only has itself to blame for a lack of wisdom bordering on imbecility which most conspicuously manifests itself in the mechanical recitation of quotations that have lost their relevance. There is also the new, "wise" Confucianism whose teaching does not differ from Marxism in its fundamentals and goals, but at most in its methods. But this second contrast is analogous to the previously described one between determinism and mechanism on the one hand, and activism and voluntarism on the other, and which so decisively shaped the communist movement in China down to our own time. For it was always inseparably associated with the problem of nationalism which had a much greater weight in modern China than we normally imagine since back of it, there lay not only an injured national pride, but the terrible experience of the self-alienation of an entire nation. Indeed, to the extent that "empire" and "world" had always been identical, it was really the self-alienation of an entire world. Only the creation of a "New China" that could achieve identity with a "New World" while yet retaining the experience, dignity and importance of a four- or five-thousand-year-old country; only the missionizing of the outside world by a teaching that was felt to be profoundly and typically Chinese, yet had been imported from that outside world; only the victory of an almost magical will over seemingly unshakable laws which yet guaranteed this victory because of their inherent developmental tendencies; only this threefold squaring of the circle would make it possible for China to set its house in order once again.

Because this necessarily complex, paradoxical relationship was simply ignored by the official leadership of the CCP as late as the thirties (and this in part because of Moscow's influence), praxis led to repeated failures as the attempt was being made to keep the theory pure. For the only alternative was to disregard Li Ta-chao and to stress the determinist aspects of Marxism. This involved the affirmation of all we have called the "outer" and the "foreign," which was fundamentally at odds with the Chinese intellectual tradition and included the priority of scientific laws over human initiative; of the city, technology and the industrial worker over the country, nature and the peasant; of the open, stage-by-stage attack over the "protracted," covert, judo-like warfare; and finally of internationalism over nationalism.

The most interesting representative of this position was the scholar Ch'en Tu-hsiu,[366] whom we have repeatedly mentioned. Born in the same year as Trotsky (1879), he was largely responsible for the founding of the CCP in 1921, and headed it as its Secretary General from that year until 1927. His critical attitude toward Chinese nationalism already manifested itself in 1902 when he was a student in Japan and refused to join Sun Yat-sen's national, i.e. primarily anti-Manchu *T'ung-meng-hui.* It was equally evident somewhat later when he became increasingly enamored of French culture. His conception of Marxism also reflected this basic orientation. Since 1915, he had been editor of the review *New Youth* which characteristically had a French subtitle *(La Jeunesse Nouvelle).* Already in the second issue of that publication, he had emphasized the superiority of the dynamic, militant, individualistic and utilitarian attitude of the West over the weak world view of China, and advocated that country's industrialization. In his interpretation of Marxism, he could visualize a socialist revolution and the building of communism only within the framework of comprehensive international cooperation and under the leadership of the urban industrial proletariat. He feared that reliance on the peasantry and the necessarily associated confinement of the Chinese communist movement to the national sphere would reintroduce the terribly heavy burden of tradition into the historical process, an encumbrance which had so often ended China's brief and desperate flights by pulling it back into the depth of a dull immobility. He therefore also opposed the organization of the peasantry, which had been stepped up since 1921. He took this stand not only because the elemental brutality of the peasants' actions offended his fragile, cosmopolitan scholar's soul (he was head of the department of Chinese civilization at Peking National University from 1917–1920), as some said accusingly at a later time, but also because he saw in them nothing more than a trite copy of the all-too familiar (and ultimately almost always unsuccessful) periodic "peasant uprisings" of the past. Rural communism seemed to him to overlook what was precisely the most important transformation of Chinese society, a transformation which he felt would not merely assure the victory of the revolution but also prevent any relapse into age-old routines after victory had been achieved. Because the countryside was mindless, a passive victim of the rhythms of nature, emphasis would have to be shifted to the city which was alive and receptive to all the changes progress would bring. But this imposed considerable limitations on the speed with which the communist movement could develop. For such a shift naturally depended on many external conditions such as the progress of industrialization and these were matters that lay beyond the control of the party. Thus the CCP began to stagnate on the course taken by Ch'en

Tu-hsiu, for even with the best possible organization, the number of industrial workers was not sufficient to carry out a successful revolution.

What was already a rather difficult problem became considerably more complex because divergent opinions within the CCP not only had to be reconciled but also brought into line with the directives from Moscow which reflected the bitter ideological dispute between Stalin and Trotsky. Trotsky's concept of a permanent revolution had the following three, interconnected implications for China: 1) the communist movement must always be viewed as an international whole. 2) As a result, the socio-economic stages of the various nations at the beginning of the revolution were of only secondary importance. International cohesion allowed for "leaps" (i.e. the omission of certain stages of development, such as capitalism), but precisely for this reason it did not permit a pause at any point but moved irresistibly toward the end of class rule. 3) Since this meant that the final goal of the revolution, the creation of a classless society, was always kept in sight, and since the revolution could only come from the revolution of the industrial proletariat, it was the workers (and not the peasants) that must claim leadership from the very beginning.[367]

Trotsky and Stalin differed concerning the tactics to be used in China because Stalin took the opposite view regarding the first two points. There was a certain agreement concerning the third since both were diffident about the Chinese peasantry, though for different reasons. Stalin saw the principal instrument of the revolution in the bourgeoisie, i.e. the KMT, while Trotsky felt that peasant leadership would jeopardize the nature of the revolution. But Stalin's conviction that the KMT should assume the leadership role during the historically prescribed stage of "bourgeois" development in China led to rather dangerous speculations about the social stage in which that country actually found itself, and what the role of the KMT should be in this context. In addition, it brought the CCP to the verge of catastrophe because for theoretical reasons and in opposition to Trotsky, Stalin ordered close cooperation between the CCP and the KMT in the government. For as it became increasingly apparent that it was not the left wing of the KMT which outmaneuvered the right with the support of the communists, as had been planned, but that it was the right wing that outmaneuvered the left and its communist allies, Ch'en Tsu-hsiu became the first victim, in August, 1927. He was not only reproached for mechanistic thinking and having failed to act with the requisite energy, but also for having been sceptical about the peasants. Actually, both of these were positions that had originally corresponded to the official line (although the second accusation should more properly have been addressed to Trotsky, which also explains why after his exclusion from the party toward the end of 1929, Ch'en founded an ephemeral anti-central committee on Trotsky's advice). But the almost hectic activity of the CCP during the years from 1927–1929, and after Chiang Kai-shek's open persecution had finally forced it underground in April, 1927 proved no less devastating. Almost all of the many uprisings in the cities (Canton Commune, September 1927, and others) and in the country (Autumn Harvest Uprising in Hunan, September, 1927, and others) which were intended to demonstrate the collaboration of workers and peasants turned into fiascoes. As a result, their instigators (Ch'ü Ch'iu-pai and Li Li-san) were subsequently condemned as "putschists."[368] These defeats almost completely destroyed all party organizations in the cities, including those of the workers. What remained were the soviets in southern China which inside a decade had developed from the peasant associations and culminated in the establishment of the National Soviet Government in Jui-ch'in (Kiangsi) toward the end of 1931. Mao's hour had come.

THE RISE OF MAO TSE-TUNG

Mao Tse-tung (born 1893) had been one of the founders of the CCP. His relatively late rise to prominence cannot be wholly explained by his comparative youth at that time. Yet compared to Ch'en Tu-hsiu (born 1879), but unlike Li Ta-chao (born 1888), he almost belonged to another generation, for this was a time of very rapid change. In contrast to the pre-World War generation made up of those leftist students in France and Japan who had barely eked out a scanty livelihood and which also included Chinese students in the United States, who were secretly envied because their living conditions were incomparably better and who inclined toward pragmatism and liberalism, Mao's generation had recovered some confidence in the strength of their own nation. Beyond that, Mao proved himself from the very beginning to be the most Chinese in the group of leading Chinese communists. Although he once mentioned having been profoundly influenced by Ch'en Tu-hsiu for a period, there was even outwardly a world of difference between him and this small, francophile professor with the great, puzzled eyes. He had no intellectual family background of any sort, and had never studied abroad (just as he hardly ever left his own country later), but merely acquired a diversified but hardly specialized education, almost resembling the traditional Chinese ideal of the learned amateur in this respect. He owed this education not so much to the rather mediocre schools he attended, but to a period of unremitting, autodidactic study from 1914–1918, and his outstanding intellectual gifts. His father, originally a peasant with relatively modest holdings, who had been a soldier for a number of years in his youth because he had been poor and had later acquired some means by trading in grain, had had different plans for him. Mao's two younger brothers, Tse-min (1896–1943) and Tse-t'an (1905–1935), and his sister Tse-hung (died in 1930) had become wholehearted members of the communist movement at an early time. The brothers were either killed in combat with the KMT or executed by it. In contrast to them, Mao was weakly at first, and his father intended to train him to keep his accounts. But the pronounced antipathy Mao felt toward his excessively strict father whom he "learned to hate" early in life and against whom he formed "a real united front"[369] with other members of the family and looked upon as his enemy, foiled this plan. After he had reluctantly learned to read the classics in the village school and secretly devoured popular novels such as the *Marsh Heroes, The Three Kingdoms,* and *Travels in the West,*[370] he prevailed upon his father to let him register at the nearby district school of Hsiang-hsiang where "western" sciences were taught. He was fourteen at that time. Being the poorest among relatively well-to-do, well-dressed fellow students, he had difficulty finding his bearings but was not without friends. With one of them, he went on extensive walks and enthusiastically worshipped nature. Practically naked, and wearing only pants, the two young students ran through pouring rain and burning sun, for which the Manchu police almost arrested them. His companion reported later that Mao supposedly said to the laughing peasants: "The sun is the source of all strength. Doesn't it make the rice grow? So why too much clothing?" He then gave the following sketch of Mao's attitude: "I think it was at that time that Mao set his face away from the townspeople. . . . He approved of the peasants; he approved of no one else. What he particularly approved of in the peasants was their courtesy and their loyalty to one another. He said that the townspeople were not really loyal to one another; and they were not courteous by nature, they simply followed accepted customs. In a sense he was split between his admiration for scholarship and scholars, and his admiration for the peasants. He thought he would be a teacher, and he would spend his time teaching peasants."[371]

At about this same time, he also became interested in the great men of history. The Chinese figures that fascinated him were the legendary emperors Yao and Shun, the emperor Ch'in Shih Huang-ti, the founder of the Chinese empire, and emperor Wu-ti of the Han dynasty, who had first extended it into Central Asia. Among western figures it was Catherine the Great, Peter the Great of Russia, Wellington, Rousseau, Montesquieu, Lincoln and George Washington, all of whom he had read about in a collection of biographies *Great Heroes of the World.* "We need great people like these. . . . We ought to study them and find out how we can make China rich and strong. . . . After six years of hard fighting, Washington defeated the British and began to build up America," he said enthusiastically to his friend after having read this book.[372]

In 1911, the year China finally shook off the yoke of the Manchus, the eighteen-year-old Mao went to the provincial capital of Ch'ang-sha to attend the considerably better middle school. In the whirl of the revolution, he heard here for the first time the name of Sun Yat-sen and immediately and with great zeal began to participate in the new movement. In a proclamation he resolutely posted on the wall of the school—a noteworthy anticipation of the "large character posters" *(ta-tzu pao)* which played such an important role during the Cultural Revolution—he pleaded for a government with Sun Yat-sen as president, K'ang Yu-wei as prime minister, and Liang Ch'i-ch'ao as foreign secretary. Spontaneously, and with many other students, he joined a rebellious army corps (an army consisting entirely of students which was also being put together struck him as "too disorderly"), but returned to his books when the first phase of the revolution seemed to have ended successfully half a year later.[373] Before, his reading of modern Chinese literature had been largely confined to Liang Ch'i-ch'ao whose writings made a profound impression on him. Now, in the well-equipped Provincial Library at Ch'ang-sha, he studied intensively on his own, familiarized himself with many other modern writers and scientists, and also read translations of works by Adam Smith, Herbert Spencer, Darwin, Montesquieu and John Stuart Mill. Having overcome certain difficulties due partly to his poverty, partly to his inadequate knowledge of foreign languages and his dislike of the natural sciences,[374] he was accepted at the Hunan Provincial First Normal Teachers' Training School in 1913, and passed his final examination there five years later.

Around this time, in 1918, he states that his ". . . mind was a curious mixture of ideas of liberalism, democratic reformism, and utopian socialism."[375] Ch'en Tu-hsiu and Hu Shih had replaced K'ang Yu-wei and Sun Yat-sen as his idols. As mentioned elsewhere, he moved to Peking during this same year to participate in the preparatory seminars for students who wanted to go to France, and which were based on anarchist ideals. But then he decided to remain at home (perhaps because he had difficulties learning French, which was naturally the core of the program). He later said he believed that "I did not know enough about my own country, and that my time could be more profitably spent in China."[376] Yang Chen-ch'i, a former teacher of ethics at the Normal School in Ch'ang-sha, and who was to become his father-in-law a short time later, recommended him to the university librarian at Peking National University, Li Ta-chao, as an assistant librarian so that he would not have to return to his parents' home which he disliked, and where a short while before his mother had died. Thus a circle closed which was to determine China's future. For although the young, brilliant and quite progressive scholars who regularly came to the library were too busy ". . . to listen to an assistant librarian speaking southern dialect who wanted to begin conversations with them on political and cultural subjects,"[377] as Mao commented bitterly, the power which would ultimately count was already in the making, and not among these scholars, but among the perhaps less scientific but more politically-oriented men around Li Ta-chao. A typical representative of those apparently somewhat smug scholars who seem to have disappointed Mao at that time was Fu Ssu-nien. Twenty years later, when the "New Life" under Chiang Kai-shek was in vogue, he became famous for his analysis of concepts of life in China. At the time of the Literary Revolution, in 1919, where he played an important role, he was impressed by an essay of Mao calling for the "great revolutionary unification of the entire people," but one year before he had thought the assistant librarian barely worth his notice.[378]

This essay, printed in the short-lived student journal *Hsiang River Daily (Hsiang-chiang p'ing-lun, The Shian Kian Weekly Review),* published by Mao himself, was not his first literary effort. An earlier essay, written under a pseudonym and characteristically dealing with physical education, had already appeared in April, 1917.[379] Organizational activity took up more and more of his time from

1919 on, and kept him traveling back and forth between Peking, Ch'ang-sha and Shanghai, but this was nothing new. Since 1915, he had been trying to set up student associations, and in April, 1919, he succeeded with the New People's Study Society *(Hsin-min hsüeh-hui)* in Ch'ang-sha. This led to the establishment of a branch organization of the CCP in Hunan province which Mao pushed through after the founding of the CCP in October, 1921. Throughout the following decade, Mao occupied a high but not a leading position in the party hierarchy, and practical and organizational work continued to predominate over purely ideological activity. What was to become decisive now was the organization of the peasants which he was not the first to promote, but pursued more energetically than others. Ignoring all those theories which counseled a different course, he engaged himself in this work from 1915 on, beginning in his home province of Hunan. As a result, the physiognomy of the party was gradually but fundamentally changed. In 1915, peasants had constituted a mere five percent of party membership. This figure had risen to 70–80 percent in 1928, and in 1930 the number of industrial workers had shrunk to two thousand (1.66 percent) out of a total of 120,000 party members. But this pragmatic procedure only had its effect when the various doctrines of the earlier party leaders—all of them either under direct or indirect western influence and men who had studied abroad—had failed and the followers of the CCP had been reduced to a kind of hopeless band of die-hards. Even Moscow could now return the freedom of ultimate decisions to that group, as one does to a mortally-ill person. The soviets, which had arisen since late 1927 in southern China, especially in the border region of Hunan and Kiangsi provinces, had been left to their own ideological and military resources. They had consolidated up to 1931, yielded before the increasing pressure of KMT troops in 1934/1935, and moved into the mountainous northwestern province of Shensi during the Long March. From the very beginning, and as a matter of course, Mao had been their leader. When, in early 1935, he also became the leader of the party which now no longer had any other base of support, this merely legalized a situation which had been existing de facto for a number of years.[380]

"CONTRADICTION" AND "PRACTICE"

In Yenan, the capital of the new soviet, which could no longer become an objective for the KMT troops because the Sino-Japanese war had broken out (July 7, 1937), Mao Tse-tung wrote two of his most important theoretical essays, "On Practice" *(Shih-chien lun)* and "On Contradiction" *(Mao-tun lun)* (1937). The subtitle of the first, "On the relations between knowledge and practice, between knowing and doing" *(Lun jen-shih ho shih-chien ti kuan-hsi, chih ho hsing ti kuan-hsi)* not only indicates that both deal basically with the same subject, i.e. contradiction, but also that the age-old problem of the opposition between "inner" and "outer" was to be reexamined and resolved in favor of "action." In

China, this problem had always been fundamental in determining where happiness lay. To a considerable extent, Mao's thought followed the course that had already been traced by Li Ta-chao (if we disregard western Marxists for the moment); yet he may not have been directly influenced by him. What was important and can be found in both of them is the curious refraction of Marxist teaching in a purely Chinese milieu.

Typical of this was first the reconciliation of the opposition between "knowing" and "acting" or, more precisely, the stress on "acting" as the primary quality that included the latter, an emphasis which already finds expression in the fact that the title of the first essay is limited to the one word "practice." For although Mao admits that "a man's knowledge consists . . . of two parts, that which comes from direct experience and that which comes from indirect experience," he yet maintains that "what is indirect experience for me, is direct experience for other people" and that "consequently, considered as a whole, knowledge of any kind is inseparable from experience."[381] Interestingly enough, however, the process of cognition built on direct experience, and which is described in orthodox Marxist terms up to this point, brings not only a qualitative change in the cognizing subject according to Mao, but also a change in the object cognized: "If you want to know the taste of a pear, you must change the pear by eating it yourself. If you want to know the structure and properties of the atom, you must make physical and chemical experiments to change the state of the atom."[382] This thesis, unique in Marxism, is vaguely reminiscent of Heisenberg's indeterminacy principle. But it was not from physics, of course, that Mao derived it, but unquestionably from the conceptual framework of the *Book of Changes* which is also merely half-determinist, as it were. For in contrast to other mantic systems which necessarily imply a rigid fatalism, the *I-ching* oracles only indicate developmental *tendencies* which could be significantly modified and indeed overcome if they and the specific counsel based on them were understood.[383]

Mao's conviction that knowledge was not only practice but also a practice that changed objective reality, also led to his doctrine that the process of cognition was necessarily infinite simply because it transforms reality (and thus the "truth" to be discovered) and constantly gives it a new appearance. Reality and cognition, object and subject, which are fundamentally inseparable, are thus in a constant process of change which does not approach a distant, fixed pole, but forms part of the nature of being and cognition. Consequently, Mao only acknowledges an "absolute truth" which consists of "innumerable" relative truths, and which thus loses its quality of absoluteness (he boldly refers to Lenin here, but knows better than to quote him, for in Lenin's thought truth consists of a *finite* number of relative truths):

> Idealism and mechanical materialism, opportunism and adventurism, are all characterized by the breach between the subjective and the objective, by the separation of knowledge from practice. The Marxist-Leninist theory of knowledge, cha-

> racterized as it is by scientific social practice, cannot but resolutely oppose these wrong ideologies. Marxists recognize that in the absolute and general process of development of the universe the development of each particular process is relative, and that hence, in the endless flow of absolute truth, man's knowledge of a particular process at any given stage of development is only relative truth. The sum total of innumerable relative truths constitutes absolute truth. The development of an objective process is full of contradictions and struggles, and so is the development of the movement of human knowledge. All the dialectical movements of the objective world can sooner or later be reflected in human knowledge. In social practice, the process of coming into being, developing and passing away is infinite, and so is the process of coming into being, developing and passing away in human knowledge. . . . The movement of change in the world of objective reality is never-ending, and so is man's cognition of truth through practice. Marxism-Leninism has in no way exhausted truth but ceaselessly opens up roads to the knowledge of truth in the course of practice. Our conclusion is the concrete, historical unity of the subjective and the objective, of theory and practice, of knowing and doing. . . . Discover the truth through practice, and again through practice verify and develop the truth. Start from perceptual knowledge and actively develop it into rational knowledge; then start from rational knowledge and actively guide revolutionary practice to change both the subjective and the objective world. Practice, knowledge, again practice, and again knowledge. This form repeats itself in endless cycles, and with each cycle the content of practice and knowledge rises to a higher level. Such is the whole of the dialectical-materialist theory of knowledge, and such is the dialectical-materialist theory of the unity of knowing and doing.[384]

The unity of cognition and reality Mao Tse-tung stresses here also had direct consequences for his conception of dialectics, which differs from that of Marx, and especially of Lenin (yet resembles Engels's). For Mao, it is not primarily, let alone exclusively a method of cognition, but an *a priori* quality inherent in all phenomena of reality. In the introduction to his essay "On Contradiction," he notes that the

> metaphysical world outlook sees things . . . as eternally isolated from one another and immutable. Such change as there is can only be an increase or decrease in quantity or a change in place. . . . But the world outlook of materialist dialectics holds that . . . the fundamental cause of development of a thing . . . lies in the contradictoriness within the thing. . . . Contradictoriness within a thing is the fundamental cause, while its interrelations and interactions with other things are secondary causes. . . . In a suitable temperature, an egg changes into a chicken. . . . There is nothing that does not contain contradiction; without contradiction, nothing would exist. Contradiction is universal and absolute, it is present in the process of development of all things and permeates every process from beginning to end. . . . Because this is the universality and absoluteness of contradiction and because there is a struggle going on between them which may be either overt or covert, and because furthermore in most phenomena there is a whole series of contradictory pairs in opposition to each other, it is necessary to distinguish between

the "universality" of contradiction and the "particularity and relativity" of contradiction.[385]

At this point, the well-known doctrine of dialectical materialism concerning the "identity of opposites" and the "leap from quantity to quality" as derived from Hegel are introduced. For the reciprocal conditionality of the pairs of opposites which Mao describes here: "without life, there would be no death; without death, there would be no life. Without 'above' there would be no 'below,' without 'below' there would be no 'above' . . . without landlords, there would be no tenant peasants; without tenant peasants, there would be no landlords" and which is reminiscent of the *Tao-te-ching,* although it is true that the latter had only proposed to demonstrate the relativity of all being, gives them a kind of common basis which makes possible that "in given conditions, each of the contradictory aspects within a thing transforms itself into its opposite, changes its position to that of its opposite."[386] But this change in position of the contradictory aspects in things which effects their qualitative change is relative in the sense that it can only occur between "identical" pairs of opposites (as distinguished from the inner contradictoriness of things): "Why can an egg but not a stone be transformed into a chicken? Why is there identity between war and peace and none between war and a stone?" It is also relative in the sense that the "identity of opposites exists only in certain necessary conditions":

> There are two states of motion in all things, that of relative rest and that of conspicuous change. Both are caused by the struggle between the two contradictory elements contained in a thing. When the thing is in the first state of motion, it is undergoing only quantitative and not qualitative change and consequently presents the outward appearance of being at rest. When the thing is in the second state of motion, the quantitative change of the first state has already reached a culminating point and gives rise to the dissolution of the thing as an entity and thereupon a qualitative change ensues, hence the appearance of a conspicuous change. . . . Things are constantly transforming themselves from the first into the second state of motion; the struggle of opposites goes on in both states but the contradiction is resolved through the second state. That is why we say that the unity of opposites is conditional, temporary and relative, while the struggle of mutually exclusive opposites is absolute. . . . The combination of conditional, relative identity and unconditional, absolute struggle constitutes the movement of opposites in all things.[387]

To find the bases for this conviction of a "dialects of nature," we need not go back to Engels, still less to Trotsky, with whose "Permanent Revolution" Mao only has the name in common. Here also, the traces lead back to the oldest Chinese book, the *Book of Changes.* For it is hardly possible to find a more exact description of the ontological system in back of the *Book of Changes* than this statement of Mao about the creative contradictions in things. In the hexagrams of the *I-ching,* which symbolize a great diversity of situations, the fundamental opposites *Yin* and *Yang* figure always in two different forms: as lines (still) at rest ("early *Yin* or *Yang*") and as changing lines ("old or what may be called 'outdated' *Yin* or *Yang*") which are about to turn into their opposites.[388] The only difference is that there also Mao prefers the infinite number of possible variations to a finite one. For while the *Book of Changes* presents in its hexagrams only sixty-four basic universal phenomena, each of which carries six "contradictions" within itself, of which in a given case one, several or all may pass from a condition of "relative rest" to one of "conspicuous change," Mao does not tie himself down in this regard. The movement of "change" thus is still the same as that of the *Yin-Yang* theories, but the closed system which necessarily entails numerical finiteness is transcended in the same way as is the spell of an "absolute truth" of cognition which, according to Lenin, was to result from a limited number of relative truths.[389] Just as in the *Book of Changes,* however, the "temporary, conspicuous changes" have, for Mao, the character of revolutions, where "revolution" is defined as something that spontaneously produces qualitative change. Connected with it—and this is of course particularly important in the social sphere—we have the emergence of "antagonistic contradictions" which Mao defines as a special, virulent form of the universal and incessant struggle of opposites in phenomena, and which lead directly to qualitative changes. This can be turned around by saying that the world could not develop without them:

> In human history, antagonism between classes exists as a particular manifestation of the struggle of opposites. Consider the contradiction between the exploiting and the exploited classes. Such contradictory classes coexist for a long time in the same society, be it slave society, feudal society or capitalist society, and they struggle with each other; but it is not until the contradiction between the two classes develops to a certain stage that it assumes the form of open antagonism and develops into revolution. . . . It is highly important to grasp this fact. It enables us to understand that revolutions and revolutionary wars are inevitable in class society and that without them, it is impossible to accomplish any leap in social development and to overthrow the reactionary ruling classes and therefore impossible for the people to win political power. . . . However, we must make a concrete study of the circumstances of each specific struggle of opposites. . . . Contradiction and struggle are universal and absolute, but the methods of resolving contradictions, that is, the forms of struggle, differ according to the differences in the nature of the contradictions. Some contradictions are characterized by open antagonism, others are not. In accordance with the concrete development of things, some contradictions which were originally nonantagonistic develop into antagonistic ones, while others which were originally antagonistic develop into nonantagonistic ones. . . . Lenin said, "Antagonism and contradiction are not at all one and the same. Under socialism the first will disappear, the second will remain."[390]

It is important to become aware of these fundamental views of Mao Tse-tung regarding the unity of practice and knowledge and the ubiquity of contradiction and movement if one wishes to determine the place of the ideal, happy society in his system of thought. For curiously enough, two seemingly contradictory demands result which could, of course, themselves be interpreted as dialectical contradictions: on the one hand, the premise of a fundamental dialectical structure constantly torn by an inner struggle precludes the reality of conceptions of the ideal, or the possibility of realizing them, for by their very nature they must always and everywhere be crystalline, frozen and immobile. At best, they can be retained as goals, although in an ideology which assigns absolute priority to practice, there attaches to them the embarrassing stigma of a bloodless insubstantiality. Not Mao, but Engels (to whom Mao is closest, as we mentioned) once characterized this situation very aptly:

> But precisely here lay the true significance and the revolutionary character of the Hegelian philosophy . . . that it once and for all dealt the deathblow to the finality of all products of human thought and action. . . . Truth lay now in the process of cognition itself, in the long historical development of science, which mounts from lower to even higher levels of knowledge without ever reaching, by discovering so-called absolute truth, a point at which it can proceed no further. . . . Just as knowledge is unable to reach a perfected termination in a perfect, ideal condition of humanity, so is history unable to do so; a perfect society, a perfect "state," are things which can only exist in imagination. On the contrary, all successive historical situations are only transitory stages in the endless course of development of human society from the lower to the higher. . . . For it (i.e. dialectical philosophy), nothing is final, absolute, sacred. It reveals the transitory character of everything and in everything; nothing can endure before it except the uninterrupted process of becoming and of passing away . . . its revolutionary character is absolute—the only absolute it admits.[391]

In Mao's writings, the unattainability of any ideal society is nowhere emphasized with the same degree of clarity, yet it can be inferred indirectly from certain comments. In his programmatic speech "On the People's Democratic Dictatorship" *(Lun jen-min min-chu chuan-cheng),* which he gave after the war and the civil war in 1949 when he seized power over all of China and many of his followers expected the inception of a kind of "Thousand-year Reich" of peace and equality, the communist ideal society is mentioned twice, and both times referred to by the familiar expression "Realm of Great Harmony." But in one instance, it is mentioned "in passing," as a "long-range perspective of human progress," and in the second, the possibility of its realization in the present is expressly rejected.[392]

Yet it is also true that precisely because it cannot find a fixed place anywhere in a perpetually changing medium, the ideal society acquires a curious presence. Just as absolute truth is only revealed "in the *process* of cognition itself," the ideal society becomes tangible reality only in the revolution, during change, which is the "only absolute." But this change is constantly at work in the incessant movement of contradictions in all phenomena (including society) and therefore can be realized at any time in the consciousness of it.[393] Happiness thus turns out to be elusive, and that in two respects. It can only be caught in flight, as it were, only in revolutionary movement. It can also always escape again unless one is ready to catch it ever anew. The blissful eternity of heaven and paradise which springs from an infinitely great, quiescent time, is replaced by the intoxicating eternity of earth which is composed of an infinite chain of infinitely small, ecstatic moments where the sudden reversal of contradictions is time and again experienced as the breathtaking rebirth of pulsating life. This "Now" is the dimension of happiness and of the ideal, not the "once" whether this refers to a distant past or a distant future.

This conception had already been largely discovered by Li Ta-chao.[394] It had something uncommonly consoling during the two decades of revolutionary struggle between 1927 and 1949 when the homeless communist partisans seemed to become engulfed in the countryside, yet derived their mobility, their strength and also a sort of precious freedom from that homelessness. The many small victories of the guerilla units, and even their many small defeats, which could easily be interpreted as steps leading to new victories, again and again gave birth to momentary experiences of happiness whose rapid extinction did not provoke dull despair but rather a curiosity about what lay ahead and the drive to move on. Besides, the unusual living conditions of the partisans obliged them to do justice to all those ideals which ensued from the demand for the unity of "practice" and "knowledge" and the primacy of "practice." All of them, and many of their leaders, were peasants, soldiers, ideologues at one and the same time, and sometimes even scientists, and gained such assurance from this that an otherwise quite favorably disposed American journalist who visited them early during the forties in Yenan, which "from the air . . . had the look of a bandits' lair . . ." could write of them: "They glowed with self-confidence, there was always a slight tinge of sanctimoniousness in their speech. You were reminded sometimes of the religious summer camps where people go about slapping each other on the back in rousing good-fellowship."[395] This headquarters of the Shensi soviet with its secluded, blooming mountain valleys reminded another foreign visitor of the cave paradise of the Peach Blossom Fountain once celebrated by the poet T'ao Ch'ien.[396] Of course, it owed its ideal aspect in large part to the involuntary primitivism of its inhabitants, and of the guerilla army more generally. Life in the country, in nature, and even more the life in the clear air of isolated mountains, the traditional dwelling place of sages, was much closer to primitive communism than to its developed form, but it was undoubtedly close to communism as such. This is the only way we can understand Mao Tse-tung's bold statement of 1937 when outwardly the CCP had become a *quantité négligeable:* "This process, the practice of changing the world . . . has already reached a historic moment in the world and in China, a great moment unprecedented in human history, that is, the moment for completely banishing darkness from the world and from China and for changing the world into a world of light such as never previously existed."[397] But this is also the only explanation why after the 1949 victory which most of his followers looked on as something definitive, he no less boldly and deliberately did everything to question, jeopardize and risk time and again all that had been achieved.

"GREAT LEAP" AND "GREAT EMPTY TALK"

This victory gave access to the cities and their industries. But it also caused problems that had been almost forgotten because of the urgency of other concerns, such as the roles to be assigned to the industrial proletariat and the peasantry during the revolution, or the middle course to be steered between "mechanism" and "activism" to emerge once again. Paradoxical though it may seem, this victory soon endangered the ideological position of the victor. For in the eyes of many critics, Mao's thought might have sufficed to seize the country, but not to administer it during times of peace since according to his doctrine of contradiction, it was a peace that not only could not be permitted to exist, but whose existence was in fact impossible. Not men who were Confucians in disguise, or counterrevolutionaries, but committed communists, if of Ch'en Tu-hsiu's type, unwittingly came to appear as enemies to Mao because they proposed to consolidate the country at the level that had been so laboriously attained, and did not wish to prolong the much praised "protracted war"[398] now that victory had so obviously been achieved. The age-old law, based not on Confucian prejudice but the necessarily complex administration of a gigantic country and according to which "the empire could be conquered from the saddle, but could not be governed from it"[399] began to exert an increasing weight during the fifties. In barely noticeable ways, it changed the spiritual climate, so that the elemental heroes of yore became venerable, yet anachronistic figures—a process that had occurred countless times before when revolutions had been successful, in China and everywhere else. What was unique was the reaction of the aging Mao Tse-tung. Rather than recant his own teachings for the sake of a well-earned rest and security, he preferred to make ready for a "Great Leap Forward" which must have appeared to some who judged from a different perspective a mad, great leap backward. For not only was energy senselessly expended, but a good deal of what had just been achieved might also be destroyed.

However one may judge this decision, its seemingly self-destructive character has a certain, perhaps a tragic greatness. Whether Mao took it principally because he was prompted by a desire for self-assertion or was motivated by loyalty to principles cannot be determined, and is ultimately unimportant. What is certain, however, is that he could neither have justified it ideologically nor carried it out, had it not been for the concept developed in the essay "On Contradiction." In February, 1957, Mao gave a speech which served as an overture to the "Great Leap Forward." The movement began with the slogan "Let a hundred flowers bloom, let a hundred schoools of thought contend" and ended with the establishment of People's communes. Mao's text "On the Correct Handling of Contradictions Among the People" *(Kuan-yü ch'üeh-ting ch'u li jen-min nei-pu mao-tun ti wen-t'i)* may be understood as a more precise restatement of the earlier, fundamental essay. It was his last, major contribution to ideology and of special importance because its most essential theses also set the course of the "Great Socialist Cultural Revolution" of 1966. It thus demonstrated that both movements were culminating points in a single process which had merely passed through a period of "relative rest" and would presumably be unending. Up to that time, its individual phases had been of eight or nine years' duration and its rhythm punctuated by countless individual campaigns. What Mao wanted to stress in this speech was the familiar but no longer heeded thesis that even the establishment of a socialist system would not mean that contradictions and conflicts would disappear either in society, among the "people," or anywhere else. More than that, they would give rise to antagonistic contradictions and could trigger a kind of revolution *after* the revolution:

> The contradictions between ourselves and the enemy are antagonistic contradictions. Within the ranks of the people, the contradictions . . . are nonantagonistic, while those between the exploited and the exploiting classes have a nonantagonistic aspect in addition to an antagonistic aspect. . . . In ordinary circumstances, contradictions among the people are not antagonistic. But if they are not handled properly, or if we relax our vigilance and lower our guard, antagonism may arise. . . . Many dare not openly admit that contradictions still exist among the people of our country, although it is these very contradictions that are pushing our society forward . . . they do not understand that socialist society will grow more united and consolidated through the ceaseless process of the correct handling and resolving of contradictions.[400]

At least outwardly, the "Great Leap" ended in failure. Mao's proposed "democratic method for resolving contradictions among the people according to the formula: 'unity-criticism-unity' " encouraged criticism among the intellectuals, but this was quickly put an end to. The People's communes, which had been launched with much enthusiasm, and allegedly greeted by many old people with tears in their eyes because they believed that the age of "Great Equality" had begun, had to be cut back significantly for economic reasons. This was also true of the famous and even notorious production of steel in millions of small furnaces which was to be the first, if indirect, demonstration of the superiority of the human will over the soulless industrial machinery. There were also ideological problems, and they had become all the more pressing because of the break with Moscow. In 1958/1959, countless essays dealt with the problem how Mao's "permanent revolution" *(pu-tuan ko-ming),* which provided the theoretical underpinning of the "Great Leap" could be reconciled with the "revolution by stages" *(ko-ming fa-chan chieh-tuan),* and how this in turn could resolve the ancient dilemma of Chinese communism.[401] The period was characterized by two seemingly contradictory developments. There was Mao's conspicuous withdrawal from public view, but this was accompanied by an increasing cult of his person, particularly in the army. At the same time, prestigious communists issued restrained warnings against the dangers of this arduous permanent revolution and the apparent stubbornness of its leader. Characteristically, these men were primarily representatives of the party intelligentsia who, together with the intellectuals, had been called upon to express their views during the first phase of the "Great Leap." The repeatedly mentioned philosopher Hou Wai-lu was a member of this group. Throughout his life, but especially after the communist takeover in 1949, he had worked on a Marxist interpretation of traditional Chinese philosophy, and made a significant contribution to the acculturation of Marxism in China, being a scholar of undisputed credentials. His book about the *Idea of the "Great Equality" in Chinese History (Chung-kuo li-tai ta-t'ung li-hsiang)* appeared in 1959, discusses the most important Chinese social utopias from the Confucian "Great Equality" to the immediate present, and contains a number of passages which can be interpreted as a criticism of hasty efforts to realize such utopias. When Hou Wai-lu was condemned during the climax of the Cultural Revolution toward the end of 1966, this somewhat risky reproach was not explicitly raised because it might have backfired. But he was accused of having written a "black book which maliciously defamed the people's society" through its quotations of the criticism of old "tyrannical rulers" by early Chinese socialists and anarchists such as Teng Mu and Pao Ching-yen in an effort to discredit Mao himself.[402]

Such a pointed attack on Hou was probably unjustified, but perhaps more plausible in the case of the secretary of the Peking Party Committee and longtime editor-in-chief of the *Peking Daily,* Teng T'o (born 1911), a much more clear-cut political personality. In a long series of essays which he published in 1961/1962 in the *Peking Evening News (Pei-ching wan-pao)* under the title "Evening Talks on Swallow Hill" *(Yen-shan yeh-hua),*[403] stories and events from antiquity were skillfully interwoven with references to the present so that what appeared to be literary trifles at first glance turned out to be solid political comments on closer inspection. One of the most aggressive essays using this age-old Chinese device bore the title "Great Empty Talk" *(Wei-ta ti k'ung-hua).* It castigated the unremitting use of political slogans which, similar to the notorious examination essays in "eight-legged prose style" during the Ming and Ch'ing dynasties, could not fail to bring about the utter inanition of all ideals:

> Some people have the gift of the gab. They can talk endlessly on any occasion, like water flowing from an undammed river. After listening to them, however, when you try to recall what they have said, you can remember nothing. Making long speeches without saying anything, making confusion worse confounded by explaining, or giving explanations which are not explanatory—these are the characteristics of great empty talk. We cannot deny that in certain special situations such great empty talk is inevitable, and therefore in a certain sense is a necessity. Still, it will be quite awful if great empty talk should be made into a prevalent fashion indulged in on every occasion or even cultivated as a special skill. It will be still more disastrous if our

children should be taught this skill and turned into hordes of experts in great empty talk. As chance would have it, my neighbor's child has recently often imitated the style of some great poet and put into writing a lot of "great empty talk." . . . Not long ago he wrote a poem entitled "Ode to Wild Grass" which is nothing but empty talk. The poem reads as follows: "The venerable Heaven is our father/The great Earth is our mother/And the sun is our nanny;/The East Wind if our benefactor-/And the West Wind if our enemy." Although such words as heaven, earth, father, mother, sun, nanny, the East Wind, the West Wind, benefactor and enemy catch our eye, they are used to no purpose here and have become mere clichés. Recourse to even the finest words and phrases is futile, or rather, the more such clichés are uttered, the worse the situation will become. Therefore I would advise those friends given to great empty talk to read more, think more, say less and take a rest when the time comes for talking, so as to save their own as well as other people's time and energy.[404]

Teng T'o feared that a dangerous trance might paralyze the entire nation if it stupidly and mechanically repeated preformed concepts. He was worried that, like Confucius in Kuo Mo-jo's story about the meeting between Marx and Confucius, the people would be hypnotized into acquiescence as the verses of political litanies were being recited, and soon let itself fall into a deep intellectual slumber, and felt that this was directly attributable to the exaggeratedly high respect paid to Mao Tse-tung's authority. It is not by chance that he begins the satiric treatment of the "ode" he quotes with the words of what is probably the most famous Neo-Confucian document, the "Western Inscription" of Chang Tsai,[405] which had ushered in an age of intolerant orthodoxy. The rather conspicuous terms "East Wind" and "West Wind" on the other hand come directly from Mao, and this circumstance led to a destructive criticism of Teng T'o's essay during the counterattack of the Cultural Revolution:

"The East Wind prevails over the West Wind" is a scientific thesis advanced by Chairman Mao Tse-tung at the Meeting of Communist and Workers' Parties on November 18, 1957. It says by way of a vivid image that the international situation has reached a new turning point and that the forces of socialism are prevailing over the forces of imperalism. The East Wind symbolizes the anti-imperalist revolutionary forces of the proletariat and of the oppressed peoples of Asia, Africa and Latin America. The West Wind symbolizes the decadent forces of imperalism and reaction in all countries. Why then should Teng T'o pick up the statement, "The East Wind is our benefactor and the West Wind is our enemy," and malign it as great empty talk and a cliché?[406]

In every revolutionary movement, social ideals are no longer merely expected from the future. There is a demand that they be implemented on the spot. Teng T'o did not believe that thoughtless and empty talk about these questions was dangerous in itself, but that the little that had been achieved might again be lost as a result (and such a possibility certainly entered into Mao's calculations). The constantly repeated demand for "everything or nothing" struck him as an illusory way of attaining the ideal, particularly when all real steps toward its implementation were at the same time being nipped in the bud. His preference for the dependable, slow, gradual approach is also expressed in the moral of one of his essays, "An egg as an asset" *(I-ko chi-tan ti chia-tang):*

> Who does not think of fairly substantial wealth when he hears the term "family fortune?" . . . We would not think that a single egg could be called a fortune. But Chuang-tzu tells of a man who "found an egg and made a fortune from it."[407] . . . So we should not think little of a fortune consisting of a single egg. Indeed, the accumulation of great wealth often begins with a very small sum. . . . This does not mean, however, that in all circumstances you have already amassed wealth when you possess only a single egg. Nothing is so simple and easy. Under Emperor Wan Li of the Ming dynasty there lived a story writer named Chiang Ying-k'o. His book, *The Stories of Hsüeh T'ao (Hsüeh T'ao hsiao-shuo)*[408] contains the following little tale: "Once there was a townsman who was so poor that he never knew where and when his next meal would be. One day by chance he found an egg. He told his wife elatedly, showed her the egg, saying 'I have found our family wealth.' Asked where it was, he showed her the egg, saying, 'Here it is. But it will take ten years to build our wealth.' Then he discussed his plan with his wife, 'I'll take the egg to the neighbor and have it hatched by his hen. When the chickens have grown up, I'll take back one of the females to lay eggs. I shall get 15 chickens a month. In two years, they will multiply and make a total of 300. Then I shall sell them for ten taels of gold, with which I can buy five cows producing calves. My cows will multiply to 25 in three years and 150 in another three years. These I shall sell for 300 taels of gold. If I lend out the money at interest, I shall have amassed 500 taels of gold in three years.' " The latter half of the story goes into rather uninteresting detail, so I would like to leave them out, except one point worth mentioning. In the end this greedy man said that he would take a concubine. At this his wife was "roused to great anger and smashed the egg with a blow of her fist." Thus his family wealth consisting of a single egg was totally destroyed. Don't you see that this story helps to explain a lot of things? This greedy man, too, realized that to build his family wealth would take a long time and hence in the discussion with his wife allowed himself ten years to do so. This seemed reasonable, but his plan was utterly lacking in any reliable basis and consisted entirely in a series of mere suppositions one piled on another. In picturing what would happen in the next ten years, he completely substituted illusion for reality, showing himself as one obsessed by greed for money. The result was that his wife flew into a rage and with a blow of her fist she destroyed all his riches.[409]

Less literary but similar in substance was a personal letter the minister of defense, P'eng Te-huai (born 1900), one of Mao's oldest fellow fighters, sent to the chairman in the summer of 1959. He wrote: "The belief that the age of communism is about to dawn has made many comrades feverish. Because people think only about realizing communism all at once and have the exaggerated idea of being the first in the world to do so, the method of looking to the facts for the truth has been abandoned. But that is something the Party has worked out over a long period of time."[410] A few months later, P'eng had to turn his post over to Mao's devoted follower Lin Piao (born 1908). This event really anticipated the victory of the Maoist line during the Cultural Revolution seven years later. But it was a victory which even from Mao's point of view (or, more accurately, precisely because of that point of view) could not be considered definitive. Although they were successfully suppressed, there can be no doubt that the opinions of Teng T'o and P'eng Te-huai reflected the views of a good many Chinese. Thus it is here, *within* communist-Chinese ideology, and not as a choice between Marxism and a warmed-up, purely Chinese world view—be it Confucian or something else—that an alternative to Maoism may well be a future possibility. This is particularly true since the Cultural Revolution resolved a number of inner contradictions in a revolutionary manner, as Mao would put it, and did not leave China's spiritual landscape unchanged. It would seem that there are arguments supporting both methods for attaining an ideal Chinese communist society, permanent revolution or a gradualist approach. But today Mao has such enormous prestige that every one of his decisions invariably tilts the scale toward the position preferred by him, and this inhibits open discussion. This prestige will unquestionably remain intact even after his death. Both sides will be able to avail themselves of it, for in cases of dispute, his writings permit as many conflicting interpretations as do those of other creators of philosophical systems throughout history.

POVERTY AND "BLANKNESS," MOVEMENT AND CLOSENESS TO DEATH

The real hub of all internal controversy continued to be the question how China could implement communism and also recover its leadership of mankind, a role in which it has seen itself throughout the course of its history. Mao's opponents, condemned as revisionists, and who included the majority of intellectuals, attempted to increase international contacts (including closer ties with the Soviet Union). At the same time, they wanted to retain whatever they could of their spiritual past as the country was being transformed into a socialist state. As far as they were concerned, China's claim to a role of leadership on the road toward communism seemed not only a necessary function of the country's size and its enormous population, but even more of its incomparably long history and its abundant historical experience. To create an awareness of this, a great deal of excellent research in history and the humanities was undertaken by a group of brilliant scholars during the period from 1949 to 1965, the beginning of the Cultural Revolution. Hou Wai-lu was only one among many. They were principally intent on shedding light on a hidden intellectual current which might offset the Confucian "Great Tradition" and serve to prove that socialism and revolution were an age-old Chinese tradition. It was also meant to show how China had suddenly outdistanced other nations in social development. This explains the favorable revaluation of the peasant uprisings, for example, of the teachings of Mo Ti and the School of Agriculture during this time, and the glorification of a diversity of "revolutionary" philosophers and writers, from the "materialist" Lao-tzu and the anarchists Pao Ching-yen and Teng Mu to the followers of the Confucian New Text School with K'ang Yu-wei as its most famous modern representative.[411] With real horror, Mao's followers observed how a group of urban Marxist scholars of impeccable intelligence was creating an ideology where a long phalanx of thinkers of the past long believed dead and buried surprisingly reentered through the back door. They decided on a counterattack of the most radical sort.

As early as the spring of 1958, during the period of the Great Leap, when it had already become evident that the conversion of the intelligentsia to the idea of a permanent revolution could only lead to rebellion, Mao Tse-tung had published an essay which energetically rejected all attempts to explain the stage of social development reached by China by its long history and its many revolutions. Boldly, and with a single stroke of the pen, China's entire past was rendered null and void. The importance of the Chinese people within the family of nations, he wrote, was due to its multitude and the fact that it was "partly poor, partly blank" *(i ch'iung, erh pai).* It was, in other words, an as yet unwritten page in world history. But in a universe where revolutionary stages were forever being superseded, it was precisely because of that "newness" that it deserved to occupy the first place, and not because it had attained one in a long series of successive stages of social development, which could not be defined in any event:

> Throughout the country, the Communist spirit is surging forward. The political consciousness of the masses is rising rapidly. Backward sections among the masses have roused themselves energetically to catch up with the more advanced, proving that China is forging ahead in her socialist economic revolution (where transformation of the relations of production has not yet been completed) as well as in her political, ideological, technical, and cultural revolutions. In view of this, our country may not need as much time as previously thought to catch up with the big capitalist countries in industrial and agricultural production. The decisive factor, apart from leadership by the Party, is our 600 million people. The more people, the more views and suggestions, the more intense the fervor, and the greater the energy. Never before have the masses been so high in spirit, so strong in morale, and so firm in determination. . . . Apart from their other characteristics, China's 600 million people have two remarkable peculiarities; they are, first of all, poor, and secondly, blank. That may seem like a bad thing, but it is really a good thing. Poor people want change, want to do things, want revolution. A clean sheet of paper has no blotches, and so the newest and most beautiful words can be written on it, the newest and most beautiful pictures can be painted on it. The *tatsepao* [opinions and criticisms written out in bold Chinese characters on large sheets of paper and pasted freely for everybody to see] is a most useful new weapon. It can be used in cities, rural areas, factories, cooperatives, shops, government institutions, schools,

> army units, and streets—wherever the masses congregate. Where it has been used widely, people should go on using it. A poem written by Kung Tzu-chen of the Ch'ing dynasty reads: Let thunderbolts rouse the universe to life. Alas that ten thousand horses should stand mute!/I urge Heaven to bestir itself anew/And send down talented men of every kind.[412] The *tatsepao* have broken the dull air in which "ten thousand horses stand mute." . . . Do the working people of China still look like slaves as they did in the past? No, they have become the masters. The working people who live on the 9.6 million square kilometers of the People's Republic of China have really begun to rule this land.[413]

The "blank" individual who, in Mao's view, is peculiarly characteristic of the Chinese people, is not only the "pure," but also the "new" man. Similar to the vision of reality the Taiping leader Hung Hsiu-ch'üan had experienced during his visit to heaven in a dream, this is a man all of whose bodily organs and old beliefs have been replaced by new ones. It is here that the spiritual transformation of the Chinese—a process referred to as "brainwashing" by a horrified West—takes on its real (but not therefore less disquieting) meaning. It deliberately penetrates all fibers of the personality, verges on the mystical, and employs all the techniques of mass psychology. The conviction that the "old Adam" has to be destroyed if a new world is to arise and that man can accomplish this more easily the closer he comes to the curious (almost Buddhist-Taoist) ideal of "emptiness," of "blankness," can also be demonstrated in the idea that with the proper reeducation, members of all classes, not just the peasantry and the proletariat, but also the intelligentsia and the "national bourgeoisie" could become fully qualified members of the new nation. This constitutes a remarkable parallel to the transformation of Buddhism in China. For in contrast to the earlier Hinayana Buddhism ("Lesser Vehicle"), its Mahayana version ("Greater Vehicle") had proclaimed that not only monks but anyone might enter Nirvana at any time. All graduations of salvation were thus negated. This idea had already made its appearance in Mao's "On New Democracy" *(Hsin min-chu chu-i lun)* (1940)[414] and continued to be championed after the communist takeover. It also conforms generally to Mao's idea of the "new man," the universal man who may be an "expert" in one respect but is "red" in all others. And this is infinitely more important because it means that he is potentially capable of any form of activity.[415] This universality expresses itself most conspicuously in the ever-repeated insistence on the combination of physical and intellectual work. As has been repeatedly mentioned, this notion pervades Chinese intellectual history as a kind of counterideal to the pure scholar and put its stamp on all oppositional currents. Through the—if need be—compulsory "practice" of physical labor, which means almost always agricultural work, this concept not only makes it possible to bridge the gap between city and country, but also to turn members of inferior classes into universal, "new men." Even the last Manchu emperor P'u-i (governed from 1906–1908) was allowed to work toward this ideal as a gardener until he died, and he had even been a traitor because he collaborated with the Japanese as emperor of "Manchuria" (Manchukuo).[416]

With this emphasis on an alleged "poverty and blankness," Mao deliberately ranged China among the underdeveloped nations. In view of their inadequate technology and short history (particularly in the case of Africa), they fully meet this qualification. In spite of this ranking, he claims a position of leadership for China because it has a large population. Interestingly enough, this claim is not direct, but indirect, and based on a curious application of the law of the leap from quantity to quality. The enormous number of "suggestions" coming from the "600 million people" will necessarily also produce the best and most elevated thoughts in this gigantic collective. In this context, the proclamations written in large characters become the characteristic form of intellectual expression in the new, constantly renewed, ideal world. For unlike practices in the "old world" where a few individuals clothed their thought in an opaque style and diffused it to an elite through use of mechanical means—printing—it is the theory here that everyone is called upon to express his ideas informally, and that in a way which differs from print since it lacks uniformity and is ephemeral. But precisely for that reason, it is filled with pulsating life and has the advantage that "knowledge" and "action," "thinking" and "practice" become one in the act of writing. This "East Wind" of an enormous, turbulent wealth of thought, created through the praxis of a nation at work, will overcome the "West Wind," the mechanically reproduced, weak and abstract thoughts of a few bloodless paper scholars alienated from that praxis. Simplicity, ever one of China's ideals, the "simplemindedness that is China's," will conquer the West, the prisoner of machine thinking by the power of the human collective. Not only in the spiritual struggle but also in armed conflict the East will unmask the West as a paper tiger. For even the spirit of the atom bomb, that ultimate, most dangerous product of the dictatorial power of the machine, will have to bow to the power of the new man who has become whole and unified through community.

These theses are curiously inconsistent with the fact that China has enormously developed its technology, and especially its arms technology, including atomic weapons (although this was due to the actions of the opposition, i.e. the sober party members of P'eng Te-huai's kind). They prove that the opposition between "inner" and "outer," between the "indigenous" and the "foreign" has not disappeared even in present-day China. In this unshakable trust in man, and even more in the trust in the great number of men in the countryside and the ultimate contempt for the machine and mechanical weapons, we see the emergence of an age-old trait of the Chinese character. It had expressed itself last—albeit in a much more naive form—in the Boxer Rebellion, which was actually modern China's only internal uprising against the West and its oppressive imperialism. For the Boxers (and to some extent the Taiping) had been convinced of the magical strength of their beliefs which they thought would even protect them against the superiority of western firearms. What is fascinating about contemporary China is precisely this contradictory mixture of a surprisingly advanced, technological modernization carried through with truly admirable consistency, and something the West cannot help seeing as an almost atavistic faith. A closer look shows that its roots actually go back to the traditional, anti-Confucian, religious traditions of the secret societies. From the tenth century on, the struggle against the icy rigidity of Neo-Confucianism had always been suffused with religious fire, even when it was waged by Confucianism itself, i.e. the religiously tinctured New Text School.[417] Naturally, this was even truer of the ideologies of the secret societies which fed on Taoist, Buddhist and West-Asian thought. Their world views always presented themselves as highly simplified, watered-down configurations of so cohesive a syncretism that its components are difficult to identify. Nor could this have been otherwise, given the backwardness of the groups involved. But these views also incorporated certain constantly recurring constituents of which some were anchored in ritual and understood everywhere as elements of movement, of change, of hope for something new that could break the "dull wind" of the reigning Confucianism. Mao's sympathies and connections with the secret societies during his youth have been documented. But during the Cultural Revolution, he did not revive their ideologies but rather these much more important behavioral models, which have something archetypical about them. He appealed to those segments of the population which by a natural disposition inclined partly to the ideal of the new, partly to the ideal of nomadism. And that meant the youth and the military.

Most striking among these models are those which can be understood directly as an expression of revolutionary *movement.* According to Mao's conception of the permanent revolution, such movement does not lead to a happy society, but already represents that happy society. This ideal found its most perfect, subsequently mythicized expression in the Long March between 1934 and 1937. It took the organized Chinese communists in a wide arc from southeastern Kiangsi province to northwestern Shensi and disseminated communist thought all over China during this flight. This march also became the legendary, great example of the countless small marches on which the Red Guards set out in 1966, and which were a form of initiation into the spirit of revolutionary unrest. But at the same time, and as certain forms of heroization show, images which had accompanied the Chinese spirit since remotest antiquity found concrete expression here. They are images of exalted personalities, of heroes and sages, who were either driven from the unjust world of ordinary men or voluntarily turned their back on it as they sought fulfillment for themselves and salvation for the world in a better sphere in the beyond. The classical example of all these is the poet and statesman Ch'ü Yüan[418] who was rejected by society and set out on his long voyage through heaven, which finally ended in disappointment and tragedy. Because he was still hero and saint in one person, we can trace back to him the two frequently entwined traditions where flight and resistance as the only possible reactions to a world experienced as inimical and perverted found literary and political expression.

The more active attitude which stresses resistance, or at least change, already comes to the fore in Sung Yü's voyage to heaven. It no longer ends in resignation, but an optimistic desire to act, although in all other respects it is an imitation of Ch'ü Yüan's.[419] In an anarchist key, it returns in the figure of "Master Great Man"[420] as described by the poet Juan Chi. He is a person who no longer roams the universe merely to find external help for transforming the world but himself appears as a cosmic force effecting an incessant reversal of all stable conditions, and can even turn heaven and earth upside down. In politics, embodiments of what are initially predominantly literary expressions of unrest and the desire for change may also be observed since the beginnings of classical Chinese culture, although they are more difficult to identify in the sources. From the sixth century A.D. on, they take form in the "wandering scholar" *(yu-shih).* In all those countless cases where it was not scholarship but the sword that constituted their capital, they could more readily be called "errant knights" or "roaming swordsmen." A connection can be established here to the numerous rebellions which caused periodic upheavals in the empire down to our time. The term "peasant uprisings" which is frequently used nowadays, too much obscures the fact that misery and mismanagement had always caused peasants to give up their sedentary life before the rebellions began. The "appearance of robbers in the mountains," always interpreted as a bad omen by Chinese advocates of the orderly conduct of government,[421] not only denoted the vexing problem of bandits that beset travelers in the mountains, traditionally the areas to which civilization had not spread, which belonged to a different world and were therefore the domain of both robbers and hermits. It also, and more generally, referred to the incomparably more dangerous internal transformation of certain segments of the population, the conversion of the "solid" aggregate of the peasantry in to the "fluid" state of vagrants and the threat of a further metamorphosis into "Robin Hoods" or revolutionaries. The rebels justified their challenge to the existing rigid social order as much by its fixity as by the injustice of prevailing conditions. But unlike injustice, this immutability was a constituent of every traditional Confucian government. Because it could not be abandoned as a matter of principle, it constituted an impassable barrier to any reconciliation with the rebels.

But from the noble bandit and robber, associations lead directly to the soldier. For in China, and especially in Confucian China, the soldier, being "rootless," was seen not so much as the rebel's adversary, but as his companion. All the virtues of the soldier were also those of the "robber." This was particularly the case when the soldier did not fight in organized military units and conventional combat, but had to choose the hit-and-run tactics of guerilla warfare, a form of combat the Chinese had repeatedly preferred in the course of their history, and which the communists were not the first to use after the Sino-Japanese War (1937–1945). The classical example of the twofold nature of these homeless vagrants—soldiers vis-a-vis the external enemy, but "robbers" and rebels vis-a-vis the government—are the figures glorified in the famous popular novel, *The Marsh Heroes,* who defended their country against the invaders from the north as vigorously as they fought for improvements in social conditions.[422] This human type, inclined toward combat and movement by natural disposition, and who also carried this orientation into the civilian sphere, is the opposite of the Confucian militiaman, the armed peasant. In the case of the latter, the military and the civilian are also closely allied, but the civilian clearly predominates. But during the Cultural Revolution, it was the former Mao Tse-tung tried to strengthen as an ideal which would combat the "demon" of passivity.

An aspect of the military is a certain closeness to death or a readiness to die, a sort of link between the combative and the escapist attitudes toward a hostile environment. The "Three Much-read Articles" of Mao Tse-tung, raised to the status of classics since 1966, therefore directly relate to death, and this is particularly striking since all of them are short pieces. In its way, each discusses the sacrifice of the self for society as a way of transcending death. The first of these documents, "Serve the People," *(Wei jen-min fu-wu)* is a speech given on September 8, 1944 during a memorial service for a worker-soldier who had died in an accident, and sounds the basic theme: "All men must die, but death can vary in its significance. The ancient Chinese writer Szuma Chien said: 'Though death befalls all men alike, it may be weightier than Mount Tai or lighter than a feather.'[423] To die for the people is weightier than Mount Tai, but to work for the fascists and die for the exploiters and oppressors is lighter than a feather. . . . Wherever there is struggle, there is sacrifice, and death is a common occurrence. But we have the interests of the people . . . at heart, and when we die for the people, it is a worthy death."[424]

The second is also an obituary (dated December 21, 1939) and entitled, "In Memory of Norman Bethune" *(Chi-nien Po Ch'iu-en).* Bethune was a Canadian physician who had been working in the Red Army since 1938 and died of blood poisoning in 1939. It also is an appreciation of death as sacrifice. But because Bethune was not Chinese, this concept is broadened to become an element in the liberation of nations or peoples which transcends all spatial barriers in the struggle against the oppressors.[425] The third document, dated June 11, 1945, "The Foolish Old Man Who Removed the Mountains" *(Yü-kung i shan)* gives a hint how death can transcend time. It recalls a story of the old book *Lieh-tzu* where we previously noted some of the most plastic early descriptions of the paradises of a primitive communism:

> There is an ancient Chinese fable called "The Foolish Old Man Who Removed the Mountains." It tells of an old man who lived in northern China long, long ago and was known as the Foolish Old Man of North Mountain. His house faced south and beyond his doorway stood the two great peaks, T'ai-hang and Wang-wu, obstructing the way. He called his sons, and hoe in hand they began to dig up these

mountains with great determination. Another greybeard, known as the Wise Old Man, saw them and said derisively, "How silly of you to do this! It is quite impossible for you few to dig up these two huge mountains." The Foolish Old Man replied, "When I die, my sons will carry on; when they die, there will be my grandsons, and then their sons and grandsons, and so on to infinity. High as they are, the mountains cannot grow any higher and with every bit we dig, they will be that much lower. Why can't we clear them away?"[426] Having refuted the Wise Old Man's wrong view, he went on digging every day, unshaken in his conviction. God was moved by this, and he sent down two angels, who carried the mountains away on their backs. Today, two big mountains lie like a dead weight on the Chinese people. One is imperialism, the other is feudalism. The Chinese Communist Party has long made up its mind to dig them up. We must persevere and work unceasingly, and we, too, will touch God's heart. Our God is none other than the masses of the Chinese people. If they stand up and dig together with us, why can't these two mountains be cleared away?[427]

THE RELIGIOUS SYMBOLISM OF SWIMMING AND THE SUN

The opposite of this energetic action against a hostile world, passivity, escape, has an interesting tradition in Chinese intellectual history as well. At least indirectly, it also extends down to the present. It does not seek to resolve the conflict between man and reality by struggle but is religious in nature. It therefore tended to express itself in aery images of fantasy rather than in actions, yet contributed its share to the launching of powerful social movements when it conbined with a revolutionary attitude. Here again, Ch'ü Yüan is the starting point from which traces lead back to the ecstatic experiences of flight of the Shamans[428] and the voyages to paradise[429] which China's religious age produced in such abundance. Even during the era of an all-powerful Confucianism, they can still be uncovered in the weary travels of Ming-liao-tzu, that resigned Taoist and "philistine,"[430] and in the wondrous voyages of T'ang Ao.[431] The criticism of the times articulated here has its ultimate offshoots in K'ang Yu-wei's teaching of "celestial peregrinations."[432] In all cases, the experience of happiness found by these wanderers between the worlds was only quite secondarily the visit to another better stable place. It was not even the final departure from this inadequate world of the here and now. What was important was the overcoming of gravity, for it was only through gravity that the world became the chain that hampered all the movements of these men that thirsted for freedom.

Not only in China, but everywhere else as well, the overcoming of this natural law, symbolic of all manmade constraints imposed by society, found its most striking form in the idea of flying, but not only there. For swimming had always had almost the same symbolic import since it also permits man to transcend the two-dimensional space within which he moves, and because it resembles flight in the sense that here also the rhythmic movement shifts from the legs to the arms. Besides, swimming was a relatively rare skill in rural, agrarian China. Something of the miraculous still attached to it since man here entered an element that had not been created for him. But for this same reason, it also carried an intimation of death. The thought of drowning was always present, much as the possibility of crashing was during flight. Both of these are clearly the real dangers for the person boldly setting out for new shores. These associations explain why so many Chinese expressions denoting more or less metaphorically such concepts as freedom, vagabondage and self-surrender are written with the signific "water." Perhaps the best known is the concept *lang,* "wave," which also means "dissolute," "to roam about" and "romantic" (when combined with the word *man,* "overflowing," which is also written with the signific "water"). Not in static Confucianism but in Taoism, this latter meaning had an indubitably positive value.

It can be shown that this curious complex of motifs runs through all of Chinese intellectual history in a kind of secret tradition. This is not a construct but is clearly present in Chinese writers themselves, such as Lin Yü-t'ang, for example.[433] Once again, the starting point is Ch'ü Yüan. Disappointed by heaven and earth, he sought to drown himself and thus became the prototype of all those who endeavored to transcend an evil world but were crushed in this superhuman attempt. The poet Li T'ai-po, of whom legend reports that he lost his life when, intoxicated, he wanted to seize the moon in the waves,[434] symbolizes the identical fate. Drunkenness and the dream of another paradisiacal world, flying and swimming, crashing and drowning all coalesce in this grandiose image. But also the many Chinese statesmen and scholars who jumped into the water not in legend but in fact when political upheaval or the ruin of their ideals had made the world so alien that they attempted to move into another belong into this context. They include the Sung loyalists who once leaped into the ocean with the last pretender to the crown, and scholars of more recent times. There were men such as the traditionally educated writer Wang Kuo-wei (1877–1927), who was fascinated by Schopenhauer, loved the modern age, yet could not detach himself from the old and therefore committed suicide in a pond of the "Summer Palace," thus becoming the symbol of an entire generation. Even Mao Tse-tung's life is not entirely free of this motif. In his oral autobiography, he reports that as a thirteen-year-old, pursued by his father after a violent altercation, he ran to the village pond and threatened to throw himself into the water. It was an act of despair which vouchsafed him a much greater measure of freedom in the family.[435] This form of suicide in the waves might have appeared attractive to all these desperate men because it held out the hope that it would cleanse them of the dust of the earth before they left it forever. But the truly strong individuals were those who really succeeded in transcending the old world without perishing in the new, unaccustomed medium they had to pass through. It is hardly surprising that we should encounter such figures almost entirely in fairy tales and legends. Examples are the sage I-liao in the book *Chuang-tzu* who encouraged the duke of Lu to set out for the "Great No-man's Land" even without a ship,[436] or the frequently recurring figure of the shipwrecked who by good fortune even travels through "light water" and whirlpools to reach the islands of the blessed.[437] It is but natural that such beliefs should exist only as rumors where we are dealing with political reality. The story about the end of the rebel Sun En in the fifth century A.D. would be an example. When we are told that he and his companions all jumped into the waves of the Yangtzu because the paradise islands were supposed to lie off its mouth, and were turned into water sprites,[438] this simply means that they had finally mastered the water and found their happiness in that unfamiliar, much more fluid element.

It is only against this background that a curious act of Mao Tse-tung from the most recent past takes on a surprising significance (his acts, which always strove to combine "knowledge" and "action" have always been much more interesting than his writings), and that is his widely acclaimed swim in the Yangtze, which was imitated by thousands in a kind of mass movement, filmed, and shown around the world. Up to this time, there have been two reports that Mao covered considerable distances in this river which has always been considered a genuine barrier within China until a huge bridge accommodating both rail and other traffic was built across it in 1957. The first time was in June, 1956, when Mao allegedly swam across the river three times, on the first, the third and the fourth of that month. The second was ten years later, on June 16, 1966. In both cases, this was not primarily intended to document the good health of the party chairman, but rather the beginning of a new, bold venture which would usher in a new, better world. It was a kind of cultic act performed by Mao with almost ritual necessity on the eve of the Great Leap Forward and again on the eve of the Cultural Revolution. His thoughts during the first crossing of the river near the place where the bridge was then being constructed have found expression in a poem which is pointedly entitled "Swimming." More clearly than anything else, it indicates the hope that the streaming movement will give birth to a new world and that this will be regretted by only one person, Confucius:

> Having just drunk the Changsha waters/Already I taste the Wuchang fish;/Swimming across the ten-thousand-li-long Yangtze/Deep I gaze my fill into far Chu skies;/Heedless of boisterous winds and buffeting waves,/Better this seemed than leisurely pacing home courtyards:/Today I have indeed obtained my release./The Master had said on the river bank:/"Thus do all things flow away."//
>
> A breeze stirs the booms,/Quiet the tortoise and snake stay,/While great plans grow apace;/A bridge flies its north-south span,/Common thoroughfare made of nature's moat./Yet to come the rocky dam athwart the western reaches,/Cutting asunder the mists and rains of Wushan,/Till a calm lake rises in the precipitous gorges/The goddess, should she still be alive,/Shall marvel at a changed world.//[439]

This connection with water recurs in one of the best known political songs which has been circulated widely, especially since the Cultural Revolution. Here, the crossing of the oceans becomes an unmistakable symbol of the revolution and the upheaval it creates: "Rely on the helmsman when sailing the seas,/All living things rely on the sun for their growth,/Moistened by rain and dew, young crops grow strong,/When making revolution, rely on the thought of Mao Tse-tung.// Fish can't live without water,/Melons can't thrive off their vine,/The revolutionary masses can't live without the Communist Party/Mao Tse-tung's thought is the never-setting sun."[440]

But in this poem, the element of water is already associated with another symbolism which also has a long-hidden, anti-Confucian tradition, namely sun and light worship. Traces of this emotional tie to the sun do not lead back directly to Chinese sources but to the influence of Zoroastrianism and Manicheism, which came to China during the T'ang. These west-Asian religions had fused so intimately with Taoist and Buddhist ideals on the level of popular religions during the eighth and ninth centuries that they were increasingly felt to be wholly Chinese from that period on. This was especially true of the lower classes where the worship of the sun, the stars, light and fire, and indeed even of the lucky color red, which was associated with these phenomena according to Han doctrines[441] constituted an ever-recurring motif in the ideology of popular uprisings. The rebellious "devil worshipers and vegetable eaters" of the Sung period had already known a cult of the sun and the moon,[442] and other rebels, such as Chang Hsien-chung, even considered themselves incarnations of stars,[443] to mention only two examples. The same belief was still alive in Hung Hsiu-ch'üan, the leader of the Taiping rebellion, who thought he was an incarnation of the sun which was in turn born of God "who is fire."[444] There is also an echo of sun worship in the enthusiasm with which Mao Tse-tung defended his unusual hunger for sunlight when he talked to the peasants during his extended wanderings through Hunan province.[445] But such associations are much more pronounced in the ubiquitous equation of the "Thoughts of Mao Tse-tung" and a "red sun" rising above a red age, as it were, an homage evident in countless pictures showing Mao's face surrounded by red rays. It is thus not nearly as rare in Chinese intellectual history as one might first believe, but can be tied in with much older intellectual currents, even if this only expresses itself in a cluster of associations which, when taken separately, seem rather vague. If one adds the fact that Mao Tse-tung's personal name *(tung)* means nothing other than "East" (*Mao* is the family name, *Tse* the "generational name" common to all children),[446] it becomes readily comprehensible how Mao could become the incarnation of the "East" for China, and this quite apart from the direct effect of his personality. He is the incarnation of a new day arising in a propitious dawn, a day which will conquer the fading West with the certainty of a natural law.

This conviction also permeates the hymn, "The East Is Red" *(Tung-fang hung)* which has probably become the song most frequently heard in China during recent times. Significantly, it carries the same message as the first Chinese earth satellite: the introductory double verse begins and ends with the word "East," which rhymes with "red" *(hung)*. In one case, it appears in its actual meaning, in the other as the component of Mao's name: "The East is red./The sun rises./China has brought forth a Mao Tse-tung./He works for the people's happiness,/he-er-hai-yo! He is the people's great savior//Chairman Mao loves the people./He is our guide./To build the new China/hu-er-hai-yo! he leads us forward."//[447]

The excessive admiration evident in these first two stanzas of the rather long hymn is so unmistakable that to demonstrate a religious component in the attitude of contemporary China hardly requires the enumeration of further indications such as the many, prayer-like letters sent in to Chinese newspapers by readers, the well-known, no less numerous reports about the miraculous effects of the "Thoughts of Mao Tse-tung," or the anthology, the "Red Bible," originally intended only for the army and published with a red cover. The billions of reprints of Mao Tse-tung's writings brought out since 1966 and whose publication took precedence over that of all other material point in the same direction. Involuntarily, one is reminded of the early period of Buddhism in China where the mass distribution of sacred writings was so firmly believed to be a good deed that it resulted in the invention of printing in the sixth century. But the reprinting of the works of an individual, which suddenly took on gigantic proportions after the Cultural Revolution, corresponds in a very characteristic manner to the propagation of the "proclamations written in large characters" which set in at about the same time. In a sense, they represent its counterpart. They are the expressions of opinions of anonymous individuals which remain manuscripts. But because they come from untold millions of authors and thus represent the people as such, they also reach the public in billions of specimen. These "proclamations" thus seem like the multitudinous echo of a tremendously rousing call, reflecting the thoughts of Mao like so many facets. At the same time, however, these thoughts are conceived of as reflections of the thoughts of the people itself which require this interplay to become clearer, more concentrated, more unambiguous.

Many different forms of a dialectical relationship of this sort can be observed in quite a few religions (and in the state systems derived from them), in China as everywhere else in the world. The beginnings of prayer, for example, have their roots here. Confronted with the enormously powerful greatness of a thou—be it a human being, a god-man or a god—the individual occupies a twofold position. On the one hand, all differences that separate him from his fellow, origin, sex, position and wealth, shrink to insignificance. The "equality before god" infuses reality and makes brothers of all those touched by it, monks of a sort, who not only wear the lowliest but the identical dress so that all individual characteristics disappear. Subjectively, identification with a great thou raises the individual to dizzying spiritual heights. Because it could never ascend to them on its own, its bliss is all the more intense. Concerned about the dangerous irrational elements, Confucianism had always rejected this almost mystical identification of the individual with the political leader. One need only recall its critical attitude toward the twelfth century cult of the popular leader Chung Hsiang.[448] The "socialist" Mo Ti, on the other hand, accepted and described in detail this communication between above and below, and this was certainly not by chance. His concept of "identification with the superior" aims precisely at that reciprocal adaptation between an eminent personality at the head of the state, and a people that has become one through a "general, reciprocal love."[449] That it should also have been Mo Ti who protested the "lack of belief of the times" and advocated a more intense religiosity accords only too well with this position. For it shows that the place religion occupied in China's spiritual landscape was quite different from that in the Occident, all outward similarities notwithstanding, and this was particularly the case where the realization of ideals was at stake. The religious ages, for which the Buddhist era between the third and the ninth centuries may serve as the most eminent example, were always those of a heightened inner and outer vitality, of intellectual and political danger and mobility, ages of expansion, exchange and experiment. The "enlightened" ages, on the other hand, among which the long period of Neo-Confucianism between the tenth and the nineteenth centuries is best remembered, were periods of intellectual calm, of concentration but also of shrinkage; of conservation but also of isolation. The causes for this curious reciprocal relationship lie in the surprising fact that China never exported religion, never missionized, but always was the target of missionizing activity coming from the outside. Taoism, the only religion it ever produced, was never carried beyond the borders of its empire. Religion was therefore always associated with the alien, the new and the revolutionary, with boldness and adventure. It was through a religion of reason that China affected its neighbors and gradually but persistently extended its culture in a process lasting thousands of years. Strictly speaking, however, Confucianism is not a *religion.* But precisely through its irresistible rationality—so clearly superior to the illusionary and utopian externalities of all religions—Confucianism time and again destroyed the seeds of new possibilities in the real world. They were seeds which are contained in all utopias, including religious ones, although it is true that ultimately the realization may differ from the seeds that were the original ideals.

In China, the religious and even the magical are thus forms of expression which are almost inevitably associated with the idea of renewal, mobility and revolution. All anti-Confucian ideals which envisaged the replacement of the hierarchical social order based on the model of the family by absolute freedom and equality arose in a religious environment, as we have seen. Some of them derived from Taoism, for at least its imaginary, rural areas of retreat (particularly the caves, less perhaps the heavens and islands) knew nothing of classes. And some came from Buddhism, of whose paradises the same holds true. Lastly, there are the secret societies which frequently absorbed other forms of western thought and often inclined toward anarchist conceptions. In a world where realism, reason and reality had been monopolized by Confucianism, these ideas thus had to survive in the milieu of an irrational underground for so long a time that they could not rid themselves of this stigma overnight.

From this perspective, the glorification of two spheres closely associated with religion becomes somewhat more comprehensible. They are the spheres of rural life and of the military. Because modern western history had a diametrically opposite orientation, we would tend to call them regressive and conservative. The many rebellions of Chinese history not only had an ideology with religious overtones, but all began quite literally in the countryside, in the smoky villages "where dogs barked and cocks crowed."[450] They were carried forward either by soldiers on duty along the borders of the empire, or by peasants who had first been desperados and robbers and then become soldiers. Given this ancestry, it may be a long time before all those Chinese determined to rebel and reform will no longer mistrust the advocates of reasonableness, moderation and a policy of small steps. For it happens too easily (although usually perhaps unfairly) that the image of those urging caution, such as Teng T'o, for example, is overlaid by that of many self-righteous Confucians of past centuries who used the identical argument to arrest all movement, for they considered the new desirable only if it was a hundred times superior to the old. Unfortunately all-too-frequently quoted in traditional China, these are the words Confucian scholars used when they objected to the Legalist Shang Yang.[451]

The shock Confucianism and almost the entire educated class suffered in the third century B.C. during the first encounter with the explicitly "New," with the unknown brutality of a "legalist" system (which we would perhaps call "fascist") under the founder of the Chinese empire Ch'in Shih Huang-ti, had such a lasting effect that during the succeeding two millennia Confucianism rather submitted than openly admit that the "New" could be something other than Legalism, that what had never existed before need not therefore be utopian. Given this trauma, there were never more than two alternatives for the educated Chinese: he could either affirm this world which appeared to be based on eternal Confucian laws, or he had to retreat into a different, spiritual, better and frequently religious world, but which was cut off from the world of reality. For the narrow connecting passage which resembled those leading from the Taoist paradises behind the caves, the transition from the utopian to the new, from what had never been realized to what would be realized for the first time had been blocked by the repellent spectacle of the Ch'in dynasty. One has to know this trauma if one wants to understand why in the past the overwhelming majority of educated Chinese tended to be conservative and to cling to the familiar. But one must also understand that modern China suffers the reverse trauma. Every step toward stabilization is now viewed with suspicion as the onset of a new stagnation, as the beginning of the end. All recourse to the past arouses the fear that, like so much mildew, the dust of the centuries will settle once again on what has newly grown. This is the reason for the constant forward thrust, those countless movements and leaps. They are meant to stay the drift into the sleep of the past.

THE KNOT THAT CANNOT BE UNTIED

Although it was probably not intended, this restlessness has also spread to western countries since the Cultural Revolution. Contrary to the concept that the industrialized nations must spearhead the revolution, China, where there was no storming of the Bastille and no Paris Commune, appears to have wanted to export the pattern of its revolution to the rest of the world: unrest begins in the countryside, in the villages, and it is in this role that today's nonindustrialized countries in Asia, African and South America see themselves. Their "poverty" and "blankness," their "calm, beauty and simplicity" surprisingly become the model for the rebels in the "cities," the part played by the rich industrialized nations. It carries the revolution into the metropolises, as peasants, robbers and soldiers had done more than once in the course of Chinese history when they overran the garrisons in the provinces. Although the West looks back on a historical experience wholly different from that of China, this seemingly archaic model is actually being adopted in certain isolated instances today. The reason for this may be that up to a point, it suffers from the same conflicting traumata which determined China's attitude toward the new, toward utopia, and thus toward revolution. For although in the West (and this includes all highly developed industrial countries) the older fear of movement and the more recent one of stagnation do not go back to such very remote events, industrialization has accelerated time in these countries to such a degree that changes that once required generations now occur from one instant to the next, so that these nations have come to resemble the visitors to the Taoist lands behind the caves. As a result, it is becoming a matter of indifference whether an experience seems outdated after millennia, centuries or after just a few decades.

In the speeding up of the pulse beat of time, the opportunities afforded the individual in the search for his happiness and that of his world unquestionably arise from the circumstance that the period of passive waiting has become short; indeed, it has ceased to exist. It is not the morrow, it is this day that becomes the Day of Judgment. Elysium is within reach, the Now demands that he act and become wholly transformed. If he has the strength, the elasticity, the inner, infinite multiformity to see in ever new metamorphoses and revolutions the dawning of an ever new day of judgment, he will time and again have the ecstatic experience of the kaleidoscopic birth of unknown worlds from seemingly tiny points, as though he were embarked on a surging flight through the starry heavens. But if he tires only once and attempts to immerse himself again in the world from which he came, to meditate there as of old on a familiar past, or to quietly await salvation, choosing paths which were never really fruitful but at least brought no harm, he will not find this world again. He will feel like all those who returned from paradise, a stranger in a world that is utterly changed, surrounded by his incredulous neighbors, and separated from them by countless generations.

Utopia and the ideal are not the same as happiness; they are too easily contaminated by lies. For those who claim to have brought utopia into existence are as far from the truth as those who maintain that it can never become reality. A life without hope for happiness is no life. But the life which is a succession of too many vain hopes is equally unbearable. With only a minor shift in perspective, the history of uncounted expectations which unrolls before the eye as one studies the development of utopias, paradises and conceptions of the ideal among a people such as the Chinese also reveals itself with a terrible clarity as a history of incessant disappointments from whose oppressive sadness the individual, having only one life to live, could hardly hope to recover. Happiness neither lies entirely where anxiety to preserve an unflawed world eternally arrests all movement, nor where the pursuit of a new world takes on an unremitting urgency. Its nature, and the nature of utopia, hold a paradoxical secret.

In 333 B.C., when Alexander the Great had set out on his campaign toward the East, he was shown an age-old knot in Gordion, on the threshold of Asia. According to legend, it had been tied by the mythical king of the Phrygians, Gordias. Whoever could untie it would be victorious and the master of all of Asia. Alexander cut it with his sword. China knows of a similar knot. The much more modest story about it also comes from the fourth century B.C., from the *Spring and Autumn Annals of Lü Pu-wei,* which we have mentioned before, and where Mohist and Taoist sources merge.[452] The story reads as follows:

> A man from Lu gave King Yüan of Sung a knot for a present. The king issued an order to all the country that skillful people should gather to attempt to untie it. But no one succeeded. A disciple of the rhetorician Erh Shuo requested permission to try. But he succeeded only in untying one half, and could do nothing with the other. He said: "It is not that this knot can be untied, and that only I am unable to do so. The knot cannot be untied." The man from Lu who had given the knot was asked about this, and he said: "It is true that it cannot be untied. I tied it myself and therefore know that it cannot be done. But a person who did not make it and yet knows that it cannot be untied must be even more skillful than I." Thus Erh Shuo's disciple untied the knot by not untying it.[453]

Perhaps nowhere else can the two extreme possibilities of solving the unsolvable be found in more pregnant juxtaposition than in these two accounts. Alexander's stroke brought the most effective, the total solution. But it did not really solve the mysterious problem; it eliminated it in almost barbaric fashion. Erh Shuo's disciple acted in a much wiser, much more civilized way. He understood the problem, he loved it and, schooled by his teacher in the use of language, he found the words to describe it. But he hesitated to act. For while the knot could not be untied, the solution of the problem did not lie in not untying it, as the scholar commented who wrote the story down. The solution was neither to cut it nor ever to desist from the attempt to untie it.

During long periods of its history, and particularly during recent centuries, the West preferred to cut the Gordian knot. During that same time, China rather put its hands in its lap and looked at a knot that had been partially untied. Today, when the ideals and utopias of both are beginning to merge, it may perhaps be possible to continue to work in common on the second uncut tied half, even if hope for ultimate success seems infinitely remote.

CHRONOLOGICAL TABLE
NOTES
BIBLIOGRAPHY
INDEX

CHRONOLOGICAL TABLE

TIME	POLITICAL HISTORY	CULTURE
2000	Legendary emperors Yao, Shun and Yü. *Hsia dynasty* (?) (traditionally 2205–1767). *Shang dynasty* (traditionally 1766–1123, historically ca. 1500–1050). Chinese nuclear area in northcentral China.	Animism and ancestor worship, Shang-ti highest divinity. Shamans and oracle priests. Mantics with bones and tortoise shells. Oldest preserved written documents.
1000	*(Early) Chou dynasty* (traditionally 1122, historically ca. 1050–770). Ideal kings Wen-wang and Wu-wang. Ideal regent: Chou-kung (Duke of Chou). Ideal military leader: T'ai-kung. Feudal state on family basis. Expansion of empire southward and westward.	Worship of heaven and stars. King highest priest, oracle priests lose position of power. Milfoil stalk oracle and creation of the *Book of Changes (I-ching).* Oldest parts of Confucian classics.
500	*(Late) Chou dynasty* (770–221). Chou kings lose political power, but remain heads of public cult. Former feudal states become independent, empire disintegrates. Multiplicity of state and royal courts	"Wandering scholars" introduce "Age of philosophy": Confucius (551–479); Mo Ti (?479–381); hermits; Taoist texts *Chuang-tzu* and *Tao-te-ching* (Lao-tzu) fifth–fourth centuries. Hedonist Yang Chu; *Lü shih ch'un ch'iu;* Mencius (372–289); Hsün-tzu (?298–238); Shang Yang (died 338); Han Fei-tzu (died 233).
250	*Ch'in dynasty* (221–206), based on "legalist" state of Ch'in in western colonial area. Founds unified empire. Feudalism abolished. "First Emperor" Ch'in Shih Huang-ti. *(Early) Han dynasty* (206–A.D. 6) adopts Ch'in administrative structure in spite of opposing ideology. Western expansion of empire to central Asia under emperor Wu-ti (governed 140–86).	Pronounced anti-intellectualism, directed particularly against Confucians. Burning of books (213). Proscription of all nonlegalist thought except *Book of Changes.* Confucianism becomes state religion. Classics edited. Cosmological-historical speculation: Tung Chung-shu (179–104). Prognostic texts. Religiously tinctured Confucianism of the New Text School. "Elegies of Ch'u" *(Ch'u-tz'u).*

0	"Usurper" Wang Mang (governed 6[9]–23) attempts restoration of Chou. *(Later) Han dynasty* (25–220) gradually disintegrates as clans assert their autonomy. Uprising of Yellow Turbans (184), state of the "Five Pecks of Rice Taoists" (186–216). Empire disintegrates: Period of the "Three Kingdoms" (220–265).	Historic-realistic Confucianism of the Old Text School gradually prevails over New Text School (Ho Hsiu 129–182). Taoism loses its profundity: prolongation of life now principal goal. Confucianism under Taoist influence, "Fin de siècle" atmosphere among the educated. Seven Sages of Bamboo Grove, among them Hsi K'ang (223–262) and Juan Chi (210–263). "Pure conversation" the ideal. Romanticism of nature; rediscovery of martial virtues. Beginnings of Buddhism (as of first century).
300	After sporadic unification by *(Western) Chin dynasty* (265–316) loss of northern half of empire to alien nomadic peoples who rule in a multiplicity of states. *Six dynasties* in the South *(Liu-ch'ao).* Mass flight to the South. Division of power between aristocratic, large land owners and military commanders. Under *Sui dynasty* (581–618) reunification of entire empire.	Alchemy: Ko Hung (284–363). Anarchism: Pao Ching-yen. Book *Lieh-tzu.* Poet T'ao Ch'ien (372–427). Buddhism comes to China by land and by sea. Simplified translations (since middle of fourth century) are replaced by enormous translating activity of high quality (beginning of fifth century.) Flowering of Buddhism first in the North (fifth century), then countless sects and monasteries (from early sixth century on). Diffusion of the Maitreya cult and also of *Ch'an (Zen)* Buddhism since 520.
600	*T'ang dynasty* (618–907): expansive foreign policy, conquest of central Asia, Korea and North Vietnam, foreign peoples as mercenaries (Uigurs). High cultural development and international life in capital of Ch'ang-an but shift of real power to the borders (military headquarters). Bloody uprisings of the military commander An Lu-shan (755–763); subsequent similar unrest and court intrigues (eunuchs) gradually destroy the dynasty.	Influx of new, foreign religions: Zoroastrianism, nestorian Christianity, Manicheanism, Islam. Propagation of Taoism but also flowering of Buddhism (middle eighth century). Golden Age of poetry (Li T'ai-po [699–762]) and science. "Old-style" *(Ku-wen)* movement as Confucian reaction against foreign cultural influences: Han Yü (769–824). Destructive Buddhist persecutions (844/845) usher in decline of Buddhism.
900	Empire disintegrates again: period of the *"Five dynasties"* (907–960), partly under foreign leadership in the north. Period of the *"Ten Kingdoms"* (907–979) in the south. Reunification under the *Sung dynasty* (960–1280). Rela-	Confucianism grows in strength; return to old, national values: interest in archaeology, establishment of libraries and schools, encyclopedia. Continuation of the *Ku-wen* movement leads to Neo-Confu-

	tively weak position vis-a-vis foreign states (Liao, Chin, finally Mongols), but disciplined centralist leadership within. Trend toward state-controlled economy. (Wang An-shih 1021–1085) stopped by Confucians. Strong emergence of secret societies. Loss of all of north China to the state of Chin (1127). Continuation of dynasties in the south.	cianism: Chou Tun-i (1017–1073), Shao Yung (1011–1077), Chang Tsai (1021–1077), Ch'eng I (1033–1107), Ch'eng Hao (1032–1085), Lu Chiu-yüan (1139–1193), Chu Hsi (1130–1200). Annalistic historiography, Ssu-ma Kuang (1019–1086). "Four Classics" as new, principal Confucian classics. Continued influence of Buddhism as Buddhism of meditation *(Ch'an)* in the scholarly community and, intermingled with Taoism and foreign religions on lower plane as popular religion in a variety of forms.
1200	Mongolian empire founded by Genghis Khan (died 1227) conquers the state of Chin (1234). Kublai Khan (governed 1260–1294) proclaims the Yüan dynasty ([1260] 1280–1368) in China and conquers all of China by 1280. The *Pax Mongolica* makes possible first direct overland contacts with Europe (Marco Polo [?1275–1292]). Privileged Mongols and their auxiliaries in power. The rebellion of a secret society results in expulsion of Mongols and establishment of the Ming dynasty (1368–1644). Centralist-totalitarian regime adopted from Mongols. First tendencies toward "isolation" in spite of continued maritime expeditions initially (1405–33).	Religious tolerance of the Mongols at first furthers Buddhism and Taoism. Dismissal of countless Chinese officials stimulates popular literature (drama, novel) and popular Confucianism. Awakening nationalism: Teng Mu (1247–1306). After the disappearance of the Mongols, revitalization of all aspects of Chinese life; further increase in schools, increasing importance of state examinations. Encyclopedia *Yung-lo ta-tien* in 11,095 volumes (1407). Neo-Confucian idealism: Wang Shou-jen (Yang-ming) (1472–1529).
1500	Portuguese merchants land in Canton (1513/1514), the Dutch follow (1610). Power struggles between officials and eunuchs produce mismanagement. Uprising of White Lotus secret society. The rebel Li Tzu-ch'eng (1605–1643) can only be suppressed with the help of the Manchus who extend their dynasty founded eight years before over all of China (Ch'ing, 1644–1911). Resistance of loyal generals ("Koxinga" [1624–1662]) crushed by 1683. Conquest of Mongolia and Tibet (1688–1751), political and cultural flowering under the emperors K'ang-hsi (governed 1662–1721), Yung-cheng (governed 1722–1735) and Ch'ien-lung (governed 1736–	Neo-Confucian "Lung-hsi school" (Wang Chi [1498–1583]) and "T'ai-chou School" (Wang Ken [1483–1540], Li Chih [1527–1602]). Liang Ju-yüan's (1527–1579) clan communism. Increasing nationalism after establishment of the Ch'ing dynasty: Huang Tsung-hsi (1610–1695). "Han School" against conservative "Sung School": Ku Yen-wu (1613–1682), Wang Fu-chih (1619–1692) and Yen Yüan (1635–1704). Tai Chen (1724–1777) introduces textual criticism and advances arguments for a criticism of Confucian classics. Increasing philological and bibliographical interest. Erosion of traditional spiritual and

	1795). Greatest territorial expansion of China.	religious ideals. Initially very successful Jesuit missions (from 1582 on: Matteo Ricci [1552–1610]), curtailment after beginning of eighteenth century.
1800	Increasing internal and external weakness of Manchu government. Economic and soon also political penetration by western powers. Increasing opium trade (since ca. 1720) leads to Opium Wars (1839–1842): England annexes Hong Kong and "opens" the most important ports. Taiping rebellion (1850–1864). "Lorcha War" with England and France (1857–1860) ushers in period of partition of China, annexations along border regions: Sakhalin (Russia), Vietnam (France), Ryuku Islands (Japan), Burma (England), Kiaochow (Germany), and loss of sovereignty within. Sino-Japanese war (1894–1895): Japan annexes Korea and Formosa. Hundred Days' Reform by K'ang Yu-wei. Boxer Rebellion (1898–1900) with direct intervention of western powers.	Ideology of Taiping, based on Christianity (Hung ʻHsiu-ch'üan [1813–1864]) anticipates numerous communist reforms by one hundred years. T'ung-chih reform (as of 1862) under Tseng Kuo-fan (1811–72) fails to revive Confucianism. K'ang Yu-wei (1858–1927) reintroduces New Text School in modified form, but becomes effective only through his ephemeral "reform movement" and his disciples. Liang Ch'i-ch'ao (1873–1929). Beginning political activity of Sun Yat-sen (1866–1925) as of 1892. Attempts to synthesize Chinese and western thought: Chang Chih-tung (1873–1909).
since 1900	Russo-Japanese War (1904–1905). Chinese students in Japan, America and Europe engage in revolutionary activity. Sun Yat-sen founds *T'ung-meng-hui* in Tokyo (1905). Rebellion of troops in Wu-ch'ang (1911) leads to abdication of Manchus (1912). *Kuo-min-tang* founded in 1913 as successor of *T'ung-meng-hui.* First World War (1914–1918). CCP develops from Marxist study societies, 1921. Civil war and division of country. Warlordism ended by Chiang Kai-shek's Northern Expedition (1926–1928). Mao Tse-tung (born 1893) organizes peasants (as of 1925). Campaigns of annihilation by Chiang against communist soviets (as of 1931) necessitate Long March (1934–1935). Sino-Japanese War (1937–1945) leads to brittle united front KMT/CCP until 1945. Civil war (1945–1949) ends with establishment of People's Republic and escape of the KMT to Formosa. "Hundred Flowers Movement" (1956–1957),	System of state examinations abolished (1905). Anarchist student organizations in France, Japan and southern China: Wu Chih-hui (1864–1954), Liu Shih-p'ei (1884–1919) and Liu Ssu-fu (died 1915). Sun Yat-sen's Three People's Principles. Discrimination against China by Versailles Treaty leads to Literary Revolution of May Fourth Movement (1919). Abolition of classical Chinese as written language: Hu Shih (1891–1962). Scientific treatment and criticism of antiquity: Ku Chieh-kang (born 1893). K'ang Yu-wei's "Lectures on the Heavens" (1927) and Liu Jen-hang's "Great Equality of the East" (1924). Liang Sou-ming's (born 1893) village cooperatives (1931–1937). Early communism: Li Ta-chao (1888–1927), Ch'en Tu-hsiu (1879–1942). Mao Tse-tung's essay on "Contradiction" and "Practice" (1937). Paralysis of intellectual and scientific activity

Great Leap Forward (1958–1959) with introduction of People's communes. Cultural revolution (1966–1968).

during war with Japan. After communist victory, attempts to find precursors of new ideology. Temporary cultural liberalization in "Hundred Flowers Movement"; Mao's "On Resolving the Contradictions Among the People" and "Poverty and Blankness" (1958). Attempt at spiritual detachment from the past during the Cultural Revolution.

NOTES

For those works where only the name of the author is listed in the notes, see the bibliography. Literature that goes beyond the specific point discussed is marked (L).

I. DEFINING THE DIMENSIONS

1. Archaeological finds have largely confirmed the traditional chronology of the Shang and Chou dynasties which have meanwhile been shown to have been historical. But these dynasties extended over somewhat shorter periods. The same probably applies to the Hsia dynasty insofar as it can be considered historical.

2. Dating was done by two rows of "cyclical characters" which determined the day within a cyclical period of sixty days. Cf. pp. 71–72.

3. A comprehensive overview of the various occasions when oracles were consulted is given with an abundance of examples in Jao Tsung-i, 73–1169.

4. Some archaic signs have no equivalents in the modernized written language introduced in the third century A.D., or at least they have not been identified so far. Consequently, they cannot be reproduced. This applies especially to names of persons and places.

5. Jao Tsung-i, 74, 300, 371, 266.

6. It is perhaps here that we have the beginning of the Chinese dualistic world view. By way of the milfoil stalk oracle and the *Book of Changes (I-ching)* that developed from it, it later became the dominant philosophical view. Cf. pp. 12–15.

7. Cf. Cheng Te-k'un (2) for an overview. The fundamental idea that life after death is merely a kind of continuation of life in a different environment is still present in burial customs practiced down to this century. Cf. Groot (1), I:241–360.

8. Particularly Carl Hentze (cf. Hentze (1) and (2)) espoused this view.

9. Since we are here dealing with oracles, this is a strikingly nonfatalistic trait, which may perhaps have some connection with the often praised "active" character of the Chinese people. It can also be shown in the *Book of Changes* whose purpose was not so much the discovery of a rigidly determined future but rather showed how to master the present with a view toward future constellations. Cf. p. 14.

10. Naturally, Chinese literature also has legends about the origin of the world and allusion to an expected end of the world. But they did not emerge until a surprisingly late period and were immediately relegated to the sphere of "popular belief." Cf., for example, Eberhard (1), 96–99 (L); (2), 2:467–470. It was not until the second century B.C. that cosmogony became a philosophical problem in in the writings of Huai-nan-tzu (Liu An [179–122]).

11. Fundamentally, written Japanese derives from Chinese in all respects. Its different appearance results from the introduction of syllabic characters which are used purely phonetically and either supplement or entirely replace the Chinese characters which were taken over without change.

12. Karlgren (2), 70, No. 377–380.

13. Karlgren (2), 61, No. 134–139; (6), No. 1125.

14. Karlgren (2), 84, No. 249–251; (6), No. 393.

15. Karlgren (2), 80, No. 176.

16. The archaic signs given here are based on Karlgren (6), where the original documents are also listed. Cf. also the relevant passages in Kuo Mo-jo (1).

17. Cf. pp. 49–56.

18. These three books on rites, the *Chou-li (The Rites of Chou),* the *Li-chi (Book of Rites)* and the *I-li (Book of Etiquette and Ceremonial)* also contain other, quite heterogeneous material. Cf., for example, pp. 69–70.

19. Legge (1), 4:309–363; Karlgren (4), 132–158; Waley (3), 304–326.

20. Legge (1), 3:173–190, 281–305; Karlgren (5), 20.

21. Cf. Waley (1). For the much more complicated milfoil stalk oracle which finally prevailed and was used for more than two millennia, cf. R. Wilhelm (1), 1:280–282.

22. Comprehensive discussion in Needham (1), 2:304–345.

23. Concerning the Chinese concept of time cf. Needham (2); Bauer (1), 57–84; Kurita Naomi.

24. Kuo Mo-jo (1), No. 115, 205, 243; 180, 206, 355.

25. Cf. Ku Chieh-kang, 3:252–308.

26. Cf. Karlgren (6), No. 134, 238; Hu Shih (2); W. Franke (2).

27. *I-ching,* 9. Cf. Legge (3), 67–68; R. Wilhelm (1), 1:17–20.

28. Legge (1), 4: 636–638; Karlgren (4), 263; Waley (3), 275–276.

29. *Hsi.*

30. Feng Yu-lan, 1–32.

31. Legge (1), 4:427; Karlgren (4), 185; Waley (3), 250.

32. Legge (1), 5:671 (Chao-kung, eighteenth year).

33. *Ch'u-tz'u,* 40–41. Cf. Hawkes, 39–40.

34. *Ch'u-tz'u,* 121–124. Cf. Hawkes, 101–109.

35. The "Axial Period" which Karl Jaspers *(Origin and Goal of History)* believes he has discovered for all of Eurasia during the middle of the first century B.C. can thus actually be verified as regards China. For the concept of "humanity" *(jen)* cf. Waley (2), 27–29.

36. *Lun-yü,* 7, 20. Cf. Legge (1), 1:201; R. Wilhelm, (3), 69; Waley (2), 127.

37. *Lun-yü,* 6, 20 and 11, 11. Cf. Legge (1), 1:191, 240–241; R. Wilhelm (3), 56, 111; Waley (2), 120, 155.

38. For conflicting interpretations, cf. Waley (2), 33; (3) 346; (4) 31; and Munro, 99–109, 185–197.

39. *Lun-yü,* 2, 1. Cf. Legge (1), 1:145; R. Wilhelm (3), 8; Waley (2), 88.

40. Concerning the concept *li,* "ritual" cf. Fung Yu-lan (1), 1:68; Forke (1), 1:131.

41. *Lun-yü,* 2, 3. Cf. Legge (1), 1:146; R. Wilhelm (3), 8; Waley (2), 88.

42. *Lun-yü,* 13, 23. Cf. Legge (1), 1:273; R. Wilhelm (3), 144; Waley (2), 177. Because of their social implications, the concepts *ho* and *t'ung* have become the subject of various treatises in contemporary China.

43. *Lun-yü,* 16, 1. Cf. Legge (1), 1:308; R. Wilhelm (3), 184; Waley (2), 203.

44. Cf. above pp. 14–16 and Hu Shih (2) and (3). The best known personalities who saw themselves in a five-hundred-year rhythm as successors of the duke of Chou (died in 1105 B.C. according to traditional chronology) were, next to Confucius (551–479 B.C.) the historian Ssu-ma Ch'ien (ca. 145–90 B.C.), the illegal emperor Wang Mang (45 B.C.–

A.D. 23) and the philosophizing emperor Yüan-ti (508–555) of the Liang dynasty. Curiously enough, men who did not live during these periods of renewal also believed that this messianic idea applied to them, particularly Mencius (372–289 B.C.). He is the first to explicitly discuss this five-hundred-year rhythm (*Meng-tzu* 2 B, 13 and 7 B, 38. Cf. Legge (1), 2:232, 501–502; R. Wilhelm (8), 48, 184) and Chu Hsi (1130–1200) (cf. pp. 209–210).

45. The curious position of the political "councillor" in Chinese intellectual history also belongs in this context. It seems that the example of the duke of Chou and of Confucius brought it about that from the perspective of humanity the "grey eminence" was often felt to rank higher than the actual ruler. Cf. pp. 124–126.

46. *Lun-yü,* 11, 8. Cf. Legge (1), 1:239; R. Wilhelm (8), 110; Waley (2), 154.

47. *Meng-tzu,* 3 B, 9. Cf. Legge (1), 2:279; R. Wilhelm (8), 69.

48. *Meng-tzu,* 5 A, 5. Cf. Legge (1), 2:354–357; R. Wilhelm (8), 104–105.

49. *Meng-tzu,* 1 B, 2. Cf. Legge (1), 2:153–154; R. Wilhelm (8), 13.

50. *Meng-tzu,* 1 A, 3. Cf. Legge (1), 2:130–132; R. Wilhelm (8), 3–4.

51. *Meng-tzu,* 3 A, 3. Cf. Legge (1), 2:243–245; R. Wilhelm (8), 51–54.

52. Cf. Levenson (2), 3:16–46 (L). Further discussions in Francis and Zen Sun (1), 25–28 and (2), 3–17.

53. In the *I-wen-chih* chapter of the *Ch'ien-Han-shu* (compiled in first century A.D.) for example, the School of Agriculture is ranked alongside the Confucian, Taoist, Mohist and Legalist schools as one of the "nine schools" *(chiu-liu).*

54. Especially Hou Wai-lu took this position, but it is also quite marked in the positive evaluation of the "peasant uprisings" which did not give way to a much more critical judgment until the middle sixties.

55. *Meng-tzu,* 3 A, 4. Cf. Legge (1), 2:246–256; R. Wilhelm (8), 54–59.

56. Cf. Fung Yu-lan (1), 1:79.

57. *Mo-tzu,* 15:64–65. Cf. Forke (2), 245–246.

58. *Mo-tzu,* 16:72–73. Cf. Forke (2), 254–255.

59. *Mo-tzu,* 11:44–46. Cf. Forke (2), 214–217.

60. *Mo-tzu,* 13:60. Cf. Forke (2), 238.

61. Cf. pp. 244–245.

62. *Lun-yü,* 18, 6. Cf. Legge (1), 1:333–334; R. Wilhelm (3), 204; Waley (2), 219–220. In Book 18 of the *Lun-yü* there are some other anecdotes which indirectly criticize Confucius's teaching.

63. Cf. above, pp. 19–20.

64. On the nearly boundless literature on the *Tao-te-ching* (translations and monographs), cf. Yen Ling-feng (1) and (2), 337–392 (comprehensive); Seidel (1), 8, note 1; Debon, 141–143; H. Franke (2), 79–82. Although, judging by internal criteria, it is reasonably certain that the final version of the *Tao-te-ching* is the work of a single author, all "biographical material" on Lao-tzu is either trivial, legendary or borrowed from other biographies. Cf. Waley (4), 99–108.

65. For literature on *Chuang-tzu,* cf. Yen Ling-feng (2) (comprehensive); H. Franke (2), 82–83.

66. *Chuang-tzu,* 9:151–152. Cf. Legge (4), 325–327; R. Wilhelm (4), 67; Watson (2), 105–106.

67. *Tao-te-ching,* 19:10. Cf. Waley (4), 166; R. Wilhelm (2), 21; Duyvendak (1), 54.

68. Waley (4), 242, note 1.

69. *Tao-te-ching,* 80:47, cf. Waley (4), 241–242; R. Wilhelm (2), 85; Duyvendak (1), 162–163. This *Tao-te-ching* passage became so much a basic element of Taoist conception of paradise that even the "barking of dogs and the crowing of cocks," which evokes the village atmosphere, recurred time and again as a cliché in later descriptions of paradise

(cf., for example, pp. 190–191). This nexus was so strong that during the Han, when paradises were increasingly localized in heaven, it was felt necessary to also have dogs and cocks ascend there (cf. for example, L. Giles, 45). This afforded more sceptical philosophers such as Wang Ch'ung an opportunity for criticism (cf. Forke [5], 1:335).

70. *Chuang-tzu,* 6:102–103. Cf. Legge (4), 285–289; R. Wilhelm (4), 46–48; Watson (2), 77–78.

71. *Chuang-tzu,* 11:165–166. Cf. Legge (4), 339–340; R. Wilhelm (4), 74; Watson (2), 114–115. Concerning similar conceptions of the ideal, cf. Needham (1), 2:127–130 (L).

72. On this entire complex, cf. especially Yü Ying-shih (1) (L), and Maspero (1).

73. Fu Ssu-nien, especially pp. 68–78, 175–186.

74. Karlgren (6), No. 762 and 823.

75. Cf. above, p. 12.

76. Karlgren (6), No. 826, 823, 827. Also Bauer (3), 35–38.

77. *Ch'un-ch'iu fan-lu,* 10 (=paragraph 35), 231–232. On the *Ch'un-ch'iu fan-lu,* cf. p. 74.

78. Cf. pp. 144–145.

79. *Chuang-tzu,* 12:199–200. Cf. Legge (4), 373; R. Wilhelm (4), 92; Watson (2), 138. The passage also describes attitudes in a Taoist ideal world: "In an age of Perfect Virtue *(Chih-te),* the worthy are not honored, the talented are not employed. Rulers are like the high branches of a tree, the people like the deer of the fields. They do what is right but they do not know that it is righteousness. They love one another but they do not know that this is benevolence. They are true-hearted but do not know that this is loyalty. They are trustworthy but do not know that this is good faith. They wriggle around like insects, performing services for one another, but do not know that they are being kind. Therefore they move without leaving any trail behind, act without leaving any memory of their deeds."

80. *Chuang-tzu,* 18:268–270. Cf. Legge (4), 441–444; R. Wilhelm (4), 135–137; Watson (2), 190–191.

81. *Chuang-tzu,* 6:116–119. Cf. Legge (4), 295–298; R. Wilhelm (4), 50–51; Watson (2), 83–85.

82. *Chuang-tzu,* 6:119–121. Cf. Legge (4), 298–301; R. Wilhelm (4), 52; Watson (2), 86–87.

83. *Chuang-tzu,* 18:272–273. Cf. Legge (4), 446–447; R. Wilhelm (4), 136–137; Watson (2), 193–194.

84. Cf. below, pp. 131–132.

85. *Chuang-tzu,* 1:12–13. Cf. Legge (4), 217–218; R. Wilhelm (4), 4–5; Watson (2), 32–33. Together with similar ones, this story appears in an extended version in Book 28 (*Chuang-tzu,* 28:414–426. Cf. Legge [4], 589–605. Watson [2], 309–322), which deals exclusively with the problem of rejecting the throne.

86. On *Lieh-tzu,* cf. p. 44.

87. *Chuang-tzu,* 18:275. Cf. Legge (4), 449; Watson (2), 195. There is a similar version of the story in *Lieh-tzu,* 1:3–4. Cf. R. Wilhelm (5), 4.

88. *Chuang-tzu,* 17:267–268. Cf. Legge (4), 439–440; R. Wilhelm (4), 134; Watson (2), 188–189.

89. *Chuang-tzu,* 2:53–54. Cf. Legge (4), 245; R. Wilhelm (4), 21; Watson (2), 49.

90. *Chuang-tzu,* 2:47–48. Cf. Legge (4), 241–243; R. Wilhelm (4), 19–20; Watson (2), 47–48.

91. Concerning the history of the text which is important here because it does not preclude direct influence by western (Indian) ideas, cf. Graham (1).

92. Chan Wing-tsit (5) and Fung Yu-lan (2), 60–67.

93. *Lieh-tzu,* 7:83. Cf. R. Wilhelm (5), 84–85; Graham (2), 148–149.

94. *Chuang-tzu,* 2:21–22; 11:168; 21:310–311. Cf. Legge (4), 224–225, 342, 486–487; R. Wilhelm (4), 11–12, F5, 157–158; Watson (2), 36, 116, 224–225.
95. *Lieh-tzu,* 7:77–78. Cf. R. Wilhelm (5), 77–78; Graham (2), 139–141.
96. *Lieh-tzu,* 7:81. Cf. R. Wilhelm (5), 82–83; Graham (2), 146–147.
97. *Lieh-tzu,* 7:83–84; Cf. R. Wilhelm (5), 85–87; Graham (2), 150–151.
98. Cf. above, p. 11.
99. Cf. below, p. 238.
100. *Hsün-tzu,* 17 (=paragraph 23):289. Cf. Dubs (1), 301.
101. *Hsün-tzu,* 5 (=paragraph 9):96. Cf. Dubs (1), 124.
102. *Hsün-tzu,* 6 (=paragraph 10):113–114. Cf. Dubs (1), 51–52.
103. *Hsün-tzu,* 6 (=paragraph 10):114–115.
104. *Hsün-tzu,* 6 (=paragraph 10):121.
105. *Hsün-tzu, ibid.*
106. *Hsün-tzu,* 6 (=paragraph 10):123–124.
107. *Hsün-tzu,* 6 (=paragraph 10):124–125.
108. Among the many translations, see especially Legge (2), 3:465–488.
109. *Hsün-tzu,* 2 (=paragraph 4), 40. Cf. Dubs (1), 61.
110. *Hsün-tzu,* 20 (=paragraph 29):347.
111. *Hsün-tzu,* 3 (=paragraph 5):50–51. Cf. Dubs (1), 72–73.
112. *Shih-chi,* 68:789a. Cf. Duyvendak (2), 9.
113. *Shih-chi,* 68:789b. Cf. Duyvendak (2), 12.
114. *Shih-chi,* 68:789b. Cf. Duyvendak (2), 12–14.
115. *Shang-chün-shu,* 8:19. Cf. Duyvendak (2), 238.
116. Concerning this entire complex, cf. Vandermeersch, 186.
117. *Shang-chün-shu,* 17:29. Cf. Duyvendak (2), 279–280.
118. *Shang-chün-shu,* 18:31. Cf. Duyvendak (2), 285.
119. *Shih-chi,* 68:790a. Cf. Duyvendak (2), 14–15.
120. Concerning these two philosophers, cf. Duyvendak (2), 68–74, 94–98; Forke (1), 1:442–450; Fung Yu-lan (1), 1:132–133, 158–159, 319; Vandermeersch, 41–55.
121. Rickett, 1:83–106, 117–150.
122. Cf. Bodde (1).
123. *Han Fei-tzu,* 19 (=paragraph 50):356. Cf. W. K. Liao, 2:306–307.
124. *Han Fei-tzu,* 19 (=paragraph 49):345. Cf. W. K. Liao, 2:286.
125. *Han Fei-tzu,* 19 (=paragraph 49):347. Cf. W. K. Liao, 2:290–291.
126. *Tao-te-ching,* 3:2. Cf. Waley (4), 145; R. Wilhelm (2), 5; Duyvendak (1), 24–25.
127. *Han Fei-tzu,* 2 (=paragraph 8):29–34. Cf. W. K. Liao, 1:54–58.
128. Concerning the intensification preceding value terms cf. below, pp. 84–85.
129. *Han Fei-tzu,* 8 (=paragraph 29):156–157. Cf. W. K. Liao, 1:279.
130. Cf. above, pp. 14–15.
131. *Han Fei-tzu,* 19 (=paragraph 49), 339. Cf. W. K. Liao, 2:276.
132. *Meng-tzu,* 2 A, 2. Cf. Legge (1), 2:190–191; R. Wilhelm (8), 29.
133. Before Ch'in Shih Huang-ti, the terms *huang* and *ti* were used separately only to designate rulers who had governed as "sage emperors" in legendary antiquity or been "eternized," i.e. had died.
134. *Shih-chi,* 6:119b. Cf. Chavannes (1), 2:151–152; 167. Cf. also below, pp. 96–100.
135. *Shih-chi,* 118: 1144a. Cf. Chavannes (1), 2:152, note 1; Watson (1), 2:374–375.
136. *Shih-chi,* 6:125a. Cf. Chavannes (1), 2:190–192.
137. Hu Shih/Lin Yutang, 89–94.

II. ON THE BOUNDARIES OF THIS WORLD

1. Cf. below, pp. 209–211.
2. Cf. above, p. 59.
3. *Shih-chi,* 47:667b. Cf. Chavannes (1), 5:327.
4. Cf. Biot. There is a considerable literature concerning the question of the extent to which the state described in the *Chou-li* corresponded to reality. Cf., for example, H. Franke (2), 126, 129; *RBS,* 2: No. 100; 4:No. 805; 7:No. 60.
5. For summary, cf. Needham (1), 2:232–253 (L).
6. For an overview, cf. Forke (4), 227–261; Eberhard (6), 40–52; Tjan Tjoe Som, 120–128.
7. Cf. Eberhard (4), 50, and Bielenstein (2), 128–129.
8. In recent years, these "apocryphal" classics have attracted the attention of a number of sinologists, most of them Japanese (cf. the research of Koyanagi Shikita, 118–135). Comprehensive western account by Dull (L). See also Tjan Tjoe Som, 95–120 and Fung Yu-lang (1), 2:88–132.
9. Tjan Tjoe Som, 105–106.
10. Cf. Koyanagi Shikita, 412–429.
11. Cf. O. Franke (2), Fung Yu-lan (1), 2:7–87 and Woo Kang who have studied the work intensively and made partial translations.
12. *Ch'un-ch'iu fan-lu,* 1:11–12. Cf. Fung Yu-lan (1), 2:62.
13. *Ch'un-ch'iu fan-lu,* 21:162. Cf. Fung Yu-lan (1), 2:61.
14. Cf. Eberhard (6), 67–75; Dubs (2), 1:35, note 2; Chavannes (1), 1:cxci–cxcii.
15. *Ch'un-ch'iu fan-lu,* 21:164–168. Cf. Fung Yu-lan (1), 2:66–67.
16. *Lun-yü,* 2, 23. Cf. Legge (1), 1:153; R. Wilhelm (3), 16–17; Waley (2), 93.
17. *Ch'un-ch'iu fan-lu,* 23:154–163. Cf. Fung Yu-lan (1), 2:58–61. On the *San-chiao, San-t'ung* and *San-cheng,* see Tjan Tjoe Som, 548–558.
18. *Ch'un-ch'iu fan-lu,* 23:154.
19. *Ch'un-ch'iu fan-lu,* 1:7. Cf. Fung Yu-lan (1), 2:81.
20. *Meng-tzu,* 3 B, 9. Cf. Legge (1), 2:281–282; R. Wilhelm (8), 70.
21. *Ch'un-ch'iu fan-lu,* 6:75–79. Cf. also O. Franke (2), 221–224.
22. Cf. Woo Kang, 1–14.
23. *Kung-yang i-su* (Yin-Kung, first year, twelfth month), 1:79–80. Cf. Fung Yu lan (1), 2:83.
24. *Kung-yang i-su,* 3:1259–1261.
25. If the character for "desire in my heart" *(chih)* is replaced by a character meaning "historical work," which sounds the same and has the identical phonetic component, a philologically unassailable interpretation adopted by some commentators, the sentence suddenly takes on an entirely different meaning: "[I thought of the time] when the Great Way prevailed and the three [past] dynasties flowered, [a time] which I did not experience but [only] know of through historical works."
26. *Li-chi,* 9: 120–121. Cf. R. Wilhelm (7), 56–57; Needham (2), 24.
27. Cf. above, p. 7.
28. The dynastic name *Hsin* actually means "new." But according to the traditional manner, it merely derives from the name of the fief which the founder of the dynasty, Wang Mang in this case, occupied before he ascended the throne. It is difficult to decide whether the "renewal" of the empire after the model of the Chou dynasty was nonetheless subliminally associated with the basic meaning of the word *hsin* that lies behind the dynastic name. The choice of a dynastic name according to the meaning of the character rather than according to an already existing name did not occur before the founding of the Yüan dynasty by the Mongols. As alien invaders, they naturally could not go back to the earlier designation of a fief. Cf. also below, p. 238.

29. Cf. above, pp. 22–23.
30. Cf. above, pp. 63–64.
31. Cf. Hu Shih (5), 218; Dubs (3), 219.
32. Most detailed discussion in K'ang's autobiography. Cf. Lo Jung-pang, 77–174. Cf. also, W. Franke (1).
33. Cf. below, pp. 302–303.
34. In his book, Ch'en Huan-chang (see bibliography) places special emphasis on the economic aspects of Confucianism, a circumstance which in itself already indicated the new approach.
35. Hu Shih (4), 89.
36. Cf. Meskill, especially pp. 25–52, and Chi Ch'ao-ting; Lin Yutang (1), 28–34.
37. Fung Yu-lan (2), 199.
38. Chung-kuo k'o-hsüeh-yüan, 1–2.
39. Cf. below, p. 231.
40. Cf. Maenchen-Helfen, and H. Franke on more recent literature (2), 194; *RBS,* 6:No. 580; 8: No. 707.
41. *Chuang-tzu,* 20:294–295. Cf. Legge (4), 468–471; R. Wilhelm (4), 147–149; Watson (2), 210–212. The idea that the soul of the dead has to cross a river or an ocean and which is naturally very intimately associated with the belief in islands or continents of the blessed is relevant here and can be documented from the Han period on. Cf. Finsterbusch, 200–201 (L). In this connection, see also the legends about the Milky Way ("Silver River") (cf. below, p. 99) and the reciprocal relations between water, death, happiness and salvation generally (cf. below, pp. 127, 182, 354, 411–414).
42. *Lieh-tzu,* 3:35. Cf. R. Wilhelm (5), 33–34; Graham (2), 67–68.
43. It is even possible that the description of the two non-Chinese continents reflects real reports, about India in the case of the southwestern region, about tribes from central Asia in that of the northeastern area.
44. *Lieh-tzu,* 2:13–14. Cf. R. Wilhelm (5), 11–12; Graham (2), 34–35.
45. *Lieh-tzu,* 5:56–57. Cf. R. Wilhelm (5), 53–54; Graham (2), 102–103. The conception of a mountain that has four nourishing streams flowing from its peak, and, more generally, the conception of a paradise situated in the North, is probably not of Chinese but more likely of Indian origin (cf. Unno Kazutaka, among others).
46. Cf. the land of Uttarakuru, also situated in the North (below, pp. 165–170).
47. Cf. Karlgren (3), 270–272.
48. *Lieh-tzu,* 3:33. Cf. R. Wilhelm (5), 30–31; Graham (2), 64; Needham (1), 2:-142–143. For the version in the *Chu-shu chi-nien,* cf. Legge (1), 3: Prolegomena, 150–151. For the version in the *Mu-t'ien-tzu-chuan* cf. Cheng Te-k'un (2), 138–140. For K'un-lun Mountains, cf. Eberhard (2), 1:245–266; Haloun, 165–169.
49. *Huai-nan-tzu,* 4:56–57. Cf. Erkes, 45–49. For representations of the "Queen Mother of the West" in art and in the various legends about her, cf. Burkhardt 2:169–170; Finsterbusch, 62–78 (L).
50. On the paradise island Ying-chou cf., for example, Eberhard (2), 2:437–438, and Stein (2), 51–54.
51. *Shih-chi,* 28:458a. Cf. Chavannes (1), 2:152, note 1; Watson (1), 2:26.
52. *Lieh-tzu,* 5:52–53. Cf. R. Wilhelm (5), 49–50. See also Graham (2), 97–98.
53. Many typical descriptions of this kind can be found, for example, in the *Hai-nei shih-chou chi* (manuscript on the ten continents in the oceans) and in the *Shih-i-chi* (manuscript of collected traditions), both of which come from the fourth or fifth century A.D. (cf. Eichhorn [4]). But the beginnings of such a mythical geography can of course already be found in the half-legendary reports of the Chou period, the *Shan-hai-ching* and the *Mu-t'ien-tzu-chuan.*

54. More extended treatment below, pp. 178–181.
55. Cf. *Hai-nei shih-chou chi.*
56. *Po-wu-chih,* 3:17. On Chang Hua and the *Po-wu-chih,* see also below, pp. 194–195.
57. *Po-wu-chih,* 3:19.
58. *Lieh-tzu,* 3:31–32. Cf. R. Wilhelm (5), 29–30; Graham (2), 61–63. See also below, pp. 188–189.
59. Numerous examples of voyages to heaven and travels through the air can be found in the collections of hagiographies, such as the *Shen-hsien-chuan,* ascribed to Ko Hung, and in the *Lieh-hsien-chuan.* The collections of hagiographies in the *T'ai-p'ing kuang-chi* still made use of this material. Typical descriptions in translation in Kaltenmark, 35, 54, 90, 109, 146, 160, 161, 170 and Giles, 64, 84–85. On ascensions to heaven generally, cf. Yü Ying-shih (1), 52–55.
60. For the abundant literature on Han and T'ang funerary statuary, see Finsterbusch, 228–244 and Roger Goepper in: Wolf-D. v. Barloewen, *Abriss der Geschichte aussereuropäischer Kulturen,* Wien, 1961/1964, 2:173–174, 182–183.
61. On the term *hsien* and the history of the concept, cf. Kaltenmark, 10–20, and Schafer (3), 79, note 14 (L). Later, Taoist magicians still wore feather garments, which makes clear the original meaning of the *Hsien* idea. (cf. below, p. 127.
62. Yü Ying-shih (1) has written the most detailed, best documented work in a European language on the problem of life and death, the prolongation of life and eternal life in China between the third century B.C. and the third cent. A.D. (summary of the most important findings also in Yü Ying-shih [2]).
63. The fundamental work here is Maspero (1).
64. Cf. Yü Ying-shih (1), 46–49.
65. *Shen-hsien-chuan,* 2:1a.
66. Cf. Yü Ying-shih (1), 36–50.
67. For examples, see Kaltenmark, 134, 142, 154.
68. Up to this time, work on Ko Hung has been done largely by Japanese scholars. But see Ware (with Ko Hung's autobiography) and Schubert.
69. There is some uncertainty whether Ko Hung was the author of these works as we have them today. But there is no question that Ko Hung did write collections of biographies.
70. *Shen-hsien-chuan,* 1:4a–5a.
71. Cf. Gulik on this (1), 135–137.
72. Cf. Bauer-Franke, 173–177.
73. *Pao-p'u-tzu,* 3:10–12; 6:26–28. Cf. Ware, 61–67, 113–119. More generally, also Yü Ying-shih (1), 96–113.
74. *Hou-Han-shu,* 112:3827a.
75. *T'ai-p'ing kuang-chi,* 58:42b. Cf. also Pfizmaier (1).
76. Cf. for example, Giles, 38, 46, 85, 97, and Kaltenmark, 51, 72, 139, 157.
77. See Balazs (1), 187–254 for a general characterization of this period.
78. Cf. Maspero (2), 138 (L).
79. Cf. Welch, 113–157; Maspero (2), 43–57.
80. According to legend, "lightwater" seas where ships supposedly went under, and quicksands which allegedly engulfed chariots, surrounded all paradise islands and lands of happiness, so that only flying beings could reach them.
81. *Hou-Han-shu,* 118:3908b–3911a.
82. See *Wei-shu,* 102, 9950b–9951a; *Pei-shih,* 97:14188b–14189a.
83. Cf. Stein (1), 8–21; Shiratori; Herrmann; Chavannes (2).
84. On the abundant literature on the state of Chang Lu and the "Five Pecks of Rice Taoists," see Stein (1) (L); Eichhorn (2); Maspero (3), 149–184; Welch, 113–123.

85. Eichhorn (5), 331. On the state of Chang-Lu, see Stein (1), 38–76 (L). The "confession" among the "Five Pecks of Rice Taoists" shows some similarity with the "self-criticism" in contemporary China. See also pp. 148–149, however.

86. Stein (1), 11–12.

87. Cf. also above, pp. 80–84.

88. *Lü-shih ch'un-ch'iu,* 1, 5:10. Cf. R. Wilhelm (6), 11.

89. *Lü-shih ch'un-ch'iu,* 1, 5:10–11. Cf. R. Wilhelm (6), 11–12.

90. *Lü-shih ch'un-ch'iu,* 1, 5:10–11. Cf. R. Wilhelm (6), 12.

91. *Tao-te-ching,* 5:3. Cf. Waley (4), 147–148; R. Wilhelm (2), 7; Duyvendak (1) 28–29.

92. *Lü-shih ch'un-ch'iu,* 1 5:10. Cf. R. Wilhelm (6), 11.

93. Cf. Stein (1), 42.

94. *Lü-shih ch'un-ch'iu,* 1, 4:8. Cf. R. Wilhelm (6), 8–9.

95. Fu Lo-shu, 72–73.

96. Cf. Pokora (1).

97. *Chuang-tzu,* 13:211. Cf. Legge (4), 385; R. Wilhelm (4), 99; Watson (2), 147. This section of Chapter 133 is nonetheless very interesting because it represents a counter-argument to the Confucian "Great Learning" *(Ta-hsüeh),* see above, p. 70 and below, pp. 210–211). Yet here, the "Great Peace" does not ultimately derive from the "investigation of things" *(ko-wu)* but from "making heaven clear" *(ming-t'ien),* i.e. understanding nature. In its entire terminology, the section clearly addresses itself to potential Confucian converts to Taoism.

98. *Shih-chi,* 6:125a. Cf. Chavannes (1), 2:189.

99. *Shih-chi,* 6:121a. Curiously enough, this written form of the character *t'ai* also means "peace." This is also its meaning as the title of the eleventh hexagram in the *Book of Changes.* Cf. R. Wilhelm (1), 1:34–38.

100. According to a quotation of the Sung Confucian Chao Ling-chih: *Hou-ch'ing-lu,* 1:11b. Cf. Eichhorn (1), 120.

101. Wang Ch'ung devotes an entire chapter of his work ("Shih-ying," *Lun-heng,* 17:171–174. Cf. Forke [5], 2:315–326) to a refutation of an excessively schematic description of the *T'ai-p'ing* state. At the beginning of that chapter, he lists all those topoi which were generally believed to be associated with this era of "Universal Peace": miraculous natural phenomena such as "red grass," "calendar grass," "fan grass," sweet dew and fountains of wine appear, sacred animals such as the yellow dragon, the unicorn and the phoenix are sighted, and especially bright stars move across the heavens. Of their own accord, mountains produce chariots, lakes, boats. The climate is temperate. The peasants do not till soil that does not belong to them, travelers do not lose their way, women and men have their own walks and identical goods are sold at identical prices on markets. White-haired people no longer have to carry burdens, gates and bridges are never closed, robbery is unknown. On this question, see also above, pp. 59, 70, and 79–80, and below, pp. 122–123.

102. Cf. Eichhorn (1), 121.

103. On the uprising of the Yellow Turbans, see Michaud (L); Levy (1), (2); Vincent Shih (2), 338–342.

104. Said by Lu Chia. Cf. *Shih-chi,* 97:989a.

105. Cf. also Eberhard (2), 2:343–441.

106. Cf. Eichhorn (1), 126–129; (2), 303–307; (6), 471.

107. Cf. Harrison, 146–147 (L), and also: Hsiung Te-chi; Jung Sheng; Wan Sheng-nan; Yü Sung-ch'ing. Cf. also Obuchi (2) and Yoshioka (2).

108. Eichhorn (1), 135.

109. *T'ai-p'ing-ching,* 126–130.

110. Cf. Bauer (4).

111. In his martial aspect, T'ai-kung Wang (also called Lü Shang), the legendary general from the founding years of the Chou dynasty, is a kind of Taoist-legalist ideal figure. He may be understood as a contrast to the Confucian ideal figure, the duke of Chou (Chou-kung) whose civilian virtues tend to be emphasized. For this reason, T'ai-kung Wang plays an important role in texts which have both Taoist and Legalist aspects, such as the *Han Fei-tzu.* Concerning the interrelations between militarism, Taoism and Legalism, see above, pp. 61–63, and below, pp. 226, 229–230, and 232.

112. Translation cf. Seidel (1), 121–128.

113. Seidel (1), 122–124.

114. Cf. Maspero (2), 176–177 (L). Concerning the various incarnations (*pien* "metamorphoses") of Lao-tzu which differ from text to text, see particularly Seidel (1), 58–69, 92–105 (L). On the various "appearances" of Lao-tzu during and after the Chou period, which are a different matter and were dealt with in many legends, see Doré, 18:62–94.

115. *T'ai-p'ing-ching,* 1–3.

116. Cf. Seidel (2), 231.

117. Cf. Eichhorn (1), 138. For a partly deviating interpretation of the expression *chung-min,* see Stein (1), 26 (L).

118. Cf. Fukui Kojun (1), 22; Eichhorn (2), 326.

119. See above, pp. 107–109.

120. Cf. Fukui Kojun (1), 23.

121. Cf. Eichhorn (6), 476.

122. Cf. Eichhorn (5), 337.

123. Cf. Eichhorn (5), 340, 350; (6), 468. It is interesting that quite similar stories are also reported about the end of the river pirates in the twelfth century. Cf., for example, reports concerning the end of Yang Yao's uprising in Sievers, 40–41.

124. Intensive research has been done on "peasant uprisings," "secret societies" and rebel ideologies since the thirties in China (see Harrison, 62–99 [L]), since the end of the Second World War in Japan (see, for example, Obuchi [1] and [2]; Kubo Noritada), and during the last decade in the West as well (see for example Chesneaux [1], [2]; Chu Yung-deh). What lies behind this, either explicitly or implicitly, is the attempt to discover a non-Confucian tradition in China which would make it possible to establish a continuing link between the ideology of a "new" China and China's extended past.

125. Cf. Eichhorn (2), 302.

III. ENTHRALLED BY THE BEYOND

1. See above, pp. 41 and 94.
2. *I-ching, Hsü-kua* commentary. Cf. R. Wilhelm (1), 2:130.
3. *Lü-shih ch'un-ch'iu,* 20, 1:255–256. Cf. R. Wilhelm (6), 346–347.
4. See above, pp. 77–78.
5. *Lun-yü,* 3, 5. Cf. Legge (1), 1:156; R. Wilhelm (3), 19–20; Waley (2), 94–95.
6. *Lun-yü,* 2, 12. Cf. Legge (1), 1:150; R. Wilhelm (3), 12; Waley (2), 90.
7. See above, p. 27.
8. *Lü-shih ch'un-ch'iu,* 1:2; 3:24. Cf. R. Wilhelm (6), 2–3, 27–28.
9. *Lieh-tzu,* 4:46. Cf. R. Wilhelm (5), 44–45; Graham (2), 84–85.
10. On Juan Chi, see Holzman (1), 336–340; (2), 29–35; (3).
11. *I-ching,* 7:1a. Cf. R. Wilhelm (1), 1:211.
12. The use of the term "a short time ago" with reference to the dynasties of remote antiquity is meant to underline the entirely different sense of time of "Master Great Man."

13. *Juan Pu-ping chi,* 230–236.
14. *Kao-shih-chuan,* 1:12–14, 15–16.
15. On Pao Ching-yen, see Forke (1), 2:224–226; Balazs (1), 242–246.
16. The combination Ching-yen occurs only once, at the beginning of the *Pao-p'u-tzu* Chapter 48, which deals with Pao's teachings. Elsewhere, Pao is introduced as "Master Pao" *(Pao-sheng).*
17. *Pao-p'u-tzu,* 48:190. Cf. Forke (1), 2:225–226; Balazs (1), 243–246.
18. Weber, 1:435–436.
19. See above, pp. 135–136.
20. *Hou-Han-shu,* 10 B: 2755a.
21. See below, pp. 187–188. On the romanticism of nature in literature, see especially Obi Koichi.
22. *Tao-te-ching,* 25:14. Cf. Waley (4), 174; R. Wilhelm (2), 75; Duyvendak (1), 65.
23. See *Huai-nan-tzu,* 1:5; 14:244.
24. See *Chuang-tzu,* 7:133. Cf. Legge (4), 309–310; R. Wilhelm (2), 59; Watson (2), 94. Soon, the Taoist "perfect man" was counted among these "things." It was precisely by the surrender of his self that he was to acquire *tzu-jan.* Cf. *Huai-nan-tzu,* 8:117.
25. Cf. Balazs (1), 247.
26. *Ch'üan Shang-ku San-tai Ch'in Han San-kuo Liu-ch'ao wen,* 89:9a–b. Cf. Balazs (1), 215–216.
27. *Ch'üan Han San-kuo Chin Nan-pei-ch'ao shih,* Han, 2, 43. Cf. Balazs (1), 217–218.
28. *Tao-te-ching,* 28:16; 55:33–34. Cf. Waley (4), 178, 209; R. Wilhelm (2), 30, 60; Duyvendak (1), 71–73, 120–121. *Pao-p'u-tzu,* 48:191. This argument, however, there appears in the speech of Pao Ching-yen's adversary.
29. Because he comes from Lu, the home state of Confucius, the scholar is identified as a Confucian.
30. *Lieh-tzu,* 3:37. Cf. R. Wilhelm (5), 36–37; Graham (2), 70–71.
31. *Lieh-tzu,* 4:44–45. Cf. R. Wilhelm (5), 43; Graham (2), 82–83.
32. On Hsi K'ang, see Holzman (2).
33. *Hsi Chung-san chi,* 19B. Cf. Holzman (2), 90–91.
34. *Ch'üan Shang-ku San-tai Ch'in Han San-kuo Liu-ch'ao wen,* section *Ch'üan Chin-wen* (Complete Chin Literature), 72:7a. Cf. Holzman (2), 95–96.
35. See above, pp. 112–116.
36. See above, p. 114.
37. *Hsi Chung-san chi,* 17a–b. Cf. Holzman (2), 130.
38. See above, p. 62.
39. Cf. Balazs (1), 249.
40. Biography in *T'ang-shu,* 192:15710. *Hsin T'ang-shu,* 196:17248. There also exist some shorter autobiographical sketches in which he praises himself as a drunkard.
41. See above, pp. 134–137.
42. This is an allusion to the story in the book *Lieh-tzu* quoted above, pp. 93–94.
43. *Tung-kao-tzu chi (Wang Wu-kung chi),* 82–84.
44. At this time, there is only one Japanese translation of this important but difficult text (Murakami Yoshimi). This is also true of almost all relevant secondary literature. The American sinologist Richard Mather is preparing an English translation. A translation with commentary of one chapter of the work has been published (see Mather).
45. *Shih-shuo hsin-yü,* 23:190.
46. On the "pure conversations," see Zürcher, 93–95, 116–119 (L); Holzman (2), 35–41; Needham (1), 2:434 (L).
47. On the introduction of Buddhism into China, see the pioneering work by Zürcher.

In order to remain within the framework of the book, the treatment of conceptions of happiness, paradise and the ideal introduced into China by Buddhism had to be limited to the most essential motifs, those that were most influential in China. A survey of the various Buddhist conceptions of happiness (consisting largely of quotations) is given by Liu Jen-hang, 6A:1–70; 6B:1–60, and about Buddhist paradises 6B:25–54.

48. Concerning the Chinese misunderstanding of the Buddhist concept of the self and the soul, a misunderstanding which resulted more or less necessarily from the translation of the concept by the term *shen,* "spirit," "soul," see Zürcher 11–12, 136, 147–148, 244 (L).

49. Discussed at length by Liebenthal (2). See also Fung Yu-lan (1), 2:284–292; Balazs (1), 255–276.

50. What is essential here is that the early Chinese Buddhist felt obviously less fervent about *ending* the cycle of rebirths than they did about the idea of *rebirth itself,* a concept which in this form had no parallel in China. It suddenly and decisively enlarged the area of application of morality, punishment and reward. Before that time, this had been limited to a single lifespan or to a few generations at most (to the extent, that is, that the acts of ancestors were believed decisive for the fate of their progeny).

51. *Sung-shu,* 97:7215b. Cf. Liebenthal (2), 369.

52. *Ch'ih-hsien shen-chou,* the "Spiritual Continent of the Red Region" was the name used by Tsou Yen (see above, p. 90) to refer to that 1/81 part of the earth (the ninth part of nine continents) which allegedly covered China. Cf. Fung Yu-lan (1), 1:160.

53. *Ming-Fou-lun,* 2 (*T,* text No. 2101:90). Cf. Liebenthal (2), 380–381.

54. *Sung-shu,* 97:7216a. Cf. Liebenthal (2), 370–371.

55. Schafer conveys a vivid impression of the cosmopolitan atmosphere of this period (1) and (2).

56. Texts (in the form of teacher-student dialogues), which deal with conditions in the "Paradise of the West" and its (fundamentally rather questionable) import within the framework of Buddhist teaching may be found, for example, in *T* among the texts No. 1957–1984. For a typical example, see the translation from the treatise *An-lo chi (Treatise About the Land of Peace and Joy)* (*T,* 47:8–11) of the patriarch Tao-ch'o (died 645) in Bary (1), 381–386.

57. *Niyuta* and *koti* are among the gigantic numbers that were used in India and which Buddhism brought to China. But commentators differed substantially in the value they assigned them. *Koti,* for example, was variously set at one hundred thousand, one million and ten million.

58. *Yojana* is the distance covered in a day's march, and may amount to forty, thirty or sixteen Chinese miles (*li*=ca. 0.6 k.m.). Concerning the precious stones motif in the paradises, see Schafer (3), especially 88–101. In the "Northend Land" in the book *Lieh-tzu,* there is a parallel for the absence of animals in paradise, an absence which makes sense only in Buddhism (see above, p. 94). But this parallel merely proves that this description was already influenced by Buddhism.

59. That the landscape in paradise is "level" is an important characteristic. It already appears in the description of the "Northend Land" in the book *Lieh-tzu* (see above, p. 94) but this was already influenced by India (see Abegg, 185, 219). But in China, where the terms for "level" evoked the idea of social equality (*chün,* for example, see above, p. 21) and, beyond that, of social peace (classical term: *p'ing,* which has the meanings of: "level," "balanced," and "peace," see above p. 116) it acquired a social and political connotation. In this context, the "leveling of mountains" also acquires a metaphoric significance (see below, pp. 410–411).

60. The beneficial effect ascribed to the rivers here has its parallel in the description

of the "Northend Land" in *Lieh-tzu.* See Unno Kazutaka.

61. [*Ta*] *Wu-liang-shou ching* (*T,* text No. 360:265c–274a). See Müller, 28–29, 36, 40–44, 51, 54–57. The translation given here is somewhat freer and occasionally condenses the many repetitive individual descriptions.

62. See, for example, *Tun-huang pi-hua-chi* (collection of mural paintings from Tun-huang), ed. Tun-huang wen-wu yen-chiu-so, Peking, 1957, plate 37.

63. On the development of the Pure Land Sect including the modern period, see Mochizuki Shinko, especially pp. 534–548, and Kenneth Ch'en, 338–350.

64. On Chih Tun, see especially Zürcher, 116–143 (L) (in its relation to the "Paradise of the West," especially p. 128), and Kenneth Ch'en, pp. 65–67.

65. Apparently deliberately, the Chinese Buddhists chose the concept *an* as a translation for "peace." For (in contradistinction to *p'ing* and *k'ang,* see above, pp. 83–84 and 116–117), it had not been used before and was therefore free of associations.

66. *Ch'üan Shang-ku San-tai Ch'in Han San-kuo Liu-ch'ao,* section *Ch'üan Chin-wen,* 157:12a.

67. Like Buddhism generally, the tea ceremony has had a much more enduring life in Japan than in China. It is therefore better known in its Japanese stylization and has more frequently become the subject of research than its Chinese form. See survey by Hammitzsch (L).

68. Cf. Kenneth Ch'en, 172 (L). Descriptions of the paradise expected with the arrival of the Buddha Maitreya can be found in Leumann, 227–282. They show a marked similarity with Uttarakuru, which is also a "western" paradise (see below, pp. 165–168).

69. See Maenchen-Helfen, 570 (L).

70. Cf. above, p. 90.

71. *Shan-hai-ching,* 18:2a–3b. See Maenchen-Helfen, 569.

72. The title of this small work by Huang Chou-hsing is *Yü-t'an-yüeh sung* (songs of praise about the land of Yü-t'an-yüeh). Yü-t'an yüeh-(chou) is the Chinese name for Uttarakuru.

73. Lin Yutang (3), 340–342.

74. In the original, the last sentence is at the end of the paragraph.

75. *Krosa* is the distance over which the bellowing of an ox can be heard. About 3.5 k.m., according to one explanation.

76. *Ch'i-shih yin-pen ching* (*T,* text No. 25:369a–372b).

77. But these forms of sexual contact all occur only in the six lowest of the twenty-eight heavens, the *Yü-t'ien.* The upper twenty-two are wholly free of these feelings.

78. Hu Shih (4), 84.

79. *T,* text No. 221, VIII:32c.

80. See Liebenthal (1), 46, note 138.

81. *T,* text No. 1858:151a–151c. See Liebenthal (1), 46–54.

82. Cf. Fung Yu-lan (1), 2:274–276.

83. *Pien-tsung-lun,* 225a.

84. The abundant literature on the Buddhism of meditation in China naturally cannot be discussed here. Kenneth Ch'en, 535–537 mentions the most important works. A brief historical survey of the Buddhism of meditation in China is given by: Fung Yu-lan (1), 2:386–406; Kenneth Ch'en, 350–364 (L); deBary (1), 386–408 (essential texts).

85. See, for example *Chen-chou Lin-chi hui-chao ch'an-shih yü-lu* (*T,* text No. 1985:-496–506).

86. [*Fu-chou*] *Ts'ao-shan Pen-chi ch'an-shih yü-lu,* in *T,* text No. 1987–526c. Cf. deBary (1), 404–408.

87. See above, pp. 151–152.

88. See above, p. 172.

89. Cf. Liebenthal (1), 40.

90. There is such a story about the nearly legendary, greatest Chinese Buddhist painter of the T'ang period, Wu Tao-tzu (Wu Tao-hsüan [died 791]), for example. With his frescoes (not preserved), he decorated the temples and palaces in the capitals Ch'ang-an and Lo-yang.

91. Quoted in Hu Shih/Lin Yutang, 65. See also above, pp.350–355.

92. Cf. above, pp. 98–100.

93. *Hai-nei shih-chou chi,* 5:169b–170a.

94. See above, pp. 95–97.

95. *Hsi-wang-mu chuan,* 1:1a.

96. *Ch'üan Han San-kuo Chin Nan-pei-ch'ao shih,* 423–425.

97. See Hightower (L); Weber-Schäfer (1). Suicide in the river as a protest against the world and particularly its relations of domination already appears in the later sections of the book *Chuang-tzu* where hermits jump into the water with disgust upon being offered the throne (*Chuang-tzu,* 28:424. Cf. Legge (4), 602–603. Watson (2), 320–321).

98. *Ch'u-tz'u,* 14–20. See Hawkes, 28–30.

99. *Ch'u-tz'u,* 118. See Hawkes, 99–100.

100. *T,* text No. 262:28b.

101. Discussed by Schafer (3), 80.

102. Schafer (3), 74–75.

103. What is meant here is the "Royal Lord of the East" *(Tung-wang-kung),* a legendary figure from the Han period, a counterpart to the "Queen Mother of the West," who was alleged to rule a paradise in the remotest East.

104. *Ch'üan Han San-kuo Chin Nan-pei-ch'ao shih,* 148.

105. Cf. Schafer (3), 81 (L).

106. *Ch'an-yüeh chi,* 1. Cf. Schafer (3), 76–79.

107. See Karlgren (3), 272.

108. The "Moon Palace" *(yüeh-kung* or *yüeh t'ien kung-tien),* abode of the moon ruler *(yüeh t'ien-tzu)* is described in Buddhism as a structure of silver and crystal. See also *Ch'i-shih ching,* in *T,* text No. 24:360b–361b, among others.

109. According to information provided by Prof. Wolfram Eberhard, Berkeley, who also observed this in an examination of dreams of a representative number of students on Taiwan.

110. In the Chinese "lunar year" which starts with spring and whose beginning may vary by as much as one month, the moon festival is celebrated on the fifteenth day of the eighth month (end of September-beginning of October).

111. *Lung-ch'eng lu,* 3b. The classical name for the fairy palace in the moon as described in the story continued to be *kuang-han.* Concerning the heavenly voyage of the Chou king Mu, see above, p. 100.

112. Of the abundant literature on T'ao Yüan-ming, we will mention only Holzman (4) (L). Even in contemporary China, there has been much research on T'ao. See, for example *RBS,* 7:No. 501; 8:No. 569 and 570.

113. Wei dynasty (220–264), Chin dynasty (265–419).

114. *Ching-chieh hsien-sheng chi,* 6, 3:1. The very similar experience of a scholar from almost the same period, Liu Lin-chih, is recounted in the *Chin-shu,* 94:5611a–b. The only difference is that the scholar only gets as far as the gate of the cave land. For further passages from a later period, see Eberhard (7), 111–112.

115. See above, p. 000.

116. Collection of the most important poems of this type in *T'ao Yüan-ming shih-wen hui-p'ing,* 338–362.

117. Karlgren (6), No. 1176 and 1185.

118. See above, p. 35.

119. Especially in conjunction with the character *chen* "true" *(t'ung-chen)* and *hsüan* "mysterious" *(t'ung-hsüan)*. Cf. the titles in the Taoist canon *(Tao-tsang)*, section *Cheng-i-pu*.

120. A collection of descriptions and stories about these cave paradises in [*Ku-chin*] *T'u-shu chi-ch'eng, Po-wu hui-pien, shen-i tien,* 313/314 *(i-ching pu)* (=514:29a–35b).

121. The "White-Tiger-Mountain" was about 150 km. south of the capital of the Shu-Han dynasty, which was one of the "Three Kingdoms" at that time. It ruled the southwestern third of the empire.

122. Ch'eng-tu was the name of the capital of the Shu-Han dynasty. The name of the cave paradise suggests that it was a kind of shadow capital of the empire.

123. *Shen-hsien kan-yü chuan,* 5:8a.

124. Red, traditionally the lucky color, not only implies joy here, but also cinnabar, the basic substance used by all alchemists in their search for the elixir of life.

125. *Shih-i-chi,* 10:8a.

126. In what is today the southeastern province of Fukien.

127. Collective term for the (largely lost), oldest, prehistorical literature. (Full title: *San-fen wu-tien pa-so chiu-ch'iu*). Traditional scholars have differed widely in their dating of it.

128. The story of the voyage to heaven via the Milky Way, quoted above, pp. 99–100, comes from the *Po-wu-chih*.

129. *Lang-huan chi,* 1:1a.

130. Legge (1), 5:6a (Yin-kung, first year).

131. The abundance of stories in Chinese literature taking place in hell is as great as their surprising monotony. Most reports about hell are told by individuals who departed this life too early because a mistake was made (names were mixed up, for example). Having been taken to hell, they were allowed to return when the misunderstanding had been cleared up.

132. See Eberhard (5), 21–23.

133. See Eberhard (5), 51 (L).

134. The famous Tung-t'ing lake in southcentral China became the center of such legends. Allegedly, there was also a floating spirit island on it (see *Shih-i-chi*).

135. For early examples, see *Shen-hsien-chuan,* 6:2b–3a and *Sou-chen hou-chi,* 1:1.

136. See above, pp. 125–126.

137. In what is today Hupei province.

138. Concerning the "Red Region," see above, p. 437, note 52.

139. *Po-i-chih,* 11b.

140. On the motif of the shift in time, see Eberhard (1), 156–157; (7), 110–111.

141. *Han Fei-tzu,* 7 (=section 22):132. Cf. W. K. Liao, 1:239–240.

142. *Yu-yang tsa-tsu,* 2:1a–b.

143. Examples in *Yu-yang tsa-tsu,* 2:1a–b.

144. [*Ming-shan*] *tung-t'ien fu-ti chi,* 1–3. The *Lu-i chi* (6:1a–4a), also by Tu Kuang-t'ing contains descriptions of cave paradises which are quite as sober and matter-of-fact as the earlier "geographical" accounts of paradise islands (see above, pp. 179–180). In this connection, also see Schafer (2), 140–145 and Soymié.

145. For survey, see Doré, 18:101–118 (L).

IV. THE DUST OF REALITY

1. This is particularly evident in the fact that Buddhism was still flowering in border areas of the empire when it was already declining in the center. See Kenneth Ch'en, 389–454.

2. On Han Yü generally, see Fung Yu-lan (1), 2:408–413; Carsun Chang (1), 1:79–100; Forke (1), 2:287–297; Hou Wai-lu (2), 4:319–337.

3. *T'ang-shu,* 160:11541a–b.

4. Translated in H. A. Giles, *Gems of Chinese Literature,* New York, 1965, 115–121. The expression "On the Origin of the Way" first appears as the title of an essay by the philosopher Huai-nan-tzu (see above, p. 95).

5. See above, p. 80.

6. See Fung Yu-lan (1), 2:469–474.

7. On Chu Hsi generally, see Fung Yu-lan (1), 2:533–571; Carsun Chang (1), 1:-243–331; Forke (1), 3:164–202; Bruce (1) and (2); Graf; Chan Wing-tsit (3); Hou Wai-lu (2), 4:595–647.

8. See James T. C. Liu (L).

9. See O. Franke (5).

10. Carsun Chang (1), 1:309–331. On Ch'en Liang also see Forke (1), 3:265–266.

11. *Chu-tzu wen-chi,* 1:14b. See Carsun Chang (1), 1:318.

12. Chapter 39 (42). On the *Li-chi,* see above, pp. 70 and 83.

13. Among the many translations, see especially Legge (1), 1:355–381; (2), 28:411–428.

14. Cf. Legge (1), 1:357–359.

15. Cf. Legge (1), 1:359.

16. See especially Eichhorn (7) (L). On Chang Tsai, also see Fung Yu-lan (1), 2:-477–498; Forke (1), 3:56–69; Carsun Chang (1), 1:167–182; Hou Wai-lu (2), 4:545–570.

17. See Eichhorn (7), 36–37.

18. Chapter 28 (31) of the Li-chi, translated by Legge (1), 1:382–434; (2), 28:301–329. An interesting revaluation of the *Chung-yung* can be found in Weber-Schäfer (2).

19. This observation cannot be documented in the *Lun-yü* (see above, p. 20). The expression "holding to the mean" appears there only once, although in a similar context (*Lun-yü,* 6, 27. Cf. Legge [1], 193; R. Wilhelm [3], 59; Waley [2], 121–122).

20. *Chung-yung,* 1, 1–2, 4–5; 2, 1–2. Cf. Legge (1), 1:383–386.

21. The entire argument is here put into Confucius's mouth, yet a corresponding passage cannot be found in the older sources.

22. *Chung-yung,* 20, 18–19; 22. Cf. Legge (1), 1:413, 415–416.

23. *Meng-tzu,* 7 A,4. Cf. Legge (1), 2:450–451; R. Wilhelm (8), 157.

24. *Meng-tzu,* 2 A,2. Cf. Legge (1), 2:189–190; R. Wilhelm (8), 29.

25. On the history of foot-binding, see Levy (3), especially 23–103. The eighth-century ballad *Mu-lan tz'u* is an eloquent testimonial to the wholly different, much freer, indeed martial ideal of the Chinese woman before the Sung period (see Barthel).

26. See above, p. 213.

27. There is no biography of Chang Pang-chi either in the official history of the Sung dynasty or in private historical works. Most data about him can be found in the introduction to his work quoted here, and which was written by himself.

28. Huang Ch'ao (died 884) provided the initial impetus for the decline of the T'ang dynasty. He pillaged Canton and conquered the capital Ch'ang-an in 880 before he could be defeated by a loyal army commander of Turkish descent.

29. P'ei Hsiu (second half, ninth century) was a statesman celebrated in large part for his carefully thought-out economic measures.

30. See above, p. 64.

31. Concerning the "eight genii," see Doré, 9:493–520; Werner, 341–352; Burkhardt, 1:158–161; 3:124–135.

32. Ginseng actually has the meaning "man's herb."

33. The *Leng-yen (Lankavatara)* Sutra is presumably the most fundamental text of Ch'an Buddhism. It proclaims that "the real teaching of truth is not a matter of words

but becomes manifest by being realized in the person of the teacher" (Gundert, *Bi Yän Lu,* Munich, 1:195). The work, which dates from the fourth or fifth century, was, according to tradition, taken to China by the "founder" of *Ch'an* Buddhism, Bodhidharma, and translated there into Chinese as early as 412–433 (there were three subsequent translations as well). English translation by D. T. Suzuki, London, 1956. See Kenneth Ch'en, 352–353.

34. *Mo-chuang man-lu,* 3:1.

35. It is especially in the figures of the brothers Po-i and Shu-ch'i, men shrouded in legend, that Confucian loyalism and eremitism had their points of crystallization. After the collapse of the Sung dynasty, they remained loyal to the fallen royal family in spite of the admitted unworthiness of its last representative. They first sought refuge in the mountains, and later refused all food and starved to death because they were even unwilling to eat wild plants which could be considered the property of the new ruler of the following dynasty. See Mote (1), (L).

36. Concerning Wang Yang-ming, see, among others, Fung Yu-lan (1), 2:596–623; Carsun Chang (1), 2:30–159; Forke (1), 3:380–399; Hou Wai-lu (2), 4:875–911. Translations by Henke and Chan Wing-tsit (2).

37. Legendary teacher of the "Yellow Emperor" (see above, pp. 93–94) who, according to one tradition, is said to have been an earlier incarnation of Lao-tzu (see Forke [1], 1:244–245).

38. "Logician" from the fourth century B.C. The writings attributed to him (translated by P. Masson-Oursel and Chu Chia-chien in *TP,* 15, 557–620, 1914) probably date from a later period (see also Forke [1], 1:421–427; Fung Yu-lan [1], 1:148–152).

39. *Wang Wen-ch'eng kung ch'üan-shu,* 21:5. See Henke, 362–364.

40. This does not preclude the possibility that the Taoists also succeeded in becoming influential at court at a later time and attempted to usurp specific aspects of court ceremonial, especially during the Ming period.

41. The religious and political influence of men skilled in the arts of healing and their connection with popular uprisings can be traced throughout Chinese history. It begins with Chang (Tao)-ling (see above, p. 113), the first Taoist "pope" in the first century A.D., who promised to save men if they confessed their sins (see L. Giles, 61, according to *Shen-hsien chuan,* 4:3b–5a) and extends down to Sun Yat-sen who had studied medicine. It was the latter K'ang Yu-wei presumably had in mind when he warned against physicians who might become powerful "religious leaders." (See below, p. 323.)

42. On Manichaeism in China and its influence on secret societies, see Vincent Shih (2), 347–352, 356, 387 (L).

43. Cf. Muramatsu Yuji, 246 (L). On the connection between popular uprisings and religion generally, and the connection to non-Chinese religions specifically, see C. K. Yang (1), 218–243.

44. See Groot (2) and Chesneaux (1) for documents on secret societies and governmental measures agains them.

45. On the *Mi-lieh chiao-hui* and the *Pai-lien chiao-hui,* cf. Chu Yung-deh; Vincent Shih (2), 355–361, and 330, 348, 355–358.

46. On the *T'ui-pei-t'u,* which is ascribed to the two T'ang scholars Yüan T'ien-kang and Li Ch'un-feng, see Koyanagi Shikita, 1:412–429; Smith, 325–339; Bauer (5), 184–185 (picture); Nakano Toru.

47. See above, pp. 73–74.

48. A collection of such prognostic texts called *Chung-kuo yü-yen pa-chung,* compiled by a certain Chu Hsiao-ch'in from Hai-ning (Chekiang) contains eight different works. One of them is said to date from the eleventh century B.C.; one from the third A.D., two from the T'ang, one from the Sung, two from the Ming, and one from the Manchu period.

Next to the *T'ui-pei-t'u,* the best known among these is the *Shao-ping ko,* ascribed to the scholar Liu Chi (1311–1375).

49. The edition of the *T'ui-pei-t'u* published by Chu Hsiao-ch'in, for example, contains a commentary by the famous prorevolutionary scholar Chin Jen-jui (executed 1661), which runs all the way through to the end and is expressed in general terms. It also contains a commentary by Chu Hsiao-ch'in himself where he attempts to correlate the various pictures and sayings with particular periods. His commentary only goes up to picture no. 39, which he took to be a symbolic representation of the Sino-Japanese war (1937–1945).

50. Of the eleven different editions of the *T'ui-pei-t'u* which this writer could collect up to this time, seven contain sixty stations, and the other four forty-eight, sixty-four, sixty-five and sixty-seven respectively. This distribution suggests that a "great end" was expected within the framework of this prognostic text, for otherwise there would presumably have been general agreement on the number sixty-four, which is the number of hexagrams in the *I-ching* (see above, p. 13), and which are indeed correlated with certain stations in some of the editions. But the "one-dimensional" concept of time found in the *I-ching,* which does not know a genuine beginning or a genuine end made a real parallel between these two systems impossible.

51. Station 34 in Chu Hsiao-ch'in's edition, which may be considered relevant for the period from 1945–1949. Occasionally, however, other editions have an entirely different sequence or completely different pictures and verses, which means that the picture does not appear in all versions of the text.

52. Cf. Koyanagi Shikita, *loc. cit.* (notes 4, 46).

53. Chuang Chi-yü's real name is Chuang Ch'ao.

54. The Diamond Sutra (*Vajracchedika-prajna-paramita* Sutra), first translated by the famous monk Kumarajiva (344–409 (or 413)), a shortened and popularized version of the *Prajna-paramita* Sutra, became extremely popular among the people, and found many readers who were not Buddhists. See Kenneth Ch'en, 58–60.

55. See above, p. 118. Since remotest times, there had been a taboo in China on the use of the personal names of venerated figures.

56. *Chi-lo-pien,* 16a–b. See Vincent Shih (2), 345–346.

57. See Vincent Shih, 347, note 54 (L).

58. See Eichhorn (5).

59. See above, p. 174, but also p. 357.

60. See Kao Yu-kung (L); Vincent Shih (2), 349–355 (L); Harrison, 152–153, 289–290 (1).

61. Vincent Shih (2), 380. The uprisings mentioned here are of course only some from the long history of China. Harrison gives a brief, practical overview, 279–304 (L), and Vincent Shih an account of typical rebel "ideologies" (2), 329–389.

62. Fang Shao's literary activity was wholly confined to descriptions of this sort. There is no biography of his in the official dynastic history of the Sung period.

63. The two collections of essays published by Li Kuang-pi and Shih Shao-pin, respectively, convey some impression of the discussion concerning the problems of these uprisings in contemporary China (for additional literature, see Harrison). While here it is usually the "feudalist" system which is held responsible for the misery leading to these uprisings, Teng-Ssu-yü (1) takes individual mismanagement and abuses to have been their real causes.

64. *Ch'ing-hsi k'ou-kuei,* 8a. See Vincent Shih (2), 353–354.

65. Whether this policy may be regarded as an intelligent form of elastic resistance or an expression of cowardly "defeatism" is even today a matter of dispute among scholars. On this question, see H. Franke (3), 217–219.

66. See, for example, the texts in *Chung-kuo k'o-hsüeh yüan,* 48. On the well field system generally, see above, pp. 24–25.

67. *Sung-shih,* 276:22476b–22477a. On Wang Hsiao-po's uprising, see Harrison, 150–152 (L); Eichhorn (3).

68. The two classical models of these novels dealing with knights and robbers are the *San-kuo chih yen-i (Romance of the Three Kingdoms)* and the *Shui-hu chuan (All Men Are Brothers).* Both are popular novels whose first, coherent version appears to date from the fourteenth century.

69. Biography see *Sung-shih,* 438:23438b–23439a. On Chung Hsiang, see especially Sievers (particularly p. vii–ix, 1–9) where the uprising of the river pirate Yang Yao, which had a connection with Chung Hsiang, is also discussed (L).

70. *San-ch'ao pei-meng hui-pien,* (*Yen-hsing hsia-chih,* 37), 3:122.

71. See *Chung-kuo k'o-hsüeh yüan,* 38–40.

72. See the devastating critical attack on Hou Wai-lu in the *Jen-min jih-pao (People's Daily),* November 22, 1966, and in the *Kuang-ming jih-pao,* August 10, 1966.

73. K'ang Yü-chih has no biography in the official dynastic history of the Sung.

74. The three capitals are Kai-feng, Lo-yang and Shang-ch'iu.

75. *Tso-meng-lu,* 12b.

76. The previously mentioned novel (see note 68) is a historical document in the sense that it embodies a number of reports about real historical events.

77. See Mote (1), 231–232.

78. *Lü-shih ch'un-ch'iu,* 14,2:140. See R. Wilhelm (6), 180–181.

79. See above, p. 137.

80. *Po-ya ch'in,* 3–5. See Fu Lo-shu, 67–71.

81. See Fu Lo-shu, 74–76.

82. See above, p. 65.

83. See Mote (2). "Expressive" dynastic names were also chosen by the following dynasties: Ming (the "brilliant") and Ch'ing (Manchu) (the "pure"). See below, p. 254.

84. See above, p. 30.

85. Survey of the various relevant teachings in Fung Yu-lan (1), 2:434–571.

86. See above, p. 208. On Shao Yung, also see Fung Yu-lan (1), 2:451–476; Forke (1), 3:18–40; Carsun Chang (1), 1:159–183; Hou Wai-lu (2), 4:521–535.

87. See above, p. 210.

88. On Lu Chiu-yüan, see Huang Siu-chi; Fung Yu-lan (1), 2:572–579; Forke (1), 3:232–248; Carsun Chang (1), 1:285–307; Hou Wai-lu (2), 4:648–691.

89. *Hsiang-shan hsien-sheng ch'üan-chi,* 33:247. See Fung Yu-lan (1), 2:573.

90. The real meaning of *hsin* is "heart." The translation "Heart School" would therefore also be possible, but this would express the actual character of this school less clearly.

91. See above, pp. 220–221 with note 36.

92. *Wang Wen-ch'eng kung ch'üan-shu,* 32:37. See Fung Yu-lan (1), 2:597.

93. *Meng-tzu,* 7A, 15. Cf. Legge (1), 2:456; R. Wilhelm (8), 160.

94. *Wang Wen-ch'eng kung ch'üan-shu,* 3:17. See Fung Yu-lan (1), 2:608–609.

95. On Wang Chi, see Fung Yu-lan (1), 2:623–629; Forke (1), 3:414–423; Carsun Chang (1), 42–43, 99–110.

96. Fung Yu-lan (1), 2:623. On Wang Ken, see Fung Yu-lan (1), 2:623–629; Forke (1), 3:399–403; Carsun Chang (1), 2:25–27, 113–118; Hou Wai-lu (2), 4:974–995.

97. On Li Chih, see O. Franke (4); Hsiao Kung-chuan (5); Carsun Chang, 2:126–127, 171–172; Hou Wai-lu (2), 4:1031–1095.

98. *Wang Hsin-chai hsien-sheng i-chi,* 1:16. Cf. Fung Yu-lan (1), 2:628; Carsun Chang (1), 2:116–117.

99. Quoted from Carsun Chang (1), 2:118. The original text could not be determined.
100. Cf. Carsun Chang (1), 2:117; Chung-kuo k'o-hsüeh-yüan, 43.
101. Quoted in *Ho Hsin-yin chi,* 1.
102. *Chung-kuo k'o-hsüeh-yüan,* 42–43.
103. Carsun Chang (1), 2:114.
104. On Ch'eng Hao and his brother Ch'eng I, two of the most important Neo-Confucian philosophers, see Graham (3) and Fung Yu-lan (1), 2:498–532; Forke (1), 3:69–104; Carsun Chang (1), 1:185–241; Hou Wai-lu (2), 4:571–584.
105. *Wang Wen-ch'eng kung ch'üan-shu,* 1:24. Cf. Fung Yu-lan (1), 2:613–614.
106. *Jen-lun* or *Wu-lun:* parents:children; rulers:subjects; man:wife; elder:younger (brother); friend:friend.
107. Mentioned only in passing in the official history of the Ming dynasty, in the biography of Wang Chi and Wang Ken (*Ming-shih,* 283:32052b).
108. *Ho Hsin-yin chi,* 24.
109. On Yen Chün (Yen Shan-nung), see Carsun Chang (1), 2:119–121.
110. Cf. Li Chih, *Ho Hsin-yin lun* (on Ho Hsin-yin), in: *Ho Hsin-yin chi,* 10–12.
111. *Ho Hsin-yin chi,* 68–69.
112. See above, pp. 81–82.
113. The passage inserted here is a necessary element in the context. As often happened in such parallel constructions, one of the copyists omitted one link in the argument by mistake.
114. The first day of each of the four seasons, the two days of the winter and summer solstice (not identical with the former in the Chinese lunar calendar) and the vernal and autumnal equinox.
115. *Ho Hsin-yin chi,* 70–71.
116. *Ho Hsin-yin chi,* 1–2.
117. See Chang Chü-cheng's biography in *Ming-shih,* 213:31263b–31269a.
118. *Ho Hsin-yin chi,* 2.
119. *Ho Hsin-yin chi,* 3.
120. *Ibid.*
121. See above, p. 231.
122. It is apparent that the introduction is partly inspired by Hou Wai-lu's estimate who devoted considerable space in his works to Liang Ju-yüan. See Hou Wai-lu (2), 4:1003–1030; (3), 29–31.
123. Immanuel Hsü, 26.
124. On Yen Yüan, see Freeman (1); Fung Yu-lan (1), 2:631–652; Forke (1), 3:-526–539; Carsun Chang (1), 2:293–316, Hu Shih (1), 3:60–69; Hou Wai-lu (2), 5:324–390; Hummel, 912–915.
125. On Ku Yen-wu, see Forke (1), 3:484–489; Carsun Chang (1), 2:216–235; Hu Shih (1), 3:57–60; Hou Wai-lu (2), 5:204–252; Hummel 421–426 (L).
126. On Wang Fu-chih, see Vierheller; Fung Yu-lan (1), 2:641–650; Forke (1), 3:-484–489; Carsun Chang (1), 2:264–292; Hou Wai-lu (2); Hummel, 817–819 (L); Teng Ssu-yü (2).
127. Immanuel Hsü, 40.
128. Immanuel Hsü, 41.
129. *Ts'un-hsüeh pien,* 1:48. See Immanuel Hsü, 41.
130. On Li Kung, see Fung Yu-lan (1), 2:631–635, 650–657, 663–672; Forke (1), 3:539–546; Hummel, 475–479.
131. On Tai Chen, see Freeman (2); Fung Yu-lan (1), 2:651–672; Forke (1), 3:-546–557; Carsun Chang (1), 2:337–358; Hu Shih (1), 3:69–82, Hou Wai-lu (2), 5:-430–464; Hummel, 695–700 (L).

132. *Meng-tzu tzu-i shu-cheng,* 1:34. See Immanuel Hsü, 60; Carsun Chang, 2:353.

133. *Meng-tzu tzu-i shu-cheng,* 1:36. See Immanuel Hsü, 60.

134. See above, p. 444, note 83.

135. The cutting off of the pigtail symbolizes a decisive turning away from all that is too traditional. During the Chinese revolution in 1911, it therefore also had a nationalist connotation since it symbolized the turning away from non-Chinese alien rule.

136. See above, pp. 80–81 and 86.

137. On Kung Tzu-chen, see Forke (1), 3:557–558; Hummel, 431–434 (L).

138. Cf. Nivison (2), 198–199.

139. *Kung Ting-an ch'üan-chi,* 81.

140. See above, pp. 72–74.

141. On Huang Tsung-hsi, see deBary (3) and (4) (L), and also Fung Yu-lan (1), 2:640–643, 650, 657–659; Forke (1), 3:474–478; Carsun Chang (1), 2:236–263; Hou Wai-lu (2), 5:144–203; Hummel, 351–354.

142. Translation in deBary (3). Translation of the title "Plan for the Prince" is in deBary (4), the translation "Until Dawn" in Carsun Chang (1).

143. *I-ching,* Wilhelm/Baynes, Pantheon Books. Thirty-sixth hexagram.

144. *Ming-i tai-fang lu,* 7. Cf. Bary (1), 537.

145. Carsun Chang (1) 2:259.

146. Although they despised the last "degenerate" ruler of the Shang dynasty, the brothers Po I and Shu Ch'i are said to have sought refuge in the mountains for reasons of loyalty, and to have starved to death there because they did not wish to eat the bread of the Chou dynasty.

147. See above, p. 238.

148. Emperor Ch'ung-chen is supposed to have said these words before he hanged himself in Peking in 1644, being surrounded by a rebel army which was later defeated by the Manchus after they had been called into the country.

149. *Ming-i tai-fang-lu,* 1–3. Cf. deBary (1), 587–588.

150. Two men made such a vain attempt, as is well known. The powerful marshal Yüan Shih-k'ai, who wanted to found a new dynasty with himself as emperor shortly before his death (in 1915/1916); and the Warlord Chang Hsün, who put the last Manchu emperor P'u-i (Hsüan-t'ung) back on the throne for a few days in 1917.

151. Lin Yutang (2) 388, footnote.

152. Lin Yutang (2), 152, 343–361.

153. Cf. the partial English translation (thirty of one hundred chapters) by A. Waley, *Monkey,* London, 1942. Eberhard (8) gives content of entire text.

154. In contemporary China where this novel has been studied intensively, Sun Wu-k'ung was interpreted as symbolic of a popular leader rebelling against the authorities. See, for example, *RBS,* 3:No. 724..

155. On Li Ju-chen, see Hummel, 472–473.

156. *Ching-hua yüan,* 32:128–131. Lin Tai-yi, 107–114. This adventurous visit to the Country of Women contributed much to making the book well known.

157. *Ching-hua yüan,* 16:57. Lin Tai-yi, 74–75.

158. *Ching-hua yüan,* 14:48–50. Lin Tai-yi, 67–69.

159. *Ching-hua yüan,* 14:48–51. Lin Tai-yi, 67–69.

160. *Ching-hua yüan,* 11:35–36. Lin Tai-yi, 57ff.

161. *Ching-hua yüan,* 43. Lin Tai-yi, 60–61.

162. On the abundant literature on Matteo Ricci and the missionary activity of the Jesuits in China, see George H. Dunne, *Generation of Giants,* Notre Dame, 1962.

163. See above, p. 223. On anti-Christian movements in early modern history between the sixteenth and the eighteenth centuries, see George Wong; Liang Si-ing.

V. IN THE TWILIGHT

1. On Christianity in China, see the standard work by Latourette (L), and Cohen (2).
2. On Li Chih-tsao, see Hummel, 452–454 (L).
3. Cf. Cohen (1) (L).
4. Some extrasensory experiences which, according to literary sources, Taoist magicians believed they had had themselves or which they induced in their disciples do suggest that occasionally opiates may have played a role. But there is no clear-cut proof of this. It is difficult to decide to what extent the burning of large amounts of incense may have induced a trance-like state which led in turn to the introduction of opium smoking. Concerning the significance of intoxicants, especially wine, in Taoism, see above, pp. 149–151.
5. Hummel, 512.
6. The curious interconnections between Coleridge, a very modern figure in many respects, and the Far East and intoxication are brought out with great clarity by Schneider.
7. Hayter, 42.
8. Hayter, 39–41.
9. What is noteworthy here is that intoxication is precisely something that did not become part of Buddhism when it amalgamated with Taoism in the Buddhism of meditation (see above, pp. 162–163). Yet in an alien milieu, this aspect emerged again.
10. See above, pp. 100, 193, and 198–199.
11. Quincey, 194.
12. Quincey, 234.
13. Hayter, 51–52.
14. See below, p. 341.
15. Cf. Holt. Waley (5) gives an interesting insight into the spiritual atmosphere of the Opium wars from the Chinese perspective.
16. As the first western country, the Soviet Union, in 1918, voluntarily renounced its rights arising from the "unequal treaties."
17. See Meadows, 25. Vincent Shih surveys the literature on the Taiping rebellion, which has enormously increased in recent decades (2), 503–525.
18. Torr, 2–3.
19. See P. M. Yap.
20. J. C. Cheng, 6–11. The sources translated by Cheng were largely unavailable in the original. The quotations here are therefore taken from Cheng's English version.
21. On Yang Hsiu-ch'ing, see Hummel, 886–888 (L).
22. On the peaches of immortality, see above, pp. 96 and 190–191.
23. On the topos of the transmission of a book by a supernatural power as the sign that a new epoch is about to begin, see above, p. 124.
24. Cf. deBary (1), 649–651; J. C. Cheng, 76.
25. See above, pp. 118–119.
26. See above, p. 150.
27. Vincent Shih (2), 136.
28. Vincent Shih (2), 239.
29. J. C. Cheng, 4.
30. See above, pp. 224–225.
31. J. C. Cheng, 84.
32. See above, pp. 222 and 227.
33. J. C. Cheng, 82.
34. J. C. Cheng, 83.
35. On Li Hsiu-ch'eng, see Hummel, 459–463 (L).
36. *Lun-yü*, 12, 5. Cf. Legge (1), 1:253; R. Wilhelm (3), 121; Waley (2), 163–164.

37. See above, pp. 211–212.

38. Vincent Shih (2), 45. Where original sources are not indicated, quotations are from Vincent Shih's English version; the Chinese text here was not accessible.

39. Wang Hui-yüeh, 20:2. Cf. Vincent Shih (2), 47–48.

40. See above, pp. 167–168.

41. See above, pp. 24–25 and 245–250.

42. See J. C. Cheng, 143, note 10.

43. J. C. Cheng, 39–41.

44. See above, pp. 70–71.

45. See above, pp. 118–119, 205–206, and 409–410.

46. Vincent Shih (2), 51.

47. On this situation, which has been recurring time and again since the uprising of the Yellow Turbans, see, for example, above, p. 127.

48. See Vincent Shih (2), 98.

49. Wang Hui-yüeh, 20:21. See Vincent Shih (2), 62, and above, p. 214.

50. See above, pp. 113–114.

51. J. C. Cheng, 49.

52. See above, pp. 111–112.

53. J. C. Cheng, 47–48.

54. Wang Hui-yüeh, 20:2. See Vincent Shih (2), 47.

55. On Ward and Gordon, see Gerald Sparrow, *Gordon: Mandarin and Pasha,* London, 1962, and Hummel, 242, 465.

56. Vincent Shih (2), 131.

57. Vincent Shih (2), *ibid.*

58. Vincent Shih (2), 6.

59. J. C. Cheng, 83.

60. See Vincent Shih (2), 50.

61. Vincent Shih (2), 88–89.

62. Vincent Shih (2), 89.

63. J. C. Cheng, 89.

64. See above, pp. 83–84.

65. See Vincent Shih (2), 119.

66. See above, pp. 22–23 and 125–126.

67. Notice that the word *hung,* "great," already appears in the fifth and sixth centuries A.D. as the name of an expected Messiah, although it is as a personal, not a family name (see above, p. 126).

68. J. C. Cheng, 82.

69. Yen-lo is the sinicized form of the name of the vedic god of the dead, Yama, which became known in China when Buddhism came to that country. In popular belief, he became the ruler of hell.

70. J. C. Cheng, 90–91.

71. J. C. Cheng, 89. Since the second century A.D. at the latest, legends frequently have reported the falling of stars as a sign that new men would appear and a new epoch begin.

72. J. C. Cheng, 11.

73. In Chu Hsia-ch'in (p. 18) as in some other editions of the *T'ui-pei-t'u* as well, we find only the picture of two interlaced circles rather than the sun and the moon in the hands of a man. The signs *hung* "red" and *pai* "white," the two colors symbolizing sun and moon, are inscribed in them.

74. Vincent Shih (2), 129.

75. S. W. Williams, 2:623.

76. S. W. Williams, *ibid.*

77. Vincent Shih (2), 438. Shih, 491–498, for a detailed discussion of conflicting evaluations of the Taiping rebellion in modern China. See also Harrison, 80–82, 247–250 (L).
78. Vincent Shih (2), 453–457.
79. Vincent Shih (2), 497–498.
80. See the standard work by M. C. Wright (1) (L), and *loc.cit.* 19, note J for name of reign title.
81. Cf. Tseng's biography in Hummel, 751–756 (L).
82. See above, pp. 250–251.
83. See below, pp. 339–344.
84. See below, pp. 341–342.
85. On Yen Fu, see Schwartz (5) (L), and more generally on Huxley's influence on Yen Fu and the China of that time, especially 91–112.
86. The term "bedside reading" has the connotation of the secret and conspiratorial.
87. On Spencer's influence on the China of the time, see Schwartz (5), 32–37, 52–62, 72–80, 155–159.
88. See Brière, 20.
89. See above, p. 255.
90. On K'ang Yu-wei, see above, pp. 86–87. For his biography, see Lo Jung-pang (L); on his "utopistic" ideas, especially Hsiao Kung-chuan (1), (2), (3).
91. Lo Jung-pang, 28–29.
92. See above, p. 86.
93. See above, pp. 83–84.
94. Quoted according to Chung-kuo k'o-hsüeh-yüan, 60–62.
95. Cf. Onogawa Hidemi, 99 (there, November 11, 1901 is given as the date of Liang's comments).
96. Over extended stretches, the text of the *Ta-t'ung shu* makes an impression of great unevenness. It seems almost impossible that it should have been written without interruptions or even have been carefully edited. Some of its "utopian" proposals could only be considered sensational if one could be certain that they really were conceived early in the century.
97. Thompson (1), 27.
98. Thompson (1), 66–67.
99. K'ang Yu-wei, 78. Thompson (1), 74–75.
100. See above, pp. 80 and 83–84.
101. K'ang Yu-wei, 121 ff.
102. *Ibid.*
103. K'ang Yu-wei, 85. Thompson (1), 85, 130, note 19.
104. K'ang Yu-wei, 111.
105. See, for example, above, pp. 179–180.
106. K'ang Yu-wei, 122. Thompson (1), 99–100.
107. K'ang Yu-wei, 383–385. Thompson (1), 230–231.
108. K'ang Yu-wei, 122. Thompson (1), 99–100.
109. Among the more consequential measures taken by emperor Ch'in Shih Huang-ti in this regard was the standardization of the track width of vehicles, of weights and measures, and especially the standardization of the script which up to that time had consisted of partly quite dissimilar local styles. In a sense, this corresponds to K'ang Yu-wei's plan to create a universal language.
110. See above, pp. 73–74.
111. K'ang Yu-wei, 122, 124–132, 134–136. Thompson (1), 103–104. The reason the year 1900 seemed especially appropriate as the starting point for a new chronology to K'ang Yu-wei was that the beginning of the century also represented a certain break for

the West. It is noteworthy that K'ang's method of dating was adopted by only one group, the anarchists in China, who used it in at least some of the issues of their journal Min-sheng. (see below, p. 357): "in such and such a year of the new century" *(Hsin Shih-chi).*

112. See below, p. 357.
113. K'ang Yu-wei, 115–116. Thompson (1), 93–94.
114. K'ang Yu-wei, 123–125. Thompson (1), 101–102.
115. K'ang Yu-wei, 388–396. Thompson (1), 233–237.
116. K'ang Yu-wei, 401–403. Thompson (1), 238–239.
117. See above, pp. 80–82.
118. See above, pp. 21 and 80 where p'ing here means both "equal" and "peace." The "great order" *(ta-chih),* however, always had a somewhat legalist connotation even when that term was used by other schools. (See above, pp. 59 and 90).
119. See above, pp. 77 and 80.
120. K'ang Yu-wei, 170. Thompson (1), 135–136.
121. K'ang Yu-wei, 180. Thompson (1), 144.
122. K'ang Yu-wei, 177, 179. Thompson (1), 141, 143.
123. K'ang Yu-wei, 184–185. Thompson (1), 146.
124. K'ang Yu-wei, 185. Thompson (1), 146–147.
125. K'ang Yu-wei, 185–186. Thompson (1), 147.
126. On the preceding page, K'ang writes that this transitional process will require "a thousand and a few hundred years."
127. K'ang Yu-wei, 178–179. Thompson (1), 141–142.
128. K'ang Yu-wei, 179–180. Thompson (1), 143–144. On physical equality as presupposition for social equality, see above, pp. 167 and 169.
129. K'ang Yu-wei, 193. Thompson (1), 150.
130. K'ang Yu-wei, 224–225. Thompson (1), 155.
131. See above, p. 214.
132. K'ang Yu-wei, 245. Thompson (1), 159.
133. K'ang Yu-wei, 246–252. Thompson (1), 160–166.
134. K'ang Yu-wei, 259–260. Thompson (1), 171.
135. K'ang Yu-wei, 265–268. Thompson (1), 174–175.
136. K'ang Yu-wei, 286–288. Thompson (1), 181–182.
137. See above, p. 210.
138. K'ang Yu-wei, 288–289. Thompson (1), 183.
139. K'ang Yu-wei, 290–291. Thompson (1), 184–186.
140. *Ta-tai Li-chi,* 3, 48. Cf. R. Wilhelm (7), 259, 261.
141. K'ang Yu-wei, 315.
142. K'ang Yu-wei, 300. Thompson (1), 190.
143. The structure of the educational system set forth in the main text of the book differs insignificantly from the basic outline quoted above, pp. 316–317.
144. K'ang Yu-wei, 328.
145. K'ang Yu-wei, 327.
146. K'ang Yu-wei, 332. Thompson (1), 199.
147. See above, p. 79.
148. K'ang Yu-wei, 339. Thompson (1), 202.
149. K'ang Yu-wei, 450.
150. K'ang Yu-wei, 350. Thompson (1), 207.
151. K'ang Yu-wei, 355.
152. K'ang Yu-wei, 354–355. Thompson (1), 212.
153. See Thompson (2).

154. K'ang Yu-wei, 373. Thompson (1), 221.
155. See above, pp. 75–76.
156. K'ang Yu-wei, 358. Thompson (1), 216. The concept *t'ien,* here translated by "nature," has the basic meaning "heaven."
157. K'ang Yu-wei, 407. Thompson (1), 241.
158. K'ang Yu-wei, 407–418. Thompson (1), 242–246.
159. K'ang Yu-wei, 377. Thompson (1), 203. On Sun Yat-sen, see below, pp. 345–350 on the connection between medicine and politics in earlier times, see above, p. 113.
160. K'ang Yu-wei, 419–425. Thompson (1), 247–253.
161. K'ang Yu-wei, 426. Thompson (1), 254.
162. K'ang Yu-wei, 427. Thompson (1), 255. This comment alludes indirectly to the legend of a Taoist hermit of the type of the "immortals on earth" (see above, p. 104) who raised himself a few feet above the ground when he was reproached for his anarchist views. In that position, he said, he need pay his respects neither to the ruler of the earth, the emperor, nor to the rulers of heaven, the gods.
163. Direct allusion to Bismarck's well-known observation of 1862. See also below, p. 321.
164. K'ang Yu-wei, 429. Thompson (1), 258–259.
165. *I-ching,* hexagram 1 *(ch'ien).* Cf. R. Wilhelm (1), 1:5.
166. K'ang Yu-wei, 427. Thompson (1), 256.
167. See above, pp. 63–65.
168. K'ang Yu-wei, 428. Thompson (1), 257.
169. See above, pp. 244–245.
170. K'ang Yu-wei, 434–435. Thompson (1), 265–266.
171. This is actually a statement of Mencius: *Meng-tzu,* 1 A, 7. Cf. Legge (1), 2:141; R. Wilhelm (8), 8.
172. K'ang Yu-wei, 438–439. Thompson (1), 268–269.
173. Liang translated Jules Verne's story *Cinq semaines en ballon.*
174. See above, p. 108.
175. K'ang Yu-wei, 431–450. Thompson (1), 271–275.
176. See above, pp. 107–109.
177. K'ang Yu-wei, 452–453. Thompson (1), 275–276.
178. On the history of this text, see Hsiao Kung-chuan (4), 377. The very rare original text was unfortunately not available to me. The translation follows the English quotations in Hsiao Kung-chuan (2) and (4).
179. See Hsiao Kung-chuan (2), 171–172. It is likely that a certain impetus was provided by the novel *Seikai so-yuki (A Voyage in Spirit to the World of the Stars)* by the Japanese Inoue Enryo, written during the eighties of the last century, and modeled on Jules Verne. It is listed in one of K'ang's bibliographies.
180. Hsiao Kung-chuan (2), 173.
181. See above, pp. 181–189.
182. K'ang Yu-wei, 5–6. Thompson (1), 66–67.
183. Hsiao Kung-chuan (4), 389.
184. Hsiao Kung-chuan (2), 175.
185. Hsiao Kung-chuan (2), 179, 181.
186. Hsiao Kung-chuan (2), 177.
187. See above, pp. 154–157.
188. See Hsiao Kung-chuan (4), 388–389.
189. Even far into our own century, some Chinese scholars do not seem to always have made clear distinctions between genuine technical achievements in the West and science fiction stories.

190. See above, p. 181.
191. See above, pp. 184–187.
192. Hsiao Kung-chuan (4), 387.
193. Forke (1), 3:597.
194. There is little biographical data on Liu. Apart from scattered remarks in the *Tung-fang ta-t'ung hsüeh-an,* which include a sort of autobiographical poem (Liu Jen-hang, 6B:69–79), only two older reference works mention him: one written in English (Shanghai, 1936) (*Who's Who in China,* 167) and one which came out in Peking in 1940, in Japanese (Hashikawa Tokio, 671).
195. Concerning Japanese translations of western literature relevant here and available during the first two decades of this century, see *Taisho Showa hon'yaku bungaku mokuroku* (index of translated literature in the Taisho era [1912–1925] and Showa [as of 1926]), Tokyo, 1959.
196. K'ang Yu-wei is mentioned in Liu's book only once, in passing.
197. See bibliography.
198. Liu Jen-hang, 6 B:40–44.
199. Liu Jen-hang, 1:95–96. On the "children's rhymes," see above, pp. 74, 225, and 284–285.
200. Liu Jen-hang, 1:97–124.
201. Liu Jen-hang, 2:15.
202. Liu Jen-hang, 1:97. See also the considerably more detailed table 1:124.
203. Liu Jen-hang, 1:101–115.
204. Liu Jen-hang, 1:132.
205. On certain fundamental polarities in Chinese thought and their continuing effect in modern China, see Bodde (2); Nivision (1); R. Wilhelm (2); Schwartz (4); Levenson (2), 1:57–78, 114–117; 2:51.
206. See above, pp. 23–24 and 49–50.
207. See above, pp. 170–174.
208. See above, pp. 240–242.
209. See above, p. 213.
210. Cf. Nivision (1), 120.
211. Cf. Nivision (1), 116.
212. Interestingly enough, a similar principle now appears in modern China as all these traditional philosophers are assigned a place in the somewhat rigid schema "idealists" and "materialists": those called "traditionalists" or "revisionists" (at least by their adversaries) believe they observe materialist aspects in almost all old thinkers, while the "progressives" always think they can discover the cloven hoof of idealism in these very same philosophers.
213. See above, p. 172.
214. *Shu-ching (Shang-shu, Shuo-ming),* 2. Cf. Legge (1), 3:258.
215. Hu Shih (1), 1:729.
216. On Chang Chih-tung, see Hummel, 27–32 (L).
217. Actually, the conviction that China would have to adopt a hybrid, eastern-western culture already appears allusively among some literati before Chang Chih-tung. But it was only the popularity of Chang's book, which was translated a mere two years after its publication into English and French, that insured the general diffusion of these ideas in the West and the East.
218. See Hummel, 705 (L).
219. Brière gives an excellent survey of the various contending intellectual currents, 45–103.
220. On Liao P'ing, see Levenson (2), 3:3–15.

221. See Levenson (2), 1:83.

222. See Wo-jen's biography in Hummel, 861–863, and Levenson (2), 1:70–77; Chang Hao.

223. Cf. Chesneaux (1), 98.

224. On the Boxer Rebellion and its intellectual background, see Purcell (L).

225. Both as philosopher and as historian of philosophy, Feng Yu-lan has had enormous influence on the conceptions that came to be held concerning traditional Chinese intellectual life. This was true both in China and the West, where a number of his most important writings appeared in English. After the victory of communism in China, he became famous through his witty scientific articles (and autobiographical writings) where he managed to both surrender and maintain his earlier positions.

226. On the May Fourth Movement, see the standard work by Chow Tse-tsung (L).

227. Survey in Brière, 19–27.

228. On Sun Yat-sen and his relationship to modern, revolutionary systems of thought, see particularly Schiffrin (L).

229. During the course of his life, Sun Yat-sen frequently repeated and contradicted himself. Because he gave a variety of definitions of his Three People's Principles, the various editors and translators of his writings could present very conflicting views of his doctrine. There mere fact that these texts appeared in selections and that condensations were inevitable made this possible. In Wittfogel (3), for example, we find a "leftist" choice of texts. As late as ca. 1930, Wittfogel was still reproaching Soviet-Russian translators with having made a selection that was too pro-KMT (p. 153 ff.). A choice of texts which is rather "rightist" is that by Price, which was published in Taiwan.

230. Sun Yat-sen, 906 (speech given January 4, 1922).

231. See Wan Tsan, 9; Wittfogel (3), 60–67.

232. The work consists of four parts: 1. psychological reconstruction, 2. material reconstruction, 3. social reconstruction, 4. reconstruction of the government. The first three chapters of the fourth part are taken up by the discussion of the *Three Principles*.

233. Cf. Wittfogel (3), 165.

234. For Sun, this conviction constitutes the basis for all other considerations. For this reason, it is discussed in the long first section of his works, and serves as a kind of introduction. Partial translations: Wittfogel (3), 251–312; deBary (1), 783–786.

235. On this question, see above, pp. 140–141.

236. Sun Yat-sen, 163. Cf. Wittfogel (3), 244–247.

237. Sun Yat-sen, 256–258. Gangulee, 85–88. Cf. Price, 151–169.

238. Sun Yat-sen, 936–937. Cf. Wittfogel (3), 313.

239. Sun Yat-sen, 271. Similar versions in the translated selections by Gangulee, 91, and Price, 183–184.

240. Cf. Scalapino/Yu, 2.

241. An illustrated journal *Shih-chieh ("World")* appeared at the same time, but published only two editions and a supplement.

242. On Wu Chih-hui, see Kwok (1) (L); Forke (1), 3:635–647; Hu Shih (1), 3:82–107. DeBary (1), 840, differs from Kwok as regards his dates: 1865–1953. Actually, Chih-hui was his "style" by which respected personalities are generally referred to in public. His real name was Wu Ching-heng.

243. Wu Ching-heng (1), 8:49–51. Kwok (1), 163.

244. See above, pp. 134–140.

245. Cf. Forke (1), 3:640–641.

246. Kwok (1), 176. The ironic tone of Wu's comments here apparently escaped Forke (1), 3:643.

247. Quoted in Hu Shih (1), 3:100. Kwok (1), 179–180.
248. See bibliography.
249. Kwok (1), 161; cf. Forke (1), 3:647.
250. Kwok (1), 173.
251. Quoted in Hu Shih (1), 3:101. Cf. Forke (1), 3:646.
252. Wu Ching-heng (2), 159. Kwok (1), 166.
253. *Hsin Shih-chi,* 8:3 (August 10, 1907). See Scalapino/Yu, 11.
254. See above, pp. 24–25.
255. *Hsin Shih-chi,* 24:2 (November 30, 1907). See Scalapino/Yu, 8–9.
256. *Hsin Shih-chi,* 5:1–2 (July 20, 1907). See Scalapino/Yu, 15.
257. See above, pp. 127 and 181–182 and below, pp. 338–340.
258. Scalapino/Yu, 4.
259. Scalapino/Yu, 15.
260. *Hsin Shih-chi,* 6:2. Scalapino/Yu, 15–16. See also the essay by Li Ta-chao, referred to by Meisner (1), 307, which was unavailable to me (cf. below, pp. 374–381): *Yüan-sha: an-sha yü tzu-sha* (analysis of killing: assassination attempt and suicide) in: *Yen-chih* journal (words on governing), 4:11–16, (September 1, 1913).
261. On Kotoku Shusui, see Bernal (2), 123–125 (L).
262. Scalapino/Yu, 30. For the models named here, see above, pp. 138ff.
263. Kotoku Shusui, for example, even translated Enrico Malatesta's *Anarchia* into Japanese. Cf. Bernal (2), 116, note 81.
264. On Liu Shih-p'ei, see Onogawa Hidemi (L); Chow Tse-tsung, 1:62, note s.
265. See above, pp. 255–257.
266. See above, pp. 26–27.
267. Onogawa Hidemi, 90–91.
268. See above, pp. 236–265.
269. Onogawa Hidemi, 97.
270. See above, p. 227.
271. Onogawa Hidemi, 99.
272. Scalapino/Yu, 70, note 93, according to a report in the journal *Min-li pao* (January 26, 1912, p. 2).
273. On Liu Ssu-fu, see Bernal (1); Scalapino/Yu, 35–44 (L).
274. It is certainly no accident that "China" is referred to here by the phonetic transcription *Chih-na* (japanese *Shina*), which is normally used only in Japanese, and not with the customary Chinese expression *Chung-kuo* ("Middle Kingdom").
275. *Min-sheng (Hui-ming-lu),* 1:1–2 (August 20, 1913).
276. *Min-sheng,* 19:6–7 (July 18, 1914).
277. See above, pp. 232–234, for example.
278. Bernal (1), 1. Only ten fundamental rules are discussed there, however.
279. Scalapino/Yu, 36.
280. Scalapino/Yu, 44–54.
281. Cf. Chow Tse-tsung, 1:190, 425, note 54–57 (L); Meisner (1), 56, 275, note 9; Lang, 55, 296, note 91 (L).
282. See above, p. 334.
283. *Hsin Ch'in-nien,* 7, 2:129–134 (January 1, 1920). Another article by him on the same subject appeared in *Hsin ch'ao (New Tide),* 2, 1:69–80 (October, 1919).
284. Liu Jen-hang, 6 B:44.
285. Liu Jen-hang, 6 B:80–82.
286. Snow, 152.
287. On Liang Sou-ming, cf. Slyke and Chi Wen-shun (L).

288. This series of lectures was published in 1929. See Slyke, 457, note 1, 460; Brière, 27–29.
289. See Slyke, 463–468.
290. Slyke, 467.
291. See above, p. 25.
292. Brilliantly discussed by Skinner (L).
293. See p. 428, note 69.
294. Lin Yutang (2), 279.
295. Onogawa Hidemi, 71.
296. Cf. Boorman (2), 1:30–35.
297. See overview in Chow Tse-tsung, 1:327–337; Brière, 29–31; deBary (1), 834–843. Sources in Chang Chün-mai.
298. Cf. Chow Tse-tsung, 192, 233, 238.
299. For typical documents of the "New Life" movement, see deBary (1), 800–812.
300. What is fascinating in this process is the "echo effect" here, which can again be observed today in the influence of "Maoism." The originally western idea seems stronger, more genuine and fresher in its east-Asian version than in its original form. This is partly due, of course, to real changes in the former.
301. See above, pp. 164–165.
302. Lin Yutang (2), 126.
303. Lin Yutang (2), 123.
304. Lin Yutang (2), 277.
305. Lin Yutang (1), 58.
306. Lin Yutang (2), 6–7.
307. Lin Yutang (2), 112–113.
308. Nothing could be found out about Li Mi-an.
309. Lin Yutang (2), 114.
310. Lin Yutang (2), 131, 134. On Chin Sheng-t'an, see Hummel, 164–166 (L).
311. Lin Yutang (3), 256–257. There is no biography of Ting Hsiung-fei either in the official or in the better known private historical works.
312. Lin Yutang (3), 91–97. There are no precise biographical data on Chang Ch'ao.
313. See Lin Yutang (2), 148–151, 206–210, 261–265. Such essays can be found primarily in Lin Yutang's most famous book, *The Importance of Living.*
314. Lin Yutang (1), 49.
315. Hu Shih/Lin Yutang, 166.
316. See above, p. 250.
317. See above, p. 234.
318. See above, pp. 181–184.
319. A frequently quoted popular legend of the death of this most famous Chinese poet of the T'ang dynasty. It still plays a role during the moon festival (on the fifteenth day of the eighth month in the Chinese calendar) and evokes the (typically Taoist) association of moon-women-wine. Cf. Burkhardt, 1:49; 2:72.
320. On Wang Kuo-wei, see Smythe; *TP,* 26:70–71, 1928/1929 (Pelliot).
321. Compare Lin Yutang's view of Legalism and its most important representative Han Fei-tzu with this glorification of the "law."
322. Differently expressed: honor, fatalism and hierarchy, which characterized Confucianism in its late phase.
323. Lin Yutang (1), 354–364.
324. Payne, 3
325. Lin Yutang (1), 361.

326. Bodde (4), 127.

327. See above, p. 355 and Chow Tse-tsung, 1:42, note a.

328. See, for example, Chow Tse-tsung, 1:248–249; Meisner (1), 114–121.

329. On Li Ta-chao, see especially Meisner (1) (L); Huang Sung-k'ang (L). On Voitinsky, cf. Chow Tse-tsung, 1:243–244, 248–249.

330. The dispute revolved around the priority of science or politics, and thus turned on the age-old question whether there could be such a thing as a science uninfluenced by socio-economic conditions, something that Hu Shih basically affirmed, and Li Ta-chao denied. See Meisner (1), 105–114.

331. *Hsin Ch'ing-nien,* 4, 4:307–308, April, 1918. See Meisner (1), 50–51.

332. See Meisner (1), 158–160, 166–170; L. A. Schneider. Even much earlier, Chinese philosophers, such as Yang Chu, for example, had stressed the value of the "Now" as opposed to the Confucian conception (see above, pp. 46–47).

333. See above, pp. 77–80.

334. See above, p. 87 and note 36 (p. 447).

335. See O. Franke (6), 1:vii–xxvi, Pokora/Skalnik and Pulleyblank, and especially Tökei.

336. See Marcuse (1), 318–319.

337. See Meisner (1), 157.

338. Li Ta-chao, 294, 465. See Meisner (1), 161, 163.

338a. Shih Chün, 1249. See Meisner (1), 148–149.

339. Li Ta-chao, 356–357. See Meisner, 151–152.

340. Li Ta-chao, 50–51. See Meisner (1), 144.

341. Li Ta-chao, 120. See Meisner (1), 142.

342. Shih Chün, 1220. See Meisner (1), 147.

343. See above, p. 213.

344. See above, p. 339.

345. Li Ta-chao, 149. See Meisner (1), 82.

346. Li Ta-chao, 236–237. See Meisner (1), 87–88.

347. See Meisner (1), 185–188. There is already a faint suggestion of a tripartite division of the world in K'ang Yu-wei (see above, p. 306) and this notion is even present in Mao Tse-tung (poem *K'un-lun*). See Schickel 24.

348. Meisner (1), 191.

349. Li Ta-chao, 553–555. See Meisner (1), 228–229.

350. See above, pp. 234–236.

351. On Kuo Mo-jo, see Boorman (2), 2:271–276.

352. The disciples of Confucius named here have become types in the popular imagination, and this is reflected in the story quoted here: Yen Hui is the gentle person who, because of his own nature, understands the Master best ("John"-type); Tzu-lu is the somewhat simple-minded, valiant figure of child-like devotion ("Peter"-type), and Tzu-kung (the characteristically Chinese disciple as shown here) is principally versed in the externals of the teaching, in ceremonial and custom.

353. Part of the humor in the story derives from the fact that some of the language used by Confucius and his disciples comes from the classics (in the translation, such comments and observations appear in quotes). The observation about Tzu-lu's ardent temper is in Lun-yü, 5, 6. See Legge (1), 1:174–175; Waley (2), 108; R. Wilhelm (3), 40.

354. See *Lun-yü,* 1, 1. See Legge (1), 1:137; Waley (2), 83; R. Wilhelm (3), 1.

355. Cf. *I-ching,* commentary *Hsi-tz'u (Ta-chuan),* 2, 1. Cf. R. Wilhelm (1), 1:250.

356. See above, pp. 83–84.

357. See above, p. 21. The Chinese text permits both the translation given above: "One

should not be concerned if the people are few in number" and also: "One should not be concerned if the people have little," which it is essential to insert here. But it is likely that the former represents the intent of the text.

358. Cf. *Lun-yü,* 13, 9. See Legge (1), 1:266–267; Waley (2), 173; R. Wilhelm (3), 138.

359. Cf. *Lun-yü,* 12, 7. See Legge (1), 1:254; Waley (2), 164; R. Wilhelm (3), 122.

360. Parody on Lun-yü, 12, 5 (see Legge [1], 1:252–253; Waley [2], 163–164; R. Wilhelm [3], 121), where it says: "Ssu-ma Niu, [a disciple of Confucius,] said with sadness: 'All men have brothers, only I have none.' "

361. Parody on the same passage where Ssu-ma's complaint is answered by Confucius with the frequently quoted words: "Within the four oceans, all men are brothers of the superior man. Why then should he be troubled that he has none?"

362. The first two passages in this speech are a quotation from the book *Meng-tzu* 1A, 7 (cf. Legge [1], 2:143; R. Wilhelm [8], [9], the third passage is an invention).

363. Judging by his "style" (Chung-ni), Confucius was the second oldest of a number of brothers. To address someone by number was customary only among close relatives and considered very impolite when used by an outsider.

364. Cf. *Lun-yü,* 19, 25. See Legge (1), 1:348; Waley (2), 230; R. Wilhelm (3), 213.

365. Kuo Mo-jo, *Ma-k'o-ssu chin wen-miao* ("Marx Visits the Ancestral Temple of Confucius"), dated November 17, 1925, in: Liu Wu-chi, *Readings in Contemporary Chinese Literature,* New Haven, 1953, p. 7–17. This is the only source known to the writer, understandably the piece of Kuo Mo-jo translated here has not been included in his "Collected Works" which were edited after 1949.

366. On Ch'en Tu-hsiu, see Boorman (2), 1:240–248; Schwartz (1); Chow Tse-tsung, 1:42, note a.

367. See Trotsky (1); Schram (5), especially 44–47.

368. On Ch'ü Ch'iu-pai and Li Li-san, see Boorman (2), 1:475–479; 2:310–312.

369. Snow, 133. In the interval, a good many biographies and biographical data on Mao Tse-tung have appeared. See especially Schram (3) (L); Payne; Grimm (2); Boorman (1) (L); Snow; Siao Emi; Siao Yü. The last two books deal especially with Mao's interesting youth. Snow contains the important autobiography, which was dictated to him and later also translated back into Chinese.

370. Snow, 133.

371. Payne, 41.

372. Payne, 35–36. On Ch'in Shih Huang-ti and Han Wu-ti, see above, pp. 64–65 and 90–91.

373. Snow, 139–143.

374. Snow, 144–145. See also, Chow Tse-tsung, 1:348–349.

375. Snow, 148–149.

376. Snow, 151.

377. Snow, 151.

378. See Chow Tse-tsung, 1:348, note c. On Fu Ssu-nien, see above, p. 36.

379. Discussed in detail in Schram (1).

380. On the history of the CCP before 1949, see especially Guillermaz.

381. Mao Tse-tung (2) 1:300. All of Mao's quotes are from the *Collected Works* since the authorized translation has as much authenticity as the original. For an interpretation of all of the following passages on "contradiction" and "praxis," see especially Holubnychy, and Doolon/Golas.

382. Mao Tse-tung (2), 1:300.

383. See above, pp. 13–14.

384. Mao Tse-tung (2), 1:307–308.

385. Mao Tse-tung (2), 1:312–319.
386. Mao Tse-tung (2), 1:338.
387. Mao Tse-tung (2), 1:342.
388. Cf. R. Wilhelm (1), 1:273–282.
389. Cf. Holubnychy, 20–25.
390. Mao Tse-tung (2), 1:343–345.
391. Engels, *Ludwig Feuerbach and the Outcome of Classical German Philosophy,* New York, International Publishers, 1941, 11–12. Cf. Holubnychy, 23.
392. Mao Tse-tung (2), 4:412. The expression "Great Equality" *(ta-t'ung)* is translated by "Great Harmony" in the official translation.
393. See above, pp. 78–79.
394. See above, pp. 375–376.
395. White/Jacoby, 229.
396. Payne, 208. See above, pp. 190–191.
397. Mao Tse-tung (2), 1:308.
398. The important essay on "protracted war" is in Mao Tse-tung (2), 2:113–194 (May, 1938). Almost all of the ideas expressed in it can be linked to the Taoist-military tradition which dates back to the Han period at the latest.
399. See above, p. 119.
400. Mao Tse-tung (5). Cf. Grimm (1), 79, 87, 89.
401. Cf. Schram (5), 147–179; Meisner (2), 104.
402. See p. 444, note 72.
403. "Swallow Hill" evokes "Peking," whose old, classical name was *Yen,* "swallow." With two friends who were also condemned in the course of the Cultural Revolution, Wu Han and Liao Mo-sha, Teng T'o published a second series of essays. They were entitled "Notes from a Three-family Village" *(San-chia-ts'un cha-chi),* appeared in the journal *Ch'ien-hsien, Frontline ("Qianxian"),* 1961–1964, and created no less of a stir.
404. Teng T'o (2), 112–114 (*Ch'ien-hsien,* 1961, No. 21). See Glaubitz, 95–98; *The Great Socialist Cultural Revolution in China,* Peking, 1966, vol. 2, pp. 13–14.
405. See above, pp. 211–212.
406. *The Great Socialist Cultural Revolution in China,* Peking, 1966, vol. 2, pp. 14–15.
407. *Chuang-tzu,* 2:47. Cf. Legge (4), 241; R. Wilhelm (4), 19; Watson (2), 47. The wording in *Chuang-tzu* is a little different: it speaks of an impatient man who "when he sees an egg, immediately also wants a cock" *(chien luan erh ch'iu shih-yeh).* The *Chuang-tzu* passage is also quoted by Chiang Yin-k'o in his story.
408. *Hsüeh T'ao hsiao-shuo,* 6a–7a (=p. 1981).
409. Teng T'o (1), 20–22; (2), 45–48. Cf. Glaubitz, 66–68; *The Great Socialist Cultural Revolution in China,* Peking, 1966, vol. 2, pp. 26–27.
410. See Glaubitz, 192–193.
411. See *Chung-kuo che-hsüeh shih wen-t'i t'ao-lun chuan-chi.*
412. *Kung Ting-an ch'üan-chi,* 321.
413. *Hung Ch'i* (Red Flag), June 1, 1958:3–4. Cf. Schram (2), 252–253.
414. Mao Tse-tung (2), 2:339ff.
415. Cf. Schwartz (6), 11; Meisner (2), 104–109.
416. This inner transformation, even if more or less involuntary (and this is likely) and therefore not entirely honest is noteworthy nonetheless because it expresses an idealized process of purification. An interesting description of it can be found in the second volume of P'u-i's autobiography, which also appeared in English (Aisin Gioro Pu Yi, *From Emperor to Citizen,* Peking, 1964).
417. See above, pp. 85–86.
418. See above, pp. 181–183. Kuo Mo-jo's very successful stage play *(Ch'ü Yüan)*

(1942) which dramatizes the fate of this "loyal" rebel demonstrates to what extent Ch'ü Yüan was seen as an idol figure by the revolutionary Chinese of that period, including the communists. One can also sense here that the old historical figures are related to much more closely by the modern Chinese than is conceivable in the West.

419. See above, pp. 183–185.

420. See above, pp. 134–137.

421. The prototype of what may not be the good, but which is at least not simply the evil robber who, not only by his mere existence but also by his views casts doubt on all the apparently indubitable maxims of (Confucian) society already appears in the book *Chuang-tzu* in the form of the "robber Chih." An entire chapter (29) is devoted to him there.

422. See above, p. 234.

423. *Han-shu,* 62:2023a. Cf. Burton Watson, *Ssu-ma Ch'ien, Grand Historian of China,* New York, 1958, p. 63.

424. Mao Tse-tung (2), 3:177–178.

425. Mao Tse-tung (2), 2:377.

426. Cf. *Lieh-tzu,* 5:55–56. Cf. R. Wilhelm (5), 51–52, Graham (2), 99–101.

427. Mao Tse-tung (2), 3:272. On the symbolic meaning of "removing the mountains," see above, p. 437, note 59.

428. See above, pp. 18–19.

429. See above, pp. 184–187.

430. See above, pp. 261–262.

431. See above, pp. 263–268.

432. See above, pp. 324–329.

433. See above, p. 368.

434. See above, p. 455, note 319.

435. Snow, 122–123.

436. See above, pp. 91–92.

437. See above, pp. 96–97 and 180.

438. See above, p. 127.

439. Poem entitled "Swimming" *(Yu-yung),* June, 1956. (From: *Poems of Mao Tse-tung,* Eastern Horizon Press, Hong Kong, 1966, pp. 50–52.) Cf. Grimm (1), 11; Schickel, 31; C.N.Tay, 645–652. The "eve" of the "Great Leap Forward" here means the "Hundred Flowers Movement" which shows particularly close parallels to the Cultural Revolution since it was also an event in the cultural sphere.

440. *China Reconstructs,* 15,10:33 (October, 1966).

441. The Han dynasty (206 B.C.–A.D. 220), the first dynasty to be considered legitimate (after the calumniated Ch'in dynasty) and under which China was unified is considered the most "Chinese" of all dynasties down to the present day. In contradistinction to alien peoples living in China (Tibetans, Mongols, Miao, etc.) who are also considered "Chinese" in a wider sense, the Chinese living within the country even today refer to themselves as *Han-jen* (Han people). Interestingly enough, however, it was precisely the Han dynasty that was associated with two different elements or colors by two different traditions of the School of Five Elements (see above, pp. 75–76). They can be considered as the most significant, opposing elements in the sequence of five. Some chose earth/yellow, others fire/red. While since that time fire/red always implied unrest, rebellion and such (the Taiping, for example, wore red headbands as a "uniform"), earth/yellow tended to evoke conservative persistence (after all, yellow was the imperial color).

442. See above, p. 226.

443. See above, p. 227.

444. See above, p. 285.

445. See above, p. 390.

446. According to Payne, 42, the personal names of Mao's brother Tse-t'an and of his sister, Tse-hung, mean "morning" and "red." (Given the frequently observable reciprocal relationship between names of brothers) this would constitute an especially clear indication of the associations connected with Mao's own name. According to other sources, however, at least Tse-t'an's name was written with a character having a different meaning, i.e. "distant," "far."

447. *China Reconstructs,* 17,1:17 (January, 1968). The poem is considerably longer, but the verses quoted here are the first and best known.

448. See above, pp. 230–231.

449. See above, pp. 28–31.

450. See above, pp. 35, 365, and 428 (note 69).

451. See above, *Shih-chi,* 68:789b. Cf. Duyvendak (2), 14.

452. See above, pp. 114–116.

453. *Lü-shih ch'un-ch'iu,* 17, 2:202. Cf. R. Wilhelm (6), 267–268.

BIBLIOGRAPHY

Only those works cited in the text, or focusing on the themes considered here, have been included in this bibliography. Most of them contain references to additional literature on related topics; the most important of these are followed by the symbol *(L)* in this bibliography. Standard procedure has been used in listing works written prior to 1900 by Chinese authors under the title of the work, rather than the author's name.

Abbreviations

JOURNALS:

AM	*Asia Major,* Leipzig; New Series, London
AO	*Archiv Orientální,* Prague
BMFEA	*Bulletin of the Museum of Far Eastern Antiquities,* Stockholm
BSOAS	*Bulletin of the School of Oriental and African Studies,* London
CQ	*The China Quarterly,* London
HCP	*Papers on China,* East Asian Research Center, Harvard University, Cambridge, Mass.
JA	*Journal Asiatique,* Paris
JAOS	*Journal of the American Oriental Society,* Baltimore
JAS	*Journal of Asian Studies,* Ann Arbor
JRASNCB	*Journal of the North China Branch of the Royal Asiatic Society,* Peking
LSYC	*Li-shih yen-chiu,* Peking
MIO	*Mitteilungen des Instituts für Orientforschung der Deutschen Akademie der Wissenschaften,* Berlin
MN	*Monumenta Nipponica,* Tokyo
MS	*Monumenta Serica,* Peiping; Tokyo; Los Angeles
RBS	*Revue Bibliographique de Sinologie,* Paris
TP	*T'oung Pao,* Leiden
ZDMG	*Zeitschrift der Deutschen Morgenländischen Gesellschaft,* Leipzig; Weisbaden

COLLECTIONS OF TEXTS:

CKHSMC	*(Tseng-ting) Chung-kuo hsüeh-shu ming-chu* (Enlarged Collection of Famous Publications of Chinese Scholars). Taipei, 1962 ff.

CTCC	*Chu-tzu chi-ch'eng* (Complete Collection of Works of Chinese Philosophers). Peking, 1954.
HWPSCC	*Han Wei Liu-ch'ao pai-san chia chi* (Collection of Works of 103 Authors from the Han, Wei, and Liu-ch'ao Periods). Taipei, 1963.
PCHSTK	*Pi-chi hsiao-shuo ta-kuan,* with *hsü-pien* (Great Survey of Notes and Tales, with Supplement). New edition. Taipei, 1960–1962.
PNP	*Erh-shih-ssu shih* (The 24 Dynastic Histories). Ed. Po-na-pen. New edition. Taipei, 1967.
SPTK	*Ssu-pu ts'ung-k'an* (Collected Prints from the Four Library Sections). Shanghai, 1927 ff.
T	*Taishō (shinshū) daizōkyō* (Buddhist Canon). Ed. Takakusu Junjirō and Watanabe Kaigyoku. Tokyo (Taishō issaikyō kankō-kai), 1914–1932.
TSCC	*Ts'ung-shu chi-ch'eng* (Complete Collection of Collected Works). Shanghai, 1936 ff.
TT	*Tao-tsang* (Taoist Canon). Reprint. Taipei, 1962 ff.
WCHSTK	*Wu-ch'ao hsiao-shuo ta-kuan* (Great Survey of Tales from the Five Dynasties). Shanghai, 1926.

Works

Abe Masao, "Fushi, eisei, fusei" (Non-dying, Eternal Life, Non-Living). *Zengaku Kenkyū* 51:88–112 (Feb. 1961).

Abegg, Emil. *Der Messiasglaube in Indien und im Iran.* Berlin, 1928.

Balazs, Etienne (1). *Chinese Civilization and Bureaucracy.* New Haven, 1964.

——— (2). *Political Theory and Administrative Reality in Traditional China.* London, 1965.

——— (3). *La Bureaucratie celeste.* Paris, 1968.

Barthel, M. "Kritische Bemerkungen zu dem Lied-Gedicht 'Mulan.' " *MIO* 8:435–465 (1963).

Bauer, Wolfgang (1). *Chinas Vergangenheit als Trauma und Vorbild.* Stuttgart, 1968.

——— (2). "Der hastende Riese." *Merkur* 231:518–535 (June 1967).

——— (3). *Der Chinesische Personenname.* Wiesbaden, 1959.

——— (4). "Der Herr vom Gelben Stein." *Oriens Extremus* 3:137–152 (1956).

——— (5). "China, Verwirklichungen einer Utopie." *Propyläen-Weltgeschichte* 13: 129–196 (Berlin, 1965).

———, and Herbert Franke (trans.). *Die Goldene Truhe.* Munich, 1959.

Bernal, Martin (1). "Liu Ssu-fu and Anarchism in China" (Foreword to the reprint of the journal *Ming-sheng* [Voice of the People]). Hong Kong, 1967.

——— (2). "The Triumph of Anarchism over Marxism, 1906–1907," in Mary C. Wright (3), pp. 97–142.

Bielenstein, Hans (1). "The Restoration of the Han Dynasty." *BMFEA* 26:1–210 (1954); 31:1–288 (1959); 39:1–198 (1967).

——— (2). "An Interpretation of the Portents in the Ts'ien-Han-shu." *BMFEA* 22: 127–143 (1950).

Biot, E. (trans.). *Le Tcheou Li.* Paris, 1851.

Bloch, Ernst (1). *Geist der Utopie.* Berlin, 1923.

——— (2). *Das Prinzip Hoffnung.* 3 vols. Frankfurt/Main, 1968.

Boardman, Eugene. *Christian Influence upon the Ideology of the Taiping Rebellion.* Madison, Wisc., 1952.

Bodde, Derk (1). *China's First Unifier.* Leiden, 1938.

______ (2). "Harmony and Conflict in Chinese Philosophy," in *Studies in Chinese Thought*, ed. Arthur F. Wright, pp. 19–80. Chicago, 1953.
______ (3). "Myths of Ancient China," in *Mythologies of the Ancient World.* Garden City, N. Y., 1961.
______ (4). *Peking-Tagebuch.* Wiesbaden, 1952.
______ (5). "The Chinese View of Immortality: Its Expression by Chu Hsi and Its Relationship to Buddhist Thought." *Review of Religions* 6:369–383 (1942).
______ (6) (trans.). "Some Chinese Tales of the Supernatural." *HJAS* 6:338–357 (1942).
______ (7) (trans.). "Again Some Chinese Tales of the Supernatural." *JAOS* 62:305–308 (1942).
Boorman, Howard L. (1). "Mao Tse-tung: The Lacquered Image." *CQ* 16:1–55 (Oct.–Dec. 1963) *(L).*
______ (2) (ed.). *Biographical Dictionary of Republican China.* New York, 1967 ff.
Brandt, Conrad. *Stalin's Failure in China.* Cambridge, Mass., 1958.
Brière, O. *Fifty Years of Chinese Philosophy, 1898–1948.* New York, 1965 *(L).*
Brock-Utne, Albert. *Der Gottesgarten: Eine vergleichende religionsgeschichtliche Studie.* Oslo, 1936.
Broman, Sven. "Studies on the *Chou Li.*" *BMFEA* 33:1–89 (1961).
Bruce, Percy J. (1). *The Philosophy of Human Nature by Chu Hsi.* London, 1922.
______ (2). *Chu Hsi and His Masters.* London, 1923.
Burkhardt, V. R. *Chinese Creeds and Customs.* 3 vols. Hong Kong, 1953–1958.
Chan Wing-tsit (1). *Religiöses Leben im heutigen China.* Munich, 1955.
______ (2) (trans.). *Institutions for Practical Living and Other Neo-Confucian Writings by Wang Yang-ming.* New York, 1963.
______ (3) (trans.). *Reflections on Things at Hand: The Neo Confucian Anthology Compiled by Chu Hsi and Lü Tsu-ch'ien.* New York, 1967.
______ (4). "The Evolution of the Neo-Confucian Concept *li* as a Principle." *Tsing Hua Journal of Chinese Studies* (new series) 4, 2:123–149 (1964).
______ (5). *Historical Charts of Chinese Philosophy.* New Haven, 1955.
Ch'an-yüeh chi. Kuan Hsiu. *SPTK.*
Chang, Carsun (1). [See also Chang Chun-mai.] *The Development of Neo-Confucian Thought.* 2 vols. New York, 1957–1962.
______ (2) (with R. Eucken). *Das Lebensproblem in China und in Europa.* Leipzig, 1922.
______ (3). *The Third Force in China.* New York, 1952.
Chang Chün-mai, et al. [See also Chang Carsun.] *K'o-hsüeh yü jen-sheng kuan* (Science and Philosophy of Life). Shanghai, 1923.
Chang Chün-yen. "Tsai lun K'ang Yu-wei ti *Ta-t'ung shu*" (Another Look at K'ang Yu-wei's *Ta-t'ung shu*). *LSYC* 8:57–69 (1959).
Chang Hao. "The Antiforeignist Role of Wo-jen." *HPC* 14:1–29 (1960).
Chang Heng-ch'ü hsien-sheng wen-chi (Collected Prose Writings of Master Chang Heng-chü). Ed. Chang T'sai. *TSCC.* [See Eichhorn's (7) translation.]
Chang Ssu-k'ung chi (Collected Writings of Chang Ssu-k'ung). Ed. Chang Hua. *HWPSCC.*
Chang Tai-nien. *Chung-kuo wei-wu chu-i ssu-hsiang chien-shih* (A Short History of Materialistic Thought in China). Peking, 1957.
Chao Feng-t'ien. *Economic Thought during the Last 50 Years.* Peiping, 1939.
Chavannes, Edouard (1) (trans.). *Les Mémoires Historiques des Se-ma Ts'ien.* 5 vols. Paris, 1895–1905.
Ch'en Hao (ed.). *Li-chi chi-shuo* (Collected Annotations to the Book of Rites). *CKHMSC.*

Chen Huan-chang. *The Economic Principles of Confucius and His School.* New York, 1911.

Ch'en, Kenneth K. S. *Buddhism in China.* Princeton, N.J., 1964 *(L).*

Cheng, J. C. *Chinese Sources for the Taiping Rebellion in China 1850–1864.* Hong Kong, 1963.

Cheng Te-k'un (1). *Archaeology in China.* Cambridge, England, 1959 ff.

——— (2). "Travels of the Emperor Mu." *JRASNCB* 64:124–142 (1933); 65:128–149 (1934).

Chesneaux, Jean (1). *Les Sociétés Secrètes en Chine (XIXe et XXe siècles).* 1965 *(L).*

——— (2). "Egalitarian and Utopian Traditions in the East." *Diogenes* 62:76–102 (1968).

Chi Ch'ao-ting. "The Economic Basis of Unity and Division in Chinese History." *Pacific Affairs,* 7, 4:386–394 (December 1934).

Chi-lo-pien (Chicken-rib Book). Chuang Ch'ao (Chuang Chi-yü). *Shuo-fu* edition (new edition in one volume). Taipei, 1963.

Ch'i-shih yin-pen ching. T, text number 25:365–420.

Chi Wen-shun. "Liang Shu-ming and Chinese Communism." *CQ* 41:64–82 (Jan.–March 1970).

Chien Yu-wen. *T'ai-p'ing t'ien-kuo ch'üan-shih* (Complete History of the T'ai-p'ing t'ien-kuo). Hong Kong, 1962.

Ching-chieh hsien-sheng chi (Collected Writings of Master Ching-chieh). Ed. T'ao Ch'ien. *Ssu-pu pei-yao.*

Ching Heng (ed.). *T'ai-p'ing t'ien-kuo ko-ming hsing-chih wen-t'i t'ao-lun chi* (Collected Articles on the Problem of the Nature of the T'ai-p'ing Revolution). Peking, 1962.

Ch'ing-hsi k'ou-kuei (The Rebellion in Ch'ing-hsi). Fang Shao. *Ku-chin shuo-hai* edition.

Ching-hua yüan (Flowers in a Mirror). Li Ju-chen. *CKHSMC.* [See Lin Tai-yi's translation.]

Chou Fu-ch'eng. *Lun Tung Chung-shu ssu-hsiang* (On the Thought of Tung Chung-shu). Shanghai, 1961.

Chow Tse-tsung. *The May Fourth Movement.* 2 vols. Stanford, 1960 *(L).*

Chu Hsiao-ch'in (ed.). *Chung-kuo yü-yen pa-chung* (Eight Chinese Prophecies). Circa 1948.

Ch'u-tz'u (The Elegies of Ch'u). *CKHSMC.* [See Hawkes' translation.]

Chu-tzu wen-chi (Collected Prose Writings of Master Chu). Chu Hsi. *Cheng-i-t'ang ch'üan-shu.* [See Chan Wing-tsit's (3) and Graf's translations.]

Chu Yung-deh, Richard. "An Introductory Study of the White Lotus Sect in Chinese History." Ph.D. dissertation, Columbia University, 1967.

Ch'üan Han San-kuo Chin Nan-pei-ch'ao shih (Complete Collection of Poems from the Han Dynasty, the Three Kingdoms, the Ch'in Dynasty and the Northern and Southern Dynasties). 2 vols. Ed. Ting Fu-pao. Peking, 1959.

Ch'üan Shang-ku San-tai Ch'in Han San-kuo Liu-ch'ao wen (Complete Collection of Prose Literature from High Antiquity, the Three Ages, the Ch'in and Han Dynasties, the Three Kingdoms and the Six Dynasties). Ed. Yen K'o-chün. *CKHSMC.*

Chuang-tzu: Chuang-tzu chi-shih (Book *Chuang-tzu* with Collected Commentaries). *CTCC.* [See Legge's (4) Watson's (2), and R. Wilhelm's (4) translations.]

Ch'un-ch'iu fan-lu: Ch'un-ch'iu fan-lu chu (Rich Dew from the Spring and Autumn Annals, with Commentary). Tung Chung-shu. *CKHSMC.* [See O. Franke's (2) and Woo Kang's translations.]

Chung-kuo che-hsüeh shih wen-t'i t'ao-lun chuan-chi (Symposium on Problems of the History of Philosophy in China). Peking, 1957.

Chung-kuo jen-min ta-hsüeh and Chung-kuo li-shih chiao-yen shih. *Chung-kuo chin-tai ssu-hsiang-chia yen-chiu lun-wen-chi* (Collected Articles on Modern Chinese Philosophy). Peking, 1957.

Chung-kuo k'o-hsüeh-yüan, Che-hsüeh yen-chiu-so, and Chung-kuo che-hsüeh-shih tsu (eds.). *Chung-kuo ta-t'ung ssu-hsiang tzu-liao* (Materials on the Concept of Ta-t'ung in China). Peking, 1959.

Cohen, Arthur A. *The Communism of Mao Tse-tung.* Chicago, 1964.

Cohen, Paul A. (1). "The Anti-Christian Tradition in China." *JAS* 20:169–180 (1960–1961).

______ (2). *China and Christianity.* Cambridge, Mass., 1963.

Dardess, John W. "The Transformation of Messianic Revolt and the Founding of the Ming Dynasty." *JAS* 29:539–558 (1970).

deBary, Wm. Theodore (1) (ed.). *Sources of Chinese Tradition.* New York, 1960.

______ (2). "A Reappraisal of Neo-Confucianism," in *Studies in Chinese Thought,* ed. Arthur F. Wright, pp. 81–111. Chicago, 1953.

______ (3) (trans.). "A Plan for the Prince: The Ming-i tai-fang lu." Ph.D. dissertation, Columbia University, 1954.

______ (4). "Chinese Despotism and the Confucian Ideal: A Seventeenth-Century View," in *Chinese Thought and Institutions,* ed. John K. Fairbank, pp. 163–203. Chicago, 1957.

______ (5). "Some Common Tendencies in Neo-Confucianism," in *Confucianism in Action,* ed. David S. Nivison, pp. 25–49. Stanford, 1959.

Debon, Günther (trans.). *Lao-tse, Tao-Te-King.* Stuttgart, 1961.

Doolon, Denis J., and Peter J. Golas. "On Contradiction in the Light of Mao Tse-tung's Essay on 'Dialectical Materialism.'" *CQ* 19:38–46 (July–Sept. 1964).

Doré, Henri. *Recherches sur les Superstitions en Chine.* 18 vols. Shanghai, 1911–1938.

Doren, A. *Wunschräume und Wunschzeiten.* Leipzig, 1927.

Dubs, Homer H. (1) (trans.). *The Works of Hsüntze.* London, 1928.

______ (2) (trans.). *The History of the Former Han Dynasty.* 3 vols. Baltimore, 1938/44/48.

______ (3). "Wang Mang and His Economic Reforms." *TP* 35:219–265 (1940).

Dull, Jack L. "A Historical Introduction to the Apocryphical Texts of the Han Dynasty." Ph.D. dissertation, University of Washington, 1966 *(L).*

Duyvendak, J. J. L. (1) (trans.). *Tao Te Ching: The Book of the Way and Its Virtue.* London, 1954.

______ (2) (trans.). *The Book of Lord Shang.* London, 1963.

Eberhard, Wolfram (1). *Typen chinesischer Volksmärchen.* Helsinki, 1937.

______ (2). *Lokalkulturen im Alten China.* Part 1: *Die Lokalkulturen des Nordens und Westens.* Leiden, 1942. Part 2: *Die Lokalkulturen des Sudens und Ostens.* Peking, 1942.

______ (3). *Kultur und Siedlung der Randvölker Chinas.* Leiden, 1942.

______ (4). "The Political Function of Astronomy and Astronomers in Han China," in *Chinese Thought and Institutions,* ed. John K. Fairbank, pp. 33–70. Chicago, 1957.

______ (5). *Guilt and Sin in Traditional China.* Berkeley, 1967.

______ (6). "Beiträge zur kosmologischen Spekulation Chinas in der Han-Zeit." *Baessler-Archiv* 16:1–100 (1933).

______ (7). *Volksmärchen aus Südost-China.* Helsinki, 1941.

______ (8). *Die chinesische Novelle des 17. bis 19. Jahrhunderts.* Ascona, 1948.

______ (9). Review of *Bull. of the Inst. of History and Philology, Academia Sinica* 10 (1948), in *Oriens* 2:190–194 (1949).

Eichhorn, Werner (1). "T'ai-p'ing und T'ai-p'ing Religion." *MIO* 5:113–140 (1957).
——— (2). "Bemerkungen zum Aufstand des Chang Chio und zum Staate des Chang Lu." *MIO* 3:291–327 (1955).
——— (3). "Zur Vorgeschichte des Aufstandes von Wang Hsiao-po und Li Shun in Sze-ch'uan (993–995)." *ZDMG* 105:192–209 (1955).
——— (4). "Wang Chia's *Shih-i-chi.*" *ZDMG* 102:130–142 (1952).
——— (5). "Description of the Rebellion of Sun En and Earlier Taoist Rebellions." *MIO* 2:325–352 (1954).
——— (6). "Nachträgliche Bemerkungen zum Aufstande des Sun En." *MIO* 2:463–476 (1954).
——— (7) (trans.). *Die Westinschrift des Chang Tsai* (*Abh. f. d. Kde. des Morgenlandes,* 22, 7:1–85). Leipzig, 1937.
Erkes, Eduard. "Das Weltbild des Huai-nan-tzu." *Ostasiatische Zeitschrift* 5:27–80 (1916–1917).
Fahrle, Robert, and Peter Schottler. *Chinas Weg: Marxismus oder Maoismus.* Frankfurt/Main, 1969.
Fass, J. "Die Anfänge des Sozialismus in China." *Sinologica* 12:109–121 (1971).
Favre, B. *Les sociétés secrètes en Chine.* Paris, 1933.
Feng Yu-lan. [See also Fung Yu-lan.] *Chung-kuo che-hsüeh shih pu* (Supplements to the History of Chinese Philosophy). Hong Kong, circa 1936.
Ferrand, Gabriel. "Le K'ouen-louen et les anciennes navigations interocéaniques dans les mers du sud." *JA* 11, 13:239–333, 431–492; 11, 14:5–68, 201–241 (1919).
Feuerwerker, Albert. *Approaches to Modern Chinese History.* Berkeley, 1967.
——— and S. Cheng. *Chinese Communist Studies of Modern Chinese History* (bibliography). Cambridge, Mass., 1961.
Finsterbusch, Käte. "Motivgruppen und Darstellungsschemata der Han-Zeit." Certification essay for university professorship. Munich, 1970.
Fokkema, D. W. "Chinese Criticism of Humanism." *CQ* 26:71–72 (April–June 1966).
Forke, Alfred (1). *Geschichte der alten, mittelalterlichen, neueren chinesischen Philosophie.* 3 vols. Hamburg, 1964.
——— (2) (trans.). *Mê Ti, des Sozialethikers und seiner Schüler philosophische Werke.* Berlin, 1922.
——— (3). "Die Neueste Chinesische Philosophie." *Sinica* 10:68–90 (1935).
——— (4). *The World-Conception of the Chinese.* London, 1925.
——— (5) (trans.). *Lun-Hêng.* Reprint in 2 vols. New York, 1962.
Francis, J. de, and Zen Sun E-tu (1). *Bibliography on Chinese Social History.* New Haven, 1952.
——— (2) (trans.). *Chinese Social History: Translations of Selected Studies.* Washington, D. C., 1956.
Franke, Herbert (1). "Volksaufstände in der Geschichte Chinas." *Geschichte in Wissenschaft und Unterricht* 2:31–40 (1951).
——— (2). *Sinologie* (bibliography). Bern, 1953.
——— (3). "Chia Ssu-tao, a 'bad last minister'?" in *Confucian Personalities,* ed. Arthur F. Wright and Denis Twitchett, pp. 217–234. Stanford, 1962.
——— and Rolf Trauzettel. *Das Chinesische Kaiserreich.* Frankfurt/Main, 1968.
Franke, Otto (1). "Die wichtigsten chinesischen Reformschriften vom Ende des neunzehnten Jahrhunderts." *Bulletin de l'Académie Impériale des Sciences de St.-Pétersbourg* 17, 3:47–59 (Oct. 1902).
——— (2). *Studien zur Geschichte des konfuzianischen Dogmas und der chinesischen Staatsreligion.* Hamburg, 1920.
——— (3). *Ostasiatische Neubildungen.* Hamburg, 1911.

______ (4). *Li Tschi (Abh. d. preuss. Akad. d. Wiss., phil. hist. Kl.).* 1937 volume, 10. Berlin, 1938.
______ (5). *Das Tse tschi t'ung kien und das T'ung kien kang mu, ihr Wesen, ihr Verhältnis zueinander und ihr Quellenwert (Sitzber d. preuss. Akad. d. Wiss., phil. hist. Kl. 4).* Berlin, 1930.
______ (6). *Geschichte des Chinesischen Reiches.* 5 vols. Berlin, 1930–1952.
Franke, Wolfgang (1). "Die staatspolitischen Reformversuche K'ang Yu-weis und seiner Schule." *Mitteilungen des Seminars für Orientalische Sprachen an der Friedrich-Wilhelms-Universität zu Berlin* I, 38:1–83 (1935).
______ (2) (trans.). "Der Ursprung der Ju und ihre Beziehung zu Konfuzius und Lau-dsi" (by Hu Shih). *Sinica* (special edition) 1:141–171; 2:1–42 (1935–1936).
Freeman, Mansfield (1). "Yen Hsi Chai, a 17th Century Chinese Philosopher." *JRASNCB* 57:70–91 (1926).
______ (2). "The Philosophy of Tai Tung-yüan." *JRASNCB* 64:50–71 (1933).
Fu Lo-shu. "Teng Mu, a Forgotten Chinese Philosopher." *TP* 52:35–96 (1966).
Fu Ssu-nien. "Hsing-ming ku-hsün pien-cheng" (Discussion of Old Theories on Nature and Life). *Fu Meng-chen hsien-sheng chi* 3:1–201 (Taipei, 1952).
Fukui Kōjun (1). *Dōkyō no kiso-teki kenkyū* (Studies on the Principles of Taoism). Tokyo, 1952.
______ (2). *Tōyō shisō no kenkyū* (Studies on the Intellectual History of East Asia). Tokyo, 1955.
______ (3). *Gendai Chūgoku shisō* (Chinese Philosophy in Modern Times). Tokyo, 1955.
Fung Yu-lan. [See also Feng Yu-lan.] (1) *A History of Chinese Philosophy.* 2 vols. Princeton, 1952–1953 *(L).*
______ (2). *A Short History of Chinese Philosophy.* London, 1948.
______ (3). *The Spirit of Chinese Philosophy.* Boston, 1962.
______ (4). *Chuang-tzu: A New Selected Translation with an Exposition of the Philosophy of Kuo Hsiang.* New edition. New York, 1964.
Gangulee, N. (trans.). *The Teachings of Sun Yat-sen.* London, 1945
Garavente, Anthony. "The Long March." *CQ* 22:89–124 (April–June 1965).
Gatz, Bodo. *Weltalter, goldene Zeit und sinnverwandte Vorstellungen.* Hildesheim, 1967 *(L).*
Giles, Lionel. *A Gallery of Chinese Immortals.* London, 1948.
Ginsburg, Norton. "On the Chinese Perception of a World Order," in *China in Crisis,* ed. Tsou Tang, vol. 2, pp. 73–92. Chicago, 1968.
Glaubitz, Joachim. *Opposition gegen Mao: Die Abendgespräche am Yenshan.* Freiburg/Breisgau, 1969.
Graf, Olaf (trans.). *Djin-Si Lu.* 3 vols. Tokyo, 1953–1954.
Graham, A. C. (1). "The Date and Composition of Liehtzyy." *AM* (new series) 8:139–198 (1961).
______ (2). *The Book of Lieh-tzu.* London, 1960.
______ (3). *Two Chinese Philosophers: Ch'eng Ming-tao und Ch'eng Yi-ch'uan.* London, 1958.
Grimm, Tilemann (1), et al (trans.). *Mao Tse-tung: Ausgewählte Schriften.* Frankfurt/Main, 1964.
______ (2). *Mao Tse-tung in Selbstzeugnissen und Bilddokumenten.* Hamburg, 1968.
Groot, J. J. M. de (1). *The Religious System of China.* New edition. Taipei, 1964.
______ (2). *Sectarianism and Religious Persecution in China.* Reprint in 2 vols. Taipei, 1963.
Grosse Proletarische Kulturrevolution in China, Die. Peking, 1966.

Guariglia, Guglielmo. *Prophetismus und Heilserwartungs-Bewegungen als völkerkundliches und religionsgeschichtliches Problem.* Horn-Wien, 1959 *(L).*

Guillermaz, Jacques. *Histoire du Parti Communiste Chinois (1921–1949).* Paris, 1968.

Gulik, Robert van (1). *Sexual Life in Ancient China.* Leiden, 1961.

——— (2). *Hsi K'ang and His Poetical Essay on the Lute.* Tokyo, 1969.

Hai-nei shih-chou chi (Report on the Ten Continents between the Seas). Attributed to Tung-fang Shuo. *Wu-ch'ao hsiao-shuo ta-kuan* edition. Shanghai, 1926.

Hail, William J. *Tseng Kuo-fan and the Taiping Rebellion.* New Haven, 1927.

Haloun, Gustav. *Seit wann kannten die Chinesen die Tocharer oder Indogermanen überhaupt?* Leipzig, 1926.

Hammitzsch, Horst. *Cha-Do: Der Tee-Weg.* Munich, 1958.

Han Fei-tzu: Han Fei-tzu chi-chieh (Book *Han Fei-tzu* with Commentary "Collected Explanations"). *CTCC.* [See W. K. Liao's translation.]

(Ch'ien-)Han-shu (History of the Former Han Dynasty). Pan Ku. *PNP.* [See Dubs' (2) translation.]

Harrison, James P. *The Communists and Chinese Peasant Rebellions.* New York, 1969 *(L).*

Hashikawa Tokio. *Chugoku bunka-kai jimbutsu sokan* (Biographical Dictionary of Cultural Life in China). Peking, 1940.

Hattori Unokichi. "Confucius' Conviction of His Heavenly Mission." *HJAS* 1:196–208 (1936).

Hawkes, David. *Ch'u Tz'u: The Songs of the South.* London, 1959.

Hayter, Alethea. *Opium and the Romantic Imagination.* London, 1968.

Henke, Frederick G. (trans.). *The Philosophy of Wang Yang-ming.* Chicago, 1916.

Hentze, Carl (1). *Bronzegerät, Kultbauten, Religion im ältesten China der Shang-Zeit.* Antwerp, 1951.

——— (2). Tod, Auferstehung, Weltordnung: *Das mythische Bild im ältesten China in der grossasiatischen und zirkumpazifischen Kultur.* 2 vols. Zurich, 1955.

Herrmann, Albert. "Ta-Chin oder das China des Fernen Westens." *MS* 6:212–272 (1941).

Hertzler, Joyce O. *The History of Utopian Thought.* London, 1923.

Hightower, James Robert. "Ch'ü Yüan Studies," in *Silver Jubilee Volume of the Zinbun-Kagaku-Kenkyusyo,* pp. 192–223. Kyoto, 1954 *(L).*

Ho Ch'i-min. *Chu-lin ch'i-hsien yen-chiu* (Studies of the Seven Sages of the Bamboo Grove). Taipei, 1966.

Ho Hsin-yin chi (Collected Writings of Ho Hsin-yin). Liang Ju-yüan. Ed. Jung Chao-tsu. Peking, 1960.

Holt, Edgar. *The Opium Wars in China.* London, 1964.

Holubnychy, Vsevolod. "Der dialektische Materialismus Mao Tse-tungs." *Der Ostblock und die Entwicklungsländer* 8/9:15–59 (Hannover, Sept. 1962).

Holzman, Donald (1). "Les Sept Sages de la Forêt des Bambous et la société de leur temps." *TP* 44:317–346 (1956).

——— (2). *La Vie et la Pensée de Hi-K'ang.* Leiden, 1957.

——— (3). "Une conception chinoise du héros." *Diogene* 36:37–55 (1961).

——— (4). "Poésie et philosophie chez T'ao Yüan-ming." *Revue de Métaphysique et de Morale* 66:286–305 (1961).

Hou-ch'ing-lu. Chao Ling-chih. *Chih-pu-tsu-chai ts'ung-shu* edition.

Hou-Han-shu (History of the Later Han Dynasty). Fa Yeh. *PNP.*

Hou Wai-lu (1). *Chung-kuo ku-tai she-hui shih* (Social History of Ancient China). Shanghai, 1949.

——— (2). *Chung-kuo ssu-hsiang t'ung-shih* (General History of Chinese Philosophy). 5 books in 6 vols. Peking, 1962–1963.

______ (3) (ed.). *Chung-kuo li-tai ta-t'ung li-hsiang* (The Concept of *ta-t'ung* in Chinese History). Peking, 1959.

______ (4). "Chung-kuo feng-chien she-hui ch'ien-ch'i ti pu-t'ung che-hsüeh liu-chi ch'i fa-chan" (Philosophical Trends in Pre-feudal China and Their Development). *LSYC* 1:15–30 (1964).

______ (5). "Shih-liu shih-chi Chung-kuo ti chin-pu ti che-hsüeh ssu-ch'ao kai-shu" (Sketch of Progressive Trends in Sixteenth-century China). *LSYC* 10:39–59 (1959).

Howard, Richard C. "K'ang Yu-wei (1858–1927): His Intellectual Background and Early Thought," in *Confucian Personalities,* ed. Arthur F. Wright and Denis Twitchett, pp. 294–316. Stanford, 1962.

Hsi Chung-san chi (Collected Writings of Hsi Chung-san). Hsi K'ang. *HWPSCC* edition. [See Gulik's (2) translation.]

Hsi K'ang chi chiao-chu (Critical Collection of Writings of Hsi K'ang). Ed. Tai Ming-yang. Peking, 1962.

Hsi-wang-mu chuan (Biography of the "Queen Mother of the West"). Huan Lin. *Wu-ch'ao hsiao-shuo ta-kuan.*

Hsia Tsi-an (1). "Heroes and Hero Worship in Chinese Communist Fiction." *CQ* 13:113–138.

______ (2). "Demons in Paradise: The Chinese Images of Russia." *Annals of the American Academy of Political and Social Science* 349:27–37 (Sept. 1963).

Hsiao Kung-chuan (1). "K'ang Yu-wei and Confucianism." *MS* 18:96–212 (1959).

______ (2). "The Philosophical Thought of K'ang Yu-wei." *MS* 21:129–193 (1962).

______ (3). "In and Out of Utopia: K'ang Yu-wei's Social Thought." *The Chung Chi Journal* 7:1–18, 101–149; 8: 1–52. (Hong Kong, 1967–1968).

______ (4). "K'ang Yu-wei's Excursions into Science: Lectures in the Heavens," in Lo Jung-pang, pp. 375–407.

______ (5). "Li Chih: An Iconoclast of the Sixteenth Century." *T'ien Hsia Monthly* 6:317–341 (Shanghai, 1938).

______ (6). "Legalism and Autocracy in Traditional China." *Tsing Hua Journal of Chinese Studies* (new series) 4, 2:108–122 (1963).

Hsiang-shan hsien-sheng ch'uan-chi (Complete Works of Master Hsiang-shan). Lu Chiu-yüan. *CKHSMC.*

Hsieh Hsing-yao. *T'ai-p'ing t'ien-kuo ti she-hui cheng-chih ssu-hsiang* (Socio-political Concepts of the Taiping). Shanghai, 1935.

Hsien-chuan shih-i (Collected Remnants of Biographies of Immortals). Tu Kuang-t'ing. *Chiu hsiao-shuo.* Peking, 1957.

Hsin Ch'ing-nien (New Youth). Journal, reprint. Tokyo, 1962–1963.

Hsin Shih-chi (New Century). Journal. Paris, 1907–1910.

Hsin T'ang-shu (New History of the T'ang Dynasty). Ou-yang Hsiu, et al. *PNP.*

Hsiung Te-chi. "T'ai-p'ing-ching ti tso-che ho ssu-hsiang chi ch'i yü huang-chin ho t'ien-shih-tao ti kuan-hsi" (The Composition and Concept of the *T'ai-p'ing-ching* and Its Relation to the Doctrine of the Yellow Turbans and the Masters of Heaven). *LSYC* 4:8–25 (1962).

Hsü, Immanuel C. Y. (trans.). *Intellectual Trends in the Ch'ing Period.* Liang Ch'i-ch'ao. Cambridge, Mass., 1959.

Hsüeh T'ao hsiao-shuo (Stories of Hsüeh T'ao). Chiang Ying-k'o. *Hsü Shuo-fu (Ssu-pu chi yao).* Taipei, 1964.

Hsün-tzu: Hsün-tzu chi-chieh (Book *Hsün-tzu,* with Commentary "Collected Explanations"). Hsün Ch'ing. *CTCC.* [Compare Dubs' (1) translation.]

Hu Pin. *Chung-kuo chin-tai kai-liang chu-i ssu-hsiang* (Reformist Ideas in Modern China). Peking, 1964.

Hu Shih (1). *Hu Shih wen-ts'un* (Collected Works of Hu Shih). 4 vols. Taipei, 1961.

——— (2). "Lun Ju" (On the *Ju*), in *Hu Shih lun-hsüeh chin-chu.* Shanghai, 1936. [Compare W. Franke's (2) translation.]

——— (3). "Buddhist Influence on Chinese Religious Life." *Chinese Social and Political Science Review* 9:142–150 (1925).

——— (4). *The Chinese Renaissance.* New edition. New York, 1963.

——— (5). "Wang Mang, the Socialist Emperor of Nineteen Centuries Ago." *JRASNCB* 59:218–230 (1928).

——— and Lin Yutang. *China's Own Critics.* Peiping, 1931.

Huai-nan-tzu. Liu An. *CTCC.* [Compare Kraft's, Morgan's, and Wallacker's translations.]

Huang Siu-chi. *Lu Hsiang-shan.* New Haven, 1944.

Huang Sung-k'ang. *Li Ta-chao and the Impact of Marxism on Modern Chinese Thinking.* Paris–Hague, 1965.

Hulsewé, A. F. P. "Texts in Tombs." *Asiatische Studien* 18/19: 78–89 (1965).

Hummel, Arthur W. (ed.). *Eminent Chinese of the Ch'ing Period (1644–1912).* Washington, D.C., 1944.

I-ching: Chou-i cheng-i (The Book of Changes of the Chou, with Commentary "Definition of Meanings"). *CKHSMC.* [Compare Legge's (3) and R. Wilhelm's (1) translations.]

Ishiguro Noritoshi. "Kyō Jichin no shunjū kūyō gaku ikō ni tsuite" (On the Reformation of the Ch'un-ch'iu Kung-yang School by Kung Tzu-chen). *Jimbun Kagaku Kiyō* 39:87–103 (1966).

Ishijima Kairyū. "Kandai shoka no shūmatsukan ni tsuite no tenbō" (Chiliastic Concepts in the Philosophy of the Han Dynasty), in *Uchino Hakase Kanreki Kinen Tōyōgaku Ronshū,* pp. 45–56. 1964.

Itō Hideichi. "Shinkaron to Chūgoku no kindai shisō" (The Theory of Progress and Modern Chinese Thought). *Rekishi Hyōron* 123:33–45; 124:44–50 (1960).

Jao Tsung-i. *Yin-tai chen-p'u jen-wu t'ung-k'ao* (Researches into the Oracle Priests of the Shang Dynasty). Hong Kong, 1959.

Johnson, Chalmers A. (1). "The Two Chinese Revolutions." *CQ* 39:12–29 (July–Sept. 1969).

——— (2). *Peasant Nationalism and Communist Power.* Stanford, 1962.

Juan Pu-ping chi (Collected Works of Juan Pu-ping). Ed. Juan Chi. *HWPSCC* edition.

Jung-Pang Lo. *K'ang Yu-wei: A Biography and a Symposium.* Tucson, Arizona, 1967.

Jung Sheng. "Shih-lun T'ai-p'ing-ching" (On the *T'ai-p'ing-ching*). *LSYC* 11:47–59 (1959).

Kaizuka Shigeki. *Catalogue of the Oracle Bones in the Kyoto University Research Institute for Humanistic Studies.* Kyoto, 1960.

Kaltenmark, Max (trans.) *Le Lie-sien Tchouan.* Peking, 1953.

Kamiya Seizo. "Chugoku kodai shisō ni okeru sei, shih, kishin, toku no igi ni tsuite" (On the concepts "Life," "Death," "Spirit," and "Virtue" in the thought of Ancient China). *(Kagoshima Daigaku)* Bunka Hōkoku 11:27–55 (1962); 12:70–122 (1963); 13:33–60 (1964); *Bunka Hōkoku* (new series) 1:53–117 (1966); 3:1–44 (1967).

K'ang Yu-wei. *Ta-t'ung shu* (Book of the Great Equality). Shanghai, 1936. [Compare Thompson's (1) translation.]

Kao-shih-chuan (Biographies of Great Scholars). Huang-fu Mi. *TSCC.*

Kao Yu-kung. "A Study of the Fang La Rebellion." *HJAS* 24:17–63 (1962/63); 26: 211–242 (1966).

Karlgren, Bernhard (1). "The Early History of the Chou Li and Tso Chuan Texts." *BMFEA* 3:1–60 (1929).

______ (2). "Word Families in Chinese." *BMFEA* 5:9–120 (1933).
______ (3). "Legends and Cults in Ancient China." *BMFEA* 18:199–365 (1946).
______ (4) (trans.). *The Book of Odes.* Stockholm, 1950.
______ (5) (trans.). *The Book of Documents.* Stockholm, 1950.
______ (6). *Grammata Serica Recensa.* Stockholm, 1957.
Kern, H. (trans.). *The Saddharma-pundarika or the Lotos of the True Law.* Vol. 21 of *The Sacred Books of the East,* ed. F. Max Müller. Oxford, 1884.
Kindermann, Gottfried-Karl (ed.). *Konfuzianismus, Sunyatsenismus und chinesischer Kommunismus.* Freiburg/Breisgau, 1963.
Koyanagi Shikita. *Tōyō shisō no kenkyū* (Studies in Far Eastern Thought). 2 vols. Tokyo, 1942–1943.
Kraft, Eva (trans.). "Zum *Huai-nan-tzu*" (On *Huai-nan-tzu). MS* 16:191–286 (1957); 17:128–207 (1958).
Ku Chieh-kang (ed.). *Ku-shih pien* (Debates on Ancient History). 7 vols. New edition. Hong Kong, 1962.
Ku-chin T'u-shu chi-ch'eng (Collection of Pictures and Writings from Ancient and Modern Times). Encyclopedia. New edition. Taipei, 1961.
Kubo Noritada. "Sodai no shin dōkyō kyōdan" (Neo-Taoist Religious Societies during the Sung Dynasty). *Rekishi Kyōiku* 12:53–59 (1964).
Kung Ting-an ch'üan-chi (Complete Works of Kung Ting-an). Ed. Kung Tzu-chen. *Kuo-hsüeh wen-k'u.* Taipei, 1963.
Kung-yang i-su (Kung-yang [chuan] with Commentaries). *Kuo-hsüeh chi-pen ts'ung-shu.* Shanghai, 1936.
Kuo Hung-nung chi (Collected Works of Kuo Hung-nung). Kuo P'u. *HWPSCC.*
Kuo Mo-jo (1). *Yin-ch'i sui-pien* (Manual of Yin documents). Peking, 1965.
______ (2). *Kuo Mo-jo wen-chi* (Collected Works of Kuo Mo-jo). Peking, 1957 ff.
Kurita Naomi. "Jōdai Shina shisō ni okeru 'ji' to jikan" ("Time" and Period in the Thinking of Ancient China). *Waseda Daigaku Daigaku-in Bungaku Kenkyū-ka Kiyō* 9:1–24 (1963).
Kwok, D. Wynn-Ye (1). "Wu Chih-hui and Scientism." *Tsing Hua Journal of Chinese Studies* (new series) 3, 1:160–186 (Taipei, May 1962).
______ (2). *Scientism in Chinese Thought 1900–1950.* New Haven, 1965 *(L).*
Lang, Olga. *Pa Chin and His Writings.* Cambridge, Mass., 1967.
Lang-huan chi (Report on Lang-huan), in *Hsüeh-chin t'ao-yüan,* ed. I Shih chen. Shanghai, 1922.
Latourette, K. S. *A History of Christian Missions in China.* New York, 1929.
Legge, James (1) (trans.). *The Chinese Classics.* 5 vols. Reprint. Hong Kong, 1960.
______ (2) (trans.). *The Sacred Books of China,* in *Sacred Books of the East,* ed. F. Max Müller, vols. 3, 16, 27, 28. Oxford, 1899.
______ (3) (trans.). *The* "I Ching": *The Book of Changes.* Reprint. New York, 1963.
______ (4) (trans.). *Tao Te Ching and the Writings of Chuang Tzu.* New edition. Taipei, 1963.
Lei Hai-tsung. "Periodization: Chinese History and World History." *Chinese Social and Political Science Review* 20:461–491 (1936/37).
Leumann, E. *Maitreya-Samiti: Das Zukunftsideal der Buddhisten.* Strassburg, 1919.
Levenson, Joseph R. (1). *Liang Ch'i-ch'ao and the Mind of Modern China.* Berkeley, 1967.
______ (2). *Confucian China and Its Modern Fate: A Trilogy.* 3 vols. Berkeley, 1968.
______ (3). "Communist China in Time and Space: Roots and Rootlessness." *CQ* 39:1–11 (July–Sept. 1969).

Levy, Howard (1). "Yellow Turban Religion and Rebellion at the End of the Han." *JAOS* 76:214–227 (1956).

——— (2). "The Bifurcation of the Yellow Turbans in Later Han." *Oriens* 13/14: 251–255 (1960/61).

——— (3). *Chinese Footbinding.* New York, 1966.

Lewis, John W. "Leader, Commissar, and Bureaucrat: The Political System in the Last Days of the Revolution," in *China in Crisis,* ed. Tsou Tang, vol. 1, pp. 449–500. Chicago, 1968.

Li-chi chi-shuo (The Book of Rites, with commentary "Collected Sayings"). *CKHSMC.*

(Ta Tai) Li-chi chieh-ku (The Ta Tai Book of Rites, with commentary "Explanations and Interpretations") *CKHSMC.*

Li Kuang-pi, et al (ed.). *Chung-kuo nung-min ch'i-i lun-chi* (Collected Articles on Peasant Uprisings in China). Peking. 1958.

Li, Lillian M. "The Ever-Victorious Army." *HPC* 21:1–42 (1968).

Li Ta-chao. *Li Ta-chao hsuan-chi* (Selected Writings of Li Ta-chao). Peking, 1959.

Liang Ch'i-ch'ao. *Ch'ing-tai hsüeh-shu kai-lun* (Outline of Scholarship during the Ch'ing Dynasty). Hong Kong, 1963.

Liang Ch'i-ch'ao. *See* Hsü, Immanuel C. Y.

Liang Si-ing. "La rencontre et le conflict entre les idées des Missionnaires chrétiens et les idées des Chinois en Chine depuis la fin des Ming." Ph.D. dissertation, Paris, 1940.

Liao, W. K. (trans.). *The Complete Works of Han Fei Tzu.* 2 vols. London, 1959.

Liebenthal, Walter (1). *The Book of Chao.* Peking, 1948.

——— (2). "The Immortality of the Soul in Chinese Thought." *MN* 8:327–397 (1952).

——— (3). "A Biography of Chu Tao-sheng." *MN* 11:284–316 (1955).

——— (4). "Chinese Buddhism during the 4th and 5th Centuries." *MN* 11:44–83 (1955).

Lieh-hsien chuan (Biographies of Immortals). Attributed to Liu Hsiang. *TSCC.* [See Kaltenmark's translation.]

Lieh-tzu: Lieh-tzu chu (Book *Lieh-tzu* with Commentary). *CTCC.* [See Graham's (2) and R. Wilhelm's (5) translations.]

Lien Chan. "Chinese Communism Versus Pragmatism." *JAS* 27, 3:551–570 (May 1968).

Lifton, Robert J. *Revolutionary Immortality: Mao Tse-tung and the Chinese Cultural Revolution.* New York, 1968.

Lin Mousheng. *Men and Ideas: An Informal History of Chinese Political Thought.* New York, 1942.

Lin Tai-yi (trans.). *Flowers in the Mirror.* London, 1965.

Lin Yutang (1). *My Country and My People.* New York, 1935.

——— (2). *The Importance of Living.* New York, 1937.

——— (3). *The Importance of Understanding.* New York, 1960.

Liu Chun-jo. Controversies in Modern Chinese Intellectual History (bibliography). Cambridge, Mass., 1964.

Liu, James J. Y. *The Chinese Knight Errant.* Chicago, 1966.

Liu, James T. C. *Reform in Sung China: Wang An-shih and His New Policies.* Cambridge, Mass., 1959.

Liu Jen-hang. *Tung-fang ta-t'ung hsüeh-an* (Outline of the *ta-t'ung* in the East). Shanghai, 1926.

Liu Kwang-ching. "Nineteenth-Century China: The Disintegration of the Old Order and the Impact of the West," in *China in Crisis,* ed. Tsou Tang, vol. 1, pp. 93–202. Chicago, 1968.

Liu Ssu-fu. *See* Shih-fu.

Lo Jung-pang (ed.). K'ang Yu-wei: A Biography and a Symposium. Tucson, Arizona, 1967 *(L)*.

Löwith, Karl. *Weltgeschichte und Heilsgeschehen.* Stuttgart, 1967.

Lu-i chi (Notes on Marvels). Tu Kuang-t'ing. *Shuo-k'u* edition.

Lü-shih ch'un-ch'iu (Spring and Autumn of Master Lü). Attributed to Lü Pu-wei. *CTCC.* [See R. Wilhelm's (6) translation.]

Lun-yü: Lun-yü cheng-i (*Analects* of Confucius, with Commentary "Definition of Meanings"). *CTCC.* [See Legge's (1), Waley's (2), and R. Wilhelm's (3) translations.]

Lung-ch'eng lu (Notes from the Dragon City). Liu Tsung-yüan. *Shuo-k'u.*

Lutz, Jessie G. *Christian Missions in China: Evangelist or What?* Boston, 1965.

MacNair, H. F. *China.* Berkeley, 1951.

Maenchen-Helfen, Otto. "The Later Books of the Shan-hai-king." *AM* 1:550–586 (1924).

Mannheim, Karl. *Ideologie und Utopie.* Frankfurt/Main, 1965.

Mao Tse-tung (1). *Mao Tse-tung hsüan-chi* (Selected Works [of Mao Tse-tung]). 4 vols. Peking, 1966. [See translation (2).]

______ (2). *Ausgewählte Werke.* 4 vols. Peking, 1968/69.

______ (3). *Mao chu-hsi shih-tz'u* (Poems of Chairman Mao). Peking, 1963. [See Schickel's translation.]

______ (4). "On Dialectical Materialism: A Fragment." *Studies in Soviet Thought* 3, 1:270–277 (March 1963).

______ (5). "Kuan-yü cheng-ch'üeh ch'u li jen-min nei-pu mao-tun ti wen-t'i" (On the Question of Correctly Resolving Contradictions among the People). *Jen-min jih-pao* (Peking *People's Daily*), June 18, 1957. [See Grimm's (1) translation, pp. 78–102.]

Marcuse, Herbert (1). *Reason and Revolution.* New York, 1954.

______ (2). *Kultur und Gesellschaft.* Frankfurt/Main, 1965.

______ (3). *Das Ende der Utopie.* Berlin, 1967.

Marx, Karl, and Friedrich Engels (1). *Manifest der Kommunistischen Partei.* New edition. Stuttgart, 1970.

______ (2). *Ausgewählte Schriften.* 2 vols. Moscow, 1950.

Maspero, Henri (1). "Le procédés de 'nourir le principe vital' dans la religion taoiste ancienne." *JA* 229:177–252, 353–430 (1937).

______ (2). *Le Taoisme.* Paris, 1950.

______ (3). *Les Religions Chinoises.* Paris, 1950.

Mather, Richard B. "Chinese Letters and Scholarship in the Third and Fourth Centuries: the *Wen-hsüeh p'ien* of the *Shih-shuo hsin-yü.*" *JAOS* 84:348–391 (Oct.–Dec. 1964).

Meadows, Thomas T. *The Chinese and Their Rebellions.* Stanford, 1953.

Meisner, Maurice (1). *Li Ta-chao and the Origin of Chinese Marxism.* Cambridge, Mass., 1968 *(L.)*

______ (2). "Utopian Goals and Ascetic Values in Chinese Communist Ideology." *JAS* 28:101–110 (Nov. 1968).

Meng-tzu: Meng-tzu cheng-i (Book *Meng-tzu* with commentary "Definition of Meanings"). *CTCC.*

Meng-tzu tzu-i shu-cheng (Explanations of Characters and Meanings in the Book *Meng-tzu*). Tai Chen. *CKHSMC.*

Meskill, John. *The Pattern of Chinese History: Cycles, Development or Stagnation?* Lexington, Mass., 1965.

Michaud, Paul. "The Yellow Turbans." *MS* 17:47–127 (1958) *(L)*.

Ming-Fou lun (On the Buddha). Tsung Ping. *T,* text number 2102. Vol. 3, pp. 9–16.

Ming-i tai-fang lu (Waiting for an Answer [to the question] Where to Go after the Darkening of Light). Huang Tsung-hsi. *CKHSMC.*

Min-sheng (People's Voice), formerly *Hui-ming-lu* (Cockcrow in the Darkness). Journal. Reprint. Hong Kong, 1967.

Ming-shan tung-t'ien fu-ti chi (Report on Cave-heavens and Countries of Happiness on Famous Mountains). Tu Kuang-t'ing. *Wu-ch'ao hsiao-shuo.*

Ming-shih (History of the Ming Dynasty). Chang T'ing-yü, et al. *PNP.*

Miyakawa Hisayuki (1). "An Outline of the Naitō Hypothesis and Its Effects on Japanese Studies of China." *Far Eastern Quarterly* 14, 4:533–552 (August 1955).

——— (2). *Rikuchōshi kenkyū: Shūkyō hen* (Studies in the History of the Six Dynasties: Religion). Kyoto, 1964.

Mo-chuang man-lu (Idle Reports from the India-Ink Village). Chang Pang-chi. *Pai-hai.*

Mo-tzu: Mo-tzu hsien-ku (Book *Mo-tzu,* with Commentary "General Interpretations"). *CTCC.* [Compare Forke's (2) translation.]

Mochizuki Shinkō. *Shina jōdo Kyōri-shi* (History of the Pure Land Idea in China). New edition. Tokyo, 1964.

Morgan, Evan (trans.). *Tao, the Great Luminant.* Reprint. Taipei, 1966.

Mote, Frederick W. (1). "Confucian Eremetism in the Yüan Period," in *The Confucian Persuasion,* ed. Arthur F. Wright, pp. 202–240. Stanford, 1960.

——— (2). "The Growth of Chinese Despotism." *Oriens Extremus* 8:1–41 (1961).

Moy, Clarence, "Kuo Mo-jo and the Creation Society." *HPC* 4:131–159 (1950).

Mu-t'ien-tzu chuan (Biography of the Son of Heaven Mu). *Ssu-pu pei-yao* edition. [See Cheng Te-k'un's (2) translation.]

Mucchielli, Roger. *Le Mythe de la Cité idéale.* Paris, 1960.

Muller, F. Max (trans.). *The Larger Sukhāvatí-vyūha and The Smaller Sukhāvatí-vyūha,* in *The Sacred Books of the East,* ed. F. Max Muller. Vol. 49. Oxford, 1894.

Munro, Donald J. *The Concept of Man in Early China.* Stanford, 1969.

Muramatsu Yuji. "Some Themes in Chinese Rebel Ideologies," in *The Confucian Persuasion,* ed. Arthur F. Wright, pp. 241–267. Stanford, 1960.

Murphey, Rhoads. "Man and Nature in China." *Modern Asian Studies* 1, 4:313–334 (London, 1967).

Naitō Shigenobu. "Chūgoku kakumei shisō no tenkai" (The Beginning of Revolutionary Thought in China). *Tōyō Gakujutsu Kenkyū* 5/6:35–50 (1965).

Nakano Tōru. " 'Suihaizu' shotan." *Tōhō Shūkyō* 36: 20–37 (1970).

Needham, Joseph (1). *Science and Civilization in China.* Cambridge, England, 1961 ff. *(L).*

——— (2). *Time and Eastern Man.* London, 1965 *(L).*

Nivison, David S. (1). "The Problem of 'Knowledge' and 'Action' in Chinese Thought since Wang Yang-ming," in *Studies in Chinese Thought,* ed. Arthur F. Wright, pp. 112–145. Chicago, 1953.

——— (2). "Protest against Conventions and Conventions of Protest," in *The Confucian Persuasion,* ed. Arthur F. Wright, pp. 177–201. Stanford, 1960.

Obi Kōichi. *Chugoku bungaku ni arawareta shizen to shizenkan* (Nature and Reflection on Nature in Chinese Literature). Tokyo, 1962.

Obuchi Ninji (1). *Dōkyō shi no kenkyū* (Studies in the History of Taoist Religion). Okayama, 1964.

——— (2). "Gotobeidō no kyōhō" (On the Religious Laws of the Five Pecks of Rice Taoists). *Tōyō Gakuhō* 49, 3:40–68 (1966).

Ogata Nobuo. "Sengoku jidai-jin no 'seimei ishiki' ni tsuite" (The "Knowledge of Life" during the Period of Warring States). *Tōkyō Kyōiku Daigaku Bungakubu Kiyō* 47 (*Kokubungaku Kanbungaku Ronsō* 9):1–31 (1964).

Onogawa Hidemi. "Liu Shih-p'ei and Anarchism." *Acta Asiatica* 12:70–99 (Tokyo, 1967).

Otake Fumio. "Chūgoku jimmin kōsha no keifu" (Genealogy of the People's Commune

in China), in *Tōhō Gakkai Sōritsu Jū-go Shūnen Kinen Tōhōgaku Ronshū*, pp. 50–62. Tokyo, 1962.
Pao-p'u-tzu (Writings of the Master Who Embraces Simplicity"). Ko Hung. *CTCC.* [See Schubert's and Ware's translations.]
Pao ts'an-chün shih-chu (Poems of the Vice-general Pao, with Commentary). Pao Chao (commentary by Huang Chieh). Peking, 1957.
Parsons, James (1). "The Culmination of a Chinese Peasant Rebellion: Chang Hsien-chung in Szechwan, 1644–45." *JAS* 16, 3:387–400 (May 1957).
______ (2). "Attitudes toward the Late Ming Rebellions." *Oriens Extremus* 6:177–209 (1959).
Payne, Robert. *Mao Tse-tung: Eine Biographie.* Hamburg, 1965.
Pei-shih (History of the Northern Dynasties). Li Yen-shou, et al. *PNP.*
Pfizmaier, August (1) (trans.). "Die Lösung der Leichname und Schwerter." *Sitzungsber. d. kais. Ak. d. Wiss. zu Wien, phil.-hist. Kl.* 65:26–57 (1870).
______ (2). "Die Lebensverlängerung der Männer des Weges." *ebenda* 64:311–376 (1870).
Pien-tsung-lun (Discussion of essentials). Hsieh Ling-yün. In *Kuang Hung-ming chi. T.* Text number 2103.4.6: 224–228.
Po-i-chih (Recollections of All Kinds of Marvels) Cheng Huan-ku. *Yang-shan Ku-shih wen-fang* (Book Chamber of Master Ku from the Yang Mountain).
Po-wu-chih (Recollections of All Kinds of Strange Things). Chang Hua. *TSCC.*
Po-ya ch'in (Po-ya's Lute). Teng Mu. *Chung-kuo ssu-hsiang shih tzu-liao ts'ung-k'an.* Peking, 1960.
Pokora, Timoteus (1). "On the Origin of the Notions T'ai-p'ing and Ta-t'ung in Chinese Philosophy." *AO* 29:448–454 (1961) *(L).*
______ (2). "Notes on New Studies on Tung Chung-shu." *AO* 33:407 (1965).
______ (3). "A Theory of the Periodisation of World History." *AO* 34:602–605 (1966).
______ (4). "The Concept of Progress in Confucianism." *East and West* 17, 3/4:302–305 (Sept.–Dec. 1967).
______ and P. Skalnik. "The Beginning of the Discussion about the Asiatic Mode of Production in the USSR and the People's Republic of China." *Eirene* 6:179–187 (1966).
Price, Frank W. (trans.). *San Min Chu I: The Three Principles of the People by Sun Yat-sen.* Taipei, n.d.
Pulleyblank, E. G. *Chinese History and World History.* Cambridge, England, 1950.
Purcell, Victor. *The Boxer Uprising.* Cambridge, Mass., 1963 *(L).*
Quincey, Thomas de. *Confessions of an English Opium Eater.* London, 1956.
Ray, David Tod. "Kuo Mo-jo: The Pre-Marxist Phase, 1892–1924." *HPC* 12:69–146 (1958).
Richards, J. A. *Mencius on the Mind.* London, 1932.
Rickett, W. Allyn (trans.). *Kuan-tzu.* Hong Kong, 1965.
Rue, John E. *Mao Tse-tung in Opposition 1927–1935.* Stanford, 1966.
Russell, Bertrand. *The Problem of China.* London, 1922.
San-ch'ao pei-meng hui-pien (Collected Documents Relating to the Northern Vow of the Three Courts). Hsü Meng-hsin. Shanghai, 1939.
San-kuo-chih (History of the Three Kingdoms). Ch'en Shou, et al. *PNP.*
Sarkisyanz, Emmanuel. *Russland und der Messianismus des Orients.* Tübingen, 1955 *(L).*
Scalapino, Robert A., and George Yu. *The Chinese Anarchist Movement.* Berkeley, 1961.
______ and Harold Schiffrin. "Early Socialist Currents in the Chinese Revolutionary Movement: Sun Yat-sen versus Liang Ch'i-ch'ao." *JAS* 18:321–342 (May 1959).
Schafer, Edward H. (1). *The Golden Peaches of Samarkand.* Berkeley, 1963 *(L).*

——— (2). *The Vermilion Bird.* Berkeley, 1967 *(L).*

——— (3). "Mineral Imagery in the Paradise Poems of Kuan-hsiu." *AM* (new series) 10:73–102 (1963) *(L).*

——— (4). "The Auspices of T'ang." *JAOS* 83:197–225 (1963).

Schickel, Joachim (trans.). *37 Gedichte* [*Mao Tse Tungs*]. Munich, 1967.

Schiffrin, Harold Z. *Sun Yat-sen and the Origins of the Chinese Revolution.* Berkeley, 1968 *(L).*

Schipper, Kristofer M. *L'Empereur Wou des Hans dans la légende taoiste.* Paris, 1965.

Schneider, Elisabeth. *Coleridge, Opium and Kublai Khan.* New York, 1966.

Schneider, Laurence A. "From Textual Criticism to Social Criticism: The Historiography of Ku Chieh-kang." *JAS* 28:771–788 (August 1969).

Schram, Stuart (1). *Mao Ze-dong: Une Étude sur l'Éducation physique.* Paris, 1962.

——— (2). *The Political Thought of Mao Tse-tung.* New York, 1963 *(L).*

——— (3). *Mao Tse-tung.* New York, 1967.

——— (4). "Mao Tse-tung and Secret Societies." *CQ* 27:1–13 (July–Sept. 1966).

——— (5). *Die permanente Revolution in China, Dokumente und Kommentar.* Frankfurt/Main, 1966.

Schubert, Renate. "Das erste Kapitel des Pao-p'u tzu wai-p'ien." *ZDMG* 119:278–301 (1969/70).

Schwartz, Benjamin (1). "Ch'en Tu-hsiu and the Acceptance of the Modern West." *Journal of the History of Ideas* 12:61–74 (1951).

——— (2). *Chinese Communism and the Rise of Mao.* Cambridge, Mass., 1952 *(L).*

——— (3). "The Intellectual History of China: Preliminary Reflections," in *Chinese Thought and Institutions,* ed. John K. Fairbank, pp. 15–30. Chicago, 1957.

——— (4). "Some Polarities in Confucian Thought," in *Confucianism in Action,* ed. David S. Nivison, pp. 50–62. Stanford, 1959.

——— (5). *In Search of Wealth and Power: Yen Fu and the West.* Cambridge, Mass., 1964.

——— (6). "Modernisation and the Maoist Vision: Some Reflections on Chinese Communist Goals." *CQ* 21:3–19 (1965).

——— (7). "China and the West in the 'Thought of Mao Tse-tung,' " in *China in Crisis,* ed. Tsou Tang, vol. 1, pp. 365–396. Chicago, 1968.

——— (8). "Ch'en Tu-hsiu: Pre-Communist Phase." *HPC* 2:167–197 (1948).

Seidel, Anna (1). *La Divinisation de Lao Tseu dans le Taoisme des Han.* Paris, 1969 *(L).*

——— (2). "The Image of the Perfect Ruler in Early Taoist Messianism." *History of Religions* 9, 2–3:216–247 (Nov. 1969–Feb. 1970).

Shan-hai-ching chien-su (Classic of Seas and Mountains, with Commentary). *Ssu-pu pei-yao* edition.

Shang-chün-shu (The Book of Lord Shang). *CTCC.* [See Duyvendak's (2) translation.]

Shen-hsien chuan (Biographies of Gods and Immortals). Attributed to Ko Hung. *Shuo-k'u.* [See L. Giles' translation.]

Shen-hsien kan-yü chuan (Sentimental Encounters with Gods and Immortals). Tu Kuang-t'ing. *TT,* 39, 2.

Shih Chün (ed.). *Chung-kuo chin-tai ssu-hsiang-shih ts'an-k'ao tzu-liao chien-pien* (Comprehensive Source Material on the Intellectual History of Modern China). Peking, 1957.

Shih Shao-pin (ed.) *Chung-kuo feng-chien she-hui nung-min chan-cheng wen-t'i t'ao-lun chi* (Collected Articles of the Debate on the Problem of Peasant Uprisings in Feudal China). Peking, 1962.

Shih, Vincent Y. C. (1). "Metaphysical Tendencies in Mencius." *Philosophy East and West* 12, 4:319–342 (1963).

______(2). *The Taiping Ideology: Its Sources, Interpretations and Influences*. Seattle, 1967 *(L)*.

Shih-chi (Historical Records). Ssu-ma Ch'ien. *PNP*. [See Chavannes' (1) and Watson's (1) translations.]

Shih-fu (1). "Wu-cheng-fu kung-chan-tang chih mu-ti yü shou-tuan" (Aims and Methods of Anarcho-Communism). *Min-sheng* 19:6–9 (July 18, 1914).

______ (2). "Wu-cheng-fu kung-chan chu-i shih-ming" (Defining Anarcho-Communism). *Min-sheng* 5:1–5 (April 11, 1914).

______ (3). "Pien-chi hsü-yen" (Declaration). *Hui-ming-lu* (or *P'ing-min chih sheng*) 1, 1:1–9 (Canton, August 20, 1913).

Shih-i chi (Record of Collected Traditions). Attributed to Wang Chia. *Ku-chin i-shih*.

Shih-shuo hsin-yü (New Analects of Talks of the Time). Liu I-ch'ing, with commentary by Liu Hsiao-piao. *CTCC*.

Shimada Kenji. *Chūgoku kakumei no senkusha tachi* (Forerunners of the Chinese Revolution). Tokyo, 1965.

Shiratori Kurakichi. "Chinese Ideas As Reflected in the Ta Ch'in Accounts," in *Memoirs of the Research Department of the Toyo Bunko*. Vol. 15. Tokyo, 1956.

Shizukuishi Kōkichi. "Jukyō no shiseikan to tōitsu no ichishiki" (The View of Life and Death and the Idea of Unification in Confucianism). *Tōkyō Shinagakuhō* 7:69–79 (June 1961).

Siao Emi. *Mao Tse-tung: His Childhood and Youth*. Bombay, 1953.

Siao Yü. *Mao Tse-tung and I Were Beggars*. Syracuse, 1959.

Sievers, Gabriele von. *Das Yang Yao shih-chi: Zur Geschichte der Rebellion des Chung Hsiang und Yang Yao*. Munich, 1969.

Skinner, G. William. "Marketing and Social Structure in Rural China." *JAS* 24:3–43, 195–228, 363–399 (1964/65).

Slyke, Lyman P. van. "Liang Sou-ming and the Rural Reconstruction Movement." *JAS* 18:457–474 (August 1959).

Smith, A. H. *Proverbs and Common Sayings from the Chinese*. New York, 1965.

Smythe, E. Joan. "The Early Thought of Wang Kuo-wei." *HPC* 18:1–25 (1964).

Snow, Edgar P. *Red Star over China*. 1st rev. ed. New York, 1968.

Solomon, Richard. "On Activism and Activists." *CQ* 39:76–114 (July–Sept. 1969).

Sou-shen chi (In Search of Ghosts). Kan Pao. *Hsüeh-chin t'ao-yüan*. [See Bodde's (6) and (7) translations.]

Sou-shen hou-chi. T'ao Ch'ien. *Hsüeh-chin t'ao-yüan*.

Soymié, Michel. "Le Lo-feou chan; étude de géographie religieuse." *Bulletin de l'École Française de l'Extrême-Orient* 48:1–139 (Paris 1956).

Stein, Rolf A. (1). "Remarques sur les mouvements du Taoisme politico-religieux au IIe siècle ap. J. C." *TP* 50:1–78 (1963) *(L)*.

______(2). "Jardins en miniature de l'Extrême Orient: Le monde en petit." *Bulletin de l'École Française de l'Extrême-Orient* 42:1–104 (1942).

Steininger, Hans. "Der Buddhismus in der chinesischen Geschichte." *Saeculum* 13, 2:132–165 (1962).

Sun Yat-sen. *Kuo-fu ch'üan-shu* (Collected Works of the Father of the Country). Ed. Chang Chi-yün. Taipei 1960. [See Gangulee's, Kindermann's, Price's, and Wittfogel's (3) translations.]

Sung-shih (History of the Sung Dynasty). T'o-t'o (Toqto), et al. *PNP*.

Sung-shu ([Historical] Documents of the [Liu] Sung Dynasty). Shen Yo, et al. *PNP*.

Ta-Wu-liang-shou ching (Great Sutra of the Immeasurable Life). *T*, text number 360: 265–279.

T'ai-p'ing-ching: T'ai-p'ing-ching ho-chiao (Critical Edition of the T'ai-p'ing-ching). Ed. Wang Ming. Peking, 1960.

T'ai-p'ing kuang-chi (Extensive Records from the T'ai-p'ing Era). Ed. Li Fang. *PCHSTK.*

T'ang Chih-chün. "Lun K'ang Yu-wei *Ta-t'ung-shu* ti ssu-hsiang shih-chih" (On the Ideological Concept of K'ang Yu-wei's *Ta-t'ung-shu*). *LSYC* 11:7–20 (1959).

T'ang Chün-i. "Ch'in Han i-hou t'ien-ming ssu-hsiang chih fa-chan" (The Development of the Concept of the Mandate of Heaven after the Ch'in and Han Dynasties). *Hsin-Ya hsüeh-pao* 6, 2:1–61 (1964).

T'ang-shu (History of the T'ang Dynasty). Liu Hsü, et al. *PNP.*

Tao-te-ching: Tao-te-ching chu (*Tao-te-ching* with Commentary [by Wang Pi]). *CTCC.* [See Debon's, Duyvendak's (1), Legge's (4), Waley's (4), and R. Wilhelm's (2) translations.]

T'ao Yüan-ming shih-wen hui-p'ing (Critical Collection of Poems and Prose Writings of T'ao Yüan-ming). T'ao Ch'ien. Edited by a Peking University study group. Peking, 1961.

Tay, C. N. "Two Poems of Mao Tse-tung in the Light of Chinese Literary Tradition." *JAS* 29, 3:633–655 (May 1970).

Teng Ssu-yü (1). "A Political Interpretation of Chinese Rebellions and Revolutions." *Tsing Hua Journal of Chinese Studies* (new series) 1, 3:91–112 (Sept. 1958).

——— (2). "Wang Fu-chih's Views on History and Historical Writing." *JAS* 28, 1: 111–123 (Nov. 1968).

——— and John K. Fairbank. *China's Response to the West.* Cambridge, Mass., 1964.

Teng T'o (1). *Yen-shan yeh-hua hsüan-chi* (Selections from the Evening Talks at the Swallow Mountain). Hong Kong, 1966.

——— (2). *Teng T'o shih-wen hsüan-chi* (Selection of Poems and Prose Writings of Teng T'o). Taipei, 1966.

Thompson, Laurence (1) (trans.). *Ta T'ung Shu: The One-World Philosophy of K'ang Yu-wei.* London, 1958.

——— (2). *"Ta-t'ung Shu* and the *Communist Manifesto,"* in Lo Jung-pang, pp. 341–354.

Tjan Tjoe Som. *Po Hu T'ung: The Comprehensive Discussions in the White Tiger Hall.* Leiden, 1952.

Tökei, Ferenc. *Zur Frage der asiat. Produktionsweise.* Neuwied/Berlin, 1970.

Topley, M. "The Great Way of Former Heaven." *BSOAS* 26, 2:362–392.

Torr, Dona (ed.). *Marx on China 1853–1860.* London, 1951.

Trotsky, Leo (1). *Die permanente Revolution.* Frankfurt/Main, 1969.

——— (2). Problems of the Chinese Revolution. New edition. Ann Arbor, 1967.

(Fu-chou) Ts'ao-shan Pen-chi ch'an-shih yü-lu (Words of the Meditation Master Pen-chi from the Ts'ao Mountain). Pen-chi. *T.* Text number 1987:535–544.

Tseu, Augustinus A. *The Moral Philosophy of Mo-tze.* Taipei, 1965.

Tso-meng-lu (Record of Dreams of Yesterday). K'ang Yü-chih. *Ku-chin shuo-hai.*

Ts'un-hsüeh pien (On the Preservation of Scholarship). Yen Yüan. *CKHSMC.*

Tung-kao-tzu chi (Collected Works of Master Tung-kao). Wang Chi. *TSCC.*

Uchiyama Toshihiko (1). "Hō Keigen (Pao Ching-yen)." *Chūgoku no Bunka to Shakai* 12:1–16 (1966).

——— (2). "Kandai shisōshi ni okeru itanteki naru mono" (On the Meaning of Portents in the Intellectual History of the Han Dynasty). *Yamaguchi Daigaku Bungakukaishi* 16:85–99 (1965).

Unno Kazutaka. "Konron shisuisetsu no chiri shisōshiteki kōsatsu" (A Geographical and Philosophical Analysis of the Legend of the Four Rivers at Mount K'un-lun). *Shirin* 41:379–393 (Kyoto, 1958).

Vandermeersch, Léon. *La Formation du Légisme.* Paris, 1965.
Vierheller, Ernst-Joachim. *Nation und Elite im Denken von Wang Fu-chih (1619–1692).* Hamburg, 1968.
Waley, Arthur (1). "The Book of Changes." *BMFEA* 5:121–142 (1933).
______ (2) (trans.). *The Analects of Confucius.* London, 1949.
______ (3) (trans.). *The Book of Songs.* London, 1954.
______ (4) (trans.) *The Way and Its Power.* London, 1956.
______ (5). *The Opium War through Chinese Eyes.* London, 1958.
Wallacker, Benjamin E. (trans.). *The Huai-nan-tzu, Book Eleven.* New Haven, 1962.
Wan Sheng-nan. "T'ai-p'ing-tao yü Wu-tou-mi-tao" (On the T'ai-p'ing-tao and the Five Pecks of Rice Taoists). *Li-shih chiao-hsüeh* 6:10–17 (1964).
Wang Erh-min. "Ch'ing-chi wei-hsin jen-wu ti t'o-ku kai-chih lun" (On Tradition-bound Reforms for the Renewal of Man in the Late Ch'ing Dynasty). *Ta-lu tsa-chih* 21, 6:14–19 (1960).
Wang Hsin-chai hsien-sheng i-chi (Collected Writings Left by Master Wang Hsin-chai). Wang Ken. Place of publication unknown (Tung-t'ai Yuan-shih), 1912.
Wang Hui-yüeh (ed.). *T'ai-p'ing t'ien-kuo yeh-shih* (Popular History of the T'ai-p'ing t'ien-kuo). Tainan, 1969. (Reprint of Ling Shan-ch'ing's edition, Shanghai, 1923).
Wang Wen-ch'eng kung ch'üan-shu (Collected Writings of Master Wang Wen-ch'eng). Wang Shou-jen. *Kuo-hsüeh chi-pen ts'ung-shu.* Shanghai, 1934. [See Chan Wing-tsit's and Henke's translations.]
Wang Yü-ch'üan. "The Development of Modern Social Science in China." *Pacific Affairs* 11, 3:345–362 (Sept. 1938).
Ware, James R. (trans.). *Alchemy, Medicine and Religion in the China of A.D. 320: The Nei P'ien of Ko Hung.* Cambridge, Mass., 1966.
Watson, Burton (1) (trans.). *Records of the Grand Historian of China.* 2 vols. New York, 1961.
______ (2) (trans.). *The Complete Works of Chuang-tzu.* New York, 1968.
Weber, Max. *Gesammelte Aufsätze zur Religionssoziologie.* 3 vols. Tübingen, 1920–1921.
Weber-Schäfer, Peter (1). "Die Himmelfahrt des Ch'ü Yüan," in *Politische Ordnung und menschliche Existenz: Festschrift Eric Voegelin.* Munich, 1963.
______ (2). *Der Edle und der Weise.* Munich, 1963.
Wei-shu (History of the Wei Dynasty). Wei Shou, et al. *PNP.*
Welch, Holmes. *The Parting of the Way.* London, 1957.
Werner, E. T. C. *A Dictionary of Chinese Mythology.* New edition. New York, 1961.
White, T. H., and A. Jacoby. *Thunder Out of China.* 1946. Reprint. New York, 1975.
Who's Who in China. Shanghai *(The China Weekly Review),* 1936.
Wilbur, Martin. "Military Separatism and the Process of Reunification under the Nationalist Regime, 1922–1937," in *China in Crisis,* ed. Tsou Tang, vol. 1, pp. 203–276. Chicago, 1968.
Wilhelm, Helmut (1). *Die Wandlung: Acht Vorträge zum I-Ging.* Peking, 1944.
______ (2). "The Problem of Within and Without: A Confucian Attempt of Synchretism." *Journal of the History of Ideas* 12: 48–60 (1951).
Wilhelm, Richard (1) (trans.). *I Ging: Das Buch der Wandlungen.* 2 vols. Dusseldorf, circa 1955.
______ (2) (trans.). *Laotse, Tao Te King.* Jena, 1941.
______ (3) (trans.). *Kungfutse: Gespräche.* Jena, 1910.
______ (4) (trans.). *Dschuang Dsi: Das wahre Buch vom Südlichen* Blütenland. Jena, 1920.
______ (5) (trans.). *Liä Dsi: Das wahre Buch vom quellenden Urgrund.* Jena, 1911.

——— (6) (trans.). *Frühling und Herbst des Lü Bu We.* Jena, 1928.
——— (7) (trans.). *Li Gi: Das Buch der Sitte.* Dusseldorf, circa 1960.
——— (8) (trans.). *Mong Dsi.* Jena, 1921.
Williams, George H. *Wilderness and Paradise in Christian Thought.* New York, 1962.
Williams, Samuel Wells. *The Middle Kingdom.* 2 vols. New York, 1883.
Wittfogel, Karl August (1). *Oriental Despotism.* New Haven, 1957.
——— (2). "Some Remarks on Mao's Handling of Concepts and Problems of Dialectics." *Studies in Soviet Thought* 3, 1:251–269 (March 1963).
——— (3) (trans.). *Sun Yat Sen: Aufzeichnungen eines chinesischen Revolutionärs.* Wien/Berlin, circa 1930.
——— (4). "Probleme der chinesischen Wirtschaftsgeschichte." *Archiv für Sozialwissenschaft und Sozialpolitik* 57, 2:289–335 (1927).
——— (5). "The Foundation and Stages of Chinese Economic History." *Zeitschrift für Sozialforschung* 4, 1:26–58 (1935).
——— (6). *Wirtschaft und Gesellschaft Chinas.* Leipzig, 1931.
Wong, George H. C. "The Anti-christian Movement in China: Late Ming and Early Ch'ing." *Tsing Hua Journal of Chinese Studies* (new series) 3, 1: 187–222 (May 1962).
Woo Kang. [See also Wu K'ang.] *Les trois théories politiques du Tch'ouen Ts'ieou.* Paris, 1932.
Wright, Arthur F. *Buddhism in Chinese History.* Stanford, 1959.
Wright, Mary C. (1). *The Last Stand of Chinese Conservatism: The T'ung-chih Restoration, 1862–1874.* Stanford, 1957 *(L).*
——— (2). "What's in a Reign Name: The Uses of History and Philology." *JAS* 18: 103–106 (Nov. 1958).
——— (3) (ed.). *China in Revolution: The First Phase 1900–1913.* New Haven, 1968.
——— (4). "From Revolution to Restoration: The Transformation of Kuomintang Ideology." *Far Eastern Quarterly* 14, 4:515–532 (August 1955).
Wu Chih-hui. *See* Wu Ching-heng.
Wu Ching-heng (1). *Wu Chih-hui ch'üan-chi* (Collected Works of Wu Chih-hui). Shanghai, 1927.
——— (2). "Chi-ch'i ts'u-chin ta-t'ung shuo" (On Bringing about the *ta-t'ung* by Machines). *Hsin Ch'ing-nien* 5, 2:158–160 (April 1918).
Wu K'ang. [See also Woo Kang.] "Man-Ch'ing Chin-wen-ching-hsüeh tai-piao K'ang Yu-wei chih kai-chih ta-t'ung ssu-hsiang" (K'ang Yu-wei's Reform and His Concept of *ta-t'ung* As an Expression of the New Text School in the Late Ch'ing Dynasty). *K'ung-Meng hsüeh-pao* 12:95–107 (1966).
Yang, C. K. (1). *Religion in Chinese Society.* Berkeley, 1961 *(L).*
——— (2). "The Functional Relationship between Confucian Thought and Chinese Religion," in *Chinese Thought and Institutions,* ed. John K. Fairbank, pp. 269–290. Chicago, 1957.
Yap, P. M. "The Mental Illness of Hung Hsiu-ch'üan, Leader of the Taiping Rebellion." *Far Eastern Quarterly* 13:287–304 (May 1954).
Yasui Kōzan (1). "Zushin no keisei to sono enyō ni tsuite no kōsatsu" (An Analysis of the Invention of Apocryphical Tablets and Texts and Their Usage at the Imperial Court). *Tōhōgaku* 27:48–63 (1964).
——— (2). "Kōkan ni okeru jumei kaisei to isho shiso" (The Mandate of Heaven, the Form of Government, and the Concept of Apocryphical Books in the Later Han Dynasty). *Taishō Daigaku Kenkyu Kiyō* 51:49–82 (1966).
Yen Ling-feng (1). *Chung-wai Lao-tzu chu-shu mu-lu* (Catalog of Chinese and Foreign Works on Lao-tzu). Taipei, 1957.

______ (2). *Lieh-tzu Chuang-tzu chih-chien shu-mu* (Catalog of Scholarly Researches into Lieh-tzu and Chuang-tzu). Hong Kong, 1961.

Yoshioka Yoshitoyo (1). *Dōkyō kenkyū* (Studies in Taoism). Tokyo, 1964.

______ (2). "Taiheikyō seiritsu no mondai ni tsuite" (On the Problem of the Compilation of the *T'ai-p'ing-ching*). *Yūki Hakase Shōju Kinen Bukkyō Shisōshi Ronshū* 341–358 (1964).

Yü Kuan-ying (ed.). *Ts'ao Ts'ao, Ts'ao P'ei, Ts'ao Chih shih hsüan* (Selected Poems of Ts'ao Ts'ao, Ts'ao P'ei, and Ts'ao Chih). Hong Kong, 1962.

Yü Sung-ch'ing. "T'ai-p'ing-ching ho Huang-chin ti kuan-hsi" (The Relations between the *T'ai-p'ing-ching* and the Yellow Turbans). *Hsin Chien-she* 75–81 (1963).

Yu-yang tsa-tsu (Mixed Plate from Yu-yang). Tuan Ch'eng-shih. *Hsüeh-chin t'ao-yüan* edition.

Yü Ying-shih (1). *Views of Life and Death in Later Han China.* Ph.D. dissertation, Cambridge, Mass., 1962 *(L).*

______ (2). "Life and Immortality in the Mind of Han China." *HJAS* 25:80–122 (1964/65).

Zürcher, Eric. *The Buddhist Conquest of China.* 2 vols. Leiden, 1959 *(L).*

INDEX